The Psychology of Education

The Psychology of Education is a textbook covering the range of contemporary psychological knowledge applied to education. Completely up to date, and written in an engaging and humorous style, this book covers

- the nature of learning
- techniques of assessment, with an emphasis on current developments in the National Curriculum
- recent findings on the impact of differences in individual pupils, schools and teachers
- ways of involving and motivating pupils
- the importance of social disadvantage, and cultural differences of ethnicity and gender, in determining attainment
- the nature of children's language, literacy development and the relationship between them
- behavioural problems and how to deal with them
- key concepts in special needs and the nature of additional provision

Suitable for those training in education, as well as those in other fields, this book emphasises the use of evidence to arrive at practical solutions. It will be an invaluable text for students on ITT, PGCE and primary teaching courses; students taking education options in first degree courses; in service teachers of CPD and postgraduates; educational psychologists and teacher trainers.

Martyn Long taught in both secondary and further education. He is currently an educational psychologist in Cambridgeshire.

This book is linked with a website at www.psych-ed.org. It contains resources to download, links, reviews and updates, as well as the opportunity to contact the author.

The Psychology of Education

Martyn Long

LONDON AND NEW YORK

First published 2000 by RoutledgeFalmer
2 Park Square, Milton Park, Oxon OX14 4RN

Simultaneously published in the USA and Canada
by RoutledgeFalmer
270 Madison Ave, New York, NY10016

Reprinted 2003 (twice), 2004, 2005 (twice), 2006 (twice)

RoutledgeFalmer is an imprint of the Taylor & Francis Group, an informa Business

Typeset in 10/12pt Goudy by Wearset, Boldon, Tyne and Wear
Printed and bound in Great Britain by Bell & Bain Ltd., Glasgow

British Library Cataloguing in Publication Data
A catalogue record for this book is available from the British Library

Library of Congress Cataloging in Publication Data
Long, Martyn, 1948-
The psychology of education/Martyn Long.
p. cm.
Includes bibliographical references and index.
1. Educational psychology. 2. Teaching. 3. Learning. I. Title.

LB1051 .L774 2000
370.15–dc21

00-042466

ISBN 10: 0-415-23906-0
ISBN 13: 978-0-415-23906-6

CONTENTS

Figures

Tables

Preface

Education is probably the largest single area of study of applied psychology. A tremendous amount is known about educational psychology which is useful to people involved with teaching and learning. Condensing and selecting from this vast body of knowledge has therefore meant that I have had to cover some areas rapidly in order to reach key ideas and conclusions. This means, I hope, that you will not have to wade through a lot of information to reach something interesting. If you want to go into more detail, there are plenty of recent references and further reading to follow up.

If you are working or training as a teacher, you should find that this book gives focused and up-to-date coverage of the research findings about many of the areas in which you are involved. If you are simply interested in education, the book describes various findings with implications for what we can expect from schooling and the ways in which it might be organised.

Perhaps the biggest problem with the educational field is that it is heavily politicised, and ill-informed and subjective interpretations abound. Politicians themselves seem particularly prone to making simplistic pronouncements and general meddling! Moreover, many people seem to have something of a chip on their shoulder about education and are very happy to read 'knocking copy' in the newspapers. This is typically very biased in order to make sensational reading and usually distorts the issues and what is known about them. There has also been a general trend over the past few years to see education as being largely responsible for many of society's ills, failing to regenerate the economy, or to overcome what is seen as increasing moral degeneracy. In fact, although schools can have an effect on social problems such as crime rates, the evidence indicates that such outcomes are much more strongly related to home background and social context. Also, international comparisons indicate that above a certain basic level of general competence, educational attainments probably do not have much of an effect on countries' economic performance.

Such blaming can be seen as a form of scapegoating, which shifts the responsibility for society's problems, and diverts attention from other causes. As part of this process, there has been something of a general reaction against the radical views of the 1960s, that social problems come from general structural aspects of society such as class divisions. Beliefs about the relative importance of education have taken root in the 'school improvement' movement and the political push for value for money in education, which has been supported by all political parties. There is little real evidence for such beliefs, however, and the situation is more complex than most of these perspectives propose.

Foster *et al.* (1996) describe the way in which a great deal of educational research appears to be largely governed by the socio-political context of its time, and is used to support whatever ideology is most current. Unfortunately, I have to say that the history of educational psychology is scarcely blemish-free itself – as witness, for example, the support for widespread ability assessment after Britain's 1944 Education Act, in the form of the 'eleven-plus'. This was a form of IQ test (advocated by education psychologists) and was used to allocate children to unequal forms of education. Despite this, psychological knowledge and research has at least the potential to provide rational and useful information that can guide educational decision making and actual teaching practice. Without such information, one can rely only on limited personal experiences and ill-informed guesswork.

One further difficulty is that a particular finding can still be interpreted in a number of different ways, according to the bias of whoever is reporting it. In the 1960s, for instance, various research studies into the effects of the teaching of grammar were widely taken to mean that this inhibited children's writing abilities. In fact, as a review of these studies by the Qualifications and Curriculum Authority (QCA, 1998) found, most of them indicated that guided written work involving the use of structure was superior to learning formal grammar in isolation. A more accurate interpretation might therefore be that it is best to teach children about different aspects of grammar in meaningful contexts, rather than doing away with any form of learning about language structure.

To avoid such misinterpretations, it might therefore be a good idea to be aware of the general nature and principal findings of actual research studies. Although it would be impossible to give details of all the studies in this book, I have given some of the main features which illustrate the design of key research studies, to enable you to assess what credibility can be given to the different interpretations.

This book concentrates on *evidence*, as opposed to opinion. As far as possible, the information I describe comes from direct applications of psychological knowledge or from the use of psychological techniques in educational research. However, there are inevitably biases, which come from the evidence which I have selected, and these are the result of attempts to reflect the balance of likely explanations in each area. I freely admit, for instance, that I am in general rather sceptical of some deterministic views, which tend to look for simple causes. These include beliefs about the importance of general cognitive abilities or ideas about certain inherited characteristics being important for children's educational progress. I am well aware that there are many people who believe otherwise and I have also therefore tried to represent evidence which supports the other side of things.

Despite this, there are certain areas where I feel strongly that the general weight of findings points in a certain direction. For instance, there is evidence that within certain wide limits, class size does not have a great effect on children's progress. Although I am sure that most teachers do not believe this, I consider that it would be dishonest of me if I did not point out such conclusions. If you disagree with my interpretations, then I hope that this book will spur you on to look for opposing evidence and develop your ideas about the area further.

I have also tried to write this book with a theoretical grounding, in order to make knowledge more flexible. This can, however, sometimes obscure any practical implications, so I have put in some additional sections with key implications and a practical scenario as a prompt for some questions. Some approaches to answering these are included in a final appendix.

If you have anything at all to do with education, you should therefore find this book factual, useful and, I hope, interesting.

Acknowledgements

I would first like to thank John Head, who encouraged the development of this book from its early stages. Without his positive comments and advice, this enterprise would never have got very far.

I would also like to acknowledge the support of Keith Melton, who was generous in reading an initial draft and giving me detailed and expert feedback. This certainly made this book better than it would have been, although the remaining faults are entirely my own responsibility.

I must finally mention the many dedicated teachers with whom I have worked, who have, I hope kept me aware of the practical realities of what education is all about. If they disagree with what I've written, I'm sure they'll let me know!

Acknowledgements of copyright material

My thanks to Nigel Paige, Bill Stott and Nick Newman for permission to use their cartoons. All of these originally appeared in the *Times Educational Supplement*.

Chapter 2

Figure 2.16 Relationship between short-term memory and speed of talking. From Nicolson, R. (1981) The relationship between memory span and processing speed. In M. Friedman, J. Das and N. O'Connor (eds) *Intelligence and Learning*. New York: Plenum Press. Reproduced by permission of the publisher and the author.

Chapter 3

Figure 3.10 Flanders' interaction analysis categories. From Flanders, N. (1970) *Analyzing Teacher Behavior*. Reading, MA: Addison Wesley. Reproduced by permission of the author.

Figure 3.11 Sequence of pupil achievement of levels, between ages 7 and 16. From TGAT (1988) *National Curriculum Task Group on Assessment and Testing: A Report*. HMSO: DES. Crown copyright is reproduced with the permission of the Controller of Her Majesty's Stationery Office.

Chapter 4

Figure 4.2 Abilities of children in different sized families. From Storfer, M. (1990) *Intelligence and Giftedness*. San Francisco: Jossey-Bass. Reproduced by permission of the publisher. Recalculated from original data in Breland, H. (1974) Birth order, family configuration, and verbal achievement. *Child Development*, 45, 1011–1019. Reproduced by permission of the Society for Research in Child Development.

Figure 4.3 Changes in mean birth order over time, and eventual A level pass rate. From Zajonc, R. and Mullally, P. (1997) Birth order: reconciling conflicting effects. *American Psychologist*, 52 (7), 685–699. Reproduced by permission of the publisher and the author.

Figure 4.4 Relationship between parenting index and IQ scores at age 3 years. From Hart, B. and Risley, T. (1995) *Meaningful Differences in Everyday Parenting and Intellectual Development in Young American Children*. Baltimore: Brookes. Reproduced by permission of Brookes Publishing Co., PO Box 10624, Baltimore, Maryland, and the author.

Figure 4.6 The Rialto, Venice. Copyright Stephen Wiltshire, from *Floating Cities*. London: Michael Joseph, 1991. Reproduced by permission of John Johnson (author's agent).

Figure 4.12 GCSE science results, 1996, in relation to school intake. From Shayer, M. (1996) *The Long-Term Effects of Cognitive Acceleration on Pupils' School Achievement, November 1996*. London: King's College, Centre for the Advancement of Thinking. Reproduced by permission of the author.

Figure 4.15 Achievements of different subjects according to their cognitive style. From Riding, R. and Pearson, F. (1994) The relationship between cognitive style and intelligence. *Educational Psychology*, 14 (4), 413–425. Reproduced by permission of Carfax Publishing, PO Box 25, Abingdon, Oxfordshire.

Figure 4.16 Overall recall scores of verbalisers and imagers. From Riding, R. and Douglas, G. (1993) The effect of cognitive style and mode of presentation on learning performance. *British Journal of Educational Psychology*, 63, 297–307. © The British Psychological Society. Reproduced by permission of the publisher and the author.

Checklist from the National Association for Gifted Children (NAGC, 1989). Reproduced by permission of the National Association of Gifted Children.

Chapter 6

Figure 6.6 GCSE performance, 1997, in relation to numbers of pupils on roll. From Funding Agency for Schools (1998) *Cost and Performance Comparisons for Grant-Maintained Schools*. York: FAS. Reproduced by permission of the Funding Agency for Schools.

Figure 6.8 Effects of individual teaching. From Bloom, B. (1984) The 2 sigma problem: the search for methods of group instruction as effective as one-to-one tutoring. *Educational Researcher*, June/July, 4–16. Copyright 1984 by the American Educational Research Association; reproduced with permission from the publisher.

Figure 6.12 Standardised gain scores for 41 teachers in Years 1 and 2. From Gray, J. (1979) Reading progress in English infant schools: some problems emerging from a study of teacher effectiveness. *British Educational Research Journal*, 5, 141–157. Reproduced by permission of the publisher.

Chapter 7

Figure 7.3 Comparison of GCSE achievements of boys and girls over time. From *Social Trends* (1997) London: The Stationery Office. Reproduced by permission of the Office for National Statistics. © Crown copyright 1997.

Figure 7.5 Educational attainments of ethnic groups, 1981–2. From DES (1985) *Education for All: Report of the Committee of Inquiry into the Education of Children from Ethnic Minority Groups*. Cmnd 9453. London: HMSO ('The Swann Report'). Crown copyright is reproduced with the permission of the Controller of Her Majesty's Stationery Office.

Figure 7.6 Average GCSE exam scores by ethnic origin, gender and social class. From Drew, D. and Gray, J. (1990) The fifth year examination achievements of Black young people in England and Wales. *Educational Research*, 32 (3), 107–117. Reproduced by permission of the National Foundation for Educational Research.

Chapter 9

Figure 9.3 Three-route model of word identification. Adapted from Buchanan, L. and Besner, D. (1995) Reading aloud: evidence for the use of a whole word nonsemantic pathway. In J. Henderson, M. Murray Singer and F. Ferreira (eds) *Reading and Language Processing*. Hillsdale, NJ: Lawrence Erlbaum. Reproduced by permission of the publisher and the author.

Figure 9.5 Fry's readability graph. From Fry, E. (1977) *Elementary Reading Instruction*. New York: McGraw-Hill, 1977, p. 217. Reproduced with permission from McGraw-Hill.

Figure 9.7 Distributions of under- and over-achievement with reading. From Rodgers, B. (1983) The identification and prevalence of specific reading retardation. *British Journal of Educational Psychology*, 53, 369–373. Reproduced by permission of the publisher and the author.

Chapter 10

Figure 10.1 Number of permanent exclusions from schools, 1990–1 to 1997–8. From Parsons, C. and Howlett, K. (1996) Permanent exclusions from school: a case where society is failing its children. *Support for Learning*, 11 (3), 109–112. Reproduced by permission of the publisher.

Figure 10.2 Levels of emotional and behavioural difficulties (EBD) in relation to social class of intake in 13 Aberdeen schools. From Maxwell, W. (1994) Figure 1, page 31, Special educational needs and social disadvantage in Aberdeen city school catchment zones. *Educational Research*, 36 (1), 25–37. Reproduced by permission of the publisher.

Chapter 11

Extract from *Education Act* (1997) London: HMSO. Part II, 4, 550A, Crown copyright.

Figure 11.3 Diagnostic criteria for attention-deficit/hyperactivity disorder (AD/HD). Reprinted with permission from the *Diagnostic and Statistical Manual of Mental Disorders*, 4th edition. Copyright 1994 American Psychiatric Association.

Chapter 12

Figure 12.1 Distributions of behavioural and literacy attainments. First graph based on Stott, D. (1971) *Manual of the Bristol Social-Adjustment Guides*. London: University of London Press. It was not possible to contact the author despite efforts to do so. Second graph based on Elliott, C., Smith, P. and McCulloch, K. (1996) *British Ability Scales II*, Windsor: NFER-Nelson, with permission of the publisher.

Figure 12.10 Percentage of 5- to 15-year-olds in special schools in England. From Norwich, B. (1997) *A Trend towards Inclusion*. Redland, Bristol: Centre for Studies on Inclusive Education. Reproduced by permission of the publisher.

1 Introduction

Chapter structure

Why do we need psychology?

Everybody seems to think that they know a lot about psychology and about how education should be run. After all, most of us have had a lot of experience with other people, and virtually all of us have been to school.

The majority of our ideas about what makes things happen are built up from personal experience, and these beliefs work well in our everyday lives. However, they are not necessarily very effective when they are applied to the particular process of educating groups of children. Here, general rules of thumb and common-sense simplifications can sometimes result in very contradictory perspectives when applied by different people. It can be impossible to prove which of two such opposing views is the more valid.

Take these sets of opposing statements, for instance. Which do you agree with?

'Formal teaching is too restrictive and puts children off learning'

versus

'Progressive teaching fails to give children discipline and doesn't teach the harder subjects well'

'Reducing class sizes would obviously result in improved learning'

versus

'Class sizes are not important; what matters most is the quality of the teaching'

'Firm discipline and punishment are important in controlling problem behaviour'

versus

'Positive behaviour comes from the examples of others; punishment is ineffective and simply brutalises children'

'Dyslexics are simply middle-class children who can't read'

versus

'Dyslexia is a genuine, important problem that is due to underlying difficulties with cognitive processes'

'Children's speech and language develops naturally and should be largely left alone'

versus

'When children use the wrong speech and language, it is important to correct them so that they don't get into bad habits'

'Children's teachers are the most important factor in their education'

versus

'Teachers aren't really important – the key things are a child's own knowledge and motivation'

It is likely that you have some existing ideas about each of these pairs of propositions. However, without getting additional information it is impossible to say which of these opposed views is going to be the most useful to us in understanding the educational process. This can be done by carrying out some form of investigation in a particular area, or by seeing what other people have found out. Each of the areas in these boxes is considered within this book, and an indication of the key findings is given later in this chapter.

What is educational psychology?

Psychology

Psychological knowledge and the techniques of psychological study can help us understand these problems since *psychology involves the logical investigation of what people think and what they do*. Psychology includes a wide range of topics and can be applied to many different areas such as education, where human thinking and behaviour are important.

Ways of investigating

A key part of psychology involves the scientific technique of developing theories and carrying out investigations to test and modify them. A theory is a way of trying to explain as simply as possible what we know (or think we know) about a particular area. For example, a theory that most people have about class size and achievement is that 'smaller classes are better for children and lead to improved achievements'. Other techniques, described later in this chapter, avoid the initial use of theories, instead allowing them to arise from the investigation itself.

An *experimental investigation* of class size could look at what happens when we change only the particular thing that we are interested in, in this case how many children are being taught together. For instance, we could investigate the effects of class size on achievement by setting up different-sized groups and measuring children's progress with their school work. For us to know that class size was the only thing having an effect, we would have to make sure that other things did not alter.

A good experimental investigation would set up different-sized classes with matched groups of pupils, to cancel out or 'control for' the effects of student ability. This has actually been done in a famous US study described in Chapter 6, called the 'STAR' investigation. This did in fact find that those pupils who were in smaller classes made better academic progress.

There is a lot to be said for directly setting up different educational experiences for children, since the outcomes may then be assumed to be closely related to what was done. However, doing so can be very difficult in practice – the STAR investigation was a massive study and cost $12 million. Interfering with children's education in this way can also be ethically questionable, since children in some of the groups are likely to learn less well. Many educational investigations therefore avoid these problems by using techniques where the investigator uses only information that is already available, or looks at situations which already exist.

Such *non-experimental investigations* are typically based on observational techniques. These can involve an investigator directly, perhaps watching children in a class, or be based on indirect data such as school records. Such approaches can sometimes be quasi-experimental ('quasi' meaning 'as if'), when it is possible to assume that a change in one thing is related to a change in something else. 'Natural experiments' can make this more likely. For instance, if a new form of educational practice (such as the literacy hour) is introduced, we can compare children's educational progress before and after the change.

One very common form of observational investigation – perhaps the least experimental – is to evaluate the extent to which one thing naturally varies along with, or *correlates* with, something else. Such investigations are often easy to carry out and can be fertile ground for developing new ideas or hypotheses about the way things work.

The main difficulty with such non-experimental approaches is that any outcomes might not necessarily be the result of any change in some other particular measure. For instance, if we looked only at existing classes of different sizes, we could be fooled by the fact that many schools use small classes for pupils of below-average ability. We might then conclude that small classes have the effect of reducing attainments!

However, since such investigations do not involve interference or control by an investigator, it can be argued that they are more likely to be valid, in the sense that they are more naturalistic, or show what normally goes on. They can also lend themselves to personal involvement, and possibly more meaningful interpretation, by an investigator. This happens in participant research, where the investigator might for instance become part of a teaching team. Observational approaches also fit well with the use of qualitative information (see below), with an emphasis on the direct experiences and interpretations of those who are involved.

Quantitative and qualitative approaches

A great deal of educational research involves measuring things. Although such *quantitative* approaches allow us to use powerful statistical techniques, they can often have the effect of simplifying and distorting what is really happening, because things have to be put into categories of some kind. Children, teachers and the processes and outcomes of education are much more than just sets of numbers. A good example is early reading skills, which emphasise decoding using sounds and letters. These are very different from more advanced skills, which involve comprehension and the use of context. It could be very misleading to compare different reading levels along a single scale, as though higher attainments were just more of the same thing.

Qualitative approaches attempt to get closer to reality by looking at information that differs in kind rather than in amount. They may involve using more direct and richer information, such as the recording of complete observations, or descriptions by teachers or pupils about what they are doing or how they feel. Mac an Ghaill (1988), for example, used interviews with African Caribbean boys to discover their characteristic ways of explaining and establishing their social identity through exaggerated cultural groupings. This information is close to the way things are, and Glaser and Strauss (1967) argue that it enables researchers to develop a *grounded theory*, one which arises from the information gathered, rather than just depending on modifying existing theories.

In reality, qualitative and quantitative approaches are closely related. Most quantitative research involves qualitative decisions about which variables to study and about what are appropriate techniques to analyse the data. An initial qualitative approach can also develop into a subsequent quantitative analysis; for example, once individuals' responses have been placed into meaningful groupings, these can then be calculated as percentages or analysed for significant differences.

Describing and analysing findings

With quantitative data, psychological and educational research often use *statistics* to describe and analyse what has been found. It is useful to have a basic idea of some key statistical concepts so that you can understand and be critical of how the information from investigations has been interpreted. Appendix 1 explains some of the terms and techniques which are referred to throughout this book.

One of the greatest errors, but a typical one, is to assume that because the results of a statistical test are significant, this automatically means that the results are psychologically or educationally meaningful. If you understand something about the basic ideas of statistics, you are much less likely to be misled about findings which are marginal or misleading.

Qualitative analysis

Qualitative information typically takes the form of direct recordings of events and their meanings, or of people's own descriptions, often referred to as 'narratives'. Interpreting such diverse information can involve selecting key themes and reporting on them by reproducing parts of transcripts. In one example, Walker (1998) carried out an analysis of the functions of secondary school parents' evenings, using parts of her interviews with parents to demonstrate that such meetings were almost invariably perceived as frustrating and distressing.

Qualitative analyses often involve setting up possible categories into which the information can be placed. One advantage of having access to the entire range of original information is that such categories can be modified if alternative groupings subsequently appear to be more meaningful. Although this may make conclusions appear rather fluid and unreliable, they can be confirmed by comparing the views found by different types of investigations ('triangulation'), or by repeating the cycle of gathering and analysing information. In any case, it can be argued that such approaches are more likely to result in findings that have some real meaning for a particular area. As discussed later in this chapter (see 'Shifting paradigms'), any categories that we use can be seen as social constructs and are therefore bound to be somewhat arbitrary.

Applying psychology

'Pure' psychology tries to arrive at general theories that can help us understand basic areas such as learning, memory, motivation, etc. However, practical education is a complex situation in which to apply psychological theories, and there are often many factors which interact or combine to give rise to a number of different effects. For example, Chapter 4 describes some evidence about the way in which academic achievement can be the outcome of the *interaction* between home- and school-based factors, with initial home-based advantages being consolidated by early educational success.

It is therefore always important to evaluate real-life applications of psychological ideas, rather than rely on ideas that are derived purely from the original abstract theories; these are often based on work that was originally far removed from the realities of real-life teaching. Some of the early psychological theories about learning, for instance, were derived largely from studying the responses of rats and pigeons in mazes and cages!

Table 1.1 Five key perspectives in the psychology of education

Perspective	Overview
Psychodynamic	An approach developed in the early twentieth century from the work of Freud. Mainly considers emotional development, and is applied in therapeutic approaches for children with problems (Chapters 10 and 11), and for deriving general educational objectives (e.g. Coren, 1997).
Behavioural	Learning theory, based on observable behaviour and developed by the psychologists Pavlov, Watson and Skinner (see Chapter 2). Although rather less popular these days, it does generate powerful techniques for analysing and modifying behaviours in school.
Humanistic	Emphasises the uniqueness and potential for self-development of individuals. Developed by Maslow (see Chapter 5) to counter the mechanistic perspectives of psychodynamic and behavioural psychology, it underlies child-centred approaches in education.
Psychobiological	Considers that basic biological structures and processes determine higher-level thought and action. A key concept in issues of nature/nurture such as the basis of intelligence (see Chapter 4), and the processes which underlie arousal and motivation (see Chapter 5).
Cognitive	Sees the individual as a processor of information, setting up an internal model of the world and developing plans and strategies to guide ways of interacting with it to achieve goals. *The most recent and productive of all the different approaches*, it can account for many of the findings and ideas in the other perspectives and applies to virtually every topic of educational study.

Source: Medcof and Roth (1979)

Table 1.2 Psychological perspectives and the theories of motivation they generate

Perspective	Motivational theories
Psychodynamic	The id, defence mechanisms (primitive drives and their management to protect conscious awareness)
Behavioural	Operant conditioning (basic learning theory, based on associating a voluntary response with a stimulus)
Humanistic	'Self-actualisation' (development to achieve a person's complete potential)
Psychobiological	Arousal and stress (levels of activation involving interactions between the mind and body and biochemical changes)
Cognitive	Attribution theory (the way in which people attempt to understand the causes for things happening)

Differing perspectives

Applying psychology to education also often involves viewing areas from a number of different psychological perspectives. Medcof and Roth (1979) consider that there are five such key approaches (Table 1.1), based upon very different beliefs and ways of analysing information.

Applying these perspectives to educational topics can generate alternative ways of approaching problems. Each of the perspectives generates a very different way of understanding the motivation for children to do things in school (Table 1.2), as we shall see in Chapter 5.

The various approaches are often complementary. For instance, achieving optimum arousal levels by using a dynamic teaching style will facilitate general involvement with learning tasks. When pupils are more alert, they are then also more likely to respond to other strategies which will focus them on their work, such as the use of praise in operant conditioning (associating a voluntary response with a stimulus).

On the other hand, some perspectives can give rise to contradictory approaches. Behaviourism, for instance, can appear rather simplistic and may encourage an approach based on rote learning. Cognitive approaches, however, emphasise the use of meaning and understanding, and seem closer to what we personally experience in learning situations. Despite this, behavioural approaches can still be very useful in analysing and managing problem behaviours, as will be described in Chapters 10 and 11. Recent developments to be reviewed in Chapter 2 consider that behavioural conditioning is the result of developing expectancies about what will happen in certain situations, and that behaviourism can therefore be seen as a particular subset of cognitive processes.

Developmental psychology

Psychology also tries to account for the ways in which children establish basic abilities such as thinking and language use. General *developmental theories* which cover these can be applied to education to help us understand learning situations. This can be seen in Chapter 2, which considers the role of theories of cognitive development such as Piaget's approach, and Chapter 8, which looks at the way in which language abilities are developed. Other areas, such as the development of social roles and identity, in Chapter 7, and the establishment of basic academic attainments such as reading, in Chapter 9, also depend to some extent on progress with other, underlying skills and abilities.

The importance of theory

There is a famous remark by Allport (1947) that the aims of science are 'understanding, prediction and control, above the levels achieved by unaided common sense'. This perspective is very useful in guiding psychological investigations, and emphasises that we should be able to use theoretical knowledge to help us with applied areas and to go beyond everyday experience and understanding.

Developments in education often lack this theoretical foundation and are frequently inspired by social processes or ideological beliefs, a fact can lead to cycles of change as the general social climate alters. For instance, in the 1940s it was commonly believed that the most efficient way of educating children was to select them for different types of schooling using the 'eleven-plus' and also to 'stream' them into different general ability groups. A later ideological emphasis on equality of opportunity subsequently led to the development of comprehensive schools and mixed-ability teaching. However, there are now signs that there is a shift backwards in this perspective, with many schools reverting to increased selection and ability grouping of pupils, even at the primary level.

A psychological perspective could help us to limit such swings of fashion by providing theories and knowledge about the realistic advantages and disadvantages of such developments. For instance, it has been shown that selection of pupils on the basis of the eleven-plus (an intelligence test) is not a very accurate or useful process. Research also indicates that streaming of children into different ability groups within schools leads to only limited improvements with the higher groups. It can also lead to pupils in lower groups receiving inferior education, partly because of teacher expectations, and the negative social groupings that can happen in such classes.

Shifting paradigms

Paradigms are general ways of looking at or understanding an area. Although it can often seem that there is only one way to understand a particular domain of knowledge, writers such as Kuhn (1962) have emphasised that paradigms often change radically over time. In the particular fields of psychology and education, earlier paradigms of learning saw the child as relatively passive, simply absorbing information transmitted by a didactic teacher. These perspectives fitted well with the then current stress on principles of conditioning, which took a very mechanistic approach to the managing of learning. According to this, the emphasis for the teacher was to deliver a standard curriculum and to evaluate stable underlying differences between children.

The most popular general paradigm at present is undoubtedly the cognitive one. This emphasises that the developing child in school is active in constructing new knowledge, skills and ways of understanding. This perspective is largely derived from the original ideas of Piaget, although there have been many substantial revisions of his approach. In particular, writers such as Wood (1998) have emphasised the social nature of this learning process, with knowledge developing as a ' "joint construction" of understanding by the child and more expert members of his (or her) culture' (p. 17). The role of the teacher can be seen as that of a facilitator of learning, by generating appropriate experiences and closely monitoring a child's changing attainments and needs.

However, a number of alternative perspectives now question the fundamental underlying premises of psychological and educational knowledge. Based on postmodernistic ideas, they propose that the classical scientific ('modernistic') approach of logical investigation using evidence, often referred to as 'positivism', is deeply flawed and outdated. The rationale for this is based on arguments generated by philosophers such as Foucault (1978) that knowledge and understanding are essentially arbitrary and socially constructed. From this perspective, scientific concepts such as 'intelligence' can be seen as functioning to legitimise the status and power of psychology within society. Language concepts and the ways in which they are used (referred to as 'discourses') also demonstrate the way in which such processes operate. For example, an investigation by Davies (1989) describes the characteristic linguistic images and metaphors in fairy stories, for example with knights rescuing damsels in distress. Davies argues that it is through such experiences that young children learn the key, socially defined constructs about what it is to be male or female in society.

The conventional social role of researchers in relation to those being studied (often referred to as 'subjects') can be seen as part of the general domination of classical scientific investigation. It is argued that the balance can be redressed by placing an emphasis on the natural experiences and reports of participants in the educational process. Such 'narratives' are of course close to the approaches of grounded theory and share their naturalistic validity.

A further perspective is that the study of education has inherent difficulties, since education takes place in a highly complex social system. Such structures may be chaotic, with processes and outcomes that are unpredictable and therefore unknowable. However, although this may be true of large-scale, open-ended systems, the educational process is arguably relatively limited and prescribed. Although single cause–effect relationships are unlikely to be meaningful, it is still possible that more complex explanations will enable us to generate useful advice. For instance, the evidence from class size effects indicates that an effective model should take account of variables such as the age range covered and school effects, as well as the type of teaching that is going on.

Some critiques can also appear rather nihilistic, undermining any attempt to arrive at explanations or prescriptions. In a review of developmental psychology, Morss (1996) argues that the very process of considering development is meaningless, and that by doing so we impose expectations and control. Despite this, it can be argued that *within* a given system, however ultimately arbitrary it may be, we can still arrive at knowledge and understanding that is useful for us. What postmodernism does in a more positive way, though, is to caution us as to the relatively local and specific nature of knowledge. Part of this is understanding that what might work in one situation may not transfer readily to others. It also guides us towards an emphasis on the direct experiences and interpretations of those most closely involved in the process of education itself.

With their emphasis on cultural determinants of knowledge and identity, these approaches are confirmed by and also have a particular relevance to issues in feminist and ethnic minority studies, and socio-economic perspectives of class. Given some caveats, a great deal of research can therefore still guide and inform debates and planning in education. As I hope that parts of this book show, it can also often lead us to reconsider the meaning and utility of some concepts and beliefs which are the foundations of educational thought.

The evidence from psychology

When psychology is applied to a number of different areas in education, it has the potential to help us to understand what is happening, and to make more logical, informed decisions about the best way to organise the educational process. Quite often, however, the findings of research or the applications of psychological theories do not give a simple answer, but qualify and extend the original debate. When the findings of educational psychology are applied to the issues that were identified at the start of the chapter, for instance, the findings summarised in this book appear to show the following.

Formal versus progressive teaching
Research indicates that these types of teaching do not lead to significant differences in attainments. Other, underlying features such as classroom organisation or the learing process encouraged seem to be much more important (Chapter 6).

Class sizes
Controlled experimental investigations have shown that reducing class sizes *does* improve attainments, but that the effect of doing so is rather limited within the realistic range of possible class sizes. Other factors such as altering the teaching approach used may have a much greater effect (Chapter 6).

Punishment
Punishment can be shown to have many negative effects such as failing to teach appropriate behaviours and leading children to regress. However, it can sometimes be justified in the context of a positive, secure relationship and when children know what it is that they should do (Chapter 11).

Dyslexia
Generally speaking, attempts to identify dyslexia as a specific form of relative underachievement have not been successful. Children whose literacy skills are significantly below their general verbal abilities may need support, but effective teaching seems to be the same for all children (Chapter 9).

Language development
Children who have difficulties with language can be helped, but simply correcting errors is likely to reverse their progress. Language mainly develops from an intent to communicate; because of this, one of the most effective approaches seems to be for adults to interact with children in an intensive but natural way and to respond mainly to the meaning behind what they say (Chapter 8).

Teacher effectiveness
Individual teachers probably do differ in their effectiveness but the differences are surprisingly small, being greatest for younger children and relatively specific to particular academic subjects. The variations in achievement due to home background appear to be much larger, and generally overwhelm any other processes (Chapter 6).

It might seem from this that using psychology and educational research is generally a good thing and that all that is needed is to go ahead and apply the approaches described here as much as possible in education.

On the other hand, there are arguments from writers such as McIntyre and Brown (1978) that psychology is *not* relevant, and that education should be based mainly on subject knowledge and expertise that is specific to the educational process. In a similar way, Schon (1983) has also argued persuasively that teachers primarily need to become 'reflective practitioners' and base their teaching largely on their own experiences and personal interpretations. These approaches have a certain 'no-nonsense' attraction and avoid what can sometimes seem to be domination and over-complication by psychological perspectives. When academic psychologists isolate an area within education for study, their lack of general knowledge of the field can also lead them to make incorrect assumptions about the validity of certain concepts. Stanovich (1994), for instance, argues that many psychologists concerned with 'dyslexia' have merely investigated its causes without questioning whether it means anything in the first place.

One answer to such criticisms is that *not* using general psychology and psychological techniques is likely to lead to even greater problems, since people will then apply their own crude theories which can only be based on, and limited by, their own experiences and ideas. Despite this, it is probably a good idea to have some healthy scepticism when applying psychology and to ensure that we 'ground' ourselves in a general appreciation of the real issues and processes of education.

Summary

Many commonly held ideas and beliefs about education are the result of limited knowledge or ideological perspectives. These can lead to fruitless arguments which can only be resolved by looking for direct evidence or other forms of relevant knowledge.

Psychology can help with the search for evidence because it involves the use of logical investigations, and theories about what people think and what they do. These can be based on the use of direct experiments, which look for effects when something is changed, as well as observation and interpretations of naturally occurring processes.

Statistics helps us to make sense of what we find in such investigations by describing and analysing numerical information. It enables us to look for differences and relationships between sets of data and to see whether they can support our theories. Observational information too can be analysed to look for meaningful relationships and trends.

Psychology includes a number of different approaches which can help us to understand what happens in education. These have changed over time, from early behavioural perspectives, to modern beliefs which emphasise that children actively construct their knowledge within a social context. When psychological understanding is applied to areas of real-life educational debate, it can help us to decide between opposing plausible explanations or to change the way in which we view those areas.

Key implications

- We cannot simply trust in common sense when making decisions about education.
- Psychology is useful in this since it is based on logical approaches using evidence.
- It is best to use a range of perspectives when considering particular areas of education.
- These can be guided by contemporary critiques which emphasise the local and constructed nature of knowledge.

Further reading

Rita Atkinson, Richard Atkinson, Edward Smith, Daryl Bem and Susan Hoeksema (1996) *Hilgard's Introduction to Psychology*. New York: Harcourt Brace.

This is a really good introduction to general psychology. It is readable and interesting, although somewhat biased towards US research and culture.

Louis Cohen, Lawrence Manion and Keith Morrison (2000) *Research Methods in Education*, 5th edition, London: RoutledgeFalmer.

This updated text covers the range of ways of carrying out studies and analysing findings. It uses lots of examples and would enable you to become an informed 'consumer of research', as well as design and implement your own investigations if you wished to.

Practical scenario

Mrs Smith has been recently appointed as the headteacher of Anytown Junior School. This has a solid middle-class intake and has done well in its Ofsted (Office for Standards in Education) inspections and with recent Standard Assessment Tests and Tasks (SATs) scores. However, she is concerned that the curriculum has become rather narrow, and is keen to foster children's wider educational and social development. Although Mrs Smith has support from most of the staff in this, the governors and many parents have very traditional views of education. They mainly want an emphasis on skill achievements, with a curriculum-centred and didactic approach to teaching.

- *How could Mrs Smith try to convince them that there are other ways of approaching education? Would academic or practical examples be more persuasive?*
- *Do you think it would be effective for her to suggest some form of action-based research in the school? How could this be set up?*
- *What would constitute proof that one approach is better than another?*
- *Who sets the agenda for educational targets and strategies? Is rational evidence part of this?*

2 Learning

Basic principles of learning

Importance of learning

Learning has a central role in education, as the whole of this book makes clear, in one way or another. In England and Wales the National Curriculum now defines the content of *what* is taught, and the teaching of literacy and of numeracy in particular are somewhat prescribed, but most of the process of *how* teaching happens is still largely left up to the individual teacher. Even with this, however, there are signs of increasing direction, with the implementation of the Green Paper proposals (DfEE, 1998f) which introduce evaluation for performance-related pay and professional development. Psychological research about what goes on during learning has established a number of different findings which have important practical implications for teaching, and some of the key aspects of these will be described in this chapter.

What is learning?

Psychologists such as Kimble (1961) have defined learning in general as *an experience which produces a relatively permanent change in behaviour, or potential behaviour*. The definition therefore excludes changes which are simply due to maturation in the form of biological growth or development, or temporary changes due to fatigue or the effects of drugs.

As Howe (1980) has pointed out, learning has the important function of enabling us to benefit from experience. It enables us to build up a progressively more sophisticated internal model or representation of our environment, and then to operate on this, rather than on the world itself. Because of this we are able to think about things, to develop strategies, and use abstract concepts such as causation when we ask ourselves what makes things happen. These abilities enable us to predict and therefore to control events which are of importance for us, giving humans an enormous evolutionary advantage over other animals.

Figure 2.1 Relative brain sizes of humans and chimpanzees

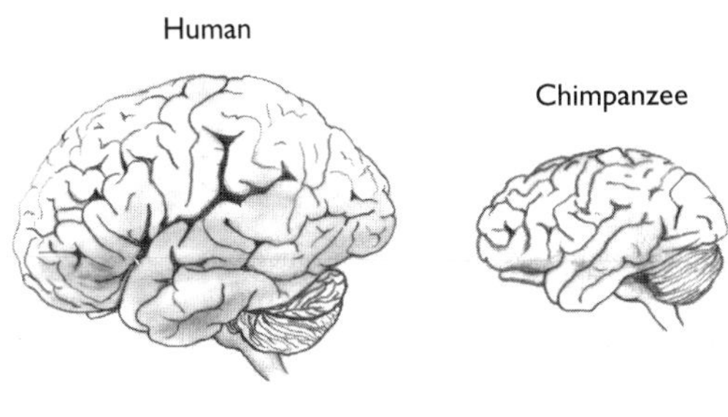

The human brain is extremely complex, with many billions of nerve cells and probably quadrillions of interconnections between them. The way in which these operate must be largely developed by experience since inheritance through our genes could encode only a tiny fraction of this number. As shown in Figure 2.1, when the human brain is compared with the brain of our nearest animal relative, the chimpanzee, the most striking differences are in terms of the overall size of the human brain and its large folded outer layer, known as the cortex. This is mostly involved with complex processes of making links between different forms of information. The more basic underlying brain structures which control the behaviour of animals are concerned with emotions and instincts.

Although we do not completely understand the biological basis of learning, our mental abilities must ultimately be based on the structure and functions of the human brain, which evidently has a huge capacity for storing and using information. A recent approach to understanding learning (considered later in this chapter) is based on systems which have similarities to the vast parallel processing capacity of the central nervous system. Implemented as 'neural networks' with computer hardware or software, these show properties such as probabilistic 'learning' and 'forgetting', as well as the derivation of complex rules which are tantalisingly similar to many of the features of natural learning.

Categories of learning

'Learning' is a relatively broad concept, and in education it can happen in many different ways, with a number of different outcomes. As Howe (1984, p. 8) describes, these include formal attainments such as new verbal concepts and early academic skills, but can also involve children developing new skills involving independence and self-help, or ways to behave and interact with other people.

In an attempt to simplify this wide range of diversity, Bloom (1956) established a well-known taxonomy of learning objectives, covering the three major domains of *cognitive*, *affective* and *psychomotor* development. (Cognitive development is concerned with memory, perception, pattern recognition and language use; affective development relates to the emotions; and psychomotor development relates to movement or muscular activity associated with mental processes.) Schools have an effect on all these, but the formal curriculum focuses on the cognitive domain, which Bloom subdivided into *knowledge*, *comprehension*, *application*, *analysis*, *synthesis* and *evaluation*. Although this has been the most popular way of categorising learning, there have been other, more recent schemes such as Gagné *et al.*'s (1988) approach, which uses the areas of intellectual skills, cognitive strategies, verbal information, attitudes and motor skills. There is evidently some overlap between these approaches, but the categories which are used in such schemes must be largely arbitrary and there does not seem to be any absolute reason why one particular approach should be preferred over another.

In practice, using the full range of such category systems can also be somewhat unwieldy and teachers will probably not be able to take them all into account when covering curriculum targets. A common approach is to simplify these using three headings, usually retaining 'knowledge', and forming two levels from the remaining categories. These often combine together Bloom's categories of 'comprehension' and 'application', and with a further heading which includes problem solving and the ability to use and transfer learning to new situations. This is similar to schemes used by the Department for Education and Employment (DfEE) and many exam syllabuses, which involve:

- knowledge (recall or recognition of specific information);
- skills (the ability to carry out meaningful, integrated tasks such as reading); and
- understanding (problem solving and the use and transfer of knowledge).

Again, however, it should be remembered that these distinctions are essentially arbitrary and that there is considerable overlap and difference in the use of many of these terms. Although 'knowledge', for instance, is often thought of as facts which can be memorised, learning of concepts depends to a great extent on understanding their meaning; in practice it is also difficult to separate out 'understanding' and the 'skills' which are involved in this. However, research and theories about the functions of memory discussed later in this chapter give some support for a meaningful distinction between 'knowledge' and 'skills' and also make the links between them more explicit.

Theories of learning

Types of learning

Psychologists have attempted to derive general principles of learning which apply to a range of tasks and situations. Simpler forms of learning include *habituation* and the two forms of conditioning, *classical* and *operant conditioning*. These emphasise behaviours and the situations in which they happen, and in their original form expressly ignore any mentalistic explanations based on thought processes.

Cognitive approaches, however, include more complex types of learning, and involve various forms of internal representation of information, and operations on these. The study of *memory* is important since it is the storage–retrieval element of learning. Cognitive approaches are applied in theories of *cognitive development* which look at qualitative changes in children's abilities.

Habituation

Habituation involves learning to ignore a stimulus (something happening) which has no importance. For instance, pupils might simply habituate to a teacher who keeps nagging them about homework if the teacher never takes any further action. This means that they will eventually learn to ignore what the teacher does in the future.

Habituation is a process that goes on all the time and is associated with attention and concentration. If we were unable to ignore most of the background features in our environment, we would not be able to focus on important tasks or events. Some children appear to have particular problems 'tuning out' unnecessary information and can have significant attention deficits and learning difficulties. Helping them may involve programmes to develop their ability to remain oriented to a specific task (see Chapter 11). Sometimes faulty or inappropriate learning means that we attend to features that are not meaningful. This happens when children develop a phobia or an irrational anxiety about something to do with school. Helping a child with such problems may therefore mean habituating or 'desensitising' them to the general school environment. However, although habituation is important, most school learning that is under the control of the teacher involves more complex and active processes.

Conditioning

Two other important forms of basic learning are called conditioning. Both of these involve forming associations between stimuli and responses. (Responses are what people do as a result of a stimulus.) These were once believed to underlie all types of learning, but, as discussed below, they are nowadays seen as specific forms which are part of a general cognitive approach. Conditioning does have a particular relevance to emotional and behavioural difficulties, owing to the structure which it gives to behaviour management approaches.

CLASSICAL CONDITIONING

In classical conditioning, an association is formed between a stimulus and an involuntary response – something that one does not have direct control over, such as heart rate. This is based on the original work by Pavlov (1927), who discovered that dogs would learn to salivate at a signal, such as a bell, which indicated that some food was about to arrive. Watson (1925) extended these ideas to humans, arguing that psychologists should confine their explanations solely to such observed behaviour – a perspective known as *behaviourism*. In a famous experiment on a little boy called Albert, Watson paired a frightening loud noise with the appearance of a white rat (which Albert did not originally fear). Albert eventually became very anxious whenever the rat appeared and had become classically conditioned to show a fear response to the stimulus of the rat.

An example of school-based classical conditioning would be a pupil's having become anxious when at school, possibly as a result of a stressful experience such as bullying. As shown in Figure 2.2, he or she might then come to associate the involuntary reactions involved in anxiety (dry mouth, racing heart, upset stomach, etc.) with the stimulus of school attendance. If the symptoms were severe enough, the case would be one of school phobia.

The original theories of classical conditioning thought of it as merely a strengthening of the mental association between the stimulus and the response. Recent cognitive theories, however, emphasise that what we are learning is to *predict* what follows the stimulus; for example, that the experience of school will follow being told to get ready for school in the morning. This *expectancy* (thinking of attending school and the things that are feared about it) appears to be what triggers off the involuntary response (of anxiety).

Involuntary responses are certainly an important part of the way in which we relate to our environment. Again, however, most school learning involves more active participation by the learner, which can be controlled and directed by the teacher.

Figure 2.2 Classical conditioning of school phobia

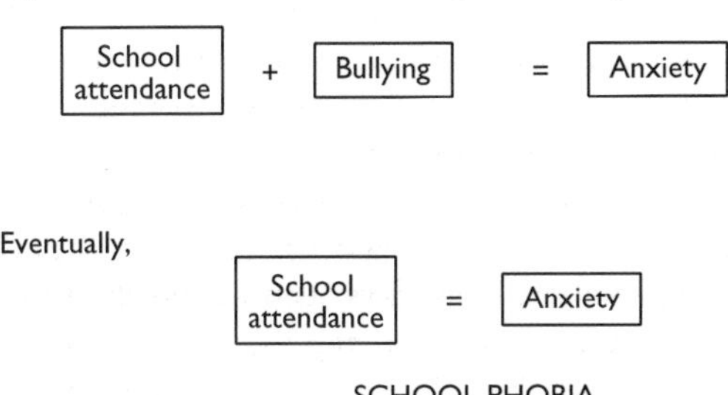

OPERANT CONDITIONING

Operant conditioning is a more important form of associative learning and involves voluntary responses. These are under conscious control and could involve a pupil working on a learning task, or alternatively a non-work activity such as calling out to his or her friends.

Skinner (1938) said that the concepts and principles involved in such learning apply when an individual acts (operates) on his or her environment to achieve a desired outcome. Three key aspects of a situation are important in such learning:

the **antecedents** (what happens before an incident)	→	the **behaviour** (what the child actually does)	→	and the **consequences** (what the results are for the child)

An example of this would be a child working in class to get praise from the teacher:

interesting work set → **pupils get on with work** → **praise from teacher**

Consequences like this, which strengthen (reinforce) the association between the situation and a response, are called *reinforcers*. An outcome which weakens the association is called a *punisher* and is typically something that is aversive (unpleasant to the individual). An example would be if a pupil was reprimanded for not doing his or her work.

Positive reinforcers strengthen the association

Figure 2.3 Effects of different behavioural consequences

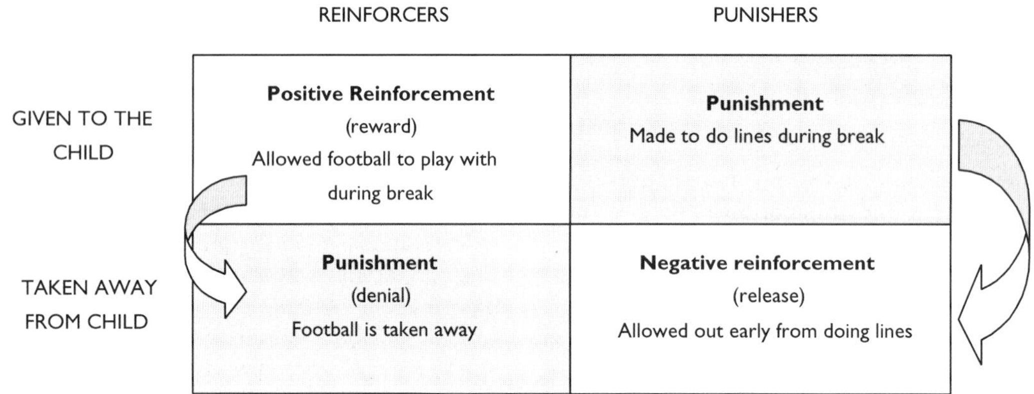

and are called *rewards*. For example, receiving praise for doing well in a test might encourage future studying. Negative reinforcers occur when something aversive is stopped, and these also strengthen an association. An example of a negative reinforcer would be making children pick up the litter around school, and then allowing them to stop doing so if their behaviour at other times has improved. As shown in Figure 2.3, giving or taking away such outcomes produces a situation which is either positively or negatively motivating for pupils.

Punishments Although the four categories shown in Figure 2.3 appear to be equally likely to be effective, there are practical reasons why both types of *punishment* are generally considered to be less desirable.

- They do not emphasise new, positive behaviours, and children might simply learn to avoid getting caught. Moreover, punishment has also been shown to lead to regression: if a pupil's present behaviour no longer succeeds in getting what the pupil wants, then he or she may return to earlier forms of behaviour. These may previously have been effective for the pupil but could nevertheless be undesirable in class.
- The person who administers the punishment also comes to be seen in a negative way. Although this means that children will be anxious and cautious about that person in the future, it also means that he or she is unlikely to generate any spontaneous co-operative behaviour; the child will just not like the teacher very much. Children who are reprimanded by teachers in front of the class are very unlikely to want to cooperate with them in the future, although they may be careful to avoid a repeat of the punishment. They may do so in a number of negative ways such as blaming others.
- Punishment also acts as a negative social model for children. Clegg and Megson (1968), for instance, found that schools which used physical punishment at that time to control pupils had much higher levels of fights and physical aggression in the playground. The use of negative control by authority figures is likely to set this up as a legitimate process for pupils as well as staff.

Rewards Positive reinforcements (rewards) can be a very powerful way of managing children's behaviour. They avoid most of the problems with punishments, since their use involves an emphasis on developing new and positive work habits; they establish a pleasant relationship between the teacher and the pupil; and they give positive social roles for pupils. In some situations, however, positive reinforcements may seem inappropriate and can appear to be rather like 'bribing a child to work', with the danger that the child rather than the teacher comes to be in control. This means that pupils can then use the situation to threaten non-cooperation to get what they want.

Also, it often seems wrong to reward a child who is on a programme because of his or her lack of effort. Other children may find it unjust if a difficult child gets extra treats and privileges, whereas they are 'behaving themselves' normally and get nothing. Ways of managing this might involve ensuring that all children are rewarded for positive behaviours, and by the use of negative reinforcement, where the reward is simply what the other children in the class are already getting for normal behaviour.

Learning principles Skinner established various principles for generating effective learning by the appropriate use of outcomes which are contingent on some form of behaviour. A key principle is that reinforcements or punishers appear to be most effective when they happen soon after the behaviour. According to this, waiting until the end of the lesson to praise students' work or to reprimand them should not be as effective as praise given just after they have completed a particular section, or verbal comments immediately after the problem behaviour.

Outcomes can also vary in frequency and timing. A very frequent, predictable reward is initially good at training for certain responses. A problem, however, is that such responses are very dependent on the reinforcer: if a pupil is working merely for frequent teacher praise and the praise suddenly stops, then the pupil will probably also stop working. If rewards are less frequent and less predictable, pupils will be more likely to continue their responses when rewards are stopped. Presumably they are less aware when rewards are finally phased out, and, one may hope, they may then develop intrinsic motivation (involvement for its own sake).

When working with a new class or a difficult child, teachers should therefore use a high level of meaningful rewards, alongside firm control. This would be aimed at establishing involvement with class tasks and routines, and at developing positive perceptions of the teacher. After a while, however, the rewards should become more intermittent and attention focused on the performance of tasks and pupils' achievements.

Uses of operant conditioning in school learning As will be described in Chapter 11, operant conditioning can be applied in the form of 'behaviour modification' to manage problem classroom behaviour and increase work involvement. However, Skinner (1954) considered that it could also be effectively used to directly alter academic progress by a process he called *programmed learning.*

At first, as shown in Figure 2.4, this often involved children initially being given some information. They were then tested on some part of the information they had been given, and a correct response was rewarded in some way (typically with praise); an incorrect response would lead to their being given either a repeat of the original information, or an alternative (simpler) presentation. Programmed learning was often implemented in expensive 'teaching machines' which presented the materials in the appropriate sequence.

The advantages claimed for such early programmed learning systems were that they

Figure 2.4 Programmed learning sequence

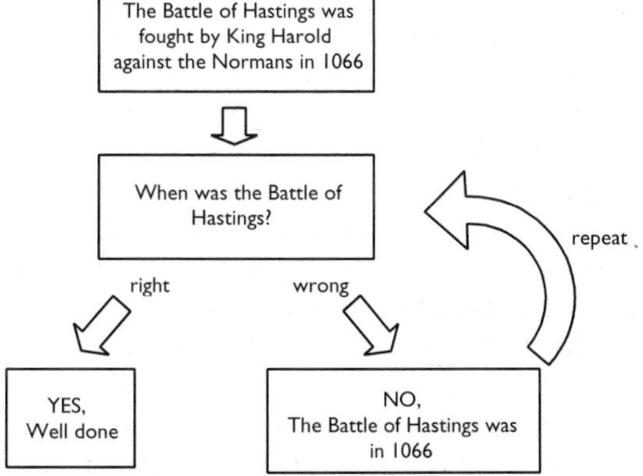

emphasised success, that the learning was sequential and structured, and that the learning was closely matched to the individual learner's pace. Unfortunately, an approach of this type is difficult to develop properly, owing to the detail involved in the programme design. Also, students often found the experience of working on such machines socially isolating and rather boring. Despite this, a review of research findings by Jamison *et al.* (1974) found that programmed learning achieved results faster than conventional, class-based learning. In a sense, such early approaches can be seen as the basis of more recent computer-based learning systems, although these are becoming increasingly based on sophisticated models of the learner's knowledge base and approach to learning.

The principles of operant conditioning have also been implemented in the *direct instruction* model of teaching, the best known of which is the DISTAR (Direct Instructional Systems for Teaching And Remediation) programme. Applied largely to basic skills work in literacy and numeracy, this approach carefully directs the teaching process by using a script for the teacher, and also specifically incorporates the use of reinforcement – mainly as verbal praise. Although DISTAR can appear over-prescriptive and possibly rather limiting, an evaluation by Kennedy (1978) found it to be the most effective of a wide range of remedial teaching techniques used at the time.

The use of operant conditioning to motivate children's work at school has been strongly criticised by Lepper and Greene (1978) as being likely to damage natural, intrinsic motivation. They argue that children have a natural curiosity and desire to find out about things; however if they perceive themselves as working only for rewards, their work becomes superficial and geared solely towards the reward, rather than for the sake of learning. Constant insistence on praising pupils can also sometimes be very disruptive to the flow of work when pupils are getting on well. The principles of intrinsic motivation imply that a better approach would be for teachers to give attention by taking an interest in the content of what pupils are doing and through this to lead them into further activities.

Skinner believed that operant conditioning ruled out mentalistic explanations based on thought processes and preferred to limit himself to describing the conditions under which learning occurred. However, it seems that individuals who have been operantly conditioned have in fact learned to *predict* what will happen in a given situation if they engage in certain behaviour, much as in classical conditioning. This learning process is a cognitive one, and Bandura *et al.* (1963) demonstrated that observational learning (which is the basis of social learning theory) depends on predictions and expectations about the consequences of behaviour, rather than direct associations. Whether or not children engaged in a particular behaviour depended on what outcomes (praise or a reprimand) they observed for other people and consequently expected for themselves.

Despite this, conditioning can still be an effective way to describe and understand basic learning situations where there is a direct and predictable link between behaviour and consequences. In many situations, however, behaviour involves more than a simple response, and can comprise a sequence of flexible and skilled activities. Such *complex learning* can be explained in behaviourism by the linking together of a number of conditioned responses, called 'chaining'. According to this view, pupils might therefore learn to enter a classroom, get out their books and start a particular activity, as a sequence which will gain the approval of their teacher.

However, early research on learning situations by Tolman (1932) demonstrated that rather than simple links, individuals often learn sophisticated internal representations, which do not show up in their immediate actions but can be used to generate different behaviours when situations alter. Tolman's original investigations were with rats, which were made to run through a maze to reach a goal of some food. When the maze was subsequently altered, they were able to take short cuts without further learning, showing that they had learned an overall 'plan' or an internal visual representation of the maze, rather than just routes.

Humans appear to do much the same thing. When first exposed to a new situation they may merely link together simple learning experiences, a process that conditioning can explain quite well. In contrast, later learning involves an overall perspective and the ability to relate parts together to derive new ways of seeing things. This approach emphasises that learning is a more active process than conditioning implies and is determined by a range of underlying mental representations and abilities.

Cognitive processes and learning

The cognitive approach in psychology sees the individual as a processor of information, in much the same way that a computer takes in information and follows a program to produce an output. But humans are much more complex and self-directing than present-day computers, and are able to develop plans and strategies to guide ways of interacting with their environment. To do this, humans also generate and test out internal models of the world, which can act as a guide for future behaviour.

Mental representations and the basis of knowledge

Such cognitive processes involve developing mental representations of events, things or ideas which can act as the basis for thought. Some of these take the form of direct experiences, such as sensations and physical movements, or visual representations which involve imagery. As discussed later in this chapter, these are particularly important at early developmental stages, or with initial learning in a new area of knowledge. 'Higher' levels of thought which develop as children become older are based on symbolic representations such as words, which stand for something else without necessarily having any direct similarity to it. Words can therefore represent concrete and abstract categories and can also express relationships between other symbolic representations.

All these categories and relationships typically take the form of *concepts*, which involve groupings of items that include the same key features or attributes. A conceptual grouping can involve living things, such as 'dogs', which share the attributes of 'four legs, barks, chases cats, can bite', and actions such as 'running', which share the attributes of 'moving fast, all legs off ground at same time'. The use of concepts is a powerful and necessary way of achieving cognitive economy and means that we do not become overloaded by the mass of information which we experience. Concepts also enable us to deal with the world rapidly and to infer attributes that we do not directly observe – in Bruner's (1957) phrase, to go 'beyond the information given'. When we meet an animal that we classify as a 'dog', we are then aware that it can bite, and will be able to treat it accordingly.

Propositions involve links or relationships between concepts. They are the smallest unit of information which can be judged either true or false, for example that 'the dog is running' (either it is or it isn't). Such propositions can make up or be assembled into *facts*, which incorporate information that is generally believed to be valid, for example that 'Hydrogen is a flammable gas', or that 'King Henry VIII had six wives'. This last fact incorporates a number of propositions: that Henry was a king, that he was the eighth king called Henry, as well as that he had six wives.

Knowledge is made up from a body of such propositions and the further relationships between them, which constitute the subject matter of domains of academic study. Propositions can also form the basis for thinking and reasoning, enabling people to make logical inferences by a process of deriving new propositional relationships.

Mental processes can be represented by 'connectionist' models, with 'learning' happening through changes in the strengths of the links between low-level units. Since these models (to be described later in this chapter) are based on the general way in which the brain is believed to function, it seems possible that similar mechanisms may represent the underlying basis of concept formation. It has also been argued that some form of 'spreading activation' links together areas in the brain and that associating concepts and propositions in this way is the basis of thought.

Such concept-based, factual information is often referred to as *declarative knowledge*, and can be contrasted with *procedural knowledge*, which refers to information about how we can do things. Procedural knowledge covers skills such as reading and writing, or fluent calculations in mathematics. Procedural memories appear to be represented as 'condition–action' rules, which are referred to as *productions*. These specify what to do under certain conditions, and involve the form of 'IF X, THEN Y'. As an example of this, most experienced teachers implicitly use the rule 'IF a student is starting to misbehave, THEN move closer to them'. A large number of such rules linked together must underlie skilled or expert behaviour.

Procedural knowledge often starts off as declarative knowledge but with practice becomes more automated, meaning that we become less conscious of the processes involved in what we are doing. When children first learn to form letters, for instance, they often learn a verbal description and rehearsal of the appropriate movements: writing an '*a*' involving the three movement sequences of 'round, up and down'. Fluent writing, however, is a relatively automatic skill, and mature writers are usually aware only of the content of what they are writing. Experienced teachers similarly would probably find it difficult to describe the many skilled elements involved in monitoring and controlling a class, which they normally achieve at the same time as organising and delivering curriculum content. Once established, such procedural knowledge is much less likely to be forgotten than declarative knowledge and, like the ability to ride a bike, skills can often be retained for years with little if any deterioration even if they are not practised.

Memory

Memory is the storage component of learning such forms of information. A great deal of education is concerned with ways of ensuring that information is input to memory (registered), for it to be subsequently reproduced or used (retrieved). The process can go wrong at any of these stages since information can fail to register or be initially processed, or there can be a failure to retrieve information (which is then available somewhere, but is not accessible). The study of memory is important to education since its models allow us to understand the processes of such losses of information, normally referred to as 'forgetting'. If we understand how forgetting occurs, we may be able to devise techniques to prevent it and to optimise learning and memory.

Short-term memory

The most popular model of memory has been the multi-store approach of Atkinson and Shiffrin (1971). In this, *short-term memory* (STM) is regarded as an initial store which has a short length of time for storage (a few seconds only) and a limited capacity, which is typically about seven 'chunks' or units of information. These are often items which can be verbally encoded, such as words, letters or numbers, and the classic test of STM involves listening to and repeating back sequences of random numbers of increasing length. Information in STM can be 'rehearsed' by a process of repeating items over, as people often do with telephone numbers while they are dialling them. With further processing or encoding, information can be transferred for further storage in *long-term memory* (LTM; see below), and can also be retrieved from it, as shown in Figure 2.5.

Because of the active nature of the short-term store, Baddeley (1986) has described it as *working memory*. This appears to have a number of processing and modality-specific components which include visual and spatial as well as auditory information. Working memory constitutes material which is being actively processed in some way, for instance the activity of carrying out the sum

Figure 2.5 The structure of memory

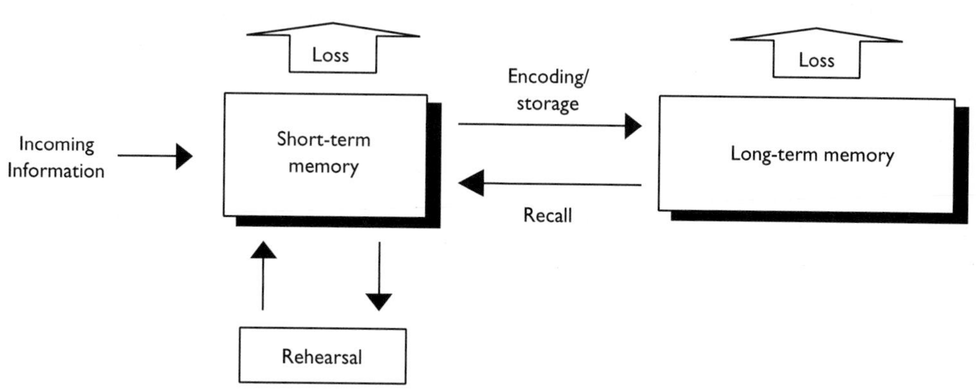

'23 × 6' in your head. Doing this can involve either visualising the outcome of successive calculations, or verbally rehearsing them. It is just about possible to do this at the same time as another task which is fluent and automatic such as reading out loud. However, anything which uses the same modality, such as counting back from a hundred in threes, produces complete interference.

Since what happens at this stage determines whether information is subsequently retained, it can be an important part of the development of general, integrated skills. Research by Byrne (1981), for instance, has shown that poor readers often appear to have a restricted STM, although there is some debate about whether this is a cause or an effect of reading difficulties. As discussed later in this chapter, one plausible argument is that apparent variations in the size of short-term memory are due to the efficiency or expertise with which we are able to encode items. When items are unfamiliar we can cope with only a few at a time and are easily overloaded. Early readers, for instance, are usually not very fluent with letter sounds and have difficulty processing many of these at the same time. When items are dealt with more automatically, then there is often only a very limited impact on capacity. For example, driving a car is normally a fluent, well-rehearsed task and can be done safely while carrying on a conversation.

Long-term memory

Short-term or working memory usually lasts only a few seconds and is in many ways closer to thinking. Long-term memory is the main way in which we store information, and it lasts over hours, weeks and years. It is this that most people usually think about when they refer to memory and forgetting. The main characteristics of LTM are:

- very large capacity (typically more than 40,000 words plus associated facts);
- very long duration (up to a lifetime);
- mainly semantic coding (by meaning);
- loss (forgetting) mainly by interference.

Most theories about the nature of representations in long-term memory see it as a system of associated concepts. Collins and Quillian (1969) originally proposed a hierarchy, with high-level concepts and features branching to lower-level subordinate concepts and features. Attributes high up in the structure would generally cover all lower concepts, so 'breathes air' would apply to all animals, and 'able to fly' would apply to all birds. Subordinate categories, however, need specific information which can either add to or modify the structure. For example, as Figure 2.6 shows, a robin has a red breast and a penguin cannot fly. Such structures have the advantage of cognitive economy since particular attributes

Figure 2.6 Concept hierarchy

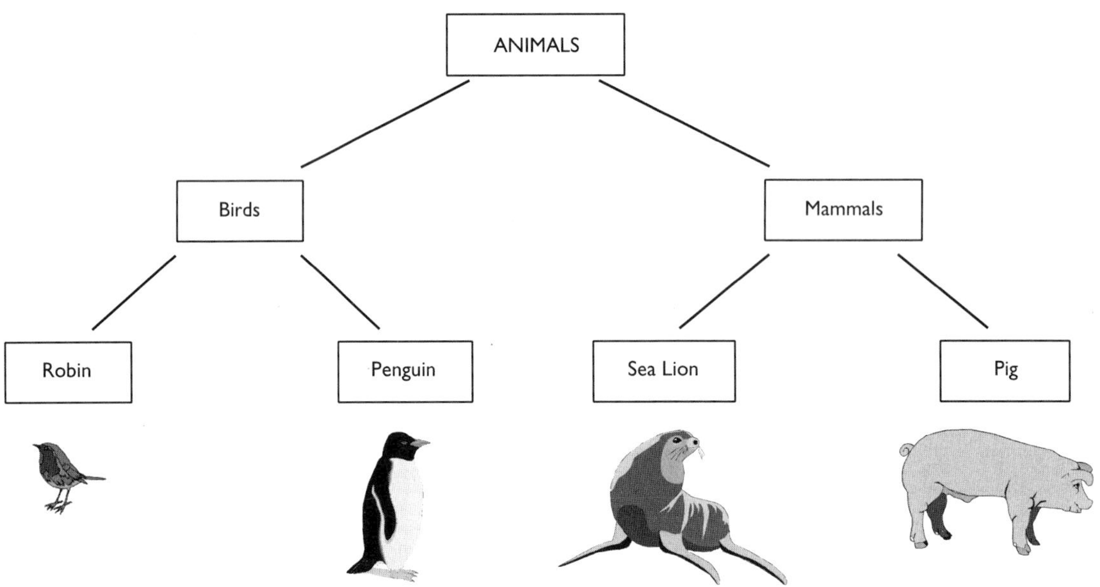

need to be stored only once, with higher attributes covering all lower categories and concepts. A hierarchy such as this is also fairly close to formal scientific classification systems and developing children's abilities to understand and use hierarchies is one of the aims of teaching.

A difficulty with this theory is that although people can adopt such structures, they often seem to prefer to use links which are based on similarity of features, rather than logical relationships. Robins and penguins are both types of birds, but the penguin is evidently not very close to what we would normally think of as being 'bird-like'. People are in fact more likely to link it with mammals such as sea lions, which come from a very different branch of classification but also live in cold areas and swim and catch fish.

Structure of long-term memory

PROTOTYPES

Such logical hierarchies also depend on concepts which can be well specified. An example of this would be a bicycle, which has the defining or *core attributes* of 'a vehicle, has two wheels, is driven by pedals'. However, the majority of the concepts which people use are generally rather 'fuzzy' and cannot be completely determined in this way. People are therefore more likely to categorise concepts according to how close they are to a typical form, known as a *prototype*. This is usually the norm, or the commonly experienced average of the features of something. The prototype for a bird would usually be something that is small, bird-shaped, has wings, able to fly, eats worms, and chirps. A typical bird would be something like a robin or a sparrow, and people will tend to judge that penguins, ostriches and chickens are not very 'bird-like'.

Although such prototypes can be identified and linked in various ways, people tend to prefer to use them at an intermediate level which is referred to as 'basic'. This is the level at which things have the most distinctive features which are of relevance to us. The word 'dog', for instance, is a basic-level verbal concept. It comes under the superordinate category of 'animals' and has subordinate categories which are the various breeds of dogs. Using basic-level concepts means that we are able to communicate effectively without being too general or too specific. In normal conversation, people would tend to say that 'the dog is barking', rather than 'the animal is making a noise' (superordinate concepts), or 'the chihuahua is yapping' (subordinate concepts).

CONCEPT DEVELOPMENT

Early conceptual development is often based on establishing prototypes, largely from initial experiences of particular instances known as *exemplars*. Exemplars become refined over time to 'average out' and represent the typical or key features of a concept. Verbal concepts such as 'doggie' may at first be used by a child to refer only to one particular dog; this is known as the 'underextension' of a concept. After the child has encountered a number of different animals, however, a partial prototype may be established and can lead to 'overextensions', with the child perhaps referring to all four-legged animals as 'doggie'. Eventually an accurate prototype will be formed, based upon the contrasts which can be made between different types of four-legged animals. Even older children or adults will establish new concepts in this way, particularly when encountering a novel area.

Older children and adults are also able to use various features to learn new conceptual categories, and Keil and Batterman (1984) found that by the age of about 10 years children tended to prefer to use the core attributes rather than the prototype when deciding on final concept classification. These attributes can be derived by children themselves, if they are able to compare members with non-members of a conceptual category, and such distinctions can also be explicitly taught.

Initial teaching of new concepts, particularly with younger children, should therefore focus on exemplars, and lead on to comparisons with other similar categories to establish distinctive features. Concepts are also generally first learned at the basic level, which is the point at which they will have greatest distinctiveness and relevance to children. If basic-level concepts are taught first, they can then lead on to the establishing of subordinate and superordinate concepts.

When teaching about metals, for example, it may be best to start with typical metals such as iron and copper, contrasting these with various non-metals. These features develop the basic-level concept of 'metal', and other exemplar metals can then be identified as subordinate concepts. In this case the superordinate concept of an 'element' is more abstract and would usually be tackled when children reach secondary age.

SCHEMAS

Schemas can be thought of as structured clusters of information which are used to represent events, concepts, actions or processes. Although this explanation may seem rather all-embracing and vague, schemas are very useful ways of understanding how we group together and simplify our general knowledge and understanding. To some extent this is achieved by the use of concepts, but schemas go further, to describe the way in which we generally organise and use conceptual information. Schemas exist because they are ways of achieving cognitive economy; although using them can sometimes lead to inaccuracies through oversimplification, they reduce complexity to a manageable level and speed up the way in which we deal with the world.

A general schema for 'school' might link together the concepts of 'teachers' and 'pupils' with 'school buildings', the fact that 'many children attend schools' and the fact that 'schools are for children to learn reading, writing and arithmetic'. We would also involve our own relationships to school – either as a past pupil or possibly as a parent or teacher. A key feature of such real-world knowledge is that we have associated emotional content and links with our past and future possible actions related to all these constituent parts of the schema.

General schemas have an overall structure which stays the same but with certain aspects that vary with specific instances. When we relate to a particular school, we then adapt the schema to take account of aspects such as its size, location and general reputation, while retaining the key aspects about what generally goes on in schools.

Some schemas cover sequences of possible actions and events, and have been described by Schank and Abelson (1977) as *scripts*. These include the key elements of what is normally carried out in certain situations. For instance, pupils are usually aware of the normal sequence of going into a class, listening to the teacher, getting their books ready and starting work. This general schema has a number of variables, and with particular subjects or teachers the process may vary somewhat. However, in most lessons the key element of the teacher managing the pupil's learning tends to stay the same.

A similar sequencing structure can be seen in written *story grammars*. In the same way that sentences have a structure which conveys meaning, bodies of text also tend to follow certain schematic sequences which enable us to follow their logic. Formal essays, for instance, usually have some form of introduction, a main body which considers evidence and ideas, and a discussion followed by a conclusion. According to Mandler (1987), stories often have the key elements of a setting, and an event structure which is composed of episodes. Each episode is made up from a beginning, a complex reaction (which sets up a state that the key character wishes to achieve), a goal path (which is the plan and consequences of attempting to achieve the goal) and a final ending. Stories which do not have such structures are hard to understand, and when they are recalled, students tend to distort them to fit them in with the more conventional form.

Schemas are useful ways of understanding general cognitive processes and probably operate at many different levels to organise general life processes, as well as more specific groupings. Schemas have been shown to be useful ways of describing a number of psychological processes, including stereotypical judgements (about what personal attributes we believe are related together), attribution processes (our assumptions of why people do things) and implicit personality theories (about underlying consistencies governing what people think and do).

Prototype concepts can also be seen as low-level schemas, which have average values. The prototype of 'bird' described earlier has the typical size, shape and features of something like a sparrow. According to this perspective, concepts will also tend to have the other attributes of schemas, such as emotional content (sparrows are 'cheeky') and how they relate to ourselves and our actions (we might feed them in the park).

Processes involved in long-term memory

As well as its conceptual structure, long-term storage can involve a number of different systems (see Figure 2.7), according to how information is dealt with. Tulving (1983) considers that declarative memory can be subdivided into the main body of *semantic memory*, which covers meaningful information such as concepts and propositions, and *episodic memory*. This involves information about an experienced event or situation and at one extreme can involve eidetic memory, when the complete experience is recalled. This is relatively rare, however, and usually only the unique or distinctive features of a situation are stored. All learning probably starts off as episodic memory and normally progresses to become semantic memory as it is processed and assimilated. A few days after a particular Christmas, the specific events are still fresh in our memory, but a few years later all Christmases can seem much the same.

Squire (1987) also considers that memory can be subdivided into two major categories relating to whether recall is conscious, referred to as *explicit* memory, or unconscious, referred to as *implicit* memory. Many forms of knowledge may initially involve conscious processes; for instance, early reading may at least partly be based on the explicit recall and use of letter sounds, which eventually becomes part of the unconscious process of skilled reading. Explicit and implicit memory also appear to involve very different brain processes. When involved in conscious recall, the brain becomes generally more active, and consumes more energy. Surprisingly, with the implicit recall involved in skilled performance, the activity of the brain is reduced, as though it were falling into a routine, 'easier' pattern.

Figure 2.7 The structure of long-term memory

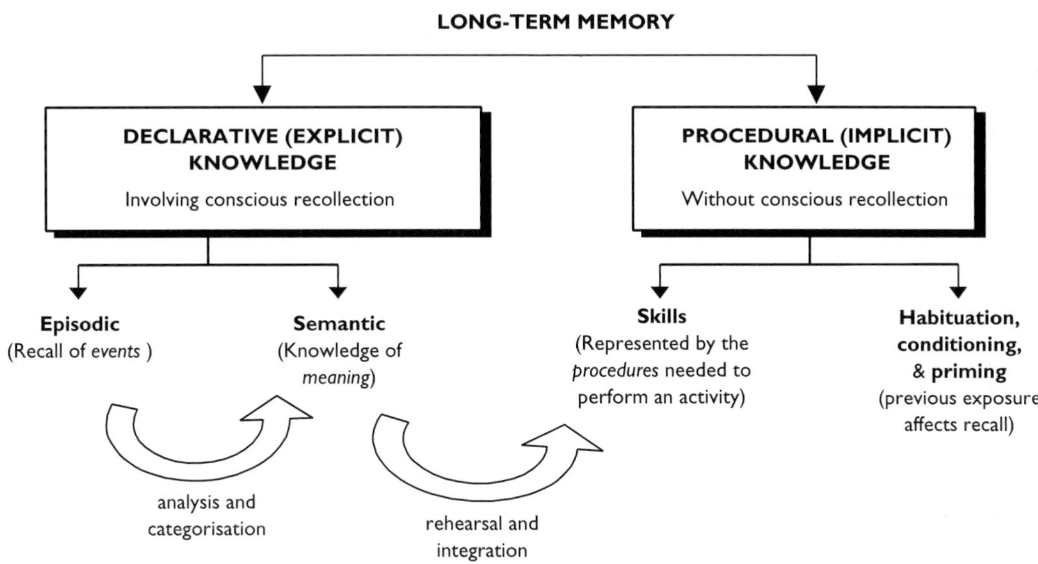

The process of learning can also be either explicit, with the use of conscious plans and strategies, or implicit, without any self-awareness that learning is actually taking place. *Explicit learning* is involved in what we would normally recognise as formal, didactic teaching, where the teacher closely directs pupils on what they are learning and (often) how they should go about it. Pupils are very aware that they are in a learning situation and of what it is that they are learning. As noted above, however, once something is learned, recall may become less conscious over time, particularly if there has been over-learning or close integration with other abilities, as in skilled performance of some kind.

Implicit learning happens when pupils are not aware that they are acquiring information. Although it may at first seem rather unlikely that such learning could occur, implicit learning does nevertheless underpin many 'natural' learning processes such as children's learning of their first language. As will be noted in Chapter 8, most vocabulary and grammar development occurs with little effort or awareness, and there is evidence that direct teaching may actually inhibit progress, by interfering with the child's own implicit hypotheses. It may seem somewhat strange to talk of high-level cognitive processes such as hypothesis formation as being non-conscious. However, there is evidence (reviewed by Baddeley, 1997) that people are able to develop rules (for example, when learning the grammar of a new language) and to control complex systems without being able to describe how they are doing this.

One possible explanation of this comes from connectionist theories, which will be discussed later in this chapter. According to this perspective, it is entirely possible for a complex system with modifiable connections to generate rules without necessarily having any high-level (conscious) controlling functions. However, if people develop such implicit knowledge to a high level, the knowledge does appear to become more accessible to conscious awareness. It seems that people are eventually able to work out what they are doing, particularly if they are helped to do so. This is shown in the way that pupils are eventually able to learn to analyse and to reflect on their use of grammar in language with formal teaching.

It can be argued that implicit learning is an effective and more natural approach to learning in many situations. As regards the learning of a second language, for instance, it is believed that 'immersion learning' is an effective approach, whereby pupils are involved in hearing and using the new language in practical situations, in much the same way as they learned their first language. Implicit learning is also a key foundation for ideas about literacy developments such as 'real reading books' and also with 'analytic phonics' (the awareness of sounds within words). According to these perspectives, literacy development is a complex and integrated skill which is best developed by enabling pupils to experience literacy and basic principles of underlying units in meaningful situations.

In general, however, the evidence tends to support the value of directed and explicit experiences in most fields of learning. Scott (1990), for instance, studied the development of French in conversational classes with students who were either given certain language rules or experienced them in stories. Even though students in the 'implicit' group were given ten times the amount of experience that those in the 'explicit' group received, their eventual learning was still inferior. Evidence to be discussed in Chapter 9 also indicates that there are significant advantages from using structured and guided approaches in developing early literacy skills, for example with the use of reading schemes and with synthetic phonics.

This should not, however, be taken to imply that teaching should involve only explicit learning. Direct experiences such as investigative work are probably very important with new work, when students are developing their general feel for a topic area. The use of learning is also very dependent on its implicit integration and links with other areas of knowledge, particularly if these are established at an early stage. In isolation, the learning of rules of grammar in a first or second language, or the developing of reading vocabulary and phonics separate from their use in reading and writing, is not the best way to develop general applied skills in those areas.

Problems with learning

Failure to register information initially or to process it subsequently for LTM storage is what we normally call 'failing to learn'. Subsequent loss or distortion of information, or the inability to retrieve it, is normally called 'forgetting'.

Initial encoding depends on the active direction and involvement of working memory, and without this, learning will not progress any further. This is effectively the process of paying attention, and most theories about attention, from that of Broadbent (1958) onwards, stress that further processing depends upon information having some form of relevance to the individual. Eysenck (1979) has also emphasised that whether information is processed into LTM depends on its 'distinctiveness' – on whether it has a special, meaningful relationship for us.

When we first transfer information into long-term storage, we do so largely in terms of its meaning. The process usually involves some form of interpretation in terms of our existing knowledge and ideas. Although interpretation can help students to contextualise new learning and to link it in with existing knowledge, it can also produce interference and distortions. This was investigated by Alverman *et al.* (1985), who directed a group of students to write down their existing knowledge of light and heat and then to learn about those topics by reading a passage. When subsequently tested for new learning, these students had acquired less knowledge than did students who had not first written down what they knew. It seems likely that doing this had activated the students' misconceptions and that they had tended to retain these as the basis for interpreting the new information.

Such findings indicate that pupils may selectively attend to parts of information to be learned, and may also distort it to fit their existing preconceptions or schemas. An important role of the teacher can therefore be to emphasise and explain unusual or unexpected aspects of new information which pupils might otherwise misinterpret.

FORGETTING

Distortion can also have an effect on information which has already been learned, to produce forgetting. This can happen when memories become progressively *reconstructed* over time to fit in with existing concepts and ideas. In a famous study, Bartlett (1932) studied subjects' recall of a Native American folk-tale called 'The War of the Ghosts'. Over a number of successive recalls, the subjects progressively shortened and distorted the content, largely to fit in with their own schemas, or ways of understanding the world.

Our expectations of commonly experienced social events can also distort our recall by 'filling in gaps' with what we expect to happen. Bower *et al.* (1979), for instance, showed that subjects would falsely recall events which were consistent with a particular 'script' (the process of going to a restaurant), but which were not included in the learned sequence.

School learning should therefore monitor recall and compare this with the original material when necessary. Teachers need to be aware of this potential for distortion of learned information; when carrying out revision programmes they should encourage pupils to check back on key points in the original material. Butler and Winne (1995), for instance, review findings that feedback is most effective when it emphasises and corrects items that students get wrong, rather than just giving grades or reinforcing their correct responses.

Early theories about forgetting focused on the idea that memories simply faded over time – the *decay theory*. This does not seem very plausible, however, since Jenkins and Dallenbach (1924) showed that when nothing else is happening (as when one is asleep), there is very little loss of information. One can in fact sometimes experience an increase in recall over time (reminiscence), and the resolving of problem areas, while not consciously focusing on the material. Despite common beliefs to the contrary, it can therefore be a good idea to study material the night before an exam, although it is also probably best to study at other times as well!

The *interference theory* has been very popular in explaining forgetting and has a number of important implications for effective teaching and learning. This essentially proposes that when similar materials are learned, it becomes difficult to distinguish one part from another. This will lead to a retrieval failure, when the information may be learned and in memory but cannot be successfully separated out. Anderson (1983) has summarised a number of investigations which show that interference can lead to a complete retrieval failure if the items to be recalled are very weak (poorly learned) or the interference (similarity) is very strong.

As shown in Figure 2.8, interference can happen when the retrieval of new information is affected by its similarity to previously learned material (*proactive interference*) and when new information affects the recall of older material (*retroactive interference*).

All learning is embedded in previous and subsequent learning and is liable to both forms of interference. This appears to be a likely explanation for the general progressive loss of information (forgetting) over time, since the longer information is in memory, the more likely it is that both types of interference will build up.

Figure 2.8 Interference processes

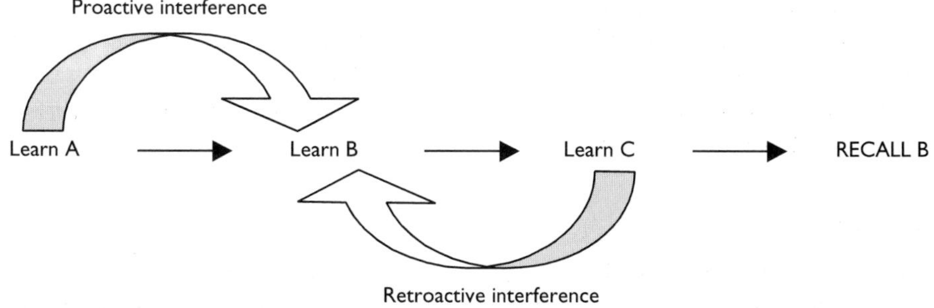

Managing learning and improving memory

The implications of the interference explanation of forgetting are, first, that teaching and learning techniques should as far as possible attempt to encode information in distinctive ways. Information which is similar to existing knowledge is hard to encode separately and will be difficult to retrieve. Second, the effective retrieval of information will depend on some form of strategy which emphasises the links it has with existing (available) knowledge.

Perhaps the most general technique which has been shown to improve memory in this way is the use of *organisation*. A classic investigation of this by Bower *et al.* (1969) gave subjects the task of learning 112 words organised into conceptual hierarchies (they were all types of minerals). The subjects learned much more effectively than subjects who simply learned the list in its unorganised form. Work by Mandler (1967) found that organising such learning material resulted in superior recall even when subjects were not explicitly instructed to learn it. Organised learning is more effective when it incorporates meaningful relationships, producing what Marton and Salijo (1976) refer to as a 'deep approach' to learning. This can be contrasted with a 'surface approach' which only reproduces information with little understanding.

Such meaningful content and organisation can be enhanced by the technique of constructing *knowledge maps*. These involve students in generating a spatial-semantic display covering a particular area of knowledge, in which the physical layout embodies meaningful relationships. The process of construction appears to activate and also to develop a schema covering that area and can form the basis for initial learning, revision or essay writing. The example in Figure 2.9 shows some concepts and connections for the role of trees in the environment. The activity of constructing this (not simply learning it from a book) would enable a student to appreciate the impact of clearing the rainforests for farming.

Such approaches often involve *visual encoding*, based on the ideas of Paivio (1969), who demonstrated that concrete imagery (visualising things) forms a much stronger basis for long-term memory than do verbal processes (when students work from written or spoken information). One important feature of visually encoding information is that it produces material that is much less likely to be similar to other items and as a result is much less liable to interference. Chmielewski

Figure 2.9 Knowledge map for trees and the environment

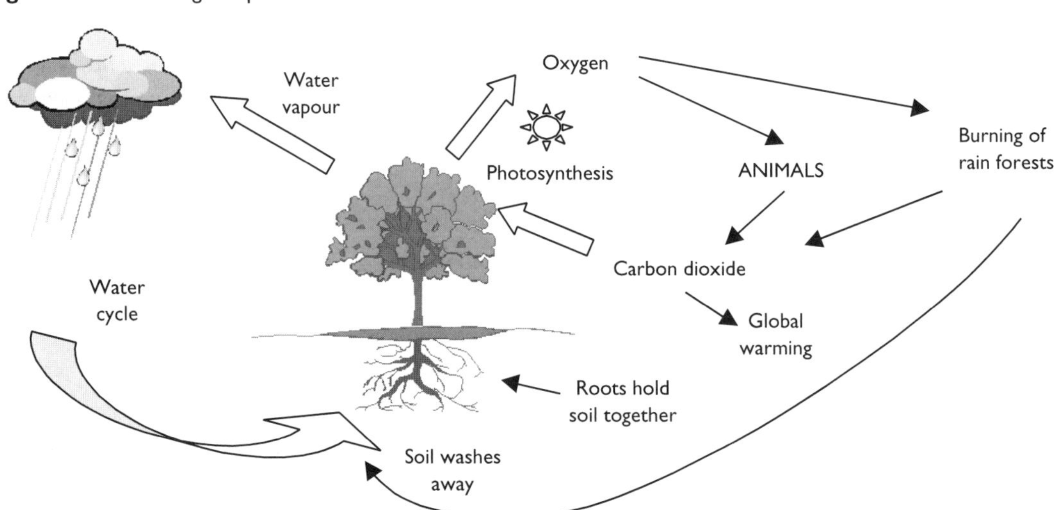

and Dansereau (1998) found that the use of such approaches not only improved students' recall of subject areas for which they had prepared knowledge maps, but also transferred to their learning in other areas. This indicates that using such maps trains students to adopt a deeper approach to learning, one which emphasises relationships and organisation.

Coding techniques can reduce the memory load, allow for specific retrieval cues and prevent the effects of both reconstruction and interference. One particular approach utilises both reduction and elaboration of information. Typically it first reduces the original information to key elements such as initial letters. These can then be elaborated into a larger structured system, such as a meaningful sentence, that can be used to reconstruct the original material when needed. In the sentence 'Richard Of York Gave Battle In Vain', the first letters of the words act as the cues for the colours in the spectrum: as red, orange, yellow, green, blue, indigo, violet. This technique is particularly popular with medical students, who have large amounts of anatomical and clinical information to learn.

The *keyword mnemonic* is another effective approach for learning associations. This works by forming a linked image between one concept and a concrete word (the keyword) representing the other concept. As shown in Figure 2.10, when a student is trying to learn that the French word for 'bald' is *chauve*, he or she could achieve this by forming an image linking a bald head with the keyword 'shaver', which is phonologically similar to the word 'chauve'.

Figure 2.10 Keyword mnemonic learning

Although such techniques can be very effective, they do require a lot of initial preparation, and the learning tends to be rather superficial. Wang and Thomas (1995) found that after only two days, keyword learning loses its initial superiority over normal learning procedures. This finding indicates that such approaches are best limited to specific areas such as the learning of foreign vocabulary, where there is limited semantic information. Even here it may be important to move rapidly into more implicit learning situations and to start to use the new vocabulary.

Massed versus distributed practice

A strong finding in learning and memory research has been that if a certain amount of study time is spread out or distributed between a number of sessions, the result usually is improved learning. When learning is combined or 'massed' together, it is likely that students will become overloaded and reduce their attention and active involvement. A classic study by Baddeley and Longman (1978) of postal workers learning to type postcodes found that daily one-hour sessions were about one and a half times as efficient than daily two-hour sessions, and about twice as efficient as two-hour sessions twice a day. A study by Solity *et al.* (1999) also looked at the effectiveness of teaching reading to children, during their first two years of schooling, with three sessions a day of 10 to 15 minutes. When tested at 6 years 4 months of age, their average reading abilities were at the 6 years, 10 months level, which supports the effectiveness of this approach. A group of children were also compared with a sample of those who had been receiving a concentrated single daily session of the literacy hour. Although the literacy hour produced some improvements over normal practice, the distributed practice group scored even higher on reading and were six months ahead of the literacy hour sample.

It seems likely that basic skill work might benefit particularly from regular and short sessions since children are more likely to become bored with such low-level activities. These skills might include early literacy attainments such as phonic skills (letters in words) and phonological abilities (sensitivity to spoken sounds), as well as numeracy development such as number bonds and multiplication tables. However, with general curriculum content it is probably more important to teach for periods which have meaningful content and to avoid too many changes during a day, which might become disruptive. More complex and integrated subject work such as investigations can be achieved only with lessons of a certain length, but again it would seem to be best if they could be spaced out during the week rather than combined into 'double periods', as often happens in the secondary school.

Reviews

If previously covered material is *reviewed* or rehearsed after a significant amount of time (but before it is forgotten), the subsequent rate of loss of information will be significantly reduced. This is probably due to a process of integrating and consolidating material by increasing or strengthening the semantic links with other knowledge and reducing the possibility of interference. If there are further, successive reviews, these will have similar effects and will be much more efficient than just putting the same amount of time into a single 'massed' revision session. As shown in Figure 2.11, Gay (1973) found that children learned mathematical rules most successfully when there were two spaced out reviews, rather than two early or two late ones together. It seems likely that early and late reviews act in different ways, with early reviews consolidating remembered material by reorganising it and linking it in with other knowledge, while delayed reviews involve relearning of forgotten information.

It seems a good idea for teachers to start off each session with a review of the key points covered in the previous teaching period and periodically to carry out reviews over longer periods. Such procedures were implemented in a teaching effectiveness project carried out by Good and Grouws (1979). This demonstrated major gains in mathematics achievements and involved the increased use of daily, weekly and monthly reviews.

Landauer and Bjork (1978) also argue that the optimum way to develop learning is by 'expanding rehearsal', whereby items are initially tested after a very short delay, then included with other items to increase the delay. If an item is wrong, then the delay is shortened again. An example of this could involve teaching the association between letter shapes and the name of things which start with those letters:

Figure 2.11 Effects of the timing of review sessions on learning

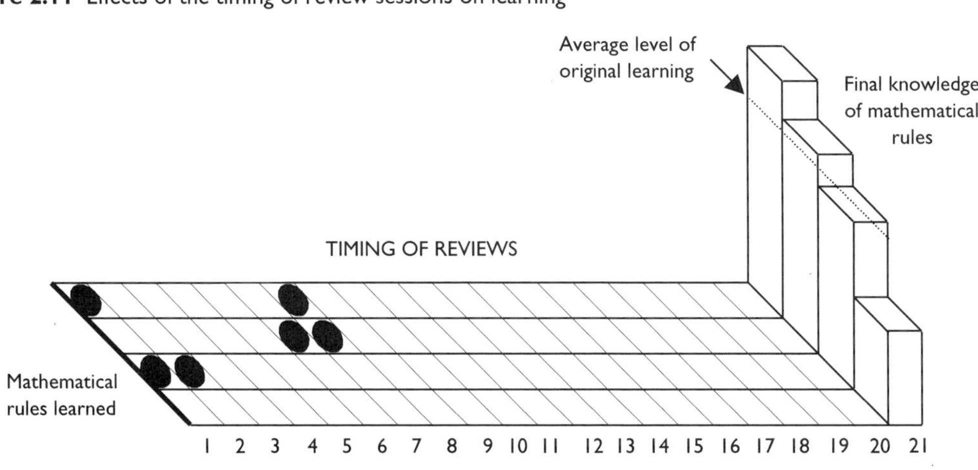

Source: based on data from Gay (1973)

Teacher [Shows '*a*', "Apple"]:	What is it?
Pupil:	"Apple"
Teacher [Shows 'm', "Man"]:	What is it?
Pupil:	"Man"
Teacher [Shows '*a*']:	What is it?
Pupil:	"Apple"
Teacher [Shows '*m*']:	What is it?
Pupil:	"Man"
Teacher [Shows '*c*']:	What is it?
Pupil:	"Cat"

Previews

Reviews at the start of lessons can also link in with a *preview* of the information that is about to be covered in that session. This can act as an 'advance organiser', and has been advocated by Ausubel (1968) as an efficient way for teachers to manage direct instruction. Advance organisers are not always very effective, however, and seem to be most important when a new topic is being introduced and where students are unlikely to have their own ways of understanding and organising the new material. Simplified models which incorporate the key elements of what is to be studied are particularly effective and can involve either drawings, animations or three-dimensional representations.

Both review and preview techniques are incorporated in the *PQRST study technique* described by Thomas and Robinson (1982). The letters stand for Preview, Question, Read, Self-recitation and Test. This approach organises and integrates information by making the learning process active and activating, and linking it with existing knowledge.

Integrated views of learning

The ideas considered so far show how the process of learning can be traced through differing levels of complexity. Gagné (1965) in particular has proposed a hierarchy of different types of learning, which progresses from simple conditioning through to concept development, rule or propositional learning and eventually problem solving. Gagné believes that children need to establish competence at earlier stages as a necessary basis for developing higher abilities. With mathematics, for instance, it would be necessary for children to establish number concepts before subsequently being able to carry out basic rule-based operations on these. This sequential and ordered view of learning is similar to the general structure of the National Curriculum, with its emphasis upon Key Stages and an ordered arrangement of skills which progress through the various levels.

Gagné has applied this approach to designing real learning sequences, and investigations by Airasian and Bart (1975) have shown that students' attainments do appear to follow this type of progression. The relationships between and within levels can, however, be very complex and can depend on how concepts are linked within a particular domain (a discrete area of associated knowledge) and what concepts are needed for further progress. This approach also tends to be most successful with skill-based learning such as mathematics, where higher stages cannot progress without competence at earlier levels. It can also be useful at certain stages in other learning domains, for instance with reading, where the knowledge and use of letter sounds does seem to facilitate early reading skills.

A very different approach sees learning as the progressive development of schemas, with their associated concepts and relationships. According to the approach known as *constructivism*, young children already have a range of schemas and use new information to actively build more complex forms. Bruner (1961a) argued that by matching in with children's abilities, it is possible to teach any subject to any child at any age in some form that is honest. Topics can be revisited at different stages in children's education to develop their knowledge and understanding further. For example, it would be possible to teach the concept of 'burning' to younger, primary-aged children, and then revisit this as 'oxidation' with older, secondary-aged children.

Simple, skill-based sequences of learning are easy to describe. However, we saw earlier in this chapter that the underlying basis of knowledge (including concepts) is generally schema based, and learning models based on these are likely to be more complex. General theories of *schema modification* described by Norman (1978) consider that there are three basic processes involved:

- *Accretion*. New knowledge is just 'fitted in with' an existing schema and takes on its structure. Learning that 'Montague's' is the name of a school would then mean that it takes on all the other implications of the schema 'school'.
- *Tuning*. Operation of the schema becomes more automatic and efficient. No new facts are acquired and the structure alters only by removal of redundant steps or adoption of new links. The schema of 'writing', for instance, becomes more fluent as it is practised.
- *Restructuring*. The schema is reorganised in some way, either by altering the relationships within a schema or by developing new schemas. The schema for 'fishy animals' can, for example, develop a new schema for 'swimming mammals' when children learn about dolphins and whales.

Such processes have also been embodied within broad theories of cognitive development that have a number of direct implications for educational processes.

Cognitive development and learning

Piagetian theory

The major theory in the area of cognitive development and learning was evolved by Piaget (1966, 1972) and is largely based around the development of the mental structures called *schemas* described earlier in this chapter. For a young child, a schema could involve the actions involved in 'reaching out and grasping an object', or for an older person it might involve the mature and complex sequence of expectations and actions involved in 'going to a restaurant'.

From an adult perspective, children's schemas appear relatively uncomplicated, and early on these involve ways of representing direct interactions with the physical world. As children mature, Piaget believed that schemas become progressively more complex and can ultimately be capable of representing abstract features, enabling older students to carry out high-level thought processes. Piaget was interested in how this development happens, in terms of children's experiences and the influence of new information on their knowledge structures.

Assimilation and accommodation

Piaget believed that much of the time, new information is only *assimilated*, or 'fitted in' with existing schemas, in a way similar to the process of accretion mentioned earlier. So, for instance, a child may have a general conceptual schema of 'fish', based largely upon early experiences of his or her own pet goldfish. This could be in the form of a prototype concept, and involve features such as 'lives in water' and 'has fins'. New experiences of different types of fishes might fit in neatly with this, and at such times schemas and incoming information are in a state of balance, known as *equilibrium*, as shown in Figure 2.12.

When subsequent information does not have quite the same attributes, there is a tendency at first to continue with assimilation. At this point, however, things do not fit together too well and there is a state of imbalance or *disequilibrium*, as shown in Figure 2.13. When young children first encounter dolphins, perhaps by seeing them on the television, they may tend to see them as being a kind of fish. The dolphins will be assigned to that concept on the basis of their most evident features, even though they may be seen to come to the surface and breathe air.

If further information does not fit too well with the existing schema, then the disequilibrium that this produces eventually becomes too great and forces a process of restructuring or adjustment to the information, known as *accommodation*, as shown in Figure 2.14. This could happen if the child then has experiences about whales, which

Figure 2.12 Assimilation of information – in a state of equilibrium

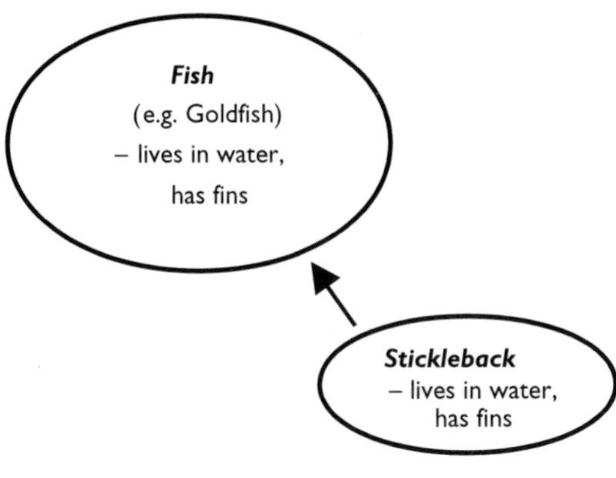

Figure 2.13 Assimilation of information – in a state of disequilibrium

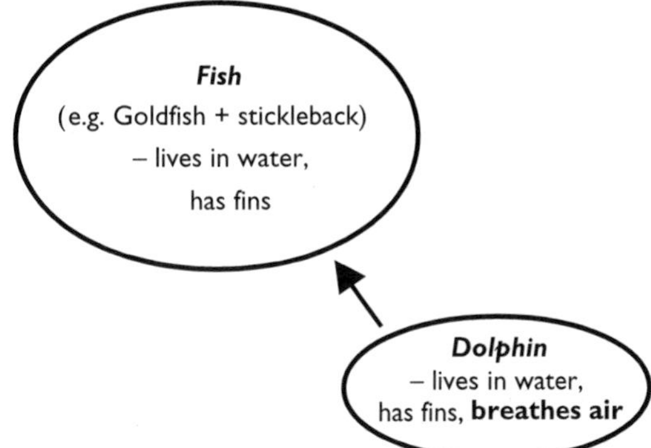

Figure 2.14 Accommodation

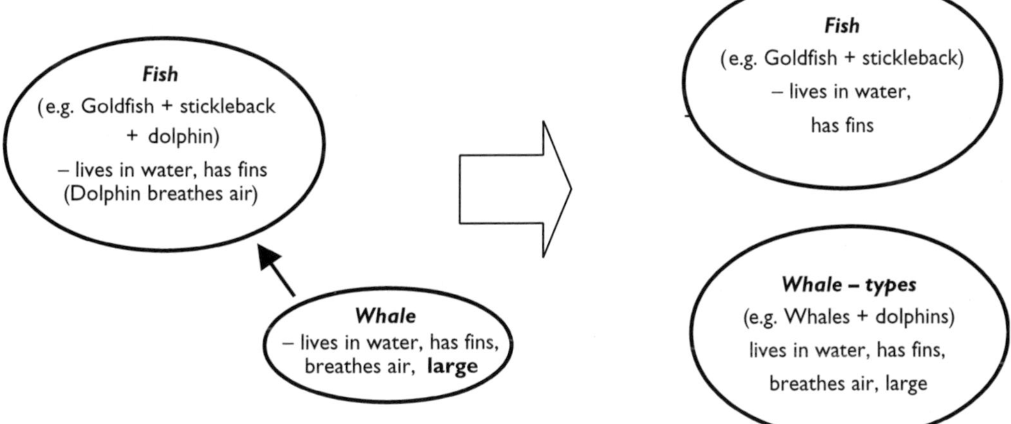

not only breathe air but are also very large and are harder fit in with the original goldfish schema. A possible resolution for this would then be to create a new category of 'whale-type' creatures.

Following this process, there is a new state of equilibrium. New information can again fit in; for instance, 'killer whales' could now be assimilated without difficulty. It will of course probably be much later before features such as 'bear live young' are incorporated and the label of 'cetacean' is used. Some people may never assimilate these latter characteristics of whales and dolphins.

Piaget developed these ideas largely from close studies of the intellectual development of his own children, including how they misapplied concepts and developed them with further experiences. His basic idea that young children have simplified schemas, which become more complex and differentiated with increasing experiences, is accepted by most people as quite plausible. It fits in with a number of psychological findings such as the overgeneralisation of early language (calling any four-legged animal a 'doggie'), and the increase in complexity of ethnic stereotype judgements when people are exposed to different cultures.

Stage theory

A less commonly accepted belief held by Piaget is that children's mental abilities go through a series of developmental stages. He proposed that these stages affect the ways in which children are able to represent the world and how they are able to use their representations of the world as the basis for thought. Piaget also believed that the various stages are due to changes in fundamental logical processes of thought and therefore affect all mental abilities at about the same time.

- The earliest, *sensori-motor stage* covers from 0 to 2 years of age. Schemas are primarily based on direct (sensory) experiences and early physical (motor) reactions and responses. At this stage, thinking is very much doing; it is only towards the end of this period that the infant is able completely to retain the identity of things when they are not present.
- The *pre-operational stage* lasts from 2 to 7 years of age. At this stage children are able to think about things in terms of consistent physical features. Their understanding depends very much on their own perspective, however; children seem to have difficulties understanding that a change in the way that something looks does not necessarily mean a change in other attributes, such as number or quantity. The ability to do this is called *conservation* and relies on children's ability to represent things to themselves and to carry out logical mental changes, referred to as operations. In the examples in Figure 2.15, children will say that there is more liquid in the tall beaker and that there are more black counters. They appear to be able to take account only of the height of the liquid, and the length of the line of counters.
- The *concrete operational stage* lasts broadly from 7 to 12 years of age. By this time children are able to think about a number of different features of things, but are still largely restricted to doing this with physical objects. Thought is now becoming more logical and shows properties such as 'reversibility', which means that things can be transformed, then returned back into their original form. Children are also able to take on different perspectives, Piaget thought, and are no longer dominated by their own experiences and needs – or no more so than adults are.
- The *formal operational stage* from 12 years of age onwards involves abstract thought processes. Children no longer need to use physical objects but can use the features and properties of things as a basis on which to reason. Scientific thought now becomes possible, with the ability to make hypotheses, to think deductively and to carry out experimental investigations by isolating variables. Piaget acknowledged, however, that many people never develop these abilities. Martorano (1977) found that only about 20 per cent of 11-year-olds had established abstract thought, progressively rising to about 60 per cent by the age of 17 years. Individuals also showed marked differences in their ability to apply logical thought in different domains, depending on their familiarity with the subject area.

Developments and modifications of Piaget's ideas

Piaget's ideas have generally been subject to a great deal of criticism and modification. First, there is considerable evidence that children are often able to carry out tasks at an earlier age than

Figure 2.15 Liquid and number conservation tasks

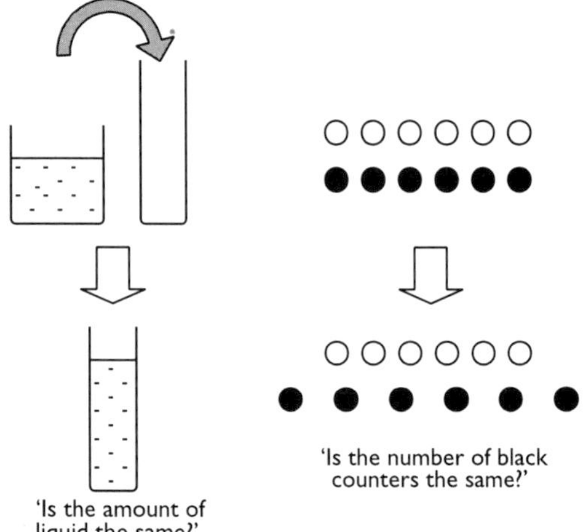
'Is the amount of liquid the same?'
'Is the number of black counters the same?'

his theory says they should be capable of. Whether they can do so seems to depend on whether the tasks have meaning or relevance to the children. Hughes (1975), for instance, found that 64 per cent of 5-year-old children were able correctly to take on the perspective of a policeman doll looking for a boy doll. Children would normally be 7 years or over before being able to show such abilities with more abstract tasks, such as identifying the correct picture showing another person's view of some model mountains.

Other work has shown that abilities with conservation also depend on what the child believes is expected of them. In a classic investigation of number conservation by McGarrigle and Donaldson (1974), a 'naughty teddy' accidentally disrupted the second row of counters and spread them out. Under these conditions, 72 per cent of 4- to 6-year-old children were able to say correctly that the number remained the same, whereas only 34 per cent of those who saw the spreading as carried out by the experimenter did so. A likely explanation for such findings is that when the experimenter asks a child in a classic conservation task if anything has changed, this is taken by the child to imply that something *must* have changed (otherwise, why ask the question?). The child therefore looks for an answer which might fit in with this, for example that there is a change in the height of the liquid or the spread of the counters. According to this, children become able to conserve when they understand that they can describe things without worrying about what other people want. This therefore represents a development in social understanding rather than logical awareness.

Children are certainly capable of carrying out many tasks earlier than Piaget would have predicted. Despite this, there are still some limits to their attainments, and one would not for example expect very young children to be capable of certain types of abstract thought, no matter what experiences they had had, or how particular tasks were presented to them.

Biological correlates

Piaget believed that although children's abilities are developed by interacting with their environment, the basis of this progress is ultimately due to the biological maturation of the nervous system. He considered that this acts as the foundation for the development of intelligence and enables the qualitative changes in logical abilities which are characteristic of each stage. There has been some support for this belief, with Hudspeth and Pribram (1990) finding that measurements of direct brain activity showed regional developmental changes which were broadly consistent with Piagetian stages. Those areas of the brain most associated with perceptual input and physical control, for instance, showed their greatest development during the first few years, whereas those most associated with higher-level processes showed a major increase in late adolescence.

Capacity limitations

Although the brain does show progressive physical maturation, it is still possible that this just results in a gradual change in the amount of processing capacity, rather than the discontinuous stages suggested by Piaget. This is supported by findings that the short-term or working memory shows progressive improvements with age. In one study by Dempster (1981), performance on the digit span task improved steadily from just over 2 at 2 years of age to just below 7 at 12 years of age. One explanation for this is that children develop more *expertise* as they grow older. Numbers evidently have more meaning for a 12-year-old than for a 2-year-old, and differences in processing may be due merely to the fact that the information is less of a load for older children. This is shown in the finding by Nicolson (1981) that the size of short-term memory is closely related to the maximum rate at which individuals are able to talk, across the age range from children to adults (see Figure 2.16). These findings are consistent with the idea that short-term memory as measured by digit span is largely due to a form of internal verbal rehearsal. Differences in our

Figure 2.16 Relationship between short-term memory and speed of talking

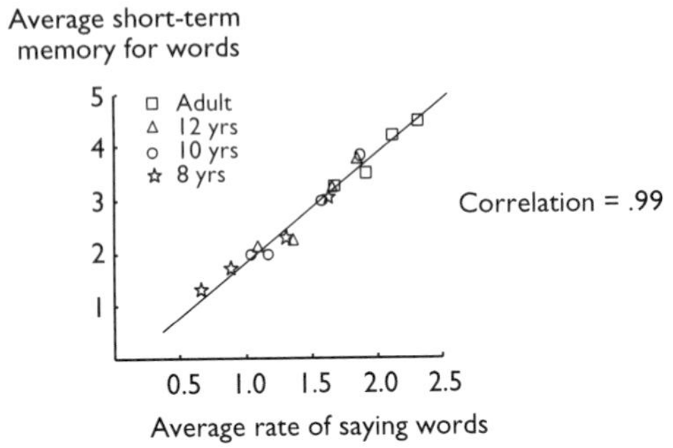

Source: Nicolson (1981)

apparent capacity with such tasks are therefore probably the result of how much we are able to rehearse in a given time.

When younger children develop greater expertise, their apparent processing abilities can become similar to or even exceed those of older, more biologically mature individuals. A classic investigation by Chi (1976), for instance, showed that children who were expert chess players were able to recall the placement of chess pieces on a board better than adults who were not so expert. Developing such high-level abilities invariably takes thousands of hours of intensive work over many years. The progressive development and the similarity of children's general abilities which Piaget noted may therefore be due to the time which it takes to establish expertise across the range of cognitive areas, rather than the unfolding of a predetermined sequence of maturation.

Consistency

Piaget's theory predicts that children's progress in different areas should generally be the same, owing to their dependence on the same underlying logical abilities. However, much evidence indicates that children's progress in different domains of knowledge or expertise often shows only a limited connection between stages. Conservation studies by Tomlinson-Keasey *et al.* (1979), for instance, found that about 60 per cent of children at age 7 were able to conserve for mass, but that conservation for volume occurred about two years later. These differences appear to be the result of the conceptual difficulty of each area. Although children's abilities to carry out conservation tasks do show overall progress from age 6 years to about 9 years, this is quite different from the single discrete stage which Piaget originally believed existed.

Children have also been shown to make great progress with specific abilities if they have additional intensive support. Gardner (1983) argues that developments in areas such as linguistic and mathematical abilities can be relatively independent, with some unusual individuals showing high levels of attainment in one area alone. This suggests that there does not have to be a single underlying process determining development. It could therefore be the case that children's apparent consistency of progress with attainments is due in part to the consistency of what happens to them. If all children have roughly the same general experiences in life, then different areas will move forward at a similar rate and it will appear that they are connected.

Within a particular domain, however, such as linguistic abilities, there can be a high level of interconnection of skills, with some attainments acting as a general basis for further progress. Focusing on specific attainments may then easily show 'stage-like' progressions. As an example of this, word-reading abilities show a relatively rapid increase in most children from about 7 years of age (see Chapter 9). This is not, however, due to the sudden onset of operational thought, but is related to the development of generalised phonic attack skills. Different areas may also interact in specific ways, as with reading and language abilities, where verbal knowledge and understanding can support reading comprehension but are also themselves developed by the process of reading.

A revised perspective on Piaget

Although there have been many criticisms of Piaget, there is still general support for his belief that cognitive progress in children can be seen as their active construction of mental structures, utilising new information from their environment.

It also seems plausible that children's thought has qualitative differences from that of adults and shows progressive development. The early years show an emphasis on direct experiences. Subsequently the child attains greater ability to represent and manipulate experiences mentally, eventually acquiring more abstract conceptual abilities. However, this progress does not appear to be dependent on underlying general logical structures and is relatively domain specific. Different areas and abilities can, however, be connected when there are necessary, dependent relationships between them.

Social constructivism

Piaget was mainly concerned with the cognitive and logical nature of children's development. Although he believed that children's abilities develop through their interactions with their environment, he tended to focus on the mental adaptations involved, rather than the role of the environment. However, other theorists, such as Vygotsky, a contemporary of Piaget, have emphasised the way in which children's experiences underlie their cognitive development. Those experiences are determined by the particular individuals (usually parents) who interact closely with children from an early age.

Vygotsky saw the progression of children's cognitive abilities as developing in a generally similar qualitative way to that proposed by Piaget, with initial abilities dependent on direct experiences and actions, leading eventually to more complex and abstract thought. He also believed that children build up or construct their own meaning and understanding of their environment. Unlike Piaget, however, he believed that they do so mainly through their ability to *internalise* experiences. The experiences themselves he saw as being largely provided by parents interacting with their own children. For example, Vygotsky (1978) described young children learning to point when they see their parents doing so in response to something that they want.

As will be discussed in Chapter 8, Vygotsky considered language to be a key feature of children's development. At first they use it mainly to interact with others, but from the age of 2 years onwards, they use it increasingly as a basis for 'thinking out loud'. Eventually a form of simplified language becomes internalised at about 7 years of age and acts to regulate and organise thought when necessary. Vygotsky saw language as the result of early socialisation, but believed that by its use in social contexts it is also the main vehicle for developing later knowledge and understanding.

Anticipating modern perspectives, Vygotsky also believed that children's development can be best understood in terms of the acquisition of their *culture*. This is embodied in language, art, and ways of seeing and understanding the world, including elements such as metaphors and other models, songs and play. This emphasis implies that there will be significant differences in the thinking of children from different cultural backgrounds, and is supported by findings that basic features such as values and attributional styles can vary widely. Kivilu and Rogers (1998), for instance, found that children from Kenya considered that their academic success depended largely on how they were taught. By contrast, children from Western and Asian countries generally consider ability and effort to be much more important.

Vygotsky particularly believed that children's early understanding came from the support that they were given by interacting with knowledgeable adults. Such support enables children to function in an area which he named the *zone of proximal development* (see Figure 2.17) and which is beyond children's normal independent abilities. When children are given such support, they are then able to internalise the actions of adults and to make further progress.

This approach implies that teaching should focus on activities within this zone, since it is here that learning progress is occurring. In

Figure 2.17 Zone of proximal development

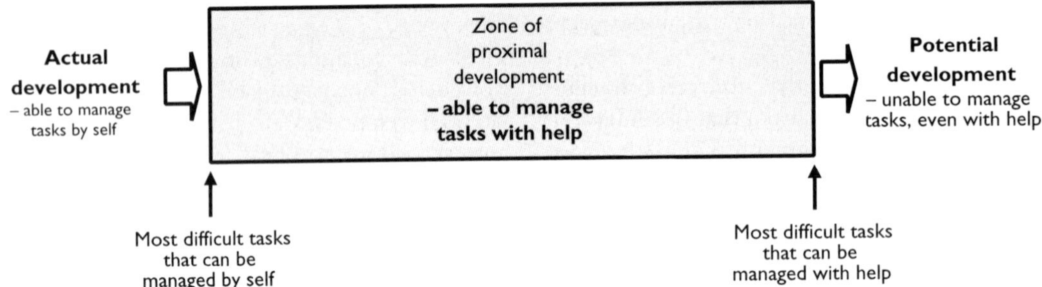

Piagetian terms, this is the area of greatest disequilibrium and accommodation, and these processes underlie children's interest, curiosity and intrinsic motivation. A further important aspect is that children with the same level of ostensible development may actually have different proximal development zones. As an example of this, two children could have the same basic word-reading vocabulary but one of them may be more likely to make progress if he or she has better abilities with speech and letter sounds. As described in Chapter 3, an assessment of children's ability to make progress could therefore involve teaching them within this zone – a procedure known as *dynamic assessment*.

Scaffolding

The process by which children can be taught within the proximal development zone has been described by Wood *et al.* (1976) as similar to the process of 'scaffolding' in building. This apt metaphor implies that the adult supplies initial support to enable children to construct their understanding, and that this support is then withdrawn when they have independent abilities. Wood *et al.* studied parents teaching 3- to 5-year-old children simple physical construction tasks. In this situation, effective teaching appeared to be based on two main 'rules':

- When a child was struggling, the tutor immediately offered more help.
- Conversely, when the child was successful, the tutor gradually reduced the support he or she provided and gave less help until the child was managing the task alone.

Another key element of scaffolding appeared to entail involving a child – 'luring' him or her into the activity. This was often done by demonstrating interesting parts of the task that the child could do straight away, such as fitting easy parts together. Also the task was often made easier, so as to fit with the child's actual abilities at that time. This could involve taking away parts, or helping the child to see things in a different way.

Unsuccessful strategies which were used by some parents involved demonstrating the whole task, which just overloaded the children. Either the children attempted to leave the situation, or the parents forced them to become more actively involved. Other parents relied almost exclusively on verbal instructions, such as 'put the little blocks on top of the big ones', which the children were not able to understand without first being shown.

When scaffolding does work well, then as Vygotsky suggested, children seem to internalise the actions that they have observed. A key role for the adult is to demonstrate or 'model' correct behaviours, as well as maintain children within their 'zone of proximal development'. Adults can also function to remind children of their overall goal or objective, since otherwise children might lose their motivation when they have completed part of the task.

Since scaffolding requires close monitoring and direction, it is difficult to apply with whole classes, and Bliss *et al.* (1996) found that scaffolding was only rarely used by most teachers. The individually based technique of 'reading recovery' mentioned in Chapter 9, however, is explicitly based on the scaffolding approach. It involves the close matching of reading material to children's abilities, at the 90 per cent success level, and by giving children minimal but sufficient prompts to enable them to function as independently as possible. This can, for example, mean encouraging children to use phonic and contextual cues, rather than just giving them the correct word when they get stuck. However, Hornsbaum *et al.* (1996) found, in direct observations of reading recovery sessions, that the zone of proximal development was constantly shifting and that there was often only incomplete learning before the child progressed to the next target.

Learning from adults does not always involve the tight structure and interactivity of scaffolding, and children can often learn by simply observing or being told what to do. Tharp and Gallimore (1988) refer to the processes of support (including scaffolding) as *assisting*. These are more applicable to class teaching and involve the techniques of *instructing*, *questioning* and *cognitive structuring*. These are recognisably what most teachers do, but Tharp and Gallimore emphasise that they should enable students to develop their own understanding, rather than merely assimilate information. For example, teachers can use questioning that leads children to think about topics, rather than just having right or wrong answers. Teachers are also an important source of information which can enable pupils to organise their own knowledge and understanding, by the use of explanations or strategies and rules.

Reciprocal teaching

Children in the same teaching group will often be at about the same level of development within a particular area. In Vygotskyan terms, they are therefore operating within the same zone of proximal development and might learn from being exposed to each other's thinking. The idea is used in a technique known as *reciprocal teaching*, whereby groups of children work together and discuss their ideas and ways of solving problems. The teacher's role in this is mainly to set up and manage the group, rather than providing a direct teaching input, since this could interfere with what the children learn from other pupils.

Although it seems surprising that children might be able to learn without being directly taught, a review of a number of studies by Rosenshine and Meister (1994) found an average effect size of 0.32 for such groups. Reciprocal teaching is also a key element of the highly effective CASE approach to be described in Chapter 4, and Askew *et al.* (1997) found that it was a strategy used by the more effective teachers of mathematics that they studied.

Implications of developmental theories for teaching

Educational limitations of cognitive development

Piaget appears to have overemphasised the possible limits to children's attainments, and it would certainly be misleading to use his stages as guides to what can or cannot be taught at specific ages. However, within domain areas there are still general qualitative differences in thought, which over the age range of pupils in school progress from the more concrete and direct, to abstract understanding. Although teachers should take account of the level of children's understanding, this will often be due to the children's underlying expertise, which can be developed to enable further progress. An example of this in mathematics is 'subtraction with decomposition', as with the sum '43 minus 17'. Children often have particular difficulties with this procedure (which is normally achieved at about 8 years of age), probably because in order to take away the unit value of 7, you need to break down (decompose or partition) the 40 into 30 and 10 and then transfer the 10 across to the units. This is much more complex than just taking away in columns, and would probably be difficult for children to achieve unless teaching had first enabled them to develop sufficient expertise with place value.

Developing new knowledge

Most developmental sequences imply that learning experiences for younger children should be based on more practical, physical (concrete) experiences, eventually leading with older children to more indirect knowledge and ideas, and should finally involve more complex and abstract information. Bruner (1966a) has extended this idea, considering that the earliest type of thought involving direct physical experience (which he has termed the enactive mode) is present at every age and that this can be the basis for all initial learning, even in adults. The principle has been applied in a number of different curriculum developments, such as the *Nuffield Science Teaching Project* (1967), which bases the initial learning of scientific principles on direct experiences by the pupil and only then goes on to develop generalisations and more complex reasoning.

Importance of active, guided involvement

The active involvement of the child is central to most recent theories about cognitive development. Piaget's original ideas on this were sometimes interpreted as implying that learning should take the form of pure discovery learning. However, this is not necessarily the case, and Piaget did state that a child's environment can involve a teacher facilitating this involvement. The ideas of Vygotsky also emphasise that learning mainly happens in the zone of proximal development and that this can happen through the guided, social interaction of a knowledgeable adult.

Play and learning

Piaget (1951) described play as essentially early, self-directed cognitive development. This is part of the process of intrinsic (self-directed) motivation, and these ideas have been successfully implemented in a number of learning programmes such as Dunn *et al.*'s (1968) approach to the teaching of language skills through structured play activities. Play therefore *is* learning, Piaget believed, and many intrinsically motivated learning activities can be described as play, even when carried out by older children or adults. Early educational experiences which are based on play have often been shown to have better long-term developmental and motivational outcomes than do more formal approaches (see Chapter 5 for a discussion of this).

Language and learning

The ideas of Vygotsky and Bruner emphasise that language is the primary medium for socially interactive learning, and that it is also the main basis of knowledge and understanding. These ideas are supported by findings such as the research of Hart and Risley (1995), which demonstrates the massive and cumulative effects of language experiences on children's long-term cognitive developments.

The role of disequilibrium

Piaget believed that development is prompted to occur when information does not fit with existing mental structures, and new equilibrium have to be formed. According to this, it should also be possible for an external agent (a teacher) to stimulate a child with new information and produce disequilibrium and cognitive change (learning). A teacher can identify a child's current level of functioning, then bring in new experiences to push along the process of assimilation (relating the new experiences to the child's existing ideas or knowledge), which should eventually lead to accommodation. Research into this process reviewed by Eckblad (1981) shows that the level of task success that generates greatest involvement is around 95 per cent. Such a level is much higher than most teachers aim for (about 60 per cent), especially when dealing with new material. The discrepancy has important implications for the matching of the difficulty level of materials for optimum learning.

The meaning of errors

Most developmental perspectives see children as actively constructing their understanding of the world. This implies that teachers, when analysing pupils' work, should treat a 'wrong' answer as a child's attempt to make sense of a difficult task, using his or her existing logical abilities and knowledge. Goodman's (1968) approach to the assessment of reading is based on such 'miscue analysis' and uses a child's errors to direct subsequent teaching targets. Effective feedback should therefore be based on the nature of children's errors and give information on how they could develop their abilities.

Use in assessment

Developmental theories have also formed the basis for a number of approaches to the assessing of children's underlying abilities. Uzguris and Hunt (1975), for instance, have devised a scale, based on Piaget's ideas, for the assessment of children with severe learning difficulties. This allows an assessor to distinguish between very early types of cognitive development – for example, from the reflex stage, at 0 to 6 weeks, to the stage of primary circular reactions (repeating actions with own body) at 6 weeks to 4 months. Another development is the Symbolic Play Test (Lowe and Costello, 1976), which has been designed to indicate whether a non-communicating child is able to develop meaningful language. This is based on Piaget's ideas that early concept formation and symbolisation are the basis for early language. The more flexible approach of Vygotsky has also been used as the basis for the development of 'dynamic assessment' (see Chapter 3), which looks at children's responses to teaching as a basis for future progress.

Optimising learning

The various findings about learning and cognitive development have a number of general implications for how teaching and learning situations should be organised.

Match

Perhaps the most important and pervasive concept is that the tasks given to an individual child should be appropriate to his or her learning needs. The simplest interpretation of match is that it involves ensuring that the work given to pupils is neither too hard nor too easy, and that the content is related to their existing knowledge, skills and understanding. In practice, it can be achieved with a specific sequential curriculum, and continuous formative assessments. As described in Chapter 3, these provide feedback for teachers, to enable them to place pupils on the curriculum and to modify subsequent learning experiences. Dockerell (1995) has described the implementation of such a system in a secondary school, which resulted in changes in teaching and significant improvements in students' learning. Specific feedback is important for students, not only to develop their sense of self-efficacy and motivation but also to guide their own learning towards work that is most appropriate for their attainments.

The *mastery learning* technique is an individualised learning approach which depends upon a close match between pupils' initial attainments and their work. Carroll (1963) believes that pupils' existing knowledge and specific abilities account for half of their subsequent progress in a particular area, and that they need to achieve at a high level of success (typically 80 per cent) before progressing on to subsequent objectives. Most reviews, such as that by Kulik *et al.* (1990), have concluded that mastery learning can be more effective than conventional teaching, where class or group work means that individuals often have to study in areas where they have a weak skills foundation.

In the normal classroom it is difficult to match

work closely to each child, owing to the range of abilities and attainments. Teachers usually compromise by pitching work at the average range, and then setting up different learning experiences for children whose needs differ significantly from this range – termed *differentiation*. This can take a number of different forms, as will be described further in Chapter 12. Although differentiation may be difficult to achieve for individual pupils, Mortimore *et al.* (1988) found that differentiating work for children grouped by ability in a particular class was an effective approach.

Withers and Eke (1995), however, criticise this view of 'curriculum match' as being mechanistic and over-simplistic, arguing for a more active cognitive developmental perspective. They emphasise the Vygotskyan perspective of learning as a social activity, with the teacher working within the 'zone of proximal development' for students and with learning being constructed rather than transmitted. According to this, 'match' becomes a more dynamic concept, with the role of the teacher being to foster learning through appropriate and responsive scaffolding, rather than just running through a curriculum sequence at what is presumed to be the right level.

High levels of success seem to be important for natural, intrinsic motivation (see Chapter 5), and curiosity and interest are generated by ensuring that the task involves some novel or challenging information. In Piagetian terms the teacher's job is to generate disequilibrium, which Withers and Eke imaginatively describe as 'putting the bit of grit into the equilibriated structure of the oyster which forces it to accommodate and produce a pearl'. Unfortunately, of course, disequilibrium does not always lead to the immediate generation of new schemas. When pupils are challenged this may sometimes be too much for them and they may need further support and direction.

Cognitive dissonance

In a similar way, Festinger (1957) has argued that development happens when two mental states conflict with each other. This cognitive dissonance appears to result in a state of unpleasant tension and arousal which motivates people to resolve the mismatch, often by restructuring their ideas or beliefs. The concept of cognitive dissonance has been particularly applied to account for the process of attitude change, which involves emotional commitment as well as the ways in which information is interpreted. For example, mixed cooperative learning groups can give pupils positive experiences of pupils from other ethnic backgrounds. These will conflict with previous prejudiced attitudes and result in dissonance, which can be resolved by developing more favourable attitudes to those ethnic groups. (The alternatives are to avoid the issue, by a process of denial; or to seek confirmatory evidence for the originally held beliefs.)

Collins and Stevens (1982) also describe how a teaching process called the Socratic technique uses cognitive conflict to develop educational goals. This involves discussion with progressive questioning to expose weaknesses and to force the student to re-evaluate and develop his or her knowledge and ideas further. These techniques can be used in class work, or with individual students. Thomas (1994) considers that learning can also occur as relatively informal ongoing dialogues between an adult and a child, called 'conversational learning'. This can be seen in the highly interactive parent–child relationship, which produces major learning gains. However, within the normal class, children have only limited direct contact with their teacher, and learning must depend to a great extent on pupils' own personal resources and involvement.

The above findings suggest that an ideal learning situation is provided by one-to-one teaching. When such teaching is carried out by a knowledgeable and experienced teacher, work can indeed be very closely matched to a child's abilities, achieving the high success levels and relevance to the child's interests that produce high levels of motivation. Studies by Bloom (1984) have demonstrated that such individual tuition can produce major learning gains, with an average effect size of 2. Individual tuition is of course normally impractical, although highly structured class teaching can achieve some of these benefits, for instance with individualised mastery learning programmes.

Connectionism

One of the problems for most of the above theories of learning is that they tend to involve the development of rather abstract features such as concepts and schemas without any links to what this could all be actually based on. The relatively new development of *connectionism* is a way of looking at thought and learning that is based upon highly complex parallel logical systems which have similarities to the structure and possible working of the human brain. The new approach can account for a range of complex functions, including concept formation and identification. It represents a radical departure from classical cognitive descriptions, which are usually couched in terms of a clear sequence of logical processes.

The human brain is made up from a huge number of cells, probably more than a trillion of the main ones, known as neurons. Each of these link with thousands of others, and together they form a dense and highly complex web of interconnections. Basic brain processes such as perceptions happen relatively quickly – typically in less time than it takes for information to pass between 10 neurons. This, combined with findings from neurophysiological research, makes it seem likely that much of the brain's processing takes place in parallel, with many neurons becoming activated at the same time and hence many processing operations occurring simultaneously. This perspective sees learning as the process by which different connections between the neurons become strengthened or weakened, producing specific patterns of pathways which are the basis for new concepts and ways of thinking.

The key elements of this process can be represented in a system called a *neural network*, which can be either a computer program or an integrated circuit. The system is made up from layers of artificial 'cells' or units, which are connected with each other. One layer acts as the 'input', rather like the initial sensory processes of the brain. Another layer usually acts as a 'hidden' or interconnecting level, where the main biasing and routing of information happens. A final layer acts as the 'output' and is the result of the combinations of the various biases in the connections. Like neurons, each unit in the network will become activated and pass on information only if the information it receives goes above a certain critical threshold.

Figure 2.18 Simplified neural network for word analysis

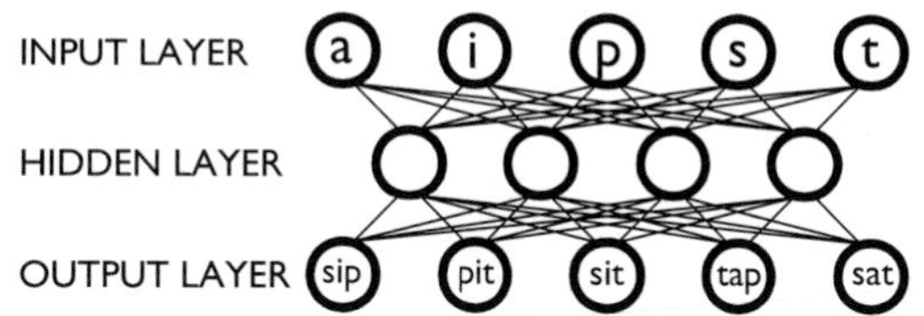

Neural networks have to be 'trained' using feedback to give the desired output for specific inputs. This is done by repeatedly giving the network a range of possible input experiences, then using the accuracy of the output to modify the biases of the connections between the units. When a particular output is incorrect, the biases are given a slight nudge in their values towards what would give a correct answer, in a technique known as 'back propagation'.

As an example, Figure 2.18 shows a basic neural network set up to receive input as five letters of the alphabet and analyse these to 'recognise' five simple words. At first, a naive network will just give random outputs. After a number of training sessions, however, the appropriate connections shown for the word 'sit' might be strengthened, as shown in Figure 2.19. If units are activated only when they receive two inputs, then the specific combination of letters in 'sit' will trigger the appropriate output unit.

Connectionism has been applied in a broadly similar way to this by Sejnowski and Rosenberg (1987) to train a neural network called NETtalk to 'read' text. This was set up to accept text input and to output phonetic codes which could be

Figure 2.19 Network trained to identify the word 'sit'

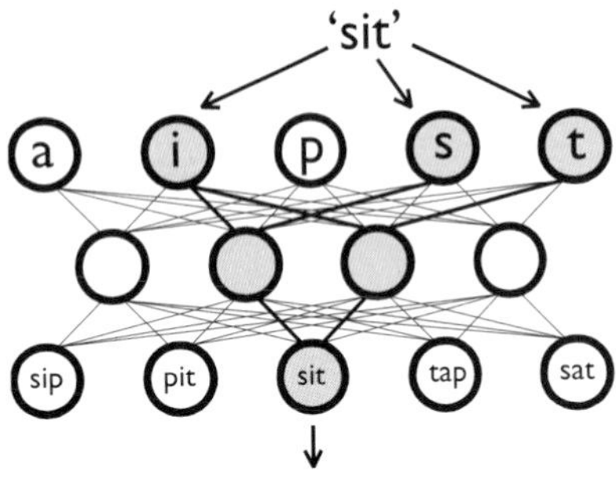

Heavy lines show the biases in connections between the cells.

turned into sounds. The training input involved a large amount of normal English text, coupled with its corresponding phonetic output. At first, the network emitted only random sounds, then went through a stage of 'babbling', which then became closer to normal speech, eventually developing a fairly accurate spoken representation of what was written. The trained network was able to 'read' new text that it had never encountered before.

Neural networks have also been used to develop language capabilities which were once thought to involve sophisticated high-level cognitive processes. Rumelhart and McClelland (1986), for instance, have developed a system which learned to identify the past tense of regular and irregular verbs, and Elman (1991) was able to train a network to make grammatical predictions for missing words.

The reason for carrying out such investigations is that they could be telling us something about how the brain may be working. One key feature is that the above networks did not need any special predisposition to learn certain types of structures. This appears to throw some doubt on the idea that humans must possess some specific inherited abilities in order to learn apparently complex behaviour. Nor do networks need any form of 'rule processing', even though the final set of connections does reflect whatever regularities and patterns there were in the original information. In NETtalk, for instance, the hidden layer units showed distinct separate patterns of activation for vowels and consonants. Combined with the fact that it is difficult to argue that such networks are 'conscious' in any meaningful way, this throws some doubt on the need for classical, 'rule-seeking' cognitive processes in basic learning.

For example, a child developing language may make what appears to be an overgeneralisation of a rule, as when saying 'mouses' instead of 'mice'. This can be taken to indicate that he or she is consciously generating and testing hypotheses about the underlying structure of adult language. However, at one stage of training, Rumelhart and McClelland's (1986) network made the very same type of error, indicating that such learning could in fact be largely automatic and unconscious, with the properties of implicit learning described earlier in this chapter.

There are large numbers of units in any practical neural network, and their connections represent a highly complex system. For this reason, it is not possible to know exactly how the various weightings in a trained system are operating. In a similar way, it may be that we cannot actually know the exact nature of human learning and can only describe possible associations between input experiences and output responses – representing a rather unexpected return to some of the original ideas of behaviourism.

It is fair to say, however, that the relevance of connectionism is still hotly debated, and there are still many uncertainties about how the brain really works. There are also difficulties in getting neural networks to reproduce *general* relationships between symbolic representations; they tend to be relatively specific to what they have been trained up on. Despite this, neural networks have many strengths which come from their distributed nature. This means, for instance, that they are able to represent complex, probabilistic concepts such as the use of prototypes or schemas (discussed earlier in this chapter). It seems likely, therefore, that connectionist approaches will continue to be a useful way of describing general learning processes, and may have a basis in the underlying biological functioning of the brain.

The promise of information and communications technology

Information and communications technology (ICT) involves the use of technology such as computers as the basis for teaching systems which use complex software programs. It also increasingly acts as the basis for communication through systems such as email and enables pupils to access a range of information via the Internet.

The use of ICT is unique in education since it is in theory capable of open-ended development. This is happening by progressive developments in the power and the cost of available hardware, and by the sophistication and availability of software systems and ways of using such technology. Ultimately, ICT-based systems appear to have the general potential to provide optimal individualised and interactive learning experiences up to and beyond the level of individual instruction.

However, at the time of writing, this still remains a possibility for the future. Although most schools now have a number of computers, a survey by the DfEE (1998h) indicated that more than a third of these were more than five years old and that each one had to be shared between as many as 18 pupils in primary schools. Moreover, the review by Harrison (1992) indicated that ICT was, at the time, largely used in the classroom simply to support existing basic educational tasks such as word processing, which at that time accounted for 37 per cent of its overall usage. Although word processing probably remains a core use, other applications have been developed. The use of adventure games can stimulate interest and involvement, and applied database projects are already part of the National Curriculum. Some of the more recent multimedia techniques use large amounts of well-presented visual and auditory information and can enable children to investigate, interactively, a particular area of knowledge. Evaluations of this approach by Moreno and Mayer (1999) found improvements in recall of 41 to 61 per cent when speech was used instead of text and when visual animations were closely linked with verbal explanations. Such systems can also encourage discovery learning as children play with and explore their content.

All schools are now being linked to the Internet to encourage communication based on the use of email, and to develop conferencing and video interaction. The use of search engines can also produce large amounts of information on a wide range of topics. Unfortunately, the difficulty with this is that the majority of what is found normally has only limited value or relevance, and younger pupils in particular will need considerable guidance to achieve a specific task.

Most computer-based learning is characterised by the fact that it is paced by users and is largely under their control. Since computers can be used on an individual basis, the learning experience may also be closely matched to a pupil's level of achievement or ability. These systems can therefore be highly motivating and lead to good progress. For example, the ImpacT study, reported by Johnson *et al.* (1994), looked at the effect of the use of ICT with 2,300 pupils from 87 classrooms in primary and secondary schools. Progress with a number of curriculum subjects was studied over two academic years, and achievements were compared between teachers using a range of different types of ICT and a comparison group who did not use any ICT. The overall results showed a significant superiority for those children who were taught using ICT, although there was considerable variation from teacher to teacher. In cases where ICT had little effect, this seemed to have been due to the use of an inappropriate software package, time constraints due to the need to cover a particular curriculum, and problems with collaborative working.

In terms of future developments, computers appear to have the potential to achieve much the same as individual personal tutoring. Self (1987), for instance, describes how intelligent computer-aided instruction could be used to model the key features of children's cognitive processes and thereby guide individually matched tuition. Anderson *et al.* (1997) have developed such an approach in an intelligent tutoring system called the Practical Algebra Tutor (PAT). This is based on Anderson's work on the development of thinking skills, and leads students through a number of applied algebraic problems, developing a model of their abilities from the responses which they make. The model is based on declarative and procedural knowledge and is used to help students when they have difficulties, using appropriate feedback which ranges from brief messages to remedial instruction. An evaluation of the educational outcomes of this approach by Anderson *et al.* (1997) demonstrated that students' basic skills improved over one year by 15 per cent, when compared with classes who were taught normally. The ability of students to solve real-world mathematical problems, which was a main objective of the curriculum, improved by 100 per cent when compared with students who followed a conventional curriculum with normal teaching techniques.

The review by MacKenzie (1990), however, notes that progress with such systems has been slow, owing to the complexity of the knowledge base, and limited understanding of the teaching and learning processes. It therefore seems likely that teachers will not be dispensed with for some time yet!

Summary

Learning is a central and pervasive concept in education and involves changes in pupils' knowledge, skills and understanding. Basic forms of learning include habituation – learning to ignore irrelevant information – and conditioning – the learning of associations between events, responses and outcomes. Most learning in schools is more active, however, and involves cognitive or thinking processes. These entail the development of internal representations from our experiences, and ways in which we can manipulate them and interact with our environment.

Memory is the storage and retrieval of information by the brain. It initially involves short-term or working memory, which has capacity limitations and depends on our encoding abilities. Long-term memory has a very large capacity, and information is mainly stored in terms of its meaning, with different forms of conceptual organisation. We can fail to learn or subsequently forget material, particularly as a result of interference, which is the result of difficulties in separating information. Learning and memory can be improved by techniques which improve the way in which we structure what we learn. The most effective and useful forms involve an emphasis on organisation and understanding. Learning is also most effective when it is spread out over time and when it involves structured reviews and relevant previewing of topics.

A popular perspective which underlies the National Curriculum sees learning as a progression through a hierarchical structure of knowledge. An alternative approach considers that learning is best seen as the active construction of mental representations (schemas) by pupils. Piagetian theory describes the key developmental processes involved in this as *assimilation* of new information, and *accommodation*, as schemas are adapted. Modifications of this perspective emphasise that pupils construct their knowledge and understanding in social contexts and that expertise can be developed in specific domains, often without any necessary logical connections between them. Applying these ideas to education emphasises that the role of the teacher is to facilitate learning. Key aspects of the facilitation of learning are to match experiences with pupils' abilities, and to encourage appropriate levels of challenge or dissonance to generate change.

Recent theories see the underlying basis of such learning structures as the formation of complex connectionist patterns, in the same way as the basic units of the brain operate. These simple systems can be very effective in producing apparently sophisticated learning, which implies that it is not necessary to consider innate predispositions for development.

The use of information and communications technology (ICT) appears to be potentially capable of optimising learning by individualising pupils' experiences. Teaching systems which develop from an understanding of the ways in which children learn are just starting to realise this potential.

Key implications

- Effective learning involves the use and application of knowledge, which takes the form of complex, interrelated internal representations.
- Such learning is best described as an active construction by pupils within a social context.
- The role of teachers is primarily to facilitate this by organising and directing experiences which are matched with pupils' abilities and attainments.
- Pupils can also construct meaning from simplified experiences involving actions and consequences (behaviourism).
- Optimal learning comes from individually matched, responsive teaching systems.

Further reading

David Wood (1998) *How Children Think and Learn*, 2nd edition. Oxford: Blackwell.

A popular classic on cognitive development and learning which has been updated. It might be best to have some existing knowledge of educational psychology before you read it, but the book would make an ideal follow-on from this chapter.

Jacqueline Bristow, Philip Cowley and Bob Daines (1999) *Memory and Learning: A Practical Guide for Teachers*. London: David Fulton.

Written by educational psychologists and with contributions by other specialists, this is a useful review of theories and practical techniques which can be applied by teachers.

Alan Baddeley (1996) *Your Memory: A User's Guide*. London: Penguin Books.

Alan Baddeley (1997) *Human Memory: Theory and Practice*, revised edition. Hove, East Sussex: Psychology Press.

The first book is an accessible general introduction to memory. The second is a more technical and in-depth review of the various topics of memory and the research evidence supporting the different theories. This may be rather heavy going by itself but would be good for reference, to develop specific ideas.

Practical scenario

For some time, Mr Jones has become increasingly worried about his teaching abilities. In the past he has considered himself to be a successful teacher, with his pupils achieving well in formal assessments. In his lessons he has usually adopted a brisk pace and aimed to cover the curriculum in some depth. Recently, however, the standard of the school's intake has dropped, owing to local changes in housing policy. Although he has slowed down the rate of teaching, his pupils just don't seem to grasp key concepts and he is wondering if there are more effective ways to develop their knowledge.

- *How would you describe the possible changes in the underlying abilities of Mr Jones's pupils? Why are such changes likely to affect their learning?*
- *Do you think that the answer might be to teach material at an earlier stage of the curriculum, i.e. for younger children?*
- *Can you think of any other ways in which Mr Jones could change the way in which he teaches to become more effective with these pupils?*
- *Is it likely that if he changes what he does and puts in more effort, he will then be able to achieve the same standards as before?*

3 Assessment

Chapter structure

Why assess?

If we did not assess pupils' attainments in some way, it would be impossible to match learning experiences with their needs. We would not be able to tell whether pupils had made any progress and whether we needed to adjust what we were teaching or how we were teaching it. It is now also increasingly clear that learning effectiveness is increased by appropriate and informative feedback to pupils and to teachers, and that, as shown in Figure 3.1, some form of assessment must be part of an effective learning–teaching cycle.

Figure 3.1 Teacher and pupil feedback cycles

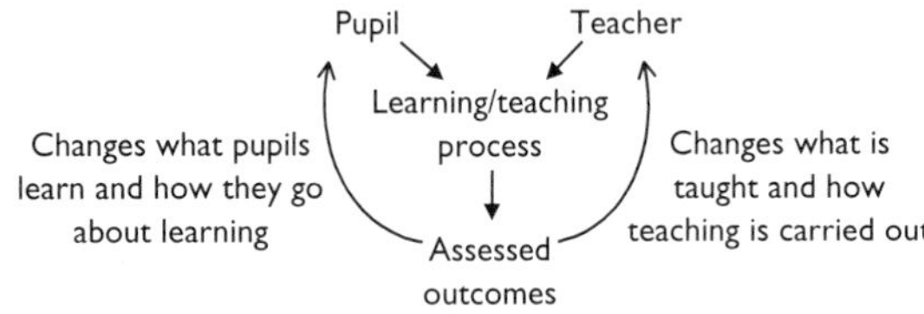

Most assessment is still relatively informal, with teachers being aware of children's performance from the work that they have done. As discussed later in this chapter, assessments should also now be carried out more explicitly as part of the National Curriculum records of achievement. More information about pupil progress or particular skills can be gathered from a range of formalised types of assessment, including specific tests. From these, teachers can make absolute as well as relative judgements about pupils' achievements. However, Gipps *et al.* (1983) found that formal test results are rarely used by teachers, and the tests are carried out by them only since they believe that the results are needed by other people.

National Curriculum assessments have also become important ways of evaluating school and

• TIME SPENT
ASSESSMENT
TEACHING
THIS IS A GOOD AREA WHERE MORE TIME CAN BE SAVED.

teacher effectiveness, and it can sometimes seem as though testing is dominating what goes on in schools. Many teachers would therefore probably support the aphorism quoted by Black and Wiliam (1998): 'Weighing the pig doesn't fatten it.'

Crooks (1988) notes that formal assessments have been found to account for from 5 to 15 per cent of the total available teaching time, with the higher figures applying to the later stages of education. Even this is probably an underestimate of the true total, since less formal assessments are often part of the general teaching process, with teachers regularly using assessments in the form of question-and-answer sessions and as part of preview and review procedures.

Assessment is therefore a major part of the educational process, and without it, teaching would be a rather unfocused activity. Despite this, a great deal of testing is probably implemented with only limited justification. Thus it is important to know about what we can assess, how assessments can be carried out and the ways in which results can be used.

What can we assess?

Attainment

The most common type of assessment looks at *attainment*, which is a pupil's present level of functioning or ability in a particular area. Most formal tests assess a specific attainment. For example, the Schonell test described later in this chapter is an old favourite which measures word-reading ability – how well a child can read a list of separate words. Such abilities can be assessed by a range of tests which cover all the main areas of general academic attainments, as well as specific abilities.

Some specialised forms of assessment are based on the concept that the range of abilities tend to be generally related to each other – if people score well on one test then it is likely they will score well on others. The quality that enables them to do so is known as 'general ability' or intelligence, and, as discussed towards the end of this chapter, it is assessed by using specialised intelligence tests.

However, the main abilities that teachers are interested in are related to the curriculum. We saw in the previous chapter how educational targets can be subdivided into a number of different categories, with the simplest and most commonly used approach covering knowledge (of factual information), skills (how to do things) and understanding (the ability to use information). Although there is general agreement about the *need* for such broad aims, research by Fleming and Chambers (1983) analysed a large number of the tests used in schools and found that nearly 80 per cent of all questions dealt only with recall of factual information. It seems likely that this is due to the ease of using simple knowledge-based assessments, since tests which incorporate children's use of skills and understanding tend to be time-consuming to design and implement. This is not such a drawback with National Curriculum assessments, which are commonly referred to as SATs (Standard Assessment Tests and Tasks), and these typically have an emphasis on questions which involve the use of knowledge.

Knowledge

Declarative, explicit knowledge can be largely thought of as a body of concepts with a structure which includes the links between concepts. Concepts can be physical, or abstract, or can express relationships. They can also be combined to form factual knowledge, in the form of propositions, such as 'A flower's stigma receives pollen', or 'Settlements tend to occur near to resources'. This factual knowledge could be assessed by means of questions such as 'What do we call the part of the flower that receives pollen?' or 'What features determine where people settle?'

Modern views of general, semantic knowledge consider it as a system of related schemas with variables which encode for specific examples. Assessment can therefore focus on the development of generalised schemas within a subject domain, as well as the knowledge of how they operate within particular exemplars. With older students, one might look at the development of the concept of a 'chemical element', with generalised notions of the nucleus and electron shell configuration determining specific valence and reactivity. The general concept could then be related to specific exemplars, and tests carried out for knowledge about particular elements showing different bonding properties, as well as their occurrence in substances of which pupils might have direct experience.

Skill

A skill involves the procedural aspects of how to do things. It normally refers to a higher-level ability that is relatively complex, being made up from a number of other abilities which are linked and coordinated. Having a skill also implies that an individual is able to function competently with it at a certain level. For instance, division is a mathematical skill which depends on the knowledge and use of number, place value and tables. The Attainment Targets at each of the levels of the National Curriculum are examples of stages of functional skill. For instance, at level 2 for Writing, part of the attainment target is: 'Pupils' writing communicates meaning . . . using appropriate and interesting vocabulary' (DfE, 1995b).

Skilled performance involves implicit knowledge and is often initially generated from the rehearsal and development of more conscious abilities. Skills would be assessed by actually carrying them out, although they can also be part of more complex activities. As an example, a reading comprehension exercise would involve a range of basic skills including reading the main text and writing down answers.

The term 'skill' is often used in a relatively loose way to describe any activity that is done well. It commonly occurs in phrases such as 'comprehension skills' or 'problem-solving skills'. Although these involve complex, integrated abilities and may be well rehearsed, they also entail conscious, planned processes and would probably be better described as abilities which involve the understanding and use of knowledge.

Understanding

At a basic level, understanding can involve the transfer and use of knowledge in new situations. This can be seen when applying simple mathematical rules in questions such as 'If Laura and Fred both need two pencils and each pencil costs 15p, how much money will they need altogether?' Other, more complex tasks place a greater emphasis on the need to recognise what knowledge is appropriate. For example, in the question 'What could you use to separate iron cans from aluminium cans?', pupils would need to be aware of the relevance of magnetic properties of different metals and how these could be used.

Higher tests of understanding involve holistic, real-life tasks where both knowledge and skills need to be used. Usually, both transfer and selection of appropriate knowledge are required, particularly in the case of problem-solving tasks. In English, for instance, creative writing will benefit from the generating of ideas and will also depend on existing knowledge and ideas. An example in mathematics which involves some understanding and application of knowledge at Key Stage 2 is shown by the question in Figure 3.2. In this example, the pupil answering it has

Figure 3.2 Mathematics question involving use of knowledge

A school with 173 children has organised a trip to the zoo. The headteacher needs to hire some buses and finds out that each bus can carry 52 children. How many buses do you think that the headteacher will need to book?

$$\frac{173}{52} = 3.3269$$

Answer: 3

just carried out the appropriate calculation on a calculator, and rounded the answer down (as he or she has probably been taught). In the real-life situation however, some children would be left behind if only three buses were available. Given that teachers and, perhaps, other adults would be present, there would need to be a total of four buses.

If problems are more open-ended, such as the use of practical tasks in the SATs, they can become a more valid test of the use of knowledge. These can involve, for instance, posing a problem for pupils to investigate, such as the early 1991 Key Stage 1 SAT task which asked pupils to look at the properties of materials which make them sink or float.

Aptitude

Aptitude assessments look at the potential for *future* attainment. The Reading Readiness Profiles (Thackray, 1974), for instance, test a child's visual and auditory discrimination, as the basis for progress with reading. Many such tests are only weak predictors, however, unless the ability assessed is a necessary precursor of the target ability. The best predictions of initial reading progress, for instance, are the skills of phonological abilities and the knowledge and use of letter sounds. The most accurate predictor at later ages is simply children's progress within a particular area, such as their present reading ability, because early reading skills are not only the basis for future progress but also, probably, an indication of ongoing positive factors such as parental support. Intelligence tests are often taken to imply general learning potential, but, as described earlier, they are really general *ability* tests. As described later in this chapter and in Chapter 4, measured intelligence also only relates weakly to future progress.

Functions of assessment

All the various forms of assessment can be placed into one of the two major categories of *summative* assessment (which gives a level of achievement) and *formative* assessment (which guides future learning). The assessment takes a quite similar form in both cases; what is important is how the results are interpreted and used. In practice, a particular assessment often has both these functions. For example, a mainly summative assessment such as a GCSE grade shows a level of achievement but can also be used to guide future studies, possibly by indicating a suitable direction for further education studies.

Summative assessment

The classic and best-recognised forms of assessment involve 'summarising' levels of achievement. As well as formal tests and examinations such as GCSEs and A levels, these include commonly used informal measures such as review tests. Such evaluations typically involve assessment of a pupil's general level of functioning on a particular curriculum. Formal assessments such as exams often have great importance to the pupils involved since they provide access to employment or higher levels of education. They are also important to schools since they are increasingly being used to evaluate the performance of schools and teachers. They are therefore often referred to as 'high stakes assessment' and bring with them pressures to achieve well.

This can result in effects such as 'curriculum backwash', whereby the content of tests comes to dominate what is taught. Although this need not necessarily be a bad thing, one cannot expect a limited test to give a realistic assessment of performance across the whole curriculum. Black (1998, pp. 67, 68) reviews evidence that to provide adequate coverage, a science assessment would need to take about 35 hours, and that 13 different assignments would be needed to obtain a satisfactory measure of writing achievement. Most formal tests therefore have to be selective and tend to focus on what can most easily be assessed in an examination situation. Teachers are of course aware of this and are influenced to deliver a narrow curriculum, focusing their coverage on the curriculum content and forms of questions that are most likely to be assessed.

General ability tests are also mainly summative, and their primary function in the past (with the 'eleven-plus' exams) was to allocate children to different types of secondary education or, within the field of special needs, to different forms of education. As discussed in the following chapter, such judgements are less likely nowadays, because the limited meaningfulness of these assessments is better understood now.

Pupils often use the results of formal evaluations to make judgements about their own competence and relative standing. Such comparisons form an early basis for establishing academic self-concept, and as pupils go through school this seems to become increasingly important in determining their involvement. When pupils perceive themselves to be successful with meaningful tasks, they are more likely to establish independent motivation and to make subsequent academic progress. When teachers emphasise the evaluative (summative) function of testing in the classroom, the tests may have short-term effects on achievements but appear to have a negative effect on children's long-term attributions and their subsequent independent involvement with school work.

Formative assessment

Formative assessments are those used to help direct or 'form' the educational process for students. They particularly apply to diagnostic assessments, although they can also have guidance, selection and prediction functions. NVQs (National Vocational Qualifications) are national assessments which are based on specific criteria and, since they are competence based, can direct subsequent learning experiences. National Curriculum assessments were initially designed to be used in this way but they have increasingly come to take on a purely evaluative function, to assess the performance of schools and teachers.

A major review of the functions and effectiveness of formative assessment by Black and Wiliam (1998) found that it can lead to significant improvements in learning when used in an appropriate way. The evidence they review indicates a possible effect size ranging from about 0.40 to 0.70, which would represent a significant impact on children's attainments. The authors note that the lowest effect size would raise the average standard of achievement to the top 35 per cent level, or increase average GCSE performance by between one and two grades.

One key feature in formative assessment appears to be the role of *feedback to pupils*. To be effective, it seems that this should focus on details of the students' work, with the assessor giving advice as to what they should do to improve, rather than merely a general evaluation or comparison with other pupils' work. In one particular study by Butler (1988), 48 students were given feedback which took one of three different forms. The first type comprised detailed comments about how the students had done, in relation to criteria for that topic of work. The second type of feedback gave merely the students' overall grades, and the third type combined grades with detailed comments.

The students given the detailed comments subsequently showed a 30 per cent improvement in their scores, while students who received only grades showed no improvement at all. Even more interestingly, those students who had received both grades and comments also made no progress. Such evidence supports the idea that any form of evaluative comment (including praise) will tend to distract attention away from informational content and will actually decrease motivation and involvement. This is similar to findings discussed in Chapter 5 about the importance of intrinsic, as opposed to extrinsic, motivation.

Since information to students about their attainments can improve learning, the *frequency of assessment* is also an important feature. When assessments are more frequent, then, generally speaking, pupils appear to do better on subsequent examination performances. A review by Bangert-Drowns *et al.* (1991) found that on courses lasting from one to four months, testing about once or twice a week had an effect size of up to 0.48. With more frequent testing, this effect is reduced, although frequent short assessments can also be effective, particularly for skill development.

The effects of the *timing of feedback* seem to vary according to the match between the original questions and what is eventually assessed. Kulik and Kulik (1988) found that immediate feedback had a positive effect size of 0.28 when the feedback items were different from those in the final test. Where the original questions were identical to those in the final test, then delayed feedback was superior, with an effect size of 0.36. One reason for these findings could be that immediate feedback tends to interfere with items which have been learned incorrectly. When feedback is delayed, interference would have decreased, enabling further distributed learning to take place.

In most classroom learning, questions and feedback only cover part of what is included in the final course assessment. It seems likely that immediate feedback is therefore normally the best bet, although delayed feedback can also give students more time to reflect on what they have learned and how they have learned it. Such delays should not be too protracted, however, and ideally should at the most only span gaps between teaching sessions, to ensure that feedback remains relevant.

Teachers regularly use *questions* to informally evaluate student knowledge and to direct subsequent instruction. The evidence does indicate that questioning can be an effective teaching technique, and a review by Rosenshine and Stevens (1986) found that teachers who use more questions tend to achieve significantly better results on subsequent formal testing. These gains appear to be a result of increases in the level of student responses and involvement, by providing rapid feedback, and by cueing students in to what the teacher considers important.

Teachers who achieve the greatest gains also tend to use questions or other forms of interactions in a general way, to include as many pupils as possible. Also, the level of difficulty is usually matched to children's abilities so that the majority of questions can be answered correctly. When children have problems with answers, an effective approach is to acknowledge what is correct but then to direct the same pupil with additional information until he or she gets the correct answer, as in the following exchange:

Teacher: 'What does an adverb do?'
Pupil: 'Tells you about a noun' (confusing it with adjective).
Teacher: 'Yes, it tells you more about something, but it's not a noun. Look at the word ad*verb* – the clue's in the word' (emphasising the 'verb' part of the word).
Pupil: 'It tells you more about a verb.'
Teacher: 'Yes, that's right.'

Rowe (1986) also found that it can be better for teachers to wait a few seconds for an answer, particularly with more complex questions (although these are rarely used). Normally, teachers will wait only briefly, and it seems that this can prevent students from thinking about what they have been asked. Samson *et al.* (1987) carried out a meta-analysis on the effects of training teachers to ask more high-level questions to assess pupils' understanding. Although teachers were able to increase their ability to do this, the effect size on academic achievements was only 0.07, which indicates that increasing the use of these types of questions is probably not a very effective strategy.

Range of functions

Assessments can be carried out for a number of different reasons, and MacIntosh and Hale (1976) have derived a number of well-known categories. As shown in Figure 3.3, these can be organised along a formative–summative continuum.

Ideally, tests should be carried out for a particular purpose, rather than simply testing for its own sake. A teacher might wish to review whether a child (or class) has made significant progress over a year, or a headteacher might wish to check whether a class or their school has a disproportionate number of poor readers.

Figure 3.3 The functions of assessment

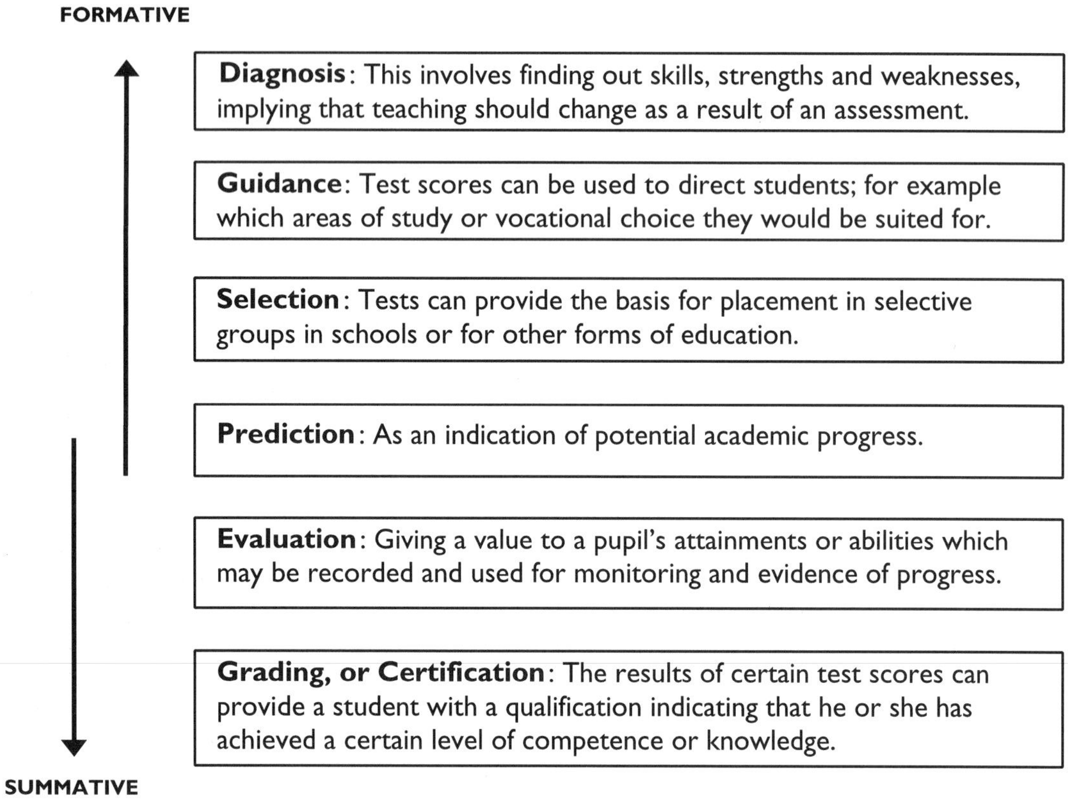

FORMATIVE

Diagnosis: This involves finding out skills, strengths and weaknesses, implying that teaching should change as a result of an assessment.

Guidance: Test scores can be used to direct students; for example which areas of study or vocational choice they would be suited for.

Selection: Tests can provide the basis for placement in selective groups in schools or for other forms of education.

Prediction: As an indication of potential academic progress.

Evaluation: Giving a value to a pupil's attainments or abilities which may be recorded and used for monitoring and evidence of progress.

Grading, or Certification: The results of certain test scores can provide a student with a qualification indicating that he or she has achieved a certain level of competence or knowledge.

SUMMATIVE

Source: based on MacIntosh and Hale (1976)

However, a large survey by Gipps *et al.* (1983) of the reasons given for testing indicated that many tests appear to exist simply for purposes of record keeping. At that time, 71 per cent of all education authorities carried out general screening for reading, but this was rarely the main basis for making further decisions. Even when teachers themselves introduced regular testing in schools, Salmon-Cox (1981) found that they relied primarily on their own judgements and observations to make assessments about children and tended to disregard the test scores. The National Curriculum assessments can also be criticised for having a poor rationale, since although they were designed with formative objectives, Wiliam (1996) points out that their coverage is too limited to achieve those objectives, and that they are also too imprecise to give summative information that is at all useful for individual pupils.

Formal versus informal assessments

Teachers continually evaluate the progress of the children whom they teach and modify the work that they do with them accordingly. Although most of these judgements are informal, they can be very accurate in terms of comparisons of children. Long (1984) found that when primary teachers were asked to assess their pupils' progress with reading, the rank order for each class was almost identical to the order shown by full formal testing. This is perhaps not surprising if one considers that primary teachers have an intimate knowledge of their pupils' daily progress and performance on a range of learning tasks.

However, a difficulty is that teachers are also liable to make substantial errors in assessing children's absolute levels of achievement. Budge (1996b), for instance, has reported on research with Year 4 pupils which found that in schools where attainments were generally all at level 4 or higher (above average), children labelled as having a reading difficulty had an average reading level of 2.28. In schools where overall attainments were at level 2 (below average), the corresponding average reading level for having a difficulty was 1.65, showing a strong effect of context on judgements.

Unlike primary teachers, subject teachers in secondary education usually teach a large number of children and therefore have a wider range of comparison. However, this also means that they cannot have the same detailed knowledge of individuals and are more liable to make errors with specific children. Formal tests can address such problems by giving additional information to teachers about absolute levels of achievement and about the relative abilities of individual pupils. They can also provide more general information, which can be used to compare schools or different types of teaching, and to monitor overall standards.

Types of tests

The two main categories of direct assessment are referred to as *criterion-referenced* and *norm-referenced* tests, and have very different rationales and functions. The purpose of a criterion-referenced test is to compare each individual's specific abilities with some form of level or criterion. The purpose of a norm-referenced test, by contrast, is to discriminate between individuals or to compare them with one another. The content and the use of these two categories is therefore also correspondingly different, although some tests overlap in their coverage.

Criterion-referenced tests

Criterion-referenced tests assess performance purely on specific features of ability attainments. With reading, this might involve whether a child knows some particular letter sounds, or whether he or she can read certain words from a list. Such assessments are closely related to the teaching–learning process and usually come from the techniques used by teachers themselves. They are therefore usually formative, since they identify skills and weaknesses and imply areas to concentrate on with subsequent teaching. A criterion-referenced maths test might identify that pupils have weak multiplication skills; this would mean that it would be fruitless to go on to division until they have developed a strong enough basis with these skills.

Criterion-referenced achievement testing is a key part of a procedure known as *mastery learning*. This is a technique that was developed from the learning theories of Carroll (1963) and which depends on the use of specific levels of achievement with key skills (typically 90 per cent or above) before further progress is possible. By ensuring that children have adequately mastered the foundations for subsequent learning, reviews such as that by Black and Wiliam (1998) have found an average effect size of 0.82 for performance on teacher-produced tests.

National Vocational Qualifications (NVQs) are also largely criterion-referenced and are mainly based on 'specific elements of competence', which are particular skills carried out in workplace conditions. In order to achieve at a certain level, a student has to be successful with a number of units, and these therefore also give summative information.

The National Curriculum assessments were originally largely criterion referenced and based on practical problem tasks. However, they have increasingly been used to evaluate the performance of schools and teachers, and the specific criteria for levels of achievement have been significantly revised over time.

Norm-referenced tests

A 'norm' is a typical or expected value for something. Norm-referenced tests are designed to allow an individual's abilities to be assessed relative to a certain population – usually all the other pupils of the same age. They are therefore mainly summative tests, although if they have the capacity to identify specific skills which can be taught, such as particular operations in a mathematical test, this would constitute a formative component.

Test construction

Norm-referenced tests are developed by first constructing a number of items that assess abilities in a particular domain. With reading, this might involve using a list of words of increasing length and complexity. The test is then checked for reliability (dependability) and validity (meaningfulness), and modified until it meets the desired criteria. Reliability and validity are discussed a little later in the chapter.

The test is then standardised by giving it to a sample of children covering an appropriate age range and general background so that they are broadly representative of the wider population. This information is then used to construct age-standardised tables that can be used to compare subsequent individual test results. Most normative tests assume that the underlying distribution of abilities is 'normally' distributed (see Appendix I), showing the classic bell-shaped curve illustrated in Figure 3.4. Scores can then be standardised, usually with 100 being the mean and 15 being the standard deviation. One standard deviation either side of the mean includes about two-thirds of the population as a whole. About 2 per cent score below 70 and 2 per cent score above 130.

Figure 3.4 Normal distribution curve

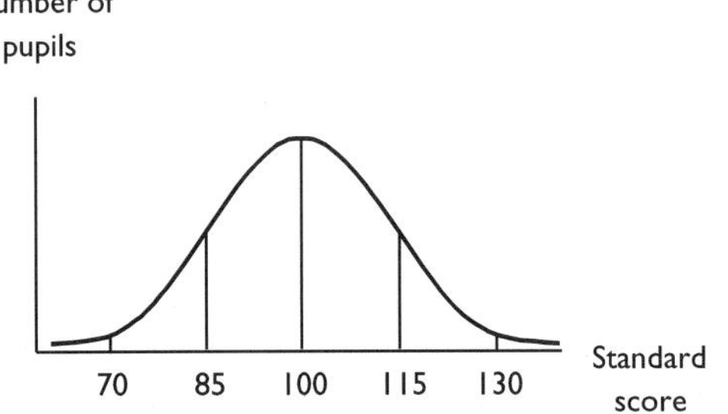

When the test is used, an individual's standard score can then be referred to tables to find out how many others in the population would score above or below that level. As an example, the British Picture Vocabulary Scale test (Dunn *et al.*, 1997) described later in this chapter involves scoring how many times children can correctly identify a picture for a word that is spoken to them. This total can then be compared with age norms to derive a standard score. This can then be used to look up a percentile rank score which tells you how many children of the same age would score above or below this level.

A raw score can also usually be referred to tables in the test manual to give a comparison skill age level, and most reading tests allow you to use the raw score to directly read off or calculate an equivalent reading age. With reading, Gipps *et al.* (1983) found that the most popular individual test in use at the time was the Schonell Graded Word Reading Test (Schonell, 1955). This uses a list of 100 words of graded reading difficulty, which the child reads out loud to a tester until he or she gets 10 wrong. The reading age is then calculated by dividing the total correct by 10 and adding 5 – from the assumption that children start reading at 5 years of age and learn ten new words from the test each year. The popularity of this test was undoubtedly largely due to the simplicity of the procedure (there was no need to refer to a separate manual).

Problems with normative tests

The standardisation of such tests is obviously very important, and the sample used should be representative of current population attainments. However, many popular tests were standardised some time ago, with rather select samples – the most recent Schonell standardisation was based on a 1971 sample of 10,000 children in Salford. This is probably not a good basis on which to assess present-day abilities or to judge other parts of the country. The rather ancient derivation of many tests also makes their validity suspect; for instance, particular words used in the test (such as 'canary' and 'shepherd' in the Schonell) may no longer be so commonly used, significantly altering the relevance of test items.

Other criticisms of normative tests reviewed by the Centre for Language in Primary Education (CLPE, 1989) include:

- the lack of diagnostic information (inevitable with a single normative score);
- the failure of a single measure to represent a complex skill such as 'real reading' which has many different interrelated aspects; and
- problems with interpreting what a single score means.

To some extent these criticisms can be answered by the development and adequate standardisation of more modern and sophisticated tests. Some of these, such as the Effective Reading Tests (1985), give simple normative information but also cover a range of real reading activities and provide diagnostic (formative) information too.

Individual and group tests

Educational tests can be designed to be administered on an individual basis or to groups of children. The advantages of an individually administered test are that it can be closely monitored and adjusted to a pupil's abilities. With some tests this means that it is not necessary to do all of the easier items and the assessment can be stopped when it is becoming too hard. Tests can also directly assess an actual skill such as reading, where the assessor may listen to a pupil reading out loud from standard texts. With some tests this can be the basis for diagnostic information, and errors can be recorded and analysed. The main disadvantage of this approach is the time involved, but this is usually compensated for by the increased accuracy of the test, since close monitoring means that there are fewer errors caused by pupils carrying out the test incorrectly. The Neale Analysis of Reading Ability (Neale, 1989) is a well-known individual test of passage reading that provides normative information and also analyses children's errors. It is meaningful, since it looks directly at the reading process, and it predicts subsequent reading abilities well, with the manual indicating that reading accuracy scores correlate at 0.83 with the same measure a year later.

Group tests are much more common in schools and can be administered to whole classes or year groups at the same time. Such tests are useful for assessing or screening many pupils in a way that is economical of the teacher's time, and all students carry the test out under the same conditions. Unfortunately, with group tests there is less control over what individual children do; such assessments are therefore inherently less accurate and provide less information than individual tests do. Also, group tests are often based on less direct outcome measures of target skills. With the popular Young's (1968) test, for instance, pupils' reading ability is assessed by their ability to choose the correct written word for a picture, and to find the missing word in incomplete sentences. However, well-designed group tests can achieve reasonable accuracy, and the results from the Young's correlate at 0.88 with results from the Neale test (Young, 1968, p. 20).

Test content and structure

Test items

The structure of assessments can vary from relatively open-ended questions (such as essays) to rather restricted questions (such as multiple-choice questions). Although essays can be a very rich source of information about an individual's knowledge and abilities, they can lack consistency in terms of the marking. Marking has been shown to be affected by the style of the writing, the length of the essay and even the name and sex of the examinee, and Wood (1991) found that correlations between markers for the same essay were typically only around the 0.6 level. However, with the use of the detailed marking schemes that are used in A level assessment, Murphy (1978) found that the correlation between the markings of different examiners was much higher, at around 0.9. This again emphasises the general importance of applying specific criteria in assessments to ensure consistency.

Multiple-choice questions have the advantage of providing a highly standardised testing and marking procedure, and certain forms can even be machine marked. Unfortunately, they can be difficult and time-consuming to design. Also, Rowley (1974) has found that their effectiveness can be affected by guessing and by the different ability of examinees to recognise ambiguity, rather than their knowledge and understanding of the subject content.

Test characteristics

When one is choosing, using or developing a test, the two aspects of *reliability* (dependability) and *validity* (meaningfulness) must be adequate so that the test can be useful in practice. Information on these can usually be found in the test manual; this should give details about how these measures were assessed, and about their interpretation, and should also refer to any other research background. Without such information, any test must be of doubtful value.

Reliability

The reliability of a test means the extent to which it is dependable, or how close a particular result is to the 'true' value of what is being measured. It shows itself in the size of the variation in scores, which is the result of various errors. These can be due to factors such as fatigue, guessing or interpreting questions differently, and variations in the administration and scoring. If pupils were given the same test on a number of occasions, then these errors would mean that sometimes they would do well and on other occasions they would not do so well. If the test is a reliable one, their scores would tend to cluster around a 'middle' value which can be thought of as their 'proper' score, the score they would achieve if there were no errors involved. The example in Figure 3.5 shows a typical scatter of scores that you might find if you carried out the same word-reading test 20 times with a child of 10. Clearly, the scores tend to cluster about the middle and usually fit in with the pattern known as the 'normal distribution'. Because it is statistically predictable how many values will fall within a certain standard deviation, this means that we can describe the spread or likelihood of errors, renaming this the *standard error of measurement* (SEM), shown in Figure 3.6.

Figure 3.5 Repeated word reading test scores with one subject

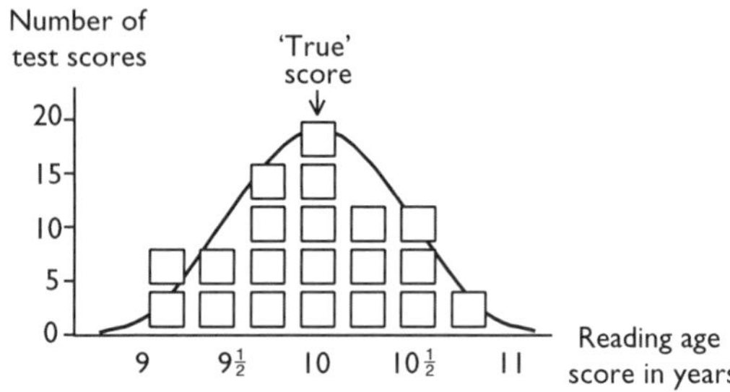

Proper, standardised tests usually give the standard error in the manual, and you can use this to work out what sort of error there will be associated with a particular score. Plus or minus (±) one standard deviation covers about 68 per cent of all values and plus or minus two standard deviations covers about 95 per cent of all values. In the example above, this means that if a child's actual score was at the 10-year level, about one time out of three that child's true score would be above 10½ years or below 9½ years. It is possible, though even less likely (about one in 20 times),

Figure 3.6 Normal distribution of test scores and standard errors

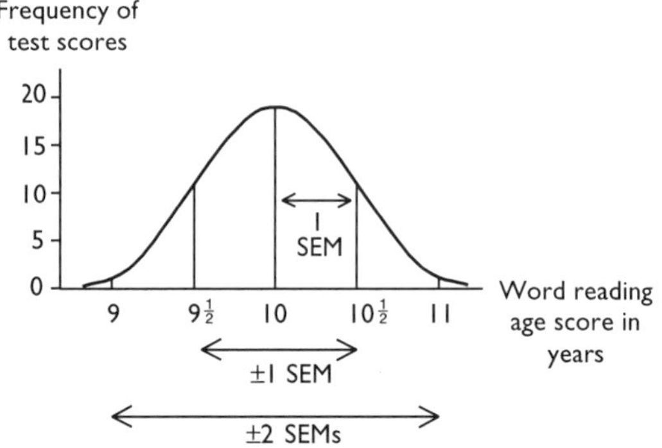

that their true score would be above 11 years, or below 9 years.

It is thus clear that the standard error of measurement is very important, in that it lets us see how much faith can be put in the accuracy of a particular test score. In the example above, it might be rather misleading to compare a child's progress over six months using this test; any real progress might easily be disguised or exaggerated by the normal run of errors. Also, most tests have errors of measurement that are greater than you would normally find with a simple word-reading assessment, particularly if the assessment involves any element of subjectivity or interpretation in the scoring. A good example of this is with reading comprehension tests, which typically have the much greater standard error of measurement of about 1 year.

If a test does not give a standard error of measurement or some other form of measure of reliability, it would be wise to be cautious about its results. Examples of this are the SATs, which, as discussed later in this chapter, probably have only limited reliability for individual children.

ASSESSING RELIABILITY

In real life, most checks for the reliability of a test cannot be carried out many times with an individual child. Improvements may come with practice, or the child's performance may deteriorate owing to fatigue. Measures of reliability therefore usually depend on correlating only two assessments with each of a number of individuals to cover the range of scores. If the value of the correlation coefficient is high enough, normally above about 0.9, then the reliability is good enough for most practical purposes. Such values can be used as a basis for the underlying correlation between what pupils actually score and an estimate of what their 'true' scores should be, as shown in Figure 3.7.

Test–retest reliability is what is assessed when a test is given to the same pupils on only two occasions and the results are correlated. This, it is hoped, minimises practice effects which can interfere with the stability of the results. Fatigue or boredom can also have a significant effect on performance, and to avoid this there has to be a significant delay between the two presentations. This can produce an underestimate in judgements of stability since there will often be some natural variation in scores. With a reading test repeated a week later, some subjects may have improved their true reading ability, while a few might have regressed.

One way round this problem is to carry the test out just once and then to split it into two equivalent halves, often by odd–even items, and then correlate these. The result is called *split-half reliability*. It depends on test items being fairly homogeneous. Although it is usually justifiable to assume that they are, on some tests certain items may not have an equivalent. In a sense, this approach compares the similarity of two tests (each being half of the overall test) carried out at the same time, and therefore gives some indication of whether pupils answer the questions in a consistent way.

An extension of this approach is to compare all possible splits, and to average these out. One popular example is 'Cronbach's alpha' test, which has been used to assess the reliability of SAT testing. Such indicators are easy to derive since they need only one administration of the test to a number of subjects. However, they will not give any idea of a number of sources of error

Figure 3.7 Correlation between actual and 'true' test scores

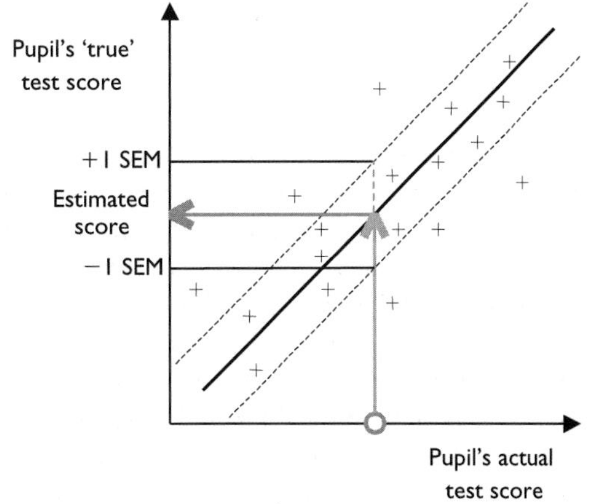

such as differing assessors and pupil variability on different occasions. Such indices can only really tell us whether the test items are generally of the same level of difficulty and whether the pupils taking the test are consistent in the way in which they perform on such test items. This will therefore give an over-optimistic value for the reliabilities of tests and should not be relied on too greatly.

A more complex but more dependable approach is for the test designer to derive two completely *parallel forms* of the same test. Correlating performance on these should give an estimate of the reliability of a single test. Although it is doubtful whether two forms can ever be completely equivalent, the approach does get round practice effects and is the most stringent of all of the reliability assessments. Well-constructed tests can achieve high correlations: the Wide-span Reading Test (Brimer, 1972), with parallel forms A and B, has a reliability coefficient of from 0.92 to 0.94 when the two forms are compared. Other advantages of parallel forms are that they can be used to monitor progress more accurately (since practice effects will be reduced), and that with group testing, the different forms can be alternated in class to prevent copying.

Validity

A test is valid if it measures what it is supposed to measure. Validity can be difficult to define and evaluate effectively, but there are a number of different ways in which this problem can be approached.

FACE VALIDITY

A test has face validity if it looks as though it is assessing what it is supposed to. Face validity can be checked by asking people who are knowledgeable in a particular area to give their impressions about the content. To do this with an early reading test, one might therefore ask for the opinions of some primary teachers, who would presumably look for such features as an early representative sight vocabulary and a progression in the knowledge of letter sounds and their combination. Face validity is typically used in the first stages of developing a test, and is needed to ensure that tests will be accepted by users.

In some cases a test may need to have its true purpose disguised and would have a low face validity. For example, in the Children's Personality Questionnaire (Porter and Cattell, 1992) the items are deliberately written to be as neutral as possible so that children taking the test will not give false responses in order to make themselves 'look good'.

CONTENT VALIDITY

Content validity refers to whether a test uses items which are part of the general area of skills and abilities that the test is designed to evaluate. Therefore, if a test is supposed to assess reading progress at the secondary level, one would expect the content to be drawn from skills appropriate at that age range; this would probably include the comprehension and interpretation of meaningful text. The Gapadol test (1973), for instance, is a group 'cloze' test for older pupils, which involves using meaningful paragraphs with missing words. In order to fill these in, the person being assessed must understand the rest of the text, which indicates that the test does involve skills which are meaningful at this age.

Content validity can also be assessed numerically, and Hoste (1981) has derived a coefficient measuring the extent to which exam items cover the stated aims and objectives of the syllabus; this has been used to show that the content validity of a test changes significantly when candidates choose between alternative questions (covering different topics), as is common in some exams. Content validity, like face validity, is concerned with what is being examined; it is more precise, however, in that it compares this with a previously defined specification, rather than with some vague notion in the mind of the test user.

CRITERION-RELATED VALIDITY

Criterion-related validities compare scores on an assessment with values from some external criterion. *Concurrent validity* is what is measured when the assessment is related to some other assessment that is already available or carried out at the same time. The easiest and most popular way of doing this is to correlate the test with the results from an existing, similar test. The APU Vocabulary Test (Closs, 1977) states in the manual that it has a correlation of 0.778 with another test, the Mill-Hill Vocabulary Test. However, these tests are constructed in virtually the same way, with a target set of words and corresponding sets of answers to choose from; the (relatively) high correlation is therefore more like a test of reliability and is of limited value in assessing general validity.

When concurrent validities are based on other measures, they can become more persuasive. For instance, Freyberg (1970) compared performance on various spelling tests with spelling mistakes in samples of some real-life written work. The correlations found were in the region of 0.9, indicating that spelling tests do relate very closely to natural spelling abilities.

Predictive validity relates an assessment to a criterion evaluated at some time in the future. This is perhaps the most stringent of all the validity tests and implies that there is something continuous over time that is affecting both sets of results. Sometimes it can also be taken to imply that the final criterion is in some way a result of the initially assessed skills, although this is not at all logically necessary.

Peers and Johnston (1994), for instance, carried out an investigation of the relationship between A level results and the criterion outcome of eventual degree level. A level results are used by university admission tutors for the selection of students, but the predictive validity Peers and Johnston found was quite weak, averaging out at a coefficient of 0.276. They interpreted this as being partly due to the different nature of studies, with A levels being largely factual, whereas degree studies are more interpretative.

In some tests which are designed to have a predictive function, this type of validity is much more important. The Bury Infant Rating Scale (Lindsay, 1981) was created to identify children who would have subsequent problems with educational progress. Longitudinal studies carried out by Lindsay to substantiate its validity in this respect found that it did in fact correlate with a range of reading tests two and four years later at around the 0.5 level. Unfortunately, this does not enable one to make very strong judgements for individual children, since the test accounts for only 25 per cent of the variance of later reading scores. As discussed below, it seems likely that baseline assessments will have similarly limited predictive validities.

CONSTRUCT VALIDITY

Construct validity is concerned with the match between the assessment and those attributes (or constructs) which are presumed to underlie test performance. To a great extent, looking for construct validity presupposes that the underlying attributes are well defined, and many tests tend to assume that there is some single global target entity such as 'reading ability' or 'mathematical ability' at which the test can be aimed. However, this may not be the case, and most educational abilities in fact show a qualitative development over time and are based upon a range of different sub-skills. In the area of literacy, Harding *et al.* (1985) have carried out an extensive analysis of reading errors in children aged from 5 to 11. They demonstrated that young children at first depended mainly upon letter sounds (phonics) and their appearance (graphophonics); later abilities depended upon whole word recognition and the use of meaning, although the earlier skills were still available. A test for younger children which looked mainly for understanding and interpretation would therefore largely miss important early skills. Accordingly, Goodacre (1979) argues that assessments should be carefully derived from a specific model of the learning process. Such construct validity has become even more important since 'high-stakes' assessments such as public exams or the SATs are currently tending to be the main goal of teaching and therefore determine the curriculum and the process of education.

There is a danger when using tests that they can sometimes be carried out for their own sake, and it is easy to become immersed in the technicalities of validity and reliability. An alternative paradigm proposed by Shinn and Hubbard (1992) argues that tests should be used as part of a problem-solving framework which emphasises the functions and outcomes of tests for individuals.

From this perspective, validity should refer to the inferences and actions which can result from an assessment, and whether these result in better student outcomes than decisions based on alternative procedures. Rather than just being a nuisance, reliability also becomes a question of how one can account for the variations in pupils' performance and of finding ways to match these with flexible and responsive teaching approaches. Such approaches emphasise the formative aspects of assessment, but have still had only limited impact on most formal testing, which is largely concerned with evaluating and categorising pupils.

Intelligence testing

Origins

The concept of general ability or intelligence has in the past been the most important single way of accounting for individual differences. It is usually assessed by measuring performance on a test of a number of different skills, using tasks which emphasise reasoning and problem solving in a number of different areas. It can be expressed for an individual as an overall IQ or intelligence quotient. Early assessments of IQ were based on work in France by Alfred Binet in 1905, as part of an attempt to identify children who needed specialist help to make educational progress. At the same time, general academic interest in the concept of intelligence was developing. Spearman (1904) in particular showed that performances on a number of performance tests tended to correlate together and believed that this could be explained by the presence of a general ability factor known as 'g'. This form of testing was continued by Cyril Burt, who became London's first educational psychologist in 1913. Burt set a convenient cut-off criterion of an IQ of 70 for special schooling, and this was subsequently widely applied for many years by psychologists working in education, both in Britain and in the United States.

Developments

There was continued academic interest in intelligence testing, and a general belief by researchers such as Louis Terman in the United States that intelligence was largely inherited and therefore stable over a child's school career. With an increase in the number of children receiving secondary education in Britain, the 1926 Hadow Report proposed that in order to achieve efficient education, there should be different forms of secondary schooling matched to children's abilities and their potential. These ideas were eventually implemented by a wide-scale form of general ability testing, known as the eleven-plus, which children sat in their last year of junior schooling. This national test selected out the most 'able' students – those who scored highest in the tests – for grammar schools, where education had a more abstract and academic basis. The eleven-plus was largely discontinued with the advent of comprehensive schooling, although such measures are still used in parts of the country where selective grammar schools remain.

There are tests available that can be used by teachers to assess the abilities of children in school; a good example is the group NFER-Nelson Verbal and Non-verbal Reasoning Test Series. The verbal assessments in this series involve a range of language-based tasks (described later), and the non-verbal assessments use picture series to assess logical reasoning, and series using abstract shapes to reduce the effects of general knowledge.

Some tests are for use with individual children, and these are often 'closed', meaning that they are for restricted use by qualified workers only, such as educational psychologists. A recent example of this type is the British Ability Scales, developed by Elliott *et al.* (1996). This test uses a number of different tasks based on the processes of speed, reasoning, spatial imagery, perceptual matching, short-term memory, and retrieval and application of knowledge.

The most commonly used form of closed individual intelligence test is the Wechsler Intelligence Scale for Children (the WISC). This is now in its third edition (Wechsler, 1992) and has been fully standardised for use in the UK. The WISC covers two overall scales with five main subtests each (see Table 3.1). The number that a child gets right for each of these subtests is referred to age-appropriate tables in the test manual and scaled scores are read off; these have a mean of 10 and go from 0 to about 30. These standard scores are totalled for the verbal and the performance scales and for the test as a whole.

By using tables, the total can then be converted to the IQ or *intelligence quotient*, which is a relative measure of an individual's score compared with that of the general population. The average IQ is 100 and scores have a standard deviation of 15. IQs can also be converted to percentile scores. For example, only 2 per cent of the population have an IQ of 70 or below.

General verbal abilities (verbal intelligence)

Although general ability is assessed by combining scores on a number of different subtests, verbal abilities contribute most strongly to the total score. With the WISC, the vocabulary subtest has the greatest single effect on overall IQ and involves both receptive language (hearing and comprehension) and expressive language (when giving the answer).

A useful test of basic receptive language which can be used by teachers is the British Picture Vocabulary Scale test (Dunn *et al.*, 1997). This is an individual test which can be used across a wide age range from 2 years 6 months to 18 years and is mainly a test of a child's underlying level of verbal concepts. The administration is relatively straightforward, and the person giving the test merely says the target word and asks the child to point to the picture which shows it, as in Figure 3.8.

This test can be particularly useful with young children who have only limited spoken language,

Table 3.1 Scales and subtests of the Wechsler Intelligence Scale for Children

Scale	Subtests	Type of problem
Verbal	Information	What is the capital of England?
	Similarities	In what way are a chair and a table alike?
	Arithmetic	If you have 12 sweets and eat 3, how many are left?
	Vocabulary	What is an elephant?
	Comprehension	What should you do if you got lost in a strange town?
Performance	Picture completion	Find missing part in pictures
	Coding	Speed test for writing matching symbols under shapes
	Picture arrangement	Put picture cards in correct order to tell a story
	Block design	Put coloured blocks together to match a pattern
	Object assembly	Put cardboard parts together to make the shape of a common object

Figure 3.8 Typical form of item in the British Picture Vocabulary Scale test

'Show me *punching*'

and with any older children who might have difficulty with the reading that is involved in some written tests of language.

Other tests assess more general verbal abilities. The NFER-Nelson verbal reasoning test series, for instance, covers the age range from 7 years 3 months to 14 years 3 months and includes vocabulary, logical verbal reasoning, relationships between words, symbol manipulation using letters and numbers, and the use of words in sentences.

Simple tests of spoken vocabulary can also give a useful quick individual assessment of general verbal abilities. An example that can be used by teachers is the vocabulary subtest from the Aston Index (Newton and Thomson, 1976), which involves the tester saying a series of words and scoring the pupil's verbal definitions. This is very similar to the vocabulary subtest of the WISC and incorporates both receptive and expressive verbal abilities, although it is unlikely to have quite the same validity.

General non-verbal abilities (non-verbal intelligence)

Most tests of general intelligence include some form of assessment of non-verbal ability. The popular Cognitive Abilities Test (Thorndike *et al.*, 1986), for instance, covers the age range from 7 years 6 months to 15 years 9 months and is promoted as a means of establishing 'value-added' information. This is done by comparing academic attainments with the abilities assessed by the test which are assumed to underlie such progress. As well as verbal and number skills, the test also incorporates a non-verbal assessment of figure classification, analysis and synthesis. There are also specific tests such as the NFER-Nelson non-verbal reasoning test series, which cover a similar age range from 7 years 3 months to 15 years 9 months. The subtests include abilities such as identifying the odd one out, discovering analogies, finding similarities, filling in gaps in series and completing unfinished picture stories.

Since non-verbal abilities appear to be less dependent on culture and experience than verbal ones are, it can be argued that they are more representative of general, underlying intelligence. This is often assumed to be innate and is referred to by Cattell (e.g. Cattell and Horne, 1978) as 'fluid' intelligence. Interestingly, abilities on such tests peak at an early age – about 14 years with the Raven's matrices test (see below), which does imply some role for biological maturation. Fluid intelligence can be contrasted with more verbally based tests which emphasise acquired knowledge, referred to by Cattell as 'crystallised' intelligence. These abilities tend to show progressive improvements during schooling and reach their highest levels from age 30 years onwards, declining significantly only for people over 60.

The Raven's Progressive Matrices test (Raven, 1993) is one of the most popular ways of assessing non-verbal intelligence. It is open to teachers and can be used either with individuals or as a group test. The various forms cover the entire school age range from 5 years to adult and give a single measure of performance which is standardised for age. As shown in Figure 3.9, the matrices involve analysing logical combinations of geometric shapes in order to select the correct missing pattern.

Although such non-verbal abilities may appear to be more valid assessments of 'true' or under-

Figure 3.9 Typical form of item in the Raven's Matrices

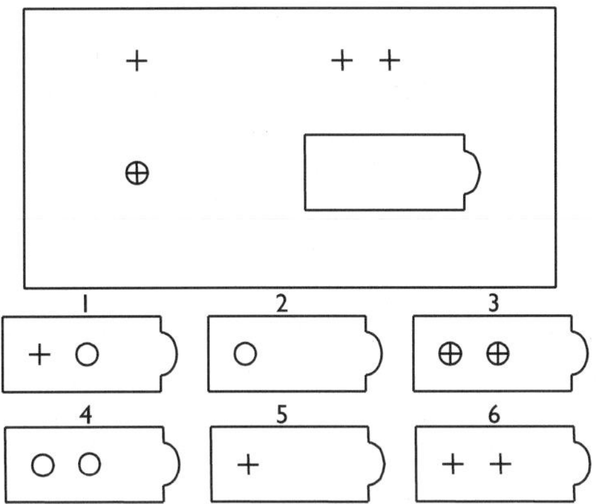

lying intelligence, they are in fact strongly affected by general experience and cultural effects. Flynn (1984), for instance, has reviewed evidence that scores on the Raven's Matrices, originally published in the 1930s, have shown major improvements over time, equivalent to about 20 IQ points per generation (each 30 years). Greenfield (1998) argues that this effect is related to aspects such as increases in the number of people receiving higher education, as well as greater experience with visual-based technology. This upward shift of standards also incidentally makes the use of any norms difficult and means that it is particularly important to base any judgements on recent standardisations of such tests.

A further reason for caution concerning the use of non-verbal assessments is that they have only a weak correlation with school achievements. The variance that can be accounted for is also usually only part of the correlation between verbal abilities and the educational target skill. As an example of this, the manual of the WISC (Wechsler, 1992) shows that the average correlation between the WISC verbal score and general literacy skills from the WORD is 0.66. Adding the WISC performance (non-verbal) score to give the full scale IQ in fact *reduces* this to 0.59. For this reason, it is best to use just verbal abilities if you want to infer some form of 'potential' for progress with literacy.

Reliability and validity of intelligence measures

The reliability of the WISC is well established and the manual gives a test–retest coefficient of 0.92, indicating that pupils tend to obtain very similar scores on different occasions. The validity of this particular test (and others like it) is, however, more open to question, which raises a number of issues related to the meaning of intelligence and the uses to which intelligence tests results are put.

One might agree that such tests have a certain face validity, since they utilise a number of different subtests which appear to cover basic mental processes and which relate to each other to some extent. Criterion validities are more debatable, however, since these depend on how well IQ relates to other attainments. The development of intelligence tests was closely related to its supposed ability to predict educational attainments or potential, an aspect that will be covered in the next chapter. In general, however, the findings show that intelligence test results correlate at only a low level with present or with future educational attainments.

Construct validity of intelligence measures

The very meaning of the construct of intelligence has been and remains the subject of debate. From a statistical perspective, there is certainly a tendency for performances on a broad range of tasks to correlate with one another, supporting the belief in a single general factor. Evans and Waites (1981), however, point out that this type of data can be alternatively explained by a number of lower-order factors which will then correlate together weakly. These low-order factors may in fact be separate mental skills, similar to Thurstone's (1938) analysis of intelligence into a number of primary mental abilities; if some mental skills were shared by the separate tasks, then this would give rise to the observed general correlations between those tasks.

Howe (1988) in particular has criticised intelligence as an explanatory concept. He has reviewed the evidence in a number of different areas as being weak; for instance, there are very low correlations between intelligence and specific learning and memory tasks. In contrast, Sternberg (1988) argues that Howe is selective of the evidence and that broader, naturalistic learning correlates more highly with intelligence. However, one particularly persuasive aspect quoted by Howe and not refuted by Sternberg is evidence of individuals who are low on measures of general ability, yet have specific areas of high achievement. Some 'autistic savants', for instance, have severely limited interpersonal development, general linguistic abilities and other cognitive skills, yet are able to function at a high level with complex mathematical calculations, on feats of memory, or complex visuo-spatial analysis – or they may have high achievements in applied areas such as music or art. If certain high-level functions are not at all dependent on a single general ability factor, then this casts severe doubt on the usefulness of the concept of a single overarching factor of intelligence.

Gardner (1983) believes that such evidence indicates that abilities are not restricted to the intellectual domain, but span at least six areas that are largely unrelated, conceptually. These include:

Linguistic Logical-mathematical Spatial	These are the cognitive abilities assessed by conventional IQ tests.
Musical	Important in cultural and aesthetic development.
Bodily-kinaesthetic	The basis for physical skills such as sport and dance.
Personal	Social abilities, including interpersonal sensitivity and skills of interacting with others.

Academic achievements appear to relate most closely to linguistic and logical-mathematical abilities. Despite this, general life success probably also depends on many other factors such as interpersonal skills and specific attainments as well as general motivation. IQ measures do correlate to some extent with general success in life, as measured for instance by people's income. However, Ceci (1990) found that this correlation was confounded by the amount of education which people had experienced. When this was controlled for, then IQ–income effects disappeared. Nor was there any correlation between measures of IQ and success within a particular occupation.

In general, there are grounds for strong doubt about the stability of intellectual abilities and questions about the use of intelligence to predict academic progress. As Howe (1989) points out, the term 'intelligence' may be useful to us in everyday life to describe general levels of functioning but probably has limited value as an explanatory concept in education. Perhaps, as he says, 'So far as attempts at scientific explanation are concerned, intelligence ... may quickly become as dead as the dodo, and belong only to history.'

Other forms of assessment

Teachers can gather further information about pupils by using a number of other techniques which include observational approaches, interviews and parental discussion. A more recent type of interactive or dynamic assessment also attempts to look at the direct process of learning and has claims to be more naturalistic and valid. These techniques are examined below.

Observational techniques

Observational techniques are particularly appropriate for gathering information about classroom processes. They are usually carried out by a separate person in the classroom. One of the most commonly used systems was developed by Flanders (1970). As shown in Figure 3.10, this looks at 10 types of interaction during a lesson, with observational judgements made every 3 seconds.

This can show differences between teacher

Figure 3.10 Flanders' interaction analysis categories

Teacher talk	*Response*	1. Accepts feeling 2. Praises or encourages 3. Accepts or uses ideas of pupils
		4. Asks questions
	Initiation	5. Lecturing 6. Giving directions 7. Criticising or justifying authority
Pupil talk	*Response*	8. Pupil talk – response
	Initiation	9. Pupil talk – initiation
Silence		10. Silence or confusion

Source: Flanders (1970)

styles, for instance whether a teacher is able to generate student involvement, or whether he or she tends to dominate classroom processes. As can be seen, however, the Flanders schedule was specifically designed to show different types of verbal interactions and would need to be modified to investigate other aspects of observable behaviour.

A more extensive approach has been used by Galton *et al.* (1980, 1999) as the basis of their long-term ORACLE (Observational Research and Classroom Learning Evaluation) study of classroom processes. This goes into great detail, with separate pupil and teacher record systems which are based on categories of behaviour observed every 25 seconds. For teachers these include the major groupings of:

- questions;
- statements;
- silent interactions;
- listening/watching;
- no interaction;
- teacher's audience; and
- curriculum area covered.

Most of these are divided into further possible groupings and specific categories, for example with some questions being task related and focusing on facts, as opposed to other questions which are related to task supervision.

The pupil record system covers the main groupings of:

- target pupil's activity;
- target pupil's location; and
- teacher's activity and location.

Again, each of these is further subdivided into a number of specific categories, for example with 14 different possible descriptors of the pupil's activity, which includes his or her level of involvement in meaningful tasks. The information gathered from such programmes can therefore be highly detailed and used to show effects in a sophisticated way. Galton *et al.* (1980, 1999) have used this approach to analyse typical styles of pupil–teacher interactions and also to investigate the detailed impact of educational changes over time.

A further approach is to focus on particular problem behaviours as a basis for the development of specific management programmes. An example is the technique developed by Wheldall *et al.* (1985), which looks at the use of positive and negative comments by teachers related to different types of specific problem behaviours by pupils. The advantage is that findings can directly imply interventions. If teachers are overusing negative comments, Wheldall *et al.*'s technique may be an effective strategy for them to monitor and attempt to reduce these.

Some systems use more inferential categories, which involve the rater making a judgement about the intended meaning underlying what an individual says or does. An example of this would be whether a teacher is more or less 'encouraging', which would not be apparent from simple behavioural descriptions. The ratings obtained can enable an investigator to make further judgements such as detecting possible biases in teacher interactions. One major difficulty, however, is that there is usually very low agreement between raters about what behaviours will fit such high-inference categories. It is impossible to give operational definitions since raters' judgements will depend to a great extent on what they believe that the teacher is thinking about. Even simple verbal praise such as 'well done' could be interpreted as a sarcastic comment if said in a certain way or in the context of a particular ongoing teacher–pupil relationship.

Raters will even have limited agreement between classification of relatively low-inference behaviours such as 'on task versus off task' unless they are given some form of training, with descriptions and examples of categories. When the rates are trained, the result can be a high level of consistency (meaning that individuals have the same standards over time), and reliability (as judged by agreement between different raters). An investigation by Wheldall *et al.* (1985), for instance, found an average of 94 per cent agreement between trained raters for non-inferential pupil behaviours.

Interviews

Teachers often interview pupils or discuss them with their parents, to report on progress or to gather information. The interviews can be intended to gather information as a basis on which to select or advise on future studies, or to investigate situations where a pupil has problem behaviour. Unfortunately, there has been only very limited evaluation of their use in schools, and most information comes from interviews in occupational selection. These have been found to have very limited reliability, and a review of a number of studies by Hunter and Hunter (1984) also found that validities were generally below 0.2, meaning that the behaviour of interviewees after the interview bore very little relationship to the judgements and predictions made by the interviewers. Explanations for the lack of validity appear to lie in the social processes which happen during such interactions, with participants following their own 'scripts' to achieve goals which are often conflicting. In schools, for instance, pupils discussing their own problem behaviour would be strongly motivated to present themselves as the innocent party. Parents who have been called into school will also often attribute problem behaviour to factors that are not their responsibility, such as their child reacting against an unprovoked attack by another pupil.

People entering interview situations have normally made critical decisions beforehand and do not change them very readily. By comparing interviewers' judgements before and after selection interviews, Dipboye (1989) reports that only one in five change their minds at all. This is also borne out by findings that interviewers will often 'correct' interviewees when what they say is counter to the interviewers' pre-formed beliefs.

One common form of interviewing is involved in parents' evenings, when pupils' achievements and needs are discussed. The typical encounter involved in parents' evenings has been reviewed by Walker (1998) as being a problematic interface between the power bases of home and school. By using typical comments and descriptions from teachers and parents, Walker established that the purpose of the meeting was unclear to the participants and that there was a basic conflict of agendas. Parents were often frustrated by not receiving information that they wanted, while teachers tended to manage the exchange and limit the need for further action.

Improving interviews

Although most interviews are probably of almost negligible reliability and validity, these qualities can be improved by using a standard structure. Such a structure can be achieved by using 'behavioural interviews' in school, which focus on pupils' behaviours, as well as the context and outcomes of what they did, rather than attributing problems to personality traits. A review by Gresham (1984) found that this approach could be very effective, particularly when carried out by trained interviewers, and as part of an overall approach to managing problems in school.

When the interview is to do with resolving a behavioural difficulty, this can be achieved by adopting a problem-solving perspective. Dowling (1985) describes a joint home and school approach that emphasises the need to delineate and analyse the problem together, and then to seek a solution and agree on positive actions. The final outcome of this might involve setting up a home–school behavioural report, with agreed actions at home and at school for certain criteria.

Dynamic assessment

A very different approach to assessment looks at the changes in child's abilities in response to a learning situation. Conventional forms of assessment are generally a form of 'snapshot' of a child's abilities or attainments at any one time. They often tend to assume that development follows a progressive and linear sequence, based upon a hierarchical structure of learning. However, as was mentioned in the previous chapter, a very different view of the learning process sees it as a form of active constructivism, with the progressive development of knowledge in the form of schemas. Vygotsky in particular has argued that children's cognitive development happens within a social context, and emphasises the importance of the 'zone of proximal development', an area where children are able to perform with adult support. This is the area where they are progressing to develop their independent capabilities, and Vygotsky argues that observing children learning with support will therefore give a much more accurate idea of their abilities and likely future progress.

These ideas have been used by Fuerstein *et al.* (1980) in Israel to assess low-achieving immigrant children's educational needs. This involves a technique known as the Learning Potential Assessment Device (LPAD), which investigates children's ability to learn new abstract problem-solving principles, using materials such as the Raven's matrices test. The assessor first sees what level a pupil is capable of without help, then goes on to teach some of the principles involved and records the pupil's response to the teaching. This evaluation then matches in with different levels of a teaching technique to develop these abilities, known as 'Instrumental Enrichment'. Fuerstein argues that this approach can be used to assess and teach general thinking skills, which are important in a range of educational areas. However, despite some anecdotal positive outcomes, an evaluation of the technique by Blagg (1991) found that there was no evidence of such transfer.

Dynamic assessment is often carried out by using the basic paradigm of 'test–teach–test'. The amount of teaching necessary to reach mastery, or the improvements in children's scores with a standard amount of teaching, can then be used as an indicator of how well they are likely to progress in the future. Unfortunately, improvement scores usually have very low reliability and have validity only when applied to a particular area of learning. An early review investigation by Woodrow (1946) found that learning could not be usefully considered a single ability since progress in any one area related only very weakly to progress in others. If this approach is to be of direct use in teaching and learning, then it would probably be best applied to known sequences or domains of skill development, where acquiring particular abilities relate strongly to other developments. With early reading, for instance, it could be appropriate to assess children's knowledge and learning of simple phonic skills. If children had difficulties with analysing words into letter sounds and also with combining these, then the assessor could directly investigate their phonological abilities and response to teaching. This approach is of course what good teaching is all about, and implementing it is probably limited only by the constraints of managing and directing whole classes.

National Curriculum assessments

Schools in England and Wales are now required to use Standard Assessment Tests and Tasks (SATs) at the specific pupil ages of 7, 11 and 14 years (Key Stages 1, 2 and 3). These are derived from the National Curriculum and involve written tests in the core curriculum subjects, as well as specific tasks, situations and judgements to be made by the teacher. The original function was to assess individual children so that the result could be used to monitor progress and to guide

Figure 3.11 Sequence of pupil achievement of levels, between ages 7 and 16

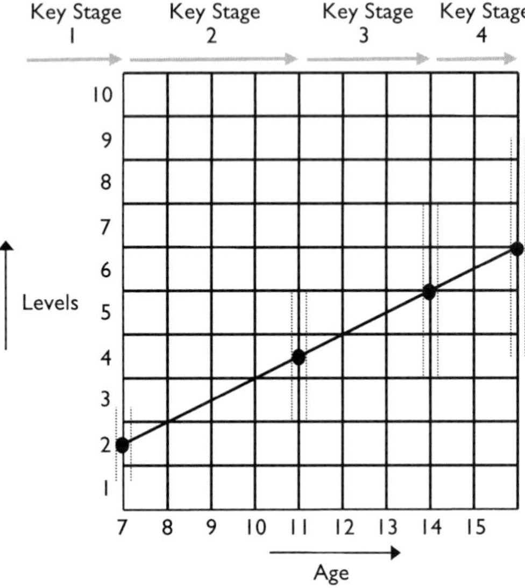

Source: TGAT (1988)

future education. The tests are based on the various Attainment Targets for the National Curriculum programmes of study; they are therefore apparently criterion-referenced assessments with formative functions, placing children within a level of the National Curriculum for each subject.

As shown in Figure 3.11, the expected levels that would be achieved by children at the different stages were originally set out by the Task Group on Assessment and Testing (TGAT, 1988). The main line gives 'the expected results for pupils at the ages specified'. The dotted lines represent '*a rough speculation* about the limits within which about 80 per cent of the pupils may be found to lie' (TGAT, 1988; emphasis added). These original and apparently arbitrary expectations have been largely retained, although the range has been lowered in later curriculum documents (DFE, 1995b) to include level 2 at Key Stage 2 (age 11) and level 3 at Key Stage 3 (age 14). These parameters appear to continue to act as the official basis for judging performances and for setting future improvement targets. These have been set for the year 2002 as 80 per cent of all pupils at the end of Key Stage 2 to be achieving at level 4 or above in English, and 75 per cent of all pupils in mathematics to be achieving at that level or above.

Reliability and validity of the SATs

The SATs have been progressively implemented over the period from 1991 onwards. During this time there has been growing debate as to their meaning and usefulness. One area of concern is the likely reliabilities associated with them, since no test–retest data have been published and there appear to be a number of likely sources of error. These can be briefly summarised as:

- the relatively short length of many of the tests, which may result in variable coverage of the curriculum. The 1998 Key Stage 2 SATs, for instance, failed to cover the key areas of 'percentages' in mathematics and 'the body' in science;
- the administration process – which is partly standardised but must vary somewhat between schools and different teachers;
- the group testing format – which will result in limited supervision and variable involvement by students; and
- the use of different assessors, who may interpret criteria in different ways.

The rather subjective nature of the assessment of many items applies particularly to Standard Tasks at the lower levels, which are heavily dependent on individual teacher administration and judgements. Abbott *et al.* (1994) found wide variations between schools in the way in which an earlier science task was carried out, sometimes with frequent interruptions and with variable prompting and support by the teacher. In order to improve the standardisation, it is important for criterion-referenced assessments to have specific directions for the criteria which are assessed. For instance, although the National Curriculum Attainment Targets include a knowledge of phonics, this is assessed at Key Stage 1 only by teacher observation of the strategies used in reading. A more reli-

NFER-Nelson Primary and Secondary Education Catalogues.

NFER-Nelson is the main supplier of tests to schools. The catalogues tell you what tests are easily available, and NFER-Nelson's own tests are professionally designed and validated. To give you an idea of what is involved, most of the tests have a specimen set which you can buy at a relatively low price.

Educational tests are also published by Macmillan, Hodder & Stoughton and LDA.

Practical scenario

Ms Peters considers that she is a competent teacher and that she helps her children to do as well as they are able. She has now become eligible for the threshold payment and would like to apply for this. However, she is worried because one of the requirements is that she has to give some proof that her pupils make good progress. Her pupils already have to do SATs part-way through the year but she feels that their attainments on these are not just due to her teaching, and she is wondering if there is any other evidence that she could gather.

- *Would the SATs be in any way a fair reflection of Ms Peters' teaching input, given that the standards of schools' intakes vary considerably? Might she be able to make some adjustment based on the children's backgrounds?*
- *How can she separate out the effects of her teaching on attainments from those of previous teachers? Should she start to carry out some formal achievement tests on her pupils at the beginning and at the end of the academic year?*
- *How could Ms Peters use the curriculum that she teaches as a basis for assessing improvements? Is this*

4 Individual differences and achievement

The importance of differences

Chapters 2 and 3 have looked at general learning principles and ways of assessing attainments. Although these can help teachers to match what they teach, each child is an individual, with a unique combination of abilities and characteristic styles. These differences are important since they can give us an idea about how we should adapt learning experiences for each child's particular needs.

In the past, one of the most important ways of measuring differences has been to focus on the 'general ability' of children, as measured by intelligence tests. It is important to know whether or not this might be a good idea since it implies that we could use general ability to categorise children and to provide appropriate education based on IQ tests. The possibility of an inherited, biological basis for intelligence would lend strong support for such an approach since it implies that children have an underlying potential which is relatively stable. This belief has many implications for the way in which education should be organised and its validity continues to be passionately debated.

More recent developments in cognitive psychology – the study of human perception, thinking and learning – have made it possible to analyse and describe thinking processes. We can now understand specific aspects of children's learning and see how to match with these to develop their achievements. Other ways of differentiating between children focus on more qualitative aspects, with an emphasis on learning style, applied to general thinking processes. Children's personality can also affect the learning process since this shapes the way in which they relate to others in learning situations.

Intelligence

Use of IQ testing

Intelligence tests have often been used in education to attempt to predict children's future academic progress, with different levels of measured intelligence being taken to imply the need for different forms of educational experiences. More able children are supposed to need abstract and academic experiences, with an accelerated rate of progress. Less able children on the other hand, are supposed to need more direct, practical experiences, with a slower rate of learning.

Another function of IQ assessments has been to indicate a child's potential for learning. When this matches achievements, then children can be said to be fulfilling their potential, whatever level this might be. When there is a discrepancy and children's achievements are below their potential level, then it can be argued that they have a specific problem. The most important problem of this type is underachieving with literacy, often being termed 'dyslexia'.

Evidence for IQ as an academic predictor

Although these arguments may seem plausible, the majority of the research findings to be discussed below indicate only a limited relationship between IQ measures and performance on academic skills. Any correspondence which does exist can also be open to a number of alternative interpretations. One such possibility is that the academic skill itself or other subskills might themselves have an effect on IQ, or that both tests may be affected by another general process such as motivation or concentration. IQ tests are also very heavily reliant on verbal abilities, and even the non-verbal subtests which are used are significantly affected by verbal processes. Verbal knowledge and understanding are often an important basis for academic progress, and correlations between IQ and school attainments may therefore exist only because they both depend on this same factor.

Reading and IQ

As reading ability is a key basic skill in education, many investigations have attempted to relate this to underlying general abilities. When IQ and reading ability are assessed at the same time, however, correlations tend to be in the region of 0.5 to 0.7, with the higher values being found only when older children are assessed. Yule *et al.* (1981), for instance, tested 82 pupils at age 16½ on the full WISC and on a sentence-reading test. The highest correlation that was found was 0.68, between the verbal scale of the WISC and reading. When the complete IQ was used (including non-verbal subtests), the correlation with reading reduced to 0.61. This is a typical finding and indicates that reading at this age level is mostly dependent on general verbal skills and comprehension. From this, a plausible explanation of the correlation is that it is merely showing that both higher-level reading and IQ tests involve underlying verbal abilities.

A further argument here is the so-called 'Matthew effect' described by Stanovich (1986), which is named after the biblical quotation in the book of Matthew, that 'for whosoever hath, to him shall be given'. Stanovich believed that children who are good at reading can use this skill to develop better verbal abilities, while poorer readers miss out. This idea is supported by Stanovich's findings of a strong correlation between measures of reading experience such as children's recognition of book titles, and their verbal abilities. An alternative explanation of this is of course that children who are more knowledgeable tend to read more. Other research however, such as that by Nagy *et al.* (1987), shows that the direct process of reading itself develops vocabulary knowledge and that this can account for a large proportion of verbal abilities. Tests of intelligence are largely based on such verbal knowledge and understanding. As summarised in Figure 4.1, it seems that intelligence itself depends upon, and is developed by, the process of reading.

Predictive correlations between IQ and reading over time are even weaker, typically less than 0.4.

Figure 4.1 Possible relationships between intelligence and literacy

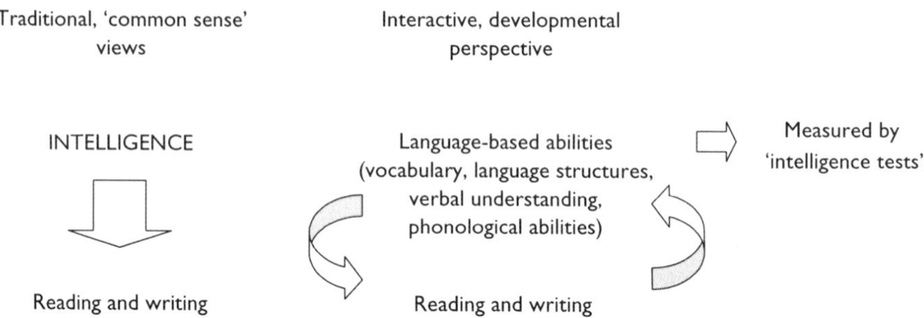

In an early longitudinal study of 53 children, DeHirsch *et al.* (1966) found a correlation of only 0.31 between Stanford–Binet IQs on starting school and reading ability two years later. Stevenson *et al.* (1976) also assessed a number of children's attainments and abilities, including IQ on starting school, and followed up their progress four years later. Verbal intelligence correlated with subsequent reading only at 0.2, and such findings indicate that there is only a weak and probably indirect effect of such measures of intelligence on academic progress.

The best way of predicting progress is to use specific rather than general abilities. When this is done in a particular skill area, correlations can be relatively high. Neale (1989), for instance, quotes research which found that early reading ability correlated at 0.83 with reading age one year later. Correlations are also relatively high if the initial ability measured forms a basis for later progress. A typical finding by Blatchford *et al* (1987) was that children's pre-school knowledge of letter sounds correlated at 0.61 with reading ability two years later. This was significantly higher than the predictive correlations from word-matching tasks or verbal intelligence and is consistent with the idea, to be discussed in Chapter 9, that early reading progress depends largely on various types of phonic skills. In this study, knowledge of letter sounds was also related to parental involvement; it seems probable that early reading abilities were helped by parents teaching letter sounds to their children, as well as their continued involvement in helping with general reading.

Heritability and abilities

As we shall see in Chapter 6, the greater part of variation in academic progress seems to be accounted for by factors outside of the educational system. One possible explanation for the importance of outside factors could be that general abilities such as intelligence are largely inherited, and that these determine subsequent academic achievements. Gill *et al.* (1985), for instance, found that twins (who have a high level of genetic similarity) scored at a very similar level on academic achievement tests at age 17, consistent with a heritability level of up to 0.7. Children also show greater similarity of intelligence with increasing genetic similarity, and Bouchard and McGue (1981), summarising 111 studies in this area, found the correlations shown in Table 4.1.

A review by Neisser at al (1996) found that further analysis of such findings showed that an

Table 4.1 IQ correlations for different family relationships

Relationship	IQ correlations
Identical twins	
Reared together	0.86
Reared apart	0.72
Siblings	
Reared together	0.47
Reared apart	0.24
Parent/child	
Natural	0.42
Adopted	0.19

Source: Based on data in Bouchard and McGue (1981)

average value of about one-half of the observed variance of IQ can be traced to genetic variation. It is important to realise, however, that most of the above correlations are relatively weak and that comparisons between them are not particularly meaningful. For instance, the parent–natural child relationship correlation accounts for just above 17 per cent of the variance between the IQs of parents and those of their children, and the parent–adopted child correlation accounts for just above 4 per cent of the variance. Since many children are adopted after already having been with their biological parent for a few years, the effects of the early home environment, as described below, might easily account for this difference.

The strongest evidence supporting heritability comes from twin studies, particularly from the high similarity of the intelligence of identical twins, even when they have been separated and raised in different environments. Identical twins are originally formed from the same fertilised egg cell, or zygote, and their cells have the same genetic information. This causes such monozygotic twins to have very similar physical structures, including the brain. These findings seem convincing but they have been subject to a considerable amount of criticism. In particular, the similar appearance of identical twins leads to their experiencing a much more closely similar environment than is usually the case with non-twin siblings. One reason for this is that identical twins who live together are often mistaken for each other and are generally treated in much the same way. Moreover, Evans and Waites (1981) review evidence showing that even when siblings are separated, they frequently continue to have similar environments. For instance, adopted siblings are usually placed with families of similar background. Indeed, they are often placed with members of the extended family (e.g. aunts and uncles), where they can remain in contact with their original siblings and families. When Ceci (1990) reanalysed some of the original data, separating out the pairs of identical twins reared in dissimilar environments such as rural versus urban, he found that the IQ correlation was massively reduced – to only 0.27, which would only give a negligible role for genetics.

Thus although there are correlations between the general abilities of relatives within families, this does not *prove* that these are inherited. Kamin (in Eysenck and Kamin (1981)), for instance, argued that the evidence at the time when he was writing was compatible with there being no heritability at all, since there are equally plausible explanations based on the effects of parent–child interactions, with more able parents just providing better-quality input for their children. As will be discussed later in this chapter, Hart and Risley (1995) have found supporting evidence for this in long-term direct investigations of family verbal interactions and their effects on cognitive development.

With recent developments in genetic analysis, there have been attempts to link specific genes directly with performance on IQ tests. Chorney *et al.* (1998), for instance, carried out a comparison of the genetic profiles of two groups of students, one with an average IQ of 101 and one with an average IQ that was above 160. If intelligence is carried by a number of genes (as many researchers believe), then the high-IQ group should have had many more of any genes which code for intelligence. An analysis of the genes in the two groups found that one particular gene called IGF2R could account for 2 per cent of the variation in intelligence test scores, being carried by about 17 per cent of the average IQ group and 34 per cent of the high-IQ group. However, given such a massive IQ difference between the two groups, one might have expected any genetic differences to be much greater, with all the high-IQ individuals possessing the better genes. The authors acknowledge that there is a possibility that the genetic findings may have been due to other differences between the two groups. For instance, the two groups might have had different ethnic compositions coming from separate gene pools. It is also unclear how IGF2R could be involved since it is an insulin-like growth factor gene with no known effects on brain mechanisms and intelligence.

If intelligence is substantially inherited, it

Table 4.2 Family context and intellectual climate

Family composition	**Total scores ÷ number in family**	**Average intellectual climate**
Single newborn child	$\frac{30 + 30 + 0}{3}$	20
Second newborn child with 2-year-old sibling	$\frac{30 + 30 + 2 + 0}{4}$	15.5

should also show high stability and would be likely to have a strong and cumulative effect on school achievements over time. As the predictive correlations between measured IQ and future school achievements are relatively low, and become even weaker over longer periods of time, it seems unlikely that heritable abilities have any major effect on academic achievements. It may still be the case that specific forms of genetic abnormalities limit intellectual abilities and academic progress. However, such abnormalities are relatively rare, and as regards the majority of the population it may be more productive to look for more direct effects related to children's immediate environments. Since children's early environment involves the context of parents and other siblings, there have been attempts to relate aspects of these to intellectual and academic progress.

Home background

Family size and birth order

One possible way in which the family context could affect an individual's abilities is by the effects of a child's position within the family. According to Zajonc's (1976) *confluence theory*, each successive child is born into a different family context. The first child receives a high level of parental attention, but subsequent children receive a reduced level of general intellectual stimulation since they are also interacting with an older sibling whose intellectual abilities are less than those of an adult. Zajonc estimates the general intellectual climate of the family by assigning a value of 30 to each adult and the actual age for each child (the newborn has a value of zero). Applying this to first- and second-born children in a family would give the outcomes shown in Table 4.2. Thus the theory predicts a reduced intellectual climate for larger families, and also suggests a birth order effect, with successive children having progressively lower abilities. These predictions have been supported by findings from a study of 800,000 pupils competing for college scholarships in the United States by Breland (1974). As shown in Figure 4.2, this found a maximum difference of 9 IQ points between the last children born in large families and the first-born in small families.

Zajonc also argues that this effect does not arise merely from depletion of the resources (intellectual or material) available to each child,

Figure 4.2 Abilities of children in different-sized families

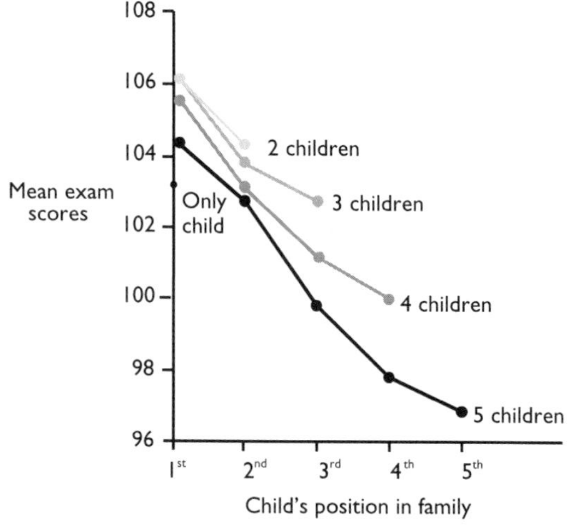

Source: Storfer (1990), recalculated from original data

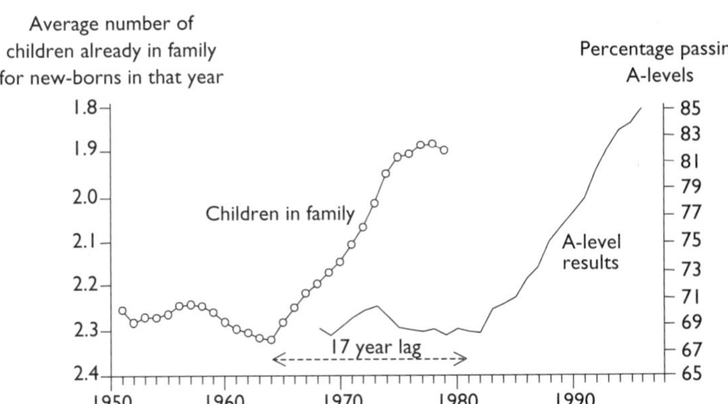

Figure 4.3 Changes in mean birth order over time, and eventual A level pass rate
Source: Adapted from Zajonc and Mullally (1997)

but is a more subtle one that depends on the particular intellectual climate that exists for each child at different ages. For instance, 'only children' would appear to have the highest possible levels of adult stimulation since this is not shared out with any others, yet they perform below all other first-born children. Zajonc's explanation for this is that children with younger siblings take on a tutoring role, and that in the process of doing this they further develop their own understanding. Although the picture of a kindly older child patiently helping their younger brother or sister may seem rather unlikely to parents reading this, children may nevertheless be able to develop their abilities by being in a more dominant role involving direction and management of their sibling(s).

One major argument against Zajonc's explanation of the effects of different family sizes is the fact that larger families are associated with lower socio-economic status and that this may cause the reduction in abilities. In an analysis of more than 10,000 American high school graduates, Page and Grandon (1979) found that social class and race accounted for most of the relationship between family size and achievements. However, in direct observations of the effects of family size, Hart and Risley (1995) found that the overall amount of verbal interactions in different-sized families stayed roughly the same but that having more children in a family led to each of them receiving a reduced share of attention.

Zajonc and Mullally (1997) argue that birth order effects occur *within* social classes, although the influence of these effects may not be as great as that of social background. They also review evidence showing that when larger groups are studied, the effects of variables such as class are cancelled out and that measures of birth order relate closely to eventual examination test scores. As shown in Figure 4.3, for British A levels, there has been an intriguingly close historical correspondence, with original birth order measures accounting for 86 per cent of the variance in exam results 17 years later.

It might be wise to be cautious about interpreting these findings since a correlation need not necessarily imply causation. The changes in both variables might, for instance, be due to changes in other social factors such as progressive improvements in living standards. Despite these cautions, Zajonc and Mullally did find similar closely matched trends in a range of other birth order and achievement data in other countries and at different times. If it is the case that A level results are dependent on the effects of birth order (and thereby student calibre), then Zajonc and Mullally consider it likely that future exam results will not continue their present rise. The 1997 and 1998 results did not, however, initially confirm this prediction, although the 1998, 1999 and 2000 results did show a certain 'levelling off'. There could of course be many other compensatory factors operating, such as the increase in modular courses, which may make it easier for students to achieve a pass, as well as improvements in children's social backgrounds and the support they get from home.

Despite these suggestive findings, family size and birth order are probably rather general effects and are unlikely to be able to account for much of the progress of individual children. To get closer to more powerful determinants, it is likely that one would need to consider those specific experiences which are likely to underlie such outcomes, and most investigations of such experiences have looked at the impact of parents on their children's development.

Direct effects of home background

Parents in different home backgrounds certainly appear to vary in the extent to which they give support for their children with early learning tasks and with school work. A study by Elliott and Hewison (1994), for instance, compared different socio-economic groups in terms of parental involvement and the academic outcome of reading ability. Those children who made the most progress with reading were helped regularly by their parents, whereas those who made the least progress came from homes where children were given little help and where there were few books. In this study, a paired reading project with working-class children and their parents brought the children's academic achievements up to those of children from the other social classes, indicating that parental support can be a direct factor leading to academic progress.

These findings are also consistent with the results of investigations by Bernstein and by Honey, to be discussed in Chapter 8, on the effects of home language on school progress, with middle-class parents typically using and fostering the use of an elaborated linguistic code. Such a code is supposed to be more capable of embodying abstract ideas and knowledge, and to be more suited for formal educational processes. A study by Tizard and Hughes (1984) also found that children from good homes experienced a higher quality of verbal interaction and stimulation with their parents than they experienced in their early schooling. In a longitudinal study Gottfried *et al.* (1994) investigated the effects of different parenting styles on motivation and eventual academic outcomes. Some of the parents used techniques that encouraged an intrinsic motivational style, for example by emphasising persistence, enjoyment and independence with school work. One year later, their children had developed significantly higher academic motivation and were also achieving at higher levels with reading and mathematics.

Hart and Risley (1995) have carried out a unique long-term investigation of the direct effects of home experiences on children's development. They looked at the verbal interactions between parents and their children and analysed, monthly, one-hour tape recordings taken from the age of about 10 months to 3 years. The 42 families involved were classified into three main groups: professional families, where parents were college professors (generally equivalent to UK lecturers), working-class families, and families who were on welfare support.

Hart and Risley's first main findings were of progressive differences in the language abilities of the children from the three types of home background. Although children from all of the groups started to speak at about the same time and also developed good structure and use of language, their vocabulary, as measured by the number of different words used, varied significantly. By age 3, the observed cumulative vocabulary for children in the professional families was about 1,100, for the working-class families it was about 750, and for the welfare families it was just above 500.

These developments happened alongside major differences in the language experiences of the children studied. In professional families, children heard an average of 2,153 words per hour; in working-class families the figure was 1,251 words per hour and in welfare families only 616 words per hour. Extrapolating these figures to cover four years of experience would give 11 million words heard by a child in a professional family, 6 million for a child in working-class family and 3 million for a child in a welfare family.

Hart and Risley also identified a number of key features of positive verbal interaction which could be applied to all of the families. They found that these could be grouped into five main categories of parent behaviours:

- 'They just talked' – generally using a wide vocabulary.
- 'They tried to be nice' – using high rates of approval and few prohibitions.
- 'They told children about things' – language had a high information content.
- 'They gave children choices' – children were asked about things, rather than simply being directed.
- 'They listened' – responding to what children said rather than just telling them what to do or making demands.

When these were combined together into a single index of parenting, Hart and Risley found that at the end of the study this had a strong relationship with children's general linguistic and intellectual development (see Figure 4.4). The correlation between these two variables is 0.78, which means that the parenting measures are able to account for 59 per cent of the cognitive accomplishments of children at this age. Given that Hart and Risley's work was based on only about 26 hours of observations for each child and that it missed out the first 10-month period, it seems likely that the true relationship between upbringing and ability could be even greater. If this is the case, then although genetics may still have some effect, its role would have to be much less than traditional estimates have indicated.

A detailed analysis of socio-economic status of the families, as assessed by parental occupation, was able to account for only 29 per cent of the variance in IQ scores. As can be seen from Figure 4.4, working-class children covered the range of attainments, the child's level of attainment being largely related to the quality of parental involvement – the child with the highest ability came from a working-class home, which also had the highest quality of interactions. Socio-economic status therefore appears to be a relatively crude proxy for what actually happens within individual families, although children with the highest levels of deprivation (on welfare) were more consistent in scoring at a low level.

When a group of 29 of the children were followed up at ages 9 to 10, the earlier parenting measures were still able to account for 61 per cent of the variance in measures of verbal ability. This is a very high value for such long-term prediction and is probably due to the fact that parenting styles were relatively stable and continued to have consistent effects on children's development. The early IQ measures at 3 years old had no discernible influence on later measures of academic achievement, and this study therefore supports the belief that quality of parenting is the key feature which determines general cognitive abilities as well as academic attainments.

One possible alternative interpretation of the above findings is that children who were inherently more intelligent evoked more verbal interaction from their parents, or that intelligent

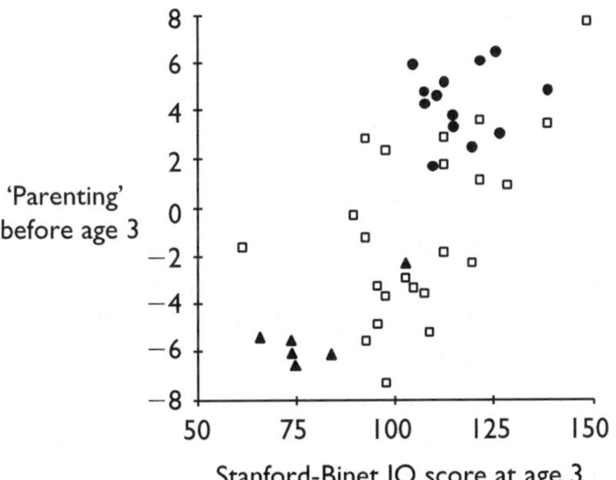

Figure 4.4 Relationship between parenting index and IQ scores at age 3 years
Source: Hart and Risley (1995)

parents (who talk a lot) simply have more intelligent children. That is to say, genetic effects could have been the underlying basis of the observed differences in performance. This does not seem likely, however, as the detailed observations indicated that parents largely set up and directed verbal interactions, and were not just responding to their children's initiatives.

Also, if intelligence were simply inherited, then children's verbal abilities and the interactions between parents and their children would arise directly from their inherited intelligence. This idea is not supported by the fact that, as discussed earlier, the correlation between the intelligence of parents and that of their children accounts for only about 17 per cent of the variance, whereas the correlation between parental behaviour and children's verbal abilities accounts for 59 per cent of the variance. It therefore seems much more likely that it is parental behaviour which causes children's verbal development, and that the correlation between parent–child intelligence could be secondary in some way.

Effects of additional early support

If children's development depends to a great extent on their early home experiences, then might additional early support also have long-term positive effects? To try to answer this question, Daniels (1995) studied the effectiveness of pre-school education on the subsequent attainments of a range of children at the age of 7 years. Those children who had attended some form of early provision did indeed show consistent and long-term gains, building on their early advantages. Children from the lowest social group who had attended nursery showed the greatest gains when compared with other children from similar backgrounds who did not have any nursery experience. This was equivalent to four to five months' schooling with their writing attainments. Intensive, school-based provision after nursery can also have significant positive effects and at least partially overcome the effects of poor early environments.

As already discussed, the long-term study by Hart and Risley (1995) showed that there are massive naturally occurring differences in the pre-school experiences of children which cannot be easily counteracted. Early compensatory programs such as Head Start during the 1960s in the United States often had only limited effects since many lasted only for about a year of part-time input or covered only the summer vacation period. Where interventions have been more long-term and intensive, and have involved changes in the home background, then more lasting gains have been made. In the Abecedarian project in North Carolina, reported by Ramey *et al.* (1984), children at risk were supported from birth with enrichment experiences which were largely language based and included helping their mothers to maintain a positive home environment. By the age of 4, these children had an average IQ of 102, compared with a control group which had an IQ of 89. These differences also continued into schooling, with significant benefits in terms of their academic progress and underlying abilities at 12 years of age.

Heritability and ethnic minorities

Children from certain ethnic minorities regularly underachieve in schools, and writers such as Herrnstein and Murray (1994) have taken this as evidence for an inherited basis for intelligence and achievement. However, various research findings to be discussed in Chapter 7 indicate that such differences are due to cultural factors rather than to any inherited differences in basic abilities. Scarr and Weinberg (1976), for instance, looked at African American children who in view of their backgrounds would have been expected to achieve at a low level but were adopted at an early age by white, middle-class American families. After being with their new families for some time (an average of about five years), these children came to be above the national average on school achievement tests, and it seems likely that they had taken on their adopted family's cultural experiences and perspectives on education.

There is therefore evidence from a number of sources that children's intellectual abilities and academic progress are strongly determined by the quality of their environments, and that environmental quality underlies differences in achievements related to social class and ethnic groupings. By the time children come to school, however, there are already substantial differences in their experiences and achievements. As Mortimore and Whitty (1997) have argued, the continuing effects of children's backgrounds will make it unlikely that education by itself will be able to achieve equality.

Gifted children

At the further end of the spectrum are children whose abilities are well above those of their peers. Rather than compensation, it seems likely that such pupils need a different level, pace and style of teaching, appropriate to their learning abilities. There is also the possibility that these differences may bring with them additional problems, owing to their effect on children's social and emotional development. In common with underachievement, high abilities are of interest since if their origins lie in certain types of early experiences, these might imply ways in which development could be fostered in all children.

What is meant by 'gifted'?

It can be argued that children with a high level of general ability ('intelligence'), or a specific ability ('talent'), should be considered as a separate group needing identification and specialised forms of education to develop their potential. Some ways of defining and identifying such children are based on teacher and parental assessments, using achievement levels; for instance, high academic attainments or creativity.

A typical checklist from the National Association for Gifted Children (NAGC, 1989) also considers that the gifted child:

- learns more quickly than others;
- has a very retentive memory;
- can concentrate for long periods on subjects that interest him or her;
- has a wide general knowledge and interest in the world;
- enjoys problem solving, often missing out the intermediate stages in an argument and making original connections;
- has an unusual imagination;
- has an odd sense of humour; and
- sets high standards for him- or herself.

A problem with such approaches is that they might fail to identify pupils who do not show their underlying abilities in school; some children might 'coast' through boredom, while others might hide their abilities so that they can fit in socially. The use of IQ testing is supposed to assess such hidden potential, and Freeman (1991) did in fact find that teachers' assessments failed to identify 24 per cent of children with high IQ scores. Intelligence tests such as the Wechsler Intelligence Scale for Children are therefore sometimes used to identify and classify gifted children.

Problems with the use of IQ to identify gifted children

An early study by Terman (1925) used an IQ of 140 or higher (achieved by only about 0.4 per cent of the population) as the identifying feature of gifted children, while others such as Freeman (1991) have used an IQ of 130 (achieved by about 2 per cent of the population). As shown in Figure 4.5, the general distribution of abilities also appears to be continuous, with no 'gap' or 'bump' at the higher end of the range; any cut-off

Figure 4.5 Gifted children and the distribution of abilities

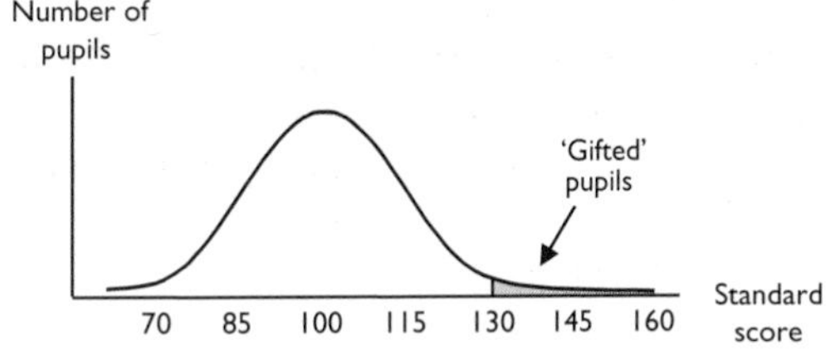

point for higher abilities therefore seems to be as arbitrary as the cut-off for identifying children with lower abilities (see Chapter 12).

In line with Gardner's (1983) theory of 'multiple intelligences', high-level achievements are often specific to one particular area such as music or art, and 'general ability' is often of little importance to these achievements. Some individuals with an outstanding ability can be severely retarded, having little language and being dependent on other people for their basic care. One such individual, Stephen Wiltshire, is able to make highly detailed architectural drawings such as Figure 4.6 from memory, after only a brief inspection. He is not simply reading off from some form of 'photographic memory' since he is able to produce extensions of complex visual themes, and interestingly, his drawings are apparently a 'mirror image' of what he sees.

Since abilities can be so specific, it therefore seems more realistic to look at children's particular attainments and the needs they may have associated with these, rather than to use arbitrary criteria and global labelling.

Why identify gifted children?

One argument for the need to identify gifted children is that they tend to have greater difficulties. For instance, one might think that their higher abilities and specialist interests could lead to their experiencing social isolation, and a mismatch of their talents with normal school work could lead to boredom and frustration.

Figure 4.6 The Rialto, Venice, as drawn by Stephen Wiltshire, an autistic person

However, an early classic study by Terman (1925–9) which followed the long-term development of a number of gifted children found that they were generally socially competent and successful in a range of different spheres. Freeman (1991), however, felt that Terman had selected relatively more privileged children (the sons and daughters of university lecturers) and that gifted children in general might have greater problems. To test this idea, she studied 70 schoolchildren who were identified by their parents as gifted (they were on the register of Britain's National Association of Gifted Children), subsequently following up their progress 10 years later. This group of children certainly appeared to have emotional and social difficulties, tending to be very sensitive, lonely and miserable. They were also generally bored and frustrated by much of the work that they experienced in school and had problems with later education. However, when Freeman included two other groups of pupils with either equally high or merely average intelligence, she found no relationship between high IQ and adjustment. This indicates that, rather than high IQ, the target gifted children's problems were more related to the fact that they were in a group which had been identified by their parents.

Marshall (1995) subsequently used a larger and less selective sample of 453 adults drawn from the Mensa membership list (Mensa is a society for people with high IQ) and found that although some of these individuals did have serious emotional problems, none of these problems was associated with their giftedness. The educational experiences of the majority of these did not appear to have been significantly different from those of normal mainstream pupils. The children studied were more concerned about enjoying being children, blending in and being one of the gang, to give much thought to how intelligent they were. A subsequent review of international evidence by Freeman (1998) has confirmed these findings, with many studies showing that intelligent children tend to be *more* stable and emotionally mature than other children their age.

Additional help for gifted children

In Britain, giftedness is not taken as being a 'special educational need' that might require the type of additional resources referred to in Chapter 12. In the United States, however, there is legislation to ensure that such children are identified and that they receive additional support, either as 'pull-out' – withdrawal for work in groups with children of similar abilities – or by attendance at special schools for gifted children. In both countries, pupils can be 'accelerated', by being placed in groups above their age level, and most secondary schools have upper sets for the most able pupils with a more advanced curriculum.

Although high-ability pupils do make more academic progress if they are given such additional help, a review of many studies by Kulik and Kulik (1992) found that such help is usually modest and is associated mainly with following a higher-level curriculum, rather than contact with other able pupils. Accelerating pupils by one or two years can provide greater benefits, but doing so often creates significant difficulties when they find themselves in groups where other children have more advanced social awareness and maturity. Even specialist schools appear to have only limited effectiveness; in one study Subotnik *et al.* (1993) carried out a review of the life attainments of 210 individuals who had attended a New York school for children with very high intelligence levels (average IQ 157). Subotnik *et al.* found that despite the high abilities of the children and the intensive nature of their education, in later life they did not generally achieve particular eminence, with most preferring moderate success in a chosen profession.

As will be outlined in Chapter 6, teachers and schools appear to have only limited differential effects on children. Above an IQ level of about 120 (achieved by 9 per cent of the population), original or high-level creative achievements appear to be strongly determined by personality and motivation, which are not easily affected by the normal educational process. It may be important to ensure an optimum match between the curriculum and a high-achieving child's abilities, but in this sense approaches to meet the educational needs of the gifted child are not different from those which should be applied to all pupils.

There is a wide range of pupil abilities, achievements and interests, and 'gifted children' are part of this general continuum, with very similar social and emotional needs. In terms of what should realistically be done to help children with higher levels of ability, Freeman (1998) concludes that rather than identify and provide for a select group of pupils, it would be better for schools to set up a range of optional extension activities which would be open to all children, according to their interests, as well as their specific abilities.

The origin of high abilities

Gifted children often show high attainments from an early age. Along with evidence which supports the possible heritability of IQ, this has been taken to indicate that such abilities are largely inherited. However, in a detailed review of the backgrounds of famous infant prodigies such as Mozart, Howe (1990) found that their abilities were invariably developed following intensive training and involvement, typically involving thousands of hours over many years. Although Mozart was supposedly a brilliant composer and performer by the age of 4, his attainments appear to be largely the result of his father's ensuring that he spent much of his early life in intensive practice. His father also lied about young Mozart's age when exhibiting him, to exaggerate his uniqueness, and his first real achievements with composing did not come about until the twelfth year of his musical career, after years of rigorous training.

Some children pay a great price for such intensive and unbalanced development. The child prodigy William Sidis, once described as 'the most remarkable boy in the United States' (Wallace, 1986), invented a new table of logarithms at 8 years and was able to speak six languages at 10. Unfortunately, this was the outcome of virtually complete domination by his psychologist father, and Sidis subsequently had severe social and emotional difficulties, eventually living an isolated, short and unfulfilling life.

Stimulating environments which are more supportive can nevertheless lead to high-achieving yet balanced individuals. Whether they then go on to make significant contributions, however, probably depends more on personality factors, chance, and the opportunities that exist within society at the time. Conventional general intellectual abilities may be an important foundation for unusual achievements but it can be argued that children also need a different type of ability to enable them to generate new ideas or solutions to problems.

Creativity

Most tests used in schools involve homing in on a single correct answer to a problem, a process referred to as 'convergent thinking'. Guilford (1950) also originally argued that it can be important for children to be creative, which involves 'divergent thinking', based upon the ability to find different ideas or solutions. Guilford analysed this as involving *fluency* (developing many ideas or concepts), *flexibility* (being able to shift direction easily), and *originality* (the ability to generate or use unusual ideas). This is similar to de Bono's (1970) ideas about lateral thinking, which emphasises the importance of following different directions, as distinct from conventional or vertical thinking. Most definitions of creativity also emphasise that new ideas or solutions should be useful; generating numerous loose or unconventional associations may be meaningless if done simply for its own sake.

Measuring creativity

Torrance (1974) developed and applied Guilford's ideas with the 'Unusual Uses Test', which involves thinking of as many uses as possible for an everyday object. When applied to a brick, such ideas might include 'building a wall', 'building a house', 'using as a paperweight' or 'using as a toy for a baby elephant'. These would score 4 for fluency (one for each of the ideas), 3 for flexibility (concepts of 'building', 'weight' and 'toy'), and 1 for originality (the 'toy' concept). However, a problem for this approach is that such measures of divergent thought show only a low correlation with performance on real creative tasks, or with ratings of creativity by other people. Torrance (1988), for instance, found that the correlations between measured creativity and later creative performance were at best about 0.3. Real-life creativity probably depends on a number of different intellectual and personality factors coming together in situations which encourage and acknowledge creative ideas.

Creativity and intelligence

Studies by Hasan and Butcher (1966) found that children's scores on divergent thinking could show a correlation as high as 0.70 with their intelligence tests results, which can be interpreted as meaning that creativity is just the result of having high general abilities. However, this relationship seems to hold only when performance is emphasised, by telling students that they should generate as many ideas as possible. It seems that intelligent students can be creative when directed to be, but that many of them are not naturally creative. Getzels and Jackson (1962) too found that creative ability in adolescents was not associated with IQ above a level of about 120. It seems likely, therefore, that a certain threshold amount of general knowledge, understanding and thinking skills can be necessary to help with generating a range of different ideas. However, once you have enough of these underlying abilities, then a creative style or personality probably becomes important in itself.

Creativity, personality and subject choice

On the basis of their analysis of personality factors, Cattell *et al.* (1970) found that individuals presumed to be creative, such as university researchers scored highly on intelligence, but that a number of personality traits were of equal importance. These involved being reserved, thoughtful and self-sufficient (introversion traits), generally imaginative and experimenting, and rather assertive and bold. It seems likely that people with these traits will be interested in and able to generate new ideas, and also will be prepared to persist with them. It is interesting to note that this profile would not necessarily make them the easiest of people to get along with, and Getzels and Jackson (1962) also found that creative students were not as well liked by their teachers as the more conforming and conventional ones.

Research by Hudson (1966) suggests that divergent thinking abilities might be important in determining pupils' choice of academic subjects. In particular, he found that arts students scored higher on divergent thought and that science students, particularly those doing physics, scored higher on convergent thought. Later research threw doubt on this finding, however, since when science students were given some examples of what was expected of them, they were then able to generate more ideas. This indicates that the initial differences in divergent thinking performance may have been due more to expectations about the task than to intrinsic abilities, and that subject choice may be related to other factors such as personality traits.

The creative process

Creativity can be seen as the coming together, or 'confluence', of a number of different features. General ability and personality are centrally involved, but domain knowledge, thinking style and motivation also figure. Lubart and Sternberg (1995) found that each of these five factors contributed separate amounts to the variance on a number of creative tasks, with a combined correlation of 0.83. General ability was the strongest correlate at 0.75, with personality being the weakest at 0.36. The creativity of individuals was moderately correlated within domain areas such as science and writing, but there was only an average correlation of 0.36 across the domains. Creativity did not appear to be a general ability and was strongly related to an individual's functioning within a particular area.

One early perspective adopted by Gestalt theorists was to see creative problem solving as reconceptualisation of either the elements of a problem, or the techniques used for solving it. This was demonstrated in a classic investigation by Maier (1931), who gave subjects the task of joining together two lengths of string which were hanging from the ceiling. The difficulty was that each string was not long enough to allow someone holding one piece to be able to reach the other. When subjects became 'stuck', Maier prompted them towards a solution by brushing against a string to set it swinging. This was usually enough to enable the subjects to restructure the problem to become one of creating a pendulum by using some handy pliers as a weight. This then enabled them to get hold of both strings when the pendulum swing brought them closer together.

According to this approach, a key element of creativity involves breaking a 'set' – a fixed way of seeing or thinking about things which limits the development of new ideas. Known as 'functional fixedness', this was also demonstrated by Duncker (1945) in a task where people were given the task of supporting a candle from a wall using objects which included a box of candles and some tacks. Since people saw the box as a holder, most of them failed to arrive at the solution, which involved pinning the inside of the box on to the wall to act as a base. This set was overcome by providing the subjects with a different verbal label that enabled them to see the box as having other possible functions.

Weisberg (1995), on the other hand, argues that creativity is normally based on essentially ordinary cognitive processes which combine to yield extraordinary products. This involves reproducing and extending previous knowledge and using techniques which have proved effective in the past. Weisberg refers to case studies of eminent creators and their work, such as Picasso's painting *Guernica* and Watson and Crick's analysis of the structure of the DNA molecule. Weisberg describes how such breakthroughs did not happen as some sudden, insightful discovery but were rather the outcome of long-term, methodical development. *Guernica*, for instance, was

Figure 4.7 Key stages in the creative process

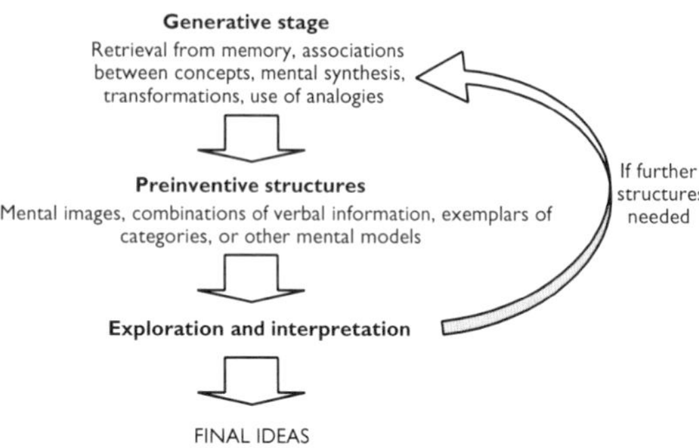

Source: Based on Fiske *et al.* (1992)

actually developed from earlier, very similar paintings, and the sudden 'discovery' of the structure of DNA in fact took a number of years and depended on a great deal of contemporary work by other researchers.

The Geneplore model derived by Fiske *et al.* (1992) describes the interplay of generative and exploratory processes in developing new and useful ideas. As shown in Figure 4.7, the 'generative stage' involves a range of normal cognitive processes which can result in 'pre-inventive structures'. These can then be explored to assess their creative possibilities, or the process can be repeated to consider more structures and possibilities. This model also emphasises that the overall process involves considering constraints about the functions of what is needed and the usefulness of what is arrived at.

The implications of this approach are that creativity does not depend on some vague form of 'insight' and that it can be developed by encouraging students to use these types of techniques and processes. There is indeed evidence that creativity and elements of the creative process can be developed in school by the use of appropriate techniques.

Facilitating creativity

Torrance (1963), however, argued that teachers tend to discourage creativity since independence and divergent thinking can interfere with the normal convergent processes of teaching. The implication is that teachers should possibly be more tolerant and aware of the need for creativity in pupils and foster it when possible. This is supported by Haddon and Lytton's (1968) investigation of the outcome of primary school teaching based on informal teaching styles which emphasised greater pupil freedom (before SATs and the literacy and numeracy hours!). They found that pupils taught in this way scored higher on measures of divergent thought and that they retained this superiority even after transfer to secondary school. Bennett (1976), however, found that there were no differences between the creative writing of pupils that depended on whether they were taught in formal or informal classrooms. Although there are doubts about the validity of his 'formal'–'informal' classification, it does seem that divergent thinking by itself might not be sufficient to improve the more complex task of creative writing and that the applying of divergent thought by pupils may need specific development work.

Creativity also appears to be related to intrinsic motivation – when children are involved in an activity for its own sake. If children perceive that they are involved only because of some form of external pressure (such as a reward), then this perception will limit their self-commitment and they will do only whatever is necessary to get the reward. In the original investigation by Lepper *et al.* (1973), children who expected a reward for doing drawings actually produced more of these but they were of lower quality than the drawings of children who did not expect the reward.

Children's creativity can also be encouraged by techniques such as *brainstorming*, which was originally developed by Parnes (1967). This involves setting up a group to generate a number of ideas on a topic, with an emphasis on fun and avoiding the use of criticism. Such ideas can then be evaluated to see which might be useful, or to develop key concepts further. Torrance (1963) also emphasised that practical creativity often involves problem solving (see 'Thinking skills', below). Maier (1933) carried out an early investigation of this by giving a group of students a 20-minute lecture on problem-solving techniques which involved flexibility, originality and avoiding becoming 'bogged down'. When given a number of unusual problems to solve, these students were then able to produce significantly more creative solutions, indicating that such academic training could be effective.

Covington and Crutchfield (1965) found that students were able to develop their ability to use creative techniques by following a course of programmed instruction. This involved 16 cartoon-text booklets, each featuring mysterious and baffling situations to be explained. As part of their explanation process, pupils were encouraged to generate ideas and then to compare these with a range of illustrative examples of relevant, fruitful and original ideas. Each lesson was designed so that students gradually worked towards the solution and were eventually brought to the stage where they could make the final discovery for themselves. An evaluation of the abilities of children who had completed this course showed that they performed better on problem solving and that this superior ability transferred well to a range of different tasks. Pupils were also subsequently much more motivated in problem situations and showed greater persistence and willingness in their general school work.

There is therefore evidence that schools can foster the development and use of creative abilities, although they might sometimes not fit too well with current achievement targets and the need for schools to cover a prescriptive curriculum. There is also an increased current emphasis on whole-class teaching in British schools and it seems likely that this will tend to discourage individuality and divergent thinking.

Thinking skills

Other, more recent ways of understanding individual differences involve analysing the processes that make up intelligent or creative thought. These approaches attempt to explain cognitive abilities and to see whether it is possible to develop these by appropriate teaching techniques.

According to Eysenck and Keane (1995), a great deal of thought depends on using existing knowledge or information, with most models of thinking incorporating the use of a storage system. As was described in Chapter 2, memory comprises a limited short-term, active store (known as working memory) and a long-term store holding a range of concepts – groups of items that share and are organised by key attributes. Long-term memory also contains a set of rules or logical relationships which are the basis for thought processes. Thinking can act on different types of representations, such as verbal categories or words, when we can literally talk to or reason with ourselves, or imagery, when we visualise a representation of what we are concerned with. Other forms of thought can involve more abstract features, and much of the time we are probably not consciously aware of the processes involved.

Whatever the form that thinking takes, much of it depends upon concepts being activated and linked together in some meaningful way. Eysenck and Keane consider that the key operations involve *reasoning*, the use of information to make *inferences*, and *decision making*, by which people evaluate likely outcomes and select between alternatives. These operations can be used to develop further concepts, and to establish additional rules about the ways in which they relate together.

Reasoning can involve logical processes, whereby inferences are made according to certain propositions. The strongest arguments are based on *deductive reasoning*, where the conclusion must be valid if the original premises are true. For example:

> A capital city is a country's seat of government.
> Lima is the capital of Peru
>
> **Therefore,** Lima is the seat of government of Peru.

People appear to be able to follow such logical processes, and Rips (1983) has shown that the time taken to arrive at such conclusions depends on the complexity of the rules involved. This is therefore one form of thought which can be used by pupils when the subject material embodies such logical relationships.

People also use *inductive reasoning*, which involves reaching a conclusion on the basis of specific instances. Such conclusions are only *probably* true, on the basis of the information given. For example:

> Mrs Smith qualified as a teacher.
> Mrs Smith works in a school.
>
> **Therefore**, Mrs Smith works as a teacher.

Although this conclusion would probably be correct, it is also possible that Mrs Smith has retired as a teacher and is now going back to help with organising the school play. Such thinking is common in everyday situations, and pupils will use their general knowledge and understanding of the world with problems in school to arrive at likely inferences. 'Wrong' answers to questions by a teacher are often due to pupils basing their reasoning on familiar premises and knowledge which are therefore logical and meaningful to them. For instance:

Teacher: 'What would you usually go into an off-licence for?' (looking for the answer 'alcohol')
Pupil: 'Some fags, sir.'

Rather than criticising or discarding such answers, it would be better for teachers to acknowledge the thinking and knowledge behind them and then to give prompts to extend the reasoning to arrive at the desired outcome, for instance by:

Teacher: 'Yes, you could, but why do you think they need to be *licensed* – what do they sell that has to be controlled?'
Pupil: 'Booze, sir.'

Decision making also appears to be based upon logical, probabilistic judgements. If pupils need to choose between possible solutions for a problem, they will assess the likelihood that each of the outcomes will achieve their goals before making a choice. Much of the time, however, the way in which people think or the decisions they arrive at are simply the result of applying knowledge or behaviour that worked in the past.

People are also able to generalise from previous situations with similar features, or even to use more complex analogies, often with models that incorporate the key elements and functions of a system. In understanding the structure of the atom, for instance, it can be useful to compare it with the solar system, with the sun representing the nucleus and the planets representing the electrons. This can help promote understanding of other features such as electron shells, as being similar to a number of planets in the same orbital sphere. In general, then, although thought can be logical, it is often based on wider knowledge and understanding. It is also often specific to domain areas which can have their own rules and principles.

Problem solving

Many educational tasks involve problem solving, such as answering higher-level questions and investigative work. Problem solving corresponds to Gagné's (1965) highest level of learning and involves both reasoning, to combine and apply concepts and rules, and decision making, to evaluate different outcomes.

Early descriptions of the problem-solving process considered that it covers a number of stages and strategies in progressing towards a final solution. Wallas's (1926) classic description of creative problem solving included:

- *preparation* – defining the problem, making first attempts to solve it;
- *incubation* – where the problem is left aside to develop;
- *illumination* – where the solution comes in a sudden, Gestalt-like 'insight'; and
- *verification* – in which the solution is evaluated to make sure that it really works.

Eysenck and Keane (1995), however, consider that this approach is rather too general and says little about what is involved. The 'incubation' and 'illumination' stages in particular are rather vague and have been largely reinterpreted in terms of general unconscious reasoning processes, with conscious 'insight' occurring when a final goal state becomes near.

Figure 4.8 Problem space for fraction to decimal conversion

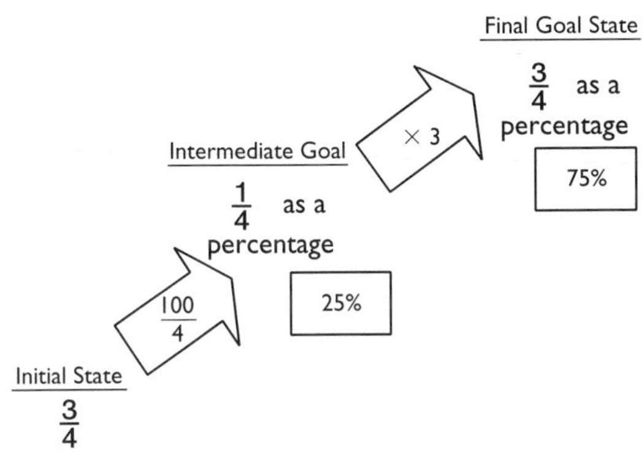

In education, many problems are relatively well defined and discrete. For instance, pupils might be given the task of working out the percentage that corresponds to a particular fraction. One way of explaining this involves the use of a 'problem space'. This is a model which is usually shown as in Figure 4.8, with initial and goal states, and indicates how the person tackling a problem can identify intermediate subgoals and appropriate strategies for achieving them.

Whenever possible, pupils should be encouraged to specify where they want to end up – that is to say, what will constitute a solution. They should also be clear about what they initially know, or need to know, and then should set up intermediate goals which will bring them closer to the final goal (see the Towers of Hanoi problem below). Often, problem solving can be helped with visual models such as drawings, but at other times it can be helped by the use of more abstract approaches.

Knowledge and rules

Problem solving which is relatively 'knowledge poor' has to depend on the use of general rules and principles. These can be investigated, and can be developed in children with logical puzzles such as the Towers of Hanoi problem (Figure 4.9). This involves moving three different-sized discs one at a time on to different pegs until they are all stacked in an identical way on the farthest peg, without ever placing a larger disc on top of a smaller one.

A generally important 'rule of thumb' principle (known as a heuristic) is to *set up an intermediate state that is part-way towards the goal, then to look for ways of solving that simpler problem.* This principle is commonly referred to as the *means–end heuristic.* With the Towers of Hanoi, applying it involves the intermediate goal of getting the largest disc on to the farthest peg, as shown in Figure 4.10; this in its turn can be achieved by first moving the two smaller discs on to the middle peg.

As shown in Figure 4.11 the problem can then be completed in three more moves.

Figure 4.9 Towers of Hanoi problem

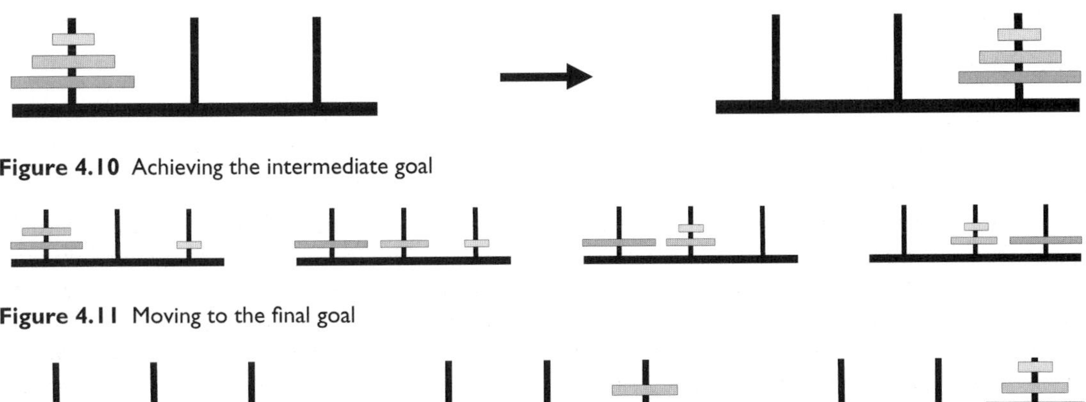

Figure 4.10 Achieving the intermediate goal

Figure 4.11 Moving to the final goal

Egan and Greeno (1974) found that experience of using this heuristic transferred to more complex problems with similar tasks. There is also evidence that it can be used across a range of other practical problem areas, and this rule is therefore an example of a 'domain independent' heuristic. These are usually relatively weak (they do not necessarily help very much), but training in them can help with general problem-solving skills. Other heuristics can be more powerful, but these are usually 'domain specific' and do not help in other areas of knowledge. With the Towers of Hanoi problem, a specific heuristic would be that 'moves often involve separating the upper discs and then combining them again'.

In school, problems and thinking are often poorly defined, without a simple goal or obvious ways of separating out intermediate stages. They are also usually 'knowledge intensive' and depend upon a great deal of initial information, and rules and stratagems that are specific to that particular domain. Progress in a particular academic area therefore normally depends mostly on closely related existing attainments since these are the knowledge and abilities that will help subsequent progress. Such attainments can operate over long periods of time, and Thomas and Mortimore (1996), for instance, found that academic attainments at secondary transfer accounted for nearly 60 per cent of the eventual variance in GCSE attainments five years later.

Schools therefore need to establish a strong foundation of subject knowledge in pupils, but it is also important for them to develop ways of using this information and to establish more general techniques which can be used across a range of subject and topic areas. These can establish greater flexibility in children's abilities and enable them to develop new knowledge and understanding more rapidly.

Use of thinking skills

A range of thinking skills can be generally useful in school work, including domain-independent strategies such as the 'means–end' heuristic. Other techniques, apart from the one of setting up strategies for achieving goals, involve ways of structuring and linking information, such as Ausubel's (1968) *advance organisers*. These set the scene for new information by reviewing the key points of earlier learning and establish the relevance of new information. Students often carry these strategies out for themselves, but Mayer (1979) found that in novel areas it can be useful for a teacher to provide prompts and an initial structure.

Analogies are a common and powerful way to develop pupils' understanding of new ideas and processes. They involve likening something that is already known to whatever is being studied, and effectively involve transfer of knowledge from one domain or context to another. Chen *et al.* (1995) investigated the way in which analogies can help understanding by studying 8-year-old children's ability to solve 'insight riddles' such as: 'A boy walked on a lake for 20 minutes without falling into the water. How did he do this?' One approach to help children with this problem might be to give them an abstract principle which does not incorporate any causal relationship such as: 'Some liquids can become hard. Heavy things can be held up.' However, when the investigators tried this, it actually interfered with the children's ability to solve the problems.

Their performance was greatly improved, however, when they were either given, or were encouraged to generate, concrete analogous examples along with the abstract principle. This involved sentences such as: 'Heavy objects can be held up by liquids when the liquids become hard. The truck drove over the hard lava without sinking.' Analogies therefore appear to be most effective when they have features which are close to those of the target problem and where a principle can be seen to work. It seems advisable that teachers who are using abstract principles to help pupils to understand a new area should either use analogous examples, or encourage pupils to generate some for themselves.

Learning and memory can also be improved by a range of general techniques, which involve organisation and coding. As was described in Chapter 2, there are a number of effective mnemonic strategies and study skills which enable students to develop their knowledge and understanding so that it is less likely that forgetting will occur.

Metacognitive skills

It is important for students, as well as having a range of thinking or learning skills, to be aware of situations when it would be relevant to use such strategies, and to select and to use appropriate ones. It may, for instance, be very effective to use a simple rehearsal technique with information which has little intrinsic meaning or which does not need to be retained for very long. Other material, however, which is more fundamental to an area of study, might require deeper learning techniques, based perhaps on links with existing knowledge (by establishing integrating principles), or by establishing an overall schema by using a 'knowledge map'.

Doing this involves conscious monitoring and planning, and Biggs (1985) found that students who were capable of such metacognitive thought had high general abilities which presumably enabled them to develop and use these skills. These students also had a belief that any progress was due to their own efforts, which appeared to motivate them to utilise their independent abilities. Although a review by Wang *et al.* (1990) indicated that metacognitive abilities are one of the most important variables which affect students' progress, Biggs found that many students did not appear to have these skills, even at the upper end of secondary school.

It is important to know whether metacognitive abilities are just a consequence of high general abilities, or whether they might be the basis of such abilities and could be taught to pupils. An investigation of this by O'Sullivan and Pressley (1984) found that teaching the 'keyword' memory strategy (described in Chapter 2) to students improved their learning with a task where they had to link the names of cities with an important industrial product. When given another task of learning Latin vocabulary, they were able to transfer this strategy, although they were helped greatly by direct instructions to use the keyword technique in the new learning situation. This indicates that such abilities may have an effect on progress in school and could be a useful target for teaching and advice on appropriate learning strategies.

Programmes to develop thinking skills

Because of their potential effectiveness, there have been many attempts to teach thinking skills. As was discussed earlier in this chapter under the heading 'Creativity', one example of a highly effective approach has been Covington and Crutchfield's (1965) course on creative problem solving. This developed pupils' abilities to manage and use thinking strategies, and significantly increased their problem solving in a number of different areas.

Fuerstein *et al.* (1980) have also developed assessment and teaching techniques based on *instrumental enrichment*, as a way of training relatively poorly functioning Israeli immigrants to improve their general thinking abilities. Early informal evaluations of this by Fuerstein were very positive, but the approach used emphasises relatively abstract principles – for instance, using concepts associated with the way in which a set of geometric shapes alter. It seems unlikely that such principles would generalise to other areas, and a subsequent evaluation of the use of this approach in the UK by Blagg (1991) found that there did not seem to be any measurable effects on pupils' academic progress. However, teachers' attitudes towards the approach were generally positive, and pupils appeared to be more active in their learning and more aware of different strategies they could use.

Blagg *et al.* (1993a) therefore developed the 'Somerset Thinking Skills Course' for 10- to 16-year-old children in school, which was subsequently extended into 'Thinking Skills at Work' (Blagg *et al.*, 1993b) for people preparing or returning to work. These courses teach a range of general skills including problem-solving techniques, organising and memorising, analysis and synthesis, the use of patterns, and the specific use

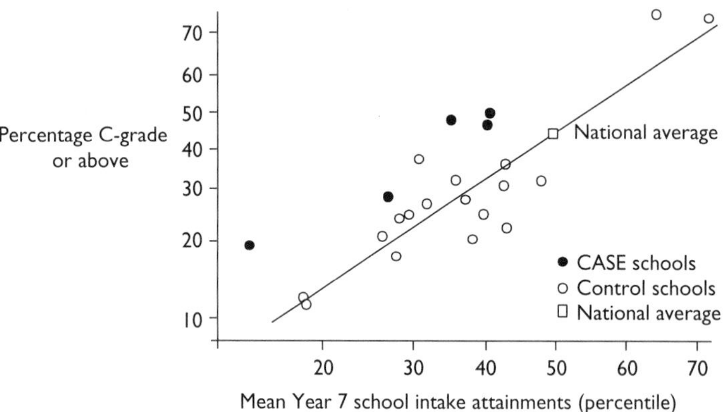

Figure 4.12 GCSE science results, 1996, in relation to school intake
Source: Shayer (1996)

of analogies and comparisons. They also emphasise the need to analyse and organise responses to the demands of new situations, and use prompts such as 'PLUG' (PLan, Understand, and Go) to trigger the necessary habits of thought. These skills are linked and applied with realistic tasks and settings to ensure transfer and generalisation. A number of evaluations of these courses by Blagg *et al.* (1994) indicate that they appear to result in significant improvements in abilities related to school learning and early vocational development.

Cognitive acceleration through science education

Shayer and Adey (see Shayer, 1996) have developed a highly effective form of metacognitive training based on developing pupils' general thinking skills in science. Known as Cognitive Acceleration through Science Education (CASE), this is based on the developmental sequence proposed by Piaget, with the aim of developing thought at the stage of formal operations. Normally, relatively few children of secondary age would be capable of such abstract thinking, which involves being able to manipulate the key features of problems, and to ask 'what if' questions. The programme runs over the first two years of secondary schooling, with a session every two weeks. The scheme's learning experiences are based on the belief of Vygotsky that learning is developed within a social context, and encourages children to reflect on their own thinking and to discuss with other children how they approach problems. These are set by the teacher and involve complex, real-life situations such as how to organise food in a larder, or predicting the force needed to raise a heavy load in a wheelbarrow.

These experiences appear to be highly effective in raising the overall long-term level of children's academic achievements, as shown by their GCSE performance three years later. Since the GCSE results for a school are normally closely related to the achievement and ability of its intake, an evaluation by Shayer (1996), shown in Figure 4.12, compared schools in terms of the performance of their intakes. These findings show that the overall effects of running the CASE programme was to increase the number of C grades or above in science by about 18.8 per cent. Achievements were also raised in other subjects such as mathematics (14.9 per cent) and English (15.6 per cent), indicating that the programme was having a generalised effect on thinking and learning skills across a range of curriculum areas. Other research by Askew *et al.* (1997) has also found positive effects on mathematics learning when teachers utilise similar teaching techniques, based on pupils making comparisons between their own problem-solving approaches and those of other students.

The CASE approach has also been found to continue to have strong and positive effects when developed by workers other than the original team, indicating that the findings are not just due to early enthusiasm and commitment. The general approach is therefore being extended by the original authors to cover mathematics education, and to develop thinking skills at earlier educational stages.

Cognitive style

The study of intellectual abilities is usually quantitative; that is to say, it is concerned with the general *level* of academic attainments. A complementary approach is to look at differences in the *way* in which individuals deal with information and how these are matched with different types of tasks. These differences are referred to as 'styles', and research has started to integrate and apply theories in this area.

Cognitive style has been defined by Tennant (1988) as 'an individual's characteristic and consistent approach to organising and processing information'. It is therefore usually seen as a stable feature and to underlie an individual's functioning in a number of different areas. It can be contrasted with cognitive *strategies*, which can vary according to the demands of particular tasks. These may vary from time to time and can be learned and developed (see 'Thinking skills', above).

An early approach by Witkin (1962) looked at *field independence–dependence*, which is an individual's ability to 'disembed' his or her perception from the effects of context. This was first investigated in tests of people's ability to judge the uprightness of a rod when the frame around it was tilted. Some people appeared to be particularly affected by the context of the frame and tended to judge that the rod was upright when it was tilted in the same direction as the frame. Although it may appear to be just a test of perception, this ability does seem to affect a range of general cognitive activities, which Witkin argues involve the extent to which people use internal or external cues.

Impulsivity–reflectivity is another style which was proposed by Kagan *et al.* (1964). This is also referred to as 'conceptual tempo' and considers the speed at which people make decisions under conditions of uncertainty. This is typically evaluated with the Matching of Familiar Figures Test (MFFT), which involves seeing how quickly a person is able to match a particular shape with the correct one among a number of alternatives.

Integrating styles

There are a large number of other styles but a factor analysis study by Riding and Cheema (1991) found that most of these tend to cluster together into a few families, with the main one being on a *holistic–analytic* continuum (Figure 4.13). This dimension is typically assessed by the ability to match different geometric shapes. For instance, a target shape may be contained within a more complex geometrical figure. As shown in

Figure 4.13 The holistic–analytic continuum

Holists	Intermediate	**Analytics**
Tend to perceive and organise information into loosely clustered wholes and to make rapid judgements based on general, impressionistic features		Tend to organise information into clear-cut conceptual groupings and take more time over decisions, basing these on logical and detailed analysis.
Includes: Field independence, Impulsivity		Includes: Field independence, Reflectivity

Figure 4.14 Embedded figure test

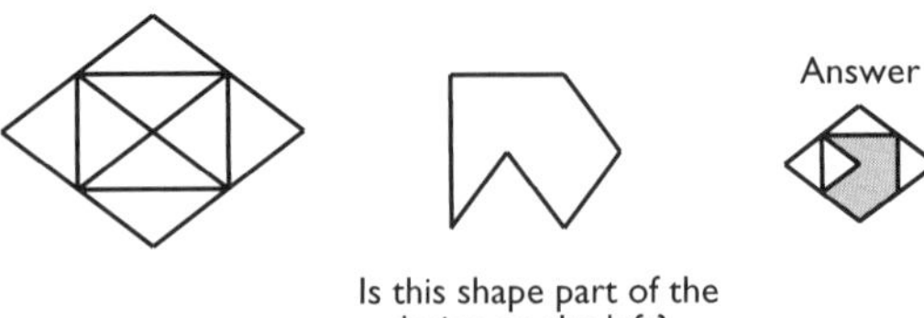
Answer
Is this shape part of the
design on the left?

Figure 4.14, this task involves the ability to 'disembed' a simpler shape from within a more complex one. Analytics are relatively superior at this, since they are less distracted by the overall context.

Performance on such tests usually correlates positively with intelligence, leading some critics such as Carroll (1993) to argue that analytic thought is really just one aspect of general ability. To counter this, Riding (1991) has devised a further test of the holistic style which involves the speed at which subjects can match simple geometric shapes. Combining this with an embedded figures test can give a ratio for wholist as against analytic abilities, which Riding and Pearson (1994) found was essentially independent of intelligence (correlating with it only at 0.05), and which also contributed independently to performance on a range of academic tasks.

Verbaliser–imager cognitive style

Riding and Cheema (1991) also found a secondary, independent style related to the way in which individuals are inclined to represent information during thinking. This can be assessed by giving subjects decisions to make which depend upon either the appearance of things, or more verbal, abstract information. 'Imagers' are people who tend to be good at dealing with information which can be represented with images, such as 'teacher'. This ability is similar to Paivio's (1969) demonstration of the importance of 'concreteness' in memory, with concepts which can be visualised well being recalled better. 'Verbalisers' on the other hand are best with tasks that involve thought using language and more abstract concepts which are difficult to represent visually, such as 'truth'.

Implications of different cognitive styles

The tests mentioned above depend largely on perceptual processes, and at first seem unlikely to relate to anything meaningful to do with higher-level studies in education. However, measures of cognitive style do in fact show a number of significant relationships with various aspects of teaching and learning, and these have important implications for educational processes. Witkin *et al.* (1977), for instance, found that field-independent (analytic) teachers tended to be generally more formal, focusing on the work content rather than the learner, being more inclined to criticise learners and explain why they are wrong. Field-dependent (wholist) students preferred group work, with frequent interactions with other students and with the teacher. Field-independent learners were likely to have more self-defined goals and to respond to intrinsic motivation, whereas field-dependent learners required more structured work by the teacher and responded more to extrinsic motivation.

With specific learning tasks, Riding and Anstey (1982) found that verbalisers were superior at initially learning to read, which is consistent with the general importance of phonological processing in early reading (see Chapter 9). Further work by Riding and Mathias (1991) also found that reading ability in 11-year-olds was significantly greater for wholist-verbalisers, with a mean reading quotient of above 120, compared with the overall mean of about 100. This is a major difference and was presumably due to the superior combination of general integrative abilities with phonological skills.

Riding and Pearson (1994) found meaningful differences between school subjects, with students who scored high on the wholist style being significantly better at school subjects such as French (Figure 4.15). A plausible explanation for this is that such subjects may depend on the ability to retain the overall meaning or to use general patterns in the information studied. The intermediate style appeared to be best for subjects such as science, where analysis is important to distinguish the effects of separate parameters, but

Figure 4.15 Achievements of different subjects according to their cognitive style

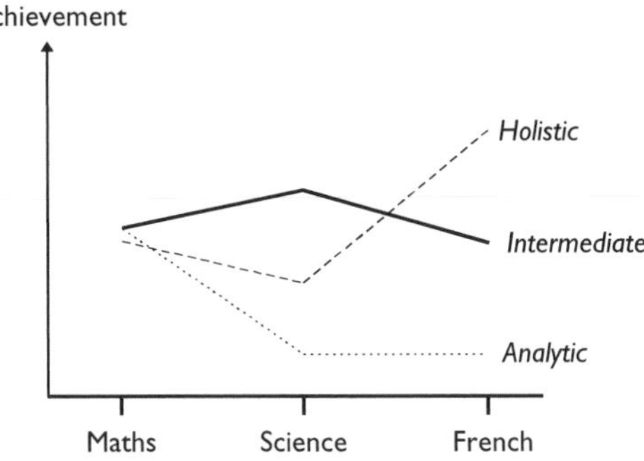

Source: Riding and Pearson (1994)

in which elements may also need to be combined into general, holistic theories. The extreme analytic style appeared to be a disadvantage for learning most subjects, although for mathematics it was equivalent to the other styles. Mathematics is a subject where specific analytic abilities probably compensate for any inability to integrate information.

Riding and Douglas (1993) investigated learning progress with a computer-presented tutorial on the topic of car brakes and found that the mode of presentation interacted significantly with the verbaliser–imager dimension (Figure 4.16). Although this is perhaps not a surprising finding, the *size* of the effect was quite large, indicating that it is generally best to present verbal information linked with a visual aid, and particularly for those students who prefer the visual mode. It is likely that any teachers who prefer the verbaliser style will tend to neglect the use of illustrations; it may therefore be a good idea for all teachers to monitor their practice to ensure that they are not over-reliant on textual explanations.

Figure 4.16 Overall recall scores of verbalisers and imagers

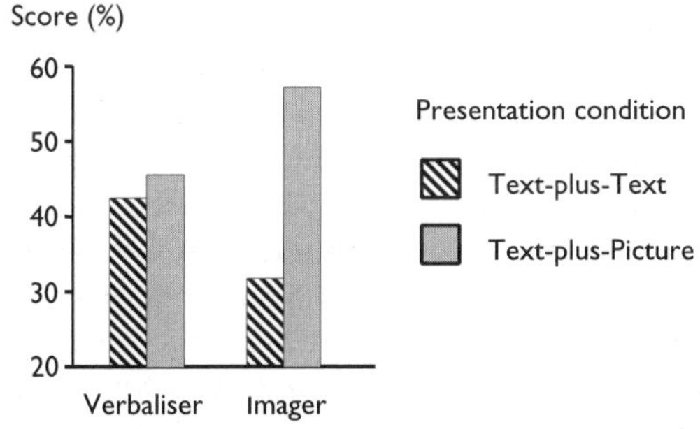

Source: Riding and Douglas (1993)

Personality

Personality refers to those stable characteristics by which individuals differ from each other and which acts as the basis for what they do. It is a label normally applied to interpersonal behaviour and we would for instance typically say that a person who is socially outgoing has an extraverted personality. It has also been used to cover cognitive and emotional differences, and Cattell *et al.* (1970) include general ability as one of 16 key personality factors. Such personality *traits* can be used to categorise or to predict behaviour, although Mischel (1968) argues that in general, individual differences are relatively small and that what we do is mostly determined by the situation that we are in. Thus, for example, a child at school is generally more likely to be sitting down and studying than he or she would be at home. Tattum (1982) also found that differences in children's behaviour in school were largely determined by the contexts of different classes, and different teachers generally do not agree very well in their assessment of separate pupils' behaviour.

Within the same situation, however (e.g. the same class), any stable differences in behaviour will be more evident. Self-report questionnaires for children also show consistent personality traits, for example with the Junior Eysenck Personality Inventory (Eysenck and Eysenck, 1975). This assesses two dimensions, which, as shown in Figure 4.17, can combine to produce different personality types. These types can have implications for education, and Eysenck and Cookson (1969) found that stable extraverts tended to do best in the primary school; however, this effect starts to reverse in secondary schooling, and by higher education, unstable introverts do

Figure 4.17 Dimensions of extraversion and introversion

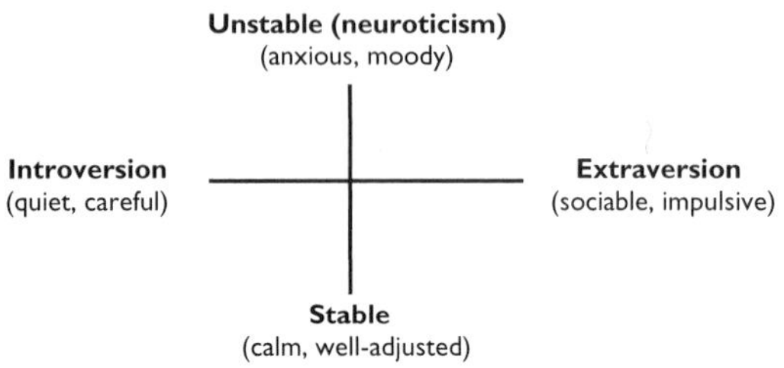

better. A possible explanation for this is that primary learning experiences are more social and therefore favour the outgoing and confident child. Later education probably involves progressively more independent, isolated working, with anxious students being more motivated to work. A longitudinal analysis by Anthony (1983) indicated that such changes probably happen as a result of academic students becoming more introverted as they progress in education, rather than by introverted students gradually doing better.

Using more factors

Although significant, these correlations are relatively weak and typically do not account for more than 4 per cent of the variance in academic attainments. In order to obtain stronger correlations, it is necessary to use a test with a larger number of low-order factors, which cover relatively specific traits. The Children's and High School Personality Questionnaire (Cattell and Beloff, 1960) is based on this approach and assesses 14 personality traits (the adult version assesses 16). Cattell *et al.* (1972) found that a combination of these (without intelligence) accounted for about 20 per cent of the variance in general academic achievements. The single-factor correlations which were significant for Grade 7 pupils are shown in Table 4.3.

Table 4.3 Correlations of personality factors with achievements

Factor	Correlation with achievements
A (warmth)	0.08
C (stability)	0.19
G (conscientiousness)	0.31
O (self assurance)	0.22
Q_3 (self-disciplined)	0.19

The big five

One problem with personality research is that using different questionnaires or ways of analysing them will give different personality factors. However, developments in personality theory have tended to converge on the importance of the 'five-factor model' (John, 1990). This combines the higher-level factors of extraversion and neuroticism with agreeableness, conscientiousness, and openness to experience. A study by Wolfe and Johnson (1995) confirmed the importance of the factor of Conscientiousness (a combination of Cattell's G and Q_3 above) in education, finding that it accounted for 9 per cent of the variance in general grade achievement for college entrants. This effect is even more impressive given that it was assessed by means of a shortened form which only used seven questions. However, these were largely based on attributes such as perseverance, carefulness and reliability, and it is perhaps not particularly surprising that students who are high on these qualities are also generally good at studying.

Motivation

It can be argued that the motivational level of pupils is a relatively stable individual characteristic and should be seen as an aspect of their personality. Higher levels of 'need achievement' (see Chapter 5) can certainly lead to better academic progress, and a study by Boyle *et al.* (1989) of the School Motivation Analysis Test found that it accounted for around 20 per cent of the variance in a range of school subjects. The key attributes for students were that they should have a keen interest in things and an integrated, conflict-free view of themselves. However, motivational levels are usually the outcome of a number of factors and are probably more subject to change than normal measures of personality.

Different frames of reference

A very different approach to personality is based on the humanistic perspective of Kelly (1955). According to this, who we are is very much a question of our system of personal constructs. Such constructs are our unique ways of categorising and understanding the world and determine how we are able to interact with it. One individual might, for instance, tend to see things in terms of how dominant or passive people are; another might see things mainly in terms of academic success or failure. Salmon (1988) considers that this approach, unlike trait theories of personality, which are relatively rigid, enables us to emphasise the possibilities and the processes of change in the ways in which pupils and teachers view things. Unfortunately, there can be difficulties if there is a mismatch between the construct systems of pupils and teachers, in particular about what is the purpose of certain types of lessons. In one example quoted by Salmon, pupils saw design and technology lessons as being about *making* something; design and technology teachers, however, saw the educational process as fostering *design*, a goal which was likely to be frustrated without the pupils' active involvement in this.

Educational implications

Many psychologists, such as Cattell and Eysenck, believe that personality is largely inherited and that it is therefore relatively stable. This would imply that in order to be effective, teachers should accommodate what they do to differences in pupils' personalities and learning styles. This might perhaps mean that teachers should ensure that the quieter pupils in primary schools get their equal share of attention. They could also make sure that such pupils are involved in tasks where learning depends on cooperation, for example by giving them positive structured roles in the type of group activities to be described in Chapter 6. Academic experiences for older pupils might also be made more social to allow the involvement of more outgoing pupils. This might involve a greater emphasis on study groups and seminar work.

The significant prediction of key personality features such as 'conscientiousness' in general academic success indicates that it may be useful to incorporate measures of this into academic and vocational counselling. Entwistle (1972) also found that certain personality factors correlate with success in certain subjects. Stable introverts were best at natural sciences or history, neurotic introverts were best at engineering and at languages, and social science students (such as psychology) were intermediate for both extraversion and neuroticism. Although these are not strong predictors, they could be useful as a basis for helping students to decide on future areas of study.

Views of personality such as Kelly's theories see it more as an active construction by people, and theories of the self argue that much of the consistency in our behaviours can be seen as an attempt to present a view of ourselves to others. This implies that education could have an impact on children's typical behaviours, although they are likely to hold on to their views of the world and self-concept unless there is a good reason to change. As described above, it may therefore be important to be aware of pupils' different perspectives and to adapt teaching to them when possible. However, one view of education, which is probably a useful perspective for teachers to adopt, is that it is all about developing these very aspects – expanding the ways in which children construe the world and developing their sense of self and belief in what they are capable of.

Summary

Differences between children are important because they indicate how learning experiences could be matched with pupils' thinking processes, cognitive style and personality. General ability or 'intelligence' tests were developed in order to separate children for different levels of educational experiences. However, there are doubts about the validity of a single measure of ability, and in any case intelligence is a relatively weak predictor of present and future academic progress.

Although there is evidence which supports the belief that intelligence is inherited and therefore biologically based, this remains an unresolved debate. There is also persuasive evidence that children's home backgrounds have a significant effect on their general verbal cognitive development. Although family size and birth order probably have only a limited impact, direct measures of early parenting appear to have a large and lasting impact on children's intellectual and academic abilities.

Children with high abilities or who have a specific strength in some area are often referred to as 'gifted'. Generally speaking, this seems to be an extension of the normal range of abilities, and such children do not necessarily have unusual social or emotional difficulties. They do appear to benefit from higher-level work that is matched with their attainments, but the effects of such matching are not great and some forms of inappropriate support can have negative social consequences.

Creativity involves generating novel ideas or solutions to problems. It appears to depend on a sufficient level of general abilities, associated with certain personality and motivational characteristics, as well as specific knowledge of the target domain. Early ideas about creativity saw it as involving a different way of thinking about an area. More recent theories emphasise the ability to extend and apply existing knowledge and abilities. Creativity in pupils appears to be encouraged by less formal teaching and an emphasis on intrinsic motivation, as well as specific techniques.

Thinking processes underlie general ability and creativity and can be based on logic as well as the use of previous experiences and knowledge. With problem solving, traditional theories have emphasised the role of the unconscious, resulting in a sudden insight into the solution. Recent developments consider that problem solving comes from deriving and achieving successive goal states, using heuristic (procedural) rules of different strengths and generalisability. In schools these include the use of 'organisers' and analogies, both of which guide and structure learning. It is also possible to develop general thinking skills with educational programmes, some of which appear to be highly effective.

People also vary according to how they typically organise and process information – their cognitive style. An integration of approaches in this area considers that two key dimensions are holistic–analytic, and verbaliser–imager styles. These have important implications for teaching, with learning being most effective when materials and teaching techniques are matched with pupils' styles.

Stable differences in behaviour are what make up personality, and variations in social orientation can affect academic progress to some extent. Personality factors which are related to effort and involvement typically account for much more of pupils' achievements, and there can also be conflicts due to the different ways in which pupils and teachers construe the educational process. It is possible for teachers to adjust to such variations between individuals, although a more positive role is for them to emphasise the ways in which pupils can develop.

Key implications

- The concept of a unitary general ability (intelligence) appears to have little value in the making of educational decisions.
- Children's specific home background and experiences have a major impact on their cognitive and educational development. These are largely beyond the influence of the school.
- It is probably not very effective to consider some children as being 'gifted'. There should, however, be a range of matched and flexible educational provision to meet the needs of children of all abilities.
- Creativity and thinking skills can be fostered by particular teaching approaches.
- Taking account of cognitive style and personality can improve the educational process.

Further reading

Michael Howe (1997) *IQ in Question: The Truth about Intelligence*. London: Sage.

Howe makes a strong case for deconstructing the concept of intelligence. He sets up and knocks down twelve apparent 'facts' about intelligence and in the process covers the key ideas and findings in this area. This is a short and readable book which goes beyond many of the accepted beliefs about general ability.

Joan Freeman (1998) *Educating the Very Able: Current International Research*. London: The Stationery Office.

A concise review of the research findings on high-ability children and their needs. An important conclusion of this book is that very able children have the normal range of emotional problems. Freeman argues for a more generally inclusive approach which gives high-level opportunities for all children.

Carol McGuiness (1999) *From Thinking Skills to Thinking Classrooms*. Research Brief no. 115. Nottingham: DfEE Publications.

A review and evaluation of research into thinking skills. Considers the key ideas in this area and evaluates the main approaches which are being used. This relatively short publication provides a rapid introduction to recent developments.

Richard Riding and Stephen Rayner (1999) *Cognitive Styles and Learning Strategies*. London: David Fulton.

A technical book which describes in some detail the justification and use of recent approaches to cognitive styles. These have a number of immediate implications for teachers, including the possibility of analysing their own style and ways in which they can become more sensitive to the cognitive styles of their pupils.

W. Ray Crozier (1997) *Individual Learners: Personality Differences in Education*. London: Routledge.

Looks at the need to account for personality theories in teaching and learning. Goes into some detail concerning the five main traits of aggressiveness, anxiety, motivation, self-confidence and shyness. Rather academic but draws out the main implications from direct research studies.

Practical scenario

Stephen's mother has just complained to the head-teacher that her son's educational needs are not being met in school. She has brought in a report from a private psychologist which assessed his IQ as being 'superior' and she asked what the school is going to do to help his particular needs. In class Stephen is doing well and is always keen to answer questions, showing that he has good general knowledge. Both the head-teacher and class teacher would like to extend Stephen's studies but do not feel that there is the time to give him separate work.

- *Is Stephen's mother right that her son has educational needs which are different from those of other children?*
- *What could the school do to ensure that work is at the right level for Stephen? Would it be appropriate to move him on to higher work, possibly by linking in with higher classes in some way? Would it be a good idea to set up a special group of high-achieving children who could receive additional help?*
- *Are there any other techniques which would meet Stephen's needs and also match in with those of other pupils in his class?*

5 Involving students

Chapter structure

Motivation

What is motivation?

Motivation refers to the psychological processes that lead us to do certain things. Common-sense views of motivation tend to see it as a single factor that we can have more or less of, and which can energise what people do. Many ideas about the role and importance of motivation in education tend to portray it as a form of personal quality, which can directly affect learning. This has been confirmed by investigations such as that by Cattell and Child (1972), who found that in addition to the effects of ability and personality, pupils' levels of motivation independently accounted for about 20 per cent of the variance in reading achievement.

Although it is possible to see motivation as a general quality, in many ways it can be relatively specific. A pupil who puts in very little effort with school work, and hence might be said to lack motivation, might spend a lot of time and energy on a complex and demanding computer game. In the same way, some pupils can also become much more involved and successful in one particular academic subject area than in others. There are many reasons why we do or do not become involved in a specific activity, and explanations for motivation encompass the complete range of perspectives in psychology.

Perhaps the best way of understanding motivation is to see it not as a single quality but rather as a process that comes into play whenever we are involved in an activity. In a sense, unless people are in a coma, they can always be said to be motivated to do whatever it is that they are doing. Part of explaining motivation therefore involves reasons for the *direction*, as well as the level, of involvement. Even if pupils are just chatting with their friends, or staring out of the window and daydreaming, we can still look at explanations for why they are involved in such intrinsically motivated activity – 'intrinsically' meaning 'for its own sake'. The problem for teachers is that such behaviours are unlikely to lead to much academic progress. For this reason, educational definitions of motivation tend to focus on academic achievement and involvement with tasks in school. These can involve more extrinsic forms of motivation; that is, factors external to the pupils themselves. We should be aware, however, that these may not necessarily be very high on some students' personal agendas.

Why is motivation important for education?

Observational studies such as those of Galton *et al.* (1999) have found that pupils work independently most of the time they are in school, showing only limited work-oriented involvement with their teacher or with other children. Whatever learning pupils do achieve is therefore likely to be heavily dependent on their own level of effort and involvement. McGee *et al.* (1986), for instance, have found that poor concentration and attention significantly limit children's educational progress when they start school. At all stages in education, progress in a particular subject is mainly determined by students' initial attainments. However, Lange and Adler (1997) found that such predictions for pupils in grades 3, 4 and 5 were significantly improved by taking into account their motivation, as measured by intrinsic goal orientation (being interested in a subject for its own sake) and academic self-perception (how pupils saw themselves as learners).

Bruner (1966b) has pointed out that school experiences differ from other forms of learning because they are *decontextualised*. This means that learning occurs separately from the actual thing or process that is being studied and therefore requires specific and conscious effort to maintain involvement. Children in school who are learning about windmills are likely to receive information from their teacher or books, but only rarely by actually visiting a windmill. Before children come to school, and in societies where formal education does not exist, learning appears to happen with little effort or external pressure. Bruner argues that this is because such learning is contextualised, meaning that children acquire knowledge which has the context of being meaningful and useful for them. All the major early developments such as walking, talking and social interaction are not taught in any formal way, but develop because they immediately enable children to interact with and to control their environment.

The decontextualising of learning is partly the product of a prescriptive curriculum and class sizes which limit the ability of teachers to respond to individual interests and needs. However, it can also be argued that education must inevitably involve the developing of abstract learning, since it is impossible to experience personally the basis of every new item of knowledge that will be useful to us. Despite this, Bruner argues that it is still possible to develop learning by some form of direct experiences in school and that a process of learning by discovery will maintain children's natural curiosity and motivation. There is some support for these ideas, although the practicalities of covering the curriculum mean that some compromises have to be made.

Despite the fact that it is the job of teachers to involve children and make sure that they learn, it is actually quite difficult for teachers to monitor their learning. Although it does not seem too difficult to check whether a child is 'on task' or not, being 'on task' is not the same as active learning. Children can be quite adept at making it look as though they are involved with their work when they are just putting on an outward show, or doing the minimum to keep out of trouble. On the other hand, children can appear to be uninvolved but may well be thinking about work. This was confirmed by Peterson *et al.* (1984), who carried out observations of pupils following a standard mathematics unit. The amount of time during which pupils appeared to be 'on task' correlated with their actual progress only at 0.31, indicating that appearances can be quite deceptive. On the other hand, pupils' reports on their own involvement were a better predictor of progress, correlating with attainments at 0.48, which accounts for more than twice the variance.

Another way to judge children's motivation is from the quality and the amount of work that they produce. However, their work also depends on ability, and it is hard to know whether pupils who have not done much work are not trying, or just do not have any knowledge or understanding of what they are supposed to be doing. Teachers try to overcome this difficulty by forming an impression of children's potential abilities, often from how well they cope with other forms of work, or by the consistency of their output. If they find that children can write well on one occasion then it is reasonable to assume that they should be able to do so at other times and that poor work is probably the result of limited effort. However, it can take some time to form these judgements, and some children adopt long-term work-avoidance strategies. Galton *et al.* (1999), for instance, found that a quarter of all children engaged in such 'easy riding', which involved giving the appearance of working while putting in only limited effort, in order to reduce teachers' expectations of them.

Academic motivation may thus be important in determining educational progress, but difficult for teachers to monitor directly. There are a number of explanations as to why pupils do or do not become involved with academic tasks in school, and most of these have direct implications for what teachers might be able to do about it.

Roles, conformity and obedience

A great deal of children's behaviour in school can be seen as conforming to their role as pupils, and obedience to the authority of teachers. Activities such as going to classes, following the instructions of the teachers and being involved with and completing work assignments are examples. Most of the time pupils rarely infringe on these expectations or do so only in minor ways, such as talking when they are not supposed to. Children evidently have the belief that they should follow these patterns of behaviour, and it is likely that this is due to a general desire to 'fit in'. People are generally rather anxious about the consequences of not conforming, and a series of classic experiments by Asch (1955) demonstrated that the feared negative reactions from other group members included being ridiculed and social rejection. Developing expectations about what is appropriate in certain situations and the need to consider the reactions of others are part of early socialisation. These can be critical in determining early academic progress, and Riley (1995) found that those children who did not show rapid and positive social adjustment to school were four times less likely to be reading by the end of their first year when compared with the average, regardless of their skills on entry.

Not all children conform to school norms or show obedience to their teachers. Some either fail to develop expectations of social roles at an early age, or subsequently adopt certain peer group roles which are directly in opposition to the work-oriented norms of schooling. Negative roles learned from peer groups can particularly affect boys, and children from certain ethnic minorities who need to establish a strong separate sense of identity. Connell (1989) has described how this can result in a subgroup ethos where academic, cooperative behaviour is seen in a negative way, with pupils who conform to this being labelled as 'swots' and 'wimps'.

The effects of peer conformity increase during secondary schooling, and can be very difficult for schools to counter. One effective approach involves the use of adults from out of school in an individual mentoring role. A study by Miller (1997) of the effects of this in a number of schools found that it improved students' self-reported motivation and significantly increased their grades at GCSE – by an average of just below half a grade for each subject they took.

Instincts, drives and needs

The simplest and earliest approaches to motivation tended to see all behaviour as being impelled by underlying forces or drives. Investigations based upon this perspective attempted to identify what these motives were, and the way in which they operated. However, one difficulty with such approaches is that they depend on a relatively circular logic and do not really explain a great deal. The existence of various instincts, drives or needs is inferred from the behaviours that we see, and the behaviours are then explained by referring to those underlying motives. Such explanations therefore tend to be mainly descriptive and do not necessarily get us much further in trying to improve children's involvement with appropriate activities in school. However, these theories are still used a great deal in education and it is worth briefly reviewing them.

Instincts

Instinct are behaviours that involve little if any learning and are the simplest form of drive state. They involve simple responses to specific stimuli and appear to be simply 'wired into' the brain. Instincts are established by exposure to appropriate situations during sensitive periods during development They are also 'species-specific', and inexperienced kittens, for instance, will spontaneously show 'chasing and catching' behaviours towards small moving objects, behaviours which can also be activated when a specific part of the brain is electrically stimulated. Although our genes differ by less than 2 per cent from those of the chimpanzee, our nearest genetic relative, the difference is sufficient to encode for a brain that is much larger, particularly the outer layer or cortex, which is able to carry out many generalised interconnections. Human behaviour may have an underlying primitive basis, but most of our behaviours are flexible and are the result of learning processes.

Despite this, some psychologists have argued that we still have a certain sensitivity or propensity to develop certain behaviours. Bowlby (1951) originally believed that babies go through a particular stage when they are able to form social bonds with their mother. He felt that if children somehow missed out on this stage, their social and emotional development would inevitably be damaged. However, this view has been modified by subsequent research, which has found that although early socialisation experiences are important, older children can still overcome quite major early social deprivation. More recently, Pinker (1994) has put the case for language development's being due to the expression of inherited abilities. However, there are alternative explanations based on socialisation processes and children's ability to learn and to generate complex systems. Although we may have the potential for certain abilities and behaviours, these involve considerable variability, and are very different from what is normally considered as instinctive.

Drive reduction

Other early theorists such as Hull (1943) argued that all behaviour is linked with the need to reduce basic biological drive states such as hunger and thirst. Although these can certainly motivate us, most of what people do is far removed from such immediate necessities, and it is difficult to see how such ideas could be at all applicable to educational experiences.

Hull did, however, attempt to explain more everyday concerns by linking basic or primary drives with secondary drives, which enable the primary ones to be achieved. In this way, earning money could be seen as a secondary drive since the money can be used to pay for food and shelter. Although this has some plausibility and may apply to some situations in life, it is still a long way from having any educational relevance. It is quite unlikely that students will regularly make the extended links between studying hard, eventually getting a job and then satisfying their primary drives. There is also the fact that many effective motivators, such as certain types of verbal feedback, or being allowed to carry out a social activity, seem to have only the most tenuous of links with such basic drive states. Although they were once popular and still have a certain simplistic attraction, Hull's theories are therefore usually nowadays considered to have little relevance.

The psychodynamic approach

Another well-known theory based on drive reduction was proposed by Freud at the start of the twentieth century. According to this approach, motivation comes from the interplay of

Figure 5.1 Mental structures as proposed by Freud

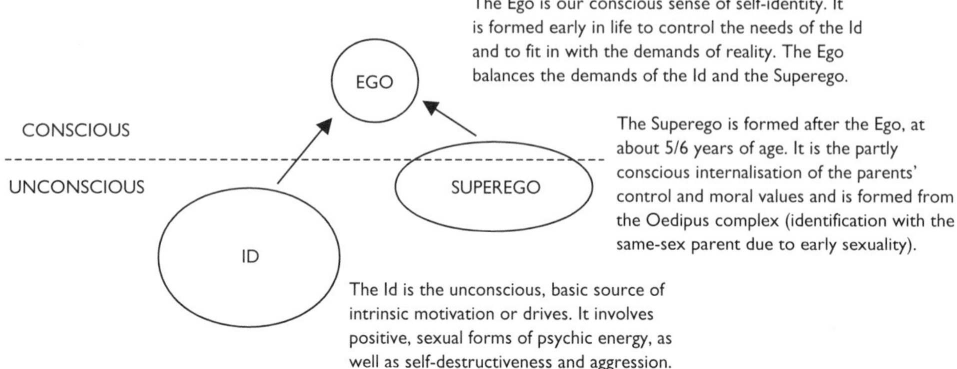

three mental structures known as the *id*, the *ego* and the *superego*. As shown in Figure 5.1, these exist at different levels of conscious awareness. The role of the ego is to balance the wilder demands of the id with the moralistic controls of the superego.

The Ego is our conscious sense of self-identity. It is formed early in life to control the needs of the Id and to fit in with the demands of reality. The Ego balances the demands of the Id and the Superego.
EGO
CONSCIOUS
UNCONSCIOUS
SUPEREGO
The Superego is formed after the Ego, at about 5/6 years of age. It is the partly conscious internalisation of the parents' control and moral values and is formed from the Oedipus complex (identification with the same-sex parent due to early sexuality).
ID
The Id is the unconscious, basic source of intrinsic motivation or drives. It involves positive, sexual forms of psychic energy, as well as self-destructiveness and aggression.

Freud believed that the action of the mind is to discharge drive states which primarily originate from the id, and to reduce them to their lowest level possible. This is achieved by processes known as *defence mechanisms*, of which we are largely unaware and which protect the conscious mind from our baser desires. Typical forms of defence mechanisms which might be seen in education include:

- *Repression* – the earliest and most common form of defence mechanism, which involves simply pushing unwanted demands into the unconscious. Repression could lead to motivated forgetting of unpleasant thoughts or knowledge.
- *Rationalisation* – creating seemingly rational causes for impulses we do not want to acknowledge. An example would be blaming failure in an exam on poor teaching rather than lack of study.
- *Projection* – transferring one's own undesirable qualities on to other people. Pupils doing this might justify their own cheating by believing that everyone else cheats at exams.
- *Displacement* – redirection of impulses to safer forms. A pupil's anger towards a teacher might therefore be directed to the safer target of another pupil. One form of this is *sublimation*, when energy is channelled into positive activities such as studying or sport.

From this perspective, motivated behaviours are normally the result of unconscious drives and adaptations. Although this can appear to be an attractive explanation, the psychodynamic approach has been heavily criticised since it is impossible to prove whether it is right or not. This is because the general complexity of the theory means that it can predict a range of contradictory outcomes. If, for instance, children have a poor relationship with their parents, then this could result either in *displacement* of these negative feelings on to their teachers, or *identification* with them, which is another defence mechanism leading to more positive feelings.

Because of such difficulties, psychoanalytic explanations have been largely superseded by cognitive perspectives. In the above example of rationalisation, the tendency to blame others can be accounted for by attribution theory (see later in this chapter), whereby we tend to have a 'self-serving bias' in our analysis of causes. There are further difficulties with applying Freud's theories to problem behaviour, and therapeutic techniques based on them have no apparent effectiveness. Despite such difficulties, Freud's ideas continue to be surprisingly popular, and Coren (1997) describes how the psychodynamic approach can be applied to a range of issues in education.

A more general criticism of drive reduction theories such as Freud's or Hull's is that they see rewards or pleasures as coming from a desire to reduce drive states. In Freud's theory in particular, he believes that the ultimate state, in which there are no more bothersome drives, is death! Apart from being a rather gloomy perspective on life, this completely fails to explain why it is that we will become involved in activities such as watching a frightening film, where there is no apparent drive reduction. Indeed, achieving a high arousal state often seems to be part of the attraction of the activity. As we shall see later in this chapter, motivation often seems to be generated and maintained just by being involved in an activity. In these situations there is no apparent separate predisposition or motive to become involved, and concepts such as instincts or drives are unlikely to be of any use.

Needs

A need implies a lack of, or a want for, something. Murray (1938) considered the way in which this can lead to motivated behaviours, originally proposing that there are two main categories of biological and social needs. An example of a biological need would be a lack of food leading to hunger, and a social need would be a lack of contact with other people leading to a desire for this.

Murray also identified a general 'need for achievement', which appears to have some relevance to education. This can be assessed using the Thematic Apperception Test (the TAT), which involves subjects' spontaneous verbal interpretations of a range of ambiguous pictures. For example, when given a picture of a woman sitting in front of a mirror, a pupil might say, 'The woman is daydreaming about doing well at her new job', indicating an interest in achievement-oriented themes. Although this test is not specifically related to education, Wendt (1955) found that students who scored high for need achievement on the TAT did much better on arithmetic tasks than other students, even when they were not directly monitored by a teacher.

The concept of underlying needs has also been developed by Maslow (1954) as part of a more general humanistic perspective, with lower levels being a necessary foundation for the higher levels of self-fulfilment. The lowest levels are similar to the basic drives of Hull and are concerned with the physical maintenance and well-being of the individual. As shown in Figure 5.2, the levels rise through social and self-concept needs before cognitive needs can be met; this level involves the

Figure 5.2 Maslow's hierarchy of needs

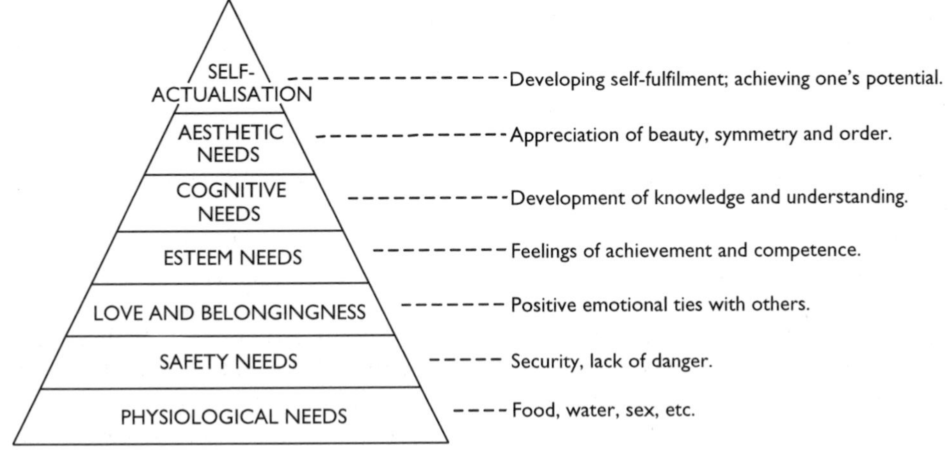
SELF-ACTUALISATION
Developing self-fulfilment; achieving one's potential.
AESTHETIC NEEDS
Appreciation of beauty, symmetry and order.
COGNITIVE NEEDS
Development of knowledge and understanding.
ESTEEM NEEDS
Feelings of achievement and competence.
LOVE AND BELONGINGNESS
Positive emotional ties with others.
SAFETY NEEDS
Security, lack of danger.
PHYSIOLOGICAL NEEDS
Food, water, sex, etc.

need for meaning and predictability, and is similar to Bandura's concept of self-efficacy, to be discussed later in this chapter. The next level involves aesthetic needs, leading to the ultimate stage of self-actualisation where individuals can realise their full potential.

According to Maslow, we are unable to proceed to higher levels before our lower needs are secure. Children who are mainly concerned about their physical needs or security are unlikely to be concerned with meeting their higher, cognitive needs at school. This seems quite plausible, and a survey by Kleinman *et al.* (1998) found that children who were regularly hungry in school were about seven times more likely to have social and emotional difficulties, and twice as likely to have special educational needs. Although the specificity of such findings is probably confounded by a number of effects, setting up breakfast clubs has been shown to be associated with significant improvements in some children's attainments.

Maslow's approach appears to bring together a number of different theories of motivation and also anticipated many of the more recent developments, such as intrinsic motivation. A number of different aspects of the theory also appear to have some validity when applied to educational settings. For example, children who have low self-esteem may fail to make progress and meet their cognitive needs, although the effects of such failure are much more specific than Maslow envisaged.

Despite these strengths, there is still the underlying problem that, like Murray's ideas, this approach tends to see needs as existing in isolation. When applied to education, it is therefore limited to techniques which only take needs into account, rather than considering their origins and how they could be modified or directed.

Before we go on to consider motivation as part of more general cognitive processes, it is worth considering a further basic perspective based on the biological functions of the brain and body. Since these underlie arousal, stress and emotions, they have important influences on behaviour, and have implications for the ways in which teachers should manage such states.

Arousal and stress

Arousal is the general level of physiological and psychological activity, and is an important aspect of the extent to which people are involved in tasks. In the first place, arousal can be a consequence of involvement, since if something is very interesting or important, it will tend to increase the mental and physiological activity of the person carrying it out.

Arousal has also been shown to cause different amounts of involvement and performance, depending upon the level of the arousal and the nature of the task. The effects are relatively generalised, and drinking a cup of coffee and just being more awake at a certain time of day would both facilitate learning. You can have too much of a good thing, however, and Yerkes and Dodson (1908) first demonstrated the classic 'inverted U shape' (Figure 5.3) that is found. Increasing arousal at first increases performance and involvement, up to a certain optimum point. Beyond this, performance deteriorates and individuals will be less likely to be effectively involved in the task.

In school, arousal states can be altered by children's level of alertness and interest in what they are doing. Dynamic and entertaining or 'enthusiastic' teaching has certainly been shown to increase the involvement and achievements of pupils. Arousal states can also be affected by children's anxiety about their performance,

Figure 5.3 Arousal and performance: the Yerkes–Dodson law

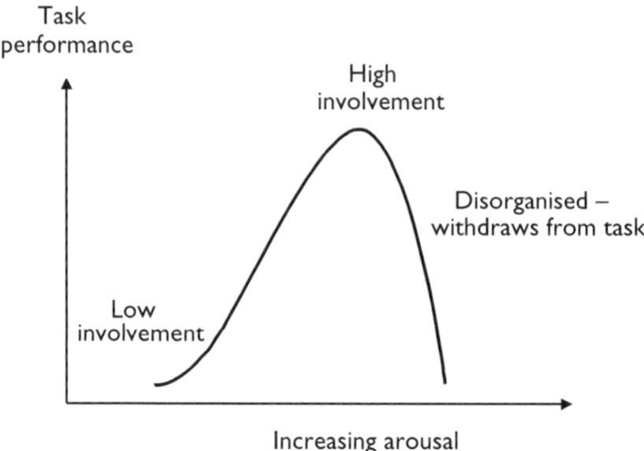

Figure 5.4 Effects of arousal on different tasks

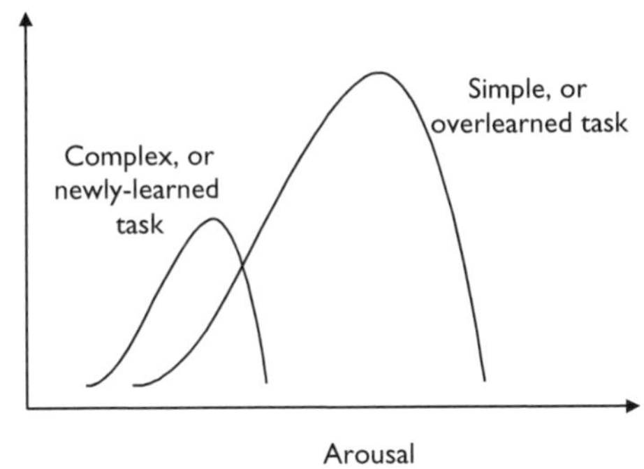

particularly in situations such as examinations. Although a certain amount of anxiety can help arousal and performance, high levels of worry can interfere with performance and lead individuals to avoid becoming involved in such situations.

The Yerkes–Dodson law also describes how different tasks can be affected by arousal. Complex tasks, or ones which have only just been learned, are most vulnerable to even moderate arousal states, such as the effects of being watched by an audience. Simple tasks, or ones which are well learned, are much more resistant to the deleterious effects of arousal, and arousal can promote higher levels of performance. The most vulnerable tasks are cognitive ones, while physical skills, which are normally 'overlearned', are least affected.

Stress

Prolonged and high levels of arousal can have disorganising, negative effects, particularly when an individual is also affected by anxiety. The anxiety can be due to a threat or a lack of perceived control and is often referred to as a state of *stress*. Although this term is rather too general for most purposes, a basic physiological process underlies most long-term arousal states. Selye (1956) originally described a *general adaptation syndrome* in which perceived stressors produce adaptations which initially allow us to function at a higher level. Following interpretation of the meaning of a stimulus, these are at first triggered by the actions of the hypothalamus, a small control centre in the base of the brain.

The 'alarm phase' then involves the sympathetic nervous system, which generally gears up the body into a higher level of activity by stimulating the adrenal glands to release adrenaline and noradrenaline into the bloodstream. These have the effect of increasing heart rate and blood pressure, dilating the pupils, diverting blood flow from the digestive system to the muscles, and generally readying the body to cope with some form of threat. The hypothalamus also activates the pituitary gland, which lies just underneath the brain, to release adrenocorticotrophic hormone into the bloodstream. This stimulates a number of glands, including the outer layer of the adrenal gland, to release a number of other hormones which are involved in the regulation of basic biological processes. These include cortisone and corticosterone, which affect glucose metabolism (to provide energy) and also influence the immune system, reducing reactions such as inflammation.

Continued stressors produce a long-term 'resistance phase', where the body reduces the level of sympathetic activity but continues to involve the stress hormones at a high level. Eventually the body reaches the 'exhaustion phase', when the adrenal glands can no longer function and the immune system and the control of glucose metabolism are no longer effective.

Long-term arousal in this way can lead to an increase in susceptibility to illnesses. Cohen *et al.* (1991) found that individuals who reported the most stressful experiences in their recent past were about twice as likely to become infected with a cold virus. Such infections appear to be particularly likely to happen about four days after emotional disruptions such as a row with someone who is close to you.

PUPILS AND STRESS

School-based stresses for children can come from academic pressures, particularly those resulting from the various forms of examinations or other assessments which are now present at all phases of education. Jemmott *et al.* (1985), for instance, found that the experience of exams significantly reduced the levels of antibodies measured in students' saliva. These substances are produced by the immune system, and such reductions make the body more susceptible to disease.

Social difficulties such as being bullied or school phobia can also cause long-term problems. These are often associated with high levels of anxiety and can be very debilitating for some children. Long-term stress has also been implicated in a number of physical problems that children may suffer from. Cleare and Wessely (1996), for instance, consider that there is a significant role for stress in the debilitating condition of myalgic encephalomyelitis (ME), also known as chronic fatigue syndrome. This is relatively common and educationally significant, with Dowse and Colby (1997) finding that it accounted for about 42 per cent of all long-term absences from school. However, most stress reactions are not usually so severe, and the most typical signs that teachers should be aware of involve headaches and stomach-aches.

TEACHERS AND STRESS

Borg *et al.* (1991) have shown that about one-third of all teachers state that they experience moderate or severe levels of stress. Because of the various pressures of the job, about one in five consider that they would not become teachers if they had their time again. As shown in Table 5.1, Borg *et al.* found that teachers associated four main factors with stress.

Pupil misbehaviour stands out as the greatest source of stress, with noisy pupils and difficult classes being the highest contributors to this factor. Teachers also have a constant and intensive load in terms of supervising and managing large groups of children, with Jackson (1968) finding that they are typically involved in more than 200 interpersonal interactions every hour. The direct demands of managing this load mean that teachers find additional administrative burdens particularly irksome and sometimes overwhelming.

Table 5.1 Factors associated with teacher stress

Factor	Variance in stress
Pupil misbehaviour	29%
Time/resource difficulties	10%
Professional recognition needs	6%
Poor relationships (staff, parents and pupils)	6%

Source: Based on data in Borg *et al.* (1991)

It can be difficult to make direct comparisons with other professions because of the unique nature of the job demands and pressures on teachers. However, Fisher (1996) found that health risk factors based on purely actuarial figures placed teachers in the highest insurance group, along with doctors and tunnelling engineers.

STRESS AND CONTROL

Many studies have shown that the key features in producing stress involve the extent to which individuals feel they have control over a situation, particularly one which makes high demands. In a classic experiment, Brady *et al.* (1958) found that many monkeys that had to press a lever every 20 seconds to avoid electric shocks eventually died of stress-induced gastric ulcers. Other monkeys that were given the same level of shocks without the possibility of stopping them were unaffected, so the stress was not simply due to the shocks. Further investigations indicated that the most important aspect was the lack of feedback to the monkeys about whether they had avoided the punisher. This meant that they could not have any real sense of being able to control the shock and therefore had to be constantly vigilant.

Seligman (1975) too found that individuals' sense of control could be limited by situations where they were repeatedly unable to affect the outcome of events. If animals were given electric shocks which they could not escape from, then they subsequently remained in the situation even when they were allowed the possibility of escaping. This is a state referred to as *learned helplessness*, and individuals who experience it become withdrawn and unreactive, which Seligman considers is similar to the normal development of depression. Hiroto and Seligman (1975) found that humans who were exposed to a loud, stressful noise over which they had no control had subsequent difficulty in learning tasks which would have led to a reduction in the noise. Like the animals, the people involved seemed to have learned that they had no control over this aspect of their environment. These particular types of beliefs about the causes of things (known as attributions) are very important in determining motivation, and are discussed later in this chapter.

Rotter (1966) has also shown that such experiences lead people to develop a sense of where control generally comes from. It can be either from within themselves, known as having an *internal locus of control*, or from outside themselves, known as having an *external locus of control*. When people have the sense of an external locus of control and the feeling that they cannot control events, they are unlikely to take an active approach to dealing with problems and will be more vulnerable to stress. The experience of externally imposed Ofsted inspections appears to be a classic example of this, and Hackett (1998) found that nearly half of all schools reported increased levels of staff sickness in the following two to three months.

In school, children who have made limited progress with basic academic skills are particularly likely to perceive that they are unable to control this aspect of their lives. Although children may attempt to avoid the area where they have problems, the process of normal schooling will repeatedly make demands on them that they cannot manage. Most lessons, for instance, involve some reading and writing, and children who do not have functional literacy skills will repeatedly experience failure. When this pressure is reduced by transferring them to a special school, children usually experience a significant reduction in the academic stress that they experience. This is of course not an option for most pupils, and in any case there is a price to pay in the effects of segregation.

If academic pressures and lack of control cause stress, then it should be possible to reduce pupils' anxiety and arousal by increasing their sense of control and effectiveness with school work. This can be done by making sure that school work is matched closely with their level of achievement and thereby increasing their overall success. Children can also be helped by giving them experiences which alter their attributions of why they succeed or fail. Dweck (1975) has developed a successful approach to improve the sense of effectiveness and motivation of students which involves setting up experiences that are moderately difficult and then encouraging pupils to persist in order to achieve success.

Other techniques include therapies based on exercises to enable children to develop a 'relaxation response'. These exercises promote both mental and physical relaxation, encouraging children to focus on a soothing image or experience and then tensing and relaxing the major muscle groups of the body. Then, experiences which would normally cause anxiety or arousal are introduced, usually at first in imagination, then by using relaxation 'triggers', such as the relaxing image, in the actual situation. This approach is technically known as *desensitisation* and is often carried out by therapists in a hospital or clinic setting. Schools can carry out the simpler elements such as relaxation with groups of pupils, who can then be encouraged to apply this approach in situations which they find difficult to manage.

The Yerkes–Dodson law shows that overlearning of information should also avoid the disruption caused by high arousal and prevent anxiety and underfunctioning. Children who were very anxious about reading something out loud in an assembly would find it much easier to cope if they had practised the reading so that it was automatic for them. A sense of control in situations such as examinations can similarly be increased by rehearsals with 'mocks' which are made as close to the real experience as possible, but with questions the children can cope with. Students can also be helped to establish greater control by using a structured approach with their revision studies and also when they sit the examination. This can involve working through old papers and identifying key areas for subsequent study, making structured notes covering these, and examination strategies which involve identifying questions and making initial notes as a basis for answers.

Emotions and their functions

Emotional states are based on primitive forms of brain–body interactions and involve a range of different types of arousal states and cognitive processes. The initial stages of developing an emotional state usually involve some form of appraisal of the meaning of a situation. Smith and Ellsworth (1987) consider that various features combine to generate a feeling. The examples shown in Table 5.2 show how these can form the foundation for four possible emotions.

Most emotional states involve some form of physiological arousal. This varies according to the emotion: the physical sensations of fear such as 'weak knees' and 'butterflies in the stomach' are very different from the angry sensations of feeling 'tense' and 'heated'. These different states are often triggered by our initial appraisal of a situation. Awareness of our physical state can then feed back to increase our emotional arousal, often setting up a self-maintaining positive feedback. Sometimes, however, the arousal can happen rapidly and without conscious thought, for example if we are startled by something. The generalised physical sensations we experience are then used as cues to develop an emotional state, and this state can then direct our appraisal of what is going on. A teacher might be surprised by an unexpected loud noise caused by a pupil accidentally knocking a chair over. In this case the teacher is more likely to become angry than if he or she had seen the pupil bump into the chair and been ready for the noise.

Once started, a state of physiological arousal takes some time to dissipate, since the various stress hormones are not broken down immediately. As well as the directly arousing effects of the adrenaline released into the blood by the adrenal bodies, the noradrenaline too has a generally stimulating indirect effect on the whole of the sympathetic nervous system. There are also psychological feedback processes that operate once a person is physiologically aroused. This means that if your body feels 'hyped up', you will often interpret the feeling as an emotional state and maintain or even increase your general arousal.

Thus emotional or arousal states can escalate suddenly but may take some time to calm down. One way of describing the sudden and discontinuous changes in arousal is with the graph shown in Figure 5.5, which 'jumps' from one level to another, depending on the direction of change of

Table 5.2 The cognitive basis of emotions

Did something happen or not?	Was it/would it have been desirable?	Who was responsible for it?	Emotion
Yes	No	Another person	Anger
Yes	No	Me	Guilt
Yes	Yes		Joy
No	No		Relief

Figure 5.5 Effects of changing stimulation on arousal

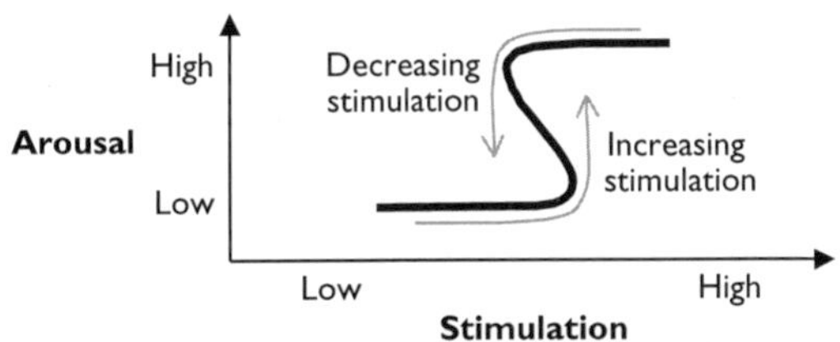

stimulation. This shows that there is an 'overshoot' in both directions before changes happen. Most people will generally avoid getting emotional until they cross a certain threshold, but will maintain their state for some time after any causes have reduced.

Calming down children who are upset or angry may take some time, and at first their heightened emotional state will probably mean that it is not possible to reason with them. In these situations it is often best to have a cooling off period during which the arousal can subdue. For similar reasons, many teachers have a short 'quiet time' when pupils have just come in from an active break or PE session, before starting a class lesson in which high arousal could be disruptive. On the other hand, once pupils are enthusiastic about a subject, their enthusiasm is likely to continue for a while, and it is therefore worth starting off lessons in an upbeat, enthusiastic way in order to generate some ongoing involvement.

'But that's illogical, Captain'

In the original *Star Trek* series, the half-Vulcan Spock was famous for his lack of emotion and his emphasis on the use of pure logic. In education this sort of cerebral approach can sometimes seem an attractive way to avoid the confounding effects of children's feelings, particularly when there is a need to cover an academic curriculum at speed. Emotions are certainly primitive mental states, and one view of them is that they are merely awkward leftovers from our evolutionary past.

Despite this, there is considerable evidence to support the belief that emotions are vital in energising and maintaining behaviour. One key function seems to be to ensure long-term commitment, which is necessary in maintaining social relationships and effective decision making. This has been shown by Antonio and Damasio's (1994) description of an individual called 'Elliott' who lost his ability to experience emotions, owing to brain damage caused by a tumour. Although he had a normal IQ and memory, Elliott's life subsequently unravelled in a series of personal and economic disasters. He was unable to maintain marriages or jobs and appeared to be unable to make effective decisions or to plan ahead for even a few hours. This was apparently related to a break in the connection between Elliott's 'knowing' things and 'feeling' things. Lacking the prompt of emotional commitment, he could weigh up and alter decisions *ad infinitum* without the 'gut feelings' which normally enable people to maintain consistent behaviour.

Emotional content is also closely involved in our long-term knowledge and understanding, and under the right conditions can facilitate recall. In general, it therefore seems that educational processes should encourage and develop emotional involvement and understanding whenever this is possible. Interest and enthusiasm for the content of lessons can be readily modelled and encouraged by teachers, which probably accounts for at least part of the large positive effects of 'enthusiastic teaching' to be described in Chapter 6.

Behavioural approaches to motivation

Operant conditioning, as outlined in Chapter 2, is a powerful way to motivate specific behaviours. It works by linking experiences that a pupil is already motivated by – a reinforcer or punisher – with an activity that we want to use in order to generate motivation. Accordingly, we can try to motivate pupils to work harder in school by using rewards such as praise and merit points, or sanctions such as detentions. For instance, a teacher might encourage pupils to complete some class work by allowing them out to play (the reinforcer being to socialise with their friends) only when they have completed their assignments.

In order for behavioural approaches to work effectively, pupils need to be aware of what is generally expected of them, in the form of 'ground rules'. These should cover classroom routines, with an emphasis on positive, work-directed behaviour. The effective behavioural approach of Assertive Discipline (Canter and Canter, 1992) emphasises a clear and unambiguous set of rules which are agreed on by staff and which should be displayed on the classroom wall. These are limited to about six in number, and it can be an effective approach to negotiate these with a new class. Pupils are normally very aware of what is expected of them in school and if anything are rather over-punitive when considering the consequences of disobedience.

In terms of motivation, pupils need to be aware of the positive and negative outcomes that are associated with such rules. Discipline procedures in schools usually focus on the failure to carry out expectations, and the most common outcome of this is a verbal reprimand. Punishers may often have unwanted effects, however, and a further danger with rebukes is that they may become reinforcing for children because of the attention that is involved. This paradoxical reinforcement can lead to even more disruptive behaviour. Despite this, Leach and Tan (1996) found that sending negative letters to parents was highly effective, increasing general on-task behaviour in a class from about 60 per cent to above the 90 per cent level. It is likely that this was due to the powerful nature of the letters as a punisher since parents control many aspects of their children's lives.

Praise

A range of rewards are possible in school, the most common form given in classrooms being teacher praise and encouragement. For most teachers, their positive comments are usually outnumbered by negative ones, although these are usually directed towards behaviour rather than achievements. Wheldall *et al.* (1985) found that when teachers were trained to give more positive comments, pupils' on-task behaviour increased significantly. Unfortunately, as mentioned earlier, such behaviour is not necessarily the same as actual learning, and a review of the effects of praise by Brophy (1981) found that it does not usually relate very well to students' achievements. One reason for this appears to be that teachers do not normally use praise in a very effective way, tending to use it only with pupils who are already doing well. Although there is a weak positive relationship between praise and achievements for younger pupils and children from deprived socio-economic backgrounds, this effect disappears with older pupils, and in some studies has even been negative.

Praise is a form of social interaction and its effectiveness therefore depends very much on the relationship between the pupil and the teacher, and whether this is valued by the pupil. In general, pupils up to the age of 8 want to please adults, so praise can be effective. After this the role of the peer group becomes progressively more important, and praise from an adult is likely to have only limited effects – or even negative ones, depending on the peer group's culture.

In order for praise to be at all effective, Brophy (1981) argues that it should emphasise information about achievements and be credible to the pupil. The use of praise should also follow the principles of learning theory, and be reliable and contingent on some specified performance. Pure behaviourists such as Skinner believe that there is no need to consider *why* such motivators work, just *how* they can be used. However, conditioning is effective because it changes individuals' expectations about what will be the outcome of their actions. If pupils are in the class of a teacher who notices good work and regularly gives praise, they should be more likely to work for such recognition.

Praise also seems to be ineffective if it generates a defensive self-concept, with limited approaches to learning. Dweck (1999) describes the way in which a great deal of teacher praise normally emphasises ability ('You're really clever') or achievement ('You've done that work well'). This encourages pupils' efforts and involvement in the short term, but, surprisingly, has long-term negative effects. Such ability- or achievement-oriented praise seems to make students most concerned about maintaining a positive image, which means that they will subsequently tackle only relatively easy tasks, in which success is guaranteed. If pupils experience work that they are less successful with, then this serves to undermine their ability- or achievement-oriented self-concept, leading to a helpless, passive orientation to future work.

Dweck argues that effective praise should emphasise effort and strategy. This might involve comments such as 'That's right – you worked really hard on that one', or 'Good – that was a really effective approach'. This type of feedback appears to encourage pupils to see their own abilities and achievements as modifiable. When they encounter difficulties, they are then much more likely to persist and to adopt different strategies. Crowne and Marlowe (1964) have, however, shown that some individual pupils have a strong need for social approval and that the use of positive personal comments can be particularly motivating. Even so, it may be more healthy for them if they are weaned off this dependence and encouraged to take a more active and flexible approach to learning.

Extrinsic versus intrinsic motivation

In most behavioural approaches, the reinforcer or punisher is usually separate from the activity, and this is said to bring about *extrinsic* motivation. Some critics consider that extrinsic motivation can interfere with the normal processes of *intrinsic* motivation, when an activity is carried out for its own sake. According to this, rewarding pupils in school is seen as a form of 'bribery' which will prevent them from developing natural interests and involvement.

Lepper and Greene (1978) argue that the majority of the activities which people normally engage in, such as sports, socialising or even vocational employment, involve such intrinsic motivation. They believe that this is a more 'natural' way for pupils to be involved with work and is likely to result in more effective learning. Their views are similar in many ways to Bruner's ideas about contextualised learning, and, as described later in this chapter, the basis of intrinsic motivation can be explained by the normal processes of cognitive development.

Lepper *et al.* (1973) carried out a classic investigation into the effects of extrinsic motivators on such natural learning in a study of children's drawing activities. First they observed a group of nursery school children in a free-play period to see how much time they spent on drawing. They chose a number of children who seemed to like drawing and split them into three groups which subsequently had different expectations and experiences of reinforcement. Only one of the groups was told that they would get a 'good-player' award for making drawings, and then all three groups were allowed to 'play' with some drawing materials. After this session, the reward was given to the group which expected it, and a reward was also given to the children in one of the other groups, who did not expect one. There was therefore one group of children remaining who did not expect, and were not given, a reward.

All three groups were then allowed a further free-play session, during which they were observed to see how much time they spontaneously spent on drawing activities. The key finding was that children in the group which had been promised and then received a reward now spent less time than the other two groups on drawing. Lepper *et al.* interpreted these results as indicating that the children who had expected a reward had come to use this as a reason to justify why they were involved in drawing. When the reward stopped, then there was no longer any reason to continue with the drawing; the children's sense of personal control or involvement with the task itself had been removed and drawing was an activity they did only to get something else.

By analogy, in normal school work it would be counter-productive to use any of the normal range of extrinsic rewards such as house points, certificates or various privileges. Although rewards may have short-term positive effects –

the group expecting a reward did more work than the other two groups on the second session – they are likely to result in superficial efforts geared solely to getting the reward. The drawings produced by the group expecting the reward were in fact of lower quality than those of the children who were drawing purely for the sake of it.

However, these findings have not always been confirmed when children have had different experiences and expectations. Cameron and Pierce (1994) point out that the group in the original Lepper *et al.* study who did not initially expect a reward, but did receive one, actually performed best of all in the final free-play session. This indicates perhaps that it was not the reward itself, but the expectation of reward which affected subsequent motivation. In a meta-analysis of 96 studies, Cameron and Pierce found that motivation is reduced only in the specific situation when a tangible reward is given merely for doing a task. When a reward is given to children for doing better on a task, a number of studies show that there is generally no damaging effect on subsequent intrinsic motivation.

These findings can be understood in terms of the way in which children interpret and use information. When pupils are rewarded whatever they do, this devalues their efforts and involvement. However, when reward or praise is contingent on what they have done, this gives feedback and is likely to increase feelings of competence and subsequent involvement. The message for teachers is clear. They should attempt to link rewards with specific achievements, and it would also seem safest initially to emphasise performance on the task, rather than the importance of the reward.

Lepper and Greene (1978) have also reviewed findings that using something as a reinforcement can have the effect of reducing its value. Suppose the reward used was being allowed to look at a book; reading would then not be so pleasant if it were regularly linked with having to do some difficult mathematics. Evidently, if this is the case, teachers should be wary of the way in which they use reinforcers so that they avoid weakening desirable behaviours.

Trying to use an intrinsically motivating activity to increase involvement in another activity can also sometimes reduce the desired target activity. Higgins *et al.* (1995) investigated the effects of emphasising different tasks when children were given a book which they could both colour in and read from. When colouring was the main activity in the first session, Higgins *et al.* found that children were subsequently less likely to want to do the reading and seemed to have developed the idea that reading was a subsidiary and less interesting activity. In general, it seems safest to develop children's interests in activities for their own sake wherever possible. However, some activities are complementary with a natural association, for example following a story in pictures with an explanation underneath which can be read. When this is done, the important aspect is to emphasise the overall task, by saying 'Let's find out what happens next', rather than 'If you read this then I'll let you look at the next picture'.

The self

A more immediate and powerful explanation for academic motivation is that it comes from a pupil's self-concept, related to school work. If pupils do not generally see themselves as successful, or feel that they are likely to fail on a particular task, they are unlikely either to get involved with the task or to put much effort into it. The findings of Dweck (1999) in relation to the effects of verbal feedback have already been mentioned, and the key aspect of these findings appears to be the effect that verbal feedback has on children's views of themselves.

Coopersmith (1967) assessed the general self-esteem of a large number of boys and found that pupils with high self-esteem achieved more in school and were generally more successful vocationally. He also found that they were the product of a parenting style which set clear and firmly enforced boundaries to behaviour but which also encouraged independence and freedom within these limits. These features seem likely to develop children's sense of control, and the ability to act within the realities of situations.

Self-efficacy

Bandura (1986) argues that our perception of our own ability to perform academic tasks is a form of esteem known as *self-efficacy*. This may be the result of past experiences, and can affect our future academic motivation. Experiences of failure tend to reduce self-esteem, whereas success tends to generate higher expectations and a more positive self-concept, leading to increased motivation, effort and success. Bandura found, for instance, that when students were given negative information about their performance on a mathematics task (irrespective of how they had done), their subsequent success and involvement in similar tasks were often significantly reduced.

Bandura considers that children's judgements of their effectiveness come, as well as from task achievement, from comparisons with the achievements of their peers, from their general arousal (see earlier in this chapter) and from advice from key others (such as teachers). Zimmerman *et al.* (1992) have also shown that children will set their goals according to what they perceive they are capable of and will avoid the emotional consequences of failure. Students with good self-esteem set themselves realistic, achievable goals and will expend considerable effort to achieve them. Students with low self-esteem, however, will either set themselves low goals, where they can be certain of success, or unrealistically high ones, where they can blame their failure on the difficulty of the task; in neither of these situations will they need to expend much effort.

Shavelson *et al.* (1976) originally argued that self-concept is a multifaceted, hierarchical concept, with general self-esteem coming from self-concept in a number of different areas. For schoolchildren, educational experiences are an important part of their lives, and children who do better at school certainly seem to have higher general self-esteem. This is not a particularly strong effect, however, and in a review of a number of studies Hansford and Hattie (1982) found a mean correlation coefficient of only 0.21 between self-esteem and academic achievements. General self-esteem can come from a number of different sources and will also depend on a child's particular context; a good footballer who is not doing too well at school will evidently have much more self-esteem when playing football.

Marsh and Yeung (1988) have found that children's sense of academic self-efficacy appears to be relatively specific to their achievements in particular subjects and that it is not very useful to talk about a general academic self-esteem. Although pupils who do well in English are also generally likely to be doing well with mathematics, a surprising finding is that pupils tend to see their achievements in these as relatively separate. Marsh explains this as being due to a combination of external and internal frames of reference. An external comparison with other children's achievements may show pupils that they are doing well in a particular subject such as mathematics. However, any sense of achievement will be cancelled out if they make an internal comparison with another subject such as English where they are doing even better, effectively saying to themselves, 'I can't be that good at maths because I'm not as good as I am in English.'

Should teachers try to boost self-esteem?

A key issue is whether self-esteem affects achievements, or whether it is mainly achievements which develop self-esteem. This is important, because if self-esteem determines academic progress, then teachers should make direct efforts to boost it in children. This aspect was investigated by Marsh and Yeung (1997) in a long-term three-year study of children's academic self-concepts and their achievements in mathematics, science and English. Using a form of path analysis to separate out the different causes, they found that academic self-concept and achievements in each of the subjects had reciprocal effects, but that the impact of achievements was much stronger. The coefficients for the effects of self-concept were of the order of about 0.1, compared with about 0.5 for specific achievements. The effects of self-esteem were related to pupils' marks, as well as teacher assessments, which were presumably fed back to pupils on a regular basis.

Chapman and Tunmer (1997) found that the effects of achievements on self-esteem were only starting to develop in the second year of schooling, as children began to perceive their progress and to make comparisons with the attainments of others around them. Rosenberg *et al.* (1995) found that later in school, the academic self-esteem for grade 10 boys had risen to give a path coefficient of 0.30 for its effects on achievements. It seems likely from this that pupils' academic self-concept develops throughout the process of schooling and may have progressively greater effects on their achievements.

Hay *et al.* (1997) also found that pupils' academic self-concept was affected by the general academic context of the class that they were in. There was a substantial overall correlation of 0.46 between pupils' self-concept and the difference between their achievements and the average of the class they were in, an observation known as the 'big fish–little pond (BFLP) effect'. The outcome of this can be that pupils who are in a group above their achievement level are likely to develop low self-esteem and reduced effort. Conversely, those in a group below their achievement level may develop high self-esteem and improved effort, although there is also the danger that they may reduce their effort to 'fit in' with their social group. These effects would, however, be less likely to happen in a secondary school if pupils were able to make comparisons with other classes.

Part of the process of self-evaluation also appears to be the extent to which pupils are able to achieve the goals to which they aspire. Dweck (1986) has distinguished between 'task goals', where pupils seek to achieve mastery of an area, and 'ability goals', where pupils set what they wish to achieve relative to other children. In general, pupils seem to show more commitment and involvement with task goals, and these seem to involve the same intrinsic motivational processes as those associated with general cognitive development (to be discussed later in this chapter).

Taken as a whole, these findings indicate that there are reciprocal effects between achievement and self-esteem, but that self-esteem usually has the minor role. The strongest predictor of progress in an academic area is actually pupils' initial attainments in that area, with Marsh and Yeung (1998) finding path coefficients greater than 0.8 for both mathematics and English test scores. These would give rise to the processes shown in Figure 5.6.

Since self-esteem usually has only a limited impact on achievement, attempts to boost it are probably not going to be the most effective way to improve motivation and achievement. In fact, it is likely that a teacher's attempts to praise pupils' work would be discounted by them if the evidence from marks or what other children were achieving went against this. Since self-efficacy is relatively specific, academic or non-academic self-esteem is also unlikely to transfer over to boost self-esteem and effort in other areas. Pupils who are competent at sports might feel better about themselves, but this would not have much impact on their efforts or achievements with reading.

The most effective ways to affect children's sense of efficacy and effort would probably be to improve pupils' real progress, and also to ensure that they value their achievements. As described

Figure 5.6 Reciprocal effects of self-esteem and achievement

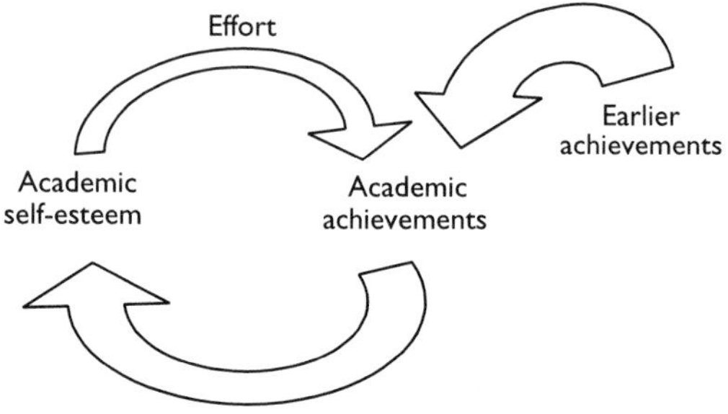

External sources:
Marks, teacher feedback, others' achievements (BFLP).
Internal sources:
Mastery, achieving own goals, relative performance in different areas.

below, some approaches are able to alter attributional styles by encouraging pupils to set worthwhile goals and supporting them in attaining these. For children in groups set by ability or achievement, the most motivating situation will be membership of a group where they can see that they are doing as well as or better than the other children around them. Although this will be impossible for some children (not everybody can be above average), teachers usually try to avoid any significant mismatches. The negative effects of context can be minimised by avoiding between-class comparisons and by emphasising pupils' individual learning goals.

Attributional processes

There is a strong general tendency for people to want to find out the reasons why things happen. This is probably part of the way in which we model and attempt to make sense of the world. It allows us to think about and plan ways in which we can interact with the various features of our environment. We particularly seek causes or attributions for the behaviour of other people, but we also seem to look for causal links between our own actions and possible effects. When we believe that we can accomplish something, this belief appears to have an important impact on our future involvement or motivation.

Rotter (1966) suggested that one form of attribution is the way in which individuals can have a sense of whether control originates from themselves – an internal locus – or from things separate from them – an external locus. In an educational setting, individuals who have an external locus of control are inclined to believe in 'luck' rather than effort attributions, which tends to result in lower effort and achievements. *Learned helplessness* has been described by Seligman (1975) as an extreme form of an external locus of control and involves a negative, apathetic and withdrawn approach to situations. As described earlier, it is likely to result when students have repeated experiences where their efforts appear to have little or no effect.

Weiner (1985) has taken this concept further by considering that there are three main dimensions for the perceived causes of success or failure:

- Stability – whether the cause changes or not. Ability or intelligence is usually perceived as a stable cause, whereas effort can change.
- Internal or external – whether the cause lies within the individual or comes from outside. External causes would be the perceived difficulty or other characteristics of tasks, whereas internal causes include ability and effort.
- Controllability – whether the result can or cannot be affected by the individual's expending greater effort. Traits such as 'laziness' are generally seen as being under voluntary control, whereas traits such as mathematical aptitude or physical coordination are not.

Some of the main categories of perceived causes are: *ability*, which is stable, internal and has low controllability; *effort*, which is unstable, internal and has high controllability; *luck*, which is unstable, external and has low controllability; and *task difficulty*, which is stable, external and has low controllability. If pupils fail on a particular task they might attribute their failure to any of these categories. If their attribution involves stable and uncontrollable causes such as a belief that they have no ability, or that tasks are always too difficult, they will feel that not much can be done to avoid future failure. The same will happen with attributions for external causes with low controllability, which is the basis for learned helplessness. Even when students are successful, attributing the outcome to 'luck' or 'low task difficulty' means that they are still going to feel that their success was not due to anything that they did, and they are therefore unlikely to be motivated in the future.

On the other hand, students who attribute success at some task to internal causes such as effort or ability are likely to feel positive about their involvement and will be highly motivated in the future. If students fail and attribute the failure to unstable characteristics such as effort or luck, they are still likely to persist in the future, since they are likely to think that they might succeed by trying harder, or by having better luck another time.

Positive attributional styles are most readily developed by successful experiences, where pupils perceive that they are competent and in control, and that it is worthwhile expending effort. Such perceptions can be encouraged and developed by teachers. Mueller and Dweck (1998) found that students who were praised for their effort at solving mathematical problems subsequently showed much greater persistence than students who had been praised for their intelligence. Praising ability led students to worry more about failure and to choose tasks only where they were certain they could be successful. The pupils who had been praised for effort, on the other hand, showed more resilience and persistence, and concentrated on ways to learn different approaches to solving problems.

Attribution retraining

Once students have established a negative attributional style, however, this will tend to persist, whatever their subsequent experiences of success or failure. Indeed, it is quite possible for it to become more ingrained over time, since they may put in decreased or inappropriate effort and will then experience even fewer successes. Even if the teacher is able to gear the work closely to a student's abilities and thereby ensure a high level of success, students are still likely to devalue this and attribute their achievements to the low level of the tasks. Cooper (1983) has found that this is particularly likely to happen with 'remedial' teaching, if the pupils see the tasks as being closely managed by the teacher, and if comparison with and comments from other children show that they are in fact doing lower-level work.

To break into this negative cycle, students can be given tasks which they perceive as difficult, but which they are encouraged to persist and to succeed with. When students are unsuccessful, the teacher can emphasise that the lack of success was due merely to lack of effort, or an inappropriate strategy, explaining where they went wrong, then encouraging them to try again. Dweck (1975) found that when treated in this way, students started to attribute success or failure to their own actions and were then able to improve their motivation and achievements. Group work can also increase the effectiveness of such training if pupils see other children making attributions to effort, thereby providing them with models for change.

Problems with self-worth

Unfortunately, some students will opt out of considering academic tasks to be of any value, in order to protect their sense of self-worth. They will be strongly motivated to avoid the possibility of failure and may focus on other aspects of their lives to achieve such positive self-esteem. One problem is that they may do so by joining social groupings whose attitudes and actions run counter to the school ethos and general social norms.

Avoidance of failure can also affect general effort and involvement with school work. In one experimental investigation, Craske (1988) was able to identify a group of pupils whose performance on a mathematics task improved, surprisingly, when they were told that the items were hard and that they were not expected to do very well. This instruction appeared to remove the need to protect self-worth since they could blame any failures on the task difficulty and could then put in effort without any risk to their self-esteem. These particular pupils did not respond to conventional attribution retraining, apparently since they were not prepared to take the risk of putting in effort in normal situations.

The involvement of such pupils can of course still be managed by behavioural approaches, but the results would be unlikely to generalise to other situations where the same rewards or punishers did not apply. Other ways of involving and motivating such alienated pupils can include alternative curriculums in off-site units. These can involve a range of individually tailored programmes of study, social and recreational activities in an environment which depends for its success on the quality of the adult–child relationship. These activities may bear little relationship to conventional school work, however, and tend to be used only with the most disaffected pupils, where a deschooling approach may be the only option.

Implications for teacher control and management

Attributional theories give rise to the rather counter-intuitive prediction that a high level of direction by a teacher might actually reduce motivation and subsequent achievements. If students perceive their own involvement and attainments at school as being mainly under the control of their teacher, then this perception is likely to reduce their own sense of control or involvement. Research summarised by Spaulding (1992) shows that motivation and achievements are decreased by teachers who emphasise their evaluative over their informative role, and who monitor students' behaviour and performance in an intrusive way.

A high level of teacher control may increase the short-term involvement and attainments of students but does not appear to produce long-term benefits. In a review of a number of different types of pre-school programmes, Miller and Dyer (1975) found that highly structured, formal approaches were associated with the greatest immediate cognitive gains. However, they were also associated with the greatest cognitive losses when the children later moved on to primary school. It is also worth noting that although the educational system puts great value on literacy, Whitehead (1977) discovered that by the age of 14, 36 per cent of all children read no books at all by choice. It seems that reading skill that is developed under the direction and control of teachers does not necessarily transfer into independent usage.

Although high student control and intrinsic motivation may be desirable, schools are organised on the basis of relatively few adults managing large numbers of students. Unfortunately, this type of arrangement tends to require a high degree of external control and direction. To overcome this problem, a number of attempts have been made to allow students to choose their own activities in schools. However, Spaulding's (1992) review indicates that such developments have generally been unsuccessful in achieving conventional curriculum goals and that they were usually rapidly replaced by traditional instruction programmes. One famous surviving British example is Summerhill, a 'free' school operating on the principles of self-direction by pupils. A study by Bernstein (1968) of the outcomes of this school found significant benefits in terms of social abilities, self-confidence and continuing personal growth. On the other hand, this study also found that parents of children at Summerhill who had themselves attended the school tended to remove their children after the age of 13 because of a lack of confidence in the conventional academic outcomes there. There have also been official pressures on the school resulting from its failure to conform to the National Curriculum.

Task involvement and cognitive development

Theories based upon self-concept and attributional theory can account for a great deal of behaviour, but they still ultimately depend on some underlying need state such as self-efficacy, or a need for achievement. As discussed earlier, a major problem with this dependence on need is that most activities that people involve themselves in appear to have intrinsic qualities that arise purely from involvement with the task. Understanding this depends on seeing motivation as part of cognitive development, rather than as just a level of activation. Earlier writers such as Hunt (1971) and Rogers (1951) have emphasised that mental activity goes on all the time, and from this perspective, motivation can be seen as involvement directed or redirected towards meaningful activities.

Even when pupils are not directly involved in 'work', they are still actively involved in something, even if it is just 'daydreaming' (a state which is in fact very productive for certain types of goals). Unfortunately, pupils' goals might not be the same as the teacher's, who has a responsibility to cover a specific curriculum. Recruiting children's natural or intrinsic involvement has the potential to develop more meaningful and effective learning experiences. Underlying theories of cognitive development, and practical findings in this area, can offer approaches which are useful for teachers.

Applying Piagetian theories

Eckblad (1981) in particular has developed Piaget's concepts of equilibrium/disequilibrium (see Chapter 2) to explain why individuals become involved in some tasks rather than others. According to Piaget's ideas, we are in complete equilibrium with our environment when new information or experiences fit in directly with existing schemas (mental structures). When that is the case, there will be little novelty, challenge or interest in such tasks, and the activation of schemas, as shown by task involvement, will be low. When new information or experiences do not fit completely with existing schemas, then we are in a state of disequilibrium, which, ideally, produces involvement with the environment or task as the schema become modified. This resolution of disequilibrium is called accommodation: changing ourselves to cope with new experiences or information. When disequilibrium is at a high level, however, then everything is new and schemas will be unable to change so as to cope, leading to low levels of involvement.

Moderate levels of disequilibrium should therefore lead to higher levels of involvement or motivation, with occasional 'leaps' when schemas undergo general reconfigurations. We see this when children make very sudden and highly motivating improvements as their reading abilities progress rapidly through the phonic skills stage at about 7 to 8 years (see Chapter 9).

Eckblad reports that spontaneous involvement in a range of different activities appears to be greatest when around 95 per cent of a task can be coped with. When the figure is higher, the task becomes boring; when it is lower, the task is too difficult for people to want to be involved. Fisher *et al.* (1980) report, however, that many class teachers aim for success rates as low as 60 per cent, and such teachers are less effective at helping their pupils learn than are teachers who programme for 90–100 per cent success rate on assignments.

Maria Montessori (1936) developed an approach to early (nursery) learning that depends on allowing children to work on simple tasks at their own level, such as physical apparatus, while introducing basic variations such as alterations in certain dimensions. She described the highly motivating quality of this with one particular little girl, who was so engrossed in repeatedly placing wooden cylinders in holes in a block that she did not appear to notice when other children were active around her, or even when her desk was picked up and moved around the room!

Cognitive involvement that is closely matched to an individual's abilities and interests also seems to capture the key features of tasks which are intrinsically motivating, with an emphasis on the process rather than the final outcome. A high level of absorption in self-directed learning tasks is essentially the state of 'flow' that Csikszentmihalyi (1975) describes as being characteristic of skilled performers such as surgeons or rock climbers – people who must be totally absorbed in what they are doing. In this state, individuals lose their sense of self-awareness and effort, and allow themselves to be carried along by the task in which they are engaged. Bowman (1982) has pointed out that such states are also characteristic of children engaged in certain computer games which have the potential to produce higher motivational states combined with more formal educational objectives. For example, Cordova and Lepper (1996) found that students made significantly greater progress with learning when a computer-based mathematics activity was made more intrinsically interesting by the use of individual choices and personalised fantasy elements.

Play and learning

'Play' can also be seen as part of this perspective on cognitive activity. Play is essentially a spontaneous, self-directed activity that involves high levels of success, involvement and progressive development. As Jay (1968) notes, it seems to be characteristic of all animals with a certain higher level of development of the nervous system (particularly humans, chimpanzees and dolphins). This appears to indicate that play is something that happens whenever there is the potential for complex cognitive activity.

Play also appears to be important in the development and mastery of skills. Hutt (1976) describes the role of curiosity and exploration in young children's mastery of a novel toy. Children who were more active in this process subsequently showed better long-term development in a number of other areas, indicating that the earlier experiences of play formed a foundation for later, more formal skills. Early theorists such as Herbert Spencer in the mid-nineteenth century saw children's play as merely a peripheral way of using up excess energy. However, recent theories view it as intrinsically motivated learning and an important part of the educational process.

Formal schooling tends to restrict the focus on play to early-years education, largely because of the need to develop certain skills such as reading or number work. Such formal skills cannot be developed by normal play experiences and need a considerable level of direction. However, it is still possible to incorporate some formal goals into less structured activities, as with number and letter rhymes and games. Such types of experiences were implemented in an American project called High/Scope described by Schweinhart and Weikart (1993), which compared groups of children receiving different early pre-school experiences. Children in the groups whose time was spent on guided play did significantly better than those in groups exposed to narrower, more formal learning experiences. These differences lasted into adult life and affected both educational attainments and social success. Schweinhart and Weikart's work is supported by findings reported on by Judd (1998) that children from countries (such as the United Kingdom) which start formal education at a relatively early age tend to be less successful with later academic achievements. All this implies that play may be a key part of initial learning experiences and that an emphasis on formal objectives can interfere with early development and subsequent progress.

Implications of cognitive development for teaching

Hunt (1971) believes that motivation is essentially the product of the *match* between the task and the individual. Rather than motivation producing learning, it is the process of cognitive development (learning) that produces the motivational state. From the perspective of the teacher, active, independent learning should come from an initial analysis of a student's abilities, then from learning experiences provided by the teacher which gradually extend these. Ideally, the learning experiences would depend on a pupil's own development, as shown in spontaneous interests and curiosity. Although this closely matched process is difficult to achieve with larger groups of children, it implies that teachers should concentrate mainly on subject matter and individuals' specific progress with ideas and concepts, rather than on gross evaluations, targets and rankings.

Spaulding (1992) in particular recommends that teachers should focus their teaching on skills that pupils can use to guide their own learning, that tasks should be moderately challenging, and that factual information should be acquired through the completion of tasks or projects. Another facet of the instructional role of the teacher should be to support pupils to generate their own subgoals and by demonstrating effective study behaviours. Extrinsic rewards can still be useful when there is no intrinsic motivation to undermine, such as when a student feels incompetent or when a task is inherently uninteresting. Also, marking should emphasise feedback, rather than evaluation, by using specific comments about work, rather than just giving a grade level.

Teacher expectations

The motivation and the achievements of individual pupils appear to be affected by what teachers believe they are capable of, irrespective of whether this belief is true or not. This is a striking finding and implies that teachers may have a significant effect on their pupils' progress, even though the teachers may not necessarily be aware of what they are doing.

The original and classic study in this area is 'Pygmalion in the Classroom', which was carried out by Rosenthal and Jacobson (1968). In this investigation they first tested all the children in one school with 18 classes, using the 'Test of Inflected Acquisition' from Harvard. This, the investigators claimed, was supposed to identify academic potential and to be particularly sensitive to children who were underfunctioning. Following this assessment, 20 per cent of pupils were identified as being capable of further intellectual progress – the 'late bloomers' – and their teachers were informed of who these children were.

The 'bloomers' were in fact selected on a random basis and the test used was not a test of potential but a new non-verbal test of intelligence. Eight months later, at the end of the school year, the children were again tested for their intelligence. The surprising finding was that the children who had simply been identified to their teachers as having potential had made significantly greater progress than the other children in the same classes. Teachers' expectations that had been formed from one piece of information seemed to be enough by themselves to alter the general intellectual attainments of pupils.

These findings were soon challenged by researchers such as Snow (1969), on the basis of poor experimental design and analysis in the original study. One criticism was that the teachers themselves administered the final intelligence test and may have biased these results by inadvertently helping or encouraging the identified students. Also, the tests used were criticised as having relatively poor reliability, which can give rise to variations in scores and is more likely to produce a 'fluke' effect. These doubts were confirmed when a subsequent replication by Claiborn (1969) failed to produce the same results as the original study.

Despite this setback, further investigations and a review of the key findings by Brophy and Good (1974) supported the basic concept of the effects of teacher expectations. Although some of the criticisms of the original study were valid, students have been shown to make differential progress in real academic skills, such as reading, which were not subject to teacher testing bias or to problems with test reliability. To a great extent the inability of studies such as Claiborn's to generate effects appears to have been due to the failure of the teachers to acquire the expectancy that the experimenter wanted them to have. When faced with too great a discrepancy, for instance being told that a low-achieving child was supposed to be quite clever, teachers appeared to discount what they were being told and acted according to their own beliefs.

Also, the size of the effect of inducing expectancies is not great and can easily be missed by investigators. An analysis of a number of experimental findings by Rosenthal (1985) indicated that teacher effects account for only about 3 per cent of the overall variance in student achievements. It is possible, however, that the effects in real life could be greater than this, since expectancies are normally formed by the teachers themselves and they are more likely to believe and act on them. Expectancies also probably act over longer periods of time than a short-term experimental investigation and their effects may be cumulative.

How expectations work

Subsequent explorations of effect of teacher expectations have looked at the effects of naturally occurring expectancies, and have moved on to consider the ways in which these operate in the classroom. Good and Brophy (1978), for instance, have identified that teachers actively construct expectations of students from their earliest contact with them. Much of this initial impression formation may in fact be accurate and appropriate; many teachers are, after all, very experienced and should be able to identify good work styles in pupils.

Teachers can form expectations about children even before they have seen them, perhaps via information from records or comments from other teachers. Baker and Crist (1971) found that teacher expectations for a child (and their subsequent achievements) could be positively or negatively affected by knowing how well an older sibling had done. As shown in Figure 5.7, the effect was confirmed by comparisons which showed that there was no effect on the pupil's progress if the older sibling was not known to the teacher.

Good and Brophy (1978) hypothesised that having formed differential expectations of students, teachers would be led to alter their behaviours. The teachers' behaviour in turn could communicate to each individual student how he or she is expected to behave in the classroom and perform on academic tasks. Good and Brophy also felt it likely that such teacher expectations would have an effect on student self-concept, achievement motivation, level of aspiration, classroom conduct, and their interactions with the teacher. Over time the result could be to reinforce the teachers' original perceptions and eventually lead to differences in student achievements.

Figure 5.7 Effects of having an older sibling on teacher expectations

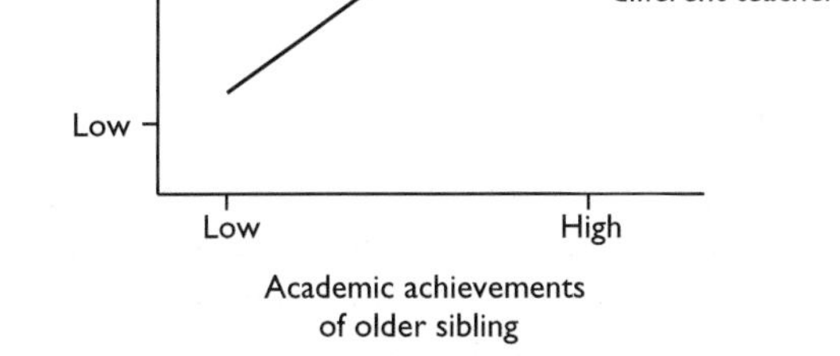

Source: based on Baker and Crist (1971)

Research summarised by Brophy and Good (1974) generally confirmed these processes, with findings that teachers do modify their classroom behaviour in accordance with how they expect pupils to achieve. With children for whom they have high expectations, teachers:

- generally pay more attention;
- criticise less often and praise more;
- seat students closer to them;
- demand more in terms of academic performance;
- give students the benefit of the doubt when marking; and
- engage in more positive non-verbal interaction.

When groups are streamed or set by ability, there is also evidence that teachers tend to give greatest attention and preparation to the higher-ability groups. This emphasises the differences between such groupings and reduces the opportunities for lower groups to achieve. Such differential treatment has also been shown to have a direct effect upon students' beliefs about their own abilities and competence. Brattesanti *et al.* (1984) found, for instance, that teacher expectations predicted 12 per cent of the variance in student expectations about their own performance, over and above the effects of prior student achievement.

Although the general findings on teacher expectancy emphasise the inequalities that can result from this, they also indicate that a generally positive approach to children's abilities and potentials could produce real effects. Research on teacher and school effectiveness by Rutter *et al.* (1979) indicated that higher expectations for student achievement were part of a pattern of differential attitudes, beliefs and behaviours characterising teachers and schools that maximised their students' learning gains. However, one should perhaps be cautious in assuming that in order to improve attainments, all that teachers need do is expect more from their students. If it were so simple, teachers would already do it, although Brophy and Evertson (1976) did identify a small proportion of bitter and disillusioned teachers who were particularly ineffective and who would probably benefit from some support to rekindle a more positive approach with their pupils, or who should consider other occupations.

Empowerment

A humanistic perspective adopted by Lefrancois (1994) emphasises that one of the most important of educational objectives is to empower students. This perspective is in direct contrast with beliefs about education which emphasise its economic role in developing a highly educated workforce in order to drive the economy along. There is in fact little evidence to support the belief that education is the basis of economic progress, and it can be argued that the true role of education should be to remove constraints holding back individuals and to increase pupils' potential.

Empowerment means that teachers should provide students with the skills and knowledge to do important things they could not do otherwise, and to develop their independent cognitive abilities and intellectual processes. Many of the approaches which develop motivation also involve giving students the power to achieve and to be in control of their own learning. Tasks which are intrinsically motivating and which involve a high level of self-efficacy and a positive attributional style enable students to become independently motivated and to extend their learning beyond formal educational experiences. Teachers have a certain moral responsibility to facilitate such development, although the realities of class teaching and curriculum coverage must inevitably to some extent limit the extent to which they can do so.

Summary

Motivation refers to whatever it is that leads us to engage in some activity. Although it is difficult to monitor directly, children's efforts and involvement with educational tasks have significant effects on their progress and it is important for teachers to find ways of facilitating this.

To a great extent children's general behaviour and involvement with work in school are the outcome of conforming to social roles and obeying the authority of teachers. There can be problems if some pupils adopt alternative norms, and education may then need to adopt alternative forms to deal with this.

Early, more individually based explanations emphasised the role of underlying forces in the form of instincts, drives and needs. However, relatively little human behaviour can be described as instinctive or the result of basic drive states. Although Freudian theory appears to offer a particularly complex explanation based on drive reduction, it has little utility or empirical support. Theories which are based on the concept of 'needs' suffer from the limitation that they tend to be mainly descriptive, although Maslow's hierarchy of needs anticipated many recent developments in cognitive science.

The general level of individuals' involvement can be partly explained by arousal levels, which are the result of interactions between the mind and the body. Prolonged arousal states where individuals lack control are often referred to as stress, and these can interfere with learning and educational performance. Stress management can include techniques to cope with physiological arousal, as well as enabling control through structured study techniques. Emotions involve more complex appraisal and physiological states and are important in generating involvement and commitment as part of pupils' educational experiences.

Behavioural approaches attempt to increase pupil effort and involvement by operant conditioning, with the use of contingent rewards and punishers. One common reward, praise, is normally less effective than people imagine when it lacks social relevance or if it gives pupils limited or inappropriate information. Moreover, the use of rewards has been criticised as damaging the natural processes of intrinsic motivation. Extrinsic motivators can be effective, however, if they provide appropriate information to pupils.

Pupils' self-concept will also motivate behaviour as they attempt to maintain a positive evaluation of themselves and to present this to other people. Self-concept in different areas of functioning appears to be relatively specific, although pupils will compare their attainments between different academic areas and with those of other pupils. It seems likely that academic self-esteem is mainly the result of achievements and that attempts to improve it in isolation would not normally be effective.

The ways in which pupils attribute causes for success or failure affect how they are likely to approach future tasks. A positive style attributes success to effort and ability, and ascribes failure to luck or task difficulty. It is possible to train students to develop such positive attributions by setting them difficult tasks where they are supported to succeed through effort and strategy, although this does not work with pupils who have a very negative view of themselves.

Involvement in tasks can be seen as part of general cognitive development. This is the basis of intrinsic motivation and depends on tasks which are closely matched with pupils' abilities and interests. Play can be seen as part of this process and is an important form of learning.

Teachers' expectations can have a significant effect on pupils' progress by generating more encouraging behaviours. These may have general and positive effects but are likely to account for only a small proportion of the variance in academic attainments.

Pupil empowerment is a key goal for education and involves developing independent motivation and bringing out students' long-term potential.

Key implications

- Teaching should focus on pupils' direct active involvement with learning tasks, rather than motivation or drives and needs.
- In the short term this can be achieved with close management and extrinsic (behaviourist) approaches.
- The use of intrinsic involvement (involvement for its own sake) is more effective as a basis for independent and long-term involvement.
- Students' active participation is greater when they have a positive view of themselves as learners.
- Having a positive view also depends on a close match between children's educational experiences and their cognitive development.

Further reading

Paul Pintrich and Dale Schunk (1996) *Motivation in Education: Theory, Research and Applications*. Englewood Cliffs, NJ: Prentice-Hall.

This gives a broad and technical coverage of the complete range of motivational theories, their developments and how they can be applied by teachers. Not the sort of book that you would want to pick up casually, but gives in-depth coverage and would be excellent for following up ideas and for reference.

Carol Dweck (1999) *Self Theories: Their Role in Motivation, Personality and Development*. Hove, East Sussex: Psychology Press.

This readable book reviews findings that just under a half of all children have a negative and defensive view of their own abilities. Carol Dweck relates this to a belief in a fixed view of intelligence and shows that children can develop more active and robust attitudes to learning from educational experiences which emphasise effort and strategy.

Practical scenario
At King Charles III secondary school, most subject teachers are finding the lowest sets in the final year difficult to motivate. Almost all these pupils have limited academic skills and few will achieve a GCSE. Some subjects do, however, aim for certification when the pupils have completed a relevant course. Although these teaching groups are relatively small (comprising about 14 pupils each), it is hard to involve them in class work and there are often behavioural problems which interfere with attempts to get through any formal work. The various subject heads are wondering if there is anything more that they could do to make this situation easier.

- *What view do you think the pupils in these classes have of themselves relative to school? How would they have formed these opinions?*
- *To what extent is it possible to alter the curriculum to match with these pupils' needs and interests? Is it necessary to continue with the whole of the normal curriculum?*
- *Would a changeover to mixed ability make any difference? Is there a danger that this might mean that the school's exam results would suffer?*
- *Could the school consider a more radical approach involving some form of deschooling?*

6 The educational context

Chapter structure

The importance of context

Children spend a large amount of time at school, amounting during term times to nearly one-third of their waking life. It seems likely that pupils' experiences there will have important effects on their development, particularly in terms of the formal academic aims of schooling.

The organisation of schools is based on a number of general features and processes. Class and school size, the use of different forms of ability grouping and the ways in which schools are laid out are some of the aspects of school life which are believed to make important differences to educational outcomes. Variables like these are frequently used for political management and direction in order to achieve improvements.

Student and teacher perceptions of the educational environment usually centre on the more immediate experiences and feelings that affect learning and social interactions. One typical measure of this is the 'Individualised Classroom Environment Questionnaire' for secondary classes (Fraser, 1986). This covers 15 scales, of which higher levels of 'cohesiveness', 'satisfaction' and 'goal direction', and less 'disorganisation' and 'friction', have been shown to relate consistently to better achievement on a variety of educational outcomes. This is supported by a key study carried out by Rutter *et al.* (1979) which identified the general ethos of a school as being the main feature associated with its apparent effectiveness. Achieving such a positive learning climate is an important goal and there have been attempts to search for the principal elements which contribute to this at school and classroom levels.

School effectiveness

Do schools make a difference?

Before we can understand which features of school life matter, a first step is to investigate whether there are existing, meaningful differences in effectiveness between different schools. If there are, it might be possible to identify the basis of such effects and then to improve schools which are low on measured effectiveness. This has very much been the underlying basis of political initiatives such as *Excellence in Schools* (DfEE, 1997c), which argued that all schools should be brought up to the level of high-achieving ones with (apparently) comparable intakes. This premise also underlies much of the role of advisers or inspectors, who are assumed to be part of this improvement process. On the other hand, if there are no real existing differences (that is, after allowing for disparities in intake) between the effectiveness of schools, then this would indicate that any basis for improvement must lie beyond existing levels and types of provision.

Although it may seem obvious that schools do differ, earlier reviews of US findings such as those by Coleman *et al.* (1966) and Jencks *et al.* (1971) suggested that there was only a minimal variation in their effectiveness. Studies at that time indicated that educational outcomes were mainly linked with children's basic abilities, their home background and community cultural resources. Even intensive early additional educational input such as the 'Head Start' project, designed to overcome social inequalities, initially seemed to accomplish little. This was interpreted as indicating that within-child features were of overwhelming importance and that further compensatory programmes would be a waste of money. In Britain the Plowden Report (1967) also reviewed existing findings, and agreed that social class and parental attitudes gave the best explanations for variations in children's performance.

However, if the effects of home background are so strong, they may mask any weaker (but real) effects of schooling. For instance, as shown in Figure 6.1, the students from school A with a poor catchment may make good progress but still ultimately achieve at a lower level than students in school B, where less progress is made, but which has a good catchment. Although one could set up a study that controlled for home background by allocating students randomly to different schools, this is evidently not feasible. Various studies have, however, attempted to try to make fair comparisons, by statistical analyses that take pupils' backgrounds or initial achievements into account, and by identifying factors

Figure 6.1 Academic progress with different catchments

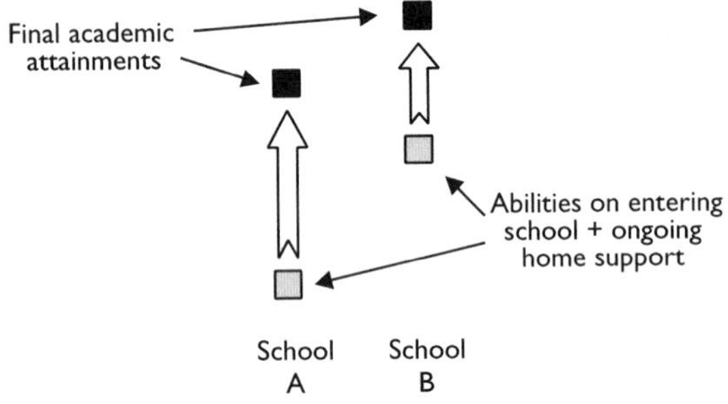

Figure 6.2 Relationship between individual pupils' initial abilities and their final achievements

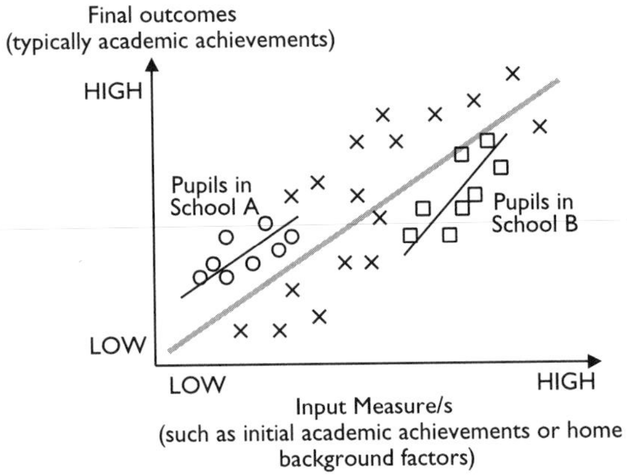

that are associated with the remaining differences between schools.

The results of this type of analysis can be shown by a graph (Figure 6.2), where the overall relationship between input variables (such as achievement and/or home background) on starting a phase of schooling can be related to pupils' final achievements. The thick central curve is the overall average for pupils in all schools and shows what one would predict, or expect from knowing the input measure(s). Figure 6.2 is essentially the same as graphs generated by the DfEE (1998b), which can be used to evaluate 'value added' effects by comparing actual progress with predicted progress. It is also similar to graphs given by attempts to equate for input by placing schools in bands according to the level of free school meals. Pupils in school A appear to be achieving better results than one would expect from their input measures, while pupils in school B appear to be achieving poorer results than one would expect. Pupils in school B who start off at a lower level also appear to be making relatively worse progress, and it might be that this school tends to place an emphasis on the achievements of the more able pupils.

One relatively recent statistical approach described by Goldstein (1995) is called *multilevel modelling* and enables researchers to separate out the various effects on pupils' academic progress. This approach can account for initial attainments and assesses the variance in final attainments which can be accounted for at pupil, class, departmental and school level. In Figure 6.2 it can be seen that schools will vary about the central curve, and in the same sort of way, pupils, classes and departments will vary within individual schools.

Primary school evidence

At the primary level, Mortimore *et al.* (1988) carried out an early form of multilevel modelling and over a four-year period followed a group of 2,000 pupils in 50 randomly selected schools. After accounting for differences in intake, this study found significant differences between the educational outcomes of different schools, seemingly associated with different factors.

In general, children made better progress in schools where class teachers kept individual records, where work outlines were forecasted, and where parents were regularly involved in progress meetings and helped in the classroom. Too narrow a focus on basic skills had a negative effect, as did an emphasis on punishment rather than praise as a motivator. Progress was greatest when teachers discussed work with children and least when teachers directed work without explaining its purpose. The most effective teachers minimised disruption (noise and movement), told stories to children, and regularly listened to children read.

Secondary school evidence

Rutter *et al.* (1979) similarly investigated the characteristics of effective secondary school education. In a study of 12 different schools, they attempted to identify those factors which had significant effects on both behaviour and academic attainments. Although the study did not use multilevel modelling, there was an attempt to balance out different intakes by carrying out adjustments based on pupils' initial attainments.

The main findings of this study were that secondary schools did have different effects on their pupils, and that these were related to differences in the overall ethos, or the general social characteristics of schools. Those schools which had a positive ethos produced both good academic outcomes and good pupil behaviours.

Features that related positively to academic outcomes included the general level of academic emphasis (shown, for example, by the amount of homework set), involvement of pupils in the school life (for example, if there were form representatives), general pupil conditions (but not staff conditions), and involvement of staff in decision making. Children in the more successful schools were also more likely to use the library and to have work put up on walls. Since these aspects tended to group together, Rutter *et al.* considered that they formed part of a general culture which could be more or less favourable to academic achievement and which had significant and long-term effects on pupils' progress.

Creemers and Reezigt (1996) carried out a review of a number of such studies which had been based on multilevel modelling and found general agreement for the importance of nine main factors. These were:

- an orderly environment/school climate;
- consensus and cooperation between teachers;
- a focus on basic skills/learning time;
- monitoring of student progress/evaluation;
- effective school educational/administrative leadership;
- having a policy on parental involvement;
- high expectations;

- coordination of curriculums and approaches to instruction; and
- quality of the school curriculums.

On the face of it, this list appears to be eminently reasonable; it would be hard to argue that schools should not be organised and run well, or that teachers should not try to manage and deliver learning. Such factors have therefore commonly been used in inspections to assess schools' effectiveness and have formed the basis for recommendations about how schools could be improved.

The full story is more complex, however, and Coe and Fitz-Gibbon (1998) have pointed out that such findings are based only on observational data. It may be a doubtful enterprise to assume causation or to allocate responsibility for any outcomes. High expectations, for instance, could be the result of pupils' attainments, rather than a cause. It is also quite likely that schools have very different tasks in terms of the balance of the quality of their intake. Research by Thrupp (1998) has found that positive organisation and management in schools very much depends on the presence of a 'critical mass' of well-behaved and able pupils. Gewirtz (1998) also describes how key staff in a school with a low socio-economic intake were overwhelmed by the daily pressures of behavioural crises, pupil turnover and inadequate funding. Accordingly, positive initiatives such as curriculum development or extra-curricular activities were difficult to set up or maintain.

The majority of schools which are judged by Ofsted to be 'failing' or which appear to be underachieving on 'value added' measures are largely those schools which have the poorest student intake. Indices such as the take-up of free school meals or even initial academic achievements are only part of the reasons for children's progress. There are many other influencing factors, such as pupil motivation and self-concept, as well as peer group membership and home background. Gibson and Asthana (1998) used a range of weighted background socio-economic factors and were able to account for 64 per cent of the between-school variance in GCSE scores, which is at least 10 per cent more than estimates based on free school meals. Plewis and Goldstein (1997) also quote findings that the take-up of free school meals accounts for only half the variance that can be accounted for by initial attainments. It is likely that DfEE-based attempts to equate for intake on the basis of free school meals alone greatly underestimate the difficulties that some schools face.

Size of school effects

Although research based on sophisticated statistics has shown that there appear to be significant differences between the effects of schools, if these are not very large they may not be too meaningful. If schools vary widely from the predicted average, as shown in graph I (Figure 6.3), then knowing which school a pupil was in would be a good predictor of his or her 'value added' progress. If, however, schools are generally close to the average, as shown in graph II (Figure 6.3), then this would mean that the overall differences between schools are slight and that they generally have the same effectiveness.

Although such studies do show that schools vary somewhat, they typically show that their effect is quite small and that the overall impact of schools is far outweighed by student characteristics. One large and representative study by Thomas and Mortimore (1996) was able to compare and quantify the effectiveness of 79 secondary schools in Lancashire after equating for different intakes, in terms of prior pupil attainments, gender effects, proportion of students on

Figure 6.3 Apparent effectiveness of different schools

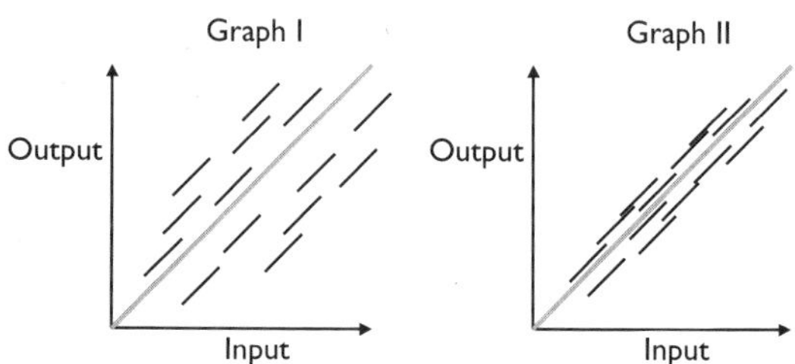

Figure 6.4 Value added effects for the range of secondary schools

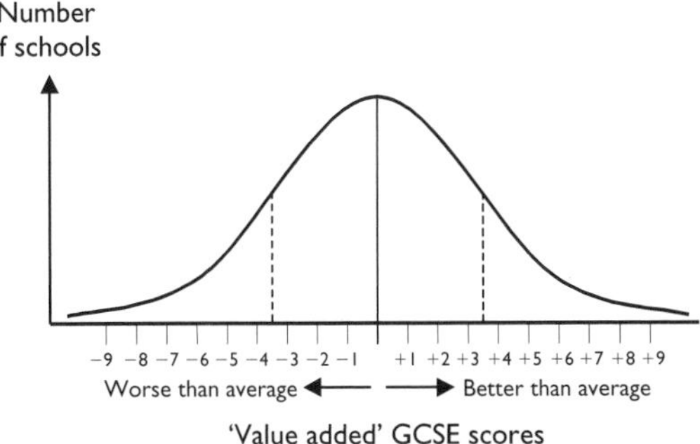

Source: Based on data from Thomas and Mortimore (1996)

free schools meals (which is related to parental income), ethnic background, and mobility between schools. GCSEs were given numerical values from A = 7 to G = 1 and added together for each pupil. The overall average for each pupil was just above 33.

An analysis of the study's findings indicates that most of the schools (±1 standard deviation, or 68 per cent) were within a band where they added or lost up to three and a half GCSE grades – the difference between three or four grade Ds and three or four grade Cs. Some schools of course achieved much better and some much worse 'value added' effects than this. The graph in Figure 6.4 shows the general distribution, which would fit these findings.

Although this effect is significant, the normal range of GCSE scores is from 0 to about 50, and Thomas and Mortimore found that the school effects accounted for only about 10 per cent of the overall variance in this. Such a finding is quite representative of the findings of school effectiveness studies, and some studies which focus on direct effects have established even lower values.

A three-year study by Zigarelli (1996) looked at more than 1,000 schools in the United States and evaluated key school variables which could be related to pupil progress from grades 8 to 12. Significant features included high expectations by staff and students, high levels of classroom learning time, positive teacher morale, head-teacher autonomy, parental support and time for teachers to prepare work. However, together these specific school factors accounted for only 5 per cent of the variance in achievements. Taken separately, student effort and ability accounted for 73 per cent and socio-economic status and parental expectations accounted for 24 per cent.

Such findings at secondary level are largely paralleled by similar studies with primary-aged children. Strand (1997), for instance, found that about 11 per cent of the variation in Key Stage 1 scores was attributable to schools. Initial attainments on school entry accounted for 39 per cent of the variance, and free school meal entitlement, gender and not having English as first language together accounted for only another 2 per cent. Bondi (1991) also looked at children's reading attainments on completing junior education and again found a very similar figure of about 10 per cent for the effects of different schools.

Such studies indicate that school effects do exist, but that they appear to be dwarfed by the initial abilities of pupils, with an additional effect due to their ongoing home environments. One might also argue from the findings of Hart and Risley (1995), discussed in Chapter 4, that initial attainments are also themselves largely due to the early home context. Mortimore and Whitty (1997) therefore argue that any realistic attempt to improve educational standards must take proper account of children's social context and that 'blaming schools for the problems of society is unfair and unproductive' (p. 12).

Positive effects of schooling

Saying that schools do not differ much is of course not the same as saying that they fail to have any effect at all. One possible interpretation of the above findings is that most schools are generally doing a similar job, in so far as they are constrained by factors such as their intake, community resources and general funding. It would also be very surprising if schools did not have positive effects on children's progress, and these can be shown when children's formal education has been limited for some reason or another.

One classic finding is the significant decrease in children's intelligence and academic attainments which happens during school holidays, particularly for children whose backgrounds mean that they are unlikely to be involved in activities similar to school work. A meta-analysis by Cooper at al (1996) of 39 studies showed that the overall summer loss was equivalent to about one month and that this was greatest for subjects such as mathematics, which pupils are unlikely to work on by themselves. Children from the lower social classes and special needs pupils showed the greatest decline, while middle-class students showed gains on reading tests, presumably due to opportunities and encouragement from their home backgrounds.

The time of year at which children start school has also been to shown to have an effect on their attainments, with Sharp and Hutchinson (1997) finding that if pupils start school two terms later than others, this reduces their end-of-Key Stage 1 attainments by about 10 per cent. A sophisticated analysis by Cahan and Coren (1989) also separated out the effects of age and the amount of schooling for children in grades 5 and 6. This demonstrated that schooling had a significant effect on general intellectual abilities such as non-verbal intelligence, but had the greatest consequences for verbal and academic attainments. The estimated impact of one year's schooling gave an effect size of 0.4 for vocabulary and 0.5 for arithmetic achievements.

Schooling does therefore appear to make a big difference to children's academic and cognitive progress. It also has a strong effect on equity, levelling up the progress of children who come from a less stimulating home background, although (as noted elsewhere) it is unlikely that it will ever be able to compensate for this completely.

Improving education

If the apparent effects due to different schools are relatively small, with overall attainments mainly due to the nature of their intake, then it may be relatively fruitless to blame schools which have problems or to attempt to improve them by grafting on features of other schools which seem more successful. However, if intake balance is important, then one possible approach would be to ensure that each school has the 'critical mass' of good students referred to earlier. This could be achieved by limiting parental choice and moving students around to balance intakes. Unfortunately, this is a political impossibility and very much against current market-led ideologies.

Alternatively, it would be possible to acknowledge that schools with a poor intake actually have a much more difficult job to do, and to allocate increased resources to them, so that key staff could be freed from crisis management in order for them to carry out more planning and development. Also, teachers could be given more time off from direct teaching to enable them to cope with the additional stresses and to prepare effective approaches. Again, this does not seem politically feasible as it would involve either massive increases in educational funding, or reallocating money away from schools which have better intakes.

One possibility is that if schools and communities are given meaningful support through initiatives such as 'Action Zones' and the pre-school 'Sure Start' programme (which will receive about £150 million a year in England), there may then be some genuine levelling up of attainments and life opportunities. Although early conclusions about the effectiveness of similar American initiatives such as Head Start in the United States were rather negative, long-term follow-ups such as those described by Barnett (1995) found significant educational and social benefits, particularly when support was long term and intensive and involved children's families. Owing to its effectiveness, Head Start received annual funding of nearly $4 billion in 1998 and supported more than 800,000 children and their families with a range of pre-school provision. If a programme in England were funded on the same basis, it would receive nearly £500 million a year.

The physical environment

Although the overall impact of schools (and teachers) normally results in only relatively minor educational differences, some physical and structural factors have been shown to have a significant relationship with pupil progress. These therefore have implications for the ways in which schools should be designed and organised if the appropriate level of resources is available.

Layout and pleasantness

Rutter *et al.*'s (1979) study of secondary schools indicated that the general physical layout of the schools (split site, age of the buildings) generally did not account for any variations in academic achievement. However, variations in the care and decorations of buildings, including the cleanliness and tidiness of rooms and the use of plants, posters and pictures, *were* related to positive outcomes. General conditions for pupils also correlated positively with academic outcomes; these included features such as pupils being allowed to use the buildings during breaks, access to a telephone, and the availability of hot drinks.

A problem here is that since these general findings are correlational, it is not necessarily the case that these environmental features caused the good outcomes; indeed, Rutter *et al.*'s interpretation is that they were part of the general ethos of the school. It does seem very likely that the generally more positive attitudes in some schools could lead to a range of effects such as better care of the buildings and privileges for pupils.

Schools usually have fairly basic levels of furnishing and decoration which are below the levels which children and adults experience in most other aspects of their lives. It would be surprising if the unattractive decor did not have any effect on pupils' comfort or sense of value. A direct experimental study by Wollin and Montagne (1981) showed that students made better progress when moved from unattractive rooms to ones which were painted in attractive colours and decorated with posters, area rugs, plants and other items. When they were moved back to the less attractive rooms, their progress also returned to previous levels, indicating that the improvements in progress were due to the environmental changes.

Open-plan designs

'Open-space' schools have few interior walls or partitions and are designed to free students from traditional barriers such as conventional seating. It is argued that this should allow them more opportunities to explore the learning environment, with different areas given over to specialist activities. Unfortunately, studies comparing and evaluating the effectiveness of this design have often been confounded by the fact that teachers tend to teach in the same way in both types of rooms. Rivlin and Rothenberg (1976), for instance, found that in many open classrooms, teachers continued to use conventional class teaching and grouped learning tasks, failing to adapt to the new opportunities there.

A review by Weinstein (1979) indicated that there were no overall differences in academic attainment between students in open-space schools and those in conventional schools. There did, however, seem to be some benefits in terms of increased persistence and involvement for children taught in open classrooms, as well as more positive attitudes towards school. On the other hand, Cotterell (1984) discovered that students who had educational difficulties found the independence and variety difficult to cope with and could need additional support.

There can be major problems with open-plan

designs due to the increased levels of noise and distractions from other pupils and classes. Evans and Lovell (1979) therefore investigated the effects of altering the general physical environment of an open-space school that was experiencing such difficulties. They used sound-absorbent partitions of varying heights, placed so as to redirect traffic away from certain class areas or to make class area boundaries more meaningful, and added several small areas to provide more opportunity for private work. Observations made before and after the changes showed that they had a significant effect, with the alterations leading to a decrease in classroom interruptions and an increase in the number of content questions.

Density and crowding

Hall (1966) has analysed four zones of personal space (shown in Figure 6.5) which affect the way in which we interact with other people. In most of our lives there appear to be proxemic rules which govern the distances which we use in our interactions. Children, however, appear to be less sensitive than adults to these rules, and can sometimes intrude on others' inner zones too readily. A teacher's role would also appear to be somewhat ambiguous, with distances depending on the nature of the task or interaction; directions to the whole class usually involve greater distances, whereas close interactions may be appropriate when working with an individual.

In the average class many children are together in a single limited space, and seating and general working arrangements usually position them within each other's casual-personal zone (see Figure 6.5). It therefore seems likely that *density* might have a significant effect on pupils' sense of being intruded upon and their ability to work effectively. Research reviewed by Weinstein (1979), however, has shown excessive density

Figure 6.5 Hall's zones of personal space

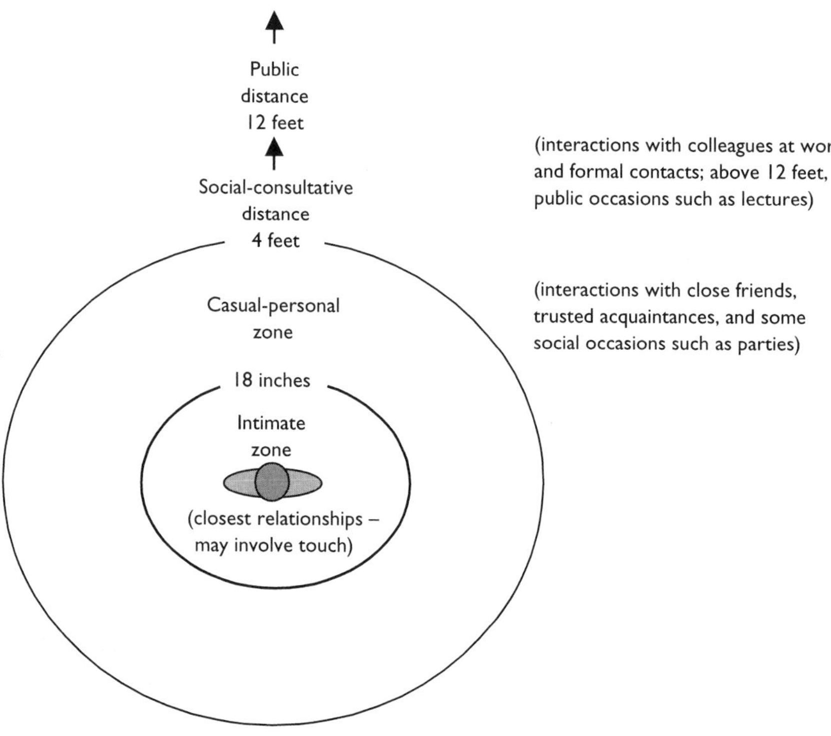

Source: Based on Hall (1966)

has only limited effects and that there have to be relatively extreme conditions before learning is affected.

The key feature appears to be whether there is a subjective experience of *crowding* and whether this affects individuals' feelings of privacy and control over their environment. When tasks are relatively constrained and passive, as in lectures, student performance is not affected by high levels of density. Even when students have contact within their intimate zone, Freedman *et al.* (1971) found that this did not seem to matter so long as the students had their own clearly separated desk space and were able to work independently. However, when tasks are more complex and require higher levels of interaction, then students are more likely to experience crowding. Heller *et al.* (1977), for instance, found that high densities *or* high levels of physical interaction were sufficient to produce perceptions of crowding, but that only a combination of the two led to poor task performance. Over a period of time such conditions can also lead students to make attributions that they are not able to control their environments. This can lead to the feelings of helplessness described in Chapter 5, and students may then withdraw from active involvement.

The overall density and relationships between pupils and the nature of the task can also affect tolerance of others. Fisher and Byrne (1975) found that students working in libraries (with a low density) were particularly disrupted by strangers' sitting close to them, even though they and the strangers were working independently. This appeared to be due to a sense of intrusion, and females especially were affected by a stranger sitting next to them – a position they would normally reserve for interacting with a friend. In school, however, pupils usually know one another well, and are more likely to tolerate close interactions. In designs of seating in public spaces in schools, it may be appropriate to limit the closeness of seating, although conversely classes may benefit from closer physical groupings, particularly when cooperative group work is being undertaken.

Noise and pupil progress

Most teachers believe that too much noise is bad for learning and will often strive for very quiet conditions to avoid pupils' being distracted. In one sense, noise can of course be an indication of low task involvement, if pupils are talking about other things or directly calling out to one another. Alternatively, some teachers will aim for more moderate levels, accepting a 'working buzz' as part of active class work. In small-group work, such as a science investigation, one would expect that there would have to be a certain amount of noise for learning to occur. Pupils would need to discuss their strategy, allocate responsibilities and coordinate the carrying out and analysis of the work.

Such short-term exposure to moderate levels of noise from within the school appears to have only limited effects. A typical investigation by Slater (1968) compared seventh-graders' performance on a reading comprehension test which required written answers, under three conditions. These were: in a quiet classroom with 45–55 dB, in an average classroom with 55–70 dB, and in an extremely noisy classroom with 75–90 dB. Surprisingly, children's performances over a class period did not show any differences between these conditions, indicating that such interfering noises can be mostly 'tuned out' when necessary.

When external noise is particularly intrusive, however, it can significantly limit progress. Bronzaft and McCarthy (1975), for instance, found significant reduction in reading scores for pupils whose classroom was next to an elevated railway, with train noise interfering for about 30 seconds every four and a half minutes. Measures to soundproof the room with acoustic tiles were associated with a subsequent improvement in reading, indicating that the noise levels had been interfering with learning.

Perhaps more importantly, McSporran (1997) reviewed findings that the typical class noise levels of 60–65 dB are louder than the normal voice levels of many teachers. Most classrooms also have reverberation effects that interfere with the intelligibility of pupils' perceptions. Because

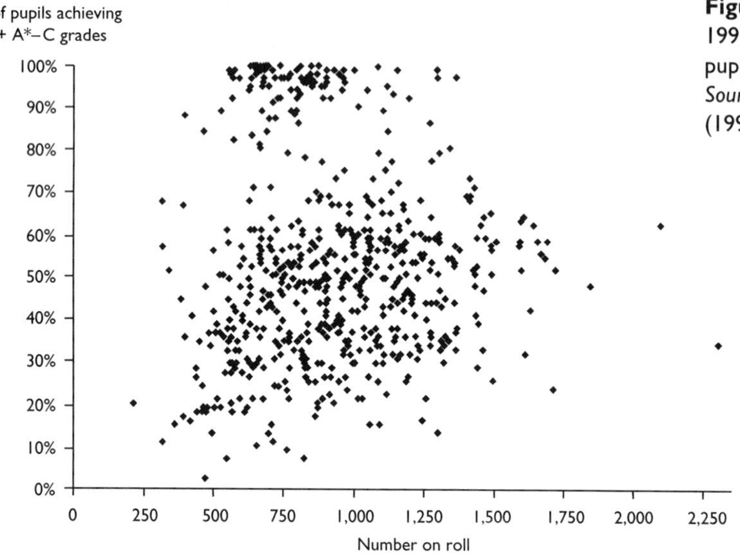

Figure 6.6 GCSE performance, 1997, in relation to numbers of pupils on roll
Source: Funding Agency for Schools (1998)

much of class learning involves teacher direction and verbal interaction such as questioning, it is important for teachers' speech to be significantly louder than the background noise, typically by at least 15 dB. Unfortunately, speaking at this level is likely to cause vocal damage, and McSporran advocates the use of a small portable wireless microphone and amplification. Reviews of the use of this indicated that it resulted in improved learning and behaviour and was liked by both teachers and pupils.

School size

In their study of school effectiveness, Rutter *et al.* (1979) also looked at the effects of the overall school size (which in this study varied from about 450 to about 2,000 pupils). Although there was a trend for smaller schools to have better academic and behavioural outcomes, this was not significant, and the sample size of 12 was probably not large enough to show any effects. Budge (1996a), however, reported on US research findings, in 789 high schools, that the most effective of these had between 600 and 900 pupils. A possible interpretation of this result comes from a study by Good and Brophy (1977), who found that as school size increased, individual participation in school life decreased, with a negative effect on educational outcomes. Smaller schools were more likely to suffer from limited specialisation and a reduction in educational variety.

Despite these plausible findings, a general review of the educational outcomes in 618 British grant-maintained schools by the Funding Agency for Schools (1998) initially found little difference according to school roll (Figure 6.6), although there was a general tendency for the smallest schools to have poorer outcomes. A closer inspection of this graph, however, reveals that it includes a separate group of schools at the top of the GCSE range. These are in fact those grant-maintained schools which had a selective intake and would generally achieve at a high level whatever their size. If one removes this group (virtually all schools above the 90 per cent level), then there is an apparent relationship, albeit still a very weak one. Smaller schools seem to achieve at a lower level and increasing size is associated with higher exam results, up to about a 1,250–1,500 roll.

It is possible, however, that pupil background factors could produce this effect. This might happen if middle-class, aspiring parents took their children out of schools which had a generally low-ability intake (and a corresponding poor reputation) and sent them to schools with a better reputation. This would have the effect of increasing the size of schools which have a good intake and reducing the size of those with a poor intake. A study by Bradley and Taylor (1998) controlled for such effects of socio-economic status, mainly by using entitlement to free school meals as a proxy measure. A significant effect of school size was still found, with an increase of 100 pupils leading to a rise of 0.7 percentage points of pupils achieving five or more A* to C GCSEs, flattening out for schools with more than about 1,000 pupils.

However, the entitlement to, or take-up of, free school meals is only a partial measure of home background and support, or of pupil abilities. When multilevel analyses have also taken pupils' initial achievements into account, school size effects largely disappear. In a study of 249 secondary schools, Gibson and Asthana (1998) found that size did have an effect on the variance in GCSE attainments, but that this was tiny compared with the effects of home background variables such as socio-economic class.

In a study of 143 primary schools, Bondi (1991) was unable to find any effect at all for school size after accounting for social class, gender, initial attainments and ability. However, Mortimore *et al.* (1988) found most effectiveness with medium to small schools with a junior roll of around 160 or fewer pupils, which would mean that there would be at least one class for each year group. Larger schools seemed to have less integration and involvement of staff, and there was more variation in the practice of individual teachers.

Organisation of pupils and teaching

Overall school structures

In terms of their general organisation, most secondary schools have a separate academic and pastoral structure, which may be organised by 'year groups' or in 'houses'. Rutter *et al.* (1979) found no differences between these, in terms of academic progress or behavioural outcomes, and it seems that either system can be operated effectively. Continuity does seem to be important, however, and Mortimore *et al.* (1988) showed that there was a significant academic superiority for primary schools which took children through from age 5 to 11 years, instead of being separated into separate infant and junior schools.

Time of day and learning

Most teachers believe that children's learning is more efficient earlier in the day; this has generally led to an emphasis on timetabling the more academic subjects in the morning, and the increasing adoption of the 'Continental day' (which involves an earlier start and finish, with a shortened lunch break).

In view of these beliefs it is surprising to learn that most work that has been carried out on arousal and general mental functioning indicates that pupil learning is likely to peak during the late afternoon. Diurnal variations such as body temperature seem to go through a general cycle of a slow rise during the morning, a short dip after lunch, then a progressive rise to higher levels during the afternoon, followed by a fall only much later in the evening. Jones (1992) has summarised the way in which such indices of arousal correspond with changes in real learning ability. In one typical investigation, Folkard *et al.* (1977) looked at the learning ability of 12- and 13-year-old children with stories read to them at either 9 a.m. or 3 p.m. After one week the afternoon group showed both superior recall and superior comprehension, retaining about 8 per cent more of meaningful material. The morning group showed only some limited short-term benefits in terms of retention of low-level factual information.

One reason put forward by Jones for the difficulty which most teachers have in believing such findings could be that in the mornings, less alert students may be more manageable and therefore appear to be more receptive. Although students may be generally aroused and capable of learning more in the afternoons, they may also be more difficult to control and less likely to be involved in more formal (boring) learning tasks. When students are older and more likely to be self-

Figure 6.7 Seating and pupil participation in lessons

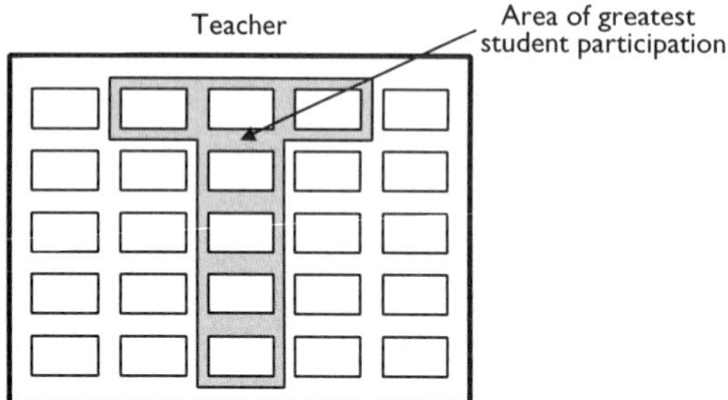

Source: Based on Delethes and Jackson (1972)

motivated, later learning sessions may be even more effective. This is supported by findings of Skinner (1985) that marks for college exams were better when courses were taught in the afternoon rather than in the morning.

Classroom location of pupils

There is also evidence to show that children respond directly to the arrangement of the space that they are taught in and their place within it. As shown in Figure 6.7, Delethes and Jackson (1972) demonstrated that roughly 64 per cent of student participation in academic discussion was by students who sat in the front row or in the strip running up the centre of the classroom.

Teachers appear to encourage the more responsive pupils to sit in these areas, but the effect can also be a reciprocal one. Schwebel and Cherlin (1972) found that when less attentive students are moved into these places, they increased the amount of time they spent on school work and became better liked by the teachers.

Seating arrangements

Students in most primary classes tend to be placed around tables in groups of four to six, to work on exercises set by the teacher. In Britain, the Plowden Report (1967) justified this seating arrangement on the basis that it would enable children to learn from each other through discussion and cooperation. Wheldall (1991), however, argued that while the seating arrangements may have changed, the style of working at that time remained largely individual, with the problem that groups give greater opportunities for pupils to distract one another. Wheldall investigated this by observing a number of classes for two weeks during which the children sat round tables, then altering the arrangement into more traditional rows for two weeks, before eventually returning to the original group pattern. The main finding was that students' on-task behaviour rose by about 15 per cent when they were seated in rows, and fell by the same amount when they returned to sitting around tables. Some children's performance rose by over 30 per cent in the row configuration, and a few of them even complained about having to go back to being seated in groups.

Despite such findings, Galton *et al.* (1999) found that the majority of classes in junior schools in 1996 continued to have grouped seating, although some classes were able to use flexible arrangements depending on the nature of the task involved. There was also a significant increase in the use of a single 'carpet area' to bring children together for whole-class instruction or discussion.

Learning in groups

Many studies have shown that with appropriate organisation, *cooperative learning* with other students can be more effective than independent learning. Johnson and Johnson (1987), for instance, reviewed 122 studies in this area and concluded that cooperative learning produced better learning, self-esteem and social outcomes than individual learning and competitive situations. Factors that were important in this appeared to be the exchange of information between group members and the use of other children's perspectives. Children also developed a sense of value that came from contributing to the group and an improved ability to interact with other children.

Although the use of grouped seating is very popular, most classroom work actually occurs on an individual basis. Observational research of junior classrooms by Galton *et al.* (1999) found that children mostly worked independently, only 13.5 per cent of the time being involved with other pupils on task-related interactions. These were also mainly restricted to practical work, with interchanges being typically brief and mostly confined to simple information giving and receiving. Pupils also interacted with the teacher as part of a group for 3.7 per cent of the time, but this was mainly to receive information and did not require much involvement with other group members.

A great deal of such normal classroom work is also *competitive*, with work marked and compared with that of other students. Far from improving effort, this is likely to decrease motivation, and may also develop oppositional interaction between pupils. Johnson and Johnson (1987) found that students often try to discourage each others' work by poor communication with their classmates and by attempts to hide information from each other.

Cooperative group work

To combat these difficulties, Aronson *et al.* (1978) have devised an alternative approach to develop more cooperative work, by the construction of what they term the *jigsaw classroom*. In this arrangement the class is divided up into groups and all of these are given a task which has a number of separate aspects to it. This could involve, say, deciding where it would be best to locate a factory, taking into account roads, workers, raw materials. Within each group, children are given separate aspects to specialise in and they then go off to find out more about this particular aspect with the members of other groups. After this, each original group then comes together again and is able to combine the knowledge and ideas from all of the specialist groups to arrive at a final solution.

Aronson *et al.* found in configurations such as this, that children from different social and ethnic backgrounds interacted in positive ways. Children with differing abilities also supported each other, with more able children becoming involved in tutoring less able children. This has been shown to benefit not only the less able children, but also the more able children, since the process of explanation means that they must organise their own understanding.

A study of the processes of such groupings by Bennett and Dunne (1989) found that children in cooperative groups showed high levels of involvement, with 88 per cent of the talk being on-task. In a further study by Bennett and Cass (1989), mixed-ability groups also showed higher levels of interaction, with high-ability children performing better than they did in homogeneous groups.

Although group work appears to be an effective teaching approach, Gavienas (1997) found that most primary teachers avoided collaborative working since they anticipated that if adopted, it would result in antisocial behaviour. Galton *et al.* (1980) also found that although one in five of a sample of teachers were enthusiastic about group work, they largely failed to implement it effectively in their teaching. One important reason is perhaps that collaborative group work requires a significant amount of preparation and organisation, and needs to develop over a period of time. Unfortunately, busy teachers have to respond to the ongoing demands of covering the curriculum, and an individualised learning approach requires less time to manage.

Mixed-ability versus ability grouping

Most primary schooling is organised with age-determined mixed-ability groupings. Despite this, a survey by Hallam (1999) indicated that nearly two-thirds of all primary schools were adopting ability grouping of some kind, largely in an attempt to raise educational standards. The extent to which this was being used increased progressively throughout the primary years, especially for mathematics lessons, for which it was used twice as much as for English. Usually, children were grouped by ability *within* classes, with the aim of helping to match work with pupils' abilities. In their comparison of school effectiveness, Mortimore *et al.* (1988) found evidence that this is an effective approach.

Secondary schools typically allocate children to classes according to their ability in a particular subject (setting), or sometimes according to their overall achievements (streaming). In some subjects, such as mathematics, this is often done early on, but in other, more practical subjects, such as art, mixed-ability groups are often retained throughout the whole school. Although grouping classes by ability can limit children's access to the full range of the curriculum, it arguably enables closer matching of work and would appear to be a justifiable way of organising teaching groups.

The evidence for its effectiveness is rather different, however, and early research by Lunn (1970) in primary schools and by Rutter *et al.* (1979) at secondary level showed little difference between the overall achievements of pupils in streamed and those in unstreamed schools. They did, however, find differences *within* schools that were using ability grouping. One particular difficulty is that there can be problems with the self-perception and behaviour of pupils in lower-attaining 'sink' classes. Also, teachers alter their expectations of lower groups and give less time to preparing work for them, with the result that pupils in such groups do worse academically than equivalent pupils in schools organised by mixed ability. Although some research, such as Lunn's (1970) review, shows that pupils in the upper sets usually do better than they would in mixed-ability groups, this effect was quite small (equivalent to about 5 IQ points). Also, a study by Boaler (1997) of mathematics groupings showed that a number of pupils in upper sets often experienced difficulties in working at the pace of the class, resulting in disaffection and underachievement. In one school, pupils in sets spent more time apparently 'working' but did not achieve as well in GCSE as equivalent pupils from another school with mixed-ability teaching.

A wide review of a number of studies by Sukhnandan and Lee (1998) found that streaming and setting had no overall positive or negative effects compared with mixed-ability teaching. Like Mortimore *et al.* (1988), they found within-class grouping to have a more positive effect, particularly for the more 'linear' subjects such as mathematics, science and modern languages.

One major justification which many schools tend to give for the use of setting is to improve the performance of higher-achieving pupils. Although a few studies have found some limited support for the belief that such pupils' performance can be enhanced in this way, a review by Slavin (1990) considers that any improvement may occur partly because students in upper groups actually follow different courses. In Britain, top mathematics groups are usually entered for the higher tier of the GCSE and as a consequence will cover more in-depth material. It is also possible that top classes will have the more experienced and better-qualified teachers allocated to them, who may be more able to coach classes to better examination results. The outcomes of setting may be real and valuable to schools, but the evidence indicates that there is probably a price to pay in terms of the wider school population's achievements and social adjustment.

Class size effects

It may seem obvious that having smaller classes would lead to more effective teaching. If teachers have more time for individual children, then they ought to be able to monitor their progress more closely and to match the work with each individual's needs. The implications of this are of course that class sizes should be as small as is feasibly possible. There are, however, major cost implications since wages are the largest single element of expenditure in education. This issue therefore has political as well as educational implications and is a regular area of public and professional attention.

One major investigation reported by Davie *et al.* (1972) was based on the National Child Development study of 18,300 children born in one week in March 1958. Information about these was gathered at ages 7, 11, 16, 21, 31 and 37. The study covered the whole of Britain and looked at the correlation between achievement and class size, after attempting to control for school size, length of schooling, parental interest and occupation. Surprisingly, pupils in larger classes appeared to be doing better than pupils in smaller classes. As in all correlational studies which study only what is already happening, there could be many factors other than the presumed one causing this unexpected result. For instance, pupils with low achievements are often put into smaller groups, and classes with the more able pupils may have fewer disruptive pupils and so can be made larger. Because of this, a lack of positive findings may be due to limitations on the range and the design of such investigations. Some of the following studies have therefore used more formal experimental approaches, or seem less likely to be affected by such confounding errors.

One-to-one and small-group effects

At one extreme, Bloom (1984) has looked at the effects of directly withdrawing individual children and teaching them separately. As shown in Figure 6.8, individual teaching showed a major and significant superiority with an effect size of 2 when compared with children taught in a conventional class of 30. The average child taught separately came to achieve at the level of the top 2 per cent for the normal class, and there was a general levelling up of achievements, with the lower-attaining children making the greatest progress.

Cashdan *et al.* (1971) also report rapid progress in a study of 1,200 children who were withdrawn and taught in different-sized small groups for remedial work. Although this was not an experimental investigation, it seems unlikely that such children would be particularly good at learning, and likely that the main effect would be the size of the group they were placed in. The average overall gain was 21 months in reading ability over an 11-month period. Cashdan *et al.* also found that readers taught individually or in pairs made no more progress than those taught in groups of three or six children, but that the gains were substantially less for groups of seven or more children.

Figure 6.8 Effects of individual teaching

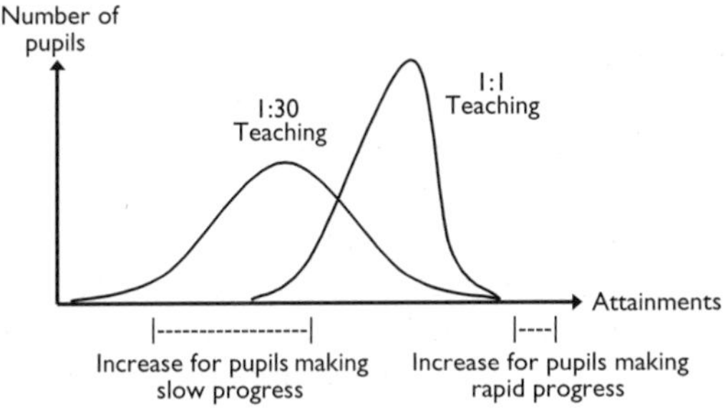

Source: Bloom (1984)

Reducing class sizes

The STAR ('student–teacher achievement ratio') project is a major US experimental study by Word *et al.* (1994), which attempted to compare learning progress in different class sizes. Costing $12 million, this covered 7,000 pupils from 300 teachers in 80 elementary schools in Tennessee. Pupils were randomly allocated to 'small' classes (13–17 pupils) or 'regular' classes (22–25 pupils) and their achievements were followed up initially over three years, from age 5 years to age 8 years. Successive improvements in basic reading and mathematics attainments showed that there was a definite learning advantage for pupils in smaller classes. With reading, 69.5 per cent of the 'small' classes passed a particular reading standard, but only 62.3 per cent of the 'regular' classes achieved the same level. This difference was statistically significant, and remained even two years after pupils had been returned to normal-sized classes.

The size of this effect is not great, however, and Prais (1996) points out that over three years, the reading advantage for the smaller classes was only equivalent to about six days of extra teaching. This is relatively minor compared with the 540 days for which the children had actually been in school. A further concern is that 108 'incompatible' children were moved out of the smaller classes at the end of the first year, which may have artificially boosted the scores of these classes.

In primary schools, Mortimore *et al.* (1988)

also looked at class size effects and found that they were most important with younger children. This is consistent with the research showing that teacher effectiveness is greatest with younger children (see later in this chapter), presumably since their independent learning skills are less developed. It is surprising that primary classes are typically larger than secondary classes, and perhaps a logical conclusion would be to reverse these ratios.

Summary of effects

In general, the above findings for different teaching groups are consistent with a model whereby small groups of up to about six show greatest effectiveness, with a subsequent rapid drop and then a slower decrease for class sizes larger than 15. This is summarised in the graph shown in Figure 6.9.

A meta-analysis of 59 different studies on the effects of different class sizes by Smith and Glass (1980) found outcomes which were very similar to this, with a rapid fall as class sizes increased from 5 to 20, then a slower fall to class sizes as large as 70. An explanation of the processes underlying these effects can be found in a study by Olson (1971), who observed the quality of interactions in 18,528 classrooms of different sizes. This found that an individualised approach was most commonly applied in groups of up to five pupils. With group sizes of between 6 and 15 pupils, rather less individualisation was possible, and less again with between 16 and 25 pupils. With more than 26 pupils, lessons consisted largely of standard exercises, question and answer, lecture and testing; with more than 36 pupils, there was virtually no group work, individual work, discussion or pupil reporting.

Figure 6.9 Hypothetical relationship between class size and pupil progress

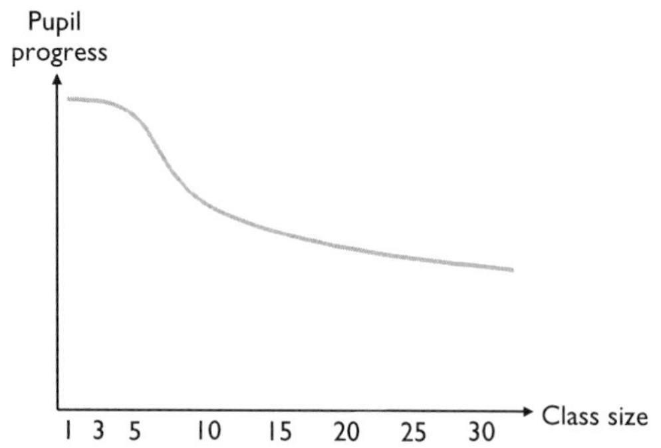

Different class sizes therefore appear to produce different levels of monitoring and matching of pupils' work and progress, and if a 'whole-class' mode of teaching is adopted, the number of pupils does not seem to matter too much. Good and Brophy (1977), for instance, quote research showing that when class sizes were reduced, learning did not improve because teachers continued to teach the same way as they had done when they had taught a larger class.

Although setting up classes of different sizes does have a statistically significant effect, its magnitude with classes in the normal range (i.e. with more than 20 pupils) is relatively small and has needed carefully controlled studies to prove its existence. Other factors such as different classroom organisation or teaching styles probably outweigh its effect. Bloom (1984), for instance, has summarised work on the use of mastery learning techniques, which involves ensuring that individual pupils achieve high levels of success before progressing to subsequent learning materials. Using this with classes of 30 was found to bring students halfway towards the effects of one-to-one tutoring, although this can in practice be a difficult approach to organise and manage.

Should we reduce class sizes?

In early 2000, average class sizes in England had decreased somewhat to 27.1 in primary schools, and increased to 22 in secondary schools (DfEE, 2000). Although changing these to very small groups of less than 10 would make a major difference, it would evidently be financially unrealistic. Altering class sizes to even 20 in primary schools would still entail a massive cost and it can be argued that the improvement in standards as a result of this would not be great enough to justify the expenditure. In passing, it should be noted that Dean and Rafferty (1996) report findings that teachers with class sizes of 26–30 work three hours more per week than those with classes of 21 or less (49.6 hours, compared with 46.4 hours), and that larger class sizes produce more stress on teachers. This is, however, unlikely to be a telling argument with those who are in charge of allocating resources!

In terms of the efficiency of educational outcomes for the use of additional resources, Wasik and Slavin (1993) have reviewed the effects of reducing class sizes and spending the same amount on periods of one-to-one tutoring for selected students. They concluded that the optimum overall approach would be to implement the best instructional programmes in classes of all sizes and to provide individual help for children who are failing. This may not address the issue of pressures on teachers, but this could be tackled separately by other approaches such as the use of periods of non-contact time during the day. In some Pacific Rim countries which do well on international comparisons, such as Taiwan, up to 25 per cent of the week is free for teachers to organise and prepare work.

Teaching effects

Teaching styles and class management

Formal versus progressive styles

Although teachers use a number of ways of organising and managing their work, two styles appear to be largely opposed and based on very different philosophies. The more traditional, *formal* approach is highly structured and based mainly on didactic or teacher-directed processes. Following the later 1960s there was arguably a swing towards more *progressive* approaches to teaching, emphasising freedom, activity, and discovery in learning. As with many developments in education, there have been attempts to evaluate the different effectiveness of these styles but these have often been confounded by weak definitions of the constructs involved and the effects of other variables. For instance, since they were the more recent development, progressive approaches have mainly been adopted by younger teachers. Any differences between the outcome of using the two approaches might therefore be due merely to the length of the teachers' experience.

One key study by Bennett (1976) tried to refine the constructs involved and to make comparisons of pupils' achievements. Bennett first used a questionnaire survey of 468 primary teachers to identify 12 different teaching styles. These appeared to be distributed across a formal–informal continuum, with most teachers using a combination of techniques. The study then looked at pupil progress over one year and compared the 12 most formal classes with 13 of the most informal classes. The main findings were that the pupils in the formally taught groups showed significantly greater gains in reading, mathematics and English. However, the achievements of a single informally organised class went against this trend and showed one of the highest gains of all. The teacher of this class was characterised by her use of structure and monitoring processes which enabled her to emphasise children's academic progress. This implies that structure and monitoring may be more important than a simple formal–informal distinction.

Bennett's study has been criticised as making incorrect statistical decisions, and for using misleading groupings of teachers. A subsequent reanalysis of the data by Bennett and co-workers (Aitkin *et al.*, 1981) found a different, more meaningful group of informal teachers whose teaching results did not differ significantly from those of the teachers who used formal techniques. Bennett also found that the largest variation was between different teachers, irrespective of teaching style, indicating that there are other, more important aspects to teaching than a simple formal–informal distinction.

Discovery learning versus direct teaching

Further research has tended to isolate more specific aspects of teaching processes and styles to evaluate their effectiveness. One important feature of progressive techniques has been the emphasis on *child-centred* approaches, which see the pupil as an active and independent learner, with the teacher facilitating his or her learning. The most important child-centred approach is the use of *discovery learning*, which emphasises that students should have experiences which lead them to find key concepts for themselves. Bruner (1961a) in particular has argued that learners must construct their own system of understanding and that didactic teaching will result in a limited ability to apply knowledge to new situations. According to this view, discovery learning will automatically match learning to the child's development as the child progresses through different stages. Bruner argues that pupils will develop their knowledge when they revisit curriculum areas, in a spiral fashion. For instance, as shown in Figure 6.10, the teacher might initially develop an intuitive concept of 'burning', with demonstrations at Key Stage 1 of a number of common substances being set on fire. At Key Stage 2, when pupils are capable of greater understanding, the concept could then be extended to include the idea of substances combining with oxygen (Figure 6.10).

Figure 6.10 The spiral curriculum

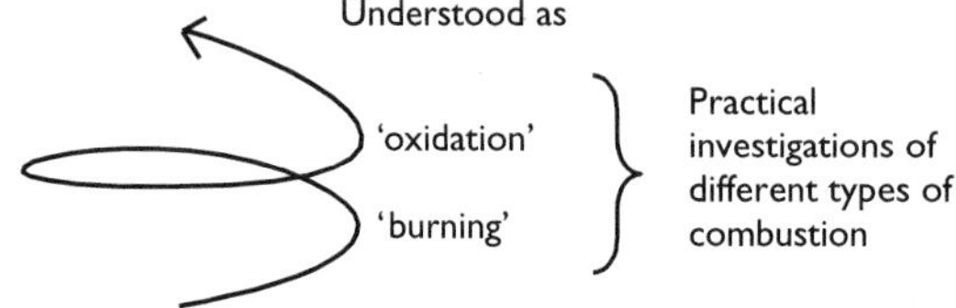

In practice, the teacher has to provide at least some direction, in the form of experiences for the pupil, but the key element is that the pupils 'find' the main principles for themselves. In one study quoted by Bruner (1961b), pupils were given maps of key geographical features and their task was to use these to decide on where settlements should be placed. Bruner found that pupils' eventual knowledge and understanding of the factors involved in settlements established in this way was more flexible and could be of more use to them than if they had merely memorised a list of key settlement features.

Such experiences can be contrasted with the more formal and conventional approaches, which are largely based upon *direct teaching*. These involve the teacher as the source and organiser of knowledge, although there is also usually an emphasis that work should be matched to the pupil's level of attainments. Direct teaching can take the form merely of having children rehearse and memorise 'facts', but, as we saw in Chapter 2, such unstructured learning is relatively inefficient. Ausubel (1968) in particular argues that the teacher's job is to organise learning for pupils and to help them progress rapidly through the structured development of knowledge. Ausubel believes that *advance organisers* can help learning by providing pupils with the necessary structure and links between knowledge; these are initial brief previews by the teacher which place the lesson in context, introduce key ideas and link them together.

Galton *et al.* (1999) have found that in practice most teachers employ a great deal of direct teaching, with the use of questions to check for understanding and to involve pupils. This is then usually followed by a period of supervised practice, with assessment by the teacher to ensure that goals have been achieved.

Although discovery learning and direct teaching may appear to be mutually exclusive, research findings indicate that each approach has different advantages appropriate to different situations, and that combining these can produce effective, flexible learning. Mayer (1987) summarises work which shows that a pure discovery approach increases motivation, as the children become deeply involved with the task, but that the learning that results can be relatively unfocused and requires a large amount of time. Direct, expositive teaching appears to need least time, with good initial learning; long-term retention tends to be poorer, however, and learning does not transfer well.

Guided discovery is a combination of approaches, and involves the teacher setting up learning situations which allow pupils to 'discover' the target knowledge or understanding. This takes longer than direct exposition but has been shown to lead to better involvement, long-term retention and transfer.

With students who have reached higher levels of (abstract) thinking, Rowell *et al.* (1969) found that direct verbal instruction led to rapid learning and good long-term retention. This implies that personal experience is not always necessary but can be most important when students do not have an initial foundation of knowledge or understanding.

Whole-class teaching versus group work

In an attempt to raise standards, there has been a major emphasis by the UK's central government on the use of whole-class teaching. This was particularly advocated in the 'Three Wise Men' discussion paper by Alexander *et al.* (1992), which has been the basis for a number of subsequent reforms of primary education. A review by Galton *et al.* (1999) indicated that primary teachers generally responded to such encouragements, with the time spent on whole-class teaching increasing from 15.1 per cent in 1976 to 31.3 per cent in 1996.

Further developments with the implementation of government-directed strategies for both literacy and numeracy also involve a large element of whole-class involvement. Guidance from the DfEE (1998n) for the 'literacy hour' indicates that 40 minutes of this should be based on activities such as whole-class reading and writing, followed by a final plenary session. Similarly, with the national numeracy strategy in primary schools (DfEE, 1998l), it is recommended that mathematics teaching should cover a daily lesson of between 45 and 60 minutes and that teachers should teach the whole class together for a high proportion of this time.

The rationale for such a prescriptive approach appears to be based on research supporting the effectiveness of direct teaching techniques as discussed above, as well as process correlates of normal class teaching. In one study by Brophy and Evertson (1976), groups with the highest gains were commonly taught via whole-class lessons. These typically began with clear presentation of material to the whole class by the teacher, followed by a practice and feedback phase. High-gain classes also had some small-group work, but this was mainly confined to practice of basic skills.

A similar study by Good and Grouws (1977) also found that children making the most progress were taught using whole-class instruction. However, this technique was also used by some teachers whose pupils made the least progress. In these classes, it seems that class teaching was more didactic, with limited involvement by pupils. Classes where there was an emphasis on small-group work consistently made intermediate progress. Such findings support the belief that whole-class teaching can be more effective than small-group work, but that it needs to be carried out in the correct way. Good and Grouws found that what was needed was good class management, a brisk pace with clear instruction, and a high level of positive involvement of pupils. The last of these can be achieved by the use of questions and feedback, as well as teaching that is enthusiastic and responsive to pupils' interests.

It is important, however, to know that these effects were relatively small and were found only by comparing the most consistently effective with the most consistently ineffective teachers. Other studies, such as the Beginning Teacher Evaluation Study (Denham and Lieberman, 1980), have found that although pupil involvement is generally higher during activities conducted by the teacher, this also means that the content and pace are inadequate for the most able pupils but excessive for the least able. In Galton *et al.*'s (1999) study, pupils were also generally more involved when they were part of whole-class activities, but some pupils, referred to as 'easy riders', opted out by using work avoidance techniques. The pupils concerned put in little effort but appeared to be working, and in a whole-class situation it was hard for the teacher to detect what was happening.

In many evaluations it can be difficult to know what is being compared and how valid any conclusions are. Both whole-class and group teaching can be done well or badly, and either might be more appropriate for certain topics or learning goals. For group teaching, pupils can be placed in ability groups, as is common in mathematics teaching, or cooperative investigative groups, which are often used in science. Both types of groups can probably be very effective in such subject areas and enable the teacher to match work with pupils' abilities and to encourage active learning styles. It is likely, however, that differentiated and cooperative group work are not usually used in the most effective way possible, because of the demands they make on teacher preparation time, and the additional difficulties with classroom management. A great many supposed group activities in class are therefore probably based merely on shared activities or parallel working.

Most of the research which supports the use of direct class teaching has typically been based on content which emphasises the development of factual knowledge and skill development. Whole-class teaching may therefore be appropriate for certain aspects of mathematics or early literacy development but may not be the most effective approach for establishing higher-level understanding. Unfortunately, the move towards the increased use of testing to evaluate the outcomes of education has encouraged an emphasis on factual knowledge and the use of direct, whole-class teaching.

INTERNATIONAL COMPARISONS

Some international studies, such as those reported by Reynolds and Farrell (1996), have shown that those countries which utilise whole-class teaching the most (notably around the Pacific Rim) also have some of the highest standards of academic attainments. However, the general culture of these countries is radically different from that of the United Kingdom, with a strong emphasis on responsibility of the individual for the group, and high levels of home support and expectations. This is supported by the findings of Caplan *et al.* (1992) that refugees from South-East Asia who migrated to the United States subsequently achieved at a very high educational level, despite their having language and economic difficulties and having to attend schools which were largely in low-income, metropolitan areas where academic standards were generally low. Detailed studies of the children's home experiences indicated that their progress was largely due to the direct influence of the family supporting them with their studies, and an emphasis on independence and academic success.

An alternative comparison could be made with Sweden, which consistently has one of the highest literacy standards in Europe and arguably has greater cultural similarities with Britain. Rather than looking for a reason in terms of a single teaching technique, we could explain Sweden's high standards by its much higher levels of educational spending and staffing, particularly at the primary stage of education (*Digest of Education Statistics*, 1995). It is tempting to argue that this comparison implies that standards in the United Kingdom could be similarly raised by employing more staff and decreasing class sizes, but there may be other critical differences between the two countries, such as Sweden's later start to formal education. As discussed earlier in this chapter, smaller class sizes alone are unlikely to alter progress very significantly, in the absence of different organisational and teaching approaches.

THE CASE OF THE LITERACY HOUR

Although it may perhaps be unsafe to draw conclusions from international comparisons, the improvements in literacy standards found by the National Literacy Project (DfEE, 1998c) lend support for some form of intensive approach based on whole-class work. Early results indicated that over 18 months the project schools improved their English results for 7-year-olds by 10 per cent, compared with gains of 7 per cent in all other schools over the same period. However, as well as having a bias towards the use of whole-class teaching, the literacy hour represented a major shift in the balance of the curriculum, with a reduced emphasis on non-core subjects. In an investigation of previous practice, Plewis and Veltman (1996) found that although literacy was involved in many aspects of the school week, many teachers based their reading strategies on individual support but were on average able to listen to each child read for only about eight minutes a week. Any improvements in attainments may therefore be at least partly due to increases in the amount of time which children spend on direct literacy activities.

When schools use a more intensive, group-based approach than is advocated for the literacy hour, it seems that they can achieve at even higher levels. Ghouri (1998), for instance, reports on an east London school where 95 per cent of the pupils had English as a second language but who achieved well above the national average for the Key Stage 1 reading SATs. None scored below 2 and half reached level 3 (nationally, one-quarter failed to reach level 2 and only 26 per cent achieved level 3). This was achieved *without* whole-class teaching, but with additional adults helping children in small groups and work centred on phonic approaches.

A final indication comes from Galton *et al.*'s (1999) study of changes in teaching practices and children's relative attainments in 1976 and 1996. As already mentioned, whole-class teaching approximately doubled over this period, to account for about one-third of all class time. Despite this, over the same time pupils' academic achievements (on the Richmond Tests of Basic Skills) fell significantly for mathematics, language and reading. The decline was greatest for reading, where the composite score reduced from 62.7 per cent in 1976 to 47.7 per cent in 1996.

To a great extent this can probably be attributed to the early effects of the National Curriculum in displacing basic skills work. The study indicated that by 1996 there had been a total reduction of 10.7 per cent in 'opportunities to learn' for English and mathematics. However, increases in the amount of whole-class teaching over this period were evidently not able to compensate for these direct limitations.

In general, it seems unlikely that altering a single aspect of teaching will have a very large effect on children's progress. It is probably more important to look in some detail at the direct process of teaching and to implement a range of flexible approaches which can involve either class, group or individual work. This should depend on a number of variables such as the nature of the task and the composition of the class, with a wider distribution of attainments (such as split year groups) needing greater differentiation. All teaching techniques can be carried out well or badly, and the emphasis should perhaps be on long-term ways of enabling and supporting teachers to develop a number of techniques from which they can choose.

Do teachers matter?

Teachers are closely involved in what and how children learn. For most people it probably seems self-evident that teachers must have an important effect on pupils' educational progress. Although schools may not differ greatly in their overall impact on pupils, perhaps the differences between good and poor teachers might be cancelling each other out. There are also many anecdotal examples of individual teachers who people believe made a significant difference to their lives, for good or ill. Questioning whether there are really any differences between the effectiveness of different teachers seems to fly in the face of common sense, and to deny people's vivid memories of the unique individuals who taught them.

Even so, it is important to pose this question, since if individual teachers are the basis of differences in children's educational progress, any improvements in the educational system should be based on what they do. This aspect has become of greater importance to teachers themselves since judgements about their effectiveness, made largely by headteachers and advisers, are increasingly the basis for assessments which determine pay and career developments (DfEE, 1998l). However, it is still the case that a large amount of the variation in the progress of individual pupils can be attributed to their initial abilities and home background factors. Thus teacher effects may be relatively insignificant, no matter how different individual teachers may be.

It would evidently be wrong to evaluate teachers only on the basis of their pupils' achievements without taking account of their initial abilities. A fair assessment should therefore be concerned with *gains* in academic achievement, by comparing pupils' final attainments with what would have been expected from their initial scores. The result can then be used to compare classes, to see whether some teachers beat expectations or fall below them. In Figure 6.11 it can be seen that although pupils in class B generally achieved at a high level at the end of the year, they did so mainly because they started ahead. Pupils in class A may have finished at a below-average level but their progress was actually greater than would have been expected from their initial scores. Although one might have assumed that the teacher of class B was doing a better job, the gain scores indicate that the pupils of the teacher in class A were in reality making better progress.

Even if there are such apparent differences in gain scores, any improvements in the overall attainments of a class may still not be due to any influence of the class teacher. The group may have a generally more positive attitude towards work for some reason, or a child who was particularly disruptive may have just moved out. Teacher effects shown in this way may also be partly due to different school contexts, with supportive schools enabling teachers to make more or less progress with children. The possibility of teacher influences becomes more likely, however, if teachers manage to achieve consistent improvements with different classes. If such consistency is low, then this might mean that any gain scores are not due to the effects of teachers, although it could also mean that individual teachers vary over time, or that teacher effectiveness tends to be relatively specific to particular classes or teaching situations.

Figure 6.11 Analysis of gain scores

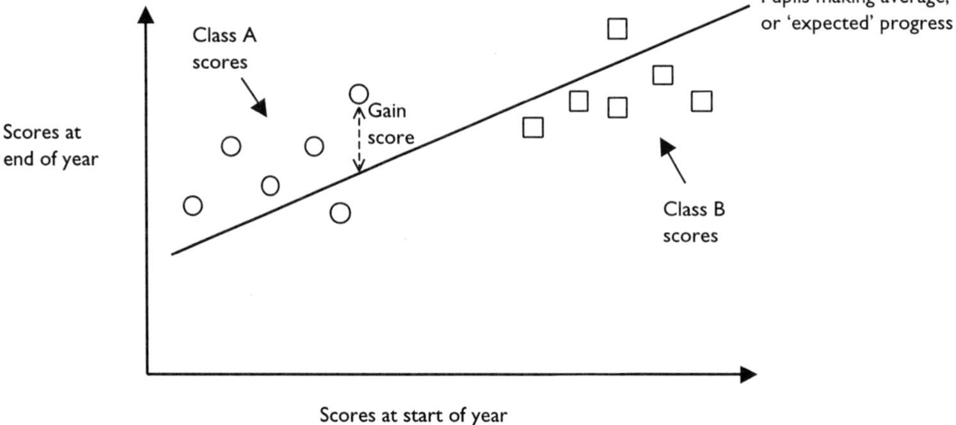

Evidence of gains

One early detailed study by Veldman and Brophy (1974), which was based upon gain scores, looked at the achievements of the pupils of 115 different teachers. To attempt to reduce any variations due to teacher experience or expertise, the study included only teachers who had at least five years' experience of teaching at their grade and who taught at the same grade level over the period of the study.

Pupils were assessed using a standard test of verbal abilities, reading and arithmetic attainments, and scores were compared over three successive years. As shown in Table 6.1, for schools with a normal intake there were significant teacher effects on overall gain scores, but these were relatively small compared with the effects of initial achievements.

The teacher effects which did exist tended to be greater with younger children and in deprived schools, where the teacher effects rose to 9.83 per cent. This is consistent with the idea that young children and children with poor home backgrounds are less independent with their learning and are therefore more affected by their teacher. If there were substantial teacher effects, then it seems likely that these would have affected 'taught' subjects such as arithmetic more than general verbal abilities, which are perhaps more likely to develop naturally. With normal schools, however, there were no significant differences between any of the achievement areas, adding support to the belief that any teacher effects are relatively limited in their impact.

Multilevel modelling is a more sophisticated way of analysing all of the different effects on pupils' progress. When it includes effects at the classroom level, it has generally confirmed such findings, explaining only a relatively small amount of the variance. A review by Creemers and Reezigt (1996) of various studies using this approach found that the effect was generally of the order of about 3 per cent. A subsequent study by Reezigt *et al.* (1999) incorporated extensive initial background information on pupils and found a similar level of about 4 per cent, the same importance as for school-level effects. Such findings indicate that the variance of about 10 per cent that is normally attributed to the effects of schools is partly due to the effects of teachers within it. Some studies have found that the class a pupil is in has a much larger effect, but these studies have typically been confounded by the effects of ability grouping or have used teacher judgements which may merely reflect differences in their perceptions.

Table 6.1 Variance in learning gains accounted for by initial attainments and teacher effects

	Initial attainments	**Teacher effects**
Grade 2	70.4%	3.0%
Grade 3	75.9%	2.2%

Source: Based on data in Veldman and Brophy (1974)

A review of eight studies of teacher effectiveness by Shavelson and Russo (1977) also looked at a range of studies on the *consistency* of teachers. This is measured by correlations between the gains of teachers with different classes. Most studies they considered showed only moderate values, with correlations usually less than 0.4, which generally tended to be highest within a particular subject area and with similar groups of pupils. Gray (1979) also carried out a comparison of the progress of teachers' classes with reading over successive years. This study was relatively well controlled since it used parallel versions of the same standardised test, which reduces the inaccuracies that come from comparing different forms of assessment. To try to maximise any teacher effects, it focused on the late infant period of education, when reading development is important, and also used a sample of 21 schools whose intake was predominantly working class (where parents would be less likely to be involved). Teachers' classes were tested at the beginning and at the end of the academic year over two successive years and academic gains were then correlated as shown in Figure 6.12.

As can be seen, only a few teachers appeared to be effective over both years and none was consistently highly effective. Rather more teachers

Figure 6.12 Standardised gain scores for 41 teachers in Years 1 and 2

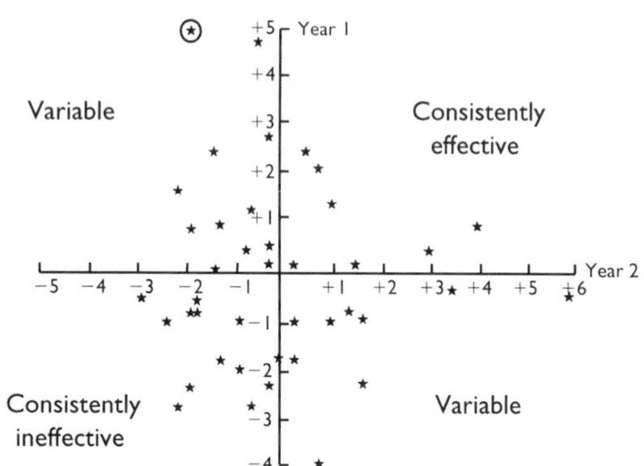

Source: Gray (1979)

were consistently ineffective, but this could be an effect of the overall random distribution of the values. Just as many teachers' classes scored high one year and low the other, with the teacher who achieved the highest gain in the first year (shown circled) obtaining one of the lowest gains in the second year. The overall correlation between year 1 and year 2 gain scores was 0.01, which means that there was no significant relationship between the two sets of scores.

Perhaps one of the best-controlled investigations of teacher effects involves comparisons based on *parallel classes*. These are quite common in secondary schools and are a form of natural experiment, since different teachers are responsible for roughly equivalent classes, covering the same curriculum material and aiming for the same end-of-course assessment. Luyten and de Jong (1998) looked at the progress made by first-grade secondary classes in 22 secondary schools on a standard mathematics course. Two teachers in each school were studied, enabling a direct comparison to be made between their classes' progress. Despite quite marked differences in instructional variables such as the use of structure and clarity by different teachers, multilevel modelling indicated that less than 1 per cent of the variance in pupils' progress was due to teacher or class effects. These findings were supported at the primary stage by Plewis (1991a), who investigated progress in mathematics in the Year 1 classes of two teachers in each of 20 London primary schools. The variation at the teacher (class) level was again very small, despite significant differences in coverage of the curriculum.

Why are there only limited differences between teachers?

One possible interpretation of these findings is simply that teachers do not matter very much. However, a more plausible explanation is that teachers are generally effective but that what they do is largely constrained by pupils' abilities, the curriculum and available resources. Teaching is a demanding, stressful job and the majority of people who start a teaching career actually leave during the first five years. It is likely that those who remain are at the very least able to cover the basic curriculum and manage classes; if they could not do this, teaching would probably be a very unpleasant experience for them. Perhaps it is not too surprising that if teachers have rather similar backgrounds and work in rather similar environments, the outcomes of teaching similar groups of children will be very much the same.

In the hurly-burly of classroom life, teachers appear to do more supervision than teaching, and as discussed earlier, they are normally able to have only very limited and superficial interactions with individual pupils. Since pupils work independently for much of the time, their progress is likely to depend mostly on their personal resources. These will include factors such as their existing knowledge and understanding, their motivation and involvement in learning tasks in school, and ongoing home support.

The fact that most people believe that teachers are important factors in pupils' learning progress may be due to the processes of 'attribution'. This is the tendency we have to assume that people and outcomes are causally related. Such assumptions may work well for us most of the time; for instance, if a pupil consistently turns up late for a lesson, then teachers will assume that he or she is doing so deliberately. The problem with this, however, is that we tend to over-attribute causes to people rather than the situation; a pupil may be regularly late because he or she has to help with clearing away in a previous lesson. When we think about teachers, we are aware of their role – to manage and educate children – and since we usually have very little other information, we simply assume that they are responsible for any educational outcomes.

Teacher effects

Although the majority of teachers may achieve more or less the same sort of pupil gains, these do cover a range, with a few teachers consistently achieving better results than others. Studies of groups of teachers who are particularly effective have shown that some specific abilities or approaches tend to be associated with better student outcomes. Such differences are difficult to demonstrate, however, and can be found only by investigations which select and compare the more stable and the more extreme types of teachers.

One study by Brophy and Evertson (1976) first selected 165 teachers who were experienced in teaching at the grade level of their class. From achievement data for second- and third-grade classes over four successive years, 31 teachers whose classes showed the most consistent gain scores were then initially chosen. Their classes were observed so as to identify any teacher characteristics or processes which could relate to eventual differences in pupils' academic gains.

The main characteristics of these teachers were that they appeared to be businesslike and task oriented. Although they seemed to enjoy working with their students, they interacted with them mainly in terms of the teacher–student relationship. Classrooms were operated mainly as learning environments and the greater part of teacher time was spent on academic activities. Many of the least effective teachers were oriented more towards personal relationships and social objectives for their pupils, while others were disillusioned and mainly concerned with authority and maintaining discipline.

Effective teachers also seemed to have a personal responsibility for their students' learning. They would increase their efforts when pupils had difficulties and change their teaching or develop new approaches when necessary. They also seemed to have a strong sense of self-efficacy and a sense of control over what they were doing.

Important teaching processes were mainly those which ensured that pupils spent the greatest possible time in active involvement with academic activities. In the classes of effective teachers, work was generally well prepared and classes ran smoothly, with only brief transitions when necessary. Assignments were also well matched with students' abilities (meaning some individualisation of work), and students who needed help were able to get it when necessary.

Behavioural difficulties were dealt with quickly and effectively, with effective teachers rarely blaming the wrong student. They were also more likely to warn than threaten students and were less likely to use personal criticism or punishment. Behavioural expectations were also made clear to students, and these were consistently followed through with reminders or demands when necessary.

Interestingly, there were curvilinear relationships between the level of difficulty of questions and pupil gains, peaking at about 70 per cent answered correctly for pupils of high socio-economic status. Optimal learning seemed to occur when students moved at a brisk pace but in small steps, so that they experienced continuous progress and high success rates. These averaged about 75 per cent when the teacher was present and 90–100 per cent when pupils were working independently.

Kounin (1970) has found that the ability to organise the various demands of the classroom and to be aware of all that is going on in it is another key element of teacher management and control. This has been termed 'withitness, and by using videotapes of teachers Kounin found a correlation of 0.62 between this attribute and the work involvement of pupils. The key to the ability of successful teachers to run effective classes was not what they did when problems occurred, but their ability to prevent and avoid problems in the first place. Teachers who did not have this quality would typically become engrossed in what they were doing and be unaware of what was happening in other parts of the room, leading to disruptions and interference with the learning process.

Silcock (1993), however, argues that such findings only confirm the need for teachers to fulfil their prescribed roles – to organise and to manage the process of education. Effective teachers are therefore those who simply provide pupils with the maximum opportunity to learn. This would imply that the main qualities which a teacher needs to develop are the ability to manage the range of social interactions which occur within school, and the basic craft, or knowledge and techniques that are involved in subject teaching.

Teacher development

One perspective proposed by Schon (1983) is that there are no real prescriptions for efficient teaching and that teachers are individually responsible for making sense of and adjusting to their own classroom environments. Desforges (1995), however, has argued that teachers in fact learn little from their experiences of teaching and that over the years all they do is to become more efficient at 'running off' their routine behaviours. A study by Bressoux (1996) compared novice (recently trained) teachers with teachers who had considerable amounts of experience. The advantage for the experienced teachers was only slight – amounting to less than 2 points for progress with language and mathematics (the tests had a standardised score of 100).

Most approaches to the training or professional development of teachers also appear to have only limited impact. Jones (1997) found no differences in the educational outcomes of trained as compared with untrained teachers for English and science, and found only small differences in the teaching techniques they used. Bressoux (1996) did, however, find that over one year trained teachers achieved an advantage of 3.37 points with mathematics, compared with untrained teachers, although there was no differential effect for language teaching. A study by Askew *et al.* (1997) of mathematics teachers also found no relationship between teacher effectiveness and attendance on short professional development courses.

Training which is more intensive and based on the use and practice of specific classroom skills does, however, seem to have a significant impact. In one project reported by Waters (1996), 15 primary schools which were given direct training and support with teaching and management skills showed gains in their pupils' reading attainments of up to 24 per cent. Moreover, Askew *et al.* (1997) found that mathematics teachers who had been part of longer-term continuing professional development (such as 20-day GEST programmes) achieved significantly higher attainments gains. One substantial programme described by Munro (1999) was unusual since it enabled teachers to link theoretical knowledge of learning theory with direct classroom practices. The programme led to major improvements in effective teaching techniques, and the pupils in the classes of these teachers made substantial gains, amounting to an effect size of 0.5 with pupils who were initially the lowest achievers.

Some studies have explicitly linked the findings from effectiveness research with improvement programmes. In the Missouri Mathematics Effectiveness Project, Good and Grouws (1979) first compared groups of effective and less effective teachers to identify important features which related to pupil gains. These were then used as the basis for training, which consisted of an initial 90-minute session to explain the programme, following which teachers were given a manual with detailed descriptions of how to implement the teaching ideas. Another 90-minute session part-way through the programme was used to respond to teacher questions and to react to any difficulties encountered. The key instructional behaviours involved were:

- the use of previews and reviews;
- basing teaching mainly around the meaning of concepts;

- the use of distributed and successful practice; and
- an emphasis on teacher presentation and explanation.

After two and a half months, the mathematical progress of classes whose teachers had received the training (the experimental group) was compared with that of other classes whose teachers were aware of the project but had received no training (the control group). Both groups made significant gains on a range of mathematical attainments, but the experimental group outperformed the control group by about 10 per cent. These gains were closely related to actual changes in teacher behaviours, indicating that such programmes can affect real-life and significant educational processes.

Individual teacher characteristics of self-efficacy and enthusiasm also appear to be related to effective teaching. Ashton and Webb (1986), for instance, report that a single question which assessed how well teachers felt they were able to affect learning accounted for 24 per cent of the variance in their pupils' scores in mathematics. Rosenshine (1970) found that teachers' traits such as enthusiasm and energy had correlations between 0.3 and 0.6 with pupil achievement gains. These effects are relatively high when one considers the generally limited effects of teachers on pupil progress. It is easy to see how teachers who have such an approach would be able to motivate children in the classroom, and one is reminded of fictional characterisations such as Jean Brody or the inspirational professor John Keating in *The Dead Poets Society*, whose effectiveness may therefore have some basis in reality. An important implication of such findings is that it may be important to ensure that teachers are empowered and enabled to perceive their own value, rather than to simply subject them to a system of externally imposed targets and accountability.

Evaluating teachers

It is worth emphasising again that the normal range of teacher effects is quite small and that the constraints of the teaching situation probably limit possible improvements. Despite this evidence, teachers are increasingly becoming subject to direct inspections and evaluations of their teaching competence. One way this happens is as part of Ofsted investigations, when inspectors observe teachers in lessons and grade their overall performance. These observations are rather brief, however, particularly in secondary schools, when they might cover only two or three lessons. Also, teachers know in advance when they are to be inspected, and such assessments are unlikely to be representative or valid measures of their normal teaching practice.

More importantly perhaps, under the new appraisal procedures (DfEE, 1998k), evaluations of teaching effectiveness by headteachers will become an important basis for judgements about competence and will be used to decide on levels of pay and future professional development. There is evidence that headteachers tend to agree about who are the most effective teachers, with Crocker (1974) finding that correlations between such ratings are generally greater than 0.7. However, research has shown that such overall assessments of teachers do not usually bear any significant relationship to the progress of pupils in their classes. In one investigation by Gray (1979), headteachers' ratings of teachers accounted for only 0.4 per cent and 0.1 per cent of the variation in infant pupils' reading gains over two successive years. Moreover, a study by Askew *et al.* (1997) found that several teachers who had been selected by heads as effective numeracy teachers turned out to be only moderately effective when compared with the remaining teachers in their schools.

One reason for such inaccuracies might be the attribution bias mentioned above. This could mean that heads might simply assume that any end-of-year results for a class are directly attributable to a teacher, without taking account of pupils' initial attainments, work habits or parental support. Such key, single judgements also tend to have 'halo effects', which means that they will tend to colour any other information. If a teacher is judged by a headteacher to have good organisation and control (if his or her pupils are rarely sent to the head to be disciplined), then he or she might be assumed to be a generally 'good teacher' and also to be managing all other aspects of the teaching process well.

Observations and judgements made by headteachers, inspectors or advisers will often have to be 'high-inference'. This means that the observer has to work out or infer what the teacher is thinking about, or means to do, from limited information. A teacher who is talking quietly to a single pupil and not paying attention to the rest of the class may appear to have poor class management skills. In reality, however, the class may be well rehearsed in a particular routine and the teacher may be using the highly effective approach of a private reprimand. In the absence of a more adequate basis, it therefore seems likely that appraisals and other evaluations will be relatively poor at discriminating between teachers.

There is also evidence that such biasing processes may be operating with general inspections, which are largely based on direct observations and judgements about the effectiveness of teachers. Pyke (1998) has pointed out that as assessed by take-up of free school meals, the 10 per cent of schools with the poorest intake are eight times more likely to fail their inspections than schools with average or below-average levels of poverty. Although one could argue that schools with poor intakes attract less effective teachers, this would not account for such a massive effect, and it could equally be argued that it is only the best teachers who can survive in such demanding schools. It seems much more likely that inspections are strongly biased by pupils' apparent abilities. When one observes a class which has a large proportion of low-achieving children whose behaviour, moreover, is problematic, it is tempting to infer that the teacher must have some responsibility for the poor state of affairs. It would be wiser, however, to base any judgements of teacher effectiveness on more objective information and to acknowledge the importance of factors which are beyond schools' control.

Summary

The school context appears to be an important factor in children's learning. However, evaluating the effectiveness of different schools and school variables depends on being able to take account of differences in the general standard of pupil intake. Techniques to help us do so depend on relating input to output measures and then comparing achievements with average (expected) gains. A more sophisticated technique known as multilevel modelling can account for variance in achievements at different levels of the educational system.

Such analyses have found significant differences between primary and between secondary schools and have related these to factors involved in organising and delivering education. The size of these differences is rather small, however, and typically accounts for about 10 per cent of the variance in pupil attainments. Such small effects are generally dwarfed by variations in pupils' abilities and initial attainments, as well as the ongoing effects of home background. But schools do have an absolute effect, and it may be possible to improve education by measures which involve balancing intakes and reallocating or increasing resources.

The physical environment of schools can have

minor but significant effects, with general layout and pleasantness facilitating pupils' progress. Open-plan designs can improve involvement and attitudes but have limited effects on attainments. Although schools usually have high densities of children, learning is negatively affected by high density only in the case of more active work, and if it is perceived as crowding. Noise also appears to have limited effects unless it is particularly intrusive. Some studies of the impact of school size indicate that larger schools are more effective, but this finding disappears when pupil intakes are completely controlled for.

Although the main types of organisational structures can be equally effective, there is evidence that learning can be better later in the school day. Also, pupils make better progress in classes if they are seated where they receive a greater proportion of teacher attention and when they are placed in rows to minimise distractions from other children. Groups can be organised to develop cooperative working and these can improve attainments, although they are difficult to set up and rarely implemented. It is more common to separate children by their abilities, and when this is done within classes it can lead to more effectively matched work. When used to set up different classes, however, separation by ability can lead to a number of negative effects, and benefits only the most able.

It is commonly believed that small class sizes are better for children's learning. Despite this belief, reducing class sizes within the normal range of possibilities has been found to have only a very limited effect. It is probably more effective to focus on effective class teaching approaches and to work with small groups (of less than six) when specific support is necessary.

Formal and progressive teaching styles are difficult to define and evaluate, although aspects of these such as discovery learning and direct teaching can bring about different learning goals. The increased advocacy and use of whole-class teaching has some limited basis in research findings, but this is only one aspect of effective teaching and is probably most suited to activities which benefit from direct instruction.

Although it may seem obvious that teachers are an important part of the educational process, differences between them account for only a small part (about 4 per cent) of the variation in pupils' progress. This is probably due to the various constraints of the teaching role and resources, as well as the overwhelming effects of individual pupils' abilities, attainments and home backgrounds. Teachers can improve their effectiveness, but only if they receive highly specific and intensive training and support. Teacher evaluations based on observation or personal knowledge have only limited validity despite the fact that they are increasingly used to determine important outcomes for teachers and schools.

Key implications

- The variation in pupils' attainments that is attributable to schools and to teachers is relatively limited.
- We should therefore be cautious in our expectations of the extent to which they can generate improvements.
- Physical and organisational factors can help, but only when they have a direct effect on the learning process.
- Major improvements in educational effectiveness are unlikely without radical changes.
- There is no evidence that the evaluation of teachers is a meaningful process.

Further reading

Maurice Galton, Linda Hargreaves, Chris Comber, Debbie Wall and Anthony Pell (1999) *Inside the Primary Classroom: 20 Years On*. London: Routledge.

This book gives a fascinating and direct insight into the processes which go on in schools and the ways in which they have changed (or remained the same) over a twenty-year period. Its examination of schools is set in the context of political and ideological pressures, and it evaluates the academic basis for aspirations towards the improving of schools' performance. Overall this is very 'teacher centred' and sympathetic to teachers' roles and the expectations made of them. A key text for anyone who is interested in learning about what really goes on in schools.

Laura Sukhnandan and Barbara Lee (1998) *Streaming, Setting and Grouping by Ability*. Slough: NFER.

Schools are increasing their use of ability grouping and yet this review finds that there is probably little to gain by doing so. This book carefully considers all the possible advantages and disadvantages of the different approaches and evaluates them using up-to-date research findings.

Practical scenario

An Ofsted visit to St Timmins' school is imminent and the head and governors are worried about what the outcome will be. A previous report was very critical of teaching and management and implied that educational standards were not high enough. SATs have actually gone down since then (because of a poor year's intake) and an initial visit made it obvious that the inspector was expecting things to have improved. The school has a poor intake (just over 30 per cent are on free school meals), but even given that fact, the head and governors feel that they have real, additional problems, given a catchment where there is very poor home support.

- *How could the school provide evidence that it is actually doing a good job? Is there anything which might persuade critical outsiders?*
- *Should the school have set up any major changes in its organisation in response to previous criticisms?*
- *Given that the pupils have relatively limited attainments, is there anything that individual teachers can do when their teaching is evaluated?*
- *What do you think that the education authority should do to support this school?*

7 Society and culture

Chapter structure

Society
Culture and schools
Sociological perspectives

Social psychology
Roles and norms
The self
Social behaviours
Developing social knowledge

The functions of education

Social disadvantage
Home background
What matters – culture or poverty?
Can education compensate?

Gender
What is gender?
Gender inequalities
Origins of gender differences
Why have girls improved so much?
Qualitative differences between girls and boys
Why aren't boys doing better?
Improving boys' attainments

Ethnicity
Race
Ethnic background
Ethnic differences in achievement
Where do differences come from?
Ethnicity and gender
Reducing discrimination
The successes of pupils from ethnic minorities

Society

Psychological perspectives often bring with them a tendency to ignore the wider social context. Most educational psychology focuses at the level of the individual and how people make sense of and react to their environment. In reality of course, the educational system is part of society and this relationship can have a strong effect on what schooling can achieve. Also, as we have seen, theorists such as Vygotsky believe that the process of education is essentially the development of children's knowledge and understanding of the social culture in which they live.

Culture and schools

According to Linton (1945), the culture of a society can be defined as 'the way of life of its members; the collection of ideas and habits which they learn, share and transmit from generation to generation'. The process of developing this in children is often referred to as socialisation, and education is an important part of it. The more *formal* and explicit aims of education are to develop the knowledge, skills and understanding laid down in the curriculum. Quite apart from what is taught in lessons, schools are also important in terms of the *informal* processes which establish the social identities and behaviours of pupils. These come from the influences of peer contact and values, the general social structure of schools, as well as the processes of management and control within the school.

The process of enculturation does more than just transmit information; it also establishes shared values and beliefs which are necessary for society to function. The relative nature of enculturation is not always apparent, and a particular perspective can seem to be obvious or 'common sense' to people who are raised within a particular culture. Much of what is learned, such as gender roles and our own relationship to them, is also quite subtle. As described later in this chapter, we learn indirectly through observations of the behaviours of others and particular forms of language. The possibility of alternative perspectives and ways of behaving is often apparent only when we look at different cultures, in other countries or at other times. Some of these differences, such as the high level of conformity in the educational systems of some Pacific Rim countries, can seem rather alien to a person who has grown up in Britain, but this is a key part of those countries' general belief in the importance of communal life rather than the individual.

Education is affected to a great extent by general cultural influences since pupils and staff bring their existing beliefs and values to schools. The pre-school years are a critical time for the establishment of basic ideas, and even when children are school age, the majority of their waking hours are still spent out of school, with powerful continuing influences from the family, peer groups and the media. The role of schools is also increasingly open to pressures from the wider society, with recent educational reforms aimed at giving more openness and greater choice to parents.

Sociological perspectives

Sociology complements individually based explanations by emphasising social structures, processes and shared meanings. These can be seen as parts of a complex and interdependent system, whose individual components have certain functions and needs and which tends to achieve and maintain an overall equilibrium. According to this perspective, known as 'structural functionalism', changes can be difficult to achieve, and what individuals think and do is largely determined by their position within society.

A problem with this sort of approach is that it tends to be rather mechanistic. It does not seem to take account of the ability of individuals actively to think about and to construct and reconstruct their social realities. An alternative perspective, known as 'social interactionism', emphasises the changeable and local nature of social experiences and the importance of processes such as discourses (how we define and talk about things) and specific narratives in defining meanings and self-concepts.

Both these perspectives are important in providing a context for psychological explanations. The earliest functionalist approaches tended to emphasise the determinism of an individual's position within society, with psychology accounting for the ways in which people adjusted to this. However, interactionist perspectives have enabled psychology to describe people as conscious thinkers who are able to define and alter their social environments. It is difficult to argue against the importance of structures in society, but these do not necessarily perform their ostensible functions. They are also made up from individuals who are able to some extent to determine their relationships to these structures and with each other.

Social psychology

Social psychology has traditionally attempted to explain social functioning by considering how individuals operate according to their immediate social context. There are a number of areas, however, where it becomes meaningless to distinguish between psychology and sociology, and the most effective approach is to use explanations which inform both societal and individually based perspectives. *Symbolic interactionism* is one important such approach, and is based on the early work of the social psychologist Mead (1934). He believed that our most important psychological features are the ability to use the *symbols* involved in language and social meanings, and that our social identity is developed from our *interactions* with other people, based on the use of these symbols.

Roles and norms

Mead also emphasised the importance of *roles* in determining such social behaviour. These are expectations about a certain position within a social structure and can be seen as the building blocks of society. Individuals can fill a number of different roles. For example, a pupil in the educational system is also usually a son or daughter, as well as a member of a peer group. Roles carry expected behaviours called *norms* that are associated with them; as far as the school is concerned, basic normative behaviour is that pupils will sit quietly and work in lessons. Behaviour which fulfils these norms is called *conformity*, and most of the time roles and norms are powerful ways of understanding and predicting what people will do. Zimbardo (Haney *et al.* 1973), for instance, carried out a role-play experiment simulating a prison, and showed that student volunteers could very rapidly take on and conform to the roles given to them. The 'guards' in particular soon behaved in a brutal way that was not typical of their normal personality, punishing and isolating the 'prisoners' for minor infractions. Their behaviour was such that although the simulation had been planned to run for two weeks, it had to be stopped after only six days owing to the severe reactions of the 'prisoners'. These included depression, uncontrollable crying and fits of rage. The students seemed to have no difficulty conforming to roles which they had never filled before, and were impelled to continue with these despite the negative experiences some of them had.

When people fail to conform to a group's norms, they are often rapidly subjected to social pressures to fit in. Early investigations by Asch (1951) placed people in situations where their judgements (about the lengths of lines) were consistently different from those of a group of other people around them. Under this pressure, the subjects regularly changed their stated opinions, even when they were right. The other people in the groups were actually stooges of the investigator and had been instructed before the experiment to make incorrect judgements. They also reacted negatively to any of the subjects' 'incorrect' judgements with non-verbal responses such as looks of surprise, or even brief noises, which the subjects appeared to find quite uncomfortable. The knowledge that other people in the group apparently had different perceptions and judgements seemed to make the subjects embarrassed and anxious. This pressure presumably forced them to agree with the main group and also to alter their beliefs if there was some ambiguity about the stimuli (when the lengths of the lines were in fact quite close).

People generally seem to be anxious about the social effects of disagreeing with normative beliefs and values, and they probably have good cause to do so. Going against a group's norms is a challenge to the identity of the group and its members and can therefore lead to extreme behaviours to either exclude the individual or to induce conformity. Many norms are of course formalised, particularly when they are part of the agreed social structure in some way. In schools these become *rules* for behaviour and are often written down and displayed for pupils to see. By law (the School Standards and Framework Act 1998), schools in England and Wales are now directed to set up home–school agreements to ensure that parents also agree about what their children should do.

Many other norms are informal and originate from peer groups, particularly from the age of about 8 years, or from wider social influences such as the media. Many of the problems in schools arise when norms are in conflict in some way – if immediate peer group pressures lead to behaviours which are a challenge to formal school expectations. Girls' developing gender roles may, for example, lead to their adopting behaviours which are hard for schools to tolerate. Measor and Woods (1988) describe how some girls refused to wear safety glasses in physical science lessons in order to maintain some distance from a non-feminine subject. As will be described later in this chapter, the norms of many boys' groups can also represent the antithesis of values which schools advocate, and such 'non-conformity' can undermine the possibility of academic progress.

The self

Goffman (1959) extended these ideas and studied the way in which people generally use roles in life, to present a conception of their self to other people. This 'self-presentation' can be seen as a kind of theatre and acts as the basis for a great deal of our social behaviour. Mead has argued that we develop this sense of self from the reactions of other people to us, and through trying out different roles. For example, young children might play at being 'parents' in the house corner of a reception class, or older pupils might adopt a style of dress or behaviour that fits with a particular peer group. Doing this enables children to see themselves as being different from other people and to understand the nature of different roles in society.

Both Goffman and Mead believed that our 'selves' are very much the combination of the roles that we adopt or are socialised into. Tajfel (1981) similarly argues that our sense of identity is largely a product of the social groups that we are part of. Known as *social identity theory*, this view means that we need to emphasise these groups in order to maintain our self-concept. This may involve denigrating an 'outgroup', with some boys' groups condemning others for being 'wimps' and by doing this emphasising their own 'toughness' and in-group identity.

Maintaining such differences between groups can entail making inferences about linked characteristics, for instance that doing well with academic work means that you are a subservient 'lick'. This type of association of beliefs is termed a *stereotype* and is the basis for prejudice (usually negative attitudes about others) and discrimination (the behaviour which can result from prejudice). Stereotypes can easily develop from obvious physical differences such as skin colour or gender. These lead respectively to racial and to sexual discrimination, both of which can be important in schools, as well as the wider society.

Social behaviours

Schank and Abelson (1977) believe that our expectations of what is appropriate social behaviour can be understood as a form of *script*. A script is a type of schema which determines the general sequence of the interactions in a given social situation. It also incidentally emphasises that in some situations we probably have limited choice about our actions. Many of the interactions in school involving teachers and pupils can be seen as fitting such scripts. A typical secondary lesson, for instance, involves pupils entering the room, listening to the teacher, getting out the appropriate books and following the normal sequences of events in that subject.

Roles, norms and scripts are useful because they enable people to predict and understand social behaviour. Secord and Backman (1964) describe the way in which roles also usually have *role partners* with shared expectations (norms) about their interactions. The teacher–pupil relationship, for instance, has the teacher in a position of authority, with the responsibility of organising pupils and passing on information. The pupil's complementary role is to accept this authority and to fulfil expectations about work and behaviour in class. Following the directions of a figure in authority in this way is known as *obedience*, and Milgram (1974) has shown that people will obey authority figures even when unusual or extreme demands are made on them. In a series of investigations, he found that the majority of people would follow instructions to administer what they were told was a dangerous electric shock, so long as they perceived themselves to be in a subordinate role.

Such power relationships are important since they enable hierarchical structures to operate. These are important in the education system since it is based upon relatively few teachers directing and managing large numbers of pupils. When a pupil (or teacher) fails to conform to the more normal behavioural expectations in school, his or her behaviour is often a cause for concern since it interferes with the normal process of transactions. Individuals who do not follow such expectations are therefore often labelled 'abnormal' and literally excluded to enable the normal social processes to continue. The 'free school' movement was an attempt to restructure such relationships in schools, although such schools have had difficulties meeting the educational expectations of normal society.

Individuals have a range of different roles, and the expectations associated with these can often be in conflict, resulting in *role strain* for the individual. An individual boy may feel that he ought to work hard to fit in with the role expectations of his parents and teachers. However, such behaviour may not match with the masculinity norms of his peer group, which view working hard as being weak and subservient to authority. The resulting mental conflict (termed *dissonance*) could be resolved by secretly working hard, or by disengaging from one of the roles and emphasising the other. As an example of this, Hargreaves (1967) has described the process by which the failure of some low-band pupils to meet the academic and social expectations of school led to the development of a negative subculture. This rejected the values of school and the wider society, and within these groupings, self-esteem was based on reacting against the norms of the predominant culture. Attempts by the formal school system to control individuals, such as formal punishments, were seen by the group as ways of achieving status. Indeed, there was often competition within the group to see how many punishments each member could get!

As summarised in Figure 7.1, behaviours can be seen as largely determined by individuals' positions within a social structure, and constructed by them to confirm and manage their sense of self-identity. Unfortunately, as mentioned earlier, a functionalist perspective of this kind tends to give a rather rigid and deterministic view of what

Figure 7.1 Social processes in schools

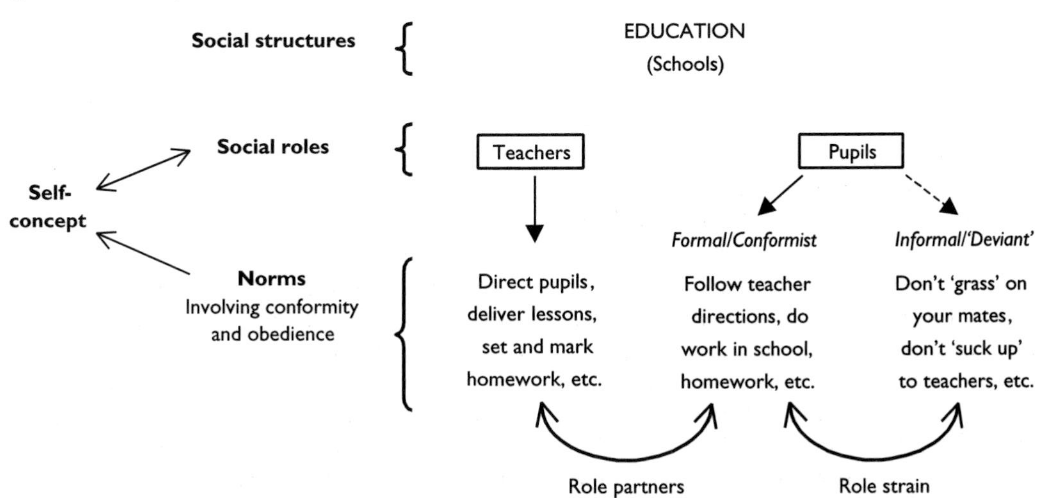

people are and what they can do. A more interactionist perspective would emphasise that our roles and identities are often open to negotiation. Teachers could therefore adopt a relatively egalitarian approach, and discuss with their classes which classroom rules are important. There are limits to such an approach, however, and pupils will usually be aware of what is expected of them and may actually find a lack of adult control and direction uncomfortable.

Developing social knowledge

Bandura *et al.* (1963) argue that children learn social expectations and behaviour largely from observing what others do. This process is called *social learning theory* and involves developing knowledge about what is appropriate or possible in particular situations. In their original investigations, Bandura *et al.* (1963) demonstrated that children were more likely to be aggressive when they had observed others behaving in this way. The studies involved showing children films of an adult either playing aggressively with a 'Bobo' doll (a blow-up toy which can be knocked down and then rebounds) or playing quietly with some other toys. Children were then shown some attractive toys, but frustrated by being prevented from playing with them. Finally, the children were allowed to play with the 'Bobo' doll and their actions were recorded.

The main findings from these studies were that children who had observed the adult acting in an aggressive way played more aggressively, and that they carried out the same actions that they had seen the adult using. Bandura *et al.* also found that whether children imitated behaviour depended on whether they saw it as relevant to them. This involved whether the model had the same gender, age or ethnic role characteristics, and what the children perceived would be the likely outcomes for them. If children believed that a certain behaviour would have negative consequences, they did not have to experience those outcomes personally for the belief to inhibit that behaviour.

Wragg (1984) has found that in schools, critical incidents that happen early on in the relationship between teachers and new classes set expectations for future behaviour. His studies found that when minor transgressions by an individual child were promptly dealt with, the teacher's response acted as a signal for other pupils about how to behave with that teacher in the future. Wragg's work therefore gives some support to social learning theory and to the common belief among teachers that it is best to start off firm and relax later, as in the saying 'Don't smile until Christmas!'

The functions of education

From a basic structural-functionalist perspective, the educational system exists to teach an agreed body of knowledge to students, in order to enable them to operate within society. This is a largely common-sense approach, and most people would agree that one of the main signs that it is succeeding is for students to pass examinations. Examinations are particularly important since they enable students to access further education and jobs, with Ceci (1990) finding that the most important factor determining people's incomes was not their general ability but the amount and level of their education.

It is often argued that educational attainments are a vital foundation for a society's success, particularly in terms of economic functioning. The logic of such arguments appears to be self-evident since people at work need to be able to manage the intellectual demands that are made on them in order to carry out their job. They require basic skills such as literacy and numeracy, general knowledge and understanding of the world, as well as certain specific technical skills. The need for educational attainments can therefore be used as a justification for the need to improve educational standards, with national and school targets being set to achieve this.

Nevertheless, Robinson (1997) argues that international comparisons indicate that above a certain basic level of general competence, educational attainments do not appear to have any significant effect on countries' economic perfor-

Figure 7.2 Mathematics attainment in different countries and their subsequent economic growth

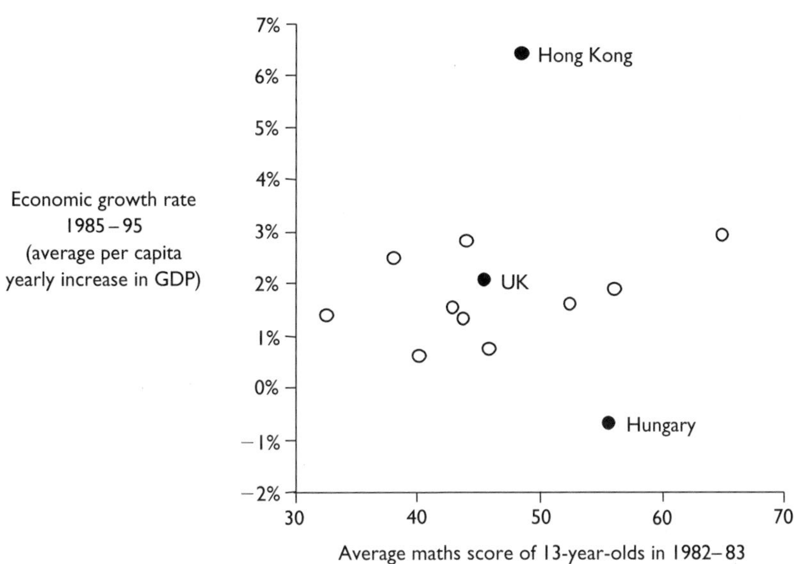

Source: Second International Maths Study (Robitaille and Garden, 1989) and *International Energy Annual* (1996)

mance. One example of this is shown in Figure 7.2, which relates secondary school achievements in mathematics in 13 different countries to those countries' later economic performance, when the individuals concerned would have become part of the labour force. Over the period covered, Hong Kong had much higher economic growth than the United Kingdom, despite having similar initial mathematics abilities. Other countries such as Hungary, however, had higher attainments but lower economic growth. It is likely that economic development in these countries was the result of a complex range of historical, structural and material factors. In many cases, such as that of Hong Kong, it is also likely that educational progress *follows* economic development, as a result of a country's increased ability to invest in education. The (apparently mistaken) belief that education is largely responsible for economic development is probably due to people's psychological need to look for simple causes of things.

This is not of course to say that education cannot, or does not need to, establish useful knowledge in its students, merely that it appears wrong to expect education to solve a country's economic problems. Some people argue that the main functions of education are quite separate from economic and even academic goals. Education, they believe, exists largely to inculcate a society's norms and values and to reproduce its general structure, in terms of economic and class relationships.

Social disadvantage

Beliefs about the economic importance of education can also lead to concerns that one's own country may be underperforming in certain basic skills when compared with other countries. In fact, it is often difficult to compare like with like, but a major survey of 41 countries – the Third International Mathematics and Science Study (1996) – found that the overall performance of children in England, for example, tended to be in the mid-range. England also had above-average scores for children's ability to apply maths and science skills in real-life situations.

What does tend to stand out, however, is a large 'tail' of underachievement for English pupils, which is generally nowhere near as marked in other countries at a similar level of economic development. Reynolds and Farrell (1996) describe the way in which this relative diversity is found with even the younger groups that have been studied in international comparisons. This indicates that this underachieving group is not just produced by schooling, although education may consolidate it. Mortimore and Whitty (1997) argue that this underachievement is related to the underlying inequalities existing within English society and is shown by increasing levels of relative social disadvantage. In 1979 about 10 per cent of all children were living in poor households (judged by having a family income at half the national average). In 1993–4 however, the proportion had risen to 32 per cent, compared with the European Union average of 20 per cent.

Home background

Children's educational progress appears to be strongly determined by their home backgrounds, as we have seen from earlier chapters. One way of evaluating the effect of home background is in terms of their families' social class, and although this can have many different meanings, it is often assessed by parental occupation or income. A number of studies have found a significant link between such measures and children's educational progress. On average, in English schools 19.8 per cent of primary children and 17.5 per cent of secondary school children are eligible for free school meals (DfEE, 1998j), which are given to families with a low income. Free school meals are therefore a measure of family poverty and can be used as an indirect measure of low social status.

Free school meals (FSMs) do account for a significant amount of the variation in children's educational abilities. Gorard (1998), for example, found a correlation of −0.87 at school level between the overall school level of eligibility for FSMs and GCSE attainments. However, the correlations between measures of social status and *individual* children's attainments are much lower than this. A typical study by Thomas (1995) found that pupil background measures accounted for only about 20 per cent of the variance at pupil level for Key Stage 1 results.

A further problem is that the majority of such effects are largely accounted for by children's initial abilities, and Plewis and Goldstein (1997) estimate that socio-economic variables account for only about half as much variation as do measures of prior attainment. A possible explanation of this is that initial attainments are more important because they are the direct basis for further progress. They are also a result of early support, which will presumably continue to some extent while children go through school. Social class and measures of poverty such as entitlement to free school meals may have only a limited direct relationship with academic attainments, but, as discussed below, they probably have significant indirect effects through their influence on children's experiences in the home.

The underlying processes which determine children's abilities and progress appear to be largely related to the quality of their home environments, in particular the nature of adult management and interaction. This is supported by findings such as those of Hart and Risley (1995), who studied the verbal interactions between parents and their children from 10 months to 3 years of age. As was described in Chapter 4, these measures showed a relatively large correlation of 0.78 with the development of general cognitive abilities. Other aspects of Hart and Risley's study showed that these early interactions also accounted for 61 per cent of the later variance in verbal abilities at ages 9 and 10 years. This is a very strong effect for long-term prediction at this age and is consistent with the idea that early language-based experiences have a continuing causative impact on general cognitive development.

Hart and Risley found that measures of socio-economic status by themselves were able to account for only 30 per cent of the variance in general verbal abilities at 9 and 10 years of age.

As shown in Figure 4.4, a large part of this effect was attributable to the fact that the poorest families on welfare almost invariably had the lowest quality of parent–child verbal interaction in the home. It involved an emphasis on negative control, parental rather than child-centred topics, and a generally reduced level of talk. From Hart and Risley's observations, this pattern of interaction appeared to be part of a culture that was concerned with established customs and where obedience, politeness and conformity were likely to be the keys for survival. Parents seemed to be preparing their children for lives which were similar to the ones which they had experienced themselves, where success would come not from knowledge and skills, but from attitudes and actual performance.

What matters – culture or poverty?

Some investigators have concluded that such patterns of interaction within the home are relatively stable and that they tend to be reproduced over successive generations. Adults who are the product of such cultural environments may therefore repeat the cycle with their own children, providing limited stimulation and low expectations. This 'cycle of deprivation' has proved resistant to compensatory programmes such as the largely school-based Educational Priority Area initiatives which were set up in the United Kingdom in the late 1960s. Initial analyses of the Head Start programme in the United States similarly indicated that early programmes of support did not improve children's progress.

A key issue, though, is whether such features are characteristic of the culture of a particular class, or whether they are an adjustment to the long-term effects of low social status and poverty. This is important, since if the main problem is that of a deviant or impoverished class culture, it should be possible to re-educate children out of this and to break into the cycle. If, however, the main driving force behind inequalities comes from the social and economic structure of society, it is less likely that this could be affected by any limited educational intervention. A famous comment by Bernstein (1970) that 'education cannot compensate for society' summarises this last perspective, and moreover it can be argued that attempts to drive up standards by setting targets for the educational system are merely a diversion from the real problems of society. Such beliefs are also supported by Mortimore and Whitty (1997), who review findings that educational improvements usually increase stratification since socially advantaged children usually benefit the most, leaving less advantaged children even further behind.

Although parent–child interactions may be the most direct cause of inequalities, it seems likely that family experiences of poverty and low status are important underlying factors. As Mortimore and Whitty (1997) describe, when there are limited and variable financial resources, it becomes pointless to plan ahead, encouraging a basic, reactive approach to life. The lack of control over key resources and careers also engenders a form of learned helplessness and a sense of apathy. It is easy to see how parents in this situation would tend to utilise negative control with their children if they feel that there is little that can be achieved in life. The parents' perceived lack of control is also likely to limit their ability to take account of their children's learning needs.

There are also more direct effects on children, in terms of poor-quality housing, heating, clothing and nutrition. These lead to an increase in health problems in low-income families which can affect general development, school attendance and learning. As we have seen, Kleinman *et al.* (1998) found that children from poorer backgrounds who were regularly hungry in school had a range of educational problems and were twice as likely to have special educational needs.

Poverty also restricts children's wider experiences, and Oppenheim (1993) has described how it can affect children socially and emotionally. Without any money, it is difficult to meet friends, and activities such as visits to the cinema or other treats are restricted. Lack of transport means that trips out are limited and many families will rarely go on holidays. Life in this situation can mean often being bored and resorting to low-level entertainment such as watching television or playing video games. Although information technology could be a liberating influence, there are signs that its uptake and usage are also strongly related to home background. Scales (1999) has reported that in 1996 only 32 per cent of the lowest-income groups had a home computer, compared with 56 per cent of the higher-income groups. Also, two-thirds of computer use in lower-income households was merely for games playing, whereas nearly half of their use in the higher-income groups was for educational purposes such as helping with homework or finding out information.

Such findings indicate that poverty is a major driving force underlying cultural deprivation and limiting educational progress. Robinson (1997) therefore concludes that 'potentially the most powerful "educational" policy might be one which tackles social and economic disadvantage. A serious programme to alleviate child poverty might do far more for boosting attainments in literacy and numeracy than any modest interventions in schooling' (p. 17).

Can education compensate?

There is a danger that such conclusions can lead to a form of paralysis since it seems unlikely that there will be any major changes in British society to prevent or to compensate for structural or economic inequality. However, if is not just poverty, but the *effects* of poverty that are responsible for educational inequalities, this leaves open the possibility of direct action aimed at the processes by which the effects occur.

Unfortunately, this is a rather daunting task and one which is generally beyond the normal remit of the educational system. From the findings of Hart and Risley (1995), the differences between the language backgrounds of children can also be quite massive, with those from the most impoverished homes having only one-third the vocabulary experience of children in professional families. The general findings about the nature of early learning and language development covered in Chapters 2 and 8 also indicate that learning is best when it forms part of children's own environments from the earliest stages and that it needs to be closely related to their personal experiences.

Given the difficulties which achieving such criteria involves, it is perhaps not surprising that many attempts to overcome inequalities have appeared to be relatively ineffective. It may also be that many of these approaches were simply aimed at the wrong level (schools rather than home background) and were not long-term enough to have an impact. Many of the initial Head Start projects, for instance, lasted only for one summer vacation and were mainly based on providing additional stimulation in a specialist centre. Subsequent analyses such as that by Barnett (1995) have shown that those parts of the programme which were more lengthy and based on home support did have significant and lasting effects.

Even short-term programmes which encourage positive involvement by parents can have a sizeable impact. Whitehurst (1994), for instance, found gains of up to 10 IQ points in the vocabulary scores of 3-year-old children when their parents worked with them using a programme of interactive picture-book reading. A more extensive early EPA project in Yorkshire described by Smith (1975) also established significant gains which were equivalent to about four months' mental age. In this case the intervention involved a one-year home-visiting programme for children aged between $1\frac{1}{2}$ and $2\frac{1}{2}$ years of age. After the programme finished, parents continued with the language interaction and play techniques that they had developed and the group maintained their developmental advantage through to schooling.

It seems likely, then, that although educational disadvantage is closely related to family class and poverty, it is still possible to compensate for this to a significant extent. Intensive school-based programmes can also have a strong effect, and *nurture groups*, as devised by Bennathan and Boxall (1996), can re-create the management and care in school that would normally be provided by an adequate family. Nurture groups are set up as classes in the ordinary school with about 12 children and 2 adults, and with an emphasis on developing predictability for the children, together with a generally stimulating environment. An evaluation by Holmes (1982) found that children in a nurture group achieved an average gain of more than 10 IQ points over one year and made good long-term adjustment to schooling. A control group of matched children who did not receive this support showed no gains in their IQs, and the majority of these eventually needed some form of special education.

Early intensive programmes such as the High/Scope project described by Schweinhart and Weikart (1993) have shown that such effects can continue through to adult life, with groups that have received this support being more successful economically and having much less involvement with crime. An analysis of these findings also indicated that this programme generated an effective overall saving of more than seven dollars for every dollar that was initially invested in it.

Gender

What is gender?

Sex refers to the biological differences between individuals. However, *gender identity*, or a person's perception of which role it is that he or she fits into, is more important in determining behaviour and the various processes of socialisation. The possibilities of gender inequalities or discrimination in education are significant since they could form the basis for long-term problems with attainments or with social roles.

Gender inequalities

There are major gender inequalities within society as a whole, which affect both occupational success and financial rewards. A British review by the Equal Opportunities Commission (1995) showed that women in general earn considerably less than men, even within the same occupational group. Also, they are under-represented in the higher levels of many occupations, including promoted posts within teaching. As regards secondary schools, Howson (1998) summarised information showing that in 1997 women made up only about 25 per cent of secondary headteachers, although 52 per cent of all secondary teachers were female. About 55 per cent of primary school headteachers were women, but this also significantly under-represented the 82 per cent of primary teachers who were female. Subsequently, the proportion of new female primary headteachers appeared to have been increasing (up to 75 per cent in 1997–8). Even so, there were probably no improvements in underlying inequalities, since headships seemed to have become progressively less attractive at this time, with a general decrease in applications for vacancies. Female success was therefore probably due to reduced competition, with male headteachers still dominating in the higher-prestige (and better-paid) positions in larger junior and primary schools.

Educational processes

Various feminist writers such as Spender (1982) have argued that the foundations for such inequalities are laid down from the earliest stages of children's educational experiences, with gender imbalances being so much a part of everyday classroom life that girls receive only about one-third of the teacher's time. However, these assertions appear to have been based on unstructured observations which were probably unrepresentative of normal classroom processes. In a review of a range of empirical British research into primary classrooms, Croll and Moses (1990) found that girls in fact received about 46 per cent of individual teacher–pupil interaction time. Moreover, the great majority of teacher interactions were whole-class (involving both boys and girls), meaning that overall, girls were involved in 49 per cent of all interactions. Also, a significant part of any increased teacher attention which boys received was to control negative behaviour, since boys generated about twice as many such difficulties as girls. Interactions which are based only on control are unlikely to help with boys' knowledge or understanding, and might in fact mean that overall, girls really get more direct support with the curriculum.

It is more likely that the general content and discourses of the classroom incorporate and socialise children into traditional gender roles. One investigation of whether that is so by Davies (1989) looked at young children's responses to the narrative of an amusing feminist fairy tale. This involved a princess saving a prince from a dragon and then deciding that she didn't want to be married to him anyway. Children were able to imaginatively position themselves as the same-sex character but often had great difficulty relating to the roles and concepts involved. Many boys could not accept the idea that the female rather than the male figure in this story was the dominant character. Instead of this they focused on the prince's smart clothes, or reinterpreted the story as showing that the princess just got things a bit wrong.

Davies (1989) argues that the normal structure of beliefs, narrative, images and metaphors which are part of children's normal everyday lives in schools reinforces inequitable male–female stereotypes. Further observations of classroom practice supported the idea that teachers also tend to use terms of address and teaching practices which position girls as being more fragile and dependent than boys.

If there are inequalities in the way in which girls and boys are treated within school, then it seems likely that these would result in different educational progress. Early investigations of whether that is the case focused on the difficulties that girls experienced, with the possibility of discrimination and restricted educational opportunities. This possibility was supported by the fact that in the past, although overall examination pass rates differed little between boys and girls, boys tended to perform better in the more technical areas, which could arguably lead on to higher-status careers. Maccoby and Jacklin (1974) also found low academic expectations about girls' achievements, from parents, teachers and the pupils themselves, which could contribute to their poorer performance in some areas. The nature of the curriculum itself has perhaps tended to exclude the experiences of girls in important areas such as science and mathematics, which often use examples that are more familiar or positive towards boys. Bilton *et al.* (1996), for instance, reviewed findings that illustrations in science textbooks and other materials portrayed four male characters for every female. There has also been evidence of many informal discriminatory processes operating, with Lees (1987) reporting that various levels of sexual abuse and harassment of girls were common features of school life.

One approach to counter such problems has been to educate girls separately. Single-sex schools for girls do tend to achieve good overall academic standards, but a review by Arnot *et al.* (1998) concluded that most of this effect is probably due to the fact that their intake is relatively selective. Most parents who seek out this type of education are relatively supportive and their children would probably achieve well whatever school they went to. Mael (1998) found evidence in some studies, however, that single-sex schools can overcome gender-typing, with girls in such schools being more likely to choose to study high-status technical subjects.

Educational attainments

Such concerns about girls' achievements have diminished with findings that since 1986–7, along with showing a general improvement in examination performances at GCSE level in England, girls began to progressively outstrip boys across the range of subjects (Figure 7.3). As can be seen, until about 1987 there were no real differences in overall achievements. Since that time a gap has developed. It stayed relatively constant over the 1990s, with a roughly 10 per cent advantage for girls. There has therefore been increasing concern about this difference, leading to various initiatives to boost the attainments of boys. As the graph shows, however, these were still to have any general impact by the time of the 1999 examination results.

Figure 7.3 Comparison of GCSE achievements of boys and girls over time

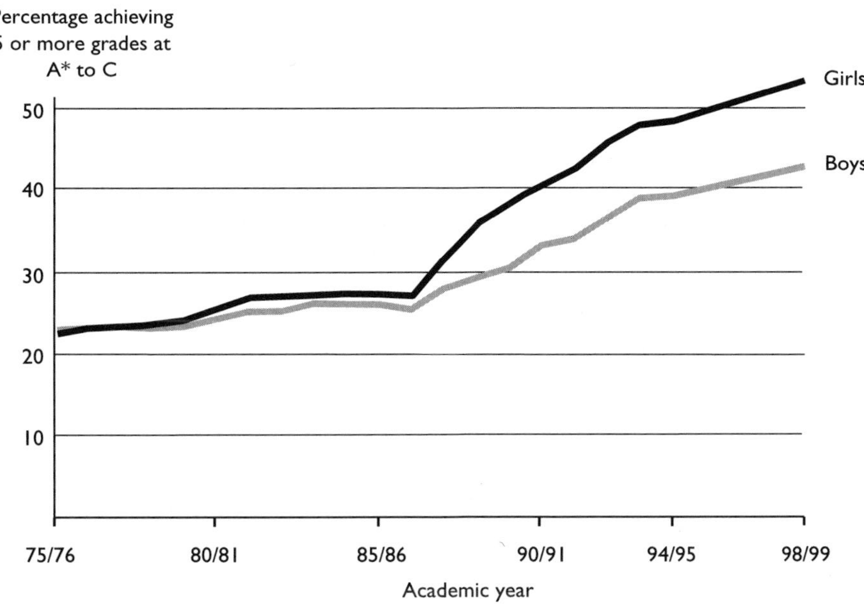

Source: Social Trends (1979, table 3.1) and DfEE (1999g)

Arnot *et al.* (1996) also carried out an analysis of trends in examination success for different subjects from 1985 to 1994 when this gender gap was developing. They found that girls had increased an initially small lead in subjects such as history and geography and reduced the lead of boys in science and mathematics to a minimal level. Girls also maintained their significant lead in subjects such as English, art and design, and social studies. By 1997 girls were outperforming boys in virtually every subject at GCSE, including mathematics and science (DfEE, 1998i). Gipps and Murphy (1994) also summarised evidence from the early SATs that girls were on average achieving above boys at the Key Stages 1 and 2 (ages 7 and 11) in all the core subjects of English, mathematics and science. There were more boys, however, achieving at the highest grades in mathematics and science, although at the lowest grades there were more boys still.

About half of 16- to 18-year-olds are in full-time education and training (*Social Trends*, 1996), which includes further academic studies (such as A levels) and also vocational courses (such as RSA, BTEC, City & Guilds, and NVQs). With A levels, the pattern of increasing female success is repeated, and in 1996–7 17.2 per cent of young women aged 17 years achieved three or more examination passes, compared with only 15.2 per cent of young men of the same age (DfEE, 1997d). For the various vocational qualifications, however, Arnot *et al.* (1996) found that females had significantly lower achievements than males, although young women's achievement levels were improving with respect to the more recent types of qualifications such as NVQs. In higher education, women's participation also overtook that of men, with women making up 38 per cent of the student body in 1980–1 but 52 per cent in 1997–8 (DFE, 1994a; and DfEE, 1998d).

Despite this, males tend to achieve a greater proportion of the higher grades and to follow higher-level courses in further and higher

Table 7.1 Higher-level qualification statistics for 1997

Qualification	Males	Females
'A' grades at GCSE A level	19.3%	18.2%
First-class degree	7.8%	6.4%
Ph.D.	6.8%	3.4%

Source: Based on data from DfEE (1998d)

education (Table 7.1). However, they also achieve an even higher proportion of the lowest grades, which brings their overall level of achievements below those of females.

Major gender differences also appear after secondary schooling, in terms of the different *types* of educational studies and vocational options. Young women start to move towards verbal and caring-oriented areas and male students towards more technical areas such as science, engineering and computing. Although these differential career paths appear to determine the foundation for the differences which exist within society as a whole, Croll and Moses (1990) argue that these are choices dictated by women's differential life chances and expectancies of their future careers, rather than just being forced on to them by educational experiences.

Origins of gender differences

Many of the behavioural differences between girls and boys are present from an early age. Croll and Moses (1990) found that by the time they reached school age, girls were generally much better than boys at subjects which involve language skills and that they were generally better motivated in school and considerably more favourably regarded by their teachers. Boys on the other hand were found to be typically more socially assertive and over-optimistic about their achievements.

Biological differences

Research reviewed by Brannon (1996) indicates that there are biological differences between the brains of males and females which appear to be due to the early presence of male or female hormones in the developing foetus. Adult males, for instance, have brains which are on average about 100 cm^3 larger than females', although the difference is probably related to body size and there is no apparent relationship between brain size and ability. Other findings are that females have a significantly larger corpus callosum (which connects the two halves of the brain), that a part of the hypothalamus (called the sexually dimorphic nucleus) is larger in males, and that male brains are more 'lateralised', with certain functions being more concentrated in one half of the brain. Unfortunately, the significance of these possible biological differences is still unclear and there are no proved links with actual behaviours.

If there were any behavioural differences between very young girl and boy babies (before upbringing could have an effect), then this could be taken as evidence for the influence of biology. Bee (1992), however, reviews evidence showing that there are no evident differences, for example in early temperament such as 'cuddliness' or 'sootheability', although baby boys are generally more active.

Differences between the sexes in more complex behaviours which develop in older children might alternatively be due to the *development* of underlying biological differences. They could also be due to children's being brought up in different ways, and this is therefore a classic 'nature versus nurture' problem that is difficult to resolve. It is a problem that has important implications for the educational process, since if differences are inherited, then perhaps education should work with and support gender specialisations. Girls could be directed towards subjects needing verbal and literacy skills and boys towards more technical subjects. However, if differences are developed by socialisation and these lead to inequalities, with girls being disbarred from high-status careers, then perhaps education should attempt to reduce these differences.

Differences in socialisation

Some 'natural experiments' support the idea that gender differences can overcome biological predispositions. This can happen where children have been socialised in the opposite gender role as a result of having ambiguous physical characteristics. Money (1986) has reviewed a number of such cases and concludes that children can successfully adopt the socialised gender role of the opposite biological sex if this begins when they are still young (before 3 years of age).

Other evidence shows that parents actively encourage what they perceive to be appropriate gender-specific behaviour in very young children. Frisch (1977) found that adults would treat the same 14-month-old infant in very different ways according to what they thought the child's sex was. If they were told that the child was female they would typically be limiting and protective, encouraging verbal interaction and reflection. Alternatively, if they were told that it was male, they allowed much greater independence and encouraged higher levels of physical play and spontaneous actions. Unger and Crawford (1992) also review evidence that from an early age boys are usually given technical, physical and construction-type toys, while girls are given dolls and drawing or painting materials. The sexes are also encouraged to develop early gender-specific recreational activities, such as boys playing football and girls going to dance lessons.

By the time they enter the infant school, children already appear to have a well-developed sense of gender role, which is reflected in the strong early bias for children to choose same-sex interactions when they are allowed to do so. Galton *et al.* (1980), for instance, found that over 80 per cent of pupil–pupil interactions in primary schools were with the same sex and that these arose from choice rather than teacher-directed groupings. Also, Croll and Moses (1990) review evidence showing that such differences are the basis for a certain amount of gender differentiation in the organisation of teaching, for example with competitive tasks divided between boys and girls. They conclude, however, that such differentiation does not result in any disadvantage to girls in the key areas of access to the curriculum and learning progress.

Why have girls improved so much?

One suggested reason for girls' improved examination attainments has been that earlier syllabus changes meant that GCSEs could be achieved mainly through coursework, which might favour conscientious and hard-working girls. This seems unlikely, however, since although coursework marks were cut back sharply in 1994, as Figure 7.3 shows, the change did not subsequently affect the relative examination advantages for girls.

Arnot *et al.* (1996) trace the relative improvement in girls' achievements as occurring after the passing of equal opportunities legislation in the 1970s, which was followed by a number of measures initiated by local education authorities and separate schools to combat various forms of inequalities. These have involved discouraging sexism by teachers and other pupils, and by encouraging equal access to the curriculum. Also, research carried out by Whyte *et al.* (1984) indicates that the perceptions of gender roles by teachers and pupils were changing at this time, a change that may have been due to these measures. On the other hand, there have also been more general changes in society's attitudes, which may have been more important, including more freedom for women and a widening of possible social and occupational roles. Whatever the reasons behind the academic improvements of girls, the very fact that they have been able to catch up with boys in traditionally male specialisms at GCSE is strong evidence for the flexibility of any underlying differences in male–female abilities.

Qualitative differences between girls and boys

Despite the overall improvement and superiority of girls' attainments, there is still a different *pattern* of male–female achievements, with girls doing relatively worse in the more technical subjects such as science and mathematics, as compared with subjects such as English. Some explanations for girls' relative lack of success in these subjects have centred on possible differences in underlying cognitive skills, with girls having better basic verbal abilities and boys having better mechanical and spatial abilities. However, although earlier research did find such differences, longitudinal research by Feingold (1988) established that over the period from 1947 to 1980 these progressively fell to non-significant levels. Moreover, Brannon (1996) reviews evidence that these abilities are strongly influenced by practice, and that if girls do worse with spatial assessments, this might simply be because they have had less experience with mechanical-type tasks.

Other explanations for differential achievements have largely been based on sex stereotypes and sex role socialisation patterns. According to such explanations, there could be generally higher social expectations for girls in verbally based subjects and a belief by girls themselves that it is more appropriate for them to do well in such subjects. Bandura (1986) has proposed that higher self-efficacy will lead to increased motivation, effort and success. One would therefore expect there to be differences between boys and girls, in terms of their academic self-concept and their achievements in different subjects. A study by Skaalvik and Rankin (1994) supports this expectation, finding that middle school girls had a higher self-concept for verbal areas which was in line with their actual superior performance. Girls also had a significantly lower self-concept in mathematics than boys, even though their achievements were in fact at the same level, which matches with the idea that maths is not an area where girls are supposed to do as well as boys.

Why aren't boys doing better?

Since boys have failed to show the same improvements as girls, an important gender issue has been to identify key reasons why they have failed and ways in which this new inequality can be addressed.

Non-conforming boys?

One argument is that for whatever reasons, boys are less likely to conform to the norms of the classroom and school. This is supported by aspects such as the generally higher level of behavioural difficulties which boys present. Evidence indicates that boys receive twice as much verbal criticism in class and they are also many times more likely to be excluded from school or to need special education for behavioural problems. Croll and Moses (1990) found that girls are generally more liked by teachers and are seen as more motivated and helpful.

The general pattern of examination achievements also supports this argument, with the distribution of males' achievements at various age levels tending to be more 'spread out' than females'. If males are less affected by educational behavioural norms than females, then this seems a likely explanation for the relatively large 'tail' of underachievers and the overall superiority for females. On the other hand, those males who are actively involved in learning may be studying more from their own personal interest than from any desire to conform. As was discussed in Chapter 5, this 'intrinsic motivation' is more likely to result in effective learning and, as illustrated in Figure 7.4, may produce the small proportion of high achievers who regularly outperform females.

Socialisation processes

From an early age, boys are certainly less motivated, are overly optimistic about their achievements, and are more likely to have difficulties with concentration and attention. Blatchford *et al.* (1985) have shown that such differences exist on school entry and are present throughout primary education, implying that they could at least partly be the result of early home-based socialisation. However, the primary school is also a largely female environment, with the majority of teachers and helpers being women. Research summarised by Mussen *et al.* (1990) emphasised the possibility that boys' low level of involvement in educational tasks at the primary level is due to the lack of appropriate male models and a curriculum that is mainly interpreted in a female gender-biased way.

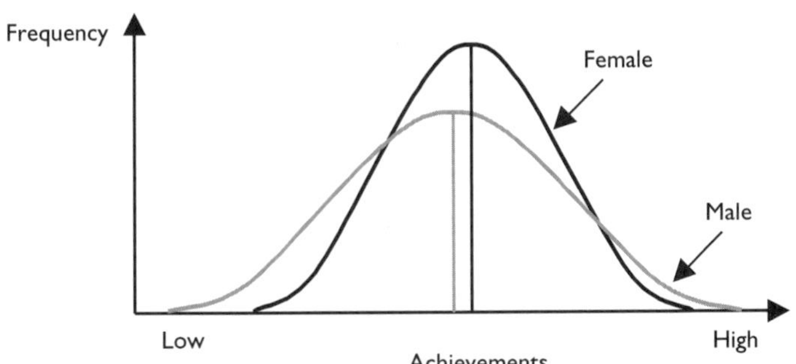

Figure 7.4 Relative distribution of male and female achievement scores

This analysis was supported by the findings that when early teaching is carried out by men, the achievements of boys become much more similar to those of girls. In an exploratory study, Woolford and McDougall (1998) followed the reading progress of two parallel junior classes, one of which had been taught by a male teacher and the other by a female teacher. Although there were no overall differences in achievements between the two classes, the boys who had been taught by a man achieved at a higher level than those taught by a woman, and the girls who had been taught by a woman achieved at a higher level than those taught by a man. One would need a broader and more controlled study to confirm these findings, but they do support the possibility that both sexes were affected by their educational context and that an optimum approach would be to balance out such gender influences in some way.

Gold (1995) reviewed evidence that in the secondary school, boys' GCSE achievements are even lower than would have been predicted on the basis of their underlying skills on secondary transfer (five years previously), implying that there are additional handicapping factors present in the secondary school. The key factors which identified underachievers were mainly poor attendance and misbehaviour, with a picture emerging of a group of boys 'generating an ethos of not working hard at school, going out in the evenings, rather than staying in to do homework' (p. 13).

This 'macho culture' has been identified by Salisbury and Jackson (1996) as a key feature preventing academic progress since boys can see hard work and achievement as running counter to the beliefs which determine their emergent sense of masculinity and group membership. Even when boys are motivated to achieve well in school, Gold (1995) indicates that they may lack the understanding and skills for additional studying. One possible reason for this is that boys identify with the male model of their fathers, who typically come home at the end of the day and do not continue with any other work. Girls on the other hand see their mothers continuing to work at home in the evenings and therefore have the expectation that effort and work continue outside formal times.

Improving boys' attainments

Bleach (1998) reports on a number of initiatives that some schools have carried out to achieve greater equality for boys. These often involve a higher level of monitoring and support with an emphasis on active involvement. One particular middle school mentioned by Gold (1995) also reverted to the use of books full of adventures and violence, which had previously been weeded out in the name of equal opportunities. The boys apparently then became more involved with reading, and at the next set of tests their achievements had caught up with those of the girls.

Since boys' achievements are probably limited by a peer group culture which emphasises non-academic values, this culture might be tackled by involving them in different socialising experiences which will link them in with the values of the school. One approach can therefore be to use successful males as academic mentors to act as credible role models and to advise on studying techniques. A review of general mentoring practices and outcomes by Miller (1997) did find positive academic and social outcomes for such schemes, with boys achieving slightly better gains than girls of just under half a GCSE grade for each subject taken.

Experiences which place more of an emphasis on positive shared values are also likely to counter any culture that might limit pupils' achievements. A review of the effectiveness of 'Outward Bound'-type courses by Hattie *et al.* (1997), for instance, found an average effect size with male-only groups of 0.40 for a range of personal and academic outcomes. Short-term outcomes were similar for female-only groups but the male groups showed a much greater 'follow-up' effect size of 0.21 compared to the female groups' 0.09. This was in addition to the original effect, and indicates that male groups particularly can benefit from subsequently using what they have learned to become part of their normal lives.

There have also been signs of some 'catching up' of boys with the 1999 Key Stage 2 English SAT results (DfEE, 1999c). Although the achievements of boys were still behind those of girls, the number achieving at level 4 or above increased by 8 per cent, whereas girls improved only by 3 per cent. One reason for this may have been the impact of the new literacy hour, which emphasises class teaching. This might have brought the involvement of boys closer to that of girls, and implies that boys may benefit from greater supervision and direction in other subjects as well as literacy.

Ethnicity

'Race'

The term 'race' is commonly used to refer to people from apparently different biological and geographical backgrounds. It has been used as the basis for comparisons of intellectual abilities and to support stereotypical judgements, in this case that certain physical features are linked with specific patterns of thought and behaviour.

One example of such comparisons is Herrnstein and Murray's (1994) review of the basis of intelligence and its population distribution, related to social factors and race. Rushton (1997) has also reviewed a number of studies which he believes support the concept of race and indicate that there is an evolutionary continuum, with Asians and Africans on opposite ends and with Europeans in the middle. Both these books conclude among other things that intelligence is largely inherited and that African Americans in particular have a lower intellectual potential. Not surprisingly, such beliefs have been widely challenged by researchers such as Kamin (1995), who argue that the majority of their evidence is flawed. One particular problem is that IQ tests tend to be based on and reflect a particular white, middle-class culture which is alien to some ethnic groupings. Labov (1979), for instance, has identified the use of different language dialects as being part of this process. Certain items, such as the Information subtest of the Wechsler Intelligence Scale for Children (WISC), certainly depend upon specific experiences and knowledge which may be unfamiliar to a child from an ethnic minority group living in an impoverished inner-city area. Because of this, Jensen (1963) has argued that we should adopt a more 'culture-fair' approach to testing and has developed paired associate tests of learning ability which appear largely to reduce the differences between various groups in society.

As was discussed in Chapter 4, there is evidence that as African Americans have generally made social progress, their results on standard tests have shown marked improvements. Grissmer *et al.* (1998), for instance, have examined the rapid rise in the academic achievements of African Americans over the period from 1970 to 1990. The gains were more than double those achieved by the rest of the school population and appear to relate to improvements over that time in educational provision as well as in family and community environments. These findings support the belief that intellectual abilities and educational progress are strongly determined by both specific and general environmental effects. This belief implies that whatever differences exist are due more to social inequality than any inherent ability.

In practice, people with apparently similar biological heritage and from similar geographical regions may come from a range of cultural backgrounds with different languages, religious groupings and economic structures. Advances in genetics, as outlined by Rose (1996), have also shown that physical characteristics which are used as the basis of a great deal of racial distinctions are in fact the result of very small genetic differences, with little if any significance for abilities or behaviour.

Ethnic background

The collection of key cultural features that distinguishes a separate group of people is referred to as their ethnic background. In Britain there are a number of different immigrant groups, including a number from various parts of Europe. However, most emphasis has been given to those who are from more distant parts of the world and who differ visibly from the majority. These are commonly classified into African Caribbeans, Africans, South Asians (Indian, Pakistani and Bangladeshi) and South-East Asians (such as Chinese). Together, in 1996–7 these grouping made up about 9 per cent of the British population up to 16 years of age (*Social Trends*, 1998). Within this group, the largest single category was Indian (22 per cent), followed by Pakistani (21 per cent) and African Caribbean (11 per cent). All other categories made up less than 10 per cent each.

Many individuals in these ethnic groupings are now second generation or later, having been, born in Britain. It is therefore more accurate to refer to a group's particular ethnic *heritage*, although I have omitted the term in the rest of this chapter as using it each time would be rather cumbersome.

In many parts of the country, the general impact of these groupings may appear to be small when compared with gender issues and social inequality. However, over two-thirds of the ethnic minority population live in the four conurbations of London, the West Midlands, West Yorkshire and Greater Manchester, and in these areas the specific needs of ethnic minorities can become more apparent.

A key issue is whether people who belong to ethnic minorities are likely to be subjected to prejudice and discrimination in schools, which could result in academic failure and other problems such as a high level of exclusions. If this happens, it could lay the foundation for long-term social inequalities for ethnic minorities such as high levels of unemployment. Bevins and Nelson (1995), for instance, report that in 1994, young black men in London had an unemployment rate of 62 per cent, which was more than three times the rate for young white men in the same area.

Ethnic differences in achievement

With educational outcomes it is difficult to get a clear picture since the progress of ethnic minorities is not officially monitored. However, general concern about the apparent underperformance of ethnic minorities led to the Rampton (1981) and

Figure 7.5 Educational attainments of ethnic groups, 1981–82

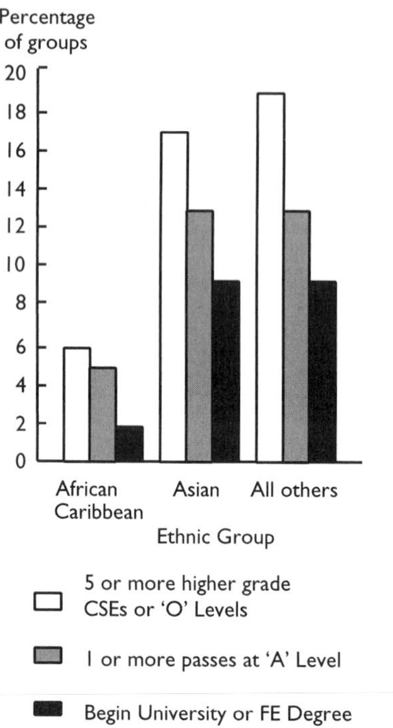

Source: DES (1985), based on data for 1981–2 school leavers, used by the Swann Report

the Swann (1985) reports, which summarised existing research in five local education authorities that had high proportions of ethnic minority students. Their main findings, illustrated in Figure 7.5, were that the general academic performance of African Caribbeans was lower at all levels but that of Asian students was quite close to the average of the population as a whole.

Drew and Gray (1990) have also reviewed ten studies covering the period from 1972 to the mid-1980s and concluded that African Caribbean students were performing less well than others, and typically achieved about one-third the average level of high-grade exam passes at 16 years of age. Nuttall (1990) also found that there were significant differences between different groups of Asian pupils, typically with Pakistani students being somewhat behind Indian students and with Bangladeshi students underperforming at all levels.

Despite the general improvements in students' GCSE results at that time, Gillborn and Gipps (1996) reviewed evidence that African Caribbean boys had not progressed at the same rate. In some areas of the country the gap had in fact widened, although Indian pupils in particular had started to achieve higher average rates of success than their white counterparts in some urban areas. Research in London, where a high priority has been given to equal opportunities, has shown an opposing trend, and Sammons (1995) found that African Caribbean students achieved as well as the white majority. This was a longitudinal study over nine years and showed that the early inequalities which were present at the junior school level had been largely overcome by the end of secondary schooling.

Difficulties with interpretation

A problem with these findings is that most studies have focused on areas containing large numbers of people of low socio-economic class, in order to achieve high representations of people from ethnic minorities. Such areas usually have examination results which are significantly worse than the national average. Comparing the achievements of those belonging to ethnic minorities with such standards will therefore underestimate their achievements relative to the country as a whole. A further interpretation could be that it is merely social class that produces educational inequalities, with African Caribbean and Bangladeshi children coming from the most socially deprived backgrounds. However, as shown in Figure 7.6, an analysis by Drew and Gray (1990) based on a nationally representative sample from all social classes showed that although social class had a major effect, there were still inequalities between ethnic groups when similar social classes were compared. African Caribbean pupils evidently did much worse than white pupils when similar social classes were compared. The effect was greatest for the lowest 'manual' grouping, which in this sample made up 59 per cent of the African Caribbean pupils and only 19 per cent of the white pupils, magnifying the differences between these groups as

Figure 7.6 Average GCSE examination scores by ethnic origin, gender and social class

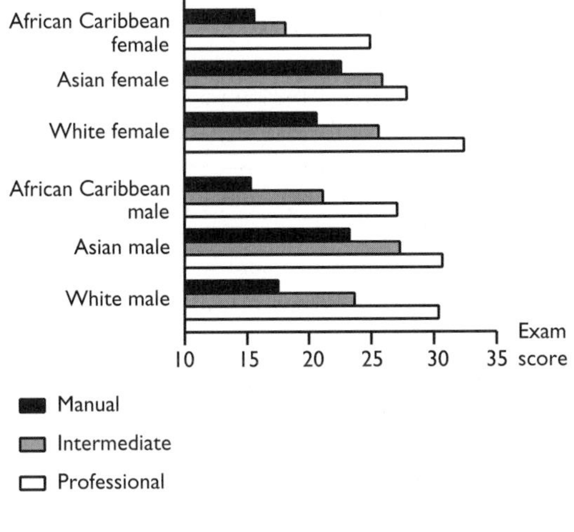

Source: Based on 1985 examination results from Drew and Gray (1990)

a whole. For Asian pupils, the picture was largely reversed since they tended to do significantly better across the social range, but particularly for the lower socio-economic groupings.

By 1998, statistics gathered on samples of 16-year-olds by the DfEE (1999e) found that the situation of some ethnic minorities had improved significantly, with Indian and Chinese/Other Asian pupils outstripping white pupils (Figure 7.7). Black and Pakistani pupils continued to lag behind, although they had closed the gap somewhat, and Bangladeshi pupils had improved dramatically from initially being at the lowest achievement levels to overtake Pakistani and black pupils. From previous statistics it seems likely that the lowest achievement levels are for the African Caribbean pupils, whose results in this study were combined within the category of 'black'.

Figure 7.7 GCSE results over time for different ethnic groups

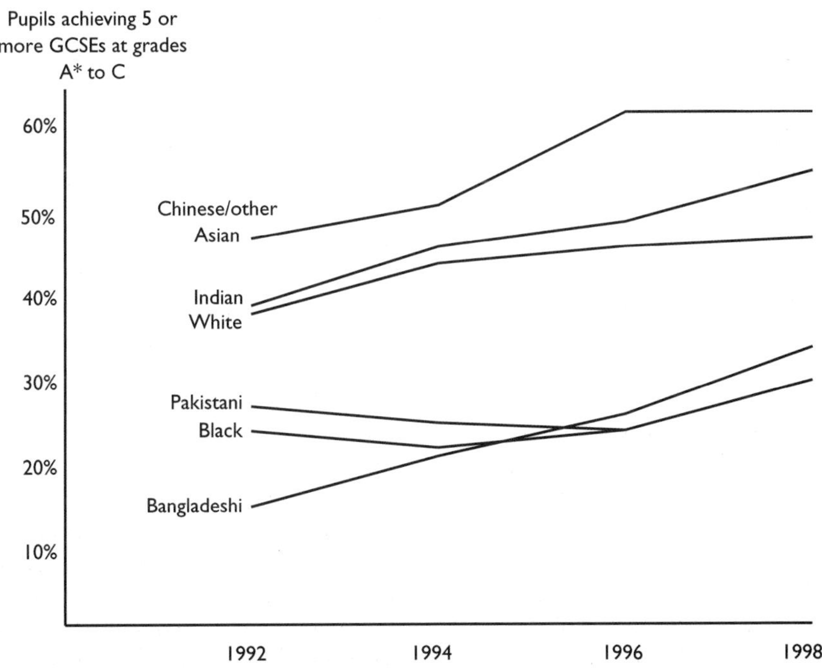

Source: Based on data from the 1998 Youth Cohort Study (DfEE, 1999e)

Where do differences come from?

The research described at the beginning of this section indicates that there are no convincing differences between the inherent abilities of different ethnic groupings. It may be, however, that there are early differences between the environments of children from different ethnic and cultural backgrounds which means they are more or less prepared for early schooling. This was not confirmed by Davies and Brember (1992), who found positive initial adjustments to nursery school for African Caribbean and Asian children; they did this better than groups of white children from the same geographical areas. Moreover, Blatchford *et al.* (1985) assessed all the African Caribbean and white children who started in 33 infant schools, and found that there were minimal differences in their early educational attainments and verbal abilities. In this study most of the differences between individual children appeared to be largely related to early parental involvement, with African Caribbean parents tending to help with reading more than white parents.

Language effects

Gillborn and Gipps (1996) have reviewed evidence that during infant and early junior schooling there were progressively greater differences over time between the educational attainments of ethnic groups. The differences seemed to be at least partly related to language background, with particular delays for South Asian pupils, who were most likely to be recent immigrants with a different home language. However, the South Asian group as a whole showed subsequent academic improvements during secondary schooling as their ability with the English language progressed. Language effects are not so much a factor with African Caribbean pupils, and some explanations for the underachievements of the latter group have centred on the possibility of negative expectations and discrimination in school.

Prejudice and discrimination

Prejudice and discrimination can certainly happen very rapidly between groups, based merely on perceived membership of one's own and other social groupings. In one famous demonstration of this, an American teacher Jane Elliot (Aronson and Osherow, 1980) divided her class into two groups simply on the basis of blue or brown eye colour. The brown-eyed children were initially assigned an inferior status, and the blue-eyed children almost immediately used this distinction to discriminate against them, with derogatory comments and social exclusion. These actions rapidly resulted in decreased self-esteem and poorer academic performance for the lower-status group. In schools there is a great deal of evidence that ethnic background forms a strong basis for such groupings, and that minorities will often react against this by exaggerating differences in order to establish a more positive self-concept. Mac an Ghaill (1988), for instance, has described a group of African Caribbean boys, 'The Rasta Heads', who used language and dress to establish a strong separate culture. Such groupings can run counter to the general ethos of the school, although Mac an Ghaill argues that they are a positive response to the pressures of racism.

Inter-group conflict also seems to be an important factor that can increase discrimination. In an early study, Sherif *et al.* (1961) studied the interactions between 11-year-old boys at a summer camp and found that setting up two groups rapidly led to the development of dangerous levels of inter-group rivalry. Brown (1986) argues that competition underlies most school processes and that equal educational status for children from different ethnic backgrounds is not possible since they are already separated by different socio-economic status. Gillborn and Gipps (1996) also review surveys which found significant levels of overt conflict between ethnic groups in schools, with the main victims being South Asian pupils. Most of this took the form of name calling but more serious incidents occurred regularly.

Although African Caribbean pupils have the greatest educational difficulties, a survey by Wrench *et al.* (1996) found that most of those in a sample they interviewed had relatively little to say about racism and harassment from other pupils. However, they did complain a great deal about problems they encountered with teachers, whom they saw as displaying a great deal of unfairness and injustice.

TEACHER PREJUDICE

Such teacher prejudice might of course be very important in determining children's educational progress, and could involve stereotypical beliefs. A teacher might believe that African Caribbean children are less able academically. This could then lead to teacher expectancy effects (see Chapter 5) which might result in discriminatory actions. Wright (1986), for instance, found that African Caribbean pupils were often placed in sets which were lower than would be warranted on the basis of their academic achievements. Moreover, various studies such as that by Gillborn (1990) have shown that teachers will typically use higher levels of negative control and criticise African Caribbean pupils more frequently than other groups, even when their behaviour is comparable. Exclusion rates for African Caribbean pupils are also much higher than for any other groups, and in 1996–7 were running at more than four times the rate for white pupils (DfEE, 1998j). Teacher attitudes are also different for particular ethnic groupings; for instance, Mac an Ghaill (1988) found that South Asian pupils were seen by teachers as more able and motivated, but also as rather 'sly'.

Foster *et al.* (1996) argue, however, that such findings do not necessarily prove the existence of discrimination. The use of negative control by teachers may be a reaction to higher levels of more assertive and difficult pupil behaviour. A study by the Runnymede Trust (1996) found that male African Caribbean pupils were more likely to question teacher requests and instructions, not as a form of insolence but from a desire to be treated with respect, which meant being given reasons and explanations, not just orders. Such behaviours are unfortunately different from typical class roles or scripted behaviours and can lead to conflict, even with black teachers. One possible reason for this may lie in the different African Caribbean family structures, with relatively more African Caribbean pupils coming from single-parent families. In 1989–91, for instance, 52 per cent of African Caribbean families with children had a lone mother, with the corresponding figure for white families being 15 per cent (Mackinnon *et al.*, 1995). A possible consequence of this could be that African Caribbean boys may have limited access to male models and roles in the home, and therefore, as they mature, they might be more likely to establish their sense of masculinity and self-esteem through peer groups. A study by Verma (1986) also indicated that African Caribbean boys received relatively limited educational advice or direct guidance from their parents and that their self-esteem was mainly derived from their peer group, with school achievements playing a smaller part. Despite these difficulties, Mirza (1993) argues, the family patterns of African Caribbeans are not pathological and the difficulties for African Caribbean children in school can be seen as mainly due to cultural mismatches. Although this may seem a rather negative perspective, it does imply that positive ways of helping African Caribbean pupils should take into account their own culture and that with boys it should emphasise ways of developing positive role models and peer groups which are able to incorporate the need for academic achievements.

Ethnicity and gender

Certain gender differences also cut across ethnic effects in an interesting way. Some early studies, for instance, found that African Caribbean girls did not appear to have the same examination handicaps as African Caribbean boys. These studies were carried out at a time before female achievements generally overtook those of males. Fuller (1980) found an explanation for this in the positive attitude of African Caribbean girls towards academic studies, which she attributed to their conscious reaction against the double discrimination of ethnicity and gender. The South Asian culture, however, appears to be much more patriarchal, with an emphasis on male achievements which is probably reflected in boys' better GCSE examination results. A study by Brah and Shaw (1992) found that a third of the parents of a group of young Pakistani Muslim women were completely against higher education for women. However, Bhachu (1985) found that other South Asian groupings such as Punjabi Sikhs do value education for women. The achievement levels summarised in Figure 7.6 also indicate that Asian girls still did as well as or better than white girls in the manual and intermediate social class categories, which at that time made up 94 per cent of the South Asian population.

A possible problem for South Asian girls is that they could be subjected to role strain since the traditional expectations of their community may be very different from the more open expectations and role models which they perceive in the ordinary school. Khanum (1995) describes the aspirations of a number of Muslim girls who resented the fact that only their brothers were encouraged to get qualifications. They saw the prospect of marriage as leading to the loss of their individual identity, and viewed their own fight for education as being a means of possible empowerment.

Reducing discrimination

Since discrimination appears to come from perceived differences and is increased by conflict between groups, Brown (1986) argues that it can be reduced by equal-status contact between members of those groupings, and by the pursuit of common goals which are achievable only by cooperation. However, as noted earlier, even when placed in direct contact in schools, ethnic groupings tend to separate out, in order to maintain their sense of group membership and identity. Moreover, ethnic groupings do not have equal socio-economic status, and the educational system is largely structured as a competitive system. One approach is therefore to accept this and to provide separate education to reduce conflict. Although American research has found that setting up ethnic minority community schools can improve achievements, Smith and Tomlinson (1989) found that British schools with a high local ethnic minority intake did not have better or worse results than other schools. There is also the problem that segregated education might perpetuate prejudice if this is based on ignorance of other ethnic groupings.

One specific approach to increase inter-group involvement has been the jigsaw classroom devised by Aronson *et al.* (1978). Within small, mixed-ethnicity groups, children are each given parts of a task which involves collaboration between the group members to complete it. Although this approach has been shown to reduce discrimination between children in the group, it tended not to generalise to members of other ethnic groups as a whole and the effects were rather short-lived. More general initiatives have emphasised the need for anti-racist and equal opportunities policies and for teacher education on these issues. This can, for instance, ensure that the curriculum takes account of the culture and experiences of ethnic minorities, that teachers are aware of the different cultural backgrounds of their pupils, and that additional resources are allocated to help areas with the greatest need. Sammons (1995) identifies major improvements in the attainments of ethnic minority children who were affected by such initiatives in the former Inner London Education Authority at a time when ethnic minorities in other parts of the country had not done so well. Targeted tuition and support can also make a significant difference, and the KWESI project in Birmingham (Klein, 1996) uses black adult male mentors to provide positive role models and counsellors for African Caribbean boys who may lack these influences in their lives. This scheme has achieved positive early results, reducing exclusions by 23 per cent (Social Exclusion Unit, 1998) and boosting pupils' self-esteem and academic success.

The successes of pupils from ethnic minorities

Although most research has focused on the difficulties experienced by ethnic minorities, South Asian and particularly South-East Asian groupings do achieve well. Caplan *et al.* (1992) carried out a detailed study of the reasons for such success with Indochinese refugee families, who initially had no exposure to Western culture or knowledge of the English language. The key feature that they found was that such children had highly supportive families in which all members participated equally in the learning process. Homework, for instance, was usually a joint family effort, and older children would often help to teach the younger ones. Clark (1983) identified African American students who were academically successful, despite low family income or only having a single parent. The key features again appeared to be that their parent(s) supported the school and teachers and that they structured their children's learning environment at home. Fuller's (1980) study of successful African Caribbean girl students identified an educationally positive subculture which accepted the need to do well at school, but which maintained their own identity. This can be much more difficult for African Caribbean boys, however, and Mac an Ghaill (1988) found, in case studies of successful male students, that their success was often at the expense of criticism from their peers.

In general, studies have tended to find that schools which are generally effective are also effective for ethnic minority pupils. One typical multilevel investigation by Strand (1999) looked at the academic progress of over 5,000 pupils in 55 primary schools. Despite the characteristic general finding that the particular school attended had a moderately significant effect on pupils' progress, there was no evidence of a differential school effect for a range of groupings, including African Caribbean pupils. However, Blair *et al.* (1998) were able to identify a group of 11 primary and 18 secondary schools which appeared to be particularly effective for ethnic minority pupils. These schools made a point of monitoring such children's progress and used a number of strategies to combat possible inequalities. Some of these involved links with the home and community, adjustment to children's needs, and strategies to improve attainments and reduce exclusions such as additional teaching and the use of mentoring schemes.

Summary

The educational system is part of the wider society. It involves enculturation and is influenced by social beliefs and values. Sociology explains this influence by emphasising structural aspects or interactionist perspectives.

Explanations in social psychology are based on people's roles, which have associated norms and generate conforming behaviour. Also, people work to present a concept of their self and to maintain the groups of which they are part. In schools, normal scripts and role expectations can lead to obedience to authority, or pupils can be influenced by peer groups to adopt a more informal and deviant role. People develop their knowledge of what is appropriate behaviour from observing and participating in social events.

The functions of education are ostensibly to transmit knowledge and to support society through educational performance. However, it is more likely that its true effect is to reproduce the norms and values and the general structure of society.

England has a disproportionally large number of underachieving pupils, a problem that is probably related to social inequalities. Children's home backgrounds are the probable cause of these inequalities and can be seen in indirect measures such as entitlement to free school meals, or more direct ones such as early abilities and parent–child interactions. Although differential expectations and values underlie such causes, these are probably generated by economic inequalities. Poverty also has more direct effects on children's experiences and life chances. It is unlikely that education can easily compensate for such differences, although intensive programmes can have a significant impact.

Gender inequalities are present within society as well as the educational system, although for school pupils inequality is mainly in the form of differential socialisation and role expectations. Academic achievements of females have progressively outstripped those of males, although there are continuing differences in the types of courses studied and at the higher levels of achievement.

There appears to be considerable overlap and flexibility in gender differences and only limited evidence of a biological basis for them. It seems likely, however, that different social experiences and expectations play an important part in their long-term development, and appear to underlie differences in achievements.

The relative underachievement and behavioural difficulties in boys are also probably due to a general lack of conformity to conventional norms and limited socialisation into roles which would support educational progress. Developing boys' attainments would therefore depend on matching educational experiences and establishing more educationally oriented masculine roles.

Although the term 'race' is commonly used to distinguish groups in society, it has no apparent biological basis, and differences largely depend on cultural background or ethnicity.

A significant proportion of pupils in British schools come from such ethnic minorities. These have been shown to have differential educational outcomes, with African Caribbean pupils and those from some South Asian groups achieving on average at the lowest levels. Their lack of success can be partly explained by low socio-economic class and language effects, but could also be due to the impact of prejudice and discrimination. However, although pupils from certain groups are more likely to have educational difficulties, this is not necessarily due to prejudice. Alternative explanations are based on a mismatch between schools' expectations and pupils' own roles, which are largely determined by peer group effects. Gender roles can also modify the experiences of ethnic groups and in particular appear to cause role strain for some South Asian girls.

It can be difficult to combat discrimination and unequal educational outcomes. However, one approach involves initiatives to acknowledge and incorporate ethnic minorities and by matching expectations with social roles. Pupils from certain ethnic minorities have shown a high level of success in the educational system, and some schools appear to be more effective than others in making their success possible.

Key implications

- Education functions within a social context.
- Social disadvantage appears to be the main factor in educational disadvantage. Schools cannot easily compensate for this.
- Gender issues in education are now focusing on the relative underachievement of boys, as well as the choice of subjects by girls.
- The educational achievements of pupils belonging to ethnic minorities have generally improved, although African Caribbean pupils continue to underachieve.
- Tackling inequalities in gender and ethnicity would need to be based on wider social roles and expectations.

Further reading

Michael Haralambos and Martin Holborn (1995) *Sociology: Themes and Perspectives*. London: Collins Educational.

Conventional psychological explanations are quite limited in accounting for the wider social context, and this book is one of the best for introducing relevant sociological ideas. Separate chapters cover education, gender and ethnicity and there is also a lot about the influence of social class and home background. As in most sociology, however, explanations tend to be somewhat generalised and abstract, and can be difficult to link with psychological perspectives.

Linda Brannon (1996) *Gender: Psychological Perspectives*. Boston: Allyn & Bacon.

A wide-ranging review of the form and basis of gender differences. Gives strong support for the role of socialisation and also looks specifically at educational influences.

Madeline Arnot, John Gray, Mary James, Jean Rudduck and Gerard Duveen (1998) *Recent Research on Gender and Educational Performance*. London: The Stationery Office.

A concise and readable review of the key research and findings in this area. It draws out implications for educational practice and evaluates possible strategies.

Dawn Gill, Barbara Mayor and Maud Blair (eds) (1992) *Racism and Education: Structures and Strategies*. London: Sage.

A collected set of readings for the Open University which give a range of approaches and opinions. Many of these attribute blame to the educational system and base possible improvements at this level.

Peter Foster, Roger Gomm and Martyn Hammersley (1996) *Constructing Educational Inequality*. London: Falmer Press.

A fascinating book which challenges many of the accepted wisdoms about the causes of inequality. It argues that a great deal of political debate has been carried out under the guise of scientific research, which has led to misinterpretations and failures to consider equally plausible explanations.

Practical scenario

Alltown Primary School is concerned about gender issues, particular the behaviour and achievements of boys. At playtimes there is often a lot of rough play, and football games can sometimes overwhelm the playground. In lessons, some of the boys are rather dominant and noisy, which can disrupt lessons. The school's overall SAT scores are generally representative of the rest of the country, with most of the boys achieving at a level somewhat below the girls. All the teachers are female apart from the head, who teaches two mornings a week.

- *Is there anything that could be done to structure and direct boys' activities at break times?*
- *Would it be possible to provide more positive male role models within the school?*
- *Should the school consider its curriculum, to make it more boy-friendly? How could this be done?*
- *Is there a danger that girls might be sidelined in these initiatives? How could this be prevented?*

8 Language

Chapter structure

The importance of language

There are many interconnected ways in which language can be seen as a central component of the educational process. Perhaps most importantly, language is the major way of forming and developing concepts, and using these to express understanding and to communicate with other people. Language therefore depends on, and is a basis for, learning and memory, as well as general thinking abilities. Because of its central role in education, English is a core subject in the National Curriculum of England and Wales, and children's progress is assessed at the end of the various Key Stages by means of SATs and the GCSE examinations.

What is language?

Harley (1995) defines language as 'a system of symbols and rules that enable us to communicate' (p. 2). Symbols are things that stand for something else. The most obvious form of language involves spoken words, although a great deal of information is also transmitted non-verbally. The use of rules involves combining those symbols in different ways, as with words in sentences. Doing so enables us to transmit the widest possible range of ideas or information from one person to another. Reading and writing are extensions of the process of verbal communication and depend upon it in different ways.

Linguistics is the scientific study of language. Part of this is the study of *grammar*, which deals with the form and structure of words (morphology) and the way in which they are combined in sentences (syntax). As shown in Figure 8.1, spoken and written language can be described at a number of different levels, ranging from the formation and use of sounds to overall structure, use and meaning.

Phonetics

There are more than 40 basic phonemes in the English language. The majority of these are con-

Figure 8.1 Structure of the study of language

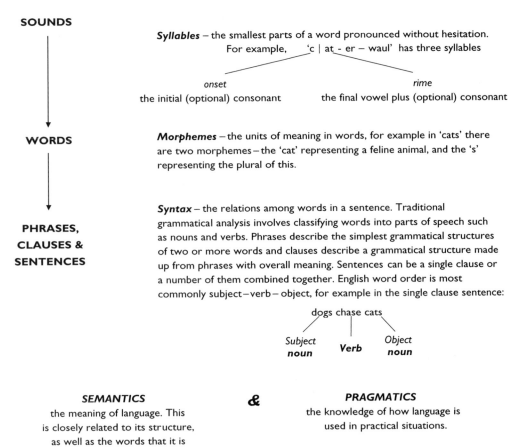

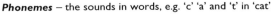

Phonemes – the sounds in words, e.g. 'c' 'a' and 't' in 'cat'
Syllables – the smallest parts of a word pronounced without hesitation.
For example, 'c | at - er – waul' has three syllables
onset
the initial (optional) consonant
rime
the final vowel plus (optional) consonant
WORDS
Morphemes – the units of meaning in words, for example in 'cats' there are two morphemes – the 'cat' representing a feline animal, and the 's' representing the plural of this.
PHRASES, CLAUSES & SENTENCES
Syntax – the relations among words in a sentence. Traditional grammatical analysis involves classifying words into parts of speech such as nouns and verbs. Phrases describe the simplest grammatical structures of two or more words and clauses describe a grammatical structure made up from phrases with overall meaning. Sentences can be a single clause or a number of them combined together. English word order is most commonly subject–verb–object, for example in the single clause sentence:
dogs chase cats
Subject **noun**
Verb
Object **noun**
SEMANTICS
the meaning of language. This is closely related to its structure, as well as the words that it is made up from.

PRAGMATICS
the knowledge of how language is used in practical situations.

sonant sounds and are formed by closing or restricting the shape of the vocal tract in some way. For instance, 'd' is formed by taking the tongue away from the alveolar ridge (just behind the teeth) while the vocal cords are active. It is known as a 'voiced' consonant; if the vocal cords were not active, the result would be the 't' sound.

The main vowel sounds are made with a relatively free flow of air and are formed by the shape of the tongue. For instance, the vowel sound in 'bed' is made with the tongue in a mid-position at the front of the mouth. Raising the tongue to a high position would instead produce the different vowel sound in 'bid'. Special types of vowels known as *diphthongs* are combined with a final glide where the tongue moves to a different position. In 'boy', for instance, the tongue moves all the way from the bottom back to the top front of the mouth.

Accents are distinguished mainly by having modified vowel sounds as in 'Received Pronunciation' ('posh' English). Dialects also make different use of consonants, as well as having a distinctive vocabulary and syntactic structures. Although a listener unfamiliar with a particular dialect may find it difficult to understand, dialects are used consistently by large groups of people and are normally as effective as other forms of the language in communicating meaning. Standard English is the dominant, high-status dialect in Britain and is required teaching as part of the National Curriculum. Whitehead (1997), however, argues that a child's dialect is a source of personal identity and self-esteem, and believes that although children should have access to Standard English (for example, through listening to stories), their own dialect should be given equal value. As discussed later in this chapter, although different social classes may use distinct forms of language, one form is not necessarily superior to another.

When sounds are distorted or missing, however, the intelligibility of children's speech can be affected, as is discussed later in the section 'Speech and language problems' at the end of this chapter. If children have problems with perceiving the sounds in words, this can also affect their ability to use sounds in early reading. Doing so appears to be particularly important in children's early use and awareness of syllables in words. Research by Bradley and Bryant (1983) showed that young children who had greater phonological sensitivity subsequently made better progress with their literacy.

Syntax and grammar

The general study of word order is known as syntax. Grammar technically refers to any form of rule-based system in language and applies to all levels of analysis, including the regularities in sounds, words, text and meaning. Traditional grammar is a particular form that is derived from classical studies of Greek and Latin. It involves analysing words into the main classes of nouns, verbs, prepositions, articles, pronouns, conjunctions, adjectives and adverbs. Rules then govern the way in which these are modified and form phrases and clauses, how these can be combined to form sentences, and the general organisation of bodies of text.

A prescriptive form of grammar can be laid down in textbooks and is currently incorporated to some extent in the National Curriculum. There is continuing debate about its value as a taught subject, in terms of the reality or otherwise of a static grammar and the value or lack of value that formal learning about grammar has for general language work.

Linguistics

The main purpose of language is communication: the transfer of meaning from one person to another to achieve practical purposes. Achieving communication must involve some structural system that is able to change thoughts into a form that can be spoken, and a reverse system of altering what has been heard, into its underlying meaning. Chomsky (1965) developed a well-known system of linguistic rules called a 'generative grammar', which governs how this can be done, involving the analysis of sentences into phrases and word classes. According to this approach, the sentence 'The boy kicks the ball' is a single clause with the basic underlying structure of somebody (the boy) carrying out an action, which is to kick the ball. This is analysed as:

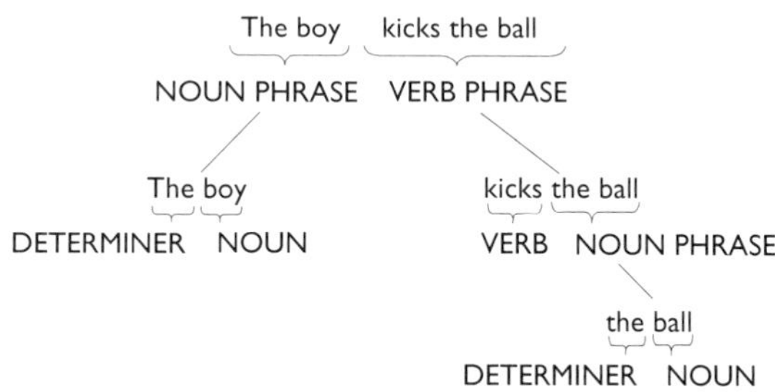

A system of rules applied in this way can account for our ability to produce grammatical sequences, and will rule out a sentence such as 'the boy ball the kicks', which is ungrammatical in English. Chomsky also believed that it is necessary for us to carry out processes called *transformations*, to simplify analyses and to relate together sentences with similar meanings but different structures. For example, the sentence 'The ball is kicked by the boy' has the same basic meaning as the sentence above but has a very different and more complex phrase structure analysis. This analysis is simplified by applying a transformational rule, which converts between the active sentence and its passive form. This particular rule is carried out by taking the second noun phrase, adding an auxiliary verb 'is', modifying the form of the verb, then adding 'by', followed by the first noun phrase.

Chomsky argued that spoken language comes from a *surface structure*, which is the output of the transformational rules and which can then be processed by the phonological system into speech. Underlying this is the *deep structure*, which is the output of the phrase structure rules and acts as the input to a semantic component. According to this approach, meaning therefore comes from the words in a sentence with information about their grammatical relationships and classes.

Early investigations gave general support to Chomsky's theory, with findings that sentences which have more transformations take longer to process. In the sentence 'Is Peter not chased by Jack?' there are three transformations, 'passive', 'negative' and 'question', and it is certainly very difficult to understand. However, Slobin (1966) showed that if there are meaningful relationships between actors and the actions they take, then the effect of this knowledge is greater than the effects of transformations. A passive sentence such as 'The cat was chased by the dog' is as easy to understand as its active form. We already have the general knowledge that dogs chase cats, so we do not have to carry out any additional syntactic work with the passive transformation to know this.

In general, it appears that we are able to use syntax for information, but that linguistic systems which rely on the use of syntax are looking only at our underlying *competence* – what we are technically capable of when necessary. Real-life *performance* with communication is likely to also be dependent on meaning, known as semantic information, and what we expect and understand from the general social context, covered as pragmatics.

Syntactic complexity does, however, affect ease of comprehension since it can interfere with our ability to use such semantic information. The use of multiple clauses, for instance, can make it particularly difficult to retain the overall meaning, particularly if they are embedded within the overall sentence. An example is:

'The dog who chased the cat which was sitting on the wall felt tired.'

By the time the receiver gets to the end of the sentence, it might be difficult to remember the initial phrase and work out which animal the 'felt tired' refers to. Since reading or listening has to be mainly sequential, this can place a load on our ability to retain such information. Frazier and Fodor (1978) therefore argue that language input is analysed by a model they named the 'sausage machine', because it divides language input into something like a link of sausages. They propose that owing to short-term memory constraints, only six words at a time can be initially processed for phrase structure, with a sentence analyser subsequently operating at a higher level.

Developments of the 'sausage machine' approach by Mitchell (1987) indicate that the first stage involves assigning words to an immediate syntactic category, and that we then make an early initial 'best guess' about what the likely phrase structure will be. The second stage then looks at consistency with other parts of the sentence and will modify the overall analysis if there is other compelling syntactic or semantic information. Such a process can account for many natural errors, such as those that occur in 'garden path' sentences. In these, we are 'led up the garden path' by the structure and meaning of the first part of the sentence; for instance:

'The cat chased round the house was tired.'

The verb 'chased' is ambiguous, and at first the simplest 'garden path' interpretation is that the cat was chasing. The final 'was tired' cannot meaningfully refer to the house and so the overall structure has to be reinterpreted. In reality, of course, people speaking or writing this would want to avoid such ambiguities and would go out of their way to make sure that the receiver understood their meaning. This can involve punctuation, by placing a comma after 'house', or even better by removing the ambiguity early on and adding the additional phrase 'that was' after 'cat'.

Speakers or writers can sometimes become overinvolved in their own understanding and lose track of the needs of the listener or reader. Young children, for instance, are very prone to simply rely on the conjunction 'and' when writing. Redrafting is therefore a useful technique, particularly if writers leave their work for some time and are then able to perceive the text from the perspective of a reader. Teachers can also be guilty of communicating in ways that are overly complex or ambiguous, and may need to monitor how they say things, or what they write.

Psycholinguistics

Linguistics by itself can only account for regularities in the structure of language and characteristics of a system which can either produce or analyse this. The complete study of language must also incorporate general psychological processes such as thought, knowledge and meaning, which are closely bound up with the nature of concepts as embodied in words. We can view word meanings as coming from a concept's place within a hierarchical structure, or as sets of linked semantic features, possibly as some form of prototype or schema. Connectionist approaches (see Chapter 2) are able to account for many of the features of schemas, with the advantages of flexibility and swift processing.

When receiving language input, we appear to rapidly identify individual words, according to Rayner and Pollatsek (1989) taking at most about 60 to 70 milliseconds for each one. This has been shown to happen by a combination of 'top-down' contextual information about what word is likely to occur in a particular place, as well as automatic 'bottom-up' analysis and synthesis of the word's structure. We then seem to have direct access to the features and associations of the concepts represented by words, which is borne out by a classic phenomenon known as the Stroop effect (Stroop, 1935). As shown in Figure 8.2, this involves asking people to read out the colour words are printed in, where the words are either the actual colour or a different one. When people are asked to say the name of the colour that the text is written in, it takes them significantly longer to do this with the top cards. The reason why that is so is that we seem to process both the colour and the word meaning automatically. When there is a difference, this produces a conflict or interference with what we are trying to do. This happens even after practice or with conscious attempts to 'block out' the unwanted information.

Once the meanings of individual words are activated, these must then be associated in some way to establish some form of thought process or conceptualisation. It seems likely that such conceptualisations can exist in a number of different forms, including direct representations of activities or as a form of imagery. As discussed later in this chapter, it also seem probable that thought can occur as a type of internal language at different levels, either as a conscious form of 'talking to ourselves' or as unconscious symbolic processing.

Constructing overall meaning from spoken or written language in this way involves a significant amount of interpretation and inferential reasoning. As well as understanding individual words, we need to form early hypotheses about the likely structure and meaning of sentences to enable us to make efficient predictions about what follows. Graesser *et al.* (1994) review evidence that people will tend to generally search for meaning in text by looking for goals and themes, for what causes things to happen and the emotional state of characters. This also apples to the structure of sentences, and one common inference is termed 'anaphoric reference', whereby a

Figure 8.2 'Stroop' cards

pronoun is used to refer to an earlier noun. For example:

'Tom hit Peter. *He* was angry.'

In this case, the word 'he' can refer to either Tom (who hit Peter because he was angry) or Peter (who was angry because Tom hit him). To decide which is meant, we would really need additional information on, say, what was already happening or the different personalities of Tom and Peter. When we do not have such information, there is a tendency to assume that a pronoun in this position will refer to the person carrying out the action; in this case that it was Tom who was angry.

Once we have derived meaning from what we have heard or read in a sentence, the specific form of the words is usually lost quite rapidly. Bransford *et al.* (1972), for instance, showed subjects sentences which incorporated certain logical relationships, such as:

'Three turtles rested on a floating log and a fish swam beneath them.'

After only a short period, they were unable to distinguish this from the following sentence:

'Three turtles rested on a floating log and a fish swam beneath it.'

It seems that when listening to the first sentence, people rapidly construct a mental representation which has the turtles on the log and the fish under the log, which is logically identical to the second sentence.

The surface content can sometimes be meaningful, however. Bates *et al.* (1978) found that people were often able to remember the specific words used in 'soap operas' when those words had a particular relevance for what had happened. This points up the fact that in natural conversations, different grammatical structures used are often used for a purpose. The use of the passive form, for instance, as in 'the dog was chased by the cat', emphasises that it was the dog that was being chased, and not the cat as would normally be the case.

Schemas

Our ability to understand text can depend to a great extent on general expectations and understanding. One way of describing such expectations is in terms of the activation of *schemas*. These have already been described in Chapter 2 as general ways of grouping together concepts or features in meaningful ways, for instance to represent particular events, situations or objects. Bransford and Johnson (1972) investigated how a schema could affect understanding of a passage where it was very difficult to work out what was happening from the text alone. Try reading this yourself and see what sense you can make of it:

> The procedure is quite simple. First, you arrange items into different groups. Of course one pile may be sufficient depending on how much there is to do. If you have to go somewhere else due to lack of facilities that is the next step; otherwise you are pretty well set. It is important not to overdo things. That is, it is better to do too few things at once than too many. In the short run this may not seem important but complications can easily arise. A mistake can be expensive as well. At first, the whole procedure will seem complicated. Soon, however, it will become just another facet of life. It is difficult to foresee any end to the necessity for this task in the immediate future, but then, one never can tell. After the procedure is completed one arranges the materials into their appropriate places. Eventually they will be used once more and the whole cycle will then have to be repeated. However, that is part of life.

When people read this passage by itself, they had great difficulty understanding what it was about and were subsequently able to remember only 2.8 ideas on average. However, when others were given the title 'Washing clothes' before they read the passage, they found it much easier to understand and were able to remember on average 5.8 ideas. The title evidently enabled them to interpret the meaning of the ambiguous information, in much the same way that advance organisers (an integrating preview of what is to be covered at the start of a study unit) have been shown to help with pupils' study and recall. Giving the title after the passage did not help with recall, indicating that the content of the passage had already been lost and could no longer be analysed.

Scripts

Interpretations about the meanings embodied within language can also come from types of schemas known as 'scripts', proposed by Schank and Abelson (1977). These are expectations of what normally happens and is appropriate in certain situations, for example in the process of 'going to a restaurant'. This would typically involve the social roles of being a customer, related to other roles such as that of waiter, and the sequence of events of entering the restaurant, sitting down, choosing from the menu, ordering then eating the food, then paying and leaving. Such expectations can have a strong effect on people's analysis and recall of verbal sequences, and when Bower *et al.* (1979) gave people different passages which described going to a restaurant, they found that people tended to distort their recall of the stories. The effect of this distortion was to make the passages fit in with what would normally happen. For example, the subjects would put in any additional features which had been missed out, such as the waiter taking the order. When the stories had additional features, such as the waiter bringing fish instead of steak, then these aspects were remembered well. This indicates that people tend to process and discard language when it fits in with what is already known, but analyse further and store information when it is new and meaningful.

Pragmatics

Pragmatics refers to the intended meaning and functions of what is said, rather than its literal meaning, and depends on our shared knowledge and understanding of social encounters. Children who are on the autistic spectrum (see Chapter 12) often have great difficulty in this respect since they appear to lack the ability to understand the thoughts and intentions of other people. A request by a teacher such as 'Can you open that window?' would therefore be treated as just a question and the child may merely answer 'Yes'. Such a reply can appear uncooperative or insolent if the teacher is not aware of the pupil's difficulties.

We evidently have to infer a great deal about what a person really means, and we do this using our knowledge of what is appropriate in certain situations, the intent of the person we are listening to, and social meanings and conventions. There are many situations where the surface meaning is unintentionally different from what is intended, but we can also make deliberate constructions, such as rhetorical questions, irony or sarcasm. The vast majority of simple requests are also indirect and become even less direct when people are trying to be polite. Rather than ask for a window to be closed, a person might therefore ask, 'Don't you find that it's getting a bit cold?' or 'Does anyone feel a draught in here?' Most people appear to understand such utterances immediately, indicating that their general knowledge of social-linguistic conventions and people's needs has primacy over direct linguistic and semantic interpretation.

In conversations there is usually a strong attempt by each participant to make sure that the other person understands what they are trying to say. This means that new content is often explicitly linked with whatever knowledge the other person already has, as in 'You know that girl in Miss Penn's class, who's always going on about her new trainers an' that, well, I saw her in town yesterday . . .'. This is also linked with a great deal of verbal information called 'prosodics' which involves emphasising different words, using pauses and different tones of voice, as well as general non-verbal behaviour such as eye contact, posture and gesture. These have a powerful effect, and have been shown by Mehrabian and Ferris (1967) to be used as the primary source about whether we believe what a person is saying. Eye contact is particularly used to structure the turn-taking of conversations, with the person who is talking looking away, then looking back at the listener to 'hand over' to them. The listener will also use eye contact as well as nods, gestures and sounds such as 'mm' to show that they are listening and in agreement. A characteristic feature of children who are on the autistic spectrum is that they make little eye contact and are often unaware that facial movements contain a great deal of information.

The development of language

The acquisition of language appears to most people to be a spontaneous and inborn process. There are in fact strong grounds for believing that humans are naturally prepared to develop some form of language and that children need only a certain level of language experience to develop basic abilities. However, there is also evidence that language development nevertheless very much depends upon experience and that young children need exposure to adequate language models as well as an interactive and supportive environment.

By the time children start school, most of them have already achieved an extensive functional vocabulary and have the basic range of grammatical abilities. Language abilities continue to develop in both these areas, however, and a key role of school can be seen as that of promoting children's general language progress, as well as language's use in studying specific areas of the curriculum. Even a subject such as mathematics, which one would imagine involves relatively independent skills is in fact dependent on words, concepts and relationships, particularly (in England and Wales) within Attainment Target 1, which often involves reading and talking about problems.

Behaviourism

One seemingly plausible explanation of the acquisition of language is that children merely imitate what they hear around them. Young children do seem to be capable of such mimicry from an early age, and Skinner (1957) has argued that this ability is developed by parents rewarding children, for instance with increased attention, when they repeat either words or phrases that they have heard. Skinner also believed that early sounds made by a child are selectively reinforced and shaped by parents' responses until they become words. The parents of a child who can say 'da-da' might respond more enthusiastically to the times when this sounds like 'da-dee', leading the child to gradually improve his or her pronunciation.

However, this process seems rather unlikely, since although parents are certainly responsive to what children say, they seem to respond mainly to the *meaning* of utterances, rather than their specific form, as we shall see. Also, learning of words and sentences does not seem to develop by a gradual improvement in accuracy, but often shows increasing errors as children develop and misapply language rules. The classic examples of this are overextending the past tense, as in 'goed', and with incorrect plurals such as 'mouses'. From the earliest stages, children also use sequences of words that they have never heard, indicating that rather than learning associations, they are building up grammatical rules that can generate novel combinations of words.

Innate theories

Children seem to learn the complex rules of language despite having only poor grammatical examples to work from. Normal speech involves much blurring of sounds and words, partial sentences, hesitations and slips of the tongue. Along with the fact that language can appear to develop largely independently of other cognitive abilities, Chomsky (1965) has therefore argued that children must have their own separate, inbuilt ability to develop grammatical principles. He refers to this as the 'Language Acquisition Device' (LAD), which he believes is inherited and operates at the level of deep structure. He also argues that its existence is shown by certain universal properties of languages, such as the fact that they all have phonological elements, and syntactic structures such as nouns and verbs. Languages differ in the rules by which they generate the surface structure, although word order still appears to show some universals, such as the fact that all languages tend to avoid placing the object first in the sentence. Pinker (1994) has also argued that humans have a unique, inherited ability to construct grammatical language for themselves. As evidence for this he uses the progressive evolution of 'pidgins', which are initially formed as simplified hybrids of more than one language with very limited grammatical structures. However, a single generation of children can develop these and establish a complete grammar, creating a language form known as a 'creole'.

One implication from this innate perspective is that language acquisition should be a relatively robust process, and Pinker (1984, p. 29) maintains that 'there is virtually no way to prevent it from happening short of raising a child in a barrel'. If this is the case, then there is little that education can or should do, other than develop the use of language in the various curriculum areas. There is, however, some doubt about this extreme view, based first on the evidence that there are major variations in language development, related to different language experiences (see under 'Language and cultural background' later in this chapter). One extreme case affected in this way was 'Jim', reported by Sachs *et al.* (1981), whose only language experience until he was 3 years of age came from watching television, since his parents were both deaf and non-talkers. Jim did have some spoken language but his grammar was unusual. He would, for example, say 'Not one house. That two house.' The use of 's' in plurals is normally one of the first morphemes that English-speaking children learn. His failure to establish such rules indicates that they depend on children experiencing language in meaningful contexts as well as some form of innate propensity.

There is also a considerable amount of evidence that progress in acquiring specific elements of a language depends very much on a combination of the complexity that is involved and a child's actual exposure to them. Allen and Crago (1996), for instance, studied the age of acquisition of the passive structure in Inuit children and found that they developed basic forms as early as 2 years of age – much earlier than in English, which starts these at about 4 years. This appears to be largely due to the structure of the Inuit language, which facilitates passive structures, as well as a generally increased use of the passive in Inuit adult–child interactions. Such findings tend to support the idea that language structures are strongly influenced by learning, rather than just following universal principles.

The most recent proponents of the innate perspective such as Slobin (1985) propose that we inherit some basic operating principles and a sensitivity to features of language, such as the beginning and end of sound strings, and sounds which are stressed. Coupled with the power of general cognitive development and an early knowledge of agency and causality, these basic abilities would enable the young child to construct language by searching for regularities and patterns in the language he or she experiences.

Cognitive ability

Although it may still be that we have some form of general specialisation to enable us to develop language, an additional explanation is that language acquisition depends on the initial development of general cognitive abilities, which tend to search for and to organise information according to patterns or logical principles. As was described in Chapter 2, if an artificial connectionist system with these properties is set up to process language input, it can learn to generate rules for complex and irregular verbs, or make grammatical predictions for missing words, without any inbuilt initial bias to process for these abilities. This does not of course prove that this is what children are doing, but it does at least show that a complex system can be capable of generating grammatical principles by itself.

Language abilities also tend to develop along with other general cognitive abilities. Piaget (1967) in particular originally argued that we need to develop our schemas, or knowledge and understanding of things and processes, before we are able to represent them symbolically. He believed that the earliest thought is dominated by direct experiences and that it is only at the stage when objects come to have a form of permanence for the child that it is possible for the child to acquire stable concepts and to name them. This happens at around the 12-month level, and it is only after this that dramatic increases in vocabulary occur. Symbolic play, which depends on the development of concepts and their functions, also happens at about this time and is closely related to the subsequent development of language. Brownell (1988) found that children would use two-word, or more than two-word, sentences in their speech only if they had previously shown sequences in their play, such as pretending to pour then drink from a cup. Such findings indicate that it is necessary to understand the logical meaning of sequences and associations to form a basis for establishing early grammar.

Although it seems very likely that language needs an intellectual basis from which to develop, there is evidence that language can itself act as the basis for the development of thought processes, and that establishing the ability to use language in such a way depends on the presence of a structured and supportive social context.

Social interaction

Children are normally closely involved in a meaningful social environment, and an interactionist perspective proposes that the main way in which language develops is through that social environment. Bruner (1983) considers that a parent provides a 'Language Acquisition Support System' (the LASS) for the child, and that this generates structured information for aspects of the LAD to operate (Bruner's little joke!). Understanding is developed and extended by the process of 'scaffolding' described in Chapter 2. This involves the parent's providing a directive and supportive framework in which the child can achieve success and develop and extend his or her concepts. By using language that is appropriate to the child's level, the adult first leads the child to use his or her existing language concepts, and later proceeds to extend the child in new situations, so that eventually the child can adopt new language and meanings from the adult's use of language. This process can then be repeated in subsequent experiences for further extension and successive development.

According to this perspective, it is early pragmatics, or the child's and parent's reciprocal knowledge and understanding of one another's intents, which drives the initial development of meaning in language. From the earliest stages, mothers have been shown to set up 'turn-taking' interactions, starting with feeding sequences where the mother will respond to pauses as a cue for verbal interaction. Any form of action by the child such as cries, burps or grimaces is interpreted as though it is meaningful, and is responded to with physical and verbal interaction. As children mature, they seem to establish an early non-verbal basis for sequences of interaction; for instance, a baby may look towards a desired object, then towards a person whom they want to get it for them. Schlesinger (1988) believes that such semantic associations lead directly to early syntactic categories, such as 'agent–action' sequences, without there being the need to consider that such specific abilities are innate.

Nevertheless, it is still likely that humans have some form of general specialisation to develop language, although this is probably less specific or innate than was originally thought. Language must depend to some extent upon aspects of cognitive development, but the relationship is a reciprocal one, with early language abilities acting as a basis for the development of thought. Most recent explanations also emphasise the importance of practical meaning and the social context of the child, implying that education has an important role to play in facilitating children's language abilities.

Characteristics of language development

The sound system

Young babies make a wide range of all the possible sounds in their early sound play, or 'babbling', but by about 1 year of age these are narrowed down to the standard set for the language that the child is being brought up with. Rathus (1988) has shown, however, that at 5 years of age (i.e. at school entry), many children are still making many errors with the use of sounds, particularly *j*, *v*, *th* and *zh*. As will be described later in this chapter, this can involve the child making substitutions which may need to be reviewed by the teacher. Many children also have difficulty with the use of final consonants, such as saying 'ge' for 'get', and with consonant combinations, such as saying 'bue' for 'blue'. By the age of 8 years, children are accurate about 90 per cent of the time, although boys take a year longer than girls to develop a mature phonological system.

Young children are not normally aware of the separate sounds in speech and just 'say words'. As discussed in the following chapter, the ability to perceive and to combine separate phonemes in early reading can be quite difficult for some children and is a strong predictor of subsequent progress with literacy.

Children starting school will also have difficulty with their ability to perceive different intonation and emphases. It can therefore still be difficult for them to resolve an anaphor, which depends upon a stressed word for meaning. In the sentence 'Peter gave a sweet to Tom and he gave one to Susan', they are likely to fail to notice when there is an emphasis on *he*, to mean that Tom gave the sweet to Susan.

Vocabulary

At age $1\frac{1}{2}$ years the average child uses about 25 words. After this stage, there is a relatively rapid growth in vocabulary, and by 2 years of age, children will be able to use about 200 words (Goldfield and Reznick, 1990). A much more rapid development in general vocabulary then takes place, and Anglin (1993) estimates that by the age of 6 years the average child knows about 10,000 words, representing the learning of about seven new words a day up to this time. By 17 years of age, Miller and Gildea (1987) consider, children have a vocabulary of about 80,000 words, which would mean a subsequent learning rate of 17 new words a day. Although such estimates can vary considerably, children's vocabularies appear to grow by thousands of words each year while they are in schooling, consistent with the rate shown in Figure 8.3. There is also usually a significant difference between the age at which children start to recognise particular words (their receptive vocabulary), and that at which they start to use them in their own speech (their expressive vocabulary). In the earlier years there is little difference, and indeed sometimes children will use words that they do not yet understand, in phrases which they have learned as a whole. Later on, children will gradually learn features and usage of words for some time before they start to use the words themselves.

Figure 8.3 Approximate vocabulary growth rate

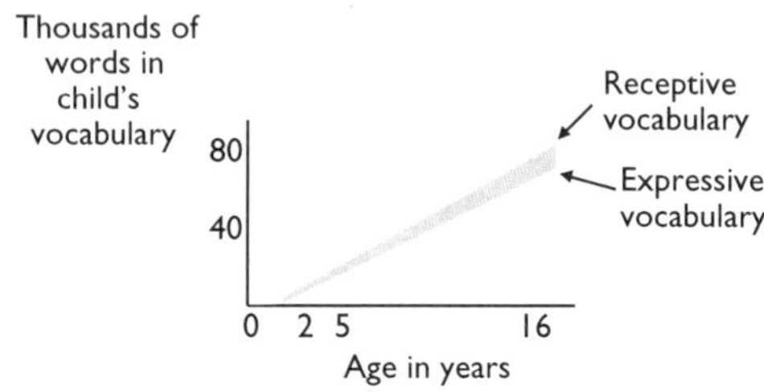

The earliest words developed up to the age of 2 are mainly nouns, with just one or two verbs. After this age there is an increase in knowledge and use of verbs, with the development of simple structural phrases. Adjectives and adverbs and some interrogative words also start to appear, as well as the simpler prepositions such as 'to', 'in' and 'on'. By the time children start school, they typically have all the main parts of speech, although they continue to develop their understanding and use of words with more difficult logical functions such as linking in complex sentences. The main development during children's time in school is now within the classes of nouns, verbs, adjectives and adverbs. These form progressively more abstract, specialised and technical vocabularies according to the subjects which are studied as the children progress through the curriculum.

In general it seems unlikely that formal teaching can account for more than a small part of this phenomenal rate of vocabulary learning. One study by Beck *et al.* (1982) gave 27 10-year-old children direct, intensive vocabulary training in school over 19 weeks. This resulted in an average gain of only 85 new words, or less than one a day, and it is likely that only very small amounts of time in schools are spent teaching and learning words in this specific way.

However, knowledge of new words seems to develop very rapidly when they are experienced in meaningful contexts. Robbins and Ehri (1994) investigated this by reading story books to 6-year-old children, which included 11 unfamiliar words such as 'irate' and 'duped' substituted for easier ones. After checking the children's initial general verbal abilities, the stories were then read twice to them over two to four days. There was no direct explanation of the unknown words and the meaning of these could only be gathered from their context. A multiple-choice test then checked whether children had made any progress with the key set of words. The key finding was that just hearing a word a few times in this way accounted for 19 per cent of the variance in their abilities on the final test, indicating that even brief experiences can significantly develop word knowledge, provided that they occur in a meaningful context.

Early reading by children themselves is unlikely to develop new vocabulary learning since first reading schemes are based on simple, high-frequency words that most children will already know. After about 8 years of age, however, children are able to tackle a wider range of words, and reading vocabulary increases greatly. Nagy *et al.* (1987) have concluded from

various studies of children's progress with reading vocabulary that an average amount of reading probably accounts for one-third of a child's annual vocabulary growth from the age of 9 years onwards, and that regular, wide reading can result in substantial and permanent vocabulary development.

Although watching television is often thought to be a passive activity and to have a negative influence on children's development, Hall *et al.* (1996) found that watching educational and informative educational programmes had a positive effect on children's general knowledge that was on average equal to the effects of their exposure to print. No such effect seemed to occur if children just watched regular television such as game shows or cartoons, and the positive effects appeared only for children who were older than 2 years.

It seems likely that children learn a great deal of their vocabulary from a range of informal sources such as conversations, or just by listening to the way in which words are used by other people. Markman (1987) considers that at first children hearing a new word attempt to map it on to an existing concept that is not yet labelled, using the context in which the word was spoken. Young children might not have developed enough concepts to enable this to happen and may have to develop novel concepts at the same time.

In a classic study, Carey and Bartlett (1978) looked at whether concept development would happen with limited exposure to the name of a colour that children could not yet identify. They first made sure that a group of 3-year-olds did not know the colour 'olive' (the children mostly called it green or brown), then exposed them to a new, nonsense name for the colour. This was done by interrupting their play and pointing to two trays, one coloured blue and the other coloured olive, and casually saying, 'Hand me the chromium tray. Not the blue one but the chromium one.' The child would sometimes pause and perhaps point to the olive tray and say, 'This one?' The experimenter would then reply, 'Yes, that one, thank you.' The children were given no further guidance and a week later they were given some colours to identify. When olive was presented to them, they were still not able to identify it correctly, but they now paused and evidently knew that the colour was not green or brown. It seems that they had started to learn that there was a new property which related to a word but had yet to develop the concept completely.

Such evidence indicates that the learning of a new word does not necessarily occur in an all or nothing way. Clark (1973) proposes that a word is normally learned by the progressive development of associated meanings – the 'semantic features hypothesis'. This is supported by early verbal errors called overgeneralisations, which indicate that the first features used tend to be the more general ones. For instance, a child may call all four-legged animals 'doggie' since he or she is using only the concept of 'animals with four legs'. When enough semantic features are acquired (e.g. 'barks', 'chases cats'), then the word can be used accurately and appropriately, and can become part of a child's active vocabulary.

As was noted in Chapter 2, it is likely that word concepts are best seen as prototypes – exemplars with classic features – or as schemas with features which are related and are relevant to the individual. Richards (1979) found that words which are good, accessible exemplars are established first: children learn 'dog' rather than 'animal' or particular breed names, and this learning is in terms of the key functions of dogs and what they mean to the child. Children will also overextend a new concept according to how similar it is to a prototype; cats might be called 'doggie', but a horse is much less likely to be. Parents and teachers probably utilise this approach intuitively and focus on words which are most accessible and relevant to children, only extending the concept once basic-level terms are established.

Structure

Alongside the development in vocabulary is an early rapid growth in language structure. At about 2 years of age, children will be putting two words together in a way that involves simple rules. This can involve using 'pivot words' such as 'more' to generate utterances such as 'more juice' or 'more tickle'. By the age of about 4 years, most children have the major elements of normal grammar involving the various parts of speech and rules for combining them.

There is still significant progress to be made during the school years. Work by Berko (1958) with 7-year-olds has shown, for instance, that they still have to develop plurals using -es at the end (rather than the basic -s) and are not yet able to form many irregular past tenses (e.g. sing/sung). It can take even longer for children to acquire the more complex constructions such as passives, which are not fully formed until about age 9. Some sentences, such as those involving double negatives and multiple embedded clauses, are logically complex and are often not mastered by even older children in secondary school.

Children's early language rules are not just parts of the adult system. They often seem to be qualitatively different and over time evolve closer towards the mature form. Children appear to develop hypotheses about useful language structures (from what they hear and experience) and test these out. For example, children in the early school years appear to establish the rule that putting -ed on a verb makes it into the past tense, as is shown by their errors, such as overextending the rule and using it with irregular verbs, such as saying 'runned' instead of 'ran'.

Brown *et al.* (1969) found that parents pay more attention to what children say (their meaning) than to how children say things (the actual structure). When adults correct children's speech, this in fact slows their progress down (Nelson, 1988), presumably since it inhibits them from developing and applying their early rule systems. For example, correcting a child for using 'runned' instead of 'ran' might lead him or her to doubt the general rule about the use of -ed.

Cazden (1965) has studied two groups of children who had their speech either expanded by an adult (repeated back to them in proper grammatical form) or enlarged (responding to and taking their meaning further). The 'expanded' group's language did improve somewhat more than a control group, but the 'enlarged' group's speech progressed much faster. This seems to indicate that children develop their early grammatical rules from the meanings inherent in adult structures rather than by merely imitating the structures they hear.

In general, the findings from normal language development strongly imply that teachers should not worry too much about children's language forms but concentrate on involving them in meaningful language work that is interesting and relevant to each child. The language used by teachers should, however, provide an appropriate model that is accessible in terms of the content and structures that they use.

Language and thought

There are probably many different ways of thinking, depending on the task involved and the individual's abilities. One useful way of categorising these is Bruner's (1966b) description of three main modes: the iconic mode, which mainly involves visual representations; an enactive mode which involves representation of physical movements or control; and a symbolic mode which uses abstractions such as words. In a similar way, Gardner (1983) considers that there are many forms of specific intellectual abilities, although linguistic intelligence is of particular importance to the educational process. A lot of thinking does seem to involve language to some extent and we are often aware of literally 'talking to ourselves'. Young children in particular will often verbalise when involved with some problem, especially when it is unexpected. At other times, however, learning or the development of ideas or solutions can arise without any awareness, and unconscious processing may be an important aspect of certain types of problem solving. At such times creative solutions might be blocked by conventional ways of thinking, including the use of inappropriate verbal labels (see Chapter 3, 'Creativity'). If language does have an important role in such ways of thinking, then we should perhaps take account of this in educational processes, by developing verbal skills where they can help children's thought in some way.

Independence of thought and language

At one extreme, linguists such as Chomsky (1965) have argued that language abilities are essentially independent of other cognitive skills. This argument is based upon such evidence as the finding that most individuals above a certain basic intellectual level appear to develop language without any apparent difficulty. One particular example is an unusual genetic disorder known as Williams syndrome. Children who have this typically achieve an overall IQ of only 85 but often have well-developed expressive verbal skills, developing complex grammar and a wide vocabulary. However, such abilities are not linked with the same level of general understanding and have only limited usefulness for individuals affected in this way. When making these arguments, linguists are therefore usually focusing only on the limited aspect of linguistic competence rather than general language performance.

Language depending on thought

A virtually opposite argument is made by Piaget (1959), that language abilities are dependent on and develop from general cognitive abilities. There is considerable evidence for this perspective, with the findings described above about the development of object permanence and different types of symbolic understanding acting as precursors to early words and grammar. Vygotsky (1962), however, has argued that Piaget's view does not take account of the developmental interrelationship between thought and language and the importance of the social and cultural context of the child. According to his theories, early language such as crying or calling out to get attention is mainly social and does not involve thought as we normally understand it. When objects are given a verbal label, this mainly functions merely as another property of that object rather than as a basis for a separate way of representation. Early thought is dominated by direct actions and experiences, and develops before any of the early forms of language.

Vygotsky found that from the age of about 2 years onwards, children appear to start to use language to 'think out loud with', particularly when they were trying to do something difficult. He argues that they do so because early thought and language have combined, with language now becoming capable of monitoring and directing internal thought, and of communicating the child's thinking to others. However, these two functions cannot yet be distinguished by the child and a great deal of language is relatively egocentric, resulting in the parallel monologues which are common in younger children.

From about the age of 7 onwards, Vygotsky believed, at the time when operational thought develops, children start to internalise such speech as a form of thought, to orient and organise their understanding. Vygotsky found that just before it 'goes underground' in this way, egocentric speech becomes less like normal social language, and is simplified and focused more on the tasks and the child's own needs. In parallel with this process, spoken language now develops separately and becomes more social and communicative, oriented to the needs of others. The two systems continue to relate to each other, with the development of spoken language leading to the assimilation of cultural knowledge, values and beliefs.

Berk (1986) found support for Vygotsky's ideas from observations of 6- and 8-year-old pupils working in class on mathematics problems. The younger children generally talked to themselves extensively when they encountered difficulties, but older children did so to a much smaller extent. The use of such 'private speech' correlated positively with intelligence for the 6-year-olds, indicating that private speech was supporting thinking. The correlation was negative for the 8-year-old children and indicates that speech which had become internalised was now the basis for thought.

Language facilitating thought

Bruner (1966b) has extended Vygotsky's ideas and considers that language is even more important in the early stages of the development of thought than Vygotsky had realised. It acts, he believes, to amplify abilities and accelerate cognitive development. Bruner sees language development as dependent on shared social understandings and support from key adults, with the process of progressive 'scaffolding' leading to new verbal abilities and increased knowledge and understanding. Investigations indicate that language used in a meaningful context which is matched with children's conceptual development can develop understanding. Sonstroem (1966), for instance, gave 6- and 7-year-old children training on a conservation task: learning that an amount of plasticine remains the same even when its shape changes. Children who merely observed and talked about the changes did not develop any new abilities. Only children who physically experienced the changes and used language at the same time to describe what was happening made progress. Sonstroem's work is therefore consistent with Bruner's ideas that new language needs a meaningful context in order to affect thinking processes.

Linguistic relativity

Bruner also believes that language acts to free children from direct experiences by providing conceptual categories which can be used as the basis for independent abstract thought. If this is the case, then it is possible that the language concepts which are available to us may have a major role in facilitating or constraining the way in which we can think. This perspective is known as *linguistic relativity*, and Whorf (1956) argued that the forms of words or grammar in a particular language generate a certain world-view which inevitably affects the type of thinking that we can do about it. Whorf based his ideas on evidence such as the existence of more than 20 words for snow in the Inuit language; this appeared to Whorf to enable Inuit to perceive and attend to the different features of snow in a way that would not be possible for English speakers.

Such strong beliefs do not appear to have much foundation. Harley (1995), for instance, found that there are in fact only two root words used by Inuit *qanik* and *aput*, to describe falling and settled snow respectively, each of which can easily be described by other languages. Even when there are apparent differences, such as Arabic languages having a large number of words related to camels, these are probably more a reflection of the fact that the culture concerned has a general bias in that direction and simply uses more words to accommodate this. All experts in a particular field will have a greater specialist vocabulary and knowledge, which will also correspond with a greater readiness to perceive and think about things to do with that area of expertise.

There has, however, been considerable support for a weaker form of the linguistic relativity argument. This proposes that rather than determining perception and the ability to establish concepts, language can rather act to *direct* cognitive processes in a more general way. A classic example of this was an investigation by Carmichael *et al.* (1932) which showed that the use of different words to label a specific picture

Figure 8.4 Reproduction of picture after verbal labelling

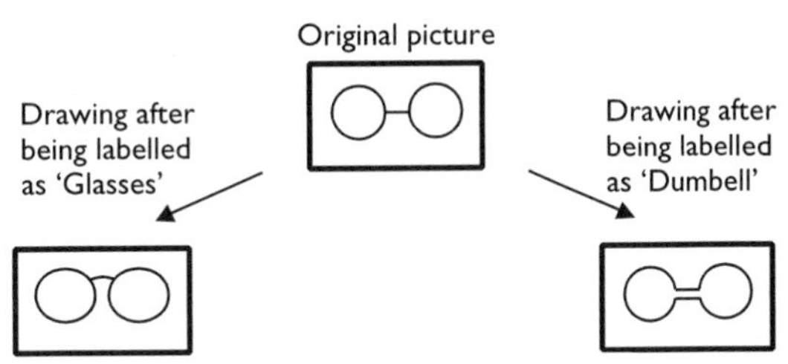

led to correspondingly different reproductions. As shown in Figure 8.4, if an ambiguous shape (of two circles joined by a straight line) was called a pair of glasses, then subsequent drawings by subjects would emphasise the curved nose piece and oval lens shapes; if it was called a dumbell then reproduction emphasised the connecting bar. The use of the word to label the picture meant that the subject did not need to retain any visual information; recall was therefore mainly from the verbal category, and the subject's drawing emphasised the features of this.

Hoffman *et al.* (1986) also found evidence that the language used by bilingual English–Chinese speakers affected their assessment of people's personalities. These tended to be biased by the availability of stereotypes in a particular language, implying that the inferences which we draw are directed by the availability of verbal concepts. As discussed later, such cultural language forms may also be present to some extent within social or ethnic subgroups, and can have an impact on children's educational progress.

Language inhibiting thought

Inappropriate use of language concepts can sometimes misdirect our attention or interfere with learning in some situations. Duncker (1945), for instance, originally demonstrated that using conventional labels for an object such as a 'box' prevented subjects from perceiving it as having another possible function; the problem was to support a candle, and people had difficulty understanding that the box the candles came in could also be used as a support. This phenomenon is known as 'functional fixedness', and can be overcome by providing subjects with different verbal labels for objects, which then enables them to be used in other ways. Certain types of learning called 'implicit learning' may also operate best when there is limited verbal awareness and control. This has been shown to happen with the learning of certain types of physical skills, and it may be that the use of language prevents the appropriate, enactive mode of thought from operating.

In general, however, language abilities have predominantly positive effects on educational progress. Although differences in language forms may not have a great effect, language in general undoubtedly has a key role as the basis for certain types of thought, and spoken language is the principal medium for communicating information between people. Language abilities depend on and also support the development of both knowledge and understanding, which are the main determinants of children's educational progress.

Language and cultural background

Bernstein (1961) has proposed that working-class and middle-class children respectively have different forms of language, and that the difference affects the way in which they think and how they react to the educational system. He believes that working-class children have a relatively 'restricted code' which is essentially simplified and limited to the immediate context. A sentence used to communicate the information that a ball had broken a window might therefore be 'It broke it.' Middle-class children, on the other hand, have an 'elaborated code' which is grammatically complex, more precise and much more capable of embodying abstract ideas and knowledge. In this case, the corresponding sentence might be 'The ball accidentally broke the window.' Parents appear to provide the models and experiences that develop this style. A working-class parent is therefore likely to say, 'Pack it in', whereas a middle-class parent might say, 'Peter, stop annoying your sister.' Bernstein believes that the language of the educational system is primarily elaborated code and that working-class children are unable to benefit from educational opportunities as much as middle-class children.

Bernstein has been at great pains to emphasise that the language capabilities of working-class children are not necessarily inferior and have the same potential to communicate ideas. In one sense this is arguing that restricted code is just a form of dialect, but it is hard to see how the loss of key elements could give the same information, particularly if writing is being used to express ideas when the context is not clear. There are also difficulties with the generalised use of the concept of 'social class', since this can refer to a number of dimensions, such as parental occupation or income, that may relate only indirectly to a child's language culture.

Labov (1979) has argued strongly against the idea that minority social groups (mainly African Americans) with lower social status have inferior language abilities. He points out that their language is often more direct and precise, and is certainly capable of expressing sophisticated concepts. Although they typically leave out some parts of speech such as the verb 'to be' in phrases such as 'They mine', this phrase has the same information content and is following the same deletion principle as 'They're mine'. Other languages also commonly contract or leave out unnecessary parts of speech, and Labov sees middle-class language as being unnecessarily complicated and often obscuring the real meaning. Labov believes that the differences between the two forms of language are mainly qualitative and cultural. If there are limits to the educational opportunities of minority groups, he concludes that this is because the control of the educational system is predominantly in white, middle-class hands. In general, Labov has made a good case for the language of African Americans to be considered at least a separate dialect, and the form of this known as 'Ebonics' has been recognised by a school district in California as being the primary language for many of its students.

Honey (1983), however, considers that Labov has overemphasised the differences in culture between groups and has glossed over the very real differences between the different forms of language in expressing meaning. Although each may be functional within its culture, he argues that the dominant form in academic fields is complex and precise, and that ignoring this fact will prevent cultural minorities from making progress.

One difficulty in this area is separating out language forms which are just different, from language experiences which are deprived. There appears to be a good case for many aspects of working-class and cultural minority languages to be seen as different dialects which are highly functional within their own cultural context. Unfortunately, restricted or socially dependent features do seem to provide a limited match with the requirements of some aspects of formal education. There is also strong evidence that the sheer amount of language experienced by children can vary significantly and that this variation is related to certain types of social class. As we have seen, an observational study by Hart and Risley (1985) found that by the age of 3, children in professional families had heard more than 30 million words. Children in working-class families, however, had heard only around 20 million, and for the children of the poorest families on welfare the figure was even lower at around 10 million. One study by Heath (1989) also set out to record the interactions between a mother in an isolated poor family with her three children over a two-year period. Over a 500-hour period of tape recording, she initiated talk in only 18 instances, other than to give some brief directions, or to ask about what the children were doing.

Such low levels of verbal stimulation seem bound to limit children's language development. Whitehurst *et al.* (1994) found that a sample of 3-year-old children from low-income families had verbal abilities which were generally one standard deviation (15 points) below what would be achieved by the normal population. However, following a six-week programme of interactive picture-book reading which emphasised language involvement and understanding, these children showed gains of up to 10 points in their vocabulary scores. This shows that even children from poor backgrounds are able to make significant progress with their language abilities, and also strongly suggests that their initially poor attainments may have been due to a previous lack of such experiences.

Educational implications of language development

If education essentially involves the development of concepts and ideas, and these are primarily taught and encoded using language, then language development must be a central issue in education. Although children starting school have already made much headway with their language abilities, they still have to establish a mature sound system and form the more complex language structures. Children also continue to develop an extensive and integrated vocabulary throughout their school careers, based essentially on meaning and understanding. From the above evidence, however, it appears that the majority of speech and language learning by children is relatively informal and comes primarily from their interest in and involvement with a broad range of experiences, rather than from directed learning.

In school it is rarely possible to provide the closely structured 'scaffolding' situations that Bruner (1983) describes as happening in a one-to-one situation between a parent and a child. Tizard and Hughes (1984), for instance, found significant differences between the conversations of 4-year-old girls at morning nursery school and at home with their mothers in the afternoon. Not surprisingly, the amount of language was much greater at home, largely owing to the greater amount of adult time that was available. More importantly, the quality of conversation at home was normally superior to what was happening in school, being based on shared knowledge and experiences. In school, language from adults was often limited and reactive, with little ongoing involvement, as shown in this typical interaction:

Child: Polly's back. Polly comed back yesterday, but she's gone home, Polly.
Staff: Polly?
Child: Yeah, my Polly.
Staff: Oh!

It is therefore perhaps not surprising that Ray and Wartes (1991) found that long-term home-based education, known as 'education otherwise', gave better outcomes than did formal school-based education. Hughes and Westgate (1997) found that even when additional help was available in school in the form of classroom assistants, the assistants adopted a 'teacherly' role, giving mainly low-level direction focused on helping the children accomplish basic learning activities. However, nursery nurses, whose training had covered the nature and importance of early language development, carried out a great deal more meaningful verbal interaction with children and focused on their interests and level of understanding.

Most of the time in schools it is of course just not possible to interact verbally with children in this way, owing to the limited amount of adult time available. Galton *et al.* (1999) show that teachers have increasingly spent their time on general class teaching and organisation, with individual children being involved with their teacher for only a few minutes each day. What involvement there is, is usually based around low-level interactions such as pupil management and information giving.

When children start at school, their interactions are often largely based on non-verbal and pragmatic understanding, with relatively egocentric language. As shown in Figure 8.5, it is therefore not uncommon to hear two very 'one-sided' conversations in parallel, where each child seems automatically to assume that others are attending to and aware of what he or she is saying.

Figure 8.5 Egocentric conversation

As children become older, they develop awareness of and sensitivity to each other's language needs and undoubtedly learn new language concepts from a range of informal verbal experiences. However, it is unlikely that pupils in school will be able to fulfil the same role as adults. In tutoring situations, children have been shown to be poor at knowing when to intervene, when to withdraw, and to tend to use simpler, didactic explanations. In a direct comparison, Shute *et al.* (1992) found that adults were better than children on all verbal tutoring measures, and although cooperative group learning may be an effective approach, this is difficult to set up and rarely used.

It seems likely, then, that a primary source of children's language and conceptual development within school must be independent and class-organised activities with curriculum studies. However, this places great stress on children's personal motivation and involvement, and so it is not surprising that these qualities are key determinants of their progress in school.

From Beck *et al.*'s (1982) study quoted earlier, it seems inefficient to spend much time teaching verbal constructs out of context, and it is probably much more effective to concentrate on general subject and content matter. New language concepts and structures should be embedded in a general structure of meaningful features and associations which will enable pupils to refine their own ability to use them. However, the National Curriculum of England and Wales requires that pupils be exposed to Standard English and formally learn parts of speech and grammar. There are dangers that doing so could become an academic exercise, and fail to develop in pupils the ability to acquire new approaches to the use of language.

Should grammar be part of the curriculum?

A specified grammar can be important in ensuring some form of conformity and stability for the language. Unfortunately, languages are constantly changing, and a static grammar will eventually become outdated. The sentence structures in common use, as well as meanings and pronunciations of words, show major changes over time. One has only to look at books written in the eighteenth century which are currently studied for GCSE to realise that phrases such as 'Lizzy has something more of quickness than her sisters' (from *Pride and Prejudice*, written by Jane Austen in 1797) may be grammatically correct in a technical sense but would not be used nowadays; a more likely expression of the same thing would be 'Lizzy is more lively than her sisters', and this would have more meaning and relevance to most children.

Formal grammar teaching involves classifying words into the various parts of speech, analysing sentences into the various types of phrases and clauses, and examining ways in which these can be combined to form sentences. The National Curriculum programmes of study for English now incorporate some aspects of this approach, and direct that children should be taught a basic range of technical grammatical terms, the functions of these and their effects. Although this may seem to be an attractive 'back to basics' approach, evidence about how we develop language structures emphasises that they are very much constructed by the child. As discussed earlier, the initial foundation of language comes from shared understandings and needs, and children appear to move through their own stages of progressively more sophisticated grammars. A child does not appear to learn that the past tense of 'to go' is 'went' and not 'goed' from direct instruction; indeed, as noted before, correcting children's language appears to destroy their developing hypotheses about how language works and can lead to slower progress.

In line with evidence of this kind, a number of research studies have shown that the formal teaching of grammar appears to have little if any effect on children's functional abilities with language. A key study by Harris (1965) compared the progress of secondary pupils who in addition to their normal English studies either had an extra period of writing, or were taught traditional formal grammar for one period a week from a standard textbook. After two years, the 'grammar' group had certainly improved their performance on a test of their knowledge of grammar, but failed to develop their performance on a writing test – which was marked according to their ability to apply grammatical principles. Furthermore, the pupils who had spent their time writing had made better progress in a number of areas of applied grammar such as the variety and complexity of sentences used. This indicates that learning formal grammar was in effect limiting children's attainments on the very principles that they had been learning about.

A review of such studies by QCA (1998), however, challenges whether there was ever any possibility of transfer from learning traditional grammar in this way to writing and composition skills. Instead, it is proposed that applied skills are more likely to develop by pupils experiencing the demands of different writing tasks, and by drawing explicit attention to the syntactic features of pupils' own writing. In the original study by Harris (1965), this less formal approach was in fact what was happening with the group who practised their writing, with teachers drawing the pupils' attention to the use of sentence structure for stylistic effect, the structure of paragraphs, and techniques for linking them together. When pupils made grammatical errors, these were corrected by example and imitation, and it seems likely that such teaching would indeed lead to improvements in writing technique.

Although the skills of formal grammatical analysis can be taught, it is likely that by itself the teaching of such skills tends to be rather an academic exercise. If the main educational objective is to develop communication skills, then this is most likely to be achieved by the teaching of linguistic features in meaningful contexts. Galton *et al.*'s (1999) study of children's relative achievements over the period when the National Curriculum of England and Wales was first implemented found that children had improved on specific features such as their use of capitals and appropriate punctuation. However, there was an overall apparent decline in children's language skills, indicating perhaps that there had been too great an emphasis on such surface techniques.

Second-language learning

Learning a first language seems to be achieved best during the early years; bilingual children also appear to achieve the relatively effortless learning of a second language by being exposed to it from an early age. This has been taken as evidence that learning a second language will be more difficult for older students and that therefore the teaching of a second language should be started as soon as possible in the primary school. Snow (1987), however, looked at the relative progress with the Dutch language of English children and adults in their first year of living in the Netherlands. Surprisingly, the adults made better progress than the children, indicating that when the learning conditions are similar, adults learn second languages more easily.

An important basis for learning a foreign language is to be consistently exposed to it in meaningful situations. However, direct, explicit teaching linked with language use has been shown to be more effective than just 'language immersion'. Bilingual children usually establish learning best when they have two parents consistently speaking different languages. Older children and adults are unlikely to experience the same type of learning, but if it does happen, then they can use their wider range of concepts and understanding to learn more rapidly.

Language and behaviour

Since young children appear to use speech to literally instruct themselves and to direct their attention, Meichenbaum (1977) has developed an approach to develop these abilities in children who have behavioural difficulties. This is called 'cognitive behaviour modification' and typically uses self-instruction to modify the behaviour of impulsive children. An adult will typically model a simple task for the child, stopping frequently to monitor his or her own behaviour and intentions out loud. The child then imitates the adult's behaviour, and after a few sessions the self-instruction is carried out covertly. When working with a young child on a letter formation task, this might involve the following when copying a letter 'a':

Model: 'STOP, What I am doing? I've got to do the rounded bit first. Start at the cross [provided on some lined paper], here I go – round, round. STOP, What do I do now? Make the line down. Down, down, finished.'

A review of findings on the effectiveness of this approach by Robinson *et al.* (1999) indicates that it has a major effect size of 0.74. Such approaches can have a very rapid effect on behaviour, and improvements are often maintained well.

Speech and language problems

By the time they enter school, most children are reasonably intelligible and have developed the majority of their grammatical structures. Unfortunately, usually because of poor home background or medical difficulties, some children have either a general delay with their progress or, less commonly, some form of abnormal development (which is often related to medical problems).

Speaking and listening are part of the National Curriculum of England and Wales, and if children have moderate difficulties, these can often be managed as part of the normal approach to teaching. In the early years, schools have a strong emphasis on involving children in language work, with listening to stories, talking as part of investigative activities, as well as early literacy activities. After Key Stage 1, problems with grammatical development will be present only in the most severe cases, but more children will have an overall relative delay with their general knowledge and understanding of language concepts. These children would normally be classified as having 'learning difficulties', and, as will be described in Chapter 12, their needs would be met with modification and matching of the curriculum, known as differentiation.

When children have more atypical problems, these are less likely to respond to such general educational approaches, and it can be important to obtain expert advice from speech and language therapists (SLTs). Although, in Britain, these are employed by health authorities, they will often visit schools and give advice to whoever is able to work with a child. Formal categories of such difficulties which are used include:

- *Voice:* Sounds originating in the larynx (using the vocal cords).
  (a) 'aphonia' – absence of voice;
  (b) 'dysphonia' – impairment of voice.
- *Articulation:* Production of speech sounds; using the lips, tongue, jaw, breathing, etc.
  (a) 'alalia' – absence of articulation;
  (b) 'dyslalia' – defects of articulation or slow development of articulatory patterns, including substitutions, omissions and transpositions of the sounds of speech. These problems are common with many young children; for example: 'me do de-a dwin', meaning 'I'm going to get a drink';
  (c) 'anarthria' and 'dysarthria' – absence of and distorted articulation respectively, caused by lack of neuromuscular control;
  (d) 'dyspraxia' – failure to perform the sequence of movements involved in articulation. Also refers to an inability to carry out various other types of sequential processing.
- *Language:* The structure and the content of what is said.
  (a) 'aphasia' – absence of recognition and use of verbal expression;
  (b) 'dysphasia' – incomplete language function. This can affect the structure – whether correct grammatical rules are present. If there is a developmental delay, these may be simple rules characteristic of younger children, for example 'more juice' for 'I would like some more juice';
  (c) 'deviant forms of language' show an uneven and atypical development. Examples include confusions in word order, inappropriate use of pronouns, adverbs, prepositions, phrase and clause patterns, and problems in modifying words as they are used with each other; for example, 'Him is going making very lots of toys';
  (d) 'semantics' – an emphasis on the meaning and knowledge involved in language. Children with a semantic disorder will often limit their conversations to known, safe topics;
  (e) 'pragmatics' – how children communicate in real situations. Children with a pragmatic disorder can therefore have problems initiating and managing conversations, as well as difficulties recognising another person's intent such as is involved in responding to questions.

  (The last two are often combined together into the category of 'semantic–pragmatic disorder', which is often considered to be part of the autistic spectrum of disorders, to be dealt with in Chapter 12).

Early speech and language difficulties can have long-term negative effects on education. Research shows how children's difficulties with sensitivity to spoken sounds have a major effect on early literacy development. Any difficulties with spoken language are likely to affect children's literacy, and there is a much higher level of educational difficulties in children with such problems. An investigation by Fundudis *et al.* (1979) studied a group of 133 pre-school children who had been identified as having retarded language. On follow-up at 7 years of age, one in five was found to have a serious educational handicap. This shows that children with these difficulties do not all spontaneously improve and should therefore be identified and given appropriate support as early as possible.

Prevalence of speech and language problems

Definitions of criteria for speech and language problems vary, but a review of surveys by Webster and McConnell (1987) indicated that about 5 per cent of all children entering school were unable to make themselves understood. Many of these children improve greatly during their early education, although the organisation AFASIC (1989) estimates that by the age of secondary schooling, one in 80 of all children continue to have a serious language disorder. Moreover, Sheridan and Peckham (1975) report that over 50 per cent of children identified as having language problems at age 7 years still demonstrated residual language problems, as well as learning, social and emotional difficulties, at the age of 16.

Turner and Vincent (1986) reviewed the progress of 60 pupils with speech and language problems and found an important distinction between children whose speech and language is simply delayed (who often make good progress) and those who have more profound difficulties which show deviance from or distortions of the normal process. These difficulties appeared to be much more difficult to overcome. Children who have problems merely with articulation are also more likely to make progress than children who have more general problems with language involving its structure and content.

Special provision

The majority of speech and language support is provided in normal schools, where any additional help in the school can work with programmes provided by SLTs. This can be an effective approach for many children since it continues their social integration and provides a meaningful context in which language can develop.

The most severe language difficulties can be part of a general delay, and educational objectives are then largely related to self-help and independence skills. Such education centres on achieving some form of functional competence in these areas. The focus is often therefore on establishing basic communication such as the expression of needs, and often uses non-verbal techniques such as picture cue cards or early signing such as Makaton.

Children with more specific problems are sometimes placed in special schools for children with speech and language problems, or in units, usually with trained teachers and SLTs. Classes are usually small (three to six children) and teaching is often intensive, using individual and structured programmes. Units are usually part of a normal school, so that children can integrate with normal-language children for at least part of the day. Many units also try to make sure that children return to their neighbourhood school for part of the week, with the aim of eventual integration. Most children enter such units in their first year of schooling (when problems become apparent) and attend for about two years.

Remediation

Articulation

Improving children's intelligibility by working with their spoken sound system can be a rather technical process and is normally best carried out by SLTs, who are particularly effective in this area. Even when children are very difficult to understand, they normally have a number of correct sounds, and there are usually other sounds which are being established. Some of these could be developed with help but others may be too abnormal to use as a basis for progress.

It is rare for children to have problems with their vowels; most difficulties are with consonant sounds. These can be missing in particular words and positions, which can be a serious problem requiring expert assessment. Sounds are often changed in some way, and the list in Figure 8.6 gives sets of common substitutions which would

Figure 8.6 Substitution immaturities

$5\frac{1}{2}$ years	
Target sound	Substitution used
t	k
d	g
k	t
g	d
f	p
v	b
sh	t
sh	s
s	t
z	d

6 years	
Target sound	Substitution used
ch	t
j	d

$6\frac{1}{2}$ years	
Target sound	Substitution used
s	th
z	th
l	y
l	w
v	w

be normal immaturities up to the ages shown; for example, saying 'kap' for 'tap' would still be likely up to $5\frac{1}{2}$ years of age. If some remain beyond these ages, they would therefore be a cause for concern.

Initial teaching often involves making sure that children are able to discriminate between different sounds. This can be done by using a number of pictures of words which start with the target and substitution sounds, and then asking them to point to the correct one for a spoken word. If children have difficulties, then they may need more experiences with listening.

The next stage can involve making the sound in isolation, for example by making a hissing noise 'like a snake' for the 's' sound. This may also involve getting children to look in a mirror so that they can see where their lips, teeth and tongue should be. This then leads on to the use of the sound in a whole word. However, if they have been substituting 't' for 's' then they may still leave the 't' sound in and say 'stun' for 'sun' – compounding their problem! A technique to avoid this could involve words where it is possible to make the 's' sound slightly separately, as in 's-poon'.

These techniques are close to the ones involved in phonological sensitivity training and the use of phonics in early reading. It is therefore an area where literacy teaching and speech work should coordinate closely and focus on the same sounds and words. It is very easy to make things worse, and if children are not making easy progress, it is always best to seek expert advice.

Language structures

It seems reasonable to assume that when children have language problems, remedial approaches should utilise goals based on the sequence of normal development. Many programmes therefore involve developing vocabulary and language structures in much the same way as happens with young children. An alternative approach is to use a more logical sequence based on the developing of grammatical rules. In practice, the two approaches are often quite similar, since normal language development involves deriving ways of expressing meaning through increasingly complex language structures.

Speech and language development work is typically done in small groups, where the child with difficulties can hear models from other children and also be part of the overall social context. Much early work to develop vocabulary and understanding is similar to normal early-years practice, with the use of interesting props or pictures to stimulate talk and generate conversations. Tough's (1977, 1981) approach is a good example of this, being based on fostering development through adult–child dialogues.

More structured assessment and teaching approaches such as the Living Language programme by Locke (1985) use a specific target vocabulary and language structures as a basis for development activities. Living Language uses small-group work with conversations and activities where a particular language construction can be used. An example of this type of approach might involve prepositional contrasts such as 'on' versus 'under', with a task where children are told where to look for a hidden object.

The Derbyshire Language System by Knowles and Masidlover (1982) is popular in schools. It uses the level of information in children's language as an initial index for a sequence of remedial approaches. These involve simple activities which are based largely on play rather than formal teaching. Target language structures are identified, and in teaching them, the emphasis is on the use of language to manage people, to obtain objects and to gain information. Once children have established comprehension, the roles are reversed, and they are then encouraged to use language to control the game themselves.

Evaluating the outcomes of such structured approaches can be difficult as there are rarely any effective comparison groups. Also, if children have an initially severe delay, it is unlikely that any form of intervention will completely overcome their difficulties. Bruges (1988), for instance, followed up the progress of 62 ex-pupils of language units where structured schemes including Living Language and the Derbyshire Language System had been used. Compared with national norms of outcomes for children with such severe initial difficulties, many but not all of the pupils did appear to have made significant progress, with 68 per cent mixing well with their peers and 60 per cent having literacy attainments in the normal range. Dockrell and Messer (1999) review research which shows that children receiving support made significant progress relative to other children who did not get help. There was also evidence that parent-administered interventions were at least as effective as direct clinician-administered treatment. However, this was not the case for articulation and phonological disorders, for which direct therapist treatment was more effective.

Harris (1984) has criticised the structured techniques that are often emphasised in language programmes as lacking the key qualities of normal, informal language acquisition. In a study of children in a special school where there was both formal and non-formal language support, he found that informal, unstructured activities produced better language interactions than structured, one-to-one language teaching sessions. It is thus important to work with meaningful tasks and children's understanding of intent, as well as to use vocabulary and structure at an appropriate level. Informal activities should involve adults becoming closely involved in shared activities with children, tuning in to their intentions and needs, and responding so that the child can understand the adult's ideas and intentions. Unfortunately, some children are not interested in tasks or social involvement, and in these cases it may be appropriate to use a more prescriptive and behavioural approach.

Summary

Language is both an important goal and a foundation for education. The study of language is mainly based on its structure and meaning, with the sound system acting as an important basis for accent and dialect. Syntax and grammar incorporate rules which determine the structure of language, and these are important in establishing the meaning of what is said. Meaning comes from processing systems which construct and revise plausible interpretations from the sequence of words using their functions and relationships. Interpretation also depends on activating systems of general contextual knowledge and understanding, which can involve the use of known scripts and schemas. In practical situations we also use our knowledge of other people's intentions to interpret what they say.

Language development appears to be natural and autonomous, and the major structures and functions are already in place when children start school. Behaviourist learning theory explains their learning as the result of a process of conditioning, with parents rewarding imitation. This explanation is unlikely, however, as children appear to use rule-based systems from an early age, and some theories argue that this ability is therefore innate. Alternative approaches emphasise the complex, pattern-seeking abilities of the human brain coupled with meaningful experiences in a social context.

The development of the sound system is completed during the early school years. Throughout education, language progress is subsequently most evident in the range and use of verbal concepts. Progress largely depends on experiencing new language in meaningful contexts, and important sources are formal education, conversations, reading and watching television. The majority of the basic structures of language are present by 4 years of age, although the more complex forms take a long time to develop. Establishing these seems to depend on experiencing language in meaningful situations and developing and modifying hypotheses about the way in which different forms are constructed and used.

Language and thought appear to be closely related, although competence with language structures is probably an independent ability. Even though it has been argued that the development of language depends upon existing cognitive abilities, it now seems more likely that thought and language combine at an early age and then take separate, more specialised forms when children become older. This seems to happen within a context of shared social meanings and shows that language-based support can facilitate cognitive development.

There is some evidence that language forms can affect thinking processes. Although it was once believed that language had a strong deterministic effect, it now seems more likely that it merely directs attention and ways of thinking. In doing so it can sometimes limit our ability to consider alternative approaches and solutions to problems. Different forms of language are characteristic of certain social and cultural groupings. The language forms used by some groups can probably result in a certain impoverishment, although some language forms are more like dialects, which are functional within their own cultural context but may be less widely understood than standard forms of the language.

It is rarely possible for education to provide the highly effective, closely monitored and directed language experiences that are possible in the home. Language development in school probably depends on participation in meaningful language-based curriculum experiences, rather than specific instruction. Teaching grammar in isolation is unlikely to be useful unless the emphasis is on its use to communicate meaning. The learning of a second language appears to take place most readily in situations which emphasise its functional usage. Internal language can be a very effective way of developing self-regulation of behaviour.

Many children have difficulties with the development of speech and language: either a delay, or, more seriously, some form of deviance. Speech and language therapists can give expert advice for children, either in the form of support in the normal school, or in special schools or units. There are specific remedial approaches for problems with articulation and language structures. These are generally effective, provided that they emphasise the meaning and practical use of language.

Key implications

- Speech and language develop naturally and informally within meaningful social contexts. Effective learning in school should follow this process.
- New language concepts should be established as part of general curriculum studies.
- Education should acknowledge and utilise children's own forms of speech and language.
- Parts of speech and grammar should be learned as ways of developing effective communication rather than as an isolated academic exercise.
- Speech and language difficulties can benefit from expert assessment, advice and support as part of situations where communication performs useful functions.

Further reading

Marian Whitehead (1997) *Language and Literacy in the Early Years*, 2nd edition. London: Paul Chapman.

Probably one of the best books available on the implications of language research for early-years education. Has a strong technical basis in modern research findings but uses lots of examples and is written in an engaging way.

Michael Forrester (1996) *Psychology of Language: A Critical Introduction*. London: Sage.

An excellent review of the main theories and developments in ideas about language. Somewhat technical but definitely readable and packed with ideas and information.

Trevor Harley (1995) *The Psychology of Language: From Data to Theory*. Hove, East Sussex: Psychology Press.

An in-depth consideration of research findings and their interpretation. This book has very wide coverage and would enable its readers to follow up any particular ideas or interests.

Julie Dockrell and David Messer (1999) *Children's Language and Communication Difficulties*. London: Cassell Education.

Covers the general basis of language difficulties and the current level of explanations in this area.

Practical scenario

Mrs Peters is a reception class teacher in a school where children often come in with very poor language abilities, scoring low on their baseline assessments. The children's home backgrounds are often poor and unstimulating, and there are probably limited language models from the parents. Although the children improve during their first year, their inadequate language development still limits their progress with the general curriculum, and particularly with literacy. Mrs Peters is therefore wondering what could be done to accelerate their language abilities, particularly where doing so would also help with their reading and writing.

- *What could Mrs Peters do to stimulate her pupils' speech and language development?*
- *Would it perhaps help to liaise with the parents? How could this be done?*
- *Should Mrs Peters perhaps concentrate on developing her pupils' language abilities and leave literacy teaching until they have a stronger foundation?*
- *Is there any form of assessment which would help guide support for these children?*

9 Literacy

Chapter structure

What is literacy?

Literacy embraces the skills of reading and writing. A useful definition, by Gibson and Levin (1975), is that '*reading* is extracting information from text' (p. 5). These authors also emphasise that reading is an active process, self-directed by the reader for many purposes and in a number of different ways. An early reader decoding words from letter sounds is functioning very differently from a mature reader who is able to use rapid word recognition and sophisticated prediction and search strategies. Goodman (1968) describes reading as essentially a linguistic process of communication, and points out that in reading we are moving from something that is unknown (marks on paper) to something that is known (our own language).

Writing, however, involves translating language into the written form – going from the known to the unknown. This is essentially a more difficult process since we have fewer cues from which to 'guess' at the unknown final form. Writing is a specialised form of communication, and because of its formalised nature and permanence it also acts to focus and direct our thinking.

Although literacy skills map on to language in various ways, in evolutionary terms they have been part of our culture for only a relatively short period. Literacy is not therefore something that is directly part of our biological make-up. Despite this, most of us certainly have the potential for reading and writing, as a result of our language system, our motor and perceptual skills and our flexible learning abilities.

The relationship between reading and spelling

Reading and writing are evidently not the same thing, although they are of course closely related. Russell (1943), for example, found a concurrent correlation of 0.88 between word reading and spelling in 116 7-year-olds. One reason for this close relationship is that we learn to read and write in parallel. There are also underlying abilities such as knowledge of letter sounds and their combinations, known as *phonic skills*, which are important in both reading and spelling. Ellis and Cataldo (1990), however, found that children's spelling ability with regular words predicted progress with reading, but not vice versa. This is consistent with the idea that early spellings depend largely on children's knowledge and use of letters, whereas reading development can start partly on the basis of visual cues.

Although progress with reading and progress with spelling are usually closely related, in English it is usually more difficult to spell a word than it is to read it. Comparisons of the words used in standard reading and spelling tests indicate that on average, children can read words about one year before they can spell them. Children may also have specific spelling problems, and in this case the gap can be much greater. Such children may have normal or good reading abilities yet underfunction significantly with spelling. They will often be aware that what they have written is incorrect since it 'reads' wrongly, but they do not know the correct letter sequence. Moseley (1989) has shown that although all children will tend to avoid words that they are unable to spell, children who have spelling difficulties are much more prone to do so. Their avoidance of problem words can rise to an underestimate of their ability, particularly in secondary schools, where written work is the main way in which attainments are assessed.

Reading development

Children entering school often have some early reading skills, such as the ability to recognise letters and some basic words. Their ability in this respect is very dependent on the home background and varies a great deal between children. When children first start school, it is estimated that on average they learn to read approximately one new word a week, and that in the early junior years their rate of learning progressively increases to many new words *a day* (Moseley, 1975).

Vocabulary development

The development of reading vocabulary was investigated by Williams (1961), who devised a specific word-reading test based on a random sample of 100 words from *The Concise Oxford Dictionary*. Using this to test a range of school-aged children, as shown in Figure 9.1 he found that there was a progressive increase in word-reading vocabulary, with a spurt starting from

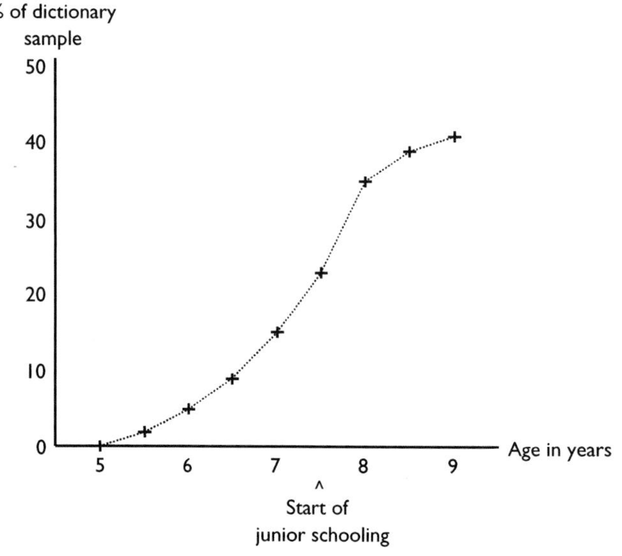

Figure 9.1 Growth in reading vocabulary
Source: Based on data from Williams (1961)

about 6½ years of age and slowing down at about 8 years of age.

Further research by Davies and Williams (1975) used a standard test of phonic skills over the period of children's most rapid reading vocabulary development. They found that whatever the type of teaching given, the spurt did not occur unless a basic level of phonic skills was initially achieved. Harding *et al.* (1985) also found that as children progressed with their reading, their attempts at unknown words were increasingly based on phonic rules, levelling off from the age of about 7 to 8 years.

Children with a reading age from about 6½ to 8 years therefore seem to be developing generalised ways of using information to work out words, known as word attack skills. These allow them to tackle a range of words that they have never met before. In this way, learning how to read '-ight' at the end of a word could enable a child to read the complete family of words such as 'fight', 'light', 'might', 'tight', etc.

When words can be worked out from their letter sounds they are referred to as 'phonically regular'. The flattening of the curve after a reading age of about 8 years probably happens as the reader comes up against words that are less phonically regular. Some of these will also be of low frequency and will not be within the reader's spoken vocabulary. An example is the word 'dough', which has a readability of just above the 9-year-level and which is both uncommon and phonically irregular. As discussed later in this chapter, it seems likely that further progress with reading after this level will depend on the development of general language abilities.

Progress with phonic skills

Reading at the very earliest stages can involve learning separate words by sight, often from limited physical features. As their reading vocabulary expands, children then seem to start to use letter sounds and their combinations to work out words. At a reading age of about 6 years, children are able to work out short, phonically regular words known as 'consonant–vowel–consonant' (CVC) words, such as 'cat'. They are also starting to identify some of the most common irregular words such as 'the', which can be identified only by visual recognition or partial phonic cues. Subsequent developments involve progressively more complex phonic skills such as consonant blends ('tr' as in 'trip') and consonant and vowel digraphs, where letter combinations result in new sounds such as 'sh' as in 'ship' and 'ou' as in 'out'. Children are eventually able to tackle clusters of letters such as 'ight' and combinations of syllables in complex words such as 'underneath', which has a readability level of just above 8 years.

The English language is not very regular, however, and Bailey (1967) found that there were about 200 rules for combining sounds. One example of these is the two-vowel rule: 'the first vowel says its name, the second is usually silent', for example with the words 'tie' and 'eat'. The difficulty is that such rules do not always work, as in the word 'field'. Bailey therefore found that even if all the 200 rules are applied, only half of all words can be tackled correctly. Many words have unique spellings, for which phonic rules would be misleading, for instance in the word 'yacht'. Others can be misleading because they have different letters but sound the same, such as 'their' and 'there'. Such words must be learned individually, although the letters that make them up are still a source of possible cues (partial information). The more gradual progress which happens after a reading age of about 8 to 9 years seems to be due to the progressive establishment of such words in children's sight vocabularies, as well as developments with general language abilities.

The process of reading

The way in which people look at print and how they identify words can be an important source of information about what we are doing when we read and how reading develops in the first place. Although it has sometimes been assumed that training up these abilities might improve reading, they mostly appear to be the outcome of the process of reading, happening as we attempt to construct meaning from what we are reading.

Eye fixations

When a person is reading, the eyes flick from one point to another in movements known as saccades, although most of the time is actually spent between movements, fixating on one part of a word. Each saccade takes about 10 to 20 milliseconds and each fixation continues for about 250 milliseconds. For good readers with material at their own reading level, each saccade jumps over about eight letters or spaces, although a beginning reader may look many times at the different parts of each word. Difficulties in interpreting the meaning of text can lead to regressions, and Rayner and Sereno (1994) found that about 10 to 15 per cent of all eye movements in reading involve a fixation on earlier text to reprocess some information there. Occasionally eye movements will also jump forward, when there is an early ambiguity which the reader believes will be resolved later on. As discussed later, eye movements can be used as an indicator of the way in which we process print and are used by researchers to study the effects of different sentence structures.

The part of the retina which has the greatest sensitivity is known as the *fovea*. As shown in Figure 9.2, in reading, the fovea can normally cover about seven to ten letters or spaces, which usually includes the start of the word currently fixated on plus about four letters to the left and to the right. The total perceptual span covers about 15 letters to the right of fixation, which means that about 11 letters to the right will be perceived outside the fovea, in an area of the retina known as the *parafoveal region* (Figure 9.2). This has less accurate perception, which means that information here can receive only a low level of analysis, such as one relating to the general shape of letters and words. Sensitivity in this region appears to develop as children learn to read from left to right. In languages such as Hebrew that are read from right to left, the perceptual span is reversed, and the parafoveal region extends to the left.

Gregory (1970) considers that general perception is often a 'top-down' process, involving the use of existing knowledge to direct our interpretations and to search for additional information particularly when we are overloaded with perceptual information or when the input is ambiguous. Although the use of existing knowledge in this way can result in misperceptions (as in illusions), it is the only efficient possibility when we have to come to some decision based on limited information. It seems likely that such a process occurs when people are reading, since they have only limited perceptual input when reading rapidly.

This postulate is supported by the fact that words fixated on are not random and appear to be those with the maximum of information. Common words such as 'the' are rarely fixated on, and words which are more informative (particularly those which are longer) are more likely to be fixated on, and for longer periods. Fixations also tend to be to the centre of words, where they will cover as much of the word as possible. It seems likely that fixations are planned on the basis of the meaning and structure of what has been read so far, as well as partial information from the right of the perceptual span, which will normally overlap to some extent with what is subsequently fixated on.

Eye movements in reading seem to be the

Figure 9.2 Text showing typical successive eye fixations and areas perceived at fixation number 3

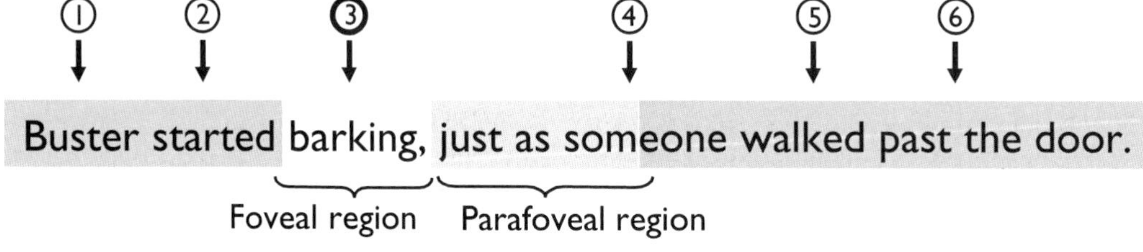

outcome of the progressive development of searching for information. Although faster readers tend to make fewer fixations, this is probably because they have better processing capabilities, and are generally more knowledgeable about the content of what they are reading. Schemes which aim to improve reading by decreasing the number of eye fixations are therefore unlikely to be effective and often merely reduce comprehension. In reviewing the effects of such training, Gibson and Levin (1975) concluded that although people can improve the speed at which they read, they can do so most effectively by developing the general cognitive abilities and strategies on which reading depends.

Word identification

Most of the letters in each word fixated on can normally be seen clearly, and the identification of individual words appears to happen relatively rapidly. Rayner *et al.* (1981) investigated how individual words are identified by using additional visual information to mask words and prevent further visual processing just after they had been fixated on. If the mask hid the words 50 milliseconds after the start of each eye fixation, the overall reading rate was reduced only slightly. Since reading involves both word naming and meaning, this implies that both processes happen within this time. The 'Stroop phenomenon' described on p. 192 shows interference from a word's meaning even when people attempt to ignore it, and also supports the idea that word identification and generating meaning are rapid and automatic processes.

Since each fixation takes about 250 milliseconds, there are therefore about 200 milliseconds of time left per word, which can be used in other types of cognitive processing. It is likely that this is used to analyse and develop the grammatical structure and meaning of what is being read, in the same way as happens with speech perception, as well as to set up the following area for fixation.

The sheer speed at which word identification occurs also implies that it is probably achieved by some form of parallel processing, with feature

Figure 9.3 Three-route model of word identification

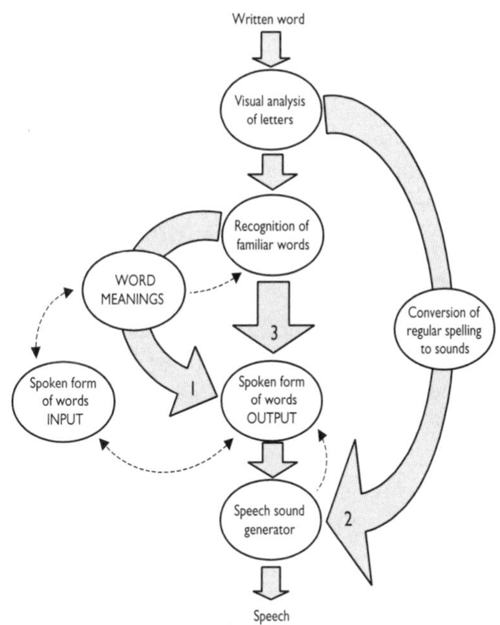

Source: Adapted from Buchanan and Besner (1995)

identification of letters and words triggering off different forms of analysis. This would fit in with hypothetical models based on connectionist approaches as described in Chapter 2. Evidence summarised by Buchanan and Besner (1995), from individuals with certain types of brain damage which cause reading problems (known as acquired dyslexias), indicates that such processing can happen through three major routes. As shown in Figure 9.3, all these routes have in common an initial visual analysis of letters and a final conversion to speech sounds.

Route

1 The main way in which words are identified and spoken by mature readers consists in the recognition that a particular word forms part of the sight vocabulary (normally numbering many thousands), leading to the identification of word meaning and subsequent verbalisation.

2 The second route initially happens without the recognition of meaning via a grapheme to phoneme conversion. Such a conversion can

handle regular spellings only and cannot therefore cope with all words. The use of this by mature readers can be shown by the ability to read regular non-words such as 'phleeck', which can be read easily even though it has no meaning. Early readers, or people encountering unfamiliar words, will also carry out a phonic analysis. This can then act as an input to word meaning via the system of dotted lines and involves generating a spoken form for identification.

3 Non-semantic whole-word reading can be seen in children who read out loud fluently but with limited understanding – sometimes referred to as 'barking at print', when children read with little intonation and make errors which show poor comprehension.

Normally when a person reads, the three routes are available at the same time, although there appears to be an emphasis on whichever is most effective for a particular task. Mature reading, for instance, mainly depends on route 1, but there is also information available from the sounds of words. This is shown by the fact that readers will sometimes be unable to detect errors if a word sounds the same as the correct one, as in the sentence 'he saw a little man only for feet high'. In this, the word 'for' sounds the same as 'four', and Daneman and Stainton (1991) found that subjects instructed to proof-read tended not to pick up such homophonic errors. This is only a weak effect, however, and the semantic route generally appears to have priority and to happen more rapidly.

Sometimes the meaning of words becomes disconnected from the actual spelling, leading to errors such as reading 'tulip' instead of 'crocus'. The word appears to directly trigger off the meaning of 'a flower' but this is not modified by direct features of the word, in order to select the correct type of flower. When this is a persistent feature for an individual, it is referred to as surface dyslexia, but it can happen occasionally with otherwise normal readers.

The psycholinguistic approach

Reading is of course more than simply the ability to read separate words. In a similar way to the perception and comprehension of speech described in Chapter 8, reading must also involve language processing capabilities – the ability to assemble grammatical structures and derive meaning from them. In this sense, reading can therefore be seen as successive identification of and 'listening to' words.

A stronger psycholinguistic perspective argues that reading involves active and high-level cognitive strategies related to the structure and meaning of language. Goodman (1968) in particular characterises reading as essentially a psycholinguistic guessing game, with readers using whatever cues are available to generate linguistic meaning. These cues can take many forms, including letter sounds and their combinations in words. What Goodman feels is more important, however, is the *meaning* that is involved in what is read, including the grammatical structure of texts. According to this approach, reading is a process of constructing meaning, using this to make hypotheses about the text and then testing them out. This is evident in a child's errors (see below on miscue analysis), which can be seen as attempts to follow a particular hypothesis, rather than just being 'wrong'. This is supported by Murray and Maliphant's (1982) findings described later, which show that word-reading errors often use a correct part of speech and make overall sense.

Goodman (1965) originally argued that such strategies were what made for good readers, finding that there was a 60 to 80 per cent improvement in reading accuracy when children read words in context, compared with when they read them in isolation. Good readers also made greater improvements by using context than poorer readers were able to. This suggests that context provides extra-semantic and syntactic cues which good readers are able to use for word identification, and that this ability improves with better reading.

However, Nicholson and Hill (1985) have

criticised Goodman's original work on the grounds that because his subjects first read the words in isolation, then in the contextual sentences, any improvement might be due just to practice effects. To test this hypothesis they ran a more stringent counterbalanced study, with 8-year-old readers on two levels of text: easy readability (8-year level) and hard readability (11-year level). Unlike Goodman, they found that context was *not* a help in reading unknown words. On the easy readability text, children were able to read all the words and did not need context. On the hard readability text, the context was simply not powerful enough to reveal the exact words.

Nicholson and Hill concluded that the main characteristic distinguishing good from poor readers (at this age) is not the ability to utilise context, but the ability to decode words independently from context. This is supported in a study by Harding *et al.* (1985) of the changing reading strategies and abilities used by children from 5 to 11 years of age. Over this time, whole-word reading strategies progressively increased, with a corresponding decline in the number of syntactic and semantic miscues made by children – the opposite of what Goodman would have predicted. Share and Stanovich (1995) also review evidence showing that when poor readers were given text that they could cope with, their comprehension abilities became as good as those of normal readers. When good readers were given text that was beyond their abilities, they too would 'plod' and were unable to use context to aid comprehension. Such findings imply that merely teaching children to guess more may not be a very effective strategy for improving early reading.

Normal reading, however, probably involves a relatively close match between children's abilities and the difficulty of the text. Such a match might then increase the effectiveness of semantic and syntactic information. The children's ability to read the harder unknown words in Nicholson and Hill's work (such as 'abdomen' and 'radii') would not have been helped by the context. For example, 'the spider tilted up her ———' gives little information unless you already know a lot about spiders. It also seems likely that many of these words were not within the children's language vocabulary at this age. The situation is probably different for older children (e.g. 9 years and above), who have wider vocabularies and well-established phonic analysis skills. In a study of the type of errors made at different ages, Murray and Maliphant (1982) found that it was not until about 9 years of age that children's errors showed higher levels of conforming to the grammatical and semantic context. When reading the sentence 'The man hit a boundary', older children were therefore likely to read 'The man hit a *baseball*'. This shows that they are aware that the final word should be a noun and that it is something that is normally hit.

In general, it seems likely that readers will use whatever strategies and information are most useful to them at any particular time. When they are reading at a matched level, most words read will probably be identified rapidly and the reader will be constructing a plausible grammatical structure and underlying meaning from this, using successive eye fixations to gather key information. On the rare occasions when words cannot be identified, the reader will make logical 'guesses', based on phonic skills as well as syntactic and semantic information. Sometimes these will be correct, but much of the time there will probably be insufficient information available, leading to errors.

When reading text which has many words at a harder level than they are able to cope with easily, readers will be forced to use contextual information more. However, it is likely to be difficult to generate an accurate context without knowing a high proportion of the key words, and readers will often need to fall back on their word-decoding phonic skills.

Reading subskills

The underlying cognitive processes involved in reading must encompass a rather complex integration of a large number of basic abilities. One popular approach proposed by Coltheart (1978) is that these can be divided into visual perceptual skills and phonological skills, involving spelling-to-sound analysis and synthesis.

Visual sequential memory

Since perceptual input involves the identification of a sequence of visual symbols, one area of investigation has been what is known as visual sequential memory (VSM). Tests of this ability, such as the Aston Index (Newton and Thomson, 1976), involve a sequence of symbols which are shown to a subject and which then have to be either identified or reproduced from memory. Performances on such tests usually show a significant positive correlation with present and future general literacy skills. Newton and Thomson (1976), for instance, found a correlation of 0.31 between children's VSM at 5½ years and their word-reading ability two years later. This implies that VSM could be an important skill in the early development of reading, and that it might be useful to develop it in children who are just beginning to read. A perceptual training programme developed by Frostig and Horne (1964) was once very popular to develop such abilities.

Unfortunately, subsequent research reviewed by Hammill and Larsen (1978) found that such training approaches were very specific in their effects, and that although children can improve on perceptual tasks, the improvement does not extend to their reading progress. One likely explanation seems to be that VSM correlates with reading abilities only because they are both dependent on verbal coding. Hicks (1980), for instance, found that when carrying out VSM tasks, subjects were actually using verbal labels to help them to remember. For example, the symbol ✧ was usually labelled 'star'. Hicks then prevented subjects from carrying out such verbal encoding by giving them the interfering verbal task of saying the word 'the' repeatedly to themselves. Under these conditions, there were *no* differences in VSM scores between good and poor readers. Telling all subjects to use verbal labelling also lifted the VSM performance of poor readers (including dyslexics) to that of good readers, indicating that the original differences between these groups were mainly due to their verbal coding strategies.

Spelling on the other hand appears to involve more definite visual sequential skills, and it seems likely that the demands of the VSM task would be close to what is required in remembering and generating a sequence of written letters. Giles and Terrell (1997) investigated whether that was the case with two VSM tasks, one of which was helped by verbal labels (a series of pictures of animals), whereas the other was a relatively abstract sequence of triangles of different shapes to which subjects tended not to attach verbal labels. They compared the performance of 13-year-old normal spellers and poor spellers and found that only the sequence which could be verbally labelled showed any difference between the two groups. Performance on the non-verbal visual sequencing task did not appear to relate to spelling ability at all. If anything, subjects seemed to be using verbal cues and techniques to help themselves with difficult spellings, for instance explicitly sounding the 'a' and 'ch' sounds when working out how to spell 'yacht'.

Phonological abilities

A knowledge of both spoken and written sounds and the ability to process them in different ways appears to be generally important for literacy progress. As will be discussed later in relation to language abilities, early sensitivity to the sounds in words has been shown to be a strong and independent predictor of subsequent progress with literacy. Even more importantly, training children in these abilities accelerates their subsequent literacy development and implies that such training should be part of early teaching approaches.

Lonigan *et al.* (1998) looked at the stability of various measures of phonological sensitivity in 2- to 5-year-old children. These included the detection of rhyme and alliteration, the ability to combine separate sounds (known as blending) and the ability to leave a specific sound out of a word (known as elision). As well as predicting reading progress, these abilities correlated together well and became more stable as children matured. Such findings imply that it is reasonable to consider such abilities as being characteristic of individual children, and that they could form the basis for assessment, for example using the Phonological Assessment Battery (Frederickson, 1995) described later in this chapter.

Short-term memory constraints

Since it can seem that we hold and analyse what we read as a form of 'inner speech', one popular theory, mentioned in Chapter 2, proposes that reading abilities are governed by the limitations of short-term memory. Short-term memory can be seen as a form of processing capacity and is known as 'working memory', with definite limits to how many meaningful 'chunks' it can deal with at any one time. In applying this idea to reading, Just and Carpenter (1992) found that subjects' ability to recall the final word in a number of sentences correlated at about 0.8 with reading comprehension. This is consistent with the idea that people's different working memory capacities may determine how well they can process information during reading.

Measures of working memory from tasks which do not involve reading or language also show significant correlations with reading. Law and Sayer (1983), for instance, found a correlation of 0.40 between reading ability and digit recall. The latter is a form of sequential memory task, and involves subjects listening to and repeating back sequences of digits of increasing length. However, such correlations vary according to how close the task is to the actual reading process. Crispin *et al.* (1984), for instance, found a correlation of 0.52 when the task involved letters instead of digits, and Share and Stanovich (1995) found a correlation of above 0.70 with letter sequences which resembled patterns found in words.

An alternative explanation of these effects is that they reflect different levels of coding skills or expertise by individuals rather than any fixed amount of working memory. According to Samuels *et al.* (1992), good readers have developed the ability to process basic reading information more automatically and efficiently, meaning that there is more capacity available for higher-level processes. Since a great part of early reading skills relates to perceiving and analysing sounds, it is likely that good readers have simply developed a more efficient way of encoding the process of doing so. They would then exhibit better performance on working memory tasks, which are heavily reliant on the way in which information is represented. This idea is supported in a study by Ellis (1990) which demonstrated that early reading experience developed auditory short-term memory, rather than the other way round. It therefore seems unlikely that the developing of short-term memory skills would by itself have any effect on reading abilities, although improving phonological expertise would probably improve both early reading and short-term memory performance.

When memory tasks involve skills which are close to those involved in reading, they can show very close relationships with reading performance. Crispin *et al.* (1984) found that combining the scores for knowledge of letter names and the memory for sequences of letters accounted for 70 per cent of the variance in early reading in 6- to 9-year-olds. This is a large effect and is consistent with the idea that knowledge and use of written letter sounds and names are very important subskills in early reading. Direct teaching of the links between speech sounds and letter sounds and their combinations in words is of course very common. As discussed below, there is considerable research evidence that this helps children's reading progress, and that it is a relatively natural strategy for children to develop.

In general, then, some subskills can be important in the process of reading and training children in them can help with their progress, so long as this relates closely to the normal process of reading acquisition. From the evidence available, the best way to proceed is to use speech sounds and link these with a knowledge of letters and their combinations. Other subskills such as the ability to perform separate memory tasks, eye fixations, or even some comprehension skills are probably themselves dependent on reading development, and attempts to develop these are unlikely to be productive.

Teaching reading

Broadly speaking, there are two major approaches to the teaching of reading, which can be characterised respectively as 'skills leading to reading' and 'reading leading to skills'. These perspectives can often become relatively polarised, and arguments between the respective proponents have sometimes been referred to as the 'reading wars'.

The phonics approach

The first of these is the more traditional perspective, one which sees reading as a 'bottom-up' process and emphasises that the basis of reading involves decoding from letter sounds. According to this, children should first be taught their alphabet and how to say the sounds for separate letters. An example of this in common use is the 'Letterland' teaching system (Wendon, 1980), which links letter shapes with pictures that start with the appropriate sounds. For example, the letter 'd' is made into the shape of a duck, with a round body on the left and a neck on the right.

This knowledge of letters can then be used to work out simple, regular words which emphasise the use of common, regular patterns such as 'cat', 'rat', 'mat', 'fat', etc. Early reading texts can also be based on such regular words, with the emphasis being on encouraging children to work out unknown words by sounding out all the letters. Children are then taught progressively more complex phonic rules to enable them to tackle a wider range of words.

A more sophisticated approach depends upon learning all the written representations for the 40-plus phonemes (spoken sounds). This means that as well as single letter sounds, children learn the consonant and vowel digraphs such as 'th' and 'ai' (as in rain). Many of the vowel digraphs have a number of different written forms for the same sound, and the 'ai' sound can also exist as 'rake', 'day', 'great', 'weigh' and 'they'. Learning all these would be quite an initial load for children, and phonemic programmes based on this approach such as 'Reading Reflex' (McGuinness and McGuinness, 1998) and 'Jolly Phonics' (Lloyd, 1998) build up their use over time.

Phonics must itself depend on children's phonological abilities. Although phonics teaching has traditionally assumed that children have the necessary ability to perceive and use speech sounds, there is now considerable evidence (discussed later in this chapter) that some children have difficulties in this area. Training for these abilities, particularly when it forms part of the approaches discussed above, provides a stronger foundation for early literacy development and enhances progress.

Analytic versus synthetic phonics

A distinction can be made between techniques which initially develop an awareness of sounds within words, known as 'analytic phonics', and those which attempt to teach sounds in isolation and then to build them up into words, known as 'synthetic phonics'. Analytic phonics is incorporated within England's National Literacy Strategy (NLS) and is arguably a more natural approach, using contrasts between whole words based on differences between them known as onset and rimes (see Chapter 8). Teaching onset involves giving children sets of words such as 'bat', 'bin', 'bun' and encouraging them to link the first sound with the letter. This approach is based on the belief that children learn by using analogies – comparing words and using patterns which they have already learned. According to this, if children have learned the words 'pin' and 'tin', they should then be able to extend their knowledge of the rime to a new word such as 'bin'.

Proponents of synthetic phonics believe that it is more effective to base learning on the 40-plus phonemes. Although it may seem that this is a lot for children to learn, it can be argued that the demands are less than the analytic approach of the NLS, which requires knowledge of many initial and final consonant clusters as well as a large number of separate rimes. Once the phonemes have been learned, they can then be used in a conventional way to build up initially simple words, progressing on to different forms for the same sounds and more complex and less regular combinations.

One programme devised by Solity *et al.* (1999) was based on the synthetic approach and used during the first two years of schooling. This found a significant advantage of six months when compared with a matched group of children who had been taught using the NLS. One reservation is that their better progress may have been at least partly the result of using a number of short learning sessions each day. However, an investigation by Watson and Johnston (1999) also found that a programme based on the synthetic approach using 'Jolly Phonics' for one session each day was highly effective. After one year of using this, pupils were 12 months ahead of other children with their reading and 14 months ahead with their spelling.

It may be, however, that the differences between the suitability of the two approaches comes down to a question of timing. Although early progress may be accelerated by the limited and more predictable synthetic approach, later progress with less regular patterns of letter combinations will probably benefit from the comparisons and generalisations which come from the analytic approach. It may be unwise to use either technique exclusively, and best to start from an emphasis on the synthetic approach and then incorporate analytic techniques once children are able to manage regular phonics.

Critics of the phonics approach often attack it on the basis of its artificiality, arguing that reading should be the process of deriving meaning from the written word, and that phonics only produces children who 'bark at print' but who are not able to use what they read. It is also argued that phonics cannot work, since isolated letter sounds are very different from sounds in words. For example, the letters 'c', 'a' and 't' are in fact sounded as 'kuh', 'ah' and 'ter' in isolation; putting them together does not result in the sound of the word 'cat'. As noted earlier, phonic rules are also often ineffective, with 200 known rules being far too many for children to learn easily, and even these apply only to about half of all words.

Real reading books

The alternative approach, based on seeing reading as essentially a linguistic process, is derived largely from the ideas of Goodman (1968) described earlier. According to this, reading should be *acquired* (not taught), just as language is. Smith (1973) in particular has argued that children should experience literacy only in meaningful contexts and that learning the finer structure of reading (letters and words) will follow from this. Any early attempt to focus on letter sounds or a limited reading vocabulary is believed to get in the way of the normal process. From the start, it is argued, this should involve immersion in *real reading books* with a complete text, governed mainly by the child's interests and without undue concern for the vocabulary or the difficulty of the words.

The evidence for the effectiveness of this approach has already been discussed and indicates that there is doubt about the power of context in enabling early readers to work out unknown words. There is, however, evidence that more fluent readers do use language structure and content to guide the search for meaning.

These two seemingly irreconcilable perspectives represent the opposite ends of a continuum, and in reality are rarely implemented by themselves. The most popular intermediate position involves an emphasis upon learning separate *whole words*, for example in the 'Breakthrough' approach (Mackay *et al.*, 1970). This particular scheme initially uses flashcards based on a child's own spoken language. The cards are used by children to assemble sentences as a basis for early writing. An early sight vocabulary can also be developed through *structured reading programmes* such as 'Reading 360' (1978). These schemes typically start off with a very limited set of words, which can involve separate flashcard learning or repeated reading from the book. Successive books gradually extend the range of words, using progressively more difficult ones. Such schemes are very popular with schools and are meant to ensure that children are always able to cope successfully with reading tasks. Children still develop phonic skills with this approach, and Davies and Williams (1975) found that they do so whatever the teaching approach used. Share and Stanovich (1995) also emphasise that a great deal of children's development in reading is self-taught and is based on the naturally occurring patterns of letter–sound correspondences in words. Although such approaches allow children to develop their own strategies, critics such as Smith (1973) still argue that reading schemes are artificial and stilted, damaging children's natural interests and involvement in early reading.

Integrating approaches

Most recent analyses attempt to integrate the two approaches into a single practical perspective. Bryant (1994), for instance, points out that the two kinds of linguistic knowledge – awareness of phonological segments, and sensitivity to semantic and syntactic constraints – can *both* be used. In a longitudinal research study of beginning readers lasting 18 months, early phonological ability was a significant predictor of subsequent letter-sound learning. In parallel with this, early semantic and syntactic ability predicted the subsequent ability to use context to decipher words. Each of these effects was also independent of the other, indicating that it can be productive in literacy teaching to develop both these abilities.

At the earliest stages of reading, it may be particularly useful to emphasise phonic abilities. Blatchford *et al.* (1987), for instance, looked at children's early knowledge of letter sounds and language abilities and found that pre-school letter–sound knowledge was the strongest single predictor of reading (with a correlation of 0.61) two years later. Taken with the general research findings on the nature of subskills (see earlier in this chapter), this does seem to indicate that in the first years of schooling it may be important to ensure that children do at least have a foundation of letter–sound knowledge, and that children's phonological abilities may need to be developed to enhance their letter–sound knowledge. The 'Sound Linkage' approach by Hatcher (1994) links phonological training and phonics with an integrated approach to early reading. A study of the effectiveness of this by Hatcher *et al.* (1994) found that over a 20-week teaching period, $7\frac{1}{2}$-year-old poor readers made one year's progress with their ability to read words in context. According to a report by HMI (1991), most teachers at that time used a fairly eclectic approach based upon a combination of early phonics, structured reading schemes and individual extension reading when appropriate. These approaches have been consolidated and standardised by the national literacy strategy, which also directs their implementation with a daily programme that is largely based on whole-class teaching.

Literacy tests

Use of tests

Testing can be a useful way for a teacher to gain additional information about pupils, either to check on overall levels of achievement (summative assessments) or to gain specific information about children's progress to help with future teaching (formative assessments). A review of the use of reading tests by Pumfrey (1979) showed that the most commonly used tests in the primary school were 'normative' ones, mostly used as a rapid test of an individual's overall level. These would have only limited value in the planning of future teaching since they do not give any diagnostic information. At one time, the simplest (and most popular) tests used for reading and spelling were the Schonell Graded Word Reading Test (Schonell, 1955) and the Graded Word Spelling Test (Vernon, 1977). These both involve a list of words of graded difficulty; with the Schonell test the child reads the words individually to the teacher, and with the Vernon's test the child writes down the words from the teacher's dictation. The spelling test can be done individually or with a group. The Schonell test covers the range from 6 to 12½ years; the Vernon's covers the range from 5 years 7 months up to 15 years 10 months. Both these tests have the virtue of simplicity, which has probably accounted for much of their popularity. As the Schonell test is now somewhat old, the best equivalent with a more modern vocabulary and standardisation might now be the Macmillan Graded Word Reading Test (1986). Another popular and rapid assessment of the accuracy of reading words, but this time using complete sentences, is the Salford Sentence Reading Test (Bookbinder, 1976).

Such tests can be useful to gain a rapid overall assessment of pupils' reading or spelling, to make sure, for instance, that they can cope with the demands of the normal range of school work. They are typically used on transfer to secondary schooling and the most common are normative group tests such as the NFER-Nelson Group Reading Test II (Cornwall and France, 1997). This takes about 30 minutes and covers the age range from 6 years to nearly 15 years. The subtests involve sentence completion and context comprehension tasks, and incorporate skills relevant to general school work at this level.

Individual and group tests

There are many different reading and spelling tests available and the particular one used will depend on the type of information needed and the circumstances in which it is used. However, individual tests are usually more reliable and often give diagnostic information. For example, on the Neale (1989) test, individual children read passages of graded difficulty, and the teacher can note the different types of errors that they make. Group tests for primary-aged children such as the Young's (1968) usually involve selecting the correct word to match with pictures and to complete sentences. Although children are less closely supervised, the Young's test does have reasonable reliability and allows the teacher to test many pupils at the same time. Such tests can therefore be very useful as a means of screening numbers of children for reading difficulties.

Most normative reading tests give relative information about children's levels of ability, such as a reading age. This may appear to be a simplistic way of summarising children's progress but it can be useful as a general indication of the type of skills that a child has developed. For instance, if children have a reading age above 9 years, then they almost certainly have a substantial range of word attack skills. Subsequent teaching should probably emphasise comprehension and the use of reading in general curriculum studies.

Criterion-referenced testing

Criterion-referenced testing is usually less formal and based upon a teacher's own understanding of the learning process. This can involve a sequence of key assessment tasks and criteria for judging whether a pupil has achieved them. For early reading, the tests might cover phonological abilities, letter sound/name knowledge, phonic skills and reading vocabulary from a set of high-frequency words. These can be easily monitored and linked directly with specific phonic teaching approaches, a large number of which have been reviewed and summarised by Hinson and Smith (1993).

Diagnostic testing

Diagnostic testing is a type of formative assessment, and its main purpose is to analyse a child's pattern of abilities and to guide future teaching support. Some diagnostic reading tests aim to pinpoint specific key abilities or skills which are weak, implying that subsequent teaching should be aimed at these areas to help to develop reading attainments. The Aston Index (Newton and Thomson, 1976) is a typical example of this approach and identifies six attainments including attainments in language vocabulary, reading and spelling. Six performance items can be related to these, including visual and auditory sequential memory, sound blending and sound discrimination. However, as discussed earlier, teaching these subskills in isolation is unlikely to be productive, although phonological abilities can be important to early readers.

A more recent diagnostic assessment is the PhaB (Phonological Assessment Battery – Frederickson, 1995), which evaluates children's sensitivity to sounds in words. This covers abilities such as the detection of alliteration and rhyme, speed of naming digits and pictures, the ability to generate spoonerisms, and a test of semantic fluency. The strongest single correlate of reading ability (with a value of 0.85) is the 'spoonerism' test, which involves replacing one sound in a word with another. For instance, a child could be asked to replace the 'l' sound in 'lip' with a 'p' sound, to make a new word. It seems likely that this test involves a number of phonological abilities, such as analysis and synthesis, and encoding in working memory, that are important in early reading. As discussed earlier, this approach has the advantage that it identifies skills that are relatively stable and characteristic of individual children, and which have been shown to improve reading when they are taught.

Choosing the appropriate test

The nature of a test depends to a great extent on what one believes that the reading or writing/spelling process is all about. As this changes at different levels of skill, the abilities looked at should also vary accordingly. As reading progress at the early stages is closely linked with establishing and using letter sounds, an appropriate test would give pupils tasks which are based upon these abilities. The Word Recognition and Phonic Skills Test, by Carver and Moseley (1994), does so by giving pupils the task of selecting among words according to sounds and their combinations, as read out by the teacher. The test has a relatively early 'floor' of 5 years and discriminates well between children at the initial stages of reading development.

With intermediate skill development at the top infant and junior level, progress depends on more complex phonic abilities. These include regular and irregular blends and digraphs as well as polysyllabic and low-frequency words with unique spellings. Most tests at this level also incorporate words in meaningful contexts and involve tasks such as selecting between a set of words to complete a sentence. These skills are covered by a wide range of available tests which can be used with groups of children in school. Popular examples of these are the Young's (1968), the Primary Reading Test (France, 1979) and the Macmillan Group Reading Test (revised, Cornwall and France, 1997a).

At higher levels of reading, it may be more appropriate to use tests which are mainly based on comprehension such as the higher levels of the NFER-Nelson Group Reading Test II (Cornwall and France, 1997b). Another type of assessment which can cover a broad range of attainments is the Informal Reading Inventory approach defined by Johnson and Kress (1964). This is a way of assessing children's errors using graded passages of real reading material. Based on 'miscue analysis', this looks for children's errors associated with the grammatical, the graphophonic (sound–symbol) and the semantic systems. Children can also be placed at different reading levels in terms of their reading accuracy. The *independent* level means getting 99 per cent or more words correct; the *instructional* level means getting 91–98 per cent correct; and the *frustration* level involves getting 90 per cent or less correct. This type of assessment therefore has direct implications for the level and type of reading material that children should be working on.

Readability assessment

The reading difficulty of texts can vary a great deal. In order for children to read independently, or to need only a low level of support, a text should be closely matched with their abilities – typically so that they can get about 95 per cent of the words correct in order to be at the instructional level. A measure of the level of difficulty of text can help the teacher to select or to check reading material so that it is in the right range for pupils.

Figure 9.4 The basis of readability

ASPECTS OF WORDS

Whether a word is high or low frequency.
For example, although it is irregular, '**the**' is one of the easiest words to read as it is very common.

The phonic regularity of words.
The simplest are short and regular, such as 'hit'. The hardest are polysyllabic and irregular, such as 'although'.

SENTENCE STRUCTURE

Complex structures make it hard to follow the meaning and to predict other parts. For example, sentences with an embedded clause such as 'The boy, *who stole the book*, ran down the road'.
The trickiest ones also involve passive verbs and negatives, for example: 'The boy, *who wasn't bitten by the dog*, had no need to avoid the kennel'.

PHYSICAL PROPERTIES

General layout (breaking text up makes it easier to read), size of print, type of font (serif is best for blocks of text), the contrast with background and levels of illumination.

MEANING OF TEXT FOR THE READER

Reading is easier if readers know about, or are interested in what they are reading. This often means that they are more able to use context to infer unknown words, as well as being more familiar with the written vocabulary that is used.

A reader's ability to manage text is affected by a number of measures. As shown in Figure 9.4, these include structural aspects such as sentence structure and the familiarity and complexity of words, as well as the physical properties of the text and how easy it is to understand the concepts involved.

Readability measures are usually based on equations which take into account the complexity of words and of sentence structures. They do so by using parameters such as the average number of syllables, the number of common words in a sentence, or the average sentence length.

One of the more reliable of such measures is the Dale–Chall index (1948), which is based on average sentence length and the percentage of words outside a high-frequency list of 3,000 words. This has been shown to correlate at about 0.7 with the average judgements of reading difficulty by groups of teachers and pupils.

However, it can be difficult to calculate such measures without the use of a computer program and the keying in of large amounts of text. The Fry Readability Index (Fry, 1977) shown in Figure 9.5 overcomes this by using word and syllable counts which are then used to read off an approximate reading level. As well as being easy to apply, the Fry index also covers the range of primary and secondary education and is one of the most popular of all such measures, with a study by Fry (1968) finding a correlation of 0.93 with reading comprehension. It is used as follows:

- Randomly select three 100-word passages from a book or an article.
- Plot the average number of syllables and the average number of sentences per 100 words on the graph to determine the readability level of the material. Choose more passages per book if great variability is observed and conclude that the book has uneven readability.
- Few passages will fall into the grey areas, but when they do, readability scores are invalid.

Figure 9.5 Fry's readability graph

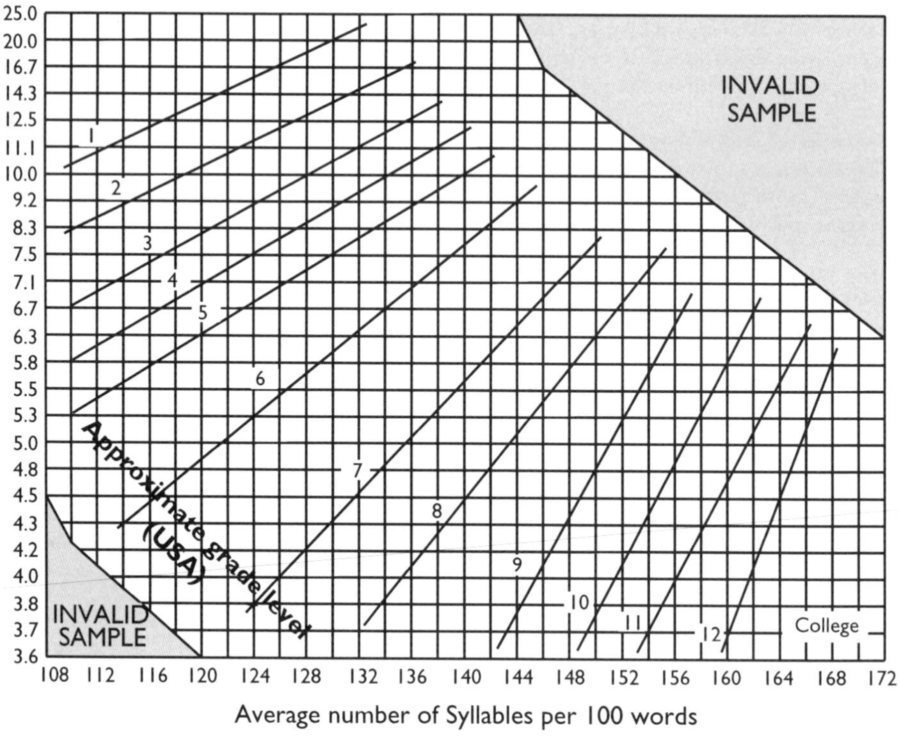

Source: Reproduced from Edward Fry, *Elementary Reading Instruction*, New York: McGraw-Hill, 1977, p. 217, with

- To convert to the reading age in years, add 5 to the American grade (between the lines).

Such measures have been heavily criticised by writers such as Goodman (1986) for their lack of consistency – limited agreement between different indices. It is also argued that they oversimplify the reading process because they fail to take account of the meaning of a text for the reader. Kintsch and Vipond (1979), for instance, found that one of the best predictors of readability was how often readers needed to search their long-term memory to enable them to make sense of what they were reading. It is also argued that readability indices encourage writing that simply involves short words and short sentences, and that such text can be stilted and actually more difficult to read.

An alternative approach, which directly links the difficulty of a text with potential readers, is the cloze procedure. Described by Rye (1982), this involves testing to see how well children can read text that has every fifth word deleted. As shown in Figure 9.6, the percentage of the missing words that the child is able to generate is then used to indicate the ease of reading and comprehension of the complete text.

Unfortunately, this approach is time-consuming and depends upon having access to the students you wish to match the text with. In a study which applied the simpler Fry and the Dale–Chall indices to 10 English textbooks, Fusaro (1988) found that they gave similar results to each other and accurate grade levels. Applying the Fry index to books from current popular schemes such as the Oxford Reading Tree also

Figure 9.6 Cloze and Readability

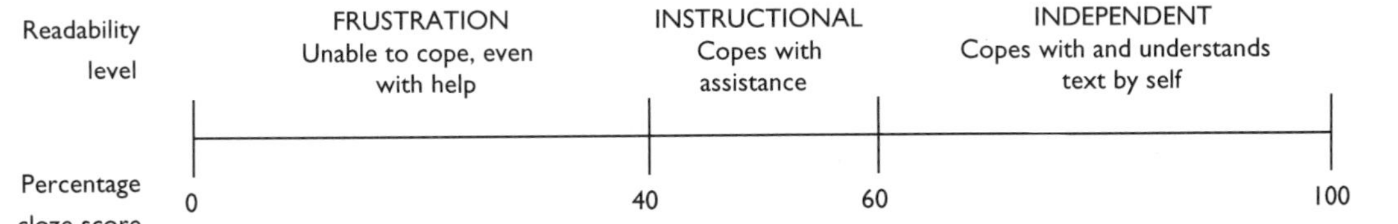

generally gives readability measures that are very close to the age levels at which they are aimed.

Although they may perhaps be only approximate measures, readabilities can be used to grade books in a library to guide 'free readers'. Without this check it is possible for children to choose books which are a poor match for their reading ability, or even for the overall level of books to be quite inappropriate. Hill (1981), for instance, found that most of the books in one particular primary school library had a readability level above 11 years, although the majority of the school's population had reading ages between 8 and 11 years. A book's readability level can also be used by teachers as a first indicator in placing a child on a reading scheme, provided that they already know the child's reading age.

A further use of readability is to check on the suitability of school textbooks. A study by Chiang-Soong and Yager (1993) used the Fry readability index on the 12 science textbooks that were most commonly used in schools. The findings from this study were typical, in that four of the books were found to be too difficult for their intended audience, which indicated that many children would have problems using them.

The difficulty of examination questions can also vary with readability. An investigation by Klare (1975) found that pupils could give a greater number of correct answers for a passage written in an easy style than if the style was more difficult to read (the subject content being kept the same). When preparing worksheets, teachers might therefore want to keep the readability level as low as possible. As previously mentioned, there are dangers in simply writing short sentences and using short words. A good technique is to think about your intended audience while writing. When you have finished, a readability measure can check whether the level that you have achieved is approximately right.

Problems with literacy

Various things can go wrong with the process of developing reading and writing skills. The most common result of any problem is a reading delay, although some children can have particular weaknesses. By definition, half of all children have literacy skills below the average for their age, and it is rather arbitrary where one chooses a cut-off point to decide that a problem exists. However, substantial numbers of children do have levels of literacy which prevent them from being able to benefit from the normal range of school work or from general literacy within society.

Language problems

As discussed later in this chapter, early language problems can be a significant factor in early reading progress. In particular, difficulties with a child's spoken sound system can delay his or her progress with phonic analysis and synthesis. Difficulties with language structure, meaning and a limited spoken vocabulary can also limit progress, particularly as reading develops above the 8-year level. Such problems may come from a restricted home environment or be related to underlying medical problems. Webster (1985), for instance, reports that otitis media, or 'glue ear', is present in as many as one-third of all children in early schooling. This has the effect of preventing children from discriminating sounds adequately, and there is a high association of subsequent reading difficulties with such conductive hearing losses.

Behavioural problems

Children's behaviour (particularly poor concentration and attention) has also been shown to have an effect on their early academic progress. McGee *et al.* (1986), for instance, carried out a longitudinal study on 925 children from the ages of 5 to 11. At school entry, those children with behaviour problems were significantly more likely to have subsequent reading difficulties. These behaviour problems also increased as the children became older, presumably at least partly because the existence of reading problems then meant that they had difficulties coping with the demands of normal schooling. Lawrence (1971), moreover, has shown that continued failure with reading leads to a loss of self-esteem and that many children decrease their effort with reading tasks. Whitehead (1977), for instance, found that 36 per cent of children of 14 and over read no books at all by choice.

Parental involvement

Parental involvement can also be a major factor in children's reading progress. A study by Elliott and Hewison (1994) of different socio-economic groups indicated that children made most progress when there was a parental helping style which emphasised comprehension and interest with reading practice. Children with the lowest achievements tended to come from lower-class homes where there were few books and where little emphasis was given to the development of literacy.

Helping children with delayed reading

Most approaches to helping with reading problems tend to focus upon developing those early skills which are missing. A great deal of research shows that failing readers tend to lack phonic abilities, and many remedial techniques such as the 'Alpha to Omega' approach by Hornsby and Shear (1974) are largely based on structured phonic teaching. Chapter 12 will describe the need to deliver such help in a regular and intensive way, with close matching of levels to the child's attainments.

In England, normal progress with reading is now largely based on class and group activities as part of the National Literacy Strategy. Unfortunately, children with difficulties may find that their achievements are no longer close to the work being done by the rest of the class. Direct involvement by the teacher is often limited, and Plewis and Veltman (1996) found that the average time infant children spent reading to their teachers at the time of their survey was only eight minutes a week. When there are problems, it is therefore important to set up a more intensive and structured approach which can involve general goals for the medium term, and from this more specific graded targets that can be achieved in the short term. For children with special needs at stage 2 or above, this can also be part of an Individual Education Plan (to be described in Chapter 12). One technique which incorporates this approach is the 'Data Pac' programme (Ackerman *et al.*, 1983), based on the principles of precision teaching. This breaks down overall goals, such as progress through a reading scheme, into manageable targets with key sets of words to be learned each week. The programme sets successive specific targets of accuracy and fluency, aimed at achieving mastery learning before children progress further. A specific daily target could, for instance, be for children to learn a set of six words so that they can identify a random set of 30 of these in one minute, with only two errors.

This technique has been shown to be highly successful, and depends upon the tight structuring and monitoring which are part of the programme. Hui (1991), for instance, looked at the effectiveness of the Data Pac programme with a range of children with early literacy problems. Over a period of 11 weeks, the group more than doubled their reading scores, with children who had specific learning difficulties ('dyslexia') making the greatest progress. However, the programme can be difficult for teachers to apply by themselves and works best when set up and monitored by a separate support teacher.

The importance of the home has been tackled by various paired teaching approaches which give parents a particular role in helping their children. A major review of 155 such projects by Topping and Whiteley (1990) showed that these can be highly effective, with an average gain in reading comprehension of 9.23 months over an average tuition period of just 8.6 weeks.

Although Lawrence (1971) has shown that older children's disaffection with the reading process can be successfully tackled by counselling, it seems more effective to try to prevent early reading difficulties developing and becoming consolidated. Unfortunately, most attempts to predict reading failure have only limited accuracy and it is relatively inefficient to base additional support on these. The best approach is probably to regularly review children's progress early in their school life, and then to apply intensive, short-term remedial techniques when necessary. This type of approach is used by the 'Reading Recovery' programme, developed by Clay (1985). This involves intensive daily 30-minute remedial sessions for 12 to 20 weeks for children who are making only limited progress with reading after their first year in school.

An evaluation of this programme in Britain by Wright (1992) found that it was highly effective, with 96.4 per cent of children reaching average levels of attainments in literacy after a mean of 16.8 weeks of teaching. Long-term follow-up three years later when the children were 9 years old showed that they maintained these gains and continued to perform as well as their own age group. Unfortunately, the training and intensive teaching are relatively expensive, and most schools are unable to make this sort of investment. Other forms of intensive teaching can be integrated with early academic work and are more realistic in terms of resources. The Early Reading Research project described by Solity *et al.* (1999) can be implemented by teachers as part of the normal teaching day and appears to have a strong preventive role. Fewer than 1 per cent of the children who were given this support were subsequently considered to have literacy difficulties, compared with just over 20 per cent of children in a comparison group.

Dyslexia

Dyslexia is a particular category of reading difficulty which has been used to refer to pupils with otherwise normal general cognitive abilities (usually assessed by means of an intelligence test). Another term for it, which is used more or less interchangeably, is specific learning disability (SpLD), although this can refer to any particular learning problem. Dyslexia is regarded by some as being different from the normal type of reading difficulty, in which children's general cognitive abilities are also delayed.

The meaning of dyslexia

The term 'dyslexia' is derived in a similar way to medical terminology from the two terms 'dys', meaning 'problems with', and 'lexia', meaning 'words'. The implication has often been that there is some form of medical problem underlying the ability to perceive and make sense of written information. In particular, the classic 'dyslexic' difficulty of reversing or confusing letters or the order of letters in words has often been linked to a basic difficulty with directionality such as distinguishing left from right, or so-called 'cross-laterality', where right-handed students may have a dominant left eye. Some investigations have shown moderate correlations of directionality difficulty with literacy problems, but general population studies such as that by Rutter and Yule (1975) have shown that difficulty with directionality is *not* more common among dyslexics and is in fact a characteristic of all poor readers.

Specific reading problems that happen as children get older are often termed *developmental dyslexia*, to distinguish the condition from *acquired dyslexia*, which can happen to previously literate people following brain injury. Acquired dyslexia can show a number of different forms, with 'phonological' dyslexia affecting letter–sound conversion, 'surface' dyslexia affecting whole-word recognition, and 'deep' dyslexia affecting reading for meaning. It has been suggested that developmental dyslexia might be subdivided in the same way, implying that there may be a similar underlying physical basis. Ellis *et al.* (1996) found that a dyslexic group of children did show similar differences, with phonological and surface patterns being apparent. However, both normal readers and generally delayed readers showed the same types of differences, which does not support a separate classification of dyslexia based on these.

Possible medical causation

Some findings have seemed to support the belief that reading problems can be due to some form of underlying brain damage or dysfunction. For instance, Galaburda (1991) found atypical asymmetry in the planum temporale (in Wernicke's area) in individuals with dyslexia. This area appears to be directly associated with phonological coding deficits which may underlie reading problems. More recently, attention has also focused on the magnocellular pathway, which is involved in attentional processes, and Best and Demb (1999) found a separate deficit in this for a group of young adults with reading difficulties.

The main difficulty with such findings is that any neurological differences could still be an effect rather than a cause. Skilled readers have had massive amounts of rehearsal in visual selection and phonological processing, and it is quite likely that this would have a direct effect on the development of specific brain areas. Also, these studies fail to distinguish between high-IQ and low-IQ pupils, and a review by Whittaker (1992) concluded that such neurological problems are just as common in children who are generally poor readers as they are in children with a reading–IQ discrepancy. There does not therefore appear to be any convincing medical basis for distinguishing a separate dyslexic reading group, and the British Medical Association (1980) has itself concluded that 'dyslexia is not a medical problem'. There may of course still be some neurological abnormalities which cause difficulties with reading for pupils at all levels of cognitive ability. Stronger evidence for this could come from studies which involved early identification and long-term follow-up.

Dyslexia as a separate distribution

Since dyslexia has usually been defined by underfunctioning with reading compared with intelligence test performance, there have been attempts to separate out a particular part of the normal range in some way. Yule *et al.* (1974), for instance, appeared to have found a particular 'hump' at one extreme of the ability–achievement distribution which would correspond to this category. However, as shown in Figure 9.7, a subsequent study by Rodgers (1983) of 8,836 10-year-olds failed to confirm this, indicating that the original findings by Yule may have been produced by range limitations in the tests used.

Figure 9.7 Distributions of under- and overachievement with reading

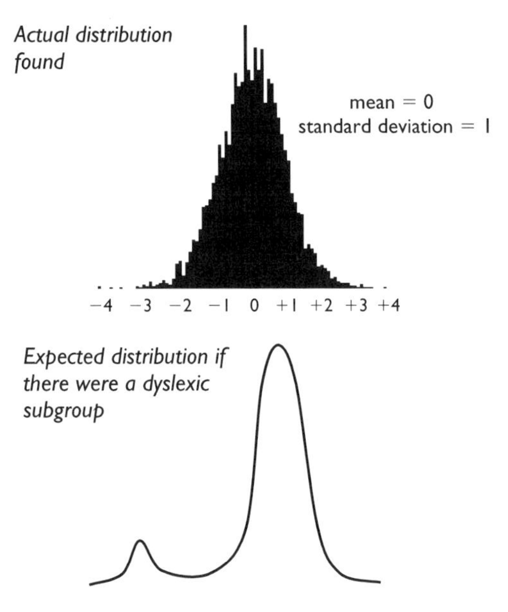

Source: Rodgers (1983), based on differences between scores on the Edinburgh Reading Test and a shortened form of the British Ability Scales. Deviations to the left one when reading skill is below general ability ('dyslexia'); deviations to the right are when reading skill is above general ability

The distribution is quite symmetrical, with no separate 'hump' which could be a separate dyslexic subgroup. It also appears to be relatively wide, which indicates there is only a weak general relationship between intelligence and reading ability.

There is also, incidentally, a condition known as 'hyperlexia', when children's reading attainments outstrip their verbal abilities. This can be the outcome of specific problems with language and comprehension disorders such as autism (when reading attainments are sometimes normal but language is retarded), but can also happen when children have very high levels of reading ability. Pennington *et al.* (1987), for instance, describe one boy aged 2 years 11 months who had a word-reading age of 9 years 3 months. He was advanced in underlying phonic skills and could also decode both regular and irregular words at the same level. Such cases indicate that word attack skills can develop in a relatively independent way, although reading for comprehension depends on verbal understanding at the appropriate level, and hyperlexic children usually cannot answer questions on the more difficult texts.

Dyslexia as a subskill deficit

There have also been attempts to identify specific processing deficits or to produce indices which are able to distinguish a particular 'dyslexic-type' learning-disabled subgroup. These have looked at various possible subskills such as visual sequential memory, or other cognitive processes involved in processing sounds. Children with reading difficulties certainly do have poorer phonological abilities, but a major review of the available research by Stanovich (1994) indicates that dyslexics cannot be distinguished from the normal continuum of reading failure on any subskills. Research by Fletcher *et al.* (1994), for instance, identified difficulties with underlying phonological awareness as being the main characteristic of children with all types of reading failure, whether they were merely behind or specifically delayed/'dyslexic'. Although children with above-average intelligence may be more able to use cognitive strategies such as the use of context, this does not seem to be important in early reading and would not affect the teaching approaches used.

There are also doubts about the use of intelligence as a unitary concept, and concerning the extent to which intelligence tests represent an individual's potential for learning. However, as Stanovich (1991) points out, it can be argued that children who have good knowledge and understanding of curriculum subjects but who cannot develop or express this with literacy *do* have particular needs. They are evidently different from those who are behind with literacy but who also have restricted knowledge and understanding of school work, but are they more deserving of extra help? It is a moot point as to where one should draw any line in terms of a definition of special needs and any additional teaching help which might have to come from resources that could be given to other children.

Although children who underfunction in this way may represent an important grouping, Presland (1991) argues that this does not imply any specific remedial technique and that one should simply use the normal range of remedial approaches. Hornsby and Miles (1980), however, argue that children with 'dyslexia' need a particular teaching technique which integrates auditory, visual and physical work: the 'multisensory approach'. Although Hornsby and Miles found that this approach was effective in helping children, it does not in fact differ very greatly from other remedial programmes. The highly effective 'Reading Recovery' approach also uses a range of techniques which involve all the senses. Evaluations of learning outcomes with this have not found any differences in its effectiveness between children of different cognitive abilities. It seems likely that if appropriate early educational support of this kind were more common, the need for the concept of dyslexia would be greatly reduced.

Most recent developments in the concept of dyslexia see it as a specific difficulty with literacy, one which is unrelated to general cognitive abilities and which can have a number of different causes. The Division of Educational and Child Psychology of the British Psychological Society (DECP, 1999, p. 8) has therefore arrived at the following definition:

> Dyslexia is evident when accurate and fluent word reading and/or spelling develops very incompletely or with great difficulty. This focuses on literacy learning at the 'word level' and implies that the problem is severe and persistent despite appropriate learning opportunities. It provides the basis for a staged process of assessment through teaching.

This definition emphasises that the primary difficulty lies with processing words (rather than more complex psycholinguistic abilities), and that dyslexia can be said to exist only when there are literacy difficulties despite normal opportunities for learning. At present, the most promising techniques to help children with such problems appear to lie with intensive and structured phonemic approaches such as 'Reading Reflex' (McGuinness and McGuinness, 1998), irrespective of children's knowledge and understanding in other domains.

Literacy and language

The relationship between literacy skills and language is dynamic and reciprocal, and changes in its nature as the two skill areas develop. At the earliest stages, a key task is for children to learn to link language and meaning with the experience of looking at books. Such a link can be established by children listening to stories read to them, and following and talking about the pictures in books. Whitehurst *et al.* (1994) found that their doing so also facilitates the development of language ability, although it should be noted that merely reading books to children does *not* teach further reading skills. Meyer *et al.* (1994) found that there was actually a negative relationship between the amount of time which kindergarten teachers spent reading to children and their subsequent progress with reading. This is apparently due to the 'displacement effect' which such activities had on more direct reading involvement by children. There is evidently a balance to be struck between reading to children, in order to develop their language abilities and interest in reading, and other activities which develop direct reading skills.

Children need to start to make early links between language, meaning and the written form of words, and in the earliest stages such links appears to relate to children's sensitivity to the sounds in words and their ability to match these to the alphabetic system. Later developments are much more dependent on general language abilities, including vocabulary and structural and semantic abilities. The whole process then also becomes more interactive, and as children progress through the junior school, literacy increasingly becomes a vehicle for linguistic and general intellectual development.

On transfer to secondary education, there is significantly less focus on developing literacy for its own sake (it is rare for reading schemes to be used), but literacy forms the foundation for the majority of academic studies. It is perhaps not surprising, therefore, that reading and writing abilities at the start of secondary schooling predict subsequent progress with the range of subjects. A study by the NFER (1997), for example, found a significant correlation of 0.55 between Year 6 scores on the London Reading Test and overall Year 11 GCSE examination scores. There were similar figures for the specific subjects of English (0.57), mathematics (0.53) and science (0.48).

Sounds

A number of children who start school have not yet developed a mature spoken sound system. Many also have difficulties with their ability to perceive the separate sounds in words, and to use them in early reading to match up with letters. This is reflected, for instance, in young children's ability to detect the odd word out that does not share a common sound. Sets of words such as 'cat', 'cap', '<u>hat</u>', 'can' involve alliteration, and this tests for sensitivity to the onset of the syllable. The set 'hat', 'fat', '<u>map</u>', 'rat' involves rhyming, and (confusingly) tests for sensitivity to the rime of the syllable.

In a key early investigation, Bradley and Bryant (1983) investigated these skills with 368 4- and 5-year-olds, none of whom could yet read. Four years later they tested the children again for their attainments with reading and writing, and, as shown in Table 9.1, they found that the earlier skills with sound categorisation correlated significantly with subsequent literacy development. These predictive correlations were higher than those for the children's early measures of receptive vocabulary or performance on a memory test and would appear to indicate that phonological development is an independent cause of early literacy progress. However, it could also be that phonological abilities and literacy are both simply the outcome of early support with literacy. It might be that children who learn to read and write at an early age develop their knowledge of sounds as a result of doing so.

To investigate whether that is the case, Bradley and Bryant carried out an investigation to see whether directly intervening with children's phonological and alphabetic skills would influence their later progress with literacy. To do this, they selected a group of 65 young children with weak sound categorisation skills and divided them up into two experimental groups and two control groups. The first experimental group received training in sound categorisation with 40 sessions over two years. This involved teaching the children that words could vary by just one sound to make alliterative or rhyming patterns. The second experimental group also learned to identify and match plastic letters which the words had in common, for example 'c' for 'cat' and 'cap'. One control group received training merely in categorising the words into similar conceptual groups, while the other control group was given no training at all. The results shown in Table 9.2 clearly show that the experimental groups made significantly more progress, with the children who had been given both alphabetic and sound training making 12.5 months more progress with reading than the children who had not been given any extra help at all (comparison 1 in the table). There was an even greater effect with spelling, which at this early stage is very dependent on knowledge of letters and their combinations. These results also show that the sound training by itself had a significant effect, one that was additional to any familiarity with the words involved (comparison 2 in the table). This gives strong support for the belief that children's initial sensitivities to sounds in words do affect their subsequent progress with literacy.

A great deal of other research has confirmed these findings, and Torgesen *et al.* (1994) found that the strongest predictor of reading in first grade was children's earlier skills with phonologi-

Table 9.1 Relationships between early sound categorisation and subsequent literacy skills (values given as correlation coefficients)

	Age	
	4 years	**5 years**
Final reading score	0.57	0.44
Final spelling score	0.48	0.44

Source: Based on Bradley and Bryant (1983)

Table 9.2 Final scores in reading and spelling for experimental and control groups given different training

	Experimental groups		Control groups	
	Sound training	**Alphabetic + sound training**	**Conceptual training**	**No training**
Reading age (months)	92.2	97.0	88.5	84.5
	②		①	
Spelling age (months)	86.0	98.8	81.8	75.2

Source: Based on Bradley and Bryant (1983)

cal analysis, measured by how well they were able to identify the sounds in words. The effect of phonological analysis was greater than the effect of early measures of language development or even of initial reading progress Later progress in second grade was, however, more dependent on phonological synthesis, represented by the ability to blend separate sounds into whole words. They also found evidence for a reciprocal relationship, with early pre-school reading abilities independently predicting later phonological awareness, although the effect was smaller than the effect of phonological skills on reading. It seems likely that the processes involved in early reading such as learning the sounds for written letters also have some effect on developing children's sensitivities to those sounds in spoken language.

Vocabulary

Language vocabulary and structure are normally far in advance of reading skills in the first two years of schooling. A child's spoken vocabulary on entering school normally runs to many thousands of words, and the sentence structures which he or she is able to verbalise and understand are usually quite complex. In early-reading books, the words used and the sentence structures are on average at least two years below this level and would be well within the range of the great majority of children.

Combining estimates of spoken vocabulary (see above) and the developments in reading vocabulary shown by Williams (1961) would give the general graph shown in Figure 9.8. It seems likely that this would show a progressive overlap of abilities, happening particularly after the 7-year level. This is borne out by the noticeable 'levelling out' of reading vocabulary progress after the 8-year level, when it is likely that there is some form of matching process between literacy and general language abilities.

The dramatic increase in word attack skills in reading that happens between $6\frac{1}{2}$ and 8 years allows children to work out a wide range of letter combinations. From this point on, the ability to work out words and meanings then depends more on verbal vocabulary, along with contextual information such as language structure and content meaning. For instance, the word 'favour' in isolation has a readability level of about 8 years. Although it cannot be worked out from the basic rules for combining letter sounds, it is cer-

Figure 9.8 Hypothetical relationship between language development and reading attainments

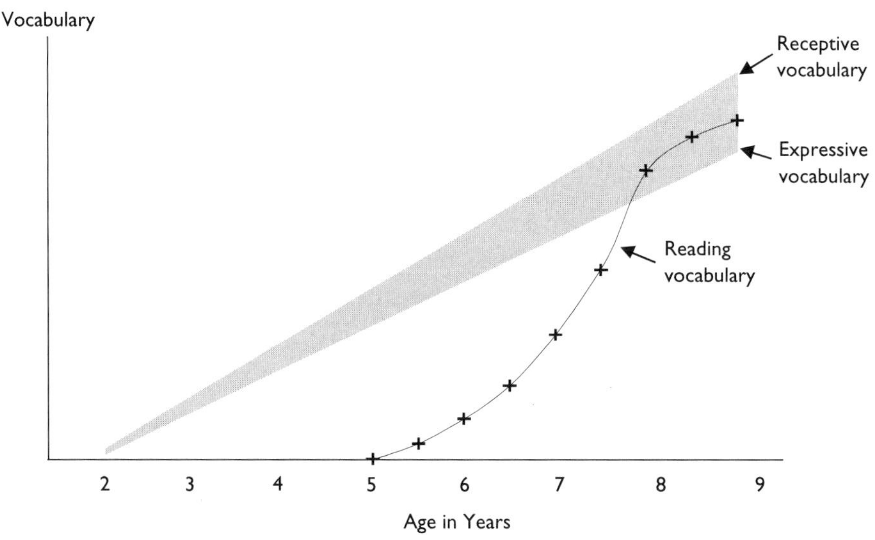

tainly in most younger children's language vocabulary. This would help with its identification in a meaningful sentence, such as: 'he helped his friend because he owed him a f———'. Goodman (1968) in particular argues that reading can be characterised as a 'psycholinguistic guessing game', driven largely by our knowledge of language. As discussed earlier, however, this does not appear to be too important since most of the time the context just does not provide enough information. In the sentence above, for example, the word 'fiver' is close to the target length and could also be a plausible fit.

A child's language vocabulary and structure are unlikely to limit reading in the early years. Once basic reading skills have been achieved, however (from a reading age of about 8 to 9 years), it is then possible for readers to be exposed to words and language structures that they can decode (i.e. read out correctly) but may not yet understand. For example, the word 'arable' is not normally understood by children until they are 15 years old but is fairly phonically regular and could be read by many children at about the 8-year level. Although coming across such words might limit reading (particularly with children who have a language delay), there is also evidence that such experiences can push along a reader's language vocabulary if he or she experiences new words in contexts which give information about their meaning.

To what extent can reading develop vocabulary?

Nagy *et al.* (1987) directly investigated the effects of reading on vocabulary development with 352 students whose ages ranged from 9 to 11 years. All students first read (to themselves) two texts, which were matched to their general educational level and included 15 difficult target words. These covered a range of different categories, such as 'cardinal', 'slunk', 'natural', 'anecdote'. The passages covered stories and extracts from textbooks and were graded for levels of readability and conceptual difficulty.

The initial reading took only about 15 minutes and the students were left with the impression that this was the end of the study. One week later, however, they were assessed for their knowledge of the target words, using multiple-choice vocabulary tests. As well as the target words, the tests also included words of similar difficulty which they had not read.

The results showed a small but statistically significant effect on vocabulary development. Those pupils who had read a text knew the meaning of 3.3 per cent more of the difficult words than those who had not read the text. Although such a small effect may not seem too important, the authors estimate that if a student reads for only 15 minutes a day in school, this will enable him or her to cover 600,000 words of text a year. Average levels of home reading also probably account for somewhat less than this (about 10 minutes a day), making a probable yearly total of about 1 million words. Of these, frequency counts indicate that about 20,000 would be unknown, and by applying the probability of learning from their study, Nagy *et al.* calculate that this would therefore account for about 1,000 new vocabulary words learned each year. If children were to read for more than 25 minutes a day, it is of course likely that they would develop their vocabularies even further. Other studies have also shown a generally positive reciprocal relationship between reading and vocabulary development, known as the 'Matthew effect'.

A further analysis indicated that the probability of learning a new word was also significantly increased by the ease of readability of the text. This was assessed by standard formulas which, as described earlier, are based on word and sentence length and word frequency. The increased probability of learning the word happened even when the texts had already been matched with children according to their grade level, which indicates that texts that are easier to read are more likely to develop new knowledge.

Word learning was also independently affected by overall conceptual difficulty. When passages were difficult to understand, they gave insufficient information to enable any unknown words to be learned. When the unknown words were themselves conceptually difficult, they needed to be part of a passage where the overall meaning was clear. These findings were taken to support the idea that the most important factor in learning from context is the degree to which the learner can integrate information in a passage into a coherent system consistent with his or her prior knowledge.

Echols *et al.* (1996) looked at the number of books read by 10-, 11- and 12-year-old children as assessed by their recognition of book titles. Even after allowing for initial verbal abilities, this measure directly predicted the subsequent growth of vocabulary and general knowledge skills over the following two years, adding further support to the belief that literacy experience does develop long-term language abilities.

The reciprocal effects between language vocabulary and reading appear to depend on whether we look at long-term development or immediate competence. The investigation by Nagy *et al.* confirms the belief that reading vocabulary of unknown words is developed by experiencing them in a meaningful context of known words. This is a long-term effect, however, and the immediate probability of increased knowledge of each single word was quite small. As we have seen, it seems likely that when a word cannot be read, the context will usually not give enough information to define it.

Although Goodman (1968) believes that the language context of words is the main means of decoding information in reading, subsequent investigations have supported the idea that immediate word-reading skills are primarily automatic. It is therefore likely that in normal reading, the use of context to predict a word or phonics to sound it out is resorted to only when this fails.

Structure and content

The way in which we use word order and meaning with reading has many similarities to how we listen to spoken language. As we have already seen, when people read they take in sequential information about word content using successive eye fixations, and most of the time spent reading is devoted to processing information. As with listening, words appear to be processed as integrated short sequences, and we develop plausible syntax and meaning as we go along. In the same way, we also rapidly discard the surface structure unless it carries particular information in some way, and we tend to construct and retain the overall meaning of what we have read. Our general knowledge and understanding of the concepts embodied in the language input also appears to be important in determining how we can develop meaning from what we read and whether we are able to avoid or resolve ambiguities.

An important difference between listening and reading is of course that in reading we do not have access to prosodic and non-verbal information. These normally tell us a great deal about the intent of the speaker, and without them we must be much more dependent on syntax and other information such as punctuation. This also means that readers must be more active in searching for information, which usually involves our frequently checking back to resolve difficulties, for instance with 'garden path' sentences. As described in the previous chapter, readers can suddenly find that their initial hypothesis about the structure or meaning of a sentence is incorrect and then need to check back to generate a new structure which will work. In sentences such as 'While the boy scratched the dog yawned', Ferreira and Henderson (1995) found that 27 per cent of eye fixations were back into the segment '*while the boy scratched*' in order to disambiguate the overall meaning. Less frequently, readers will also check forward to resolve uncertainties, for instance if an initial pronoun is clarified later in the text as in 'It was the first time that *he* had been to the seaside and *Peter* did not know what to expect.' When readers come across 'he', they will often skip across until they find the noun 'Peter', and then return to where they were originally reading.

Kintsch (1994) argues that when we are dealing with larger bodies of text, we use ongoing information known as propositions, derived from the phrases and clauses within each sentence, which activate associated knowledge and ideas from long-term memory. Any information that then forms a coherent and meaningful whole can subsequently be stored as a form of episodic memory. This approach predicts that as in other forms of language processing, we will tend to remember overall meaning rather than particular information from the structure or the logical propositions within sentences. The prediction is borne out by Kintsch *et al.*'s (1990) findings that over four days, subjects' recall of the situation described by a story that they had read showed no loss at all, whereas other forms of information such as the surface structure fell off quite rapidly.

This model emphasises the importance of meaningful relationships between sentences and larger units of text. There is certainly evidence, for example from Trabasso and Sperry (1985), that sentences and paragraphs which are causally linked with each other and the main story concept are read more rapidly and are better remembered.

The writing process also appears to operate according to overall principles of general meaning and organisation. In this case, of course, the writer has first to generate some form of concept or plan which can be translated into continuous text. Initial goals are first generated, for instance with a general title which guides the general content. Bereiter *et al.* (1988) describe how, according to expertise, the writer will then either set up a simple knowledge-telling strategy or a more complex knowledge-transforming strategy. Younger children will often simply put down all that they know on a topic, whereas skilled writers attempt to fit what they know with general themes or arguments. Kellogg (1988) demonstrated that generating an initial outline can help with this process more than can just producing a rough draft, apparently because it focuses the attention of the writer on higher-level integrating propositions. Final sentence generation happens by constructing linked and meaningful phrases and clauses, and can involve a high level of ongoing revision.

The dynamic and conceptually driven nature of the writing task can evidently be constrained if children go straight to writing down a final version without any further modifications. The use of word processors, however, allows much easier planning and redrafting, and Bangert-Drowns (1993) found that their use can significantly improve both the quantity and the quality of children's writing.

Speech and reading

When children are at the earliest stages of reading, they will typically focus on decoding words and directly translate them into spoken language as they go along. When word decoding becomes more skilled and automatic, reading becomes more silent, typically from a reading age level of about 8 years onwards. Older children or adults will nevertheless often go back to verbalising to some extent when they encounter difficult text or words. People will also sometimes inwardly rehearse the way in which the author would have probably said the text, to give themselves prosody cues, or simply to enjoy what they are reading.

Making individuals read out loud when they are capable of silent reading appears to slow their reading down to about half their normal rate. The subvocalisations or inner speech which people often use in skilled reading are therefore probably only a partial representation of actual language, used to support the analysis of surface structure when necessary. Hardyck and Petrinovich (1970) found that preventing such subvocal speech interfered with comprehension of text only when the meaning was not clear. With easy text there seemed to be a relatively direct route to meaning, presumably with no need for language-type processing. Complex texts seem to place a greater load on short-term memory, as we need to hold possible syntactic and semantic interpretations, as well as previous surface structure features. Any form of forced verbalisation is then likely to interfere with normal comprehension processes.

When children 'read out loud' or say parts of the text quietly to themselves, this is normally a natural result of the reading level they are at, and the match of their abilities with their current reading material. Although preventing them from doing so would normally reduce children's comprehension, McGuigan (1970) demonstrated that six particular children or young people with ages from 7 to 19 appeared to vocalise purely by habit. In this case an operant programme rapidly reduced subvocalisation, with an increased reading rate and no loss in comprehension.

Summary

Literacy is a form of communication based on print and includes reading and writing skills. These are normally closely related, although writing can sometimes fall behind.

Progress with reading vocabulary is initially slow, but there follows a rapid increase from 6 years on. This comes from generalised word attack skills which are based on phonic abilities. The process of reading involves successive eye fixations which build up information about words and enable the search for overall meaning. The identification of separate words happens relatively automatically, with the main route leading to rapid activation of meaning.

Psycholinguistic explanations of the reading process argue that readers mainly depend upon information from grammatical structure to identify words. This explanation seems unlikely, however, since context does not usually provide enough information. Words are therefore usually identified separately using letter combinations and context when necessary. Reading does, however, use grammatical structure to guide the selection of words for identification and to construct plausible sentences.

Reading appears to mainly involve visual skills but the role of these is essential to generate information as a basis for what words sound like. The ability to use such phonological information depends on expertise with separate and combined sounds, leading to differences in short-term processing capacity.

Teaching reading involves learning to use the separate letters and sounds in words, known as phonics, as well as the use of structures and meaning in complete text. Phonics does appear to accelerate early reading progress, particularly when it is based upon techniques which build up learning in a careful way. Also helpful, however, are an emphasis on the use and meaning of reading, and the encouraging of later active searches for common word structures.

The use of literacy tests can help teachers to match learning experiences with children's needs. Such tests can be carried out with individuals or groups and may involve either normative or criterion-referenced comparisons. The usefulness of tests such as diagnostic assessments depends very much on whether they are based on appropriate models of the reading process.

The readability of text depends on a number of factors but can be estimated using measures such as equations based on word and sentence length. These can be useful to match reading materials with children's abilities.

Children can have difficulties with literacy because of language problems, limited involvement or poor home support. Helping them can involve developing underlying skills such as phonic abilities using structured programmes with specific targets. Enabling parents to help their children can be highly effective, and counselling can overcome some difficulties with disaffection. However, prevention is more effective, and early and intensive support appears to have the greatest impact.

'Dyslexia' refers to specific difficulties with developing literacy. It is often assumed to have a medical basis, but any biological causes for reading problems appear to be equally likely to happen over the range of underlying abilities. Children considered to have dyslexia do not appear to have subskills different from those of non-readers generally, and the same remedial techniques appear to be equally effective. Recent definitions emphasise a failure to develop word reading and/or spelling despite appropriate learning opportunities.

Language and literacy are interdependent, and there is now strong evidence that sensitivity to sounds supports early literacy and that training such phonological sensitivity improves literacy progress. Language and literacy vocabulary probably become closely related from about 8 years onwards, as children start to read more words that are new to or beyond their language vocabulary. Experiencing new words in reading appears to have a long-term and substantial facilitating effect on the development of language vocabulary. When reading, we use the structure of sentences to construct meaning in much the same way as we do for heard language. Written text is more open to checking, however, and writing in particular enables children to modify and refine their ideas. Early readers or pupils with some difficulty will sometimes read aloud, and although their resort to such a strategy is usually temporary, it can interfere with their progress.

Key implications

- An important emphasis in early reading should be on developing the rapid identification of words.
- A child starting reading is helped by the ability to analyse and to combine the various sounds which are represented by letters. The training up of any other supposed subskills or abilities does not appear to be effective.
- Literacy difficulties benefit from early intensive support and can possibly be prevented by the general use of structured teaching.
- Recent definitions of dyslexia consider that it has little to do with intelligence, but can be considered as a failure to develop word reading and/or spelling despite appropriate learning opportunities.
- Later reading depends upon language and is also important in developing general verbal abilities.

Further reading

Keith Rayner and Alexander Pollatsek (1994) *The Psychology of Reading*. Hove, East Sussex: Lawrence Erlbaum.

This is a technical and detailed book which covers the main areas of psychological research and key findings and theories related to reading. Useful for reference or for further study.

Jane Oakhill and Roger Beard (eds) (1999) *Reading Development and the Teaching of Reading*. Oxford: Blackwell.

The chapters in this book are written by a range of active researchers and provide an in-depth review of current findings and implications for teaching literacy. They emphasise that reading is not simply some form of guessing game, that phonological skills are important in reading, and that the use of any form of text depends upon the links between orthography and the phonology of English.

Practical scenario

James is a Year 5 boy who had problems with his early literacy development despite having normal general knowledge and understanding. Although he has now established basic phonic skills, his reading age is about three years behind and he has problems coping with the level of literacy that is part of normal class work. James receives some help with his reading and writing, but this is limited to two sessions a week in a group with a support assistant and one 20-minute session with a learning support teacher. James's parents are worried about his progress, particularly in view of secondary transfer after next year. They are supportive of school but would like to know if he is dyslexic and if he should get additional help.

- *What should school do to help James? Is it likely that continuing the present approaches will make much difference?*
- *Will it help to see if James has dyslexia?*
- *Would it be possible to get extra help for James through a statement of special educational needs?*

10 Behavioural problems

Chapter structure

What are behavioural problems?

All teachers are bound at some time or another to experience children whose behaviour can be a problem. Surveys have generally indicated that behavioural problems have become progressively more important to schools, with Figure 10.1 showing that in England the level of permanent exclusions rose more than four times over the period from 1990–1 to 1996–7. The reduction that seems to have begun after this period is probably due to increased pressures on schools to retain pupils rather than to any improvements in underlying behaviour.

A review by the Children's Society (1998) showed that the level of temporary exclusions

Figure 10.1 Number of permanent exclusions for English schools, 1990–1 to 1997–8

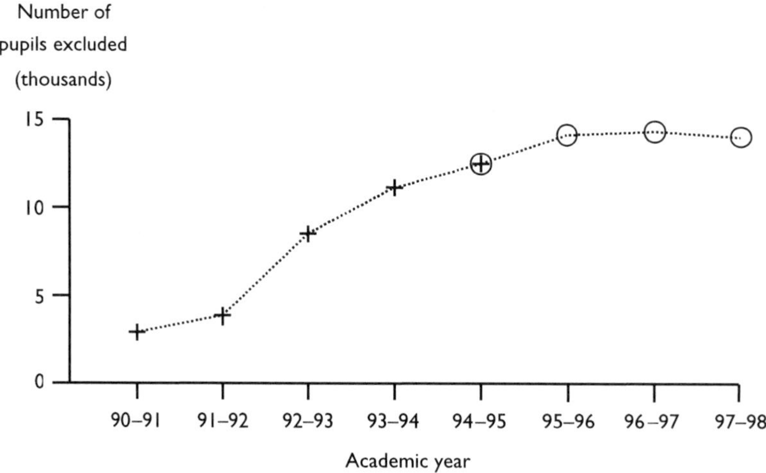

Source: Data for 1990–1 to 1994–5 from Parsons and Howlett (1966); subsequent changes from DfEE (1998k, 1999b)

was even higher, at more than ten times this number. Although the majority of exclusions are from secondary schools, the highest rate of increase over this period was for primary-aged children, indicating that all types of schools are affected.

There are of course many possible reasons for this rise, other than an actual increase in problem behaviours. One of these could simply be that schools became less tolerant over this time, owing to changes in the curriculum and increased pressures on them to achieve academic standards. However, there is also evidence that there has been a real increase in underlying difficulties. Rutter and Smith (1995), for instance, carried out a major review of changes in a range of indices of psycho-social disorders of youth in the post-war period. They found significant increases in crime, alcohol and drug abuse in young people, and a range of psychiatric disorders such as depression, anorexia and suicide. The number of children requiring psychiatric help also rose by a quarter in the second half of the 1980s, and the number of those under the age of 10 with such difficulties doubled over this time. Rutter and Smith concluded from such evidence that there were generally more children with difficult behaviour and that the overall level of pressures and problems experienced by young people in Western society was on the increase owing to factors such as family difficulties and increased expectations.

Although such findings suggest that behaviour problems might be rampant in schools, it should be emphasised that the vast majority of schools and classes are well managed and orderly. In their observational review of a range of primary classrooms, Galton *et al.* (1999) found that disruptive behaviour was infrequent and that in the majority of cases teachers were able to deal rapidly with any problems by techniques such as moving pupils or by gently cautioning them.

Unfortunately, behaviour problems at any level can have a significant impact upon children's educational progress. McGee *et al.* (1986), for example, found that poor concentration and attention seemed to have a particularly damaging effect on subsequent learning progress. Moreover, in a review of teachers' concerns, Tattum (1986) found that disruptive pupils were a major source of personal stress. This is therefore an important area in education, and one where psychology has developed a number of practical and useful approaches.

Categories of behaviour problems

Although the term 'maladjusted' was used for some time to describe children with problems, nowadays this is seen as having strong medical overtones. The term *emotional and behavioural difficulties* (EBD) is now more commonly used in education. This implies that as well as showing the more obvious disruptive behaviours, children can be affected by emotional difficulties such as anxiety or depression. These may not affect the class or the teacher so much, but Borg and Falzon (1990) found that experienced teachers consider that they are much more serious for the child's long-term development.

What is EBD?

Most definitions of EBD, such as that by Chazan *et al.* (1994), tend to cover three major aspects. These authors consider that a child shows EBD:

- when the child's behaviour is *a danger to themself, other people or property*. This is the most obvious category and can involve physical aggression or less direct problems such as running out of school;
- when the child's behaviour *interferes with efficient education* of other children or with their own educational progress. Difficult children can deliberately interfere with or distract others, and withdrawn or anxious children may have difficulties concentrating on their work;
- when the child has *difficulty with social relationships* or interferes with the relationships of other children. Again, this might be a deliberate process or it could be simply due to lack of interpersonal skills.

Each of these difficulties can exist by itself or combined together, for instance when children are involved in bullying. This is a common problem and involves prolonged social or physical intimidation, with the added dimension that there is usually the direct intent to have this effect on the victim.

The concept of EBD

There are various ways of construing problems in school, and this area overlaps in an interesting way with the field of abnormal psychology. As in abnormal psychology, an unusual behaviour in school is not necessarily a problem. For example, very creative or intelligent children may do their work very differently from the other children around them, but their doing so would usually be seen as desirable rather than a problem.

THE 'MEDICAL' MODEL

There is a strong tendency for people to see behavioural problems as being primarily located within the child, although such a view is probably less common than it used to be. By implication, any problems should be dealt with by simply considering the child as a difficult individual. (Similarly, the medical model in abnormal psychology sees problems as being due to an 'illness' of the individual.) According to this perspective, problems are the result of an individual child's behaviour, which can be diagnosed and classified and then treated by some expert. From the teacher's perspective, this can mean that the child should be removed from the classroom and educated or 'treated' in some form of specialist provision, away from the school, in the hope that the treatment can 'cure' the behaviour. However, despite a large rise in off-site behaviour units, Topping (1983) summarised research which indicated that at the time of writing, they were not as effective in improving problem behaviour as teachers believed.

A more popular perspective nowadays considers that problems are best seen as an interaction between children and their past and present environments, both at school and at home. This implies that overall it may be more effective to manage children and the situation they are in rather than simply remove them.

DEVIATION FROM THE NORM

Behaviours which are different from what is usually expected (the norm) are often used as the basis for categorisation. For instance, if children fail to obey normal classroom rules, there is certainly a problem, since their behaviour will result in difficulties for teachers in carrying out their job. However, some teachers will have rigid expectations of conformity whereas others will expect (or tolerate) a certain amount of individuality. This will inevitably lead to inconsistencies between teachers in their judgement of an individual child, and, as discussed later, the reliability of behavioural assessments tends to be quite low between different teachers and different situations.

FUNCTIONAL DEFINITIONS OF PROBLEM BEHAVIOUR

In fact, the judgements of individual teachers are the most common basis for determining whether a problem exists. When they are asked to give examples of difficulties, teachers will usually talk about behaviours which interfere with class work. A typical survey by Merrett and Wheldall (1984) found that these included:

- disturbing others (31 per cent);
- talking (28 per cent);
- non-attending and disobeying (14 per cent); and
- making a noise (11 per cent).

Teachers will also include behaviour which is physically dangerous to the child causing the problems, and aggression towards other children or the teacher. However, these are seen as being much less frequent than the above behaviours, which are mainly important because they make it difficult for the teacher to carry on with the process of teaching.

Formal teacher-based assessments of problems

which are discussed later in this chapter typically focus on disruptive and aggressive behaviours, despite their generally low frequency. However, anxiety (phobic states, shyness, etc.) and depression (withdrawn behaviour, unhappiness) can be more important for the individual child. Although they are not necessarily a direct problem for the teacher, these are certainly significant for children in terms of their personal and educational development. It seems advisable to broaden the concept of EBD to cover 'maladaptiveness in the school situation', which includes these types of problems and emphasises the goal of adaptive behaviour. In school this would mean being able to use cooperative social behaviours and to adjust to differing situations. Again, the concept has similarities with perspectives in abnormal psychology based on humanistic approaches, which focus on the ability of people to develop and to fulfil their potential.

Background and causes of educational and behavioural difficulties

Psychological theories

Many psychological explanations tend to focus on individuals and try to explain problems from what is going on inside them. However, possibly more powerful approaches take into account the social context and look at the way in which long-term environments develop individuals' strategies and predispositions.

Frustration–aggression

Aggression was originally proposed by Dollard *et al.* (1939) to be mainly an innate response that is *always* triggered by frustrating situations and events. Although there is some support for this approach, it was subsequently modified by researchers such as Berkowitz (1989) to take account of differing emotional states, environmental cues and cognitive factors such as attributions. According to this, the emotional state of anger towards somebody can result when an individual has an aversive (unpleasant) experience that is perceived to be due to the deliberate intent of another person.

Our existing emotional state, can significantly affect the likelihood of aggression. People who are already upset will easily become more aggressive, whereas people who are happy or amused are less likely to become aggressive. Many teachers are of course already well aware of this, and use humour to avoid or defuse tense situations. All emotions are at least partly mediated by arousal, whatever the cause, and an individual who has recently experienced a strong emotion is particularly likely to react in an aggressive way. Zillmann (1988) argues that this happens because physiological arousal takes some time to dissipate; a subsequent minor annoyance can then become intensified by our assuming that it has caused our arousal.

Environmental cues which are associated with aggression can also increase the likelihood of aggressive behaviours occurring. Berkowitz (1989) originally studied this effect by showing that the presence of a gun would increase the likelihood of subjects' giving a confederate of the investigator what they believed to be an electric shock (the apparatus was in fact only a dummy). Although this particular cue is unlikely to occur in British schools, similar effects have also been shown to operate with other associations with violence, for example when people believe that the person they are shocking is more or less belligerent.

Another important feature is whether we attribute an aversive or unpleasant experience to another person, particularly if we believe or perceive that they intended it to have a negative effect. Such attributions are particularly likely when direct physical or verbal provocation, such as insults, is involved. For example, Geen (1968) gave subjects a difficult puzzle which they were sometimes unable to complete. A confederate then proceeded to insult them, attacking both their intelligence and their motivation. Even when they were able to complete the puzzle, the insults led to levels of aggression towards the confederate which were higher than when the subjects had simply been frustrated by being unable to complete the task. Evidently, teachers should be careful in their use of negative feedback and criticism towards pupils. It is also likely that some children have social difficulties due to their use of provocation as an interpersonal style, and such children might be helped to develop more positive ways of getting on with people.

Kelley (1967) has argued that we use logical ways of deciding whether a person's actions are intended to have a certain effect. Attributions of perceived intent are most likely when we believe that another person's actions are different from what other people would do in that situation, when they act consistently in this way (on different occasions), and when they act in the same way with different people. Therefore, if Mrs Smith criticises Peter (but other teachers do not), if she criticises him each lesson, and if she also criticises other students, then Peter is likely to say that Mrs Smith is a generally negative teacher. Similarly, in the case of aggressive behaviours we are likely to be most upset and retaliate when a person repeatedly behaves in an atypical negative way towards us. However, if we are given mitigating information – for example, that the person was upset about something, or that they did not realise the effect that they were having – we are much less likely to be negatively affected.

Although frustration can lead to aggression, Berkowitz (1989) argues that it does so only when it produces negative, unpleasant feelings which result in emotional arousal. Emotional arousal can be strongly reduced by higher thought processes, but these may be undeveloped in some children in schools. It can be difficult to rationalise causes and intents with some pupils, and in these cases it may be appropriate to use a more direct behavioural framework.

Behavioural causes of aggression

Like most other behaviours, aggression (or other problem behaviours) can be seen as the result of *operant conditioning*. If people act aggressively and receive some reinforcement as a result, they will be more likely to be aggressive on other occasions. Deaux and Wrightsman (1988) have reviewed the evidence that there are a number of effective reinforcers which have been found to increase aggression. These include:

- social approval;
- increased status; and
- evidence of a victim's suffering.

There is considerable evidence (to be discussed later) of aggressive behaviour being reinforced by processes that take place in the homes of some children. These sometimes involve direct approval for negative acts, for example with attention, laughter or verbal comments. The most important type of reinforcement, however, consists of 'escape-conditioning'. This involves a child learning to use negative behaviour to escape from aversive intrusions from other family members. Within such families, aggressive and manipulative behaviours are highly functional since they make it possible for the child to survive in a negative social system.

Patterson *et al.* (1967) found that such processes can similarly operate from an early age in school. When aggressive acts by nursery children were followed by rewarding consequences, such as passivity or crying by the victim, the aggression was much more likely to be repeated. Children who were non-assertive were often victimised in this way. Eventually, some of them began to copy the aggressive behaviours of other children, and the positive consequences that they then experienced increased the likelihood of these behaviours being used again. Although it seems certain that children are motivated by the consequences of their actions, it also seems to be the case that they develop what they do from the behaviours of others around them.

Social learning theory

Social learning theory proposes that many behaviours develop as a result of our observing what other people do. An investigation by Bandura *et al.* (1963) of behaviour learned from observation showed that children were more likely to be aggressive when they had observed another person behaving aggressively. They were also more likely to be aggressive when they had observed the person being praised for what he or she had done. This indicates that they had learned the social expectations and the likely outcomes for this type of behaviour.

Such *observational learning* is a key concept in understanding how children develop their knowledge of social roles and their sense of identity in school. Wragg (1984) has shown that children do seem to learn from the behaviour of other children in class, particularly about what the consequences would be for themselves if they were to misbehave. These are often critical incidents which set the scene for future expectations and behaviour. The first time that a teacher takes a new class, he or she may see a child being naughty but decide to do nothing about it. However, the other children in the class will see the child's bad behaviour being ignored, particularly if the behaviour is a deliberate challenge to the normal rules of the classroom. In these circumstances, children will often recruit attention from those around them and make sure that the teacher is aware of what they are doing. On future occasions, the children who observed that naughty behaviour goes unchecked will therefore be more likely to become involved in similar difficult behaviour themselves.

A similar approach can be applied to the influence of the media, where studies have shown the general way in which social learning occurs. Huesman (1988), for example, argues that when children watch media characters deal with interpersonal problems by using violence, they develop ideas about *scripts* – what events are likely or appropriate in a given situation. When children are confronted with similar situations in their own lives, these scripts are then likely to be activated and increase the probability of overt aggression. An important feature which increases the likelihood of children believing that such behaviour would be appropriate for themselves seems to be the extent to which they identify with the aggressor. This is the perceived similarity of the model, or the ideal role which the model represents, to themselves. They are also more likely to use aggressive behaviour which they have seen as being justified in some way, which has not had upsetting or negative consequences, and, perhaps most importantly, if they see the context and behaviour as being close to reality.

TELEVISION AND AGGRESSION

There has been a great deal of controversy about whether children's viewing of violence on television can be causally linked with subsequent aggressive behaviour. British children certainly watch a great deal of television, more than 20 hours a week for most schoolchildren (Broadcasters' Audience Research Council, 1995), and a great deal of aggression is portrayed. Cumberbatch (1991) found that there were on average 1.68 violent acts per hour, which equates to children typically observing more than 20,000 violent acts over their school career.

Long-term studies have shown that children who watch more violence on television tend to be aggressive later in life. However, these findings are merely correlational, and may just reflect the fact that such children are from backgrounds which encourage this type of viewing and at the same time foster the development of aggressive behaviour. In an attempt to investigate whether that is the case, Huesman (1986) carried out a 22-year long-term study which considered the relative importance of a range of different factors. Huesman looked at aggression and the amount of violent television watched at 8 years of age, and related these factors to aggression and criminality (including the seriousness of the crimes committed) at 30 years of age. The investigation found that early television watching was a better predictor of later difficulties than early ratings of aggression, indicating that it was the television watching that caused the later difficult behaviour. However, the study found that there were a number of other long-term mediating effects including family background, social integration and academic achievements. It may therefore be that the key feature was in fact the continuity over time of a family background which fostered progressively more aggressive behaviour, as well as poor supervision permitting the viewing of violence. Stronger evidence would need to show a direct effect of watching violence, by comparing the behaviour of groups of children who had either watched or not watched violent television or films, while holding other factors such as home background constant.

Josephson (1987) carried out such a study with groups of boys who watched either an exciting film about a bike-racing team, or one in which members of a special police team either killed or knocked unconscious a number of criminals. In a subsequent game of 'floor hockey', the boys were then observed and rated for the aggressiveness of their actions. These included hitting other players with their stick, elbowing them and verbal insults. The interesting finding here was that such aggression increased after viewing the violent film, but only in boys who had already been rated by their teachers as normally aggressive in the classroom. One explanation is therefore that the aggressive children had weaker pro-social norms which were more easily altered, whereas the non-aggressive children had well-established norms which remained consistent despite the violence portrayed in the film. Although these explanations are plausible, such investigations can be criticised for being rather short term and not showing natural patterns of television and behaviour.

Perhaps the ideal way of studying the effects of television would be to carry out a long-term experiment in a real-life situation. This would involve assembling two similar groups of people who had been prevented from seeing television in their lives. One group would then be exposed to television and studied over time to see whether the level of aggression in that population changed, relative to the other control group. Although such an experiment is impossible to arrange, it has been approximated by some 'natural experiments'.

Natural experiments in television watching In 1973 a small Canadian town (called 'Notel' by the investigators) became able to receive television for the first time when problems with reception were overcome. Joy *et al.* (1986) investigated the impact of television on this community and used as controls two similar communities which already had television.

Using a double-blind research design, 45 first- and second-grade students were observed over a period of two years for rates of different forms of aggression. Although the behaviour in the two control communities stayed the same, the rates of physical aggression among children in Notel dramatically increased by 160 per cent, indicating that television viewing had a strongly negative effect on behaviour.

However, there were very different findings in a similar study by Charlton and O'Bey (1997), who looked at the effects of introducing television to the isolated island of St Helena in the South Atlantic. In this case the behaviour of children in school, as assessed by direct observation and by teacher ratings, did not worsen over time. There were in fact some improvements among younger children, with a reduction in teasing and fighting behaviour.

These differences may be due to the fact that other general real-life cultural and socialising factors such as the family can sometimes be more important than viewing negative models on television. In this context, the St Helena population may have been rather atypical, since it had very close community links, ensuring monitoring and accountability for behaviour. When home and the general community (including schooling) are less cohesive (as in Notel), then it may be that the influences of viewing television can be more negative.

Television and pro-social effects A further interesting possibility is that some television, particularly programmes specifically made for children, can have pro-social effects, since they often portray positive moral principles and outcomes. Sprafkin and Rubinstein (1979), for instance, found that children who prefer and watch more pro-social programmes tend to behave more positively in school. Also, Baran (1979) showed that

8- and 9-year-olds who watched an episode of *The Waltons* where helping behaviour was emphasised later showed more helping behaviour than other children who had not seen the programme.

The implications of these findings for parents and schools appears to be that the media can affect children's behaviour, but that the effects can be mediated by children's general social and cultural context and that television watching can have positive effects if managed appropriately.

Social roles and expectations

Chapter 7 described how behaviour in school can be seen as the result of a set of norms and scripts, with pupils and teachers acting to present their concepts of their own self in social situations. In school there are *role expectations* for both pupils and teachers, and these determine a great deal of normal behaviour. The role of the teacher is to control, organise and to exercise authority. Pupils will normally show obedience to the teacher's authority, and conformity to the norms of the normal classroom situation. 'Normal' behaviour can be seen as the process of generally following these expectations, with 'scripts' which govern the processes that happen in different situations in school.

In lessons, pupils are expected to enter the class, sit down at their desks, attend to the teacher and get on with their work. Teachers are expected to complement this behaviour by organising and directing the children. Even informal times of the day such as breaks have their own expectations, with limits on where children can go and the type of games that they can get involved in. It is not surprising that problems with non-teaching supervisors are particularly likely at these times. They are unlikely to be perceived by the pupils as having the same authority role as teachers, but have the role responsibility of directing and managing behaviour, which leads to role conflict.

Hargreaves (1967) has shown that problem behaviours in school can often be seen as a general social process, with pupils acting against the organisation's norms in order to meet the alternative norms of their own peer group. Meeting the norms of the peer group can lead to challenges and activities which are deliberately in opposition to school rules and expectations of behaviour. For example, they may subvert the school's dress codes or, at the extreme, actively seek punishment to confirm to their peers that they are in opposition to the formal rules.

The implications of such explanations are that behaviour will be more positive when pupils perceive themselves to be part of the social structures of school and identify with groupings such as their own tutor group or 'house'. They are also more likely to feel commitment when they are part of the processes of decision making and in establishing rules and regulations. These approaches are incorporated in a number of techniques to be described in Chapter 11, such as 'circle time' and the 'no blame approach', which depend on developing pro-social behaviour through group activities. Cooperative involvement by pupils out of school can be particularly effective in setting up relationships which transfer well to the normal school situation. A review of a number of studies by Hattie *et al.* (1997) found that the shared experience of going on an 'outward bound' type of activity resulted among other things in significant improvements in pupils' behaviour when they were back in school, with an overall long-term effect size of 0.51.

Deindividuation

Deindividuation happens when individuals lose their sense of personal identity. This is likely to happen when people are part of a crowd, or when they feel anonymous. People can, for instance, lose their sense of individual responsibility if they believe that others will not be able to attribute their actions to them.

Behaviour in such situations and experiences can be understood from the perspective of people becoming free from the normal roles and scripts which govern what they do. Such situations can sometimes lead to impulsive and aggressive behaviour, if there is even a low level of motivation to behave in this way. Zimbardo (1970), for instance, found that subjects would follow instructions and deliver greater electric shocks to an innocent victim when they were part of a group or when they were wearing disguises (the 'shocks' and the victim were actually pretence).

School classes involve relatively large groups of pupils, and in secondary schools in particular there can be relatively high levels of anonymity. These circumstances are likely to lead to a decreased sense of responsibility by pupils and a tendency to join in with class misbehaviour. A key technique to prevent such deindividuation and its consequences is for a teacher to be able to identify individual pupils as soon as possible, and to make sure that they are aware that the teacher knows them as individuals. Marland (1993) describes practical ways of achieving this, which include insisting on regular seating positions with a key kept by the teacher and regular rehearsal of children's names in the early stages with a new class. Incidentally, a useful technique here is to use the mnemonic strategies mentioned in Chapter 2. For example, a pupil's key visual features can be identified and linked with the pupil's name in some way – for example, the name of a child called Paul could be remembered if he happened to look a bit like Sir Paul McCartney.

It also seems probable that the use of a standard school uniform could deindividuate pupils and that it might therefore be best to allow individual dress styles. However, such a policy might also encourage the use of clothing as the signals for subgroup membership with a general ethos counter to that of the school. The best option might be to allow some variation but with limits to the more extreme and challenging forms of clothing.

Bystander apathy

Aggression also becomes more likely when children who are not directly involved fail to act to help an evident victim. Maines and Robinson (1991) consider that such bystander apathy is particularly important in the case of bullying and must be tackled when one is trying to reduce such behaviour problems. Bystander apathy has been extensively studied, since it can seem rather surprising that people will fail to act helpfully in such situations.

Latane and Darley (1970) emphasise that individuals appear to carry out an evaluation of the situation, in terms of whether there is a real problem and whether they could actually do something to help. Piliavin *et al.* (1981) also found that people will weigh up the costs and benefits of helping. On the one hand, helping another pupil who is being bullied might result in social approval from adults and a boost to one's self-esteem. However, becoming involved could also expose a child to social pressures from other children and perhaps some physical danger. At the very least it would involve some inconvenience, for instance if the child had to be involved in reporting the incident. Owing to such concerns, children in school will often fail to act and may then seek to rationalise their non-action in order to protect their own self-esteem. They may do this by saying that it was the victim's own fault, or that the incident was not really as serious as it seemed.

As already described, being part of a group can also lead to a decrease in individual responsibility and assumptions that somebody else will act. People also tend to conform and take cues for appropriate roles and actions from others round them. Such conformity can have the effect of inhibiting action unless children become aware of their own responsibilities and the need for action. This aspect is part of some approaches to reducing bullying, and it has been shown that when students are aware of the processes of bystander apathy they are much more likely to help others in need.

The social skills perspective

Some children can have behavioural difficulties that appear to be due to problems with social interaction. These may involve an inability to structure social exchanges, with the normal turn-taking and reciprocity that the structuring of social exchanges entails. Some children appear to misread social cues and situations, causing faulty peer group entry, misperception of peer group norms, inappropriate responses to provocation, and misinterpretation of pro-social interactions. Inappropriate understanding and responses may lead to aggression, or alternatively to withdrawal and subsequent rejection by the normal peer group. This can in its own turn lead to membership of more deviant peer groups where children with such problems are even less likely to develop positive interaction skills.

Since many behavioural difficulties are present before school and persist when pupils are there, it seems likely that some children fail to develop social skills as a result of faulty social experiences in the home. Observations by Patterson (1982) in the homes of some families have shown that children's pro-social acts are often ignored or responded to inappropriately. Also, the parental models for positive behaviours can often be limited, with an emphasis on inconsistent, restricted and punitive interactions with children. Through poor supervision, children can also frequently be intruded upon by others in the family, which can lead them to develop reactive and coercive behaviours such as shouting and hitting as a form of substitute social skill (see 'The home', below).

Studies of pupils in school by Dodge *et al.* (1986) have found that many children who are ignored, neglected or rejected by their peers are unhappy and lacking in social skills, and Dunn and McGuire (1992) found that such children are particularly at risk of continued maladaptive behaviour such as aggression, disruption and hypersensitivity. It seems likely that an effective way to help some children with such behavioural difficulties would be to focus on the development of specific social interactions skills, and some of these approaches are described in Chapter 11.

The role of gender

Boys are much more likely than girls to have behaviour problems in school. Croll and Moses (1990) review evidence that boys receive 68 per cent of criticisms directed at classroom behaviour, implying that low-level problems are twice as prevalent in boys as girls. Also, more serious problems which involve difficult, acting-out behaviour are much more likely to happen with boys. Ofsted (1996), for instance, reports that about four times as many boys are excluded from school, typically for aggressive behaviour. MacKinnon *et al.* (1995) report that boys make up 87 per cent of the pupils in types of EBD special schooling which take children with the most severe difficulties, a ratio of nearly seven to one.

Some explanations for this difference focus on the possibility of biological differences in the aggressiveness of males and females, for instance due to the effect of the male hormone testosterone. Although males with higher levels of testosterone are more likely to commit antisocial acts (Dabbs and Morris, 1990), aggression itself boosts the levels of testosterone, and this is probably unlikely to be a simple cause of difficult behaviour. Cairns *et al.* (1989) found that boys and girls in school did not differ in their experiences of anger or aggression in different situations, but that they did differ in the behavioural expression of anger. Boys tended to use physical confrontation but girls were much more likely to use 'social aggression' that involved attempts to alienate or ostracise a girl from a social group or to defame her character. These differences appear to be strongly influenced by the development of sex roles and stereotype expectations, described in Chapter 7.

The home

A large number of studies have shown that children with behavioural problems at school also have unusual and stressful home backgrounds. Sears *et al.* (1957) originally interviewed nearly 400 mothers of 5-year-old children and concluded that children's aggression was related to:

- severity of punishment by the parents,;
- disagreement between the parents; and
- lack of warmth on the part of the mother.

Subsequent studies by Olweus (1993) have confirmed the importance of these aspects, and have extended them to include

- lack of supervision; and
- inconsistent management.

Such experiences appear to give children only partial and inconsistent boundaries for their behaviour, with limited internalisation of values. They also give children poor models for interpersonal relationships and behaviour, and prevent them from developing understanding and feeling for the needs of others.

However, since these findings are only correlational, it could be that children's behavioural difficulties cause changes in their parents' handling of them and might also generate stresses within the family. To investigate this, a longitudinal study by Farrington (1978) looked at the development of behavioural difficulties in 411 males from age 8 until they were 22 years old. Among other factors, this looked at the outcomes for harsh parental attitudes and an emphasis on the use of discipline.

The findings shown in Table 10.1 indicate that there was a significant relationship between early behaviour problems and long-term delinquency, but that parents' attitudes and discipline had an even stronger effect. This is consistent with the possibility that the children's home background had a progressively greater impact on them over time. Evidently, many children who were not originally difficult at age 8 years eventually became so, although, also, some must have improved over time.

How children learn to be aggressive

Patterson (1986) found that parenting practices and family interactions by themselves account for 30 to 40 per cent of the variance in general antisocial behaviour. Direct observations and analyses of family interaction processes indicate that aggressive and non-compliant behaviours are developed from an early age by a process of social learning. At first, the occurrence of relatively trivial behaviours such as whining, teasing and temper tantrums is reinforced either by attention or by positive outcomes if the child gets what it wants. As children become older, parents may then continue to use reinforcers and punishments inappropriately and inconsistently.

Table 10.1 Prediction of delinquency by early aggression and parental background

Measures at 8–10 years	Delinquents at 22 years, identified by earlier measures
Aggression	48.2%
Harsh parental attitudes and discipline	61.5%

Source: Based on data from Farrington (1978)

Various intrusions or forms of attack on children are common in some families and may occur hundreds of times each day. These can include simple verbal name-calling, the taking of a toy or other object away from a sibling, and direct physical interference. In such families, children rapidly learn that the only way to handle such events is to counterattack, and Patterson (1982) found that about one-third of children's coercive behaviours were a reaction to aversive intrusions by other family members. The child's counterattacks were also functional, in that about 70 per cent of the time they were followed by the attacker's withdrawal, resulting in a positive or a neutral outcome. As children learn to use high rates of negative behaviours, other family members also acquire the same skills, and chains of reciprocal behaviour can build up. Analyses have shown that as the lengths of these increase beyond 18 seconds, family members are at increased risk of hitting each other.

Patterson (1986) argues that such patterns of learned negative and coercive behaviours extend to outside the family and lead to rejection from normal peer groups. Allied to lax parental supervision and academic failure in school, this can then predispose children to join with similar individuals, forming deviant peer groups. The norms that are then established by these groups appear to become the main socialising process for their members and can lead to delinquent activities and substance abuse. Members of such groups can provide considerable positive reinforcement for deviant behaviour and will punish others for socially conforming acts.

Incorporating such family, peer group and academic factors into a general model enabled Patterson to account for 54 per cent of the variance in delinquency. This is a strong effect and indicates that there is likely to be a causative process operating. There is also support for this perspective from family intervention studies. These show that when it is possible to change towards more positive directions the ways in which families interact, the likelihood of children developing aggressive behaviour is greatly reduced. Kazdin (1987) found that such parental training was most effective with younger children, and also when it was combined with social skill development programmes.

Early problems

A major review of various studies by Campbell (1995) found that difficult home backgrounds were associated with the emergence of problems in early childhood and predicted their persistence to school age. Stott (1981) also carried out some longitudinal research of 1,100 children entering school and found that those with behaviour problems before starting school were very likely to continue to have difficulties three years later. These difficulties had a significant effect on later educational attainments, in particular slowing down their progress with reading.

However, a poor start does not guarantee that all such problems will continue; McCaffrey and Cumming (1969), for instance, showed that only one out of three emotional disturbances persisted over a two-year period in early education. Also, Topping's (1983) review finding of a 'spontaneous remission rate' of about two-thirds over 4 years, has been replicated in most longitudinal research, across all age ranges.

Along with this recovery rate, however, new behavioural problems can develop, particularly when there are significant changes in the home environment. Common events include moving house, loss of employment or separation of parents. Pagani *et al.* (1997), for instance, found that divorce before a child was 6 years old resulted in long-term increases in anxious, hyperactive and oppositional behaviour during later childhood. Apart from the direct disharmony which precipitates and is the result of such major changes, some children can be subsequently faced with adapting to a new family if their parent remarries. Although children may eventually learn to adjust to such situations, they may take some time to do so, and new behaviour problems might develop.

Different backgrounds, different problems

There is also evidence that different sorts of behaviour problems come from particular types of experiences. For example, in a study by Farrington (1978), subsequent violence in children was best predicted by harsh parental attitudes and discipline. Other studies reviewed by Gotlib and Hammon (1992) show on the other hand that depression is associated with backgrounds where children experience neglect, criticism or maternal rejection within the family. As well as supporting the general concept that behaviour is strongly influenced by their home environment, these findings are also consistent with social learning theory, that children learn appropriate behaviour from their parents or other close family members.

School factors

Children spend a great deal of their lives in school and it seems almost inevitable that they will be affected by their social experiences there. However, the home is the main early socialising influence for children, and the social environments of different schools are likely to vary less than children's home backgrounds. Nevertheless, schools with a roughly similar intake can still show significant differences in the overall level of general behavioural difficulties. This indicates that schools do vary to some extent in their effectiveness in dealing with children's behaviour.

Maxwell (1994), for instance, looked at the social intake of 13 secondary schools in Aberdeen and related this to the level of behavioural difficulties in each catchment. The level of free school meals uptake was taken as a measure of social disadvantage since although free school meals uptake relates only indirectly to the processes in individual families, it does give some indication of the overall levels of social pressures and difficulties. Emotional and behavioural difficulties were assessed by the number of children who were being educated out of school as a result of such problems.

As shown in Figure 10.2, this correlation is in fact quite high at 0.89, and evidently children from the most disadvantaged areas are much more likely to have emotional and behavioural difficulties. General home background therefore appears to account for the greater part of the variation between schools over this range. Most schools also tend not to be too extreme on either count and it is difficult to separate them. However, schools A and B appear to have roughly similar intakes, yet school A has at least four times the level of this type of behavioural difficulty as compared with school B.

Reynolds and Sullivan (1981) have shown in a comparison of eight secondary schools in south Wales that such differences could be related to the ways in which schools view and deal with their intake. When schools had a perspective they designated *'incorporation'*, both children and their families were encouraged to take an active and participative role in school. These schools used prefects and monitors, and had good interpersonal relationships between pupils and staff, with minimal use of overt institutional control. Parental involvement was helped by the regular sending home of information, and there was close informal contact with teachers.

Schools using the alternative perspective of *'coercion'* tended to view problems as being

Figure 10.2 Levels of emotional and behavioural difficulties (EBD) in relation to social class of intake in 13 Aberdeen schools

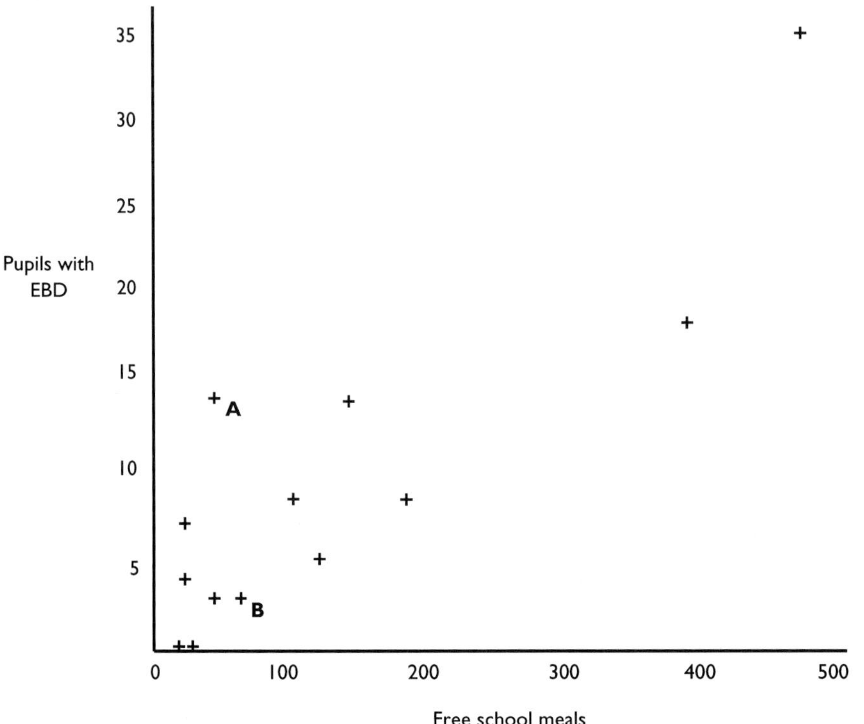

Source: Maxwell (1994)

mainly due to children's home backgrounds and largely relied upon institutional control, strict rule enforcement and the use of punishment. Pupils were not involved in the authority structure of the school, since teachers felt that they would abuse that power, and parents were not involved since it was felt that they would not support the school.

In a controlled comparison of a number of secondary schools, Rutter *et al.* (1979) also identified a number of similar school features which had a significant effect on children's behaviour at school and on levels of delinquency after leaving school. Factors which positively influenced outcomes were the degree of the school's academic emphasis, teacher actions in lessons, the availability of incentives and rewards, good conditions for pupils, and the extent to which children were able to take on responsibilities in school.

However, a caution about such findings is that they are unlikely to account completely for the differences in intakes between schools. Although measures such as entitlement to free school meals may be an indicator of home background, these are likely to be affected by factors such as the local possibilities of employment and cannot accurately account for the general social culture and practices in bringing up children. Also, it is likely that what schools are able to do is strongly affected by their catchment and that factors such as the levels of parental support are mainly affected by a school's social intake. Randall (1997), for instance, describes how interpersonal aggression is very much part of the culture in some school catchments and how some parents encourage their children to continue with aggression in school.

Achievement and behaviour

At first glance there appears to be a strong association between learning difficulties and behaviour problems. Older children with behaviour problems of the sort that can lead them into subsequent delinquency (trouble with the law) often have low levels of basic academic skills. A typical study by Wilgosh and Paitich (1982) found that more than 60 per cent of a sample of 99 girls and boys who were delinquents at about 14 years of age were underachieving by two or more years in at least one area of academic skills. Similarly, Meltzer *et al.* (1984) found that as early as second grade, 45 per cent of children who eventually became delinquents were already significantly behind with their reading. Williams and McGee (1994) carried out a long-term investigation with a large sample of boys from the beginning to the end of their schooling. They found that children's early failure with literacy was significantly associated with a subsequent diagnosis of conduct disorder at 15 years of age.

Unfortunately, a difficulty in interpreting such findings is knowing whether it was in fact the learning problems which caused the behavioural difficulties. One possibility is that low literacy skills mean that pupils are frequently unable to cope with the work in school and therefore look for other (more deviant) ways in which to boost their self-esteem. However, there is an alternative and plausible explanation which is the complete reverse. This is that early and persistent behavioural difficulties cause learning problems.

There is some support for this explanation in that the literacy attainments of older children with behaviour problems are in fact generally not particularly far behind: in the Wilgosh and Paitich (1982) study, which included children with the most severe behavioural difficulties, the overall delay with literacy was only about one year. Although significant, this would hardly limit their ability to cope with the majority of school work. As will be discussed in Chapter 12, such delays are in fact quite common, and the majority of children with such literacy difficulties do not automatically have behavioural problems.

The relationship between the long-term development of literacy and behavioural problems was investigated by McGee *et al.* (1986) with 925 boys from 5 to 11 years of age. The main finding was that those children who had early behaviour problems at the age of 5, particularly poor concentration/attention, subsequently had low levels of learning progress. As they became older, the type of their behavioural difficulties changed and they became more antisocial. This gives support for the idea that early behaviour problems which prevent children from being involved with school work will limit their progress with literacy skills.

However, an alternative explanation is that something else might be causing both the eventual conduct disorder and the long-term reading difficulty. Various types of evidence suggest that this something might be the ongoing effects of negative home environments, coupled with early difficulties with attention and concentration. According to this perspective, children can fail to make initial progress with reading owing to a combination of home environment factors including limited parental involvement. Early difficulties with concentration and attention would interfere with initial learning and are also strongly associated with conduct disorder, frequently acting as a basis for its later development (see Chapter 12).

When allowance is made for the effect of such background variables, attainments no longer appear to have a direct effect on behaviour. Fergusson and Lynskey (1997), for instance, followed a birth cohort of 1,265 children in New Zealand from the point of school entry to the age of 16. Children with early reading delays were found to have many negative features in their lives, including high rates of attentional difficulties and conduct problems. They also generally had poor home backgrounds, including a high chance of belonging to a low social class, a high chance of coming from a single-parent family, and a high chance of coming from a poorly managed home. When these effects were accounted for, there was no longer any association between the reading skills and behaviour of the children when they were 16 years old.

Finally, if literacy difficulties did cause conduct disorders, one would expect that academic remediation would lead to a reduction in antisocial behaviour. In fact, a number of studies reviewed by Wilson and Hernstein (1985) have repeatedly demonstrated that this does not happen. Having one's skills boosted and experiencing success in school do not appear to be sufficient in themselves to generate improved behaviour. It could of course still be the case that the help was given too late and that it is difficult to overcome established patterns of negative behaviour.

In general, behavioural problems do not seem to be a simple outcome of learning difficulties, although they probably share some causes in terms of poor early adjustment to school and long-term home environmental factors. It still seems likely, however, that the most severe forms of literacy difficulties, such as a reading age below 8 years later in the secondary school, will have a direct effect on behaviour. If children are unable to manage any formal work in class, they might easily become involved in other activities such as talking to other children, which would be generally disruptive. Even in such extreme cases, it is still not certain that problems would extend beyond academic situations. It is possible, though, that failure would have a negative effect on pupils' self-esteem and that they might seek alternative (deviant) social groups to boost this.

'Giftedness'

It is often assumed that children with high abilities may have behaviour problems, owing to their becoming bored and disaffected with the normal curriculum. However, this does not appear to be the case, and Freeman (1998) has reviewed a number of studies which show that able children tend if anything to have better adjustment than most children and usually also have high self-esteem. When they do have problems, these seem to be primarily related to family difficulties, just as do those of other children. High creativity does, however, appear to be associated with unusual backgrounds and personality development. Such children are more likely to have difficulties in school as well as longer-term social and emotional difficulties.

Medical causes of children's behaviour problems

Various workers have proposed a medical basis for children's problems, and various formal psychiatric categories have been proposed. These include the possibility of an inherited or genetic component, brain abnormalities, dietary factors, and also psychodynamic explanations of developmental problems. Although some children can appear to have symptoms characteristic of adult psychiatric states such as psychotic behaviour, such symptoms are relatively rare, although it is sometimes tempting to look for an underlying cause in this way.

Even so, some major disorders such as autism are characteristically present from an early age and can have important educational implications if they involve difficult social behaviours. As will be discussed in Chapter 12, there is now convincing evidence that autism has a genetic basis and that difficulties with social interaction arise from a specific cognitive deficit which limits empathy.

Genetic basis

Some long-term studies, such as that by Thomas and Chess (1977), have found that newborn babies show stable differences in their general dispositions, such as being 'easy' or 'difficult'. They also found that these characteristics persisted at least until the children were 14 years old, which indicates that there could be an inherited basis for such underlying general behavioural predispositions.

Subsequent investigations have attempted to quantify the extent of the amount of inheritance for different types of specific behavioural difficulties. The investigations are similar to investigations of heritability of intelligence discussed in Chapter 3, and in the same way the heritability of behavioural difficulties has been studied by comparing the behaviour of different types of twins with varying levels of genetic similarity. In one major study of a range of different behavioural disorders, Eaves *et al.* (1997) compared identical twins (who are genetically the same) with non-identical twins, whose genetic similarity is the same as for any other siblings. Table 10.2 summarises part of their findings.

Table 10.2 Average correlation coefficients for parents' assessments of twins' behaviours

	Identical male twins	**Non-identical male twins**
Attention-deficit/ hyperactivity disorder	0.47	−0.045
Conduct disorder	0.69	0.43

Source: Based on data from Eaves *et al.* (1997)

If one assumes that the only difference between identical and non-identical twins is their genetic similarity, then these findings indicate that there is a strong genetic effect on the two behavioural categories, particularly for attention-deficit/hyperactivity disorder (AD/HD). However, it is likely that twins share very similar environments and that they will be treated the same, especially if their appearance is similar and people confuse them with each other. They are also likely to imitate each other's behaviour, and any conflicts are likely to be with each other. These effects would lead to an increase in the perceived similarity of their behaviour, and the above correlations could therefore be somewhat misleading.

A further difficulty with such findings comes from a study by Levy *et al.* (1996), who found a higher rate for AD/HD among twins in general, which would inflate the correlations for this category. They also found that most of the variance in AD/HD could be accounted for by language difficulties. These are more common in twins and may be due to the decreased adult involvement with each individual or the tendency of twins to develop their own alternative systems of communication. Language has a close relationship with thought and behaviour, and could underlie any difficulties with attention.

In general, therefore, genetic effects remain controversial and difficult to prove conclusively. Even if they are shown to have a significant effect, it is still likely that they will show interactions with other factors. This might happen for instance if traits that involve being more difficult to manage evoke less positive parenting styles.

Brain abnormalities

It is possible that problem behaviours may have a physical basis such as abnormal electrical activity in the brain (as shown by an electroencephalogram), some form of (minimal) brain damage or structural abnormality, or a biochemical imbalance which affects mood.

One particular theory reviewed by Harris (1978) is that difficult behaviour may be related to abnormal brain activity in the temporal lobes, since structures in these areas are associated with emotional states. There is often some evidence of abnormal 'spiking' activity in the EEGs of children with behavioural difficulties, and treatment can involve anticonvulsant medication even if there is no evidence of seizures. A problem with this theory, though, is that only about 68 per cent of all children have a totally 'normal' EEG, and there can in fact be many reasons for abnormal brain electrical activity. Known clinical problems with brain function can affect behaviour, however, and a study by Ounsted (1969) of 100 children with diagnosed temporal lobe epilepsy found that 36 suffered from episodes of rage.

Mood and behaviour can certainly be affected by specific forms of known brain damage. These include tumours, infections and various types of direct physical trauma. Such causes are relatively rare, but it has also been proposed that low-level or 'minimal brain damage' can result in difficulties with learning and with behaviour. Such low-level brain damage is often assessed by means of so-called 'soft' neurological signs such as clumsiness or impulsivity. Despite this, an epidemiological study by Schmidt *et al.* (1987) of 399 8-year-old children indicated that the range of supposed features failed to 'cluster' together. Various neurological features, skill development, and physical and psychological features were all relatively independent; doing badly on one of these did not mean that there was a significant risk for any of the others.

With developments in direct imaging techniques such as nuclear magnetic resonance, it is now possible to view soft tissue structures in the brain and to compare normal and abnormal populations. Such evidence has been used to indicate the existence of abnormalities in certain parts of the brains of children classified as having AD/HD. However, the level of variation that can be found in the brains of children with normal behaviour means that such tests cannot be used to make a valid diagnosis with an individual child.

The cells of the brain transmit information by passing small amounts of transmitter chemicals, and some of these are specific to certain structures involved in mood and behaviour. One of these, dopamine, is believed to affect behavioural inhibition and may be involved in AD/HD. Another key candidate for behavioural problems is serotonin, which is involved in mood and emotions and appears to be at a low level in aggressive individuals. Unis *et al.* (1997), for instance, found these types of serotonin abnormalities in 45 juvenile offenders. There was also a positive correlation between low serotonin levels and the severity of their crimes, as well as how young they were when their difficulties began. On the other hand, negative environmental influences have also been shown to depress serotonin levels, and one would need to carry out long-term controlled studies to prove any causation. If there is a biochemical abnormality, it could perhaps be treated, and drugs such as Prozac, which increase the levels of serotonin, do have positive effects on mood and behaviour in children. However, there are doubts about the advisability of using such drugs routinely with children, particularly if their problems are mainly the result of difficult environments.

Dietary factors

There has been considerable interest in the possibility raised by Feingold (1975) that a number of (mostly artificial) food additives have an effect on hyperactive behaviour. The diet he recommended, which is still in current use, involves exclusion of:

- synthetic colours, particularly tartrazine (yellow – E102) and amaranth (red – E123);
- synthetic flavours, such as vanillin – not usually listed by name;
- antioxidant preservatives, in particular butylated hydroxyanisole (BHA – E320), butylated hydroxytoluene (BHT – E321) and tertiary butylhydroquinone (TBHQ – E319); and
- salicylate and aspirin (salicylic acid).

The Feingold Association provides a list of foods which it believes are safe to eat, and it is emphasised that even small amounts of the above substances could trigger a negative reaction.

Early research by Feingold (1976) indicated that 32 to 60 per cent of children with behavioural difficulties improved dramatically on this diet, implying that these substances were affecting sensitive children. However, critics have noted that many of the foods on the recommended list do in fact contain salicylates, and that it excluded others which were low in them. More importantly, people's expectations may have influenced how they interpreted or managed subsequent behaviour. There is also the possibility that the apparent effectiveness of the diet may have been mainly due to the different parental management involved in administering the diet; restricting what children eat can involve very firm monitoring and handling, which may improve general behaviour.

A number of subsequent studies were therefore based on the strict experimental 'double-blind' design. This means that the diet was set up and run within a clinic and neither the families nor the person administering the diet knew when additives were included in or removed from the diet. Wender and Lipton (1980) carried out a review of seven such well-designed studies involving about 190 children. They found *no* instances of any consistent, dramatic deterioration in behaviour in hyperactive children who had been challenged with artificial food colourings under these conditions.

Since then, however, there have been criticisms that the dose levels of additives used in such studies were too low, in order to disguise their presence. The actual amount of colorants in the diets of some children can be as high as 250 milligrams, whereas the earlier studies mostly used doses of only 25 milligrams. Other substances, such as 'whole foods', have also been implicated in affecting behaviour, particularly with children who have some form of allergy. These have included egg, milk, peanut, wheat, fish and soya.

Breakey (1997) has reviewed 13 more recent studies which used good experimental designs and also used levels of additives and whole foods that would normally be in children's diets. All these found substantial and significant effects on children's behaviour, often with more than half of the children concerned being affected in some way or another. One interesting finding was also that the difficulties were not specific to the hyperactive syndrome (now subsumed under AD/HD), but appeared to be affecting mood, particularly irritability.

Most of these studies were based on children who had already been identified as having behaviour problems, but in many of the cases food problems were already suspected; for instance, there was a family history of allergy or migraines. It is difficult to know to what extent these findings could be applied to the normal population, but it does seem likely that for some susceptible children food difficulties could be involved, affecting mood and making a range of behavioural problems more likely.

However, for the majority of children with behavioural problems there is normally no known physical basis. Also, the fact (mentioned earlier) that most behavioural difficulties are relatively temporary, with a high rate of spontaneous remission, makes such biological explanations unlikely in the majority of cases and might distract parents and teachers from other explanations.

Psychodynamic causes

The psychodynamic approach is based on the work of Freud, and was largely developed to account for neurotic behaviour in adults. His daughter Anna Freud (e.g. 1964) later extended and developed his work with children, to explain the different ways in which they might have problems.

As shown in Table 10.3, Freud's theory proposes that children develop through five distinct psychosexual stages where they have key tasks to achieve. Children progressing through school should mainly be at the latency stage, eventually progressing to the genital stage at puberty. They should have already progressed beyond the oral and anal stages and have developed internal self-control through the Oedipus complex.

The psychodynamic perspective proposes that problems can arise from early experiences which disrupt normal development and lead to fixation at an earlier stage. Children who were weaned early might therefore show signs of being orally fixated, with self-centred behaviour; if they were weaned too late, they would show greed and envy. If a child is fixated at the anal stage, he or she might show an over-concern with orderliness.

As was described in Chapter 5, the mental structures of the id, the ego and superego were seen by Freud as the main sources of motivation, with the ego channelling and balancing the demands of the id and the superego. It does so by utilising a range of defence mechanisms which prevent us from being aware of the true nature of our drives.

Apart from repression (the most common form in general), behavioural difficulties in particular may involve:

- *displacement* – by transferring aggression from a threatening to a safer target;
- *identification* – adopting aspects of another's personality when threatened by them; and
- *regression* – returning to an earlier fixated stage

Neuroses are seen as the outcome of ineffective, short-term defence mechanisms (usually repression) which eventually cannot protect the ego and lead to neurotic symptoms such as anxiety. Displacement can lead to irrational anxiety about experiences such as school attendance (school phobia) when the real problem could be something completely different and often based on events at home.

When children have problems in school, the psychodynamic approach argues that the causes lie in early home-based experiences and that these must be tackled in an intensive, specialist way (usually in a clinic). It also implies that behavioural techniques will fail as they do not tackle underlying causes. It is nowadays rare for such approaches to be the only ones used by child psychiatrists, but there is often a belief in the dynamic processes underlying problems.

Freud's theories have been heavily criticised for being unscientific; they were largely his own ideas and developed only from clinical practice. Some aspects are also simply unbelievable, such as his emphasis on infant sexuality and aspects such as penis envy by little girls. However, it is difficult to ignore Freud's ideas and his terminology completely since they have become part of our language and culture. Also, some of his ideas such as those relating to unconscious processes

Table 10.3 Freud's proposed developmental stages

Stage	Age	Erogenous zones	Main developments
Oral	0–1	Mouth, lips and tongue	Weaning
Anal	2–3	Anus	Toilet training
Phallic	4–5	Genitals	Oedipus complex
Latency	6–12	None	Defence mechanisms

and defence mechanisms do seem interesting, although there are probably more useful explanations for these based on cognitive approaches.

The origins of anxiety and depression

Anxiety

Anxiety in school can happen when a child is fearful of things which have happened or which might happen. These could include social difficulties such as bullying, or problems with work such as a feeling of inability to cope with examinations. School phobia is an example of a seemingly irrational anxiety, and its development and continuation can be explained by Gray's (1975) two-process theory. An initial precipitating event, such as being bullied at school, may produce a negative involuntary emotional state, which becomes classically conditioned to thoughts about or attendance at school. If the pupil then avoids attending, this can result in operant conditioning of this behaviour in the future since the non-attendance is effectively being rewarded with reductions in anxiety.

According to Ullman and Krasner (1975), anxiety can also be reinforced by interpersonal rewards. Teachers or parents can sometimes inadvertently reinforce anxiety by giving children attention for anxious behaviour or thoughts, thereby increasing such attention-seeking behaviour and leading to even greater difficulties. Although it may sometimes be tempting to ignore an anxious child, in the short term the child may then step up the behaviour until he or she does get some attention, sometimes with dangerous consequences. It is important to ensure that such situations are closely supervised.

Depression

One explanation of depression is that it can be the result of a loss of self-esteem or self-effectiveness, which may be related to school processes. If children experience long-term failure, they may come to feel that they have no control over events, a condition known as *learned helplessness*. Seligman (1975) has found that individuals who develop this remain passive and have a low sense of self-worth. This can continue even if they subsequently experience success, since even their success is attributed to external processes such as luck. Although self-esteem appears to be relatively specific, children spend a lot of their lives in school and it is likely that long-term academic failure will have a significant impact in this way.

Another theory elaborated by Lewinsohn (1974) is that depressed individuals are simply not receiving enough positive experiences in their lives. The lack of positive experiences can lead them to reduce the levels of behaviour that were previously reinforced and generally become more passive. If the person continues in this state, they will label themself 'depressed' and may then go on to use this label to explain their lack of activity. As with anxiety, a danger is that others may give some attention and sympathy for the abnormal behaviour, which may then reinforce it.

Medical explanations for anxiety and depression

Some medical explanations are based on the belief that such disorders are due to biological malfunctioning of the brain. Anxiety might be the result of an overactive autonomic nervous system (the system that manages general physiological arousal), for instance by releasing adrenaline into the bloodstream. Depression on the other hand is believed to be due to a lack of certain chemical transmitters in the brain which are to do with mood, in particular a substance called noradrenaline which is mainly found in the brain stem. These theories are supported by the effectiveness of drug therapies, with diazepam (known as Valium) acting as a tranquilliser to reduce anxiety by acting on the parts of the brain to do with arousal. Tricyclic antidepressants such as imipramine (known as Tofranil) also appear to work by increasing the amount of noradrenaline which is present in the brain.

However, it is also possible that any such biological malfunctions could be a result of psychological factors, since repeated stresses or a perceived lack of control may themselves bring about specific physiological changes. Nevertheless, medication can still be useful and bring about rapid and positive changes for some individuals, particularly when other techniques have not been effective.

Categories of emotional and behavioural difficulties

In a review of the various perspectives, Chazan *et al.* (1994) consider that there is a general tendency to put problem school behaviours into two major groups. The first of these is the category of antisocial/overreacting behaviour, often termed 'acting out', which includes aggression and hyperactivity, or behaviours which are generally disruptive. The second category involves withdrawn/underreacting behaviour and includes anxiety, such as school phobia, and depression, which can involve unhappiness, passivity and social isolation. Like the classification systems used in abnormal psychology, however, this approach is largely based on what can be observed of the behaviour. It is not necessarily linked with a knowledge of specific causes or with particular techniques to help with the behaviour.

Psychiatric classifications of childhood disorders are also based on the use of symptoms and use similar categories. These come from two main schedules, the *American Diagnostic and Statistical Manual of Mental Disorders*, 4th edition (DSM-IV, 1994), and the *International Classification of Diseases*, 10th revision (ICD-10, 1993), which is mainly used in Europe. Diagnosis is based on a clinical interview with a child's parents and this is used to assess whether a child has a certain number of problem behaviours, as set out in a standard list, and for a significant length of time – usually 6 months. Both schedules separate out emotional difficulties from disruptive behaviours, and the major categories which cover behavioural problems of children are shown in Table 10.4.

There is evidently some overlap between these two systems, for example with the common use of the category 'conduct disorder'. Also, hyperactivity disorder in the DSM is similar to hyperkinetic disorder in the ICD. However, there are also major contrasts between the two approaches, which points up the fact that these systems probably reflect different medical customs and practices, and there must be a certain arbitrariness about the use of categories.

There are also many shared features and associations between categories within the classification systems. For example, most children who have AD/HD have other disruptive behaviours as well. Because of this imprecision, specific diagnoses should perhaps be viewed with some caution and interpreted in terms of their usefulness for helping children with such problems.

Table 10.4 Psychiatric classification of childhood disorders

DSM-IV	ICD-10
Attention-deficit and disruptive behaviour disorders	Hyperkinetic disorder
	Conduct disorders
Attention-deficit/hyperactivity disorder (AD/HD)	Mixed disorders of conduct and emotions
Conduct disorder	Emotional disorders with onset specific to childhood
Oppositional defiant disorder Disruptive behaviour disorder	Disorders of social functioning with onset specific to childhood and adolescence
Anxiety disorders are now included with adult categories as they are not considered to be specific to childhood, apart from separation anxiety disorder.	Other behavioural and emotional disorders with onset usually occurring in childhood and adolescence

Assessment of behavioural problems

Teacher questionnaires

A common way of identifying and categorising behaviour problems in schools has been by the use of a behavioural checklist administered by a teacher who knows the child well. One of the most popular of these techniques has been the BSAG (Bristol Social-Adjustment Guides – Stott, 1971), which covers the age range from 5 to 16 years. Each guide is made up from 33 categories of behaviour, such as 'paying attention in class' and 'ways with other children'. All these categories have a number of possible descriptors such as 'attends to anything but his work' or 'on the whole attends well'. A teacher goes through the questionnaire, circling the statements which he or she judges are most appropriate for each of the categories. The questionnaire is then scored by using an overlay which puts these responses into two general groupings, as shown in Table 10.5. The assessment therefore results in two scores which can be referred to normative tables to see how often they are likely to occur. These tables are adjusted to take account of the higher levels of behaviour problems for boys. So, for example, an Over-reaction score of 21 would be achieved by only 4 per cent of all boys and by 1 per cent of all girls.

The BSAG is rather old now and it is becoming difficult to get the test materials. A more modern variation on this approach which covers the same age range is the Devereux test (Naglieri *et al.*, 1992), which uses 40 statements with five rating categories. The statements use specific problem behaviours, similar to 'During the last four weeks, how often did the child . . .' 'act aggressively to others?' or 'seem anxious or distressed?' Each of the behaviours is rated for frequency with the categories 'never', 'rarely', 'occasionally', 'frequently' and 'very frequently'. Scoring is similar to that for the BSAG, with answers placed into the subscales of Interpersonal Problems, Inappropriate Behaviours/Feelings, Depression, Physical Symptoms/Fears, as well as an overall total problem score.

Two other popular behaviour rating scales which can be used with primary-aged children are the Rutter (1967) Child Behaviour Scale and the Conners (1973) Teacher's Rating Scale. Both these involve a number of items describing problems behaviours, which are rated by the teacher for a particular child. The Rutter scale is primarily designed to be used as an initial screening instrument, but the Conners scale enables scores to be grouped into four subscales of Conduct Problems, Inattentive–Passive, Tension–Anxiety and Hyperactivity.

Table 10.5 Major dimensions of British Social-Adjustment Guides

Under-reaction	Over-reaction
Includes the core syndromes of unforthcomingness, withdrawal and depression	Includes the core syndromes of inconsequence and hostility, as well as the associated grouping of peer-maladaptiveness

Pupil questionnaires

There are alternative approaches, including questionnaires which are filled out by the pupil instead of a teacher, such as the Behaviour in School Inventory (Youngman, 1979). This involves 34 questions about school such as 'Are you usually quiet in class?' and 'Do you answer back if a teacher tells you off?' The answers are grouped into the three categories of Studiousness, Compliance and Teacher Contact, and are added together to give a single overall score. Scores can again be compared with norms to see how likely it would be for a particular pattern of responses to occur.

Classroom observation

A further type of approach avoids all concepts of classification and instead just records observations of problem behaviours. Identification in this way is often part of an overall approach to dealing with behaviour problems. An example is the Behavioural Approach to Teaching Package (Wheldall *et al.*, 1983) in which standard schedules are used to record observations of both pupil and teacher behaviours. Observation categories are specified beforehand and involve positive and negative teacher behaviours and on- or off-task pupil behaviours.

Sociometry

Sociometric techniques can also be used to establish the social links and organisation in classes. As described by Cohen (1976), such techniques involve first asking all the children in a class to nominate those other children whom they like, or some other index of the same thing, such as naming two other children they would want to work with. As shown in Figure 10.3, the results are typically analysed by drawing a visual representation of the groupings and the popularity of each individual.

The technique can then be used to establish groupings, key individuals and individuals' social situations. For instance, if the individual pupil C is disruptive, his or her behaviour might have a disproportionate effect because of C's influence on a number of other children. The general behaviour of the whole group might be improved if that child's role could be modified to become more positive. The approach can also show up children who are relatively isolated (such as D) and are not chosen by any others. This could give the opportunity to set up some limited social engineering or social skills work (see Chapter 11), to encourage the formation of relationships.

Although sociometry can be a very useful approach, it can cause problems if the results are not kept confidential since there is the possibility that it could expose isolated children.

Figure 10.3 Sociometric analysis

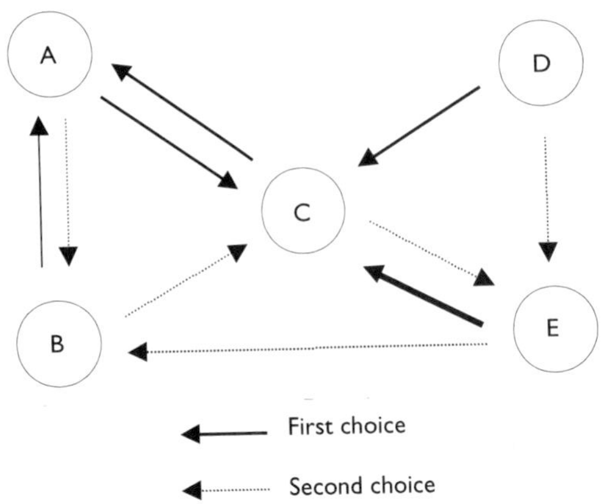

Prevalence of behavioural problems

In all the various assessment techniques referred to above, there is no single obvious cut-off criterion beyond which a behaviour suddenly becomes a problem (see Chapter 12). This means that there cannot be a definitive value for the frequency of problems. A high criterion score on a questionnaire such as the BSAG will result in relatively few children being identified as having problems, a low criterion score will identify many more.

In one study reported by Sue at al (1990), when all possible types of problem were identified, a surprisingly high level of about 56 per cent of 101 pre-adolescents (6- to 12-year-olds) received a medical diagnosis of one type or another, on the basis of the DSM-III-R. The diagnoses were based on interviews with the parents and children, none of whom had a prior history of psychological or psychiatric disturbance. Many children have transient problems, and a study by Moore (1966) of a sample of 164 primary-age children in London indicated that most children will have a school-based behavioural difficulty at some time or another.

Most of these problems would be relatively minor or a reaction to some temporary circumstances. What is more important, perhaps, is the number of children who teachers find are a significant problem for them in school. A review by Laslett (1977) of a number of such studies found that the range was from about 5 to 15 per cent of all children. This means that in most classes teachers will have from one to four pupils whose behaviour is of concern to them at any one time.

Reliability of assessments

In order for any form of assessment to be of use, it must reach a certain level of consistency or reliability, as measured by whether different parts of an assessment agree with each other, whether running the assessment again will give a similar result, and whether different forms of the assessment agree with each other. Most research findings show that when scores on two halves of a behavioural checklist are compared with each other, they typically show a high level of agreement. The BSAG, for instance, has an internal reliability of the order of 0.82 for the grouping of Under-reaction, and 0.91 for the grouping of Over-reaction. Retesting of children tends to show lower reliabilities, although they are still fairly substantial. Again, a typical result in the case of the BSAG for reassessment one year later gives coefficients of 0.74 for Under-reaction and 0.77 for Over-reaction.

Such consistency between such assessments could indicate that a test is accurately evaluating some stability in behaviour problems. An alternative interpretation, however, would be that instead of assessing the fixed attributes of the child, it is demonstrating the fixed attitudes of the teacher. Teacher attitudes and judgements have been shown to be stable over time, and there is evidence that a negative set towards a child can actually generate and perpetuate success or failure, as was described in Chapter 5.

Another explanation of consistency might be that the test is assessing merely the specificity of the situations which children find themselves in. This means that consistencies in a teacher's assessments might be due to a child's responding to that particular teacher and class in a specific way. Tattum (1982), for instance, found that problem pupils chose certain teachers and lessons to misbehave with. This would produce a high level of consistency for individual teachers' ratings even though the children's behaviours were actually quite variable between different teachers and lessons.

The reliabilities for assessments between different raters and different situations tends to be relatively low. The more different either of these factors are, the lower the coefficients become. For example, in a study by St James-Roberts (1994) there was only 38 per cent agreement between different staff about which children posed definite problems. This was despite the fact that the test–retest reliability coefficient of the test itself was 0.88 over two weeks.

When very different situations such as home and school are compared, there is usually only limited agreement. With the Devereux test the correlation between assessments by teachers and by counsellors who saw children in a residential setting was only 0.40 (Naglieri *et al.*, 1992, p. 45). In the Isle of Wight study by Rutter *et al.* (1970), 2,193 children were screened by means of both a parent questionnaire and a teacher questionnaire, each of which had been previously piloted extensively. Of these, 157 were selected as being 'maladjusted' on the basis of the teacher questionnaire, and 133 were selected as being 'maladjusted' on the basis of the parent questionnaire. As shown in Figure 10.4, only 19 children (less than 1 per cent) were selected on the basis of both teacher and parent questionnaires. It seems likely that this minimal overlap could be due to the different role expectations for children in the two situations. At home, children have relatively few constraints, and self-centred behaviour can often be tolerated. At school, on the other hand, firm role expectations and management can limit behaviours that would cause difficulties if they happened at home.

When behaviour assessments are carried out by pupils themselves, these can achieve much greater reliability coefficients. Jesness (1966) report test–retest coefficients over an eight-month period of as high as 0.79 for subscales of a

Figure 10.4 Overlap between problems identified by teacher questionnaires and problems identified by parent questionnaires

7.2% Identified by parents	.87% overlap	6.1% Identified by teachers

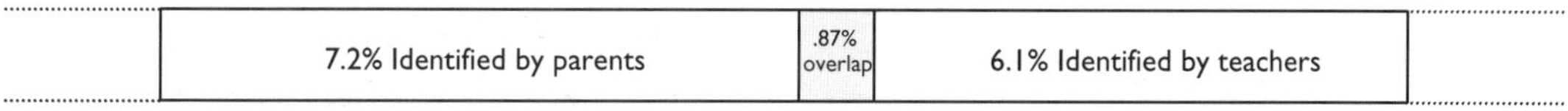

Source: Based on data in Rutter *et al.* (1970)

pupil self-report test. This is not surprising if we consider that this type of test is probably assessing an individual's self-concept, which is more likely to be stable than the judgements of different people. The difficulty with such assessments is of course that teachers are often more concerned about a pupil's behaviour as they see it. Also, there are likely to be significant differences between teachers' behavioural assessments and pupils' own self-ratings. The differences are at least partly due to a tendency for pupils to see their own behaviour as a reasonable response to the particular situation they are in, avoiding responsibility when things go wrong. This is an example of 'self-serving' bias, and is one of the different types of attribution which people use to preserve their self-esteem.

Reliabilities are also affected by the level of specificity of the behaviour described. For example, many descriptions in the BSAG such as 'a good mixer' are vague and open to different interpretations. Reliabilities are greatest when an assessment technique identifies specific observable behaviours, uses agreed categories, and has trained and experienced assessors. In one such investigation, for instance, Wheldall *et al.* (1985) carried out a study in which inter-rater agreements for specific pupil behaviours achieved an average of 94 per cent.

Validity of EBD assessment

In order for such assessments to be of any use, it is also essential that they have validity, and evaluate something to do with behavioural problems.

Content validity

Content validity refers to whether a test focuses on the appropriate problem behaviour. One would expect that a questionnaire that is supposed to be evaluating problem behaviour at school would consider things like 'attitudes to school and school work' and 'relationships with teachers'. If some items involve more general problems with adjustment such as sleep problems, it is less likely that they will have much to do with school behaviour. Most tests initially generate many of their items from teacher reports, and the BSAG is based almost exclusively on this approach. They can also be based on previous educational research findings which have themselves been validated, for example the Jesness inventory (Jesness, 1966). Both these approaches can reasonably claim to have validity of this sort.

Concurrent validity

Concurrent validity involves relating scores on a test to other features which are already present and which most people would agree show problem behaviour. Sometimes this is done simply by correlating the test scores with other assessments of behaviour or personality. Most tests correlate fairly well, particularly if they are of the same type, and St James-Roberts (1994) found a correlation of 0.83 between the Child Behaviour Checklist (the most commonly used US teacher checklist) and the Preschool Behaviour Checklist (a similar device for young children). However, a more persuasive assessment of the concurrent validity of a behavioural test would relate it to a range of current problem behaviours such as absenteeism or disruptive behaviour. Unfortunately, these relationships tend to be low, and in a study by Youngman and Szaday (1985) the Youngman's self-report inventory correlated at only around the 0.5 level with the number of times that a pupil was sent out of the room in a particular year.

Predictive validity

A more stringent test is predictive validity, the extent to which an assessment relates to problem behaviours that happen later in time. The BSAG, for instance, has been shown to relate significantly to subsequent delinquency and criminality. These validities tend to be the lowest of all, however, and Rutter *et al.* (1979) found a correlation of only 0.4 between a teacher-rated questionnaire of behaviour problems and delinquency after leaving school. The best predictors are usually measures which are closest to the eventual target behaviour. If one wished to predict disruptive behaviour in a child when he or she gets older, the best measure will probably be an assessment of the child's present behaviour. An exception to this, however, is when other factors such as home background can be shown to act as a basis for behaviour development. As already described, detailed models which incorporate home management, peer group influences and school attainments predict later delinquency better than do measures of early behaviour.

Construct validity

Construct validity refers to how meaningful are the basic constructs identified in the assessment. The criterion of meaningfulness could apply to the very concept of measuring a 'behavioural problem', or to particular dimensions from a behavioural assessment. Since much of behaviour is situation specific and measures of it have the poor reliability mentioned above, it can be argued that 'behaviour problems' do not have much construct validity.

As many of the assessment devices depend upon factor analysis, they are also subject to some basic criticisms of this approach that will be mentioned in Appendix 1: namely, that the factors derived depend largely on what items are included and the technique of analysis that is utilised. One might finally consider whether an assessment is of any value in allowing one to deal with problem behaviour. Although assessments may be useful in general research, such as in determining how stable behaviour problems are over time, the ultimate pragmatic evaluation is how far they will allow a school or teacher to directly help or deal with a child with problem behaviours. In order for the child to be helped, perhaps any assessment needs to be derived from a particular treatment or management approach.

Approaches such as direct behavioural evaluations or social analyses would appear to be most valid in this respect since, as Chapter 11 will show, there are immediate implications for setting up a programme of behavioural management or some form of social manipulation.

Summary

There are signs that schools have become increasingly concerned over pupils' behaviour and that modern life puts children under greater pressure. Severe problems are still relatively infrequent, however, although low-level difficulties can significantly limit children's educational progress.

The most common term is nowadays *emotional and behavioural difficulties* (EBD), which covers aggressive and disruptive as well as disturbed behaviours. These can be seen as related to individual differences or to failure to conform, although teacher concerns tend to focus on direct difficulties with adapting to the educational situation.

Most psychological theories emphasise individual experiences and reactions, such as frustration and attributions of responsibility for unpleasant experiences. Children also seem to be more likely to use problem behaviour when it has positive outcomes for them. However, it is likely that they learn more from observing others and judging what is appropriate and likely to succeed for themselves. The media can have similar effects, particularly if children see events as being realistic and relevant, although appropriate experiences can also have pro-social effects.

Social causes may be pupils' conforming to deviant peer group norms, and teachers can combat these by strengthening positive school norms. Group effects can lead to deindividuation and bystander apathy, when pupils may have a weakened sense of responsibility and fail to conform to normal behaviours or to help others in trouble. Owing to their home background, some children seem to lack positive social interaction skills. Boys are much more likely to have behavioural difficulties than girls, and although there may be a biological reason, their greater incidence of problems appears to be largely due to the development of gender roles.

A poor home background appears to be strongly linked with the development of behavioural problems such as aggression. These appear to be learned as a coping strategy within the home and can later be perpetuated in negative peer group membership. Such difficulties start early and are affected by different types of home situations.

Schools appear to have differential effects on behaviour, although their effect is much less than the impact of their intake's social background. Although it is widely believed that low achievement can cause poor behaviour, it is likely that early and long-term behavioural difficulties cause both the low achievement and later behaviour problems. 'Gifted' pupils do not seem to have any higher level of behavioural or emotional difficulties.

There are some suggestive findings which indicate that there is a biological basis for certain types of behavioural problems such as attention-deficit/hyperactivity disorder (AD/HD) and mood disorders. Dietary factors may be important in affecting AD/HD, although the way in which it works and the number of children affected is not yet clear. For most behavioural difficulties there is no known medical cause. Psychodynamic explanations are based on the ideas of Freud and propose that problems are the result of ineffective defence mechanisms. Anxiety and depression can result from past learning experiences and a perception of lack of control. They can also be associated with certain biological factors, although these could be a result as well as a cause.

Problem behaviours can be grouped as 'acting out' or as anxiety and depressive states. Psychiatric classifications break these down into further groupings which have some overlap. Problem behaviours can be assessed using techniques such as teacher and pupil questionnaires, direct observation and sociometry. Although there is no absolute criterion for such categories, most teachers find about one to four children in their class to be of some concern.

Such assessments usually have low reliabilities, owing to the varying effects of different contexts and relationships with whoever carries out the assessment. Most assessments have reasonable content and concurrent validities but are poor at predicting future behaviour, and their meaningfulness depends on how they are going to be used.

Key implications

- Home background and peer group influences appear to be the main causes of behavioural difficulties.
- Education can probably have only a limited impact on these.
- The possibility of medical or biological causes remains uncertain.
- We should not place too much reliance on classifying individual children as having behavioural problems. The must useful approaches are those which are directly linked with management strategies.

Further reading

Maurice Chazan, Alice Laing and Diane Davies (1994) *Emotional and Behavioural Difficulties in Middle Childhood*. London: Falmer Press.

A general review based upon research findings, which applies to all ages of pupils. Uses case studies and examples to make the ideas more real and also tells you which techniques have been found to be effective.

Rita Wicks-Nelson and Allen Israel (1991) *Behavior Disorders of Childhood*, 2nd edition. Englewood Cliffs, NJ: Prentice-Hall.

A medically oriented text which covers all the main categories and syndromes. Some of these, such as conduct disorder, will be familiar to all teachers, but others are rarer, and this book would be an excellent reference from which to find out more. Although somewhat American, it is very readable and considers the educational implications of many of the behavioural disorders which children experience.

Practical scenario

Tom has significant behavioural problems in school which mainly involve calling out and attention seeking in class. He also regularly gets involved in physical aggression, when he reacts against minor social problems if he does not gets his own way. Tom's teacher is concerned about his behaviour and would like to know the reasons for his difficulties. Tom was adopted three years ago and his teacher believes that he has seen a child psychiatrist a number of times. His adoptive parents are always supportive of school and appear to have similar difficulties managing Tom at home.

- *What could be some possible reasons for Tom's difficulties? To what extent should these guide the way in which his teacher manages him in the future?*
- *Is it likely that it would help his teacher to find out more from Tom's child psychiatrist? What would the psychiatrist's perspective be?*
- *If Tom has had early damaging experiences, does this 'excuse' his disruptive behaviour?*
- *Is it at all likely that Tom will improve? Is normal school the best place for him?*

11 Dealing with behaviour problems

Chapter structure

Behaviour support

Behavioural approaches to problem behaviour
Classical conditioning
Operant conditioning
Implementing a behavioural programme

Other techniques for managing behaviour
Social skills training and social manipulation
Circle Time
Television and pro-social development
Cognitive approaches

Medical approaches to problem behaviour
Psychodynamic techniques
Drug therapies

Educational psychologists and behaviour problems

Specific problems
Bullying
Non attendance
Attention-deficit/hyperactivity disorder (AD/HD)

School-based behaviour programmes
Assertive Discipline
Building A Better Behaved School (BABBS)
Preventive Approaches to Disruption (PAD)
Behaviour recovery

Special needs provision for behaviour problems
Sporting schooling
Alternative approaches

Behaviour support

The general background of behavioural problems has been covered in Chapter 10, along with the various explanations for what might cause them. Many of these explanations directly imply ways of managing and changing what children do, although some of the most important factors such as home background are beyond the influence of schools or teachers.

All education authorities must now have behaviour support plans which detail the strategies and resources that can be used and the roles of the various agencies. These can include behaviour support services, educational psychologists, education welfare, social services and various types of health authority provision. The latter are often based in clinics which specialise in child and family problems and have workers such as child psychiatrists, specialist nurses, counsellors and other therapists. Their role is often focused on the home, but some centres are able to link in with schools, their services sometimes being partly funded by the education authority.

Many authorities have a specialist behaviour support service which is made up from teachers with particular expertise and experience in this field. They normally work directly with schools, mainly with individual cases, although they can also be involved in projects with groups of pupils such as in social skills development and whole-school and in-service training activities.

Schools in England are now responsible for implementing 'pastoral support programmes' (DfEE, 1999d) for pupils who do not respond to the normal systems of management and are in danger of permanent exclusion. These programmes should be developed with external services and involve appropriate targets, strategies and resources.

Children who are permanently excluded can attend pupil referral units (PRUs). These have the difficult job of providing a general curriculum for a number of pupils with the most extreme behavioural problems, at the same time as working with their emotional and behavioural difficulties. Pupils in PRUs can also be registered with a school, and an objective of these units can be to reintegrate them, although with older pupils it may be more appropriate to prepare them for other life experiences.

However, the majority of the large number of children who have problems are in normal classes and are the day-to-day responsibility of the class teacher. Although there is now a particular emphasis on the academic curriculum with targets to be achieved, achieving targets is possible only if classes are manageable and if the teacher does not have to spend too much time on dealing with behavioural problems. It is therefore important for all teachers to be aware of what are appropriate techniques and to develop effective behavioural strategies.

Behavioural approaches to problem behaviour

A behaviouristic perspective can be particularly useful for understanding and managing difficult behaviours. Behaviourism, as we have seen, gives a set of rules and principles for describing and manipulating learning. If problem behaviours have been learned in the first place, they can be altered by applying the principles of conditioning. Even if some behaviours are due to inherited or biological factors, it should still be possible to learn other behaviours which could take their place.

Behavioural techniques can appear somewhat simplistic and mechanistic, largely ignoring children's thoughts and feelings. However, as was described in Chapter 2, they are in fact part of a broader cognitive perspective since they work by altering children's expectations about what will happen in certain circumstances. Their simplicity can also be a major advantage when one is designing and running a behavioural programme, as they avoid the distractions and interference of supposed causes and processes. Children are often not consciously aware of why they do things and just repeat actions which have been effective in the past. Asking children to explain the reasons for something that they have done can lead to their making up a plausible cause, or rationalisation. This could be very misleading if it was used as the basis for any further action.

Although operant conditioning is generally the most important approach that is used in behavioural programmes, classical conditioning also underlies many learning experiences.

Classical conditioning

Both anxiety and phobias in school involve involuntary behaviours and can be the result of classical conditioning. When one is trying to manage such problems, it might therefore be appropriate to attempt to break down the learned association. With school phobia (described later in this chapter), this could involve exposing the child to situations which become progressively closer to the reality of school, while reducing their anxiety, a technique called *systematic desensitisation*. This might involve the use of relaxation techniques, combined with trips which gradually get closer to school, home visits from teachers, other pupils, and any other links with school. If a child was anxious about going into the school hall for assemblies (a common problem with young children), the desensitisation could involve experiences such as brief play sessions in the hall or attendance for only part of class assemblies. It is important that if the child becomes anxious at any stage, the process is halted until he or she is able to cope. This can be a very time-consuming therapy and it may take weeks until a child is able to tolerate the difficult situation.

An alternative approach called *flooding* is much more rapid and involves forcibly exposing the child to the feared experience and keeping him or her exposed to it until the anxiety decreases naturally. With school phobia, parents would need to physically take children in and keep them there, no matter how extreme their behaviour became. Allowing children to escape the situation on even one occasion will undermine the process since their behaviour will have been reinforced by the reduction in anxiety. They will then have an expectation on future occasions that their anxiety/escape behaviour might be reinforced again.

This technique can be very effective, since it normally works quickly, typically after a few days. When carried out for school phobia with a pupil's parents, it can also give them encouragement in positive techniques for handling their child. Unfortunately, it does place great strains on parents, who may be very anxious about their child. As described later in this chapter, they have often inadvertently generated the problem in the first place by excessive concern and by allowing the child to stay away from school for minor problems.

Operant conditioning

Operant (or instrumental) conditioning involves learned voluntary behaviours. When it is applied to children's problem behaviours, it should be possible to reduce negative behaviours and increase the positive ones by altering the outcomes and antecedents for these.

Figure 11.1 shows the three key elements in the process of *behaviour modification*. Consequences (see Figure 11.1) can affect the likelihood of a child's engaging in a behaviour. They are termed reinforcers if they increase the behaviour and involve experiences which are positive, such as getting house points, stickers on a chart or attention from a teacher. Punishers are aversive and decrease a behaviour, and include experiences such as detentions or cleaning the board.

The use of rewards/reinforcers and punishments

Reinforcers can take many different forms and their use is often purely empirical. That is to say, you use whatever seems to work with a particular child in a particular situation. This can often be completely different for different children. Some young children really like to hold a teacher's hand during break, but doing so could be highly aversive to another child, particularly an older one.

As a general rule, effective reinforcers with younger children tend to be more direct and physical, and can involve adult attention, whereas older children tend to prefer reinforcers which give them more freedom and control and contact with their peer group. Studies of the effectiveness of different reinforcers in school by Harrop and Williams (1992) indicate that the most powerful ones involve sending information to parents, although teachers tend to reserve this for the most important problems.

As described in Chapter 2, the use of punishers is generally frowned on in most behavioural approaches. Nevertheless, there are arguments for their use in some situations.

SHOULD WE EVER USE PUNISHMENT?

Most teachers (and parents) mainly use punishments such as reprimanding children, keeping them in at break and so on. Although training as used in 'Assertive Discipline' (covered towards the end of this chapter) can reduce the use of such negative control, there seems to be a natural tendency to regress, and the effect of Assertive Discipline will normally fall off after a couple of years unless there is some maintenance support.

Figure 11.1 The key elements in behaviour modification

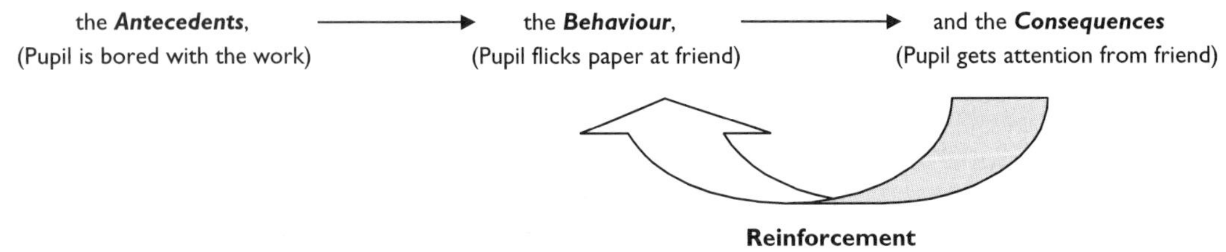
the ***Antecedents***,
(Pupil is bored with the work)
the ***Behaviour***,
(Pupil flicks paper at friend)
and the ***Consequences***
(Pupil gets attention from friend)
Reinforcement

Punishment has traditionally been seen as ineffective by psychologists, and it seems strange that people naturally tend to prefer to use something that is not supposed to work very well.

One reason why negative control is favoured could be that it is a 'quick fix', and that it is easier to be negative than positive. With negative control, you respond only to the misbehaviour, whereas with positive control, you have to go out of your way to look for and reward the good behaviour.

Another reason may be that in many situations, negative approaches can work quite well. O'Leary *et al.* (1970), for instance, found that *private individual reprimands* were an effective way of reducing disruptive behaviour with specific disruptive children when the following criteria were met:

- there is an alternative behaviour known to the child;
- the feedback is consistent and specific; and
- the teacher has a positive relationship with the child.

Most children are probably aware of what they should be doing, and it should also be possible for teachers to ensure that they respond in the same way to problem behaviours. It is also possible for teachers to establish positive relationships with children, and it has been consistently found that teachers who have the personal quality of 'warmth' are generally more effective and are less likely to have behavioural problems in their classes.

Negative reinforcement is another effective approach which involves some negative experiences. It initially involves the use of a punisher, which is then removed when the child behaves in an appropriate way. Although this also involves negative control of children and at first has the same negative consequences as punishment, it eventually produces positive results which are, effectively, rewards. Negative reinforcement involves first taking away things from children that are normally given to or allowed them. These can include favourite activities (sports, playing with certain toys, free play during breaks, or sitting on a chosen table), which can then be given back for normal, reasonable behaviour. This has the advantage of normalising behaviour; nothing extra is given and the child is working to receive positive feedback. Unfortunately, the most difficult part is taking away the desired activity or objects in the first place. This is usually seen by the child as particularly undesirable and can at first lead to even more difficult behaviour which must be dealt with.

Children who feel that they are losing control will often step up their problem behaviours, to put on more pressure to get what they want. If, for example, they have been told that from now on they cannot sit at their preferred table, they may then have a temper tantrum if this behaviour has been effective in the past.

A particular procedure known as '*time-out* from positive reinforcement' is often used in behavioural programmes to prevent such problem behaviour being reinforced. Rather than just ignoring problem behaviour (which might sometimes be dangerous), the child is removed from the room to somewhere less reinforcing for about 5 to 10 minutes. The approach is intended to prevent the child from getting the immediate reinforcement of attention or control that the behaviour usually generates. Longer periods of exclusion can sometimes be used with difficult behaviour. In removing the child, however, one is doing so either as a punishment (with the inherent dangers and drawbacks involved) or as a form of negative reinforcement. In this case the child should be given explicit directions about what he or she needs to do to win back normal social contact.

When using negative approaches, one must be quite clear about why one is using them and what are the strategies being used. When carried out properly they can be highly effective and ultimately humane, since a child can quickly come back into more normalised and positive experiences. Unfortunately, there have been instances where negative techniques have been applied inappropriately, as in the 'Pindown' approach once used in social services homes in England. This involved children being effectively imprisoned in their bedrooms for long periods of time (Levy and Kahan, 1991). In this situation staff were not effectively trained and there was no guidance for them about what was effective and safe for the children involved.

Implementing a behavioural programme

Most teachers naturally use a number of rewards and punishers in their classes without much thought about how this is done. However, when something is going wrong, they may need to analyse the situation and to use a more specific approach. Such an approach is often referred to as a *behaviour modification programme* and involves the following sequence:

- The first stage involves identifying the specific *problem behaviour(s)*. These must be directly observable and capable of being assessed. For example, the category 'Stands up and shouts in class' is better than the rather fuzzy (imprecise) category of 'being disruptive'.
- The next stage involves identifying *alternative behaviours* which are appropriate and which would displace the problem behaviour – that is to say, ones that cannot be done at the same time. Again, this would have to be specific, such as 'On-task behaviour, involving writing, reading or attending to the teacher'.
- An *effective reinforcement* now has to be identified. This can involve either observing what individual children will do when they have a free choice of activities, asking other people who know them well, or asking children directly. With younger children it might involve being allowed to play a particular game and with older children it often involves more freedom or control, such as break sessions. As described earlier, either positive or negative reinforcements may be used.
- An ideal behavioural programme would involve an initial set of *baseline observations* so that it is possible to see whether the behaviour does improve. In practice it is often important to get a rapid improvement, for instance to prevent an exclusion from school, so this stage is often left out.
- *Running the programme* now involves setting targets, monitoring the positive behaviour(s) and applying the reinforcer(s) consistently. So, for example, a positive behaviour could involve 'being on task' and the reinforcer might be 'being allowed to play with a favourite toy'. A realistic target should first be set for the child, such as 70 per cent of the time on task. The child's behaviour is then monitored, which could involve the teacher checking the child on regular occasions. If the target is reached by playtime, then the child would be allowed to play with the toy. Although negative behaviours sometimes have to be dealt with, as far as possible they should be ignored, to avoid inadvertently reinforcing them with attention.

It is important that children are aware of the target that they are aiming for and exactly how they are doing. For the latter, they need some form of regular feedback. With younger children this can take the form of a chart system, for instance with stickers for good behaviour. Some form of tokens can be used such as plastic counters or coloured table tennis balls placed in a large container in front of the child. These would be given for positive behaviours and can then be counted up at the end of a lesson and exchanged for desired rewards. Older children will be able to operate with less immediate reinforcers and their behaviour can be reviewed at the end of each lesson. The normal reports that are commonly used in secondary schools can be modified for daily monitoring and linked in with outcomes such as being given weekly pocket money or being allowed out to a youth club.

This type of approach can be used effectively with individual pupils and also with whole classes. Reviews such as that by O'Leary and O'Leary (1977) show that it is an effective approach for dealing with a range of school-based problems, and that it results in generally more positive classroom environments, cooperative behaviours and improved learning.

Following the principle of operant conditioning, initial reinforcement schedules should involve a high, constant ratio; that is to say, the child's behaviour should be reinforced frequently and predictably. As one does not usually wish to continue a behavioural programme indefinitely, as soon as possible the schedule should be switched to a low-frequency variable ratio; this means reinforcing less often and less predictably. The reason for the change is that although there will be a fall in the positive behaviour, this is then much more likely to become stable and to be maintained in the long term without the reinforcers.

Strict behavioural theory states that the key feature of a conditioning programme is the close matching of reinforcers with particular behaviours. More recent developments in learning theory, however, emphasise the cognitive nature of this process, with the individual developing expectancies about what will happen in certain situations. This implies that it would be useful to involve individuals as much as possible in the process, possibly by monitoring their own behaviour and deciding on desirable behaviours, targets and rewards. This can be particularly effective with older pupils, and McNamara (1979), for instance, has shown how such self-rating systems can be used with secondary pupils. Self-rating systems involve the use of reports where pupils make assessments of their own behaviours during lessons. Their assessments are usually surprisingly close to teacher assessments and encourage pupils to acknowledge their difficulties and to enter into a discussion about what they are doing.

Physical control

It is no longer legal for British teachers to use physical punishment with children, and such approaches have in any case been shown to be largely ineffective. School records of children who were caned demonstrated that the same children continued to be punished regularly, with no evident deterrent effect on their misbehaviour.

Unfortunately, some children may need to be physically restricted in some way, to prevent them from physically harming themselves, other people or property, or from disruption of the educational process. The 1997 Education Act gives members of staff the *power to restrain*, using

> such force as is reasonable in the circumstances for the purpose of preventing the pupil from doing (or continuing to do) any of the following, namely –
>
> (a) committing any offence,
> (b) causing personal injury to, or damage to the property of, any person (including the pupil himself), or
> (c) engaging in any behaviour prejudicial to the maintenance of good order and discipline at the school or among any of its pupils, whether that behaviour occurs during a teaching session or otherwise.
>
> (Part II, 4, 550A, Crown copyright)

The power to restrain evidently has a very broad coverage and would appear to enable a teacher to (safely) restrain a child who was causing significant problems in school. Such restraint is of course likely to be aversive to the child and perceived by them as a punishment. If at all possible, the use of such physical approaches should therefore be carefully thought out and used as part of a behavioural programme that is aimed at developing positive behaviours, rather than just controlling negative ones. With a young child who enjoys playing on the computer, this might mean preventing his or her access to it, so that being allowed to use it once more can be used as a reinforcer for cooperative behaviour. Limiting children in this way could of course lead to disruptive attempts by them to get their own way. It might then be appropriate to consider using physical restraint (in line with the guidance mentioned above) to prevent their behaviour interfering with the educational process. If it looks as though this procedure might be necessary with a child, it is important for teachers to inform senior staff and to involve parents so that they are aware that what is being done is in their child's best interests. If schools are concerned, it may sometimes be appropriate to involve an educational psychologist or specialist support teacher, who would usually be able to advise on the best approaches to be used.

It can also be difficult to know quite what forms of restraint are safe for the child and for the person applying them. Merely holding a child by one arm could be damaging if he or she then struggles against the restraint. To help teachers avoid hurting children and to protect staff from legal repercussions, the DfEE has clarified, in Circular 10/98 (DfEE, 1998c), what staff are allowed to do. Safe restraint procedures are also described in a video inset training package by Lucky Duck (1998), which includes advice from a physiotherapist about appropriate and safe physical techniques. These can involve preventing children from hurting themselves or others, for example by standing (or sitting) behind children and holding both their arms across their body.

Antecedents

A number of studies have emphasised the role of the context in determining problem behaviour. Context acts as the antecedent stage in behaviour modification and provides cues and information for the pupil. These might simply alert children that a certain type of behaviour from them is likely to have a desirable outcome. For instance, when a particular teacher enters the room, pupils might anticipate that shouting out will confuse him or her and delay the start of the lesson.

There are other effects which are more than a signal for the opportunity for misbehaviour. These include the pupil's active involvement or lack of involvement in more positive activities, such as concentrating on the lesson. Teachers vary, for instance, in the amount of time which they spend setting up and changing activities. Teachers who are alert to the processes going on in the classroom and who minimise the opportunity for problems certainly appear to experience fewer behavioural difficulties in their lessons. The study by Rutter *et al.* (1979) compared different schools and showed that behaviour problems were less likely when work was well organised and at the right level for pupils, when staff were themselves prompt in starting lessons, and when the student–staff relationships were positive. Certain peripheral school features also appeared to have a positive effect on general behaviour, including the use of carpets and the presence of plants in classrooms.

Criticisms of behavioural approaches

Although the behavioural approach has been shown to be very powerful in changing behaviour, some criticisms can be made of it. It is often said that its superficiality may miss the true underlying difficulty in a child. For example, children who have behaviour problems in school may be acting in a particular way because they are the victim of abuse or bullying. Failing to take account of such difficulties can of course be a real problem, and any possible causes should first be investigated. However, it should also be borne in mind that behaviour can be relatively specific to particular situations. A major long-term study by Leiter and Johnsen (1997) of 967 children with proven physical and sexual abuse showed that their subsequent school behaviour and progress were only moderately affected. A positive school management programme is also likely to improve a child's self-esteem, despite whatever may be happening to him or her elsewhere.

A similar criticism from the psychodynamic perspective argues that suppressing one problem behaviour will lead only to 'symptom substitution', with other difficult behaviours arising, since the underlying problems will seek an alternative outlet. However, an effective positive behavioural programme with a whole class by Ward and Baker (1968) did not find any evidence of adverse effects, even when assessed using psychodynamic techniques such as an assessment of fantasy to explore children's unconscious mental processes.

A further criticism of behavioural approaches is the effect that they may have upon children's motivation. Lepper and Greene (1978), for instance, showed that the use of extrinsic rewards was effective in changing behaviour but that the behaviour became dependent on it. However, provided that rewards are not overemphasised, appropriate behavioural techniques should probably bring the child back to normal motivators. Bornstein and Quevillon (1976), for example, showed good long-term maintenance following a behavioural programme, which they interpreted as being due to the 'behavioural trap' of the normal classroom. This means that when children's behaviour becomes more positive, they gain from increased task involvement and naturally positive teacher responses.

Other techniques for managing behaviour

Social skills training and social manipulation

If children's behavioural problems appear to be related to social difficulties, it seems reasonable to train up specific abilities or to modify children's social situation in some way. In an approach devised by Spence (1995), children's abilities can first be analysed and then programmes run to work on areas of deficit. These areas of deficit can include non-verbal abilities such as making appropriate eye contact and having good posture and good listening skills. Role-play situations can also be used to structure and deal with problem situations such as teasing, bullying, or confrontation by an adult (to model some pupil–teacher interactions).

A review evaluation of a wide range of research in this area by Ogilvy (1994) found that children can make progress with these specific abilities but that they are unlikely to transfer these skills to other situations. Most research on the outcomes of social skills training has failed to demonstrate any changes in children's normal social functioning, which may be partly due to the rigidity of peer expectations and stereotypes. When social development is carried out in a meaningful social context, it is much more likely to have a generalised impact. In one programme by Bierman and Furman (1984), children with social difficulties were trained in conversational skills, either individually or as part of a task with peers which required coordination to achieve a superordinate goal. Children who were trained individually showed no transfer of conversational skills, whereas those who had developed them in a group situation continued to use them in other situations. It is, however, rare for social training to be carried out in this way, and the evidence generally indicates that there will be little transfer of skills unless considerable effort is put into developing their use in a child's normal social context.

Difficulties with social organisation in the classroom can be elicited by the sociogram technique outlined in Chapter 10 (Figure 10.3). The technique might make it possible to reduce the impact of key disruptive individuals who have a disproportionate effect on the class through their range of contacts, perhaps by moving their seating position or changing their teaching group for some lessons. The converse is also true: socially isolated children might benefit from setting up greater contact for them with other children who are likely to be open to social involvement. This could be achieved by setting up small adult-directed games groups during break times or by seating children together. However, in a five-year longitudinal study, Coie and Dodge (1983) found the social dynamics of classrooms was a complex process, with many problem situations resolving naturally. Social status also tended to change over time without any intervention, which indicates that such social engineering may be difficult to achieve.

Circle Time

Circle Time is a specific technique described by Bliss *et al.* (1995) which aims to promote prosocial behaviour and positive climates in schools by means of regular class work with groups of children. The actual session involves an interactive process which has firm ground rules whereby children (and staff) are required to listen to each other with respect and to take turns in speaking. Children can, for instance, each identify positive aspects about other group members, or commit themselves to specific ways in which they could help a child who is having difficulties. A complete circle of turns can lead on to children working in small groups on key social areas which they can then bring back to the main group. As with general counselling approaches, the emphasis is on commitment to and resolution of problems, but this time in the form of the overall social group.

Television and pro-social development

As we have seen, although television can provide negative examples and cues for behaviour, watching pro-social programmes can have positive effects. Forge and Phemeister (1987), for instance, have shown that *Sesame Street*, as well as developing young children's knowledge and ideas, led to an increase in positive helping behaviours on the part of those who watched it.

Other work has indicated ways in which the negative effects of watching violence on television can be reduced. Hicks (1968), for instance, found that the presence of an adult who condemned the violence meant that children were subsequently less likely to behave aggressively. Also, Eron (1982) has experimented with three-hour training sessions in which children were helped to distinguish television fantasy from real-life events. They learned, for example, how special effects are used to simulate violence and the real effects that such violence has. These children were followed up one year later and were found to be less aggressive than children who had not been through the programme. This indicates that schools could use such approaches to 'inoculate' children against the long-term negative effects of the media which some of them experience.

Cognitive approaches

Some approaches such as counselling and cognitive behaviour modification involve individual work with children. These attempt to modify ways in which children with problems think about and deal with their difficulties.

Counselling

Originally based largely on the work of Rogers (1951), school-based counselling is a helping process which depends on the development of a relationship between a counsellor and a child. This should be sufficiently supportive to enable children to explore aspects of their life more freely. A final goal should be the possibility of arriving at more adequate ways of coping with whatever children perceive as a problem in their life.

Counselling is normally based on uncritical acceptance of what children have to say, and matching in with their 'frame of reference' – the way in which they construe the world. The frame of reference incorporates views about the roles and motivations of others, and children with problems will often have a very different perspective compared with other people in the school. However, this can be a difficult stance for teachers to take, as they have to uphold the rules and regulations of school. As far as possible, counselling is therefore carried out by a neutral person, and some schools employ professional counsellors or counselling services.

As shown in Figure 11.2, counselling starts with listening and reflecting back what the child has said. This is followed by a number of questions, mostly open-ended to allow the child to expand on his or her perceptions. During this time, the counsellor is trying to build up an understanding of the child's situation using non-verbal as well as verbal information. He or she will often then try to interpret the problem, via a remark such as 'So perhaps a lot of your problems start with your friends?' The final stages involve the counsellor prompting for solutions. Although it is very tempting for counsellors to impose their own ideas at this stage, it is important for them to be non-directive. The key element here is for children to generate their own realistic options, since they are then more likely to be committed to them.

Some schools using this approach allow pupils to refer themselves. Counselling can be an effective way to help pupils with anxiety and/or depression, and Lawrence (1971) used volunteers

Figure 11.2 Key elements of the counselling session

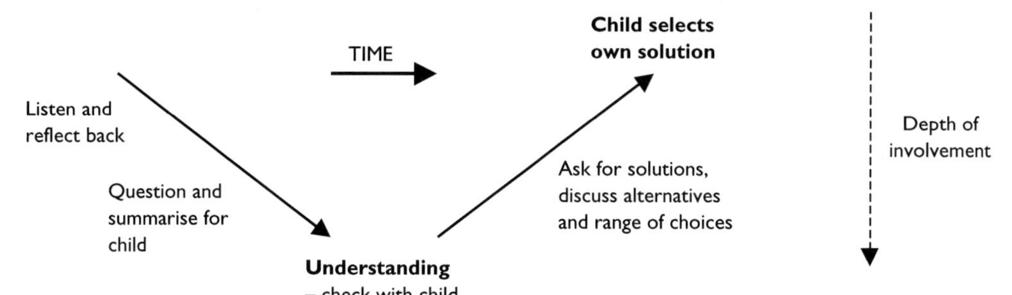

to visit schools and talk regularly with underachieving children. This counselling was shown to help them with adjustment difficulties and resulted in improved self-esteem and improvements in academic skills such as reading.

Referrals can also be made by senior staff, whose concerns are often prompted by challenging or worrying behaviours. In these situations children may be less motivated, and it can be difficult for the counsellor to get pupils involved in considering the need to change. Bergan and Tombari (1976) found, however, that once pupils had committed themselves to implementing a plan, there was then a very high correlation (of 0.977) with eventual resolution of the original problem. In this study the effect of the counsellors was greatest at the stage of problem identification, and counsellors who did not have very good interviewing skills were the least effective.

A recent development allied to traditional counselling is *solution-focused brief therapy*. Rhodes and Ajmal (1995) describe this approach, which can be used with individuals or groups in schools. It involves only about four sessions, and from the start it emphasises solutions, rather than what the problem is, or what caused it.

The solution-focused approach is largely congruent with research on the nature of effective problem-solving techniques, as described in Chapter 4. The key elements of this are to first identify or construct the goal end-state, then an intermediate achievable goal which can be linked with the final one. In solution-focused therapy, the therapist starts off by asking the child about what the child's life would be like if there were not a problem. Ways of working towards this desired state are then identified by looking for 'exceptions' – times when the problem is not present. A child might, for instance, find that there are no problems in school on days when the child did not first have a row with his or her parents. Small changes in a child's life may then lead to many other positive changes through a 'ripple effect'. This happens as children realise that there are different ways of seeing and doing things, ways which are under their control.

As with conventional counselling, there is an emphasis on adopting the frame of reference of the client. Some children who have been forced to see the therapist are described as 'visitors' (and will probably have little commitment to change), and others, such as teachers, who perceive problems with a child are described as 'information givers'. A third category who believe that their actions can bring about change are described as 'customers', and following a session they can be given tasks to carry out. For example, parents might be asked to make a positive comment to their child each morning.

Rhodes (1993) has reviewed findings which indicate that the effectiveness of this approach is similar to that of other forms of therapy. In view of the short-term nature of the approach, combined with its simplicity and respect for the client, he argues that solution-focused brief therapy should therefore be a first choice for most interventions.

Cognitive behaviour modification

Cognitive behaviour modification has been developed by workers such as Meichenbaum (1977) who believe that various problems can be modified by altering the way a pupil thinks. Cognitive behaviour modification usually involves attempts to use verbally mediated self-control to direct attention and to modify behaviour. Therapists will first model a task, which involves 'talking out loud' to themselves about what they are doing and what is going to be done next. The child then imitates the therapist's actions and progressively internalises the verbal instructions.

Such approaches have often been shown to be highly effective with impulsive behaviour. An early study by Bornstein and Quevillon (1976) used this approach with three young hyperactive boys and showed a dramatic increase in on-task behaviours which transferred well to classroom behaviours and was well maintained over time. A meta-analysis of 23 such studies by Robinson *et al.* (1999) also found an overall effect size of 0.74 on reducing hyperactive–impulsive and aggressive behaviours in school settings, indicating that this could be a useful routine approach for children with such behavioural difficulties.

Non-verbal behaviour and authority

Non-verbal information comes from a range of aspects such as posture, gesture, general body positioning and eye contact. Paralanguage also involves the volume, tone and rhythm of speech. All these have a great influence on communication processes, and Mehrabian and Ferris (1967) have shown that people give relatively more credibility to non-verbal information when there is conflict between this and verbal information. Teachers who *say* that they going to carry out some discipline behaviour, and yet at the same time physically *act* in an indecisive way, are unlikely to be believed and will have less impact. A teacher who threatens a detention unless a child stops a particular behaviour will not be given much credibility if he or she stands well away, has no eye contact and also 'fidgets'.

The effects of teacher non-verbal communication used to be investigated by showing pupils photographs of teacher postures and asking them to rate these. This method lacks validity, however, and more complex and realistic techniques now utilise videotape analysis of classrooms, which enables researchers to identify common features of teachers with good classroom control. Reviews such as that by Neill and Caswell (1993) find that effective teachers have non-verbal behaviour which is appropriate to their authority role and which is matched with the information content of what they say.

Appropriate teacher behaviour covers the general use and control of space, with effective teachers greeting and directing classes at the door as they come in. According to Hall (1966), every individual pupil has his or her own zone of personal space, which extends to a little over 1 metre around them. If teachers avoid entering this and stay at the front of the class, this can give a message of insecurity to pupils. When there is a minor problem such as inappropriate talking, then if a teacher merely enters the zone of personal space, it can send a message to a pupil that the teacher is aware of what he or she is doing and will usually stop the behaviour progressing. Confident use of pupils' territory by the teacher implies high status and also enables the teacher to monitor their work.

Eye contact can also have the same effect, and high-status individuals are able to control interactions by dictating how and when gaze is used. When the encounter has little emotional content, the high-status person is able to give and withdraw eye contact when he or she wishes. With high emotional content, however, the high-status person will concentrate their gaze on the low-status person, who has to either return the gaze or look down.

A high-pitched voice is characteristic of stress or anxiety, and again gives a signal to pupils that the teacher lacks confidence and has limited control. A low-pitched voice has been shown to be characteristic of a relaxed and authoritative style, and is also generally more trusted and believed. Other signs of insecurity and tension which pupils unconsciously detect can involve 'grooming' such as hair or arm stroking, and defensive postures, such as arms, or objects such as a book, held across the body. Even effective teachers appear to have such characteristics, particularly when directing a class to change from one activity to another. However, they are usually able to control these involuntary signs at critical points of the lesson.

Effective teachers were found by Neill and Caswell (1993) to show warmth, enthusiasm for their subject, and decisiveness. They used smiles, positive interactions with pupils, and a wide variety of facial expressions, gestures and tones of voice. They used these to illustrate the content of what they were saying and made lessons more vivid and interesting for the class. Effective teachers also showed a keen interest in what pupils had to say, with good eye contact and appropriate head and facial movements such as the 'eyebrow flash' – a strong signal involving raising the eyebrows briefly, which shows interest. When effective teachers watched their performances, they were often surprised at their own exaggerated style, but these ways of interacting with classes had the effect of involving students and prevented them from initiating inappropriate behaviour.

Pupils will often make challenges to the teacher's authority, and effective teachers will monitor for these and act appropriately. 'Closed' challenges are just limited rule breaking, for instance two children talking, and can often be safely left. 'Open' challenges on the other hand are a direct test of the teacher's authority and are characterised by 'control checks' by pupils. These involve rapid glances at the teacher just before and after an incident to see if the teacher is monitoring what is going on. A teacher who has 'withitness', as described in Chapter 6, will be aware of the first control check by pupils and will respond with a low-level non-verbal control. This can involve eye contact or moving towards them, to let them know that the teacher is aware of what is going on.

Neill and Caswell (1993) found that when confrontations do occur, the behaviour of effective teachers was both more decisive and more relaxed than that of ineffective teachers. They used more controlling and illustrative gestures and they used animated intonation, showing a lively and often humorous involvement in what they were saying. They also used a loud voice less often, and, although forceful, did not adopt a threatening tone or posture.

In general, the most effective control is achieved by teachers who are relaxed and authoritative, who monitor and are aware of classroom behaviour, who take on the right to control and direct pupils' behaviour, and who show their control by means of matched verbal and non-verbal behaviour.

Medical approaches to problem behaviour

Many treatment approaches based on the medical perspective take place in a clinic setting, often with child psychiatrists in charge. These are doctors who have become qualified in studying and dealing with abnormal behaviour in young people. Referrals are usually made from within the health service, and are usually triggered off when parents go to see their GP and complain about problem behaviours. The focus of these centres is mainly on individual children and their family, and there is normally little contact with the school. Teachers may know that a pupil is attending a clinic of some kind but are often unaware of what approaches are being used. Occasionally centres are set up in conjunction with education, and these can sometimes be particularly effective in drawing together different types of expertise and in setting up joint management approaches.

Psychodynamic techniques

One technique has been to use *psychodynamic psychotherapy*, based originally on the mental structures and theories proposed by Freud. According to Freud, problems are the result of a child's having inappropriate techniques for dealing with unconscious drives. Such maladaptive defence mechanisms may produce behaviours which can appear to be unrelated to what is causing them. The classic example of this described by Freud is the case of a child called 'Little Hans', whose irrational fear (phobia) of horses was analysed as being really due to displaced fear of his father. Simple behavioural approaches are therefore supposed to be unlikely to solve such a problem. Since they tackle the symptom and not the cause, they will only lead to 'symptom substitution', which means that one form of problem behaviour is merely exchanged for another.

Psychodynamic therapy typically involves talking with a patient and analysing his or her unconscious processes. With adults, this can be done by studying a patient's dreams, which are supposed to show unconscious desires. There can also be lapses of control, as in 'Freudian slips', when we make revealing errors, such as calling a disliked teacher Mrs Hate, when her name is really Mrs Hite. Using such information, the therapist analyses and reflects back patients' mental processes, enabling them to develop insight into their own mental processes. This then enables patients to experience catharsis (an emotional release from tension) and to change themselves – if they want to.

Children are less likely to be able to understand and talk about their mental processes in this way. *Play therapy* was therefore developed as a way of studying children's unconscious motivations and enabling them to understand and to cope with their underlying difficulties. It involves placing the child in a room with some age-appropriate playthings and encouraging their use. If, say, a boy buries a toy soldier in some sand, this could be interpreted as an unresolved tension concerning his father, and further directed play might encourage him to work through these difficulties.

Freudian theories were derived about a hundred years ago and are nowadays viewed with some scepticism, owing to their unscientific nature. More importantly, many studies of the outcomes of such therapeutic approaches with children have indicated that they are not effective. In a classic early review, Levitt (1957) looked at a range of studies which covered almost 8,000 child patients, and found that those who were treated made only as much progress as those who dropped out and were not treated. Despite this, some elements of psychodynamic approaches are still used, and play or art can be useful ways for children to show their feelings about abuse when they are unable to verbalise them.

Steinberg (1986) has pointed out, however, that nowadays much of the work in child psychiatry involves a range of different approaches. One important technique described by Sue *et al.* (1990) is *family therapy*, when the therapist(s) will attempt to analyse and change the way in which the members of a family interact. Based on systems theory, family therapy argues that the different roles of individuals within the family can contribute to an individual's problem behaviour. For instance, underlying conflicts between a husband and wife might result in their child's misbehaviour. Although parents might bring children to a clinic and say that they want to improve their behaviour, the family system might in fact need to maintain these difficulties. Resolving them might mean that the key relationship of the marriage would be threatened if the parents would no longer be able to blame any problems on the behaviour of their child. Changing the system means encouraging the family members to develop new roles, sometimes by carrying out particular tasks which will force them to realise what is happening. One such technique is the 'paradoxical instruction' whereby the therapist tells the family to try to make things worse. It is hoped that success in doing so will show them how they can also make things better.

It can be difficult to evaluate the effectiveness of such techniques as target outcomes will vary. With some families, for instance, it may be impossible to resolve any difficulties, and the best resolution would be for the parents to separate and then reconstruct their lives. Some intensive and structured programmes can, however, achieve positive outcomes with standard measures. One example of such a programme is the

Functional Family Therapy Program (Alexander *et al.*, 1998), which is based upon improving communication skills and identifying solutions to family problems. Long-term evaluations of this have found that the reoffending rate of older children was reduced by up to 75 per cent and that there was also a preventive influence on younger siblings.

Drug therapies

Since child psychiatrists normally have a medical orientation, children are sometimes prescribed drugs to alter their mood or behaviour. Drugs would typically only be used for the more severe disorders where other approaches are not effective, for instance when the child's behaviour appears to be beyond his or her own control, or when there is some real physical danger to the child (such as a danger of suicide). Children who are highly impulsive and overactive are increasingly often prescribed Ritalin (methylphenidate); the use of this is covered later in the chapter. Antidepressant drugs are also popularly prescribed, and these include the tricyclic group of drugs such as imipramine (known as Tofranil). This is one of the most commonly used antidepressants for children and works by increasing the amount of the brain chemical noradrenaline, which transmits information between cells in parts of the brain to do with mood. Such drugs do unfortunately have some side effects: imipramine can cause dry mouth, blurred vision, drowsiness and constipation, and also affects the cardiovascular system.

Perhaps more important are the doubts about whether some of these drugs really work, since an inactive substance that the patient believes will help them (called a placebo) can have much the same effect. A review by Sommers-Flanagan and Sommers-Flanagan (1996) of five placebo-controlled studies of tricyclic antidepressants with children found that although they were effective with between 8 per cent and 45 per cent of individuals, placebos were effective for 17 to 68 per cent.

More recently, doctors have begun to use selective serotonin reuptake inhibitors (SSRIs), such as fluoxetine (known as Prozac), with children. These tend to have fewer medical side effects but can still cause agitation, nausea and loss of appetite. Some children taking these, particularly younger children, also become disinhibited, saying and doing things they would not have before. The SSRIs work by preventing the reuptake by cells of the brain chemical serotonin, which again is involved in mood. However, critics of this drug argue that the use of fluoxetine is largely unproved with children and that interfering with the biochemistry of developing brains could have long-term negative effects.

There is another natural brain chemical to do with mood called dopamine, which can boost energy and initiative. It is therefore likely that the use of a dopamine reuptake inhibitor could increase dopamine levels and improve children's effort and attention. Unfortunately, the most common such inhibitor is cocaine, and I have yet to hear of anyone advocating its therapeutic use with children!

As well as these largely medical approaches, many clinics also use techniques such as behavioural and social interventions. These could be linked in with schools, but Gillham (1981) has criticised clinic-based approaches since they usually deal with cases in isolation from other agencies. Within clinics there is often an emphasis on problems as coming from the individual child and even when the family is included, only infrequent contact outside the home is involved. Even so, there is no doubt that clinics and child psychiatrists tend to be used as a final resort for the more severe cases, where it is difficult to make progress with the techniques and resources available elsewhere.

Educational psychologists and behaviour problems

A large number of the children referred to educational psychologists have behavioural difficulties and are usually those children whose 'acting out' behaviour is disruptive to the general process of education. A review by Miller (1996) found that most psychologists involved with such children carry out an overall assessment of the situation and then set up behavioural programmes. Although practices differ in different parts of the United Kingdom, many psychologists monitor the programmes for up to about three visits, and the whole process can last for about half a term to a term. A detailed review of a number of such interventions found a high level of success, with teachers reporting satisfaction with the outcome in 90 per cent of cases. Miller estimates that nationally, a minimum of about 12,500 such cases are dealt with by educational psychologists each year, which represents a significant impact on this problem area.

Berger (1979) has pointed out that such behavioural approaches have the danger of being applied as a 'mindless technology', using simplistic techniques which could be unresponsive to the needs of individual cases and would therefore be likely to fail. The programmes reviewed by Miller were, however, closely tuned to the needs of children and their schools, with sophisticated emphases on altering the specific context of each child. This could involve altering seating arrangements or an emphasis on certain rules which were particularly important for the individual. The majority of reinforcers used in such programmes were also social and activity based rather than material rewards which could be criticised as a form of 'bribery'.

Cases referred to psychologists are usually the more severe ones, and these are often the source of earlier conflict between home and school. The school has often reflected children's problems back to their parents, who might then have felt threatened and reacted against any further contact. The role of the educational psychologist in this is difficult and usually involves gaining the cooperation of home and school in a positive programme. Long (1988), for instance, describes the way in which parents can be encouraged to support their child by a combined interview in school. This is structured to avoid any criticism, and after the situation has been reviewed, cooperation can be gained by describing the benefits from a combined programme. Resolving such situations can require a high level of interpersonal skill from the psychologist when home–school relationships have become confrontational.

Specific problems

Bullying

Bullying is a form of aggression which goes on over a period of time and which is focused on a particular individual. When the Department for Education and Employment carried out a questionnaire survey of pupils in a range of different British schools (DfEE, 1994), it was found that 27 per cent of children in primary schools and 10 per cent in secondary schools said that they had experienced being bullied. Bullying can of course involve direct physical confrontation, but it can be more insidious, with 66 per cent of children saying that they had been subjected to teasing or to some form of victimisation leading to social exclusion and isolation.

Bullying can have a major negative impact on a child's academic and social development. In the most severe cases the result can be removal from school or attempted or actual suicide. Bullies themselves are also likely to experience long-term negative consequences, and a study by Olweus (1993) found that 60 per cent of bullies in grades 6–9 had at least one criminal conviction by the age of 24 years.

Characteristics of bullies and their victims

BULLIES

Olweus (1993) carried out a series of questionnaire surveys and in-depth investigations of bullying with many thousands of children, staff and parents. He found that in contrast to what is often believed, bullies generally have little anxiety and possess strong self-esteem. They are normally stronger than average and often enjoy physical confrontation. The stereotype of the bully as a coward who will cave in at the first sign of resistance is therefore a dangerous myth to promote among children.

Bullies appear to derive satisfaction from inflicting injury and suffering on others. They seem to have little empathy or feeling for their victims and will often rationalise their actions by saying that their victims provoked them in some way or another. Olweus found that the home background and general environment of such children was typically characterised by:

- limited love and care;
- too much 'freedom' in childhood;
- the use of 'power-assertive' child-rearing methods such as physical punishments and violent emotional outbursts.

When children are brought up in this way, they are likely to fail to establish limits to their own behaviour and will also learn that interacting with others involves the use of control. This type of home background also seems less likely to enable children to develop an understanding of their own mental states and those of others, known as a 'theory of mind'. A failure to develop this ability appears to lead to limited understanding by children about the effects of their actions on others' feelings. Dunn (1984) argues that the normal process of early pro-social development is very dependent on the capacity to feel for others. The developing of this capacity appears to be largely dependent on the quality and quantity of social interactions with parents in particular, as well as the level of development of general thought processes.

Bullies will often claim that they were 'only having a laugh' and play down the importance of their actions. Although this may be an attempt to divert responsibility, it may also be that they do in fact have limited appreciation of the effects of what they are doing.

VICTIMS

Victims are characteristically less physically strong than average but it has been shown that they do not usually differ in any extreme way. Although bullies will often focus on one particular characteristic, 75 per cent of all children have an 'unusual' feature such as red hair, weight problems or glasses. Victims are, however, typically more anxious and suffer from low self-esteem, although this might at least in part be because of the experience of being bullied. A key feature appears to be that they are much less likely to react in a positive way when bullied, tending to withdraw, and they often fail to communicate their difficulties to either teachers or their parents. Because of this they become 'easy targets', and attacks can escalate over time. Victims are also much less likely to have adequate social skills and tend to be socially isolated, lacking the protective effects of a supportive social group.

The home background of victims tends to be overprotective, often with particularly strong relationships between the mother and the child. Although it is tempting to assume that an overprotective background is a cause of poor relationships with the child's peers, it could also be at least partly a consequence of the child's isolation.

General environmental factors

Olweus found that school size did not seem to be an important factor and that there was the same incidence of bullying in small, single-class primary schools. The broader social context does appear to be a key feature, and Randall (1997) has found that in some geographical areas with a generally high level of aggression, bullying is imported into schools and is very resistant to change. Aggressive or conflicting families will often encourage their children to react violently and parents themselves will sometimes bring disputes into school.

Although bullying can happen on the way to and from school, Olweus found that two-thirds of incidents occur within school. Out-of-school bullying was linked to within-school bullying, and it is therefore possible that school events are the main precipitating factor. Bullying incidents happen particularly during breaks and lunch time and Olweus found that the greater the number of teachers supervising at breaks, the lower the level of bully/victim problems.

Staff awareness of likely problems also seems to be important, since it can be difficult to distinguish between general processes such as 'play fights' and low-level complaints by children, and more serious difficulties. Where the range of staff, including teachers, assistants and supervisors, have awareness of such problems and are involved in a common policy, bullying is much less likely to go unnoticed.

Techniques to reduce bullying

To reduce bullying, Olweus argues that the key aspect is to promote principles which are the opposite of the child-rearing dimensions that research has shown produce the problem in the first place. He gives details of an approach that involves intervention at the school, class and individual levels. This process involves the following:

- An initial questionnaire is administered to students and adults. This raises awareness of the problem, justifies interventions, and serves as a benchmark for subsequent improvements.
- A parental awareness campaign is launched. This can be done through conference days, newsletters and PTA meetings. The goal is to increase awareness (by using the questionnaire results) and to point out the importance of parental involvement and support.
- Teachers are encouraged to work at the class level to develop rules against bullying. Techniques include formal role-playing and assignments that teach pupils alternative ways of interacting. The aims are also to show other students how they can help victims and create an anti-bullying school climate.
- Interventions with bullies and victims are made at the individual level. Cooperative learning activities to reduce social isolation are implemented. Adult supervision at key times are increased.

Olweus carried out an evaluation of this approach in 42 junior and high schools with approximately 2,500 children. Comparing questionnaire data before and after the intervention, he found that there was a 50 per cent or more reduction in bully/victim problems, with the effects becoming more marked after two years. There were also other positive changes affecting general behaviour, social relationships and school ethos. Similar approaches have also been recommended in the DfEE's (1994) publication *Bullying: Don't Suffer in Silence. An Anti Bullying Pack for Schools*.

Assertiveness training

Since a key component of bullying is the victim's vulnerability, some approaches aim to strengthen children's ability to cope with social pressures and typical problem situations. Programmes such as Sharp *et al.*'s (1994) social training can be carried out with individuals or small groups and equip victims with verbal and social skills that they can then use to defuse harassment when it actually takes place. The objective in these approaches is that the situation becomes less rewarding for the bully and that the child will no longer be seen as vulnerable.

Assertiveness is developed by social skills training and starts by emphasising a child's own needs and rights as being equal to those of others. Using safe role-play practice, techniques are then developed which are neither passive nor aggressive. These include:

- *Broken record* – just repeating an assertive statement, for example:

  'Lend us your football.'
  'I don't lend my football.'
  'We'll pay you for it afterwards.'
  'I don't want the money, I don't lend my football.'

  This avoids becoming involved with social pressuring and the logic which others will use to manipulate another child into giving in. In the example above, there was almost certainly no intent to actually pay the child. If this had been challenged, then it could have led on to further pressure, such as 'Are you accusing me of being a cheat?'

- *Fogging* – this involves responding with a neutral statement that de-escalates the situation. For example, a child might challenge with 'Are you a swot then?' and the victim could reply 'It might look that way.' This does not attack the original statement but doesn't agree with it either and prevents the tormentor from making any progress.

As part of these techniques, children may need to rehearse non-verbal behaviour such as appropriate eye contact, body language and tone of voice in these situations. They also need to be aware of the need to get out of the situation and to inform an adult as soon as possible.

Children can also practise ways of overcoming bystander apathy (see p. 252), by calling out to others and enlisting support. Such direct requests can lead on to more general supportive networks, with children looking out for each other.

Should we punish the bullies?

From a common-sense and behaviourist approach, it would seem logical to focus on bullies as the source of the problem, and to attempt to modify their behaviour. In practice, this often means the use of punishments after incidents have happened, for instance with reprimands and detentions.

However, as pointed out before, the use of punishments is not very effective in developing positive behaviours. In the case of bullying, punishments also run the risk of making the situation worse if the bully then attempts to 'get back' at the victim and to threaten them so that they will not tell again.

Maines and Robinson (1991) argue that the basis of much of bullying lies in general social processes, with groups excluding and victimising individuals to enhance their own sense of identity. Techniques to reduce bullying should therefore avoid focusing on an individual as a 'bully', but instead restructure the perceptions and interactions in the whole social system. This 'no blame' approach involves bringing a group of children together, sometimes including the victim, but usually the other children directly involved, and any others around at the time – the 'colluders' and the 'onlookers'.

The teacher then explains what the victim has been experiencing and asks the others to comment on this, about their own similar experiences, and in particular about what they think could be done to help the situation. Each group member is then seen alone, one week later, to discover how things are going.

When this technique is applied in schools, the findings have shown it to be highly successful. In a review of 51 cases, Young (1998) reported immediate success for 80 per cent of them, with the victim and other children involved reporting few or no difficulties, and the parents being happy that the bullying had stopped. A further 14 per cent also improved to a similar level over the following three to five weeks. Such experiences led the support team to advise schools always to adopt this approach, unless there were compelling reasons why it would not be appropriate.

Non-attendance

Non-attendance at school is a very different type of problem but one that is very serious as it limits children's educational opportunities. Children who do not attend school may be *phobic*, where the main reason for their non-attendance is anxiety about school, or just *truants*, where children have unjustified absences with or without the knowledge of parents. In either case the role of the parent(s) is critical, both since they have a legal duty to ensure their child is educated, and because they have the key role in managing their child's behaviour.

School phobia

School phobia involves an anxiety state about attending school which is (like all phobias) assumed to be irrational or without a present basis. The phobia involves involuntary fear responses which become worse when a child thinks about or approaches school. This anxiety is reduced by avoiding school, so if the child stays away, his or her non-attendance is effectively receiving operant negative reinforcement.

Although school phobia can be triggered by an unpleasant school-based experience such as bullying, a range of other factors can be a part of its development and help to keep it going. Many of these are home based and involve anxieties about separation (from the home or from the mother) rather than a fear of something to do with school. Such anxieties are typically increased by parental management which gives more attention to anxious behaviour from the child. Various family stresses can trigger this off, such as the loss of a relative. A very common starting point is when a grandparent dies, particularly if the child knew them well. This death also has a major effect on parents, who are then themselves less able to cope. For various reasons children may also become anxious about the possible loss of a parent and fear that being away from home may make this more likely.

Non-attendance is also much more likely after periods of absence due to illness or holidays. At these times the child will often become progressively more anxious as the prospect of school comes closer. Since each non-attendance effectively reinforces the phobia, approaches to dealing with this should therefore attempt to get the child back to school as soon as possible. In early research by Waldfogel *et al.* (1959), in 25 out of 26 cases where treatment was begun promptly, school attendance was normal within a few weeks. However, in the cases where it was delayed beyond a term, it persisted for months or even years.

Approaches involving progressive desensitisation or flooding can be used, as described earlier in this chapter, but the critical element is often the home environment and the way in which the parent deals with the child. Since the home is usually seen by the child as more rewarding than the school, this can be made less attractive by the parent's removing privileges: preventing the child from just lying on the sofa all day and watching television. Parents must also be convinced that they have to deal firmly with their child, ignoring his or her anxiety and giving attention/reward only to positive behaviour.

Practitioners such as Blagg (1987) have shown that when such firm programmes are implemented, rapid progress can be made in the majority of cases, far exceeding the results obtained with traditional, clinic-based therapies. This particular approach used by Blagg involved an educational psychologist working with parents to encourage positive and firm management to overcome children's anxieties.

The key role for the psychologist here is the use of persuasive techniques to direct and encourage parents to use strategies which they will often find very upsetting when their child shows emotional distress. It is important for the psychologist to adopt a positive, problem-solving perspective as outlined by Dowling (1985), for example by talking with parents about examples of cases which have worked in the past and by setting up and monitoring achievable goals.

Truancy

Truancy involves unauthorised absence from school, with or without parental knowledge or consent. Although Galloway (1976) found that only about 0.05 per cent of primary pupils truant, the proportion can rise to about 0.4 per cent in the final year of secondary schooling, and studies have found that about 1 million children in England and Wales truant each year (Social Exclusion Unit, 1998). As shown in Table 11.1, a study of secondary pupils in Sheffield by Galloway (1982) found that truants had a range of significant difficulties in their home background, as well as problems with their relationships with teachers and other pupils at school. Academic failure is often a contributory factor, but Galloway found

Table 11.1 Features of truants and non-truants

	Truants	**Non-truants**
Neither parent employed	52.6%	9.1%
Social worker involved	46.2%	8.7%
Fear of teachers	66.7%	21.7%
Social difficulties with other pupils	12.8%	4.3%

Source: Based on Galloway (1982)

that the attainments of truants were similar to those of other pupils in lower sets, implying that their main difficulties were with social relationships and emotional adjustment.

Truancy would normally be dealt with by education welfare officers, who have the ability to take legal action, as well as support parents and schools with advice and direct intervention. Educational psychologists can sometimes be involved with individual truancy cases, and one approach is to set up behavioural programmes. These can involve monitoring direct behaviour and ensuring that there are sufficient ways of ensuring that pupils attend.

Normally, however, children are simply monitored with a registration card, which goes between school and home, and links attendance with reinforcers. Other effective techniques can include phoning parents the same morning that a child does not arrive, or loaning pagers to parents if they cannot be contacted by telephone. Again, parental involvement is critical, and support workers will need to plan an effective programme and gain their cooperation and involvement. As an alternative, Lewis (1995) describes a whole-school approach whereby the educational psychologist was involved in training, planning and implementing an attendance programme in a secondary school and four primary schools. This involved the use of merits, credits, certificates, keyrings and pens for good attendance, with mugs being given for 100 per cent attendance records. Social skills groups were set up for children with early difficulties, and an intensive reading support scheme aimed to help pupils manage their school work. These changes had a significant effect, with attendance in the secondary school rising by 15 per cent, along with a 50 per cent reduction in pupil lateness.

Attention-deficit/hyperactivity disorder (AD/HD)

Children who have attention and concentration problems often also have a general level of overactivity, particularly when they are young. AD/HD is a clinical diagnostic category in the American Psychological Association's *Diagnostic and Statistical Manual* (DSM-IV), and estimates of its prevalence indicate that it is a significant problem. In a review of research on this syndrome, Tannock (1998) found that it occurred in 3 to 6 per cent of children from a range of different cultures and regions, with boys outnumbering girls by approximately three to one. Children with these problems can be particularly demanding and difficult to manage in school.

A long-term study by Fergusson *et al.* (1997) found that if children have difficulties with attention, they often make limited educational progress. About 1,000 children were evaluated for attentional difficulties at 8 years of age and their educational progress was subsequently assessed when they were 18 years of age. Thirty-five per cent of those children initially in the top 5 per cent for attention problems eventually scored six years or more behind with their reading, which constitutes a major interference with their educational progress.

DSM-IV lays down specific criteria for diagnosing a child as having AD/HD. Figure 11.3 gives the symptoms and criteria which are necessary for such a diagnosis.

Many children with AD/HD have a combination of most of these features but some may have primarily Inattentive type, or primarily Hyperactivity–Impulsivity type. In order to meet the diagnosis, two out of three of the symptoms must be present for at least six months, and they must

Figure 11.3 Diagnostic criteria for attention-deficit/hyperactivity disorder (AD/HD)

Source: From the *Diagnostic and Statistical Manual of Mental Disorders*, 4th edition, with permission. Copyright 1994 American Psychiatric Association

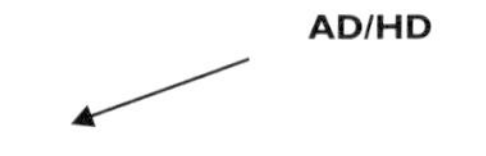

Inattention

Often fails to give close attention to details or makes careless mistakes in schoolwork, work or other activities.

Often has difficulty sustaining attention in tasks or play activities.

Often does not seem to listen when spoken to directly.

Often does not follow through on instructions and fails to finish schoolwork, chores, or duties in the workplace (not due to oppositional behaviour or failure to understand instructions).

Often has difficulty organising tasks and activities.

Often avoids, dislikes, or is reluctant to engage in tasks that require sustained mental effort (such as schoolwork or homework).

Often loses things necessary for tasks or activities (e.g., toys, school assignments, pencils, books, or tools).

Is often easily distracted by extraneous stimuli.

Is often forgetful in daily activities.

Hyperactivity

Often fidgets with hands or feet or squirms in seat.

Often leaves seat in classroom or in other situations in which remaining seated is expected.

Often runs about or climbs excessively in situations in which it is inappropriate.

Often has problems playing or engaging in leisure activities quietly.

Is often 'on the go' or often acts as if 'driven by a motor'.

Often talks excessively.

Impulsivity

Often blurts out answers before questions have been completed.

Often has difficulty awaiting turn.

Often interrupts or intrudes on others (e.g., butts into conversations or games).

have been present from an early age (before 7 years). Also, symptoms must be at a relatively severe level and present in at least two settings (usually both school and home), and they should not be the outcome of another mental problem.

About 40 to 50 per cent of children diagnosed as having AD/HD also have associated behavioural difficulties such as conduct disorder, or oppositional defiant disorder. Despite this overlap, factor-analytic studies have found that attentional and behavioural difficulties appear to be distinct domains. Moreover, a longitudinal study by Fergusson *et al.* (1997) found that behaviour problems at the age of 18 years were largely unrelated to earlier specific attentional problems at age 8 years.

Drug therapy

An approach to the treatment of AD/HD that is increasingly widely adopted in the United Kingdom involves the use of stimulant drugs, in particular methylphenidate (known as Ritalin) and dextroamphetamine (known as Dexadrine). Antidepressants such as imipramine (known as Tofranil) are also sometimes used, as well as anti-hypertensive drugs with sedative effects such as clonidine (known as Carapres). According to Leutwyler (1996), 5 to 6 per cent of all children in the United States (approximately 2 million) were being treated with Ritalin. Its use in the United Kingdom has been catching up with this, roughly doubling every year, from 3,500 prescriptions in 1993 to 126,500 in 1998 (TES, 2000).

Such drug therapy does appear to have a positive effect, one that rises to about 80 per cent of all cases when the range of possible drugs are tried. However, there is a significant placebo effect, with up to 30 per cent of children showing behavioural improvements when they are given an inactive substance which they believe will be effective. Moreover, widespread use of medication is controversial as there are side effects which for the stimulant drugs include insomnia, decreased appetite, weight loss (usually temporary), headaches, irritability and stomach-ache. Moreover, the effectiveness of the drugs lasts only as long as they are being taken; they do not 'cure' the behaviour. Ritalin taken in the morning will usually wear off during the day, and this can mean that the child must take another pill at midday while at school.

Using stimulant drugs to treat children who are already overactive seems rather paradoxical.

Figure 11.4 Hypothetical arousal states for children with AD/HD and normal children

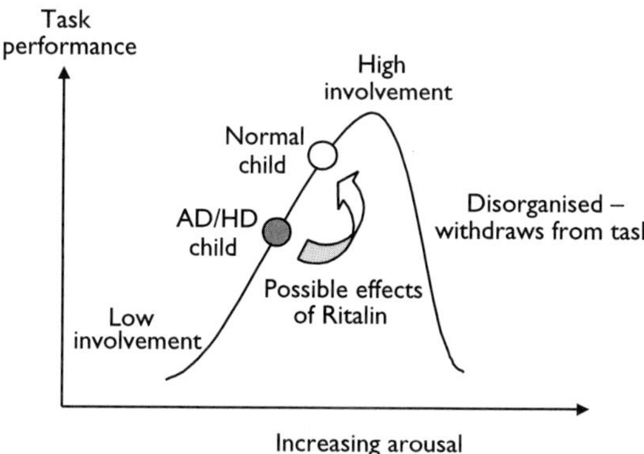

One possible explanation for their effectiveness is that the brains of children with AD/HD lack arousal. According to this, their difficult behaviours are an attempt to seek more stimulation to enable them to function at an optimal arousal level. As shown in Figure 11.4, the stimulant effect of Ritalin is supposed to 'normalise' their brains and allow them to function like everyone else. Rapoport *et al.* (1978), however, found that when Dexedrine was given to normal boys, it increased the general ability of these boys too to focus their concentration and attention, rather undermining the idea that there is a specific difficulty with arousal for AD/HD children.

Ritalin has the effect of increasing the levels of noradrenaline and dopamine in the brain. These are substances which transmit information between the brain cells and particularly affect arousal and mood. Tannock (1998) has reviewed extensive evidence which indicates that children with AD/HD may inherit a weakness in the dopamine circuits of the brain in the frontal region. This area is believed to be particularly involved with higher thought processes and the inhibition of responses.

There is also increasing evidence of structural differences which may underlie such difficulties. Castellanos *et al.* (1996), for instance, carried out a study of the brains of 57 children with AD/HD, using magnetic resonance imaging (MRI). When they compared these with 55 healthy matched controls, they found that the AD/HD children had a significant reduction in the size of the right frontal lobe. Unfortunately, there is quite a large normal variation in the size and shape of children's brains, and it is unlikely that such scans would be at all reliable in diagnosing individual cases.

Children with AD/HD are often presumed to have a long-term disabling condition that will need long-term treatment. Hill and Schoener (1996), however, brought together the findings from nine studies in which children with AD/HD were followed up 4 to 16 years later. They found that the incidence consistently declined for individuals by about 50 per cent every five years. Since this is similar to the spontaneous remission rate for all behavioural problems, it does perhaps imply that the causes are not necessarily a long-term biological abnormality, or that if they are, children can learn to adjust in some way over time.

Dietary changes

It is possible that a general category of behaviour such as AD/HD may have a number of different causes. There is also now evidence (reviewed in Chapter 10) that different types of foods and additives may have an effect on the behaviour of some individuals, particularly in terms of their mood and general irritability. A number of apparently well-designed studies show that significant numbers of children diagnosed with AD/HD improve if they are put on 'exclusion diets', although it is unclear just how many children would benefit from this. A review by Madsen (1994) has indicated that estimates of the prevalence of food additive intolerance in school-aged children vary from 0.026 per cent to 2 per cent.

Behavioural approaches

The majority of children's difficulties with attention and hyperactivity/impulsivity are short-term and are just a reaction to circumstances in their lives. Lessons which children find boring will lead to attention lapses, and emotional trauma in children's lives may make it difficult for them to focus on a particular activity.

Woodward *et al.* (1998) studied the home backgrounds of 28 9-year-old boys with pervasive hyperactivity disorder and compared these with the home backgrounds of 30 normal boys of the same age. They found that the parents of the children with hyperactivity were significantly more likely to use disciplinary aggression, and they also had more difficulties coping with their children. These effects were still significant when associated conduct disorder was controlled for. One possible explanation of this is that poor behavioural management may have generated the hyperactivity, although it is equally likely that this style of parenting was actually a reaction to the frustration and difficulties of having a child with hyperactivity. Whatever the causes, this type of management is unlikely to generate positive behaviours, and there is evidence that parental training based on establishing proactive and authoritative child management can bring about behavioural improvements.

Simple and effective behavioural approaches for both school and home behaviour can be set up by psychologists and teachers. These can involve operant conditioning with targets for self-control and work completion, as well as cognitive behaviour modification as described earlier. In an evaluation of this approach, Hinshaw *et al.* (1984) found that self-control training was more effective than medication. However, a combination of medication and individualised psychological intervention provided both academic gains and better psychological adjustment.

School-based behaviour programmes

In recent years a number of programmes have been designed and evaluated which implement many of the factors that have been shown to help with behaviour problems. Most of these involve whole-class and whole-school approaches and can be delivered by a process of in-service training. Some of the better-known approaches used in the United Kingdom are the following.

Assertive Discipline

The Assertive Discipline approach (Canter and Canter, 1992) is a commercial (franchised) course developed in the United States which presents teachers with a classroom and school-wide discipline programme. This includes many behavioural objectives, such as the frequent use of positives, clear and stated boundaries to behaviour, clarity of instruction, and the use of non-verbal communication. One particular controversial technique is the process whereby misbehaviour (breaking one of the five classroom rules) results in a child's name being written on either the board or (more recently) a separate clipboard, and sanctions being taken against the child. More misbehaviour results in checks being added to the child's name, and further sanctions are carried out. Other elements are the involvement of parents, and the establishment of a school 'discipline squad' to deal with problem situations.

The firm behavioural rationale behind the programme has resulted in a number of positive evaluations. In a typical study, Swinson and Melling (1995) found the statistically significant results shown in Table 11.2 after implementing the programme in two schools. Other writers such as Robinson and Maines (1994) have, however, voiced some disquiet about the negative, control-oriented aspects of the overall approach, and the way in which students are seen as the sole cause of misbehaviour.

Building A Better Behaved School (BABBS)

The authors of the Building A Better Behaved School (BABBS) approach (Galvin *et al.*, 1990)

Table 11.2 Outcomes for Assertive Discipline training

	Pre-training	Post-training
Mean pupil time on task	75%	89.1%
Mean disruptive incidents per lesson	4.8	0.8
Mean teacher praise statements per lesson	7.3	15.4

Source: Based on data in Swinson and Melling (1995)

have built up a set of extensive resource materials which cover nine units dealing with the range of problems in school and effective management techniques. There are three main tiers, which cover, respectively, the levels of the whole school, classrooms and individual pupils.

Early units deal with the way in which schools can review behavioural issues and move from this to set up whole-school discipline plans, manage parental involvement and organise the curriculum to minimise behavioural problems. At the level of the classroom, there is an emphasis on the 'lightest possible' approach with organisation and management. With more difficult classes, this can progress on to the use of firmer guidelines and teacher responses. The final level is a highly structured and behavioural approach for use with the most difficult individual pupils.

The BABBS materials can be used by schools as a basis for their own development and in-service training, but they have also formed a basis for the extensive 'Positive Behaviour Project' in Leeds (Galvin and Costa, 1994). This initially included 21 schools covering the primary and secondary age range, which were given training and ongoing support over two years.

The approach is strongly based on research findings and has generally been found to be effective. At the end of the Positive Behaviour Project, 69 out of a sample of 100 teachers said that they felt more confident of their ability to control those factors that influence classroom behaviour.

Preventive Approaches to Disruption (PAD)

Preventive Approaches to Disruption (PAD), devised by Chisholm *et al.* (1986), provides materials for use in the in-service training of teachers in secondary schools. It is made up of six units, which consist of handouts to introduce the main ideas, and additional activity materials. The content covers how to describe behaviours accurately, lesson organisation, non-verbal communication, the management of pupils, and developing teaching skills.

The programme utilises general behavioural principles as well as known features of effective teaching such as organisation and relationships with children. The in-service teaching methods include personal reflection, group discussion, video or classroom observation, and role play.

A review of the usage of this approach by Knight *et al.* (1989) indicates that it has a good uptake by schools and has been given a range of positive evaluations.

Behaviour Recovery

Behaviour Recovery (Rogers, 1994) is a whole-school approach for primary schools and describes a range of strategies and techniques which can be used by teachers. The emphasis is on practical approaches to a number of common problems such as inattention and disruption in class, as well as aggressive behaviours and problems at break times. The programme is based on researched and valid interpersonal techniques and behavioural principles.

The approach has proved to be very popular with teachers, and Rogers' general approaches (Rogers, 1990) can also be used with children in secondary schools.

Special needs provision for behaviour problems

Special schooling

In Britain, when a school's own approaches are not effective, they may *exclude* a child for a fixed number of days in any one school year. Under the 1997 Education Act this number is 45 days, which can all be taken in one term. Intractable problems may warrant permanent exclusion, and the child will then have to be educated at another school with available places. If this also fails, then a mainstream school may legally refuse to take the child and he or she may attend a Pupil Referral Unit. This is usually a small off-site provision, generally with only part-time attendance. Alternatively, as a result of the statementing procedure that will be described in Chapter

12, pupils can be placed in special schools which deal with behavioural problems. The placement can be a residential one if it is felt that there needs to be close coordination between the care of the child and his or her education.

The ratio of pupils to adults in specialist EBD schools is usually very low, typically 6:1 or less. As this low pupil to staff ratio is often combined with residential provision, this type of education is one of the most expensive of all. The Audit Commission (1992), for instance, reported that the cost per child for EBD schooling was more than twice that for children with moderate learning difficulties (which was itself three times mainstream costs).

Although EBD provision takes up a lot of resources, and one would therefore expect it to be effective, this has been questioned by a range of studies. Lloyd-Smith (1985), for instance, reviewed the development of off-site unit provision in a Midlands education authority. Although schools were each able to exclude a few children, this did not solve their problems in the long term, since other children appeared to take on the 'problem role' in schools, leading to even more exclusions. Also, a major review by Topping (1983) showed that pupils who had been excluded made poor educational progress and that they were usually not reintegrated. Most importantly of all, he found that the subsequent adjustment of pupils attending the various types of EBD provision was well below spontaneous remission rates (over about four years, only one-third of problem pupils continue to be difficult). Even intensive (and expensive) long-term residential provision does not seem to beat this normal rate of improvement.

Alternative approaches

One conclusion from these findings is that it may be best to maintain children in their normal school as far as possible. However, merely waiting for the normal spontaneous improvements to happen can evidently lead to stresses on teachers and interfere with the social and academic development of other pupils. One behavioural approach which aims to maintain the most difficult children in schools yet avoid these problems has been described by Long (1988). This used a positive daily school report with grades for each lesson, which were totalled and linked with home rewards and management. Of all the cases dealt with in one year, 64 per cent of pupils made virtually immediate progress, with tolerable behaviour and continued attendance. A further 18 per cent made some progress and a similar proportion did not respond at all. The pupils for whom this approach was not effective were usually older ones, for whom 'deschooling' approaches such as further education vocational courses and work experience may be more appropriate. Such alternative experiences have also been implemented in programmes such as the 'Bridge Course' as part of a charitable programme known as Cities in Schools. This aims to provide meaningful experiences for 15- and 16-year-olds whose mainstream secondary education has completely broken down. The effectiveness of this approach is currently being reviewed by the DfEE, but for some children this is the only realistic option that is open to them.

Schools are ultimately limited in what they can do, and have the task of coping with large numbers of children in crowded conditions. They are also increasingly judged in rather mechanistic terms, with targets set for the number of children who reach particular academic goals, with little thought for the work that schools do to develop children's social abilities. In view of this, it is perhaps surprising that problems are generally at such a relatively low level – even with the increase in exclusions during the early 1990s, the highest level was only 0.16 per cent of the school population in 1996–7. Galton *et al.* (1999) found that most teachers they observed showed highly effective personal and management skills and were able to deal rapidly with the majority of difficult behaviours by the use of low-key but firm strategies.

Summary

One of the main ways of dealing with difficult pupils is to use a behavioural approach. For some problems, such as anxiety, this can use classical conditioning but the main approach is based on operant conditioning using rewards and punishers to encourage positive behaviours. Despite some concerns, punishers can be effective if used in the right way, and negative reinforcement can be a powerful way to normalise behaviour. Programmes need to be carefully implemented and can if necessary involve the appropriate, and legal, use of restraint. It can also be important to improve the way in which work is organised and monitored. The behavioural approach can be criticised for being superficial and damaging natural motivation but it is likely that these negative effects can be largely avoided.

Social skills and ways of interacting can be trained directly, with groups and by guided watching of television programmes. Counselling in schools develops children's abilities to solve their own problems, and some approaches work on the links between thought and behaviour. Non-verbal behaviour by teachers and pupils is a powerful source of unconscious information and establishes role relationships.

Medical approaches tend to see problems as related to the individual, and psychodynamic techniques aim to develop insight into maladaptive defence mechanisms. There is an increasing use of drug therapies to deal with problems such as AD/HD as well as depression and anxiety.

Many of the cases referred to educational psychologists involve behavioural difficulties and these are often dealt with effectively by behavioural programmes.

Bullying is an important problem which affects a large number of pupils in schools. Bullies often have limited empathy and victims are more socially vulnerable; these features are probably related to early home backgrounds. Most bullying happens within schools, and techniques to reduce it which involve awareness, training and monitoring can be very effective. Individual pupils can learn to be more socially assertive, but the most effective approaches involve managing the social dynamics of groups.

Non-attendance at school can be due to anxiety about school, and managing this effectively involves an early return with measures to reduce children's fears. Truancy is often related to social and emotional difficulties with school and problems with home backgrounds. Effective management of this involves a positive support system with close monitoring.

AD/HD is a medical diagnosis, and the behaviours involved have important negative effects on children's socialisation and their educational progress. An increasingly popular treatment approach is to use drug therapy such as Ritalin, which appears to bring about significant improvements. This may operate by activating areas of the brain which are involved with inhibiting behaviour, and there is some evidence that certain brain structures are less active in children with this disorder. Most children grow out of AD/HD, although it can take a number of years for them to do so. Dietary changes may help a few children, but home factors appear to be important in maintaining problems, and behavioural and cognitive behaviour modification programmes can be highly effective.

There are a number of whole-school approaches which can improve general ways of dealing with problems. Assertive Discipline involves techniques which emphasise rules and positive management, and has been positively evaluated. Building A Better Behaved School is a set of resource materials covering the range of school problems and has been shown to improve teachers' perceived control. PAD (Preventive Approaches to Disruption) is a general in-service basis for improving class management. Behaviour Recovery is a skill-based set of practical techniques which are based on research findings.

When children cannot be maintained in their normal school, they can attend special schools or units. These are expensive, and outcomes are not better than spontaneous remission rates. The most effective approaches concentrate resources and techniques on the early stages to maintain pupils in the ordinary school.

Key implications

- Behaviour modification is a simplified and effective way of improving problem behaviour in school.
- A range of other techniques can also have positive outcomes. Many are based on children's active involvement, supported by adults in school. Clinic-based medical approaches tend to have less of a direct impact.
- Schools should take an active approach to bullying. The most effective approaches increase monitoring and tackle the social processes involved.
- Children who have difficulties with concentration and attention may benefit from medication. However, this is still a controversial approach, and cognitive/behavioural techniques are also effective.
- If at all possible, children with behaviour problems should be maintained (with appropriate support) in their normal school.

Further reading

Michael Marland (1993) *The Craft of the Classroom*. London: Heinemann Educational.

This incredibly useful book tells teachers how to get through the day-to-day work of setting up and organising their classes. It has been available for some time now and has been consistently popular.

Thomas Zirpoli and Kristine Melloy (1993) *Behaviour Management: Applications for Teachers and Parents*. New York: Macmillan.

Although this book has rather an American flavour, it does give an excellent coverage of the theory and practice of behavioural approaches. Teachers should find this very relevant and useful for setting up programmes.

Peter Gray, Andy Miller and Jim Noakes (eds) (1994) *Challenging Behaviour in Schools: Teacher Support, Practical Techniques and Policy Development*. London: Routledge.

A range of interesting articles by psychologists and teachers which consider different levels of organisational support.

Sean Neill and Chris Casswell (1993) *Body Language for Competent Teachers*. London: Routledge.

A fascinating book which gives insights and practical pointers into the largely unconscious non-verbal processes which teachers use for class control and management. Incorporates a number of illustrative drawings and has training exercises for new teachers to try out.

Practical scenario

Mr Gray is a newly qualified teacher in his first term who is having difficulties with a new class. Although most of the pupils can be well behaved, some are particularly difficult and regularly disrupt his carefully planned lessons with boisterous and noisy behaviour. The usual approaches, such as keeping them in at breaks, do not seem to be very effective and if anything make them more resentful. He is rather reluctant to send pupils out or to ask for support as he would be seen as having poor classroom control. Because of these problems he is starting to dread taking the class and is wondering whether he should continue with his teaching career.

- *Is Mr Gray in the wrong job?*
- *Should he try to get help from senior staff or attempt some different stratagems himself?*
- *Could it be that he has just got a difficult class and that things will get better next year?*
- *What techniques could Mr Gray use to achieve more positive control? Is it likely that some form of behavioural approach could be used?*

12 Special educational needs

Chapter structure

What are special needs?

Children are said to have special needs when they have difficulties which prevent them from making normal progress in school. Many different types of difficulties can do so, including learning problems, emotional and behavioural difficulties, and physical problems of various types.

The education of children with special needs often involves resources and expertise that would not be part of the range of normal provision. In Britain, the levels of additional support increased significantly during the 1990s, and the Audit Commission (1998) found that it then accounted for about 15 per cent of all the money spent on schools. The aims of this support are to allow children with these needs to benefit appropriately from their educational experiences. Educational psychologists have a major role in identifying children's special educational needs, and advising on ways in which they can be helped.

The law

Various forms of legislation have attempted to make provision for special needs, and the most recent of these is the 1996 Education Act. Section 312(2) of this identifies a child as having special needs if 'he has a significantly greater difficulty in learning than the majority of children of his age'. This can lead to the education authority maintaining a Statement of Special Educational Needs, which is a document that describes a child's needs and how they will be met. As discussed later, getting a 'statement' is an important way in which children can gain extra educational support, and guidance on the implementation of the law to achieve this is set out in a *Code of Practice* (DFE, 1994b). This has five stages, with the first three involving support from school and external agencies, and the two further stages leading to assessment and issuing of a statement.

The problem with the legal definition of special needs is that it is open to various interpretations since the term 'significant' does not have an exact meaning. In a statistical sense it means 'unlikely to happen by chance', but here it refers to whether there is a difference which is meaningful in some way. Although none of the legislation lays down any specific criteria for determining this level, the Department for Education and Employment (DfEE, 1998f) will publish guidance drawing on a range of examples of current practice. This guidance will, however, be non-statutory, and some guidelines, such as those issued by the Audit Commission (1994), have stated that it is not possible to lay down exact criteria. This is because schools have different levels of resources, and 'having special needs' is often just defined as 'needing help that is not normally available'. There is, however, an existing, historical level of provision which tends to determine criteria and there have also been studies of the number of children whom teachers consider to have special needs.

Much of the present philosophy about special education comes from the Warnock Report (*Special Educational Needs*, 1978), which attempted to set up meaningful descriptions of needs, rather than simple categories, and to identify the proportion of children with such needs. The report found that at the time, separate special educational provision was catering for 1.8 per cent of the school population, and it also reviewed the existing knowledge about what proportion of children had some form of special needs. In particular, it looked at how many children teachers felt would benefit from additional provision. From this it identified *one in five* (20 per cent) of all children as needing some form of special educational provision at some time during their school career. In January 1999 the actual proportion of children registered as having special educational needs was 19.9 per cent (DfEE, 1999f), although the total percentage over time would probably be greater, with some children phasing in and out of the lower levels. This value also showed a progressive increase from a level of 16.4 per cent in 1996, and there were indications that the rise was continuing.

Concepts of special educational needs

Special needs as a continuum

The distributions of the various types of abilities or problems that are relevant to education are almost invariably continuous, without any evident part that can be labelled as special in some way. As examples of this, the plots shown in Figure 12.1 are based on data from the manuals for Behavioural Problems – from the Bristol Social-Adjustment Guides (Stott, 1971) – and

Figure 12.1 Distributions of behavioural and literacy attainments

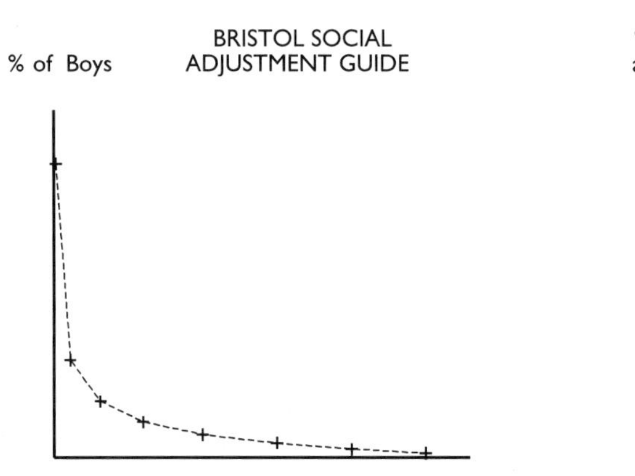

Source: Based on data from Stott (1971) and Elliott *et al.* (1983)

Reading Ability – from the British Ability Scales (Elliott *et al.*, 1983). If there were parts of these curves which were a separate 'special needs' population, then there would be a discontinuity or a 'bulge' somewhere in the lower range; however, these plots show continuous and smooth curves. The only exception to this general principle happens with the distribution of general intelligence, where there is a small 'bump' somewhere below the IQ 50 level. A plausible explanation for this is the presence of specific biological problems such as brain damage or genetic disorders, which would account for only a small proportion of the overall special needs population.

Special needs as a criterion

Although Warnock's cut-off point at the bottom 20 per cent level appears to be a useful guide for establishing a level of moderate needs, this was based only on studies of teachers' subjective opinions. It is therefore likely that the figure was affected by what teachers considered realistic. This could only have been a relative judgement and might just as easily have been 30 or 10 per cent if more or fewer special needs resources had been available at the time of the report.

An alternative statistical approach which has been used to define more severe special needs is a criterion of the bottom two standard deviation points of the distribution of a particular ability. If the ability you are looking at has a normal distribution, this identifies a percentage (about 2 per cent) that is not far different from the proportion of children who are in special schools. In fact, Gipps and Stobart (1990) discovered that this figure (which corresponds to an IQ figure of 70) was originally advocated as a criterion by Cyril Burt, the first educational psychologist, who was employed by the former London County Council. The reason he gave for doing this was as follows: 'For immediate practical purposes the only satisfactory definition of mental deficiency is a percentage definition *based on the amount of existing accommodation*' (Burt, 1921, p. 167; my italics). It is only from then onwards that quotients of 70 (which correspond to two standard deviations below the norm) were taken to imply some critical level of need. It can be seen, then, that this is essentially an arbitrary level, and again is really dependent only on the level of special needs provision available.

Special needs as functional abilities

In order to arrive at a more meaningful definition of special needs, some workers, such as Hillerich (1976), have attempted to relate skills to the ability to function in school or within society. Applying this approach to literacy, Hillerich identifies key points along a continuum of skills (Figure 12.2). Using this, one could argue that 'use for basic life functions' should be a minimum level for as many people as possible. This would involve the ability to use key signs for information, such as danger signals or public facilities. In fact, children who would have difficulties eventually achieving this level would normally be recognised as having special educational needs, within the category of 'moderate or severe learning difficulties'. Above this level, the criteria for special needs become more difficult to define, although 'Use for social concerns' should also perhaps be a desirable outcome for the majority of people and could be a reason for identifying special needs. This might involve the ability to read basic newspapers, reading and writing letters, and filling out forms. A study in 1995 of 1,714 adults aged 37

Figure 12.2 Levels of functional reading

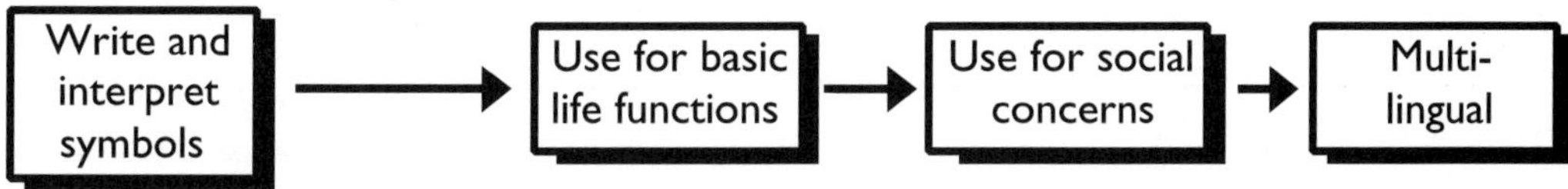

Source: Based on Hillerich (1976)

Table 12.1 Levels of reading ability at different stages of the education system

Stage	Levels of reading ability
End of infant schooling, age 7½	About one in 25 children will have failed to have made significant progress and will still be reading below the 6-year level.
End of junior schooling, age 11½	About one in 20 children will still not be (basic) free readers, with a reading age of 8 years or below.
End of secondary schooling, age 16½	About one in 20 children will have a reading age of 10 years or below; one in eight children will have a reading age of 12 years or below.

from the long-term National Child Development Study by Bynner and Parsons (1997) found that many people failed to achieve these skills, with 6 per cent scoring below the 9-year level on such basic literacy tasks.

Table 12.1 illustrates the varying levels, as children progress through the educational system, of functional reading problems from the norms of current reading tests. Some people might say that things were better in the past and that these levels are simply evidence for lowered standards. However, a long-term review of the scores on reading tests over time by the National Commission on Education (NCE, 1995) found that reading levels had hardly changed since the end of the Second World War.

Unfortunately, even if things are not actually getting worse, the levels of reading problems shown in Table 12.1 still mean that a number of children will have difficulties with tasks that are important for them. Sawyer *et al.* (1991) found, for instance, that the reading age needed for GCSE exams was generally from the 10-year level upwards. The reading age needed for daily tabloid newspapers is from about the 12-year level upwards, with many passages such as descriptions of football skills exceeding this by a wide margin. These levels are evidently beyond the capabilities of a significant number of children at the end of their schooling, and, as mentioned above, many adults fail to make any further progress after leaving school.

Within-child perspectives

The use of ability measures such as IQ testing, and placing children into special needs categories, tend to locate the explanation for special needs within the child. A strong 'within-child' belief would be that such difficulties have a biological basis and that little can be done to overcome them. If this is the case, then special education can have only a coping function, educating children at their level and allowing them to achieve only up to their supposedly limited potential.

At the lower end of the ability range, below an IQ of 50, there is strong evidence that many children do have intrinsic biological problems. Simonoff *et al.* (1996), for instance, review evidence that about a third of individuals with severe learning difficulties have a known genetic abnormality (such as Down syndrome) and about a fifth have multiple congenital anomalies, with most of the remainder having some clear evidence of brain damage. However, the majority of children above this level who have mild and moderate learning difficulties do not have any known physical problems, although Simonoff *et al.* argue that unidentified genetic conditions such as the fragile X syndrome also exist within the moderate learning difficulties population and may lead to a reduction in IQ levels.

In a review of the processes which maintain disadvantage in society, Rutter and Madge (1976) argue that there is a strong heritable basis for general intelligence, and that this has a significant effect on learning at the lower end of the normal range. Research on the similarity of IQ of family members is consistent with this belief and indicates that the general heritability of intelligence across the range is about 50 per cent. However, as was noted in Chapter 4, the studies on which this finding is based can be criticised for not taking sufficient account of environmental effects, and the level of heritability of intelligence for the majority of children with special needs therefore remains a controversial area.

Gender may also affect special educational needs since boys tend to be over-represented in most measures of special provision. A review by Male (1996), for example, found that more than twice as many boys as girls were attending schools for children with moderate learning difficulties. This higher proportion could be interpreted as being due to some underlying biological difference which affects learning, such as the known greater vulnerability of the male foetus to various stresses. However, evidence reviewed in Chapter 7 indicates that there are alternative plausible explanations based on the cultural effects of boys being less actively involved in the educational process.

Less strong 'within-child' views of the basis of general special needs see difficulties as the outcome of *stable* individual abilities, whatever the cause. Therefore, children with low educational achievements can be seen as having limited general knowledge and understanding, poor general motivation, and ineffective learning styles. If these are likely to be long-term characteristics, then they can be taken to imply the need for long-term differences in the type of education that they should receive.

Environmental perspectives

If one excludes those children who have a known physical basis for their difficulties, the majority of children with special needs are consistently found to come from the more deprived sectors of the community. In a classic review of such findings, Dunn (1968) argued that moderate learning difficulties were mainly the outcome of social deprivation and that the process of (segregated) special education was not justified as it was effectively discriminatory. However, if special needs are the outcome of a limited home background, it may still be justifiable to attempt to make up for this with whatever form of provision is most effective (although, as discussed later, the role and effectiveness of special schools are open to debate).

Early compensatory programmes for disadvantaged children, such as the Head Start project in the United States, did not initially appear to be effective, and led Jensen (1973) to conclude that low educational attainments were mainly the result of inherited abilities. However, later assessments such as that by Barnett (1995) found long-term positive effects and identified that a critical aspect was the involvement of parents. Clark (1983) carried out a comparison analysis of the home processes in socially and economically disadvantaged homes, where children were either successful or unsuccessful in school. This study found that the home lives of all of the unsuccessful children were characterised by much higher levels of social stress, with loose social ties between parents and children, and with limited effective support for education.

As we saw in Chapter 4, parental involvement affects language development, general learning style, and achievements with basic academic skills. The effects of this appear to be cumulative, and Clarke and Clarke (1974) summarise findings that although there are only minor developmental and cognitive differences between children from different social classes before about 18 months of age, children in deprived social groupings then become progressively further behind, the longer they are in such home environments.

Interactions and limits to progress

Rutter and Madge (1976) argue that such environmental effects can interact with inherited abilities, generating a 'cycle of disadvantage' as parents with low abilities provide an unstimulating environment for their children, who will in turn raise their own children in similar circumstances. There is also some evidence from Plomin (1995) that the environment of children can itself be modified by their genetic potential. This can happen if an inherited disorder means that children are not very responsive, since their parents will often reduce their level of involvement as a result of the low level of feedback they receive.

When children with low abilities fail to make progress in school, their lack of progress can also lead to different educational experiences. For instance, they may be placed in low sets or even into segregated special education. Although these are normally justified as providing education that is matched to children's attainments and rate of progress, this provision may actually result in a rather restrictive and unstimulating environment. There is evidence covered in previous chapters that pupils can make less progress in these situations, owing for instance to the limited verbal abilities of other pupils, reduced expectations from teachers, and the poor self-perceptions and negative social groupings that can arise.

Failure to make progress with basic skills such as reading can also limit a pupil's progress with general knowledge and understanding – a reversal of the 'Matthew effect' discussed in Chapter 4. Lack of progress can also have negative effects on attribution and motivation – failure leading to apathy and withdrawal from learning situations. Similarly negative interaction effects might occur between learning and behaviour as limited success leads to disaffection, reactive behaviour and reduced involvement and success in learning. However, there does not appear to be a strong independent effect of learning failure on behaviour, although they probably share similar causes.

Categories of special needs

The Warnock Report (*Special Educational Needs*, 1978) attempted to change the general philosophy of special education away from simplistic groupings of children within categories such as 'Educationally Sub-Normal (Moderate)', which merely records the fact that they are not coping with normal work, and towards terms such as 'Moderate Learning Difficulties', which puts more of an emphasis on pupils' learning needs. However, there are still a number of categories of special needs in common use, usually when a particular problem has direct implications for the type of educational experiences needed. In practice, many categories are ill-defined or overlap, and with many individual children there is a combination of factors which makes it unsafe to generalise from a particular diagnostic classification.

Learning difficulties

The largest single group of children with special needs are those with learning difficulties, a category that is further subdivided into mild, moderate, and severe. These subcategories are often determined by levels of key abilities or functional attainments and there are different educational approaches associated with each of them.

Children with *mild learning difficulties* have some difficulty with normal school work but are able to cope with the normal curriculum. According to the Code of Practice, they would be placed at stages up to 3, which means that their needs should be met in the ordinary school with some additional support and differentiation of work.

As we shall see, about 3 per cent of all British children have a statement of special educational needs. In 1999 (DfEE, 1999f), nearly 20 per cent of all children were identified as having special needs, which leaves about 17 per cent of all children in the category of having special needs without a statement. Although some of these would have other separate difficulties such as behavioural problems, there are probably four or five children in most classes who have mild learning difficulties and who are mainly the responsibility of the school and external support agencies.

Children with *moderate learning difficulties* are those who make very limited progress with basic academic skills, for example failing to achieve basic functional skills with literacy, despite the help available in school or from the support agencies. They normally need additional help, and for many this would result from a statement of their special educational needs. According to a review by Coopers & Lybrand (1996), new statements for children in this category made up about 1 per cent of the school population. Special education for these types of learning problems can take place in either ordinary or special schools, although, as described later in this chapter, there is an increasing emphasis on mainstream support.

Children with *severe learning difficulties* are functioning at a low level with a range of basic skills, including self-help and independence. Their communication skills and formal academic attainments would normally be very limited and the curriculum that they follow is often based upon early developmental sequences. New statements for these are issued to about 0.2 per cent of the school population, and children with such needs normally attend special schools. They can often have some integration, however, particularly in the early years when the mainstream curriculum is more developmental and child-centred.

A large number of children are diagnosed as having *specific learning difficulties*, often referred to as 'dyslexia'. The Coopers & Lybrand (1996) review found that new statements for such children made up just above 0.4 per cent of the school population, which was the second highest category at that time. Such cases are often controversial, however, and constituted the largest single group at first dealt with by the appeals tribunal. Although the current code of practice (DFE, 1994b) considers that dyslexia has criteria which warrant making a statement (pp. 56–57), the DfEE (1997b) Green Paper on special needs proposes that this should happen only in 'exceptional circumstances' (p. 15), and, in line with the findings discussed in Chapter 9, considers that the same teaching approaches help all children.

Emotional and behavioural difficulties (EBD)

Children with emotional and behavioural difficulties make up the next largest single category, one that has been increasing in size. It mainly includes children whose behaviours are disruptive, although there are also many children with problems such as anxiety or depression. About 5 to 15 per cent of all children are judged by teachers to have some level of emotional and behavioural difficulties, and the Coopers & Lybrand (1996) review found that new statements for the more severe cases made up just below 0.4 per cent of the school population.

Special provision for children with EBD covers the range from within-school support to specialist residential provision. The latter was discussed in Chapter 11, but it is worth emphasising again that problem behaviours are bound up with children's social context at home and at school, and that there is strong evidence for a high 'spontaneous remission rate'. This indicates that any interventions should be the minimum necessary either to ensure the safety and well-being of pupils and staff or to prevent disruption of the educational process. Although it is tempting for teachers to assume that disruptive children should be educated elsewhere, it is usually best to first explore all the possibilities in the normal school, including parental involvement, additional in-school support, and specialist advice.

Speech and language difficulties

A significant proportion of children have significant speech and language difficulties on starting school, and many of these difficulties continue throughout their education. As speaking and listening are part of the National Curriculum of England and Wales, statements sometimes consider problems in this area as educational, although severe communication problems can also be classified as a medical need. The difficulty with making such a classification is that in Britain, almost all speech and language therapists (SLTs) are employed by health authorities. This means that there is sometimes conflict between the recommendation in a statement for SLT support and the ability of the therapists' often overstretched services to meet this. It is proposed (DfEE, 1997b) that the new code of practice which is due in 2001 should address these problems, probably by giving local education authorities some influence over the allocation of SLT time and an emphasis on joint planning.

Difficulties with speech and language have a major impact on children's ability to access an appropriate curriculum, to make progress with basic literacy skills, and to interact socially. As was described in Chapter 8, there are a number of different types of approaches and forms of provision, depending on a child's particular difficulties. The key features, however, are an emphasis on developing communication in contexts which are meaningful for children. If possible, therefore, support should be integrated into a child's daily experiences in school, although there is no doubt that the expertise of SLTs to assess and advise on programmes plays a vital part in such support.

Physical or medical problems

There are many types of physical difficulties which can affect the nature of a child's education. Some of these have direct and obvious effects, such as limits on mobility and access to parts of the school building, or restrictions on working within certain areas of the curriculum. A child in a wheelchair, for instance, may need ramps, special toileting facilities, and support in some lessons such as technology, where he or she may not be able to reach certain equipment.

Other disabilities, such as epilepsy, may not be so obvious, particularly when well controlled with drugs. Unfortunately, some forms of medication at high doses have the effect of producing unsteadiness, drowsiness or withdrawn behaviour, which can limit educational progress. As many as 5 per cent of all children will have a fit at one time or another, although only about 2 per cent of children have long-term epilepsy, with its incidence tending to reduce as children get older. There are many different types of epilepsy, but in the more extreme form of 'tonic-clonic seizure' (previously known as grand mal) there can be a loss of consciousness, difficulty in breathing, convulsions, incontinence and drowsiness on recovery. Certain types of epilepsy which affect the temporal lobe may be less obvious and involve behavioural problems such as tension, irritability, bad temper, aggressiveness and hyperkinesis (DES, 1962). Other types of epilepsy, called 'absences' (previously known as petit mal), may also be difficult to detect since they are transitory and have little outward effect on the child. They often disrupt concentration, however, and may leave the child feeling rather dazed and confused, and liable to react inappropriately. Structured learning programmes can be useful to ensure continuity in such cases, since children can then quickly pick up where they left off.

Epilepsy is the result of cells in parts or all of the brain firing in synchrony, rather than separately. The cause may be some form of abnormality or brain damage, with a focus that triggers the fit, or by high temperatures in the brain. In susceptible children a fit can be triggered by flashing lights or by general stress. Although children with epilepsy are somewhat more likely to have reading difficulties than other children, their difficulties are often associated with other problems, rather than the epilepsy itself. A review by Bagley (1971) of 118 cases of children with epilepsy uncomplicated by other handicaps found that they had a mean IQ of 99.2, indicating that epilepsy does not by itself limit intellectual development. Epilepsy is, however, quite common among children with severe learning difficulties, when it is often due to general physical problems in the brain.

When poor physical control and coordination are the result of early brain damage, the condition is called *cerebral palsy*. This affects around two to three in a thousand children, and is often (but not always) associated with other problems such as difficulties with speech and language or learning problems. Damage to different parts of the brain produces different problems:

- *Spasticity* is the most common form and is the result of damage to the motor cortex. This produces poor movement control and stiff or weak limbs.
- *Athetosis* affects far fewer children and is caused by damage to the basal ganglia, which

organise the body's motor activity; there are therefore often involuntary movements such as grimacing, dribbling and difficulty with speaking.

- *Ataxia* is caused by damage to the cerebellum, which controls the body's equilibrium. Children often have problems with walking and negotiating their environment, and can appear rather clumsy and accident-prone.

About half of all children with cerebral palsy have communication problems. These may be due to the effects of the damage on the language areas of the brain, or due to poor control over the speech organs. Children with cerebral palsy also have a higher level of problems with vision (associated with central damage or with control of the eyes), as well as with hearing.

If the damage is limited to areas of the brain associated with physical control then there may be no significant intellectual impairments. However, the damage can often be more widespread, and Cockburn (1961) found that about half the children with cerebral palsy whom she studied had IQs below 70. Children with greater physical handicaps were also more likely to have cognitive and educational problems. Despite this, Cockburn's study showed that about half the children were able to cope in ordinary schools with appropriate support, and the figure has probably risen since then. Assessments of children with such physical difficulties must therefore look for evidence of learning or understanding that does not depend on normal physical responses. Many children will therefore benefit from the use of technological aids such as speech synthesisers, page-turners, and writing aids such as modified word processors.

Sensory problems

Sensory problems are usually not so evident as other physical difficulties but they often have the most profound effects on the process of education.

Hearing difficulties in particular are quite prevalent in young children, and Murphy (1976) found that as many as 20 per cent of primary-age children suffer from temporary conductive hearing loss – when the inner ear is not able to transmit information owing to poor drainage and/or infections. These can affect early speech and language development, and Gottlieb *et al.* (1980) found that 46 per cent of children referred for special help with reading problems had suffered from such middle ear disorders. However, many children with conductive hearing loss do not have subsequent reading problems. Such difficulties are therefore probably due to a combination of hearing problems along with other factors such as a poor home background.

Permanent problems are less common, and as noted later, are in the region of 1 per 1,000 for moderate and severe losses combined. Such difficulties can have a major effect on communication skills and educational attainments. Conrad (1977) found that the average reading age of school leavers with a profound hearing impairment was only at the 9-year level, and that these abilities depended largely on children's use of visual representations of words.

Hearing loss is measured on the decibel scale, and this is usually assessed and shown by an audiogram of the type shown in Figure 12.3. This shows the intensity of the sound that can be heard at different frequencies. Normal (modal) hearing ability is at the zero decibel level, and different levels of hearing loss occur at levels greater than this. The audiogram shows the range of normal speech in the shaded central portion; when hearing loss is greater than parts of this speech curve, then those sounds cannot be heard. A mild hearing loss cuts out the lower and higher frequencies, producing a 'muffled' sound. With a severe hearing loss one can hear only shouted speech, and with a profound hearing loss, even this cannot be heard. High frequencies are the most likely ones to be lost, and a specific hearing loss often means that many sounds such as 's' and 'th' will be lost, reducing overall intelligibility.

As with other abilities, hearing appears to exist as a continuum, as shown by the graph in

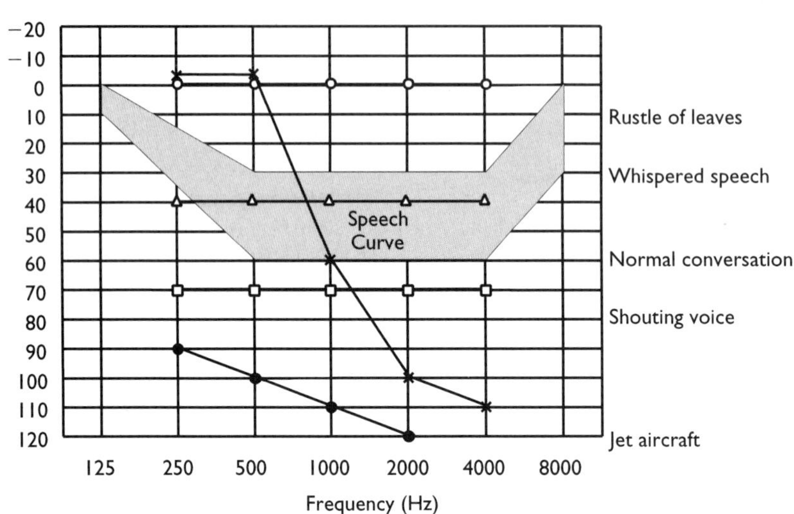

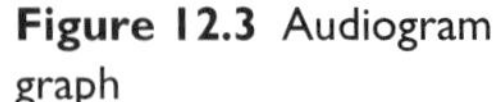
Figure 12.3 Audiogram graph

Figure 12.4. In terms of hearing sensitivity, there are no particular cut-off points that can distinguish separate categories. The trend recently has therefore been away from categorising children as 'deaf' or 'hearing impaired', towards a more functional classification in terms of what can or cannot be perceived. This mainly considers the extent to which children are able to pick up speech, since this has direct relevance to their educational needs.

Figure 12.4 Distribution of hearing abilities

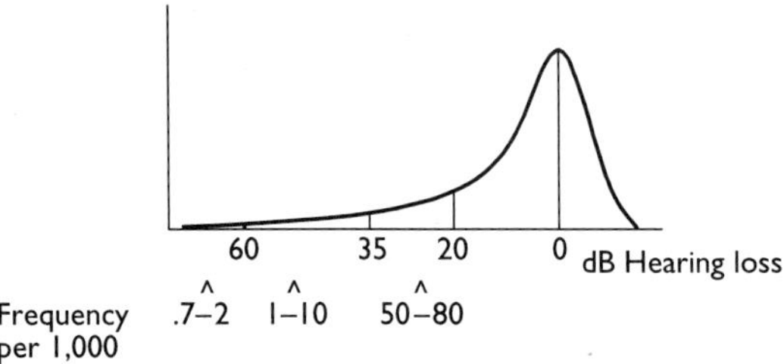

Source: Advisory Council on Education in Scotland (1950) and Scottish Council for Research in Education (1956)

Conductive hearing losses are normally temporary and improve as children get older and the drainage of the inner ear improves. However, about one in 200 children suffer from permanent conductive losses. Treatment of conductive hearing loss usually involves dealing with any infection, removing fluid from the inner ear and making a semi-permanent hole in the eardrum with a small plastic 'grommet'; this allows air into the inner ear and improves drainage.

Permanent loss of hearing is often due to sensori-neural damage, causing the cochlear or the auditory nerves to fail to function, or due to problems with the fine structures of the inner ear. These can be inherited, or due to perinatal (birth) problems or disease. Webster and Ellwood (1985) found that about five children in 10,000 have a moderate sensori-neural loss, with a slightly lower figure of four per 10,000 for more severe losses.

Many children with long-term hearing problems can benefit from the amplification of sound, using a range of different types of hearing aids. As we have seen, language develops from verbal experience and interactions very early on in a child's life. It is therefore important that hearing aids are used as soon as possible. Unfortunately, detection can sometimes be late, and if the early foundations are missed, long-term problems are likely to result.

In an educational setting there is often a great deal of background noise such as chatter from other children and scraping of chairs. When amplified, this can all mask a teacher's voice, so a more effective approach can be to use a radio transmitter microphone worn by the teacher. By itself, use of such a microphone can limit a child's exposure to incidental communication with other children, and some aids can therefore be switched between radio and local reception to compensate for that fact.

With a mild hearing loss, amplification can be very effective and produce good speech perception. Children with this level of loss can therefore usually develop spoken (oral) language and can be taught in the normal way with only limited monitoring and support. With profound hearing loss, amplification is much less effective, and children with this level of difficulty have often been educated in specialist schools or units using manual techniques. These involve the use of a signing system, such as British Sign Language. This is a complete language that is partially separate from spoken English, with some differences in grammatical structure and words/meanings; for example, there is no sign for the word 'the', since it is implied by context.

Many children, however, fall between these two extremes, and there has been a historical bias to attempt to develop normal (oral) communication with them so that they can function as independently as possible in the wider (hearing) society. The techniques to achieve this can involve an emphasis upon the use of amplification, periods of one-to-one speech training, and tuition with lip-reading. Schools or units adopting this approach have often banned the use of signing since it was felt that it would prevent pupils from developing spoken language.

The proponents of signing argue that when this is developed from an early age, it establishes language concepts which form a basis for later language-based skills. A typical study by Stuckless and Birch (1966) compared two groups of children with a profound hearing loss: those who had been brought up with sign (because their parents had hearing impairments), and those who used spoken language (because their parents had normal hearing). The main outcomes were that children who had learned sign at home were half a grade ahead with their reading and writing, and that there were no significant differences in speech intelligibility.

Conrad (1979) has reviewed a number of studies which indicate that if children with a profound hearing loss use sign from the earliest ages, their subsequent intellectual abilities are above those of children with a similar loss who do not sign. In his sample, the average age of being fitted with a hearing aid was about 2½ years. Conrad therefore argued that if children did not sign, they were likely to suffer from early linguistic deprivation, limiting the development of those cognitive abilities which use language components.

Although Conrad argues that it would be best to aim to develop sign with all children who have a significant hearing loss, only about 5 per cent of hearing parents are actually able to use or learn to use sign effectively. Webster and Wood (1989) therefore argue that in practice there is no overall superiority for manual or oral training, and that the key feature is the quality of interaction, whatever the mode used. The method adopted should therefore depend very much on individual children's abilities and their situation. For instance, a child with parents who do sign might well benefit from a combined approach and will certainly not suffer from developing signing. However, a child with limited access to sign and only a moderate hearing loss is likely to get greatest meaning and information from an emphasis on the development of spoken language.

Visual difficulties can cover a wide range of capabilities, and according to Best (1992) there are about 4.2 partially sighted and 3 blind children per 10,000 of the school age population. Far vision can be assessed by the use of a Snellen test

Figure 12.5 A Snellen test chart (not to scale)

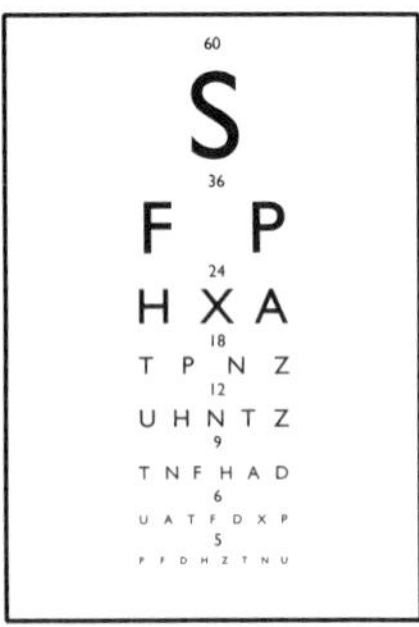

6/6 normal vision
6/9 mild loss of vision
6/12 child needs to be near to blackboard
6/18 lowest level of visual acuity for blackboard work
6/36 will need low vision aids and specially prepared texts
6/60 legally partially sighted; only limited vision
3/60 legally blind; education mainly depends on non-sighted approaches

chart (Figure 12.5), and a child's visual abilities will be expressed as the distance that a child needs to be from the chart (usually 6 metres) in order to read print of a certain size. A child at 6 metres who can read only the size 18 therefore has a visual acuity of 6/18.

Near vision can be assessed by simple reading tasks using print of different sizes, as in the example shown in Figure 12.6. The finding that a child has problems with near vision has direct implications for the type of text that should be used in a child's normal reading, or for the need to magnify normal reading texts. This can be done using lenses, or with a video system which can also be used to enhance the contrast.

Figure 12.6 Test of print size reading ability (not to scale)

36
tom has a cat
24
she is not very big
18
he likes to play with her
12
when it is warm she goes out
10
the cat likes to drink milk
8
she has a long tail and black feet
6
tom can make a bed for his cat to sleep in

When children have reading difficulties or a severe visual impairment, which means that they cannot read or identify letters, the ability of the lens to focus light on the retina can be assessed directly using special instruments. Other tests can also assess a child's field of vision, which in school work can be important to pick up peripheral information. An assessment of children's colour vision can indicate whether they will be able to respond to information involving the use of different colours.

The educational implications of these different levels of ability depends to a great extent upon children's understanding of available visual cues, their ability to respond to different types of moving and stationary objects, as well as their field of vision (which is important in reading). When children have some sight, however limited, there has been an increasing emphasis on training residual vision, which means learning to interpret the imperfect or incomplete information that is received. This approach is supported by Gregory's (1970) 'top-down' theory of perceptual processing, according to which normal perception depends on limited visual input, and can be interpreted only according to expectations built up from previous experiences. Gregory thus believes that we construct our perceptions according to higher-level concepts and expectations.

Children with limited visual input may have not learned the relevance of certain types of visual information. They will often have had limited experience of different situations, since it is common for parents of children with visual problems to be very protective towards them. Visual training therefore involves extending children's experiences and encouraging them to independently interpret and use partial visual information in different contexts.

The process of special education

Special education exists to support children who have educational problems and, if possible, to prevent such problems from developing. The present guidelines for identifying and meeting the needs of children requiring special education are laid down by the 1996 Education Act, covering England and Wales, which is interpreted by a code of practice (DFE, 1994b, to be updated in September 2001) and by various circulars on specific areas of need.

Together these cover the administrative stages that can lead to a *statement of special educational needs*. This is a document maintained by the education authority for children whose needs cannot be completely met within the normal range of provision. It is based upon assessment information from three main sources: the school, an educational psychologist and a school medical officer. It also includes information from any other agencies that might be involved, such as social services. The statement itself summarises the child's functioning, his or her educational needs, and how those needs will be met, including which school he or she should attend and the nature of any additional provision.

Statements are therefore the way in which children with special needs can gain additional resources in the normal school and how they are placed in special schools. Not surprisingly, therefore, as shown in Figure 12.7, there has been an increasing demand for statements and such resources. This has outstripped the advice from the original code of practice (DFE, 1994, p. 38), that provision should be required only 'in a minority of cases, perhaps two per cent of children'. The increase seems to be due to the combination of a general desire to get additional help for children who have problems, and the lack of any adequate definition of what constitutes special needs. It is also probably due to a perception in schools of a general underfunding for children with problems, with statements seen as a way of redressing this somewhat. In itself, the increase is unimportant and would be of general benefit to children with special needs if it meant that more children received additional help. There was in fact a rise in funding of 25 per cent from 1992–3 to 1996–7 (Audit Commission, 1998), which was close to the rise in the number of statements of about 26 per cent over this period. Unfortunately, this probably mostly represents a diversion of funding from normal education budgets, which did not grow so rapidly.

Figure 12.7 Percentage of children receiving statements

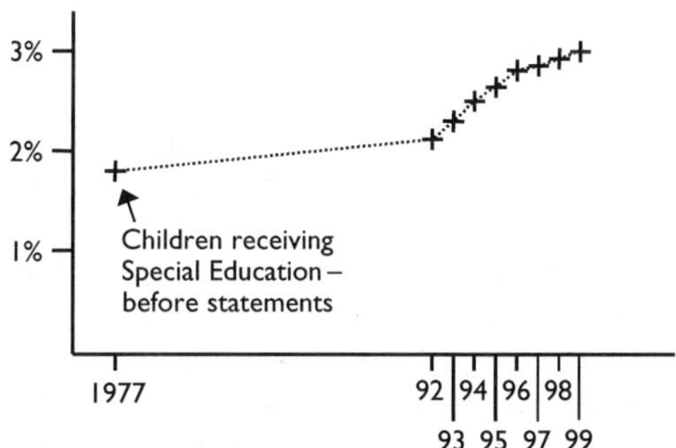

Source: Based on data from *Special Educational Needs* (1978) and DfEE (1996b, 1997a, 1998g, 1999f)

One alternative is for schools periodically to assess all children with special needs and to allocate children to specific bands within the schools' special needs funding. This 'special needs audit' can avoid the lengthy and costly procedure of statementing, and Marsh (1997) found that the use of this and code of practice stages as a basis for funding had spread to 22 per cent of education authorities in 1996. However, some authorities had concluded that the problems of administering an audit, such as achieving moderation within and across schools, were too great to justify its use.

A more expedient measure would be to allocate special needs funding to schools on the basis of a 'proxy' measure – one that is a general indication of need, such as the level of free school meals. Marsh (1997) found that this was used by 92 per cent of all education authorities, often in conjunction with other indices such as educational achievements and measures of pupil turnover. Although these are mainly used to allocate resources at stages before statementing, they could be extended to this level and would give greater stability to funding, which would help with schools' planning and staffing. When a number of background and school-based factors are taken into account, they can account for a large proportion of the variance in pupils' achievements and discriminate between schools quite well.

There remains, however, a significant variation in the philosophies and practices of different education authorities. In 1997 (DfEE, 1998g) this resulted in a wide range for the level of statementing which included figures of 1.2 per cent in Nottinghamshire (where there was an emphasis on initial provision in schools) and 5.0 per cent in Doncaster (with a high level of social and economic deprivation).

Identification of special needs and levels of provision

The code of practice (DFE, 1994b) lays down successive stages (Figure 12.8) in identifying children with special needs and providing for them. Involved are:

- the class teacher;
- the special educational needs coordinator – the 'SENCO' – a teacher in each school who is responsible for special needs;
- external agents – such as specialist support teachers and educational psychologists; and
- the special needs section of the education authority.

Parents are supposed to be closely involved at all stages and children's progress is reviewed regularly to see whether any changes need to be made to the type of support or the stage they are at. Following a review of the implementation of the code of practice (DfEE, 1998f), a revised code is planned for September 2001. It is proposed that this will remove stage 1 and rename stages 2 and 3 with simple descriptions (probably 'school action' and 'school action plus'). The word 'stage' will no longer be used, to avoid any expectation that there will be a natural and inevitable progression towards the child's receiving a statement.

If parents disagree with the outcome of a statutory assessment, they can appeal to a *special educational needs tribunal*. This is chaired by a lawyer and is independent of the education authority. Reviews of tribunals' findings indicate that although the proceedings can be rather lengthy, they are mainly focused on how the child's needs can be met properly in the future, rather than simply encouraging a legalistic confrontation.

Individual Education Plans

Under the code of practice (DFE, 1994b), schools have the responsibility for meeting the needs of the majority of children with special needs who have low-level problems. They are accountable for their actions in this respect, with reports to parents and in their school policy, and are monitored as part of the regular, statutory school inspection process.

A key element in the meeting of a child's special needs is his or her Individual Education Plan (IEP), which is used from stage 2 onwards. An example is given in Figure 12.9 and shows the key information which it is useful to include. IEPs normally last for about a term and should be brief but set up specific targets which can be eval-

Figure 12.8 The formal process of special education

STAGE ONE (removed in 2001)
The class teacher becomes concerned that a child may have some problems, monitors his or her progress, seeks support from the special educational needs co-ordinator and alters teaching approaches to help the child.

↓

STAGE TWO (renamed in 2001)
If a child continues to have problems then the responsibility passes to the special educational needs co-ordinator. An ***Individual Education Plan*** (IEP) is now generated which can utilise resources and expertise available in the school as a whole. This might for example involve teaching or non-teaching time out of the school's own budget.

↓

STAGE THREE (renamed in 2001)
If problems continue, then the child is referred for assessment and help outside of the school and this would result in a further IEP. This advice or support would at first be from a peripatetic support teacher who would assess the child's level of problems and give advice on teaching approaches and/or some teaching time. Educational psychologists tend to become involved in cases which are either more severe or where a number of factors are involved; they carry out assessments of level of functioning and give advice on teaching and management.

↓

STAGE FOUR
With the more severe and intractable problems, the child is referred to the education authority to consider whether statutory assessment is appropriate. If this is agreed (and the majority are at this stage), then reports are gathered from the proffesionals involved.

↓

STAGE FIVE
The various reports and assessments are now considered by the education authority who usually issue a *Statement of Special Educational Needs*, with the appropriate support or school placement. Statements are regularly reviewed (at least yearly), and these can be modified if the child's needs change.

Source: Based on the code of practice (DfEE, 1998)

uated. It is not very effective to use descriptions such as 'to improve reading' since it is impossible to know when the pupil will have done so. It is also important to specify what is going to be done to help the pupil, with details of the resources to be used, who will help and when. The example given (*see* p. 314) largely fits this, apart from the area of verbal abilities which is rather vague.

Each school must keep a *special needs register* of all children who are on the various stages of the code of practice. At a basic level this will include the names of the children, the nature of their problem and their stage or category of special needs. Ofsted inspections of special needs in a school involve selecting children from this and following up their IEPs or statements and then ensuring that the provision is being made for them.

Educational psychologists

Educational psychologists in the United Kingdom are employed by education authorities to help children having educational difficulties in some form. They have a degree in psychology, a teaching qualification (for example, a PGCE – postgraduate certificate of education), a minimum of two years as a teacher, and finally a one-year master's degree in educational psychology. The shortest time that the qualifying process can take is therefore currently seven years.

There are just over 2,000 educational

Figure 12.9 Example of an Individual Education Plan

ANYTOWN PRIMARY SCHOOL **Individual Education Plan** – Stage 3 I.E.P. No. 5

Started 11/12/99

Name: Peter Jenkins

Date of Birth: 26th October 1991 R Y1 Y2 (Y3) Y4 Y5 Y6 First on SEN register 7/7/98

Cause for concern	Specific Targets (up to 5)	Strategies & Resources	Effectiveness Review 30/3/00
No functional progress with literacy (no sight vocabulary or knowledge of letter sounds)	Learn letter sounds: a, c, s, t, m	Use 'Letterland' system 15 mins each day during literacy hour with Support Assistant. Learn names, then link with sounds, then sounds alone.	Learnt sounds, started on new set.
	Learn to match a set of five personal words with pictures: Peter, mummy, daddy, baby, dog,	Matching games during literacy hour using photographs and set of printed words.	Consistently able to match five words with pictures. Now starting to use verbal labels.
Poor number skills. Inconsistent counting.	Develop ability to count along a physical sequence of up to five objects in a row.	Daily practice of simple counting rhymes, use of set of five cubes to practice counting along during numeracy hour. Practical counting opportunities, e.g. sweets, money, register, etc.	Consistently counting to 5 and able to follow physical sequence of blocks. Starting to match with written numbers.
Poor attention and concentration	Develop ability to repeat back to an adult the next major objective on the work he is doing.	Regular monitoring on at least one task each day. Prompting and cueing each 5 minutes to verbalise what he is doing and what he is about to do.	Regularly reports back on current activity. Not always accurate in identifying what he should do next.
Limited verbal abilities	Extend vocabulary on key concepts in curriculum studies.	Involve in discussion work at own level. Small group language experience work with adult in class when possible.	Participates in 1:1 discussions well. Starting to contribute in small group.

Outside agencies involved:	Suggestions made:	Parental views:
Learning Support Service Educational Psychologist	Consider for Statutory assessment Moved to Stage ... 4 on ...30/3/00 Remain at Stage ... on ...	Mr & Mrs Jenkins are very concerned about Peter's slow progress although they appreciate school's efforts.

psychologists in the United Kingdom, and a review by Coopers & Lybrand (1996) found that there was on average one psychologist for about 4,400 pupils. The majority of referrals come from primary and secondary schools, and these tend to cover learning problems, usually with a bias towards primary-age children, and behavioural difficulties, mainly involving secondary-age children. Many children are referred before they enter school and these tend to have the more severe learning difficulties which affect general development. Referrals can also come for pupils up to the age of 19, or above for students in further education colleges. However, as these colleges are independently funded, they would need to 'buy in' psychological services, and some colleges use private-practice psychologists.

Most psychologists carry out assessments of children's educational attainments using individual normative tests. These usually involve tests of reading, spelling and mathematical abilities. Many psychologists also assess various cognitive abilities such as those involved in intelligence tests. The most popular of these continues to be the Wechsler Intelligence Scale for Children (Wechsler, 1992), although many psychologists also use the British Ability Scales. However, some psychologists focus more directly on the nature of a child's learning processes – for example, using teaching–learning tasks, or an analysis of learning subskills. These might, for instance, involve an evaluation of phonological abilities as the basis for the development of literacy skills. It can be argued that this is a more useful approach since it can directly imply appropriate teaching procedures. However, such assessments can as easily be carried out by trained teachers, who are also likely to be the people setting up and delivering subsequent teaching programmes. A more effective use of psychologists' time and expertise may be to research and develop such teaching approaches and then pass them on to those who are involved in teaching children.

When children have behavioural problems, an assessment may involve observations of their behaviour, or personality assessments. These can lead to the development of a programme involving techniques such as behaviour modification or social skills training. A review of the work of educational psychologists in this area by Miller (1996) found that such approaches were often highly effective and that psychologists deal with a large number of such cases over the whole of Britain.

Educational problems can be found at a pre-school age, when the assessment would involve developmental criteria, and the range of physical disabilities. Psychologists also deal with complex difficulties such as cases where behaviour and learning problems are present at the same time. In most of these situations, a knowledge of psychology can give a particular insight into the nature of a child's problems and avoid over-simplistic labelling.

A psychological assessment can be part of the development of an Individual Educational Plan for a child, at stage 3 of the code of practice (DFE, 1994b). At stage 4, the assessment would be part of the statutory procedure for a statement, when it should outline a child's educational needs and how those could be met. A great amount of educational psychologists' time is therefore taken up carrying out assessments and writing reports, which must be accurate and useful for all those involved. The Coopers & Lybrand (1996) review found that psychologists spent 32.1 per cent of their time on stages 1–3 and 26.9 per cent of their time on stage 4 (assessment for statements). Nowadays, psychologists' assessments are being increasingly queried in legal or semi-legal situations (such as in a special educational needs tribunal). They must therefore be justified in terms of the evidence they are based upon and the logic of their arguments, rather than on 'clinical experience'.

A key part of an assessment is often to give advice about the appropriate educational environment for a child, including the nature of provision. This involves a detailed and expert knowledge of what are effective approaches for a range of special needs problems, as described in this chapter and elsewhere in the book. With a literacy problem, a psychologist might therefore give advice about the teaching techniques to be used, the learning group size, and the frequency of teaching. The advice might also cover specific psychological strategies to increase success, such as mastery learning or mediated learning techniques. Some students may also need a particular emphasis on high levels of meaningful success to improve their attributional style and motivation, as described in Chapter 5.

Although psychological advice cannot name a particular school, it can describe key features, such as the nature of the general school curriculum and the social context, which might be characteristic of a certain type of learning environment. Again, however, the psychologist should be aware of the effectiveness of segregated schooling, and its advantages and drawbacks as described later in this chapter.

Psychologists have a relatively ambiguous role since they have the responsibility for identifying needs, but do not normally have the direct power or resources to go with this. Only a proportion of children seen by psychologists are able to get additional support through statements, and schools do not have unlimited resources available for children with special needs. Since psychologists normally have many cases referred to them, they are often limited to making recommendations, and busy, overstretched schools can have difficulties carrying them out. Also, many children with special needs come from home circumstances where there is little support for their educational development.

Problem pimps and crocodile hunters

These constraints can lead to psychologists' carrying out assessments and writing reports which serve only to confirm children's difficulties.

Reynolds (1987), for instance, argues that there is a danger that educational psychologists may function as 'problem pimps', living off their ability to provide an apparently legitimate attribution for failure by using general ability testing.

An allegory attempts to illuminate this scenario by describing how a village that was plagued by crocodiles hired an expert crocodile hunter. Every day the hunter would go off into the swamps around the village and devise traps for the crocodiles or shoot them with a special powerful rifle. The crocodiles kept breeding, however, and although the hunter kept their numbers down, it seemed that crocodiles simply had to be accepted by the villagers as being part of their lives.

In this story, the role of the psychologist can of course be likened to the crocodile hunter, using ever more specialised techniques and devices to deal with the result, rather than the causes of the problem. Evidently, what the villagers really needed was a civil engineer to drain the swamps and destroy the crocodiles' breeding grounds.

It is however, not quite so simple to identify or to deal with the causes of educational failure. It seems likely that schools and teachers have fairly similar levels of effectiveness, given the major constraints under which they operate. Overall improvements are therefore normally unlikely to occur, unless there are dramatic changes in key factors – which would generally involve additional funding. If, as seems likely, home background and economic inequality are the main causes of educational problems, then these factors are also unfortunately well beyond the control of any individual, or even of the educational system as a whole.

It is possible, however, that psychologists may be able to influence some parts of the educational system in a developmental or training role. Such a role can involve working with individual schools or across the whole education authority to develop particular techniques or general systems to help children with problems. Burden (1978) in particular has argued that it is more effective for psychologists to adopt this approach than simply to label and assign children to different forms of schooling. One positive and effective example of this is the 'Sound Linkage' programme developed by Hatcher (1994) to establish phonological abilities as part of general reading development. The 'no blame' approach to bullying by Maines and Robinson (1991) described in Chapter 11 has also been shown to be highly effective.

A move away from the traditional approach is also seen in the *consultancy model* as described by Wagner (1995). According to this, psychologists are more likely to be effective if they work in a collaborative way with schools to address individual or more general problems. The idea is that they do not simply give advice but take something akin to a counselling approach, involving a dialogue with schools to seek information and to analyse and reflect back the present situation. This can then act as the basis for a school to develop new ways of solving difficulties or problems. Using this approach seems more likely to generate involvement and commitment to change than the traditional process of 'test and tell'.

Special needs support

Mild learning difficulties

The largest single category of special needs is that of children with mild learning difficulties, which covers children who are failing within the normal class situation. One of the main ways of helping such children to make progress is simply by providing one-to-one support. Bloom (1984) found that with individual teaching, 99 per cent of all pupils were able to achieve above the normal class average. The improvement is most marked with low-achieving pupils, who are effectively brought closer to the class average.

Unfortunately, teacher time is often limited, but individual help can sometimes be achieved by using non-teaching assistants, parent helpers and even other children. Parents can be very effective in helping children make progress, and peer tutors can also have a dramatic effect. Topping (1992) has reviewed the main research findings, which indicate that the key factors are a good relationship between the child and his or her tutor, and that the child doing the tutoring should have a skill level at least two years above the child he or she is tutoring. Surprisingly, the child doing the tutoring has been shown to make the greater progress, illustrating the dictum that 'to teach is to learn something twice'. This finding has also been capitalised on to successfully motivate low-achieving secondary school pupils by involving them in remedial help in local primary schools.

Cashdan *et al.* (1971) also found that backward junior readers made most progress when taught in groups of six or less. This is consistent with the findings discussed in Chapter 6 on the influence of class sizes on teaching effectiveness, and is related to the difficulty for teachers in monitoring the progress of individual pupils when group sizes are above this critical number.

Structured learning programmes have also been shown to be very effective at bringing the progress of slow learners closer to the class norm. An example of this is the mastery learning approach based on work by Carroll (1963), which emphasises complete learning of one stage before going on to the next one. Teaching also seems to be most effective when it is targeted at key skills that are part of the direct learning process; in early reading, for example, this often means the progressive development of word attack skills through phonics teaching allied to phonological awareness, as described in Chapter 9.

It also seems to be important for learning sessions to happen regularly enough to have an impact. A typical finding here is that of Rigley (1968), who found that with two one-hour remedial sessions a week, a group of secondary pupils with learning difficulties made only 10½ months' progress with reading over about 15 months. However, with more sessions a week, an effective threshold can be crossed, and Rushworth (1974), found that when underachieving secondary pupils were given four sessions a week of additional help, they made an average reading gain of one and a half years over a one-year period.

An important caution, however, is the research finding that pupils can make progress even when no additional help is given. Clift (1970), for instance, discovered that the average gain for 112 backward readers over the second year of junior school (with no additional remedial help given) was actually one year in reading age. This implies that when additional teaching help is given, it should be evaluated against such control group expectations and should aim to achieve greater progress. Secondary pupils, however, seem much less likely to make progress by themselves than primary pupils. Ablewhite (1967), for instance, showed that when a group of secondary pupils were left in lower streams, their average rate of progress over four years was a mere seven months! It is probable that pupils failing in the secondary school are more likely to become disaffected with the whole process of education and to have only limited motivation to achieve in this area.

The main characteristics of effective help are therefore, first, that it should be given early in a pupil's school life, to avoid the loss of motivation that happens with older pupils. It should also be done within a small group – ideally one to one and at most in groups of six. Finally, it should be delivered on a regular, daily basis with a structured programme based on skills matched to the child's level of attainment.

These criteria are met by the 'Reading Recovery' programme developed by Clay (1985). In children's second year of schooling, those failing are given half an hour's daily individual teaching, based on the development of a progressive sight vocabulary and word attack skills. Evaluations of this approach have been very positive, for example with Beckett (1995) finding that 400 children on reading recovery from seven different British local authorities made around 17 months' progress in reading in the space of the eight or nine months between pre-test and first follow-up. Unfortunately, Reading Recovery can be relatively expensive to set up and deliver, but similarly intensive approaches can be based on other effective programmes such as 'Reading Reflex' and 'Jolly Phonics', described in Chapter 9.

Differentiation

Children with special needs are likely to have problems coping with the normal curriculum in school. It may be that the work is not at their general level of understanding, they may lack specific knowledge in an area or they may not have functional basic educational skills such as literacy. This means that the nature of educational experiences and tasks may need to be altered or differentiated to match in with such children's abilities.

The most common form of differentiation is simply by *outcome*. This means that the actual task is the same for all children, but there are different expectations according to children's abilities. Although children's achievements will naturally vary, the key element is that the teacher sets different goals for children and judges their work in terms of their own capabilities.

Work can also be differentiated according to the *level* at which a child is functioning. In England and Wales, the National Curriculum allows material to be selected from earlier Key Stages when necessary, and some reading or mathematics schemes are organised so that each child follows material that is matched closely with his or her abilities.

Children can also be given different *teaching delivery*, or *tasks* which cover the same area of knowledge but with a different type of conceptual understanding. Bruner (1961a) argues that it is possible to teach any concept to any child in an intellectually respectable way. In investigating oxidation, a practical lesson might therefore involve direct experiences which depend on describing chemical combinations with oxygen. Other children who have not reached this level of understanding might have differentiated tasks which depend on the concept of 'burning'.

Experiences can also be differentiated in terms of the *rate* at which children complete tasks set for them, the nature of the *organisation* of teaching groups, for example with ability sets, and in terms of the different physical *resources* and teaching *support* that is available.

Children with literacy difficulties may also need different forms of *reading*, for example with worksheets written to match their abilities, group work where other children can read any directions, or adult help to prompt with unknown words. Alternative approaches to *recording* can involve using a tape recorder, an adult to copy a child's dictation, the use of summary drawings or just copies of another child's work.

The developing of differentiated approaches is a key basis for inclusive education, and its principles also apply to the more able children. There are a range of actual abilities even in classes which have been put into sets by achievement. In an ideal world, teachers would differentiate their lessons to match with the needs of every individual child. However, practical reasons limit the extent to which they can do so, and differentiation is mainly reserved for those children who are deemed to have significant levels of special needs.

Moderate learning difficulties

For children who have moderate learning difficulties and who have statements but are taught in normal schools, the provision and the teaching approaches used are often very similar to those used for children with mild learning difficulties, sometimes with additional individual or small-group help with specific skills. One significant difference, however, is that such children often need support with the general curriculum. This can be achieved by additional help in class – for example, with an assistant interpreting the normal subject matter or helping with literacy demands. An evaluation of such assistance by the schools inspectorate HMI (Audit Commission, 1992), found that it improved the quality of learning above the level of even withdrawal work (teaching children in small, separate groups). Such support is expensive, however, and is usually possible only for some of a pupil's lessons.

Special schools for children with moderate learning difficulties

Although most British children with statements are educated in mainstream schools, some are educated in special schools which are separate from the normal school population. Reintegration from these is possible, but pupils are usually placed in such schools only when they are having significant difficulties, and the majority stay within them for the whole of their education. Class sizes are much smaller than in the normal school (typically 10–12), and teachers often have specialist qualifications and experience. The curriculum is more closely matched to the achievements and the rate of learning of the children who attend there. However, small class sizes and specialist provision means that the cost of educating children in such schools is about three times the level of the cost of normal education (Audit Commission, 1992). Also, Crowther *et al.* (1998) found that special schooling costs were about 58 per cent higher than the cost of special needs support for equivalent children in the ordinary school.

The need for such segregated provision has been the subject of a great deal of concern and debate. Some people argue that children with low abilities need such support and protection, whereas others argue that segregation can be divisive and limiting. There have certainly been changes over time in the philosophy about the need for segregated provision, and as shown in Figure 12.10, these changes have been reflected in changes in the numbers attending such schools. From 1982 to 1996 the proportion of all children in special schools progressively decreased from 1.72 per cent down to 1.40 per cent (Norwich, 1997), and continued to fall over the years 1997–9.

Figure 12.10 Percentage of 5- to 15-year-olds in special schools in England

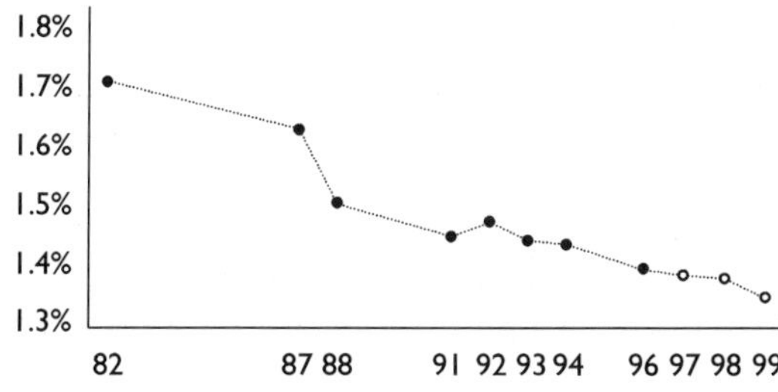

Source: Data from 1982 to 1996 from Norwich (1997); subsequent data shown as relative changes based on DfEE (1998j, 1999f)

One possible explanation of this decrease is that it was due to an emphasis on integrated education since the Warnock Report (*Special Educational Needs*, 1978), which moved away from certain categories of special need being automatically associated with segregated schooling. As described below, official policy has also emphasised the need for the inclusion of children with special needs whenever this is possible.

Why segregate?

A principal argument for segregated provision is that children who have ostensibly failed in the normal educational system need to be helped in a very different (separate), specialist type of schooling. The opposing argument against the use of segregated provision is that it does not necessarily result in better learning outcomes. A review of the research on educational effectiveness by Crowther *et al.* (1998), for instance, found few differences between the progress of children with special needs in special schools and the progress of similar children in normal schools, with some research actually showing better progress in the ordinary school. An evaluation by HMI (Audit Commission, 1992) also found no differences in outcomes between the two types of placements. The relative lack of progress in special schools, was attributed to a lack of pace in lessons, a general absence of assessment and a lack of response to pupils' individual needs. To some extent these failings may be due to the class sizes, which, although significantly smaller than those in mainstream schools, still do not allow teachers to monitor individual pupils closely, and restrict them to class teaching. Teaching is probably made even more difficult by the generally limited motivation of pupils with such problems, many of whom will have poor educational self-esteem and associated difficulties with concentration on school tasks. Also, research such as that of Hargreaves (1967) shows that putting a number of children with such difficulties together in this way can make classes disproportionately more difficult to organise and to monitor.

A further important argument against segregated education is that it tends to isolate children socially, separating them from their normal local peer group. A follow-up study by Marra (1982) of children who had attended special schools demonstrated that such isolation does happen, and that over half of the children studied said that they felt a definite inferiority and stigma as a result of having attended a special school. A counter-argument, however, is the general finding by Lewis (1972) that when special needs children are integrated into the ordinary school, they have lower self-esteem and tend to have poorer social integration than children in segregated special schools. Special schools therefore appear to protect children to some extent, giving them a context that does not constantly emphasise their failure or expose them to social demands that they cannot cope with.

Placements in special schools are in reality made not just on the basis of educational or intellectual attainments, but more on a child's ability to cope with the overall demands of normal schooling. For instance, some pupils may be very much behind with their attainments but have good social coping skills, which might enable them to get help from other children when they have problems in lessons. Such children may not need the general protection of a special school and could even be limited by its segregation. However, other children, who do not have such coping abilities, would be much more evident in their failure and often respond with behavioural difficulties and anxieties about school attendance.

Integration and inclusion

Integration involves meeting the needs of children in normal schools, as opposed to the traditional policy of segregated education. This approach emphasises the particular needs of children, and ways of managing these within the mainstream school, rather than placing them into categories and assuming that specialist schools are the best place for them to be educated. The concept of integration still tends to see children with special needs as being separate in some way, but proposes that schools need only to make certain accommodations to them, such as individual teaching support. *Inclusion*, however, has progressed from these ideas and considers that schools should be able to meet the needs of all children without needing to identify any of them as forming a separate category. Children who present problems are therefore included in the normal life of the school, rather than having separate specialist support. This approach emphasises individual needs and that the same principle of matching educational and social experiences to children's abilities applies to *all* pupils. Developing this approach involves considering different organisational structures and curriculums which do not automatically exclude children with certain abilities. It can be argued that such approaches benefit the entire school community and are relevant to all schools.

In a study of inclusion in four secondary schools, Clark *et al.* (1999) found that despite the good intentions and rhetoric, there were still dilemmas inherent in this approach. Contradictions were apparent between meeting individuals' needs (which can involve significant differentiation) and attempting to treat all children in the same way. Such dilemmas are impossible to resolve but can be managed to some extent, for instance by the use of ability grouping or additional within-class support.

There appears to be a general trend in Britain towards increased integration, as shown by the graph in Figure 12.9, with a reducing proportion of children who attend segregated schools. The DfEE has strongly advocated the philosophy of inclusion in documents such as the 1997 Green Paper (DfEE, 1997b), and some local education authorities have already made significant progress with such approaches. The education authority of the London borough of Newham, for instance, reduced the proportion of children in special schools from 1.05 per cent in 1992 down to 0.32

per cent in 1996, with a deliberate policy to integrate children with special needs whenever possible (Norwich, 1997). This happened despite its having a general school population with significant levels of social and economic deprivation and overall levels of statements which were rising along with national trends.

Severe learning difficulties

Some children with learning difficulties have more severe needs to do with the basic skills of self-help and establishing independence. Children with such needs usually attend segregated special schools, where the curriculum is based upon the range and sequence of skills which children normally develop at a much earlier age. These can be grouped into areas such as communication, mobility, coordination, feeding, toileting, dressing/undressing and social abilities. A sequence of targets can then be identified with each of these areas, according to the child's level of functioning. With feeding this might first involve a child's swallowing liquidised food from a spoon, then holding on to a spoon and feeding him- or herself with guidance, then eventually doing so independently. In practice, such skills normally take many more stages to achieve and progress can be very variable. It usually depends almost entirely on the specific abilities of individuals, rather than their age.

At one extreme there are children with profound difficulties. These pupils may need work to develop basic responses such as simple eye or limb movements, or generalised responses to sound or to light. At the other extreme are those who overlap with the moderate learning difficulties population and who can achieve functional targets with basic academic skills such as reading. Usually, however, much of the curriculum in special schools is geared towards enabling individuals to operate as independently as possible within their care situation or the wider society.

The teaching and management of children with severe learning difficulties is often demanding and intensive, and usually takes place in classes with up to six pupils, with one teacher and one non-teaching assistant. Placements in these special schools are usually made on the basis of early skills, for instance by using developmental checklists. These should not, however, be taken to imply a simple overall developmental level, since children often have an uneven pattern of abilities, which imply different learning needs in each area of attainment. Children with Down syndrome, for instance, typically show higher levels of verbal comprehension than verbal expression, whereas children with autism have particular difficulties understanding social meanings. Both of these categories are relatively common and raise key educational issues for educational targets and curriculum experiences.

Down syndrome

The largest single group of children who attend schools for children with severe learning difficulties have Down syndrome. This affects about one in every 800 children and is the result of additional genetic material (mostly from the mother), usually in the form of an additional chromosome number 21. Among other things, this affects the central nervous system, and IQs are typically in the range from 40 to 80. Like children with many other types of severe learning difficulties, children with Down syndrome often have associated medical problems such as hearing and visual impairments, breathing disorders and heart defects.

For various reasons, children with Down syndrome usually have a relative delay with their expressive language. This can make communication difficult and frustrating for them, and so signed communication systems such as Makaton (a simplified form of sign language) are often utilised from an early age. As was described earlier in this chapter, sign does not displace language but acts to establish concepts which can eventually be developed into a spoken form.

Children with Down syndrome seem particularly likely to learn by imitation from other children. Their learning can also tend to plateau in adolescence, although this may be due more to lack of appropriate learning experiences than to any intrinsic limitation at this age. It can therefore be a good idea to start group educational experiences as early as possible and to maintain integration whenever possible. A study by Cuckle (1997) has indicated that in Britain an increasing proportion of children with Down syndrome are being educated in mainstream schools, although in 1996 the majority (60 per cent) were still educated in special schools.

Autistic spectrum disorder

Autism is characterised by difficulties with socialisation, communication and imagination – the so-called 'triad of impairments' (Wing and Gould, 1979). Associated with these are often ritualistic or obsessional behaviours as well as generally limited cognitive abilities. Since all these can exist along a continuum of severity, the condition is often referred to as autistic spectrum disorder (ASD). There are many similarities between high-functioning autism and a condition known as *Asperger syndrome*, in which there are the same obsessional and social-communicative difficulties but relatively normal cognitive skills and language development.

Wing (1996) estimated the prevalence of 'classic' autism to be about five per 10,000, and children with this level of difficulty are usually diagnosed before they start school. However, with Asperger syndrome, epidemiological studies by Gillberg (1989) found levels for children as high as seven per 1,000, with the majority not having a diagnosis and functioning within the normal school. From family studies, it seems likely that there is a strong genetic component with all forms of ASD. When one member of an identical twin had ASD, Bailey *et al.* (1995) found that there was a greater than 90 per cent chance that the other twin would also have some significant level of autistic features. The possible chromosomal and biological basis for ASD is still unclear, however.

Children with ASD may sometimes possess normal or even high-level abilities in isolated areas such as computation, musical or mechanical skills. Their difficulties therefore appear to be relatively specific, and a theory put forward by Frith (1989) attempts to explain this by hypothesising that autistic children somehow lack the ability to understand what is going on in another person's mind. This ability or 'theory of mind' is shown in tasks which involve their understanding of another person who is fooled in some way. In an investigation by Frith (1989), the sequence of events shown in Figure 12.11 was enacted for a child by two puppets. Normally, children as young as 4 years of age are able to realise at the end that Sally will look in the wrong container because she does not know that the marble has been moved. A group of Down syndrome children who had a mental age of 6 years were able to correctly answer questions about what Sally would think. However, of a group of 20 autistic children who had a mean mental age of 9 years, 16 failed the task. This was despite the fact that they showed that they knew what had happened to the marble and that Sally had not seen the

Figure 12.11 The autistic puppet show

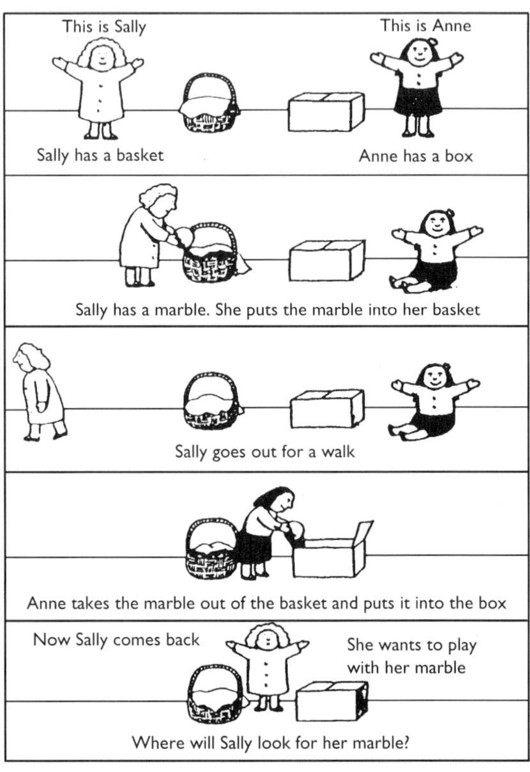

Source: By Axel Scheffler, 1989

marble move. The key difference seemed to be that they could not grasp the concept that Sally believed something that was not true.

The inability of children with ASD to appreciate another person's understanding and intent has a profound effect on their social functioning. Since language develops from early social interaction, it is also likely that their lack of language abilities comes from this basic difficulty. As this deficit can be relatively specific, however, other, non-language or non-social abilities can develop independently.

It can therefore be very difficult and frustrating to educate children with ASD since they do not respond very well to normal interpersonal interaction. They also tend to have difficulties in generalising learning to different situations, presumably since they are not aware of the way in which people generally construe them. Queuing for lunch may seem very different from queuing for a bus unless you are aware that this is an agreed social convention. One approach can therefore be to teach children with ASD how to react in specific situations, using basic learning that does not depend on social understanding. Lovaas *et al.* (1973), for instance, has demonstrated that an appropriate behavioural approach can be effective, reducing unusual behaviours and developing basic independence skills. Lovaas (1996) has described how this can be the basis for a highly intensive approach which takes about 40 hours a week with younger children from 2 to 4 years of age. Other highly structured and intensive programmes include the Japanese-based 'Daily Life Therapy' at the Higashi schools, based largely on physically oriented experiences. The 'Options' method of Kaufman (1981) emphasises the need to limit the range of experiences of children with ASD, and for adults to participate in the children's own behaviours to establish social understanding. Such approaches often claim dramatic improvements, although a review by Howlin (1998) has found that there is still only limited evaluation of their effectiveness.

The TEACCH programme (Treatment and Education of Autistic and related Communication handicapped CHildren) is, however, largely developed from research findings as to the best ways to structure learning experiences. It is based on the relative strengths in the visual processing of children with ASD, for example by using picture prompts, and also has a major emphasis on routines and contextual cues. For example, reading tasks can always be done in a particular place and at a particular time of day. Evaluation of the long-term outcomes of TEACCH has generally been positive, with Schlopler *et al.* (1981) finding that 96 per cent of autistic adolescents and adults who had been educated in this way were able to live in their local community, whereas 39–74 per cent would normally need to be in residential care programmes.

Behavioural teaching approaches

Behavioural techniques in the management of learning are commonly used in schools for children with severe learning difficulties, since many of the individuals are not able to communicate effectively or to otherwise appreciate learning goals. One particular programme, known as the Education of the Developmentally Young project (EDY – Farrell *et al.*, 1992), uses the principles of conditioning to teach learning goals, with major skills areas broken down into achievable targets and key reinforcers identified for individual children. Teaching sessions then use operant conditioning procedures as described in Chapter 2, along with modelling when necessary. This approach can also be used with the more problematic behaviours such as obsessive or self-injurious behaviours.

There is, however, some concern, as expressed for example by Wood and Shears (1986), that this general approach results in a reduction of children's rights, owing to its emphasis on conformity and simplistic learning approaches. Against this it can be argued that within the present framework of educational care, behaviouristic approaches usually bring about positive progress for many children, with increased levels of functioning and independence.

Summary

Children have special needs when they have difficulties which prevent educational progress. These are formally recognised when they are significantly greater than those of other children. Usually about 20 per cent of all children are identified as having special educational needs. These are part of the normal distribution, and any cut-off points are arbitrary, although one useful way to define special needs involves describing the ability to function with certain key skills. Many approaches consider that special needs are centred within the child, but there is also considerable evidence that children's backgrounds affect their progress and that there are interactions between children's environments and their abilities.

The major category of 'learning difficulties' includes groups whose problems range from slow progress with the curriculum and academic skills, to limited self-help and independence. Children with 'emotional and behavioural difficulties' form the second largest group; for these children provision ideally is centred in the normal school.

Medical problems such as physical difficulties, epilepsy and cerebral palsy can affect children's educational progress and require environmental and teaching modifications. Hearing difficulties are quite common and affect language and educational progress. Children with hearing difficulties can benefit from specialist oral and manual communication techniques which match with their needs. Visual difficulties limit children's access to the curriculum, which means they may need specialist equipment and support to develop their use of information.

Special education procedures identify children who need additional support. About 17 per cent of children receive help from the normal range of resources while about 3 per cent receive statements of special educational need. The level of statements has been increasing but there are alternative resourcing approaches which are being developed to limit this. Identifying and providing for needs mainly occurs in schools and involves the class teacher, the special educational needs coordinator and outside agencies. There are currently five progressive stages (due to be simplified in September 2001). A key element of dealing with a child's special needs is the use of Individual Education Plans for children.

Educational psychologists have experience and training in education and in psychology, and they assess, advise on and support the range of children's needs in schools. They can also have a developmental and training role, and increasingly utilise a more consultative approach.

Effective special needs support for children with mild learning difficulties is based on early, regular and intensive teaching, aimed at key skills such as modern phonics programmes. Differentiation for such children involves matching general curriculum experiences with their abilities. Some children with moderate learning difficulties are educated in segregated special schools. Although the educational effectiveness of these is not necessarily greater than that of provision based in mainstream schools, they can offer a protective environment for some children. The use of special schools has declined significantly over recent years and there is an increased emphasis on integration and inclusion in an ordinary school.

Children with severe learning difficulties need an early, developmentally based curriculum to achieve self-help and independence goals. The largest single group have Down syndrome, which is a genetic disorder affecting general development. Autistic spectrum disorder is related to an inability to appreciate the thoughts and understanding of other people, and can severely limit social abilities, language and cognitive development. Successful teaching approaches for children with severe leaning difficulties are often based on direct behavioural approaches.

Key implications

- Special educational needs should be seen as a relative judgement about the level of educational difficulty and the allocation of resources.
- Teachers and parents need to be aware of the

formal process of special education so that they can ensure that their pupils'/children's needs are being met.

- The range of children's problems and needs means that teachers may need additional advice and support with specific cases.
- There is some controversy over the role of special (segregated) schools, although they may be particularly effective in providing supportive environments for some children.

Further Reading

Paul Widlake (ed.) (1996) *The Good Practice Guide to Special Educational Needs*. Birmingham: Questions Publishing Company.

Written by a range of experts, this guide can be used for reference or for in-school training with photocopiable pages. A number of topics are covered, with an emphasis on practical ways of covering the curriculum for children with various types of special educational needs.

Michael Farrell (1997) *The Special Education Handbook*. London: David Fulton.

A useful A to Z reference which gives a quick review of all the main topics in special education as well as addresses of key contacts. The final section gives brief summaries of the most recent legislation in this area.

Michael Alcott (1997) *An Introduction to Children with Special Educational Needs*. London: Hodder & Stoughton.

An introduction to the field that has been written as an initial guide for training teachers. It is concise and readable, and brings out the key concepts in an accessible way. There are lists of specialist readings which cover the various types of needs and provisions.

Sheila Wolfendale (1998) *Meeting Special Needs in the Early Years*. London: David Fulton.

The various chapters in this book cover the range of different special needs which young children might have, with suggestions for support and management. A good overall introduction to special needs, the book covers general themes of professional roles and organisation of support.

Mel Ainscow (1999) *Understanding the Development of Inclusive Schools*. London: Falmer Press.

The author has worked for some time to develop theories and practices related to inclusive education. In this book he reviews the development of the field and features of effective projects.

Practical scenario

A new family has just moved into the catchment of St Marshall's Junior School and the parents have approached the headteacher about their daughter Susan attending there. Susan has Down syndrome and previously attended a special school for children with moderate learning difficulties. Although she has limited educational attainments, she is sociable and has basic language abilities. The school are concerned about whether they can meet Susan's needs or whether she would be better off in a school that has specialist teachers and resources.

- *How would Susan benefit from going to St Marshall's?*
- *What would be the problems? How might the class teacher feel?*
- *Do you think that the school might benefit from Susan going there?*
- *Would Susan be better off in a special school?*

Appendix 1: Statistics

Things that we measure can be described and analysed using mathematical techniques. Doing this with a set of numbers is useful because it summarises and simplifies the data and lets us see what it means.

Describing data

Most things that we can measure in education vary quite a bit, and sets of data usually take the form of a bell-shaped curve known as the normal distribution. For instance, children's reading at age 10 years covers a wide range of attainments (Figure A1.1).

The extent to which the data is spread out or varies is referred to as the *variance*; and a measure of this is the *standard deviation* (Figure A1.2), which always includes about one-third of all the values. The middle of the distribution is where most of the scores are and is usually the *mean*, or average, of all the scores.

This sort of distribution is usually the result of the combination of a large number of factors that have come together in a random way. Children's reading abilities, for instance, can be the result of the interaction between how they have been taught, how much they were helped by their parents, their ability to perceive separate sounds in spoken language, and their motivation and involvement with reading (see Chapter 9).

Analysing data

A statistical analysis can also assess whether what an investigation has found is *significant*, or whether it is likely to have simply happened by chance. We make a statistical analysis because we have to be careful that any effect that we discover is not just part of the variation in scores that normally occurs.

If we found that using a new reading scheme with 10 children increased their average reading ability, then we would need to compare their abilities with the range of reading abilities on the normal reading scheme. In the example in Figure A1.3, there is a considerable amount of overlap;

Figure A1.1 Normal distribution of reading abilities at 10 years of age

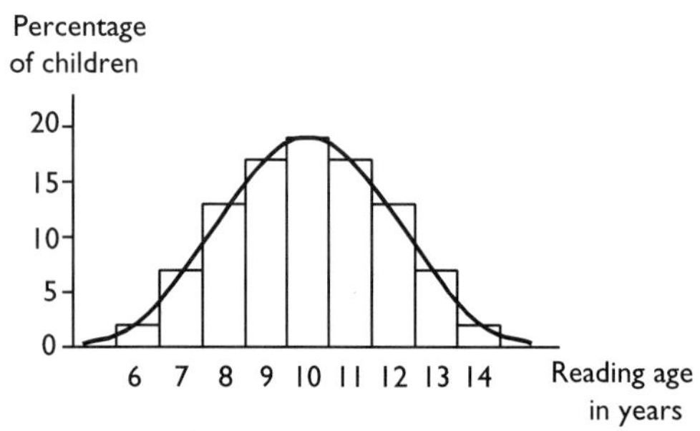

Figure A1.2 Distribution showing the standard deviation

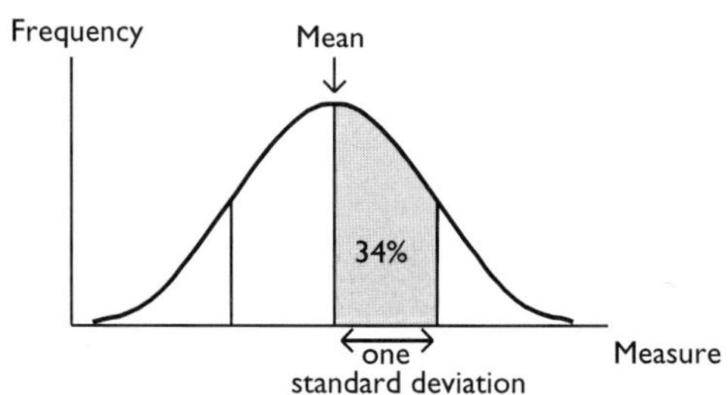

Figure A1.3 A sample that is part of the normal range

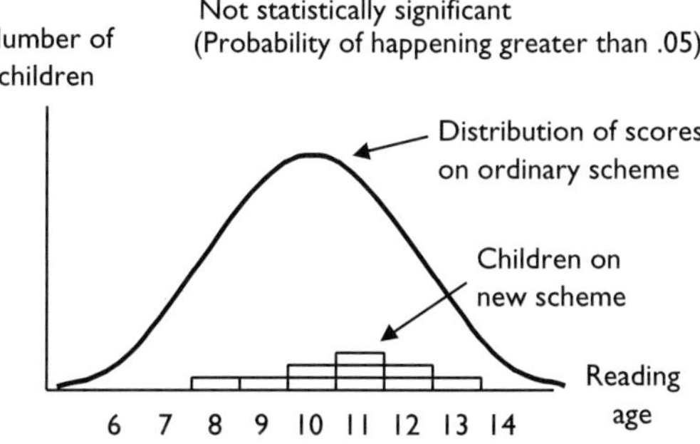

it could easily have been chance that there were a few more children above the normal average of 10 years.

If the effect were greater, or if there were more children on the new reading scheme (as shown in Figure A1.4), then it is less likely (or probable) that the improvement only happened by chance. The criterion for significance in statistical testing is usually set at a probability of 0.05 (a probability of 1 means that something is certain to happen). A result is therefore said to be statistically significant when it would have happened by chance only five times or less in a hundred.

Effect size

There can be problems interpreting the result of this sort of analysis, since a statistically significant effect is not always meaningful in practical educational terms. A good example of this can be seen in the area of school effectiveness. Research since the 1970s began to show that there were significant differences between the effectiveness of different schools. A problem with this research, as discussed in Chapter 6, is that the size of this effect is quite small compared with that of other factors such as home background, and to ignore these can be rather misleading. A lot of educational research therefore looks at *effect size*. This compares the size of a particular effect with the range of scores that you would normally expect to find, as measured by the standard deviation. For example, as described in Chapter 6, one-to-one teaching has a relatively large effect size of 2 (see Figure A1.5), when compared with the variation of attainments in normal teaching groups.

Effect sizes can also be used to combine and summarise the results of a number of different studies in an area by using a technique called *meta-analysis*. A meta-analysis gives a more reliable indicator of the general effect size than the result of just one study, which is more likely to have been affected by some form of inaccuracy. An example is a review by Fuchs and Fuchs (1986) of 21 studies into the effectiveness of formative assessment and feedback to children (letting them know how well they had done and how they could make progress). The overall effect size they found was 0.7, which means that teachers can have confidence that the proper use of feedback is likely to have a meaningful effect on children's progress.

Figure A1.4 A sample that is different from the normal range

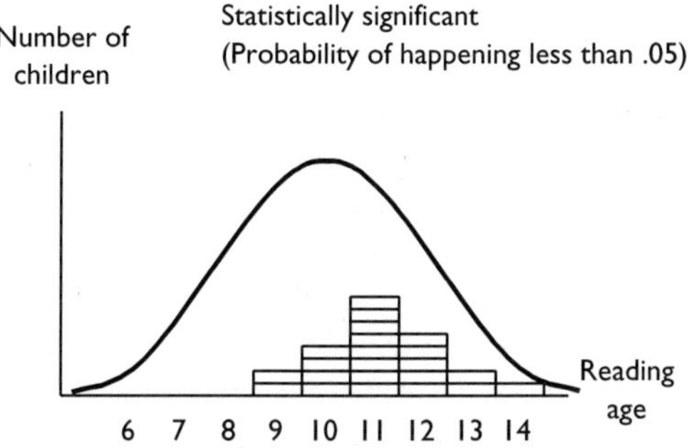

Figure A1.5 Effect size of 2

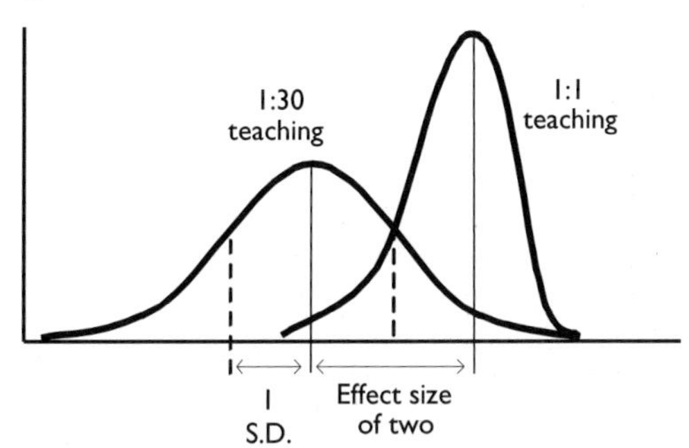

Correlation

Another technique that is used a great deal in psychology and education is to look at how two measures relate together. This relationship is known as *correlation* and is shown by a single value that can vary between −1 and +1. A positive correlation means that as one measure increases, the other increases as well. A negative correlation means that as one measure increases, the other decreases. A correlation of zero means that there is no relationship between the two measures. For example, reading attainments tend to improve along with scores on intelligence tests. The correlation between reading attainments and intelligence tests is usually around +0.7, as represented in Figure A1.6.

Although correlations are useful and popular ways of showing such relationships, they can be rather misleading and are often assumed to have too great an importance. The correlation of 0.7 at first sounds as though it should explain most of an effect. However, this value will allow one measure to account only for 49 per cent of the variance in the other one (this is calculated by multiplying the correlation by itself, then by 100). If you knew a child's intelligence score at the point shown by the circle in Figure A1.6, then as the vertical line on the graph shows, this would cover a relatively wide range of possible reading attainments, albeit with some clustering towards the central part.

Figure A1.6 Correlation between intelligence and reading attainments

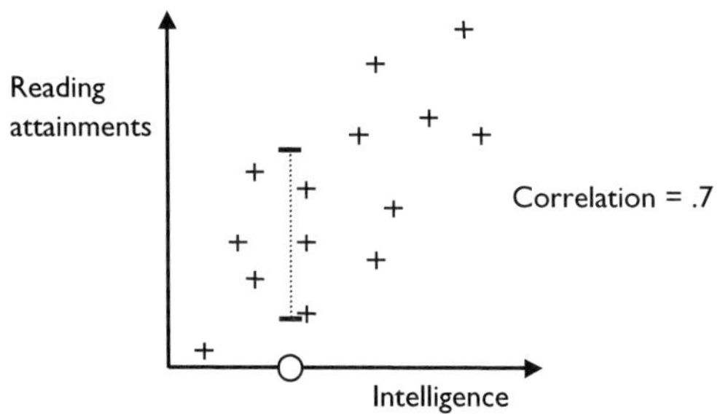

Causation

In a great deal of behavioural research it can be difficult to know what it is that *causes* things to happen, and how such processes occur. With correlations in particular, it is often tempting to assume that changes in one measure cause changes in the other measure; for instance, that intelligence directly determines reading attainments. However, this sort of inference is not logically valid, and there is good evidence that reading (and being read to) itself develops verbal abilities and thereby improves children's performance on intelligence tests. It is also possible that another, entirely separate variable such as motivation is affecting both reading and intelligence test scores at the same time.

Rather than relying upon observations and possibly misleading correlations, it is much safer to carry out direct interventions and see what the effect of doing something is. In the STAR investigation of class size effects, children were randomly allocated to one of two different-sized groups. The better performance of the smaller groups was then much more likely to be due to the group size, rather than pupils in smaller groups somehow having better learning abilities.

Another problem with drawing conclusions is that causation can sometimes go in both directions. Using the example again of literacy and general language abilities, research in this area covered in Chapters 8 and 9 indicates that speech and language abilities are important as a basis for the development of literacy, and that language abilities in turn are extended by wide reading experiences.

Path analysis

The existence of correlation does not necessarily prove that one thing causes another. However, it can be used to help support or reject a particular theoretical model. In most areas studied in education there are a number of possible variables and effects, and the theoretical relationships between them can be represented by a structured diagram. This should be derived from existing theoretical ideas and show the direction of effects.

Figure A1.7 Path diagram of factors related to reading

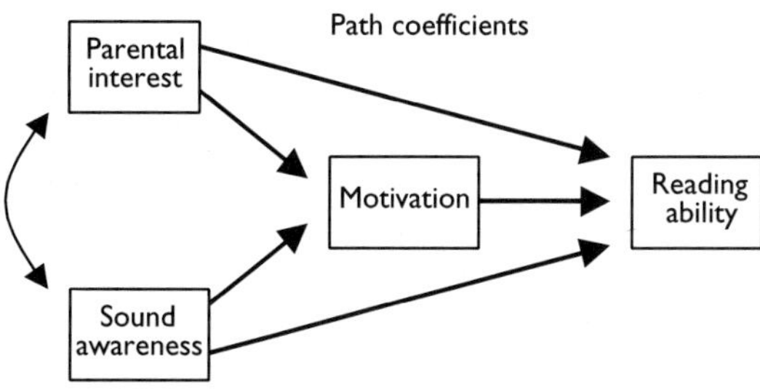

For example, there is good reason to believe that a child's awareness of speech sounds and parental interest in reading both affect the child's motivation towards reading tasks and subsequent reading attainments. This would lead to the path diagram shown in Figure A1.7.

A path coefficient is a value which is similar to a correlation coefficient and shows the direct effect that one variable has upon another one. It would normally be written next to each straight arrowed line, and an observed correlation is usually the result of a number of path coefficients. In this example the correlation between motivation and reading ability will be the sum of the direct path coefficient between them and the various indirect effects of parental interest and sound awareness.

A correlation study might support the above model, but it is important to remember that it still cannot prove the structure or the causal links. It might be that we would want to consider the mutual influences between motivation and attainments, giving the structure the rather different, but possibly more plausible, form shown in Figure A1.8.

Figure A1.8 Path diagram showing reciprocal effects between motivation and reading

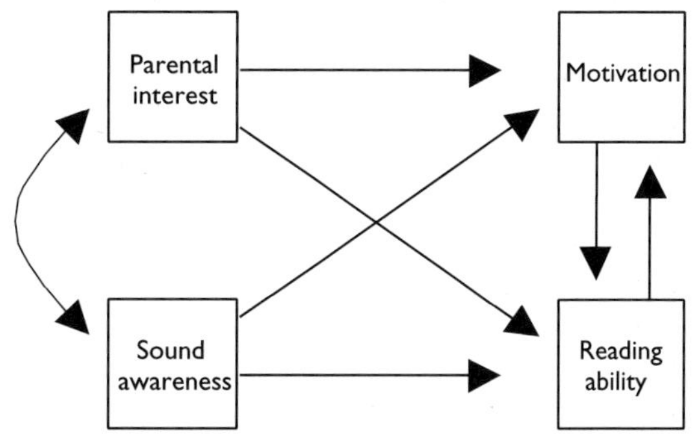

Factor analysis

Information can sometimes involve a large number of items such as responses to a questionnaire or answers on an intelligence test. Factor analysis is a way of simplifying and summarising the relationships between these, usually in terms of the correlations between the ways in which items are responded to. This technique assumes that if some of the questions tend to be answered in the same way, then they might be measures of the same underlying *factor*.

If we made up a basic personality questionnaire and gave it to a few people, we might get the answers shown in Figure A1.9. Answers to three of these questions seem to be strongly linked: if people in this sample say YES to liking parties, then they will also dislike reading and have many friends. If people say NO to liking parties, then they will like reading and not have many friends. The question about getting bored does not seem to link in with these at all, so it looks as though the other three items form a factor which we could call 'sociability'. The two questions on liking parties and having many friends are both important positive questions for sociability all the time, so each is given a loading on this factor of +1. The reading question has to be answered negatively to increase this factor, so has a loading of −1.

Figure A1.9 Answers to a simple personality questionnaire

	Susan	Peter	Fred	Jane	Sociability factor loadings
Do you like parties?	YES	NO	YES	NO	+1
Do you get bored easily?	YES	YES	NO	NO	Zero
Do you like reading?	NO	YES	NO	YES	−1
Do you have many friends?	YES	NO	YES	NO	+1

If we asked a wider range of questions, we would of course probably find more factors. Also, in real life, answers to questions do not go together quite so exactly, and factor loadings are usually fractions rather than whole numbers.

When there is a large amount of information to analyse, specialised computer programs can be used to look for likely factors. They can be set to find either a few factors which are relatively independent of each other, called orthogonal factors, or a larger number which have some overlap, called oblique factors. In practice, most investigators tend to go for oblique factors, combining their analysis with techniques to find the simplest or most economical way of describing the data.

Although factor analysis can seem to discover real, underlying processes, it must be remembered that the technique is only a mathematical simplification of whatever data is fed in. The factors that are found will change with different sets of questions or techniques of analysis; with intelligence tests, for instance, factor analysis can show either a single general ability factor or a large number of interrelated mental skills, as described in Chapter 3. As with all statistical techniques, the psychological reality of the concepts involved should still depend on other ideas and knowledge rather than our assuming that the analysis shows us some form of ultimate reality.

Appendix II: Comments on practical scenarios

Chapter 1 Introduction: The new headteacher

This is a common dilemma nowadays, with many teachers being forced into a narrow approach to teaching, but feeling powerless to counter this. One approach could be to look for applications of theories and research evidence about the effectiveness and limitations of purely skills-based approaches. However, practical evidence is more likely to persuade people, particularly if other schools can be shown to be using a more eclectic approach and achieve more rounded pupils who also have good skills. Another way would be to set up an investigation within school, to compare different techniques over time.

If there are differences between schools or classes taught in different ways, then it would be important to control for the effects of a number of variables, particularly varying initial abilities or achievements (see Chapter 6). The size of any effect is also important to evaluate and although an approach might work, it is possible that the effort or resources involved would be too great to warrant continuing with it.

A final underlying issue is that the educational agenda may be largely considered as politically driven. From this perspective, initiatives have little basis in reality but originate from politicians pandering to the simple prejudices of the majority of the population. Although the result could be to generate feelings of helplessness, individual schools and teachers can operate creatively within the constraints that they face and achieve intrinsic satisfaction from achieving what they define as real goals.

Chapter 2 Learning: Teaching different pupils

It seems likely that the children Mr Jones now teaches have lower levels of personal resources, in terms of their existing knowledge base, orientation to learning and home support. They will probably have difficulty with learning experiences if these are not matched with their level of knowledge and understanding, and if topics have limited relevance to their own lives.

Using parts of the earlier curriculum might be a partial answer, but there is a danger this will also reduce the coverage of key areas. It might be better to search for ways in which to cover the age-appropriate curriculum but using approaches which are more accessible and relevant to his pupils.

One approach might involve an emphasis on more experimental work, using pupils' own background and interests where possible. Some work might involve broadening out pupil's general knowledge in order to make specific information more relevant. He could also look at the possibility of peer group tutoring, cooperative learning (see Chapter 6) and programmes to develop children's thinking skills (see Chapter 4).

Given the constraints of learning time and the wide variations in pupils' initial abilities, it seems unrealistic to expect all children to achieve at the same level. Goals should be realistic, and should be relative to where children start from.

Chapter 3 Assessment: Going for the threshold payment

It is likely that SAT results are the outcome of a number of factors, such as children's initial achievements and home backgrounds, as well as the input of previous teachers. Attempting to control for the effect of home background would be rather limited, particularly if this were done only by using free school meal categories.

Using 'before and after' measures is probably the closest that one can get to direct teacher effects. However, when this has been done, it has shown only very limited differences between teachers. The section on teacher effectiveness in Chapter 6 goes into these findings in some detail, and they cast some doubt on the whole meaning of payment by results.

It can, however, be very persuasive to give direct examples of children's actual achievements, for example by contrasting samples of work done at the beginning and the end of the year respectively. This is a form of criterion-referenced assessment and therefore has high validity, although one would have to accept that it has limited reliability. One would hope that all teachers who do a reasonable job could be assessed in this way and that their efforts would be valued.

Chapter 4 Individual differences and achievement: The gifted pupil

It is arguable as to whether there is a separate group of gifted children who should be identified and given special provision. Moreover, it is not possible to get additional help through a statement (see Chapter 12) for children with high abilities. Although one might sympathise with Stephen's mother's concerns, if her son is generally getting on well in school, she could be reassured that high-achieving children are usually socially adjusted and go on to achieve well.

It is probably possible to provide some level of differentiation of work, for example using some more open-ended tasks and independent study work, which should also be open for all children achieving at that level. Putting him in with higher classes or setting up a special acceleration group would probably push him forward academically to some extent (by covering more curriculum). However, there might be social pressures on him, and school would also have to decide on the fairness of giving a few children additional support.

It might be worth considering using some class approaches based on developing creativity and thinking skills. Such approaches often involve small groups in cooperative learning situations, where high-achieving pupils benefit from supporting the learning of other pupils. This could also possibly be extended to a more formal peer-tutoring scheme of the kind described in Chapter 12, from which (surprisingly) the tutor particularly benefits.

Chapter 5 Involving students: Difficult secondary classes

It is very likely that the academic self-perception of these pupils is quite negative. By this age it has been formed over a long period of time involving comparisons between their own achievements and other pupils', as well as the fact of their placement in lower sets.

Modifying and matching the curriculum might go some way to help improve pupil involvement. However, account would need to be taken of the pupils' limited skills, and curriculum matching would probably be difficult to achieve in an academic setting. Although it is possible to be quite creative with the normal curriculum, parts of this can be formally disapplied if necessary, and a broader view of what constitutes education could be adopted.

Using mixed-ability teaching would avoid having 'sink groups', and is likely to give pupils the message that they are worth including. There is, however, the danger that their low achievements might be even more exposed, although some teaching approaches might ameliorate this danger to some extent. These could include using different levels of work and cooperative investigations. As reviewed in Chapter 6, the grouping system used probably does not greatly affect academic standards.

One approach is to consider that for these pupils, less academic experiences would be more relevant, such as extended work experience and college-based vocational courses. This may seem like getting rid of the problem, but could be much more valuable to the pupils concerned.

Chapter 6 The educational context: The imminent Ofsted inspection

The school could certainly make sure that Ofsted is aware of any value-added information that is relevant. An investigation by Goldstein *et al.* (2000) which was actually commissioned by Ofsted found that using the uptake of free school meals as a criterion is a very poor way of doing this. It is much better to track individual attainments over time. Doing so would, one hopes, show children making significant progress.

Any organisational changes should be based on firm evidence that they will be effective. Since changes are likely to be disruptive, it might even be that they will initially have an adverse effect and may need some time to bear fruit. It would, however, be wise for the school to show that it is actively addressing any issues which have been brought up in the past.

It is likely that observers who see pupils struggling with work will form a negative bias which will colour any other perceptions. It might be safest to teach a lesson that the class can cope with, although this might also lead to (unfair) criticisms of low expectations.

It is hoped that the authority would be aware of this school's difficult intake and give ongoing support, according to their own policies and resources. Sometimes schools can be given time to explore different approaches and develop new initiatives. To be effective, support would probably have to be relatively long-term and focused.

Chapter 7 Society and culture: Problems with boys

Some schools have set up directed activities (such as organised games) and clubs (such as board game clubs and computer clubs), particularly at lunchtimes. These can reduce negative peer group effects and encourage some cross-gender socialising.

It would probably be a good idea to try to get more male mentors to come into school, particularly to model academic and cooperative behaviours (not just helping with games). The volunteers could perhaps help with reading or practical activities. Some schemes have used older male pupils from a local secondary school as well as adult volunteers.

It might be worth looking at the books available in school, as well as other curriculum materials, to see whether they incorporate any of the interests of boys – whether, for instance, there are stories which involve boys and activities or topics which might appeal to them (adventures, ghost stories, cars, football, etc.).

Although primary schools are already quite 'girl friendly', it is probably a good idea to incorporate girls in any developments, so as to avoid any overcompensation and encourage cross-gender social interaction. Some activities are relatively gender neutral, and girls too will benefit from any additional support that is made available in school.

Chapter 8 Language: Language in the reception class

Children's speech and language can benefit from a range of activities where communication is necessary and where they are involved with the meaning of what is going on. Examples include turn-taking play activities, role play ('dressing up'), listening to stories, and joining in with rhymes and simple songs. Ideally the activities would have an adult closely involved with small groups of children to prompt and to model good language.

It would certainly be a positive idea to try to encourage parents to be more actively involved with their children. One relatively simple and effective approach is to base this on shared picture books or story book reading by the parent. Ideally, this would be done with pre-school children and would need a supply of appropriate books and periodic meetings with the parents.

It may be tempting to leave literacy until children are 'ready', but this might then produce a double handicap of both academic and language delay. Unless children have a severe problem, they can usually start to work on some words and letter sounds. Moreover, the process of developing early literacy skills is likely to improve children's sensitivity to sounds and their general language abilities (see Chapter 9).

It would be possible for teachers to check on pupils' underlying vocabulary comprehension by using the British Picture Vocabulary Scales test (see Chapter 3). This would indicate whether they have basic abilities which can be built on. The Derbyshire Language System by Knowles and Masidlover (see Chapter 8) uses an assessment procedure which is directly linked with teaching approaches.

Chapter 9 Literacy: The reading problem

During his time in school, James has made less than half the normal rate of reading progress. To improve his progress will probably need a significant change. At James's reading level, he is still developing word attack skills. One key alteration would be to ensure that he works on his reading more often to generate greater fluency with these. It is possible that after a year of more intensive support he could break through to a level where his verbal abilities would help his reading. Reading should be closely matched to his level of attainments (95 per cent-plus accuracy) and linked with a more advanced phonics programme, and with spelling techniques if necessary (the learning support teacher could advise on these).

A particular diagnosis is of use only if it implies a different teaching approach. According to the definition used by the Division of Educational and Child Psychology of the British Psychological Society (failure to progress despite learning opportunities), he does have dyslexia, but effective teaching approaches are the same for all children with problems with literacy.

If James had a statement, this would almost certainly help since it should bring additional support. However, getting one will depend on the criteria applied by the education authority. A reading age of 7 years at 10 years of age is at the bottom 5 per cent level, and statements are usually given only to children in the lowest 2 per cent. Some authorities would also take a pupil's general ability into account, although that is not part of the DECP definition.

Chapter 10 Behavioural problems: The pupil with a difficult background

It is quite likely that earlier negative/inconsistent and possibly abusive parental management has prevented Tom from developing normal social and emotional behaviours. He probably focuses mainly on his own short-term needs and becomes frustrated when these are not met. Managing Tom in school will therefore involve close monitoring and direction with counselling about appropriate behaviours and ways of relating to others.

It is relatively rare for child or family psychiatrists to directly inform or involve schools; any advice which they give is more for the home and parents. Child psychiatrists usually focus on children: their main care situation and long-term mental adjustment.

It is often tempting to be less strict with children who have suffered early trauma. In this case, difficult behaviour is less likely to be deliberate and liable to be due more to problems coping emotionally. Other children may still require protection, however, and disruptions need to be controlled.

Children can show good recovery from even severe early problems, particularly if their new environment is positive. If at all possible, ordinary schooling should be maintained in order to provide a social context with normal expectations and models.

Chapter 11 Dealing with behaviour problems: The difficult class

Mr Gray might ultimately decide that he is in the wrong career, but he should try out some other approaches first. Class control skills can be developed, and a few different techniques should make life much easier.

Unfortunately, the support he gets will depend on the nature of his senior staff. If a mentor can observe and offer constructive advice, this will be an enormous help. If this fails, however, he might find himself very much on his own.

It may be that this class is particularly difficult. However, there are potentially disruptive pupils in most classes, and if he gets better control with this group it will stand him in good stead for the future.

A 'quick fix' might be to set up a report system and link in with the parents of a few of the more problematic children. Mr Gray should also look at the overall classroom dynamics and whether he needs to move pupils. Seating in rows can also work well (see Chapter 6). He should also probably look at his overall approach to this class. It may be that a difficult start means that he has been forced to adopt a rather negative style with them. He could also possibly think about a class-based behaviour modification technique. This should emphasise positive behaviours and link in with individual and group rewards such as free-choice activities. There are also specific programmes and video tapes which he could look at for techniques of class management – the Bill Rogers videos are particularly good.

Chapter 12 Special educational needs: The pupil with special needs

Going to the normal local school would mean that Susan could develop contacts with local children. It would probably be quicker and less disruptive for her to get to school (attending special school often means using special transport). Susan might also benefit from the higher levels of language stimulation in the normal school, as well as a wider curriculum which might stretch her more.

On the other hand, there may have been some good reasons why she did not attend the normal school in her previous authority. For example, she may have had particular needs with early self-help/independence which the normal school might have found difficult to manage. Also, for children with significant special needs, the normal curriculum might also be at too high a level and Susan might need to be taught separately or in small groups for much of the time, which might rather isolate her. Class teachers often feel concerned that they lack the expertise and time needed to help children with such difficulties. However, many mainstream schools have found that meeting the needs of children with the range of special needs gives them greater depth and is also a positive experience for all children, leading to greater understanding and tolerance.

Special schools give a more protected environment with expert staff who can provide a matched curriculum. However, bear in mind that educational outcomes tend to be similar for both types of school and that when inclusive education is possible (with appropriate support), it enables children with special needs to experience normal socialisation.

References

Abbott, D., Broadfoot, P., Croll, P., Osborn, M. and Pollard, A. (1994) Some sink, some float: National Curriculum assessment and accountability. *British Educational Research Journal*, 20 (2), 155–162.

Ablewhite, R. (1967) *The Slow Reader*. London: Heinemann.

Ackerman, T., Gillett, D., Kenward, P., Leadbetter, P., Mason, I., Matthews, C., Tweddle, D. and Winteringham, D. (1983) Daily teaching and assessment: primary-aged children. In *Post Experience Courses for Educational Psychologists*, 1983–4, 33–52. University of Birmingham: Department of Educational Psychology.

Advisory Council on Education in Scotland (1950) *Pupils Who Are Defective in Hearing*. Edinburgh: HMSO.

AFASIC (1989) *Breaking Down the Communication Barrier*. London: AFASIC.

Ainscow, M. (1999) *Understanding the Development of Inclusive Schools*. London: Falmer Press.

Airasian, P. and Bart, W. (1975) Validating a priori instructional hierarchies. *Journal of Educational Measurement*, 12, 163–173.

Aitkin, M., Bennett, S. and Hesketh, J. (1981) Teaching styles and pupil progress: a re-analysis. *British Journal of Educational Psychology*, 51, 170–186.

Alexander, R., Rose, J. and Woodhead, C. (1992) *Curriculum Organisation and Classroom Practice in Primary Schools: A Discussion Paper*. London: Department of Education and Science.

Alexander, J., Barton, C., Gordon, D., Grotpeter, J., Hansson, K., Harrison, R., Mears, S., Mihalic, S., Parsons, B., Pugh, C., Schulman, S., Waldron, H. and Sexton, T. (1998). *Blueprints for Violence Prevention*, Book Three: *Functional Family Therapy*. Boulder, CO: Center for the Study and Prevention of Violence.

Alcott, M. (1997) *An Introduction to Children with Special Educational Needs*. London: Hodder & Stoughton.

Allen, S. and Crago, M. (1996) Early passive acquisition in Inuktitut. *Journal of Child Language*, 23, 129–155.

Allport, G. (1947) *The Use of Personal Documents in Psychological Science*. New York: Science Research Council.

Alverman, D., Smith, L. and Readence, J. (1985) Prior knowledge activation and the comprehension of compatible and incompatible texts. *Reading Research Quarterly*, 20, 420–436.

Anderson, J. (1983) *The Architecture of Cognition*. Cambridge, MA: Harvard University Press.

Anderson, J., Hadley, W., Koedinger, K. and Mark, M. (1997) Intelligent tutoring goes to school in the big city. *International Journal of Artificial Intelligence in Education*, 8, 30–43.

Anglin, J. (1993) Vocabulary development: a morphological analysis. *Monograph of the Society for Research in Child Development*, 58, 10.

Anthony, W. (1983) The development of extraversion and ability: analysis of data from a large-scale longitudinal study of children tested at 10–11 and 15–18 years. *British Journal of Educational Psychology*, 53, 374–379.

Antonio, R. and Damasio, A. (1994) *Descartes' Error: Emotion, Reason, and the Human Brain*. New York: Avon Books.

Arnot, M., David, M. and Weiner, G. (1996) *Educational Reforms and Gender Equality in Schools*. Manchester: Equal Opportunities Commission.

Arnot, M., Gray, J., James, M., Rudduck, J. and Duveen, G. (1998) *Recent Research on Gender and Educational Performance*. London: The Stationery Office.

Aronson, E., Blaney, N., Stephen, C., Sikes, J. and Snapp, M. (1978) *The Jigsaw Classroom*. Beverly Hills, CA: Sage Publications.

Aronson, E. and Osherow, N. (1980) Co-operation, prosocial behaviour and academic performance:

experiments in the desegregated classroom. In L. Bickman (ed.) *Applied Social Psychology Annual*, vol. 1. Beverly Hills, CA: Sage Publications.

Asch, S. (1951) Effects of group pressure upon the modification and distortion of judgements. In H. Guetzkow (ed.) *Groups, Leadership and Men*. Pittsburgh, PA: Carnegie Press.

Asch, S. (1955) Opinions and social pressures. *Scientific American*, 193, 31–35.

Ashton, P. and Webb, R. (1986) *Making a Difference: Teachers' Sense of Efficacy and Student Achievement*. New York: Longman.

Askew, M., Brown, M., Rhodes, V., Johnson, D. and Wiliam, D. (1997) *Effective Teachers of Numeracy*. London: King's College.

Atkinson, R., Atkinson, R., Smith, E., Bem, D. and Hoeksema, S. (1996) *Hilgard's Introduction to Psychology*. New York: Harcourt Brace.

Atkinson, R. and Shiffrin, R. (1971) The control of short-term memory. *Scientific American*, 224, 82–90.

Audit Commission (1992) *Getting In on the Act*. HMI. London: HMSO.

Audit Commission (1994) *The Act Moves On: Progress in Special Educational Needs*. London: HMSO.

Audit Commission (1998) *Getting In on the Act: A Review of Progress on Special Educational Needs*. London: HMSO.

Ausubel, D. (1968) *Educational Psychology: A Cognitive View*. New York: Holt, Rinehart & Winston.

Baddeley, A. (1986) *Working Memory*. Oxford: Oxford University Press.

Baddeley, A. (1996) *Your Memory: A User's Guide*. London: Penguin Books.

Baddeley, A. (1997) *Human Memory: Theory and Practice*, revised edition. Hove, East Sussex: Psychology Press.

Baddeley, A. and Longman, D. (1978) The influence of length and frequency of training sessions on the rate of learning to type. *Ergonomics*, 21, 627–635.

Bagley, C. (1971) *The Social Psychology of the Child with Epilepsy*. London: Routledge & Kegan Paul.

Bailey, A., Le Couteur, A., Gottesman, I., Bolton, P., Simonoff, E., Yuzda, E. and Rutter, M. (1995) Autism as a strongly genetic disorder: evidence from a British twin study. *Psychological Medicine*, 25, 63–78.

Bailey, M. (1967) The utility of phonic generalisations in Grades One through Six. *Reading Teacher*, 20, 413–418.

Baker, J. and Crist, J. (1971) Teacher expectancies: a review of the literature. In J. Elashoff and E. Snow (eds) *Pygmalion Reconsidered*. Worthington, OH: Jones.

Bandura, A. (1986) *Social Foundations of Thought and Action: A Social Cognitive Theory*. Englewood Cliffs, NJ: Prentice-Hall.

Bandura, A., Ross, D. and Ross, S. (1963) Imitation of film-mediated aggressive models. *Journal of Abnormal and Social Psychology*, 66, 3–11.

Bangert-Drowns, R. (1993) The word processor as an instructional tool: a meta-analysis of word processing in writing instruction. *Review of Educational Research*, 63, 69–93.

Bangert-Drowns, R., Kulik, J. and Kulik, C. (1991) Effects of frequent classroom testing. *Journal of Educational Research*, 85, 89–99.

Baran, S. (1979) Television drama as a facilitator of prosocial behaviour. *Journal of Broadcasting*, 23, 277–285.

Barnett, W. (1995) Long-term effects of early childhood programs on cognitive and school outcomes. *The Future of Children*, 5, 25–50.

Bartlett, F. (1932) *Remembering*. Cambridge: Cambridge University Press.

Bates, E., Masling, M. and Kintsch, W. (1978) Recognition memory for aspects of dialog. *Journal of Experimental Psychology: Human Learning and Memory*, 4, 187–197.

Beck, I., Perfetti, C. and McKeown, M. (1982) Effects of long-term vocabulary instruction on lexical access and reading comprehension. *Journal of Educational Psychology*, 74, 506–521.

Beckett, F. (1995) Pioneer's fears are realised. *Times Educational Supplement*, 21 April, 5.

Bee, H. (1992) *The Developing Child*. New York: HarperCollins.

Bennathan, M. and Boxall, M. (1996) *Effective Intervention in Primary Schools: Nurture Groups*. London: David Fulton.

Bennett, N. (1976) *Teaching Styles and Pupil Progress*. London: Open Books.

Bennett, N. and Cass, A. (1989) The effects of group composition on group interactive processes and pupil understanding. *British Educational Research Journal*, 15, 1, 19–32.

Bennett, N. and Dunne, E. (1989) *Implementing Cooperative Groupwork in Classrooms*. Exeter: University of Exeter School of Education.

Bereiter, C., Burtis, P. and Scardamalia, M. (1988) Cognitive operations in constructing main points in written composition. *Journal of Memory and Language*, 27, 261–278.

Bergan, J. and Tombari, M. (1976) Consultant skill and efficiency and the implementation and outcomes of consultation. *Journal of School Psychology*, 14, 3–13.

Berger, M. (1979) Behaviour modification in education and professional practice: the dangers of a mindless technology. *Bulletin of the British Psychological Society*, 32, 418–419.

Berk, L. (1986) Relationship of elementary school children's private speech to behavioural accompaniment to task, attention, and task performance. *Developmental Psychology*, 22, 671–680.

Berko, J. (1958) The child's learning of English morphology. *Word*, 14, 150–177.

Berkowitz, L. (1989) Frustration–aggression hypothesis: examination and reformulation. *Psychological Bulletin*, 106, 59–73.

Bernstein, B. (1961) Social class and linguistic development. In A. Halsey, J. Flaud and C. Anderson (eds) *Education, Economy and Society*. London: Collier-Macmillan.

Bernstein, B. (1970) Education cannot compensate for society. *New Society*, 387, 344–347.

Bernstein, E. (1968) What does a Summerhill old school tie look like? *Psychology Today*, 2 (5), 37–41.

Best, A. (1992) *Teaching Children with Visual Impairments*. Buckingham: Open University Press.

Best, M. and Demb, J. (1999) Normal planum temporale asymmetry in dyslexics with a magnocellular pathway deficit. *NeuroReport*, 10, 607–612.

Bevins, A. and Nelson, D. (1995) Blacks stranded at the back of the jobs queue. *Observer*, 12 February, p. 5.

Bhachu, P. (1985) *Twice Migrants: East African Sikh Settlers in Britain*. London: Tavistock.

Bierman, K. and Furman, W. (1984) The effects of social skills training and peer involvement in the social adjustment of preadolescents. *Child Development*, 55, 151–162.

Biggs, J. (1985) The role of metalearning in study processes. *British Journal of Educational Psychology*, 55, 185–212.

Bilton, T., Bonnett, K., Joines, P., Skinner, D., Stanworth, M. and Webster, A. (1996) *Introductory Sociology*, 3rd edition. London: Macmillan.

Black, P. (1998) *Testing: Friend or Foe? Theory and Practice of Assessment and Testing*. London: Falmer Press.

Black, P. and Wiliam, D. (1998) Assessment and classroom learning. *Assessment in Education*, 5, 7–75.

Blagg, N. (1987) *School Phobia and Its Treatment*. London: Croom Helm.

Blagg, N. (1991) *Can We Teach Intelligence? A Comprehensive Evaluation of Fuerstein's Instrumental Enrichment Programme*. Hillsdale, NJ: Lawrence Erlbaum.

Blagg, N., Ballinger, M. and Gardner, R. (1993a) *Somerset Thinking Skills Course Handbook*. Taunton: Nigel Blagg Associates.

Blagg, N., Ballinger, M. and Lewis, R. (1993b) *Thinking Skills at Work*. Taunton: Nigel Blagg Associates.

Blagg, N., Lewis, R and Ballinger, M. (1994) *Thinking and Learning at Work: A Report on the Development and Evaluation of the Thinking Skills At Work Modules*. Sheffield: Department of Employment, Research Series no. 23.

Blair, M., Bourne, J., Coffin, C., Creese, A. and Kenner, C. (1998) *Making the Difference: Teaching and Learning Strategies in Successful Multi-ethnic Schools*. Research Briefs Report no. 59. Sudbury, Suffolk: DfEE Publications.

Blatchford, P., Burke, J., Farquhar, C., Plewis, I. and Tizard, B. (1985) Educational achievement in the infant school: the influence of ethnic origin, gender and home on entry skills. *Educational Research*, 27, 1, 52–60.

Blatchford, P., Burke, J., Farquhar, C., Plewis, I. and Tizard, B. (1987) Associations between pre-school reading related skills and later reading achievement. *British Educational Research Journal*, 13, 1, 15–23.

Bleach, K. (ed.) (1998) *Raising Boys' Achievement in Schools*. Stoke-on-Trent: Trentham Books.

Bliss, J., Askew, M. and Macrae, S. (1996) Effective teaching and learning: scaffolding revisited. *Oxford Review of Education*. 22, 37–61.

Bliss, T., Robinson, G. and Maines, B. (1995) *Coming Round to Circle Time*. Bristol: Lame Duck Publishing.

Bloom, B. (ed.) (1956) *Taxonomy of Educational Objectives*. Handbook 1: *Cognitive Domain*. New York: David McKay.

Bloom, B. (1984) The 2 sigma problem: the search for methods of group instruction as effective as one-to-one tutoring. *Educational Researcher*, June/July, 4–16.

Boaler, J. (1997) Setting, social class and survival of the quickest. *British Educational Research Journal*, 23, 575–595.

Bondi, L. (1991) Attainment at primary schools: an analysis of variations between schools. *British Educational Research Journal*, 17, 203–217.

Bookbinder, G. (1976) *Manual for the Salford Sentence Reading Test*. London: Hodder & Stoughton.

Borg, M. and Falzon, J. (1990) Teachers' perceptions of primary schoolchildren's undesirable behaviours: the effects of teaching experience, pupil's age, sex and ability stream. *British Journal of Educational Psychology*, 60 (2), 220–226.

Borg, M., Riding, R. and Falzon, J. (1991) Stress in teaching: a study of occupational stress and its determinants, job satisfaction and career commitment among primary schoolteachers. *Educational Psychology*, 11, 59–75.

Bornstein, P. and Quevillon, R. (1976) The effects of a self-instructional package on overactive pre-school boys. *Journal of Applied Behavior Analysis*, 9 (2), 179–188.

Bouchard, T. and McGue, M. (1981) Familial studies of intelligence: a review. *Science*, 212, 1055–1059.

Bower, G., Black, J. and Turner, T. (1979) Scripts in memory for text. *Cognitive Psychology*, 11, 177–220.

Bower, G., Clark, M., Lesgold, A. and Winzenz, D. (1969) Hierarchical retrieval schemes in recall of categorised word lists. *Journal of Verbal Learning and Verbal Behaviour*, 8, 323–343.

Bowlby, J. (1951) *Child Care and the Growth of Love*. Harmondsworth: Penguin.

Bowman, R. (1982) A 'Pac-Man' theory of motivation: tactical implications for classroom instruction. *Educational Technology*, September, 14–16.

Boyle, G., Start, B. and Hall, J. (1989) Prediction of academic achievement using the School Motivation Analysis Test. *British Journal of Educational Psychology*, 59, 92–99.

Bradley, L. and Bryant, P. (1983) Categorising sounds and learning to read: a causal connection. *Nature*, 301, 419–421.

Bradley, S. and Taylor, J. (1998) The effect of school size on exam performance in secondary schools. *Oxford Bulletin of Economics and Statistics*, 60, 291–324.

Brady, J., Porter, R., Conrad, D. and Mason, J. (1958) Avoidance behaviour and the development of gastroduodenal ulcers. *Journal of the Experimental Analysis of Behaviour*, 1, 69–72.

Brah, A. and Shaw, S. (1992) Working choices: South Asian young Muslim women and the labour market. *Research Paper no. 91*. London: Department of Employment.

Brannon, L. (1996) *Gender: Psychological Perspectives*. Boston: Allyn & Bacon.

Bransford, J., Barclay, J. and Franks, J. (1972) Sentence memory: a constructive versus interpretative approach. *Cognitive Psychology*, 3, 193–209.

Bransford, J. and Johnson, M. (1972) Consideration of some problems of comprehension. In W. Chase (ed.) *Visual Information Processing*. New York: Academic Press.

Brattesanti, K., Weinstein, R. and Marshall, H. (1984) Student perceptions of differential teacher treatment as moderators of teacher expectation effects. *Journal of Educational Psychology*, 76, 236–247.

Breakey, J. (1997) The role of diet and behaviour in childhood. *Journal of Paediatrics and Child Health*, 33, 190–194.

Breland, H. (1974) Birth order, family configuration, and verbal achievement. *Child Development*, 45, 1011–1019.

Bressoux, P. (1996) The effects of teachers' training on pupils' achievement: the case of elementary schools in France. *School Effectiveness and School Improvement*, 7, 252–279.

Brimer, A. (1972) *Wide-span Reading Test Manual*. London: Nelson.

Bristow, J., Cowley, P. and Daines, B. (1999) *Memory and Learning: A Practical Guide for Teachers*. London: David Fulton.

British Medical Association (1980) Dyslexia is not a medical problem. *BMA News Review*, January.

Broadbent, D. (1958) *Perception and Communication*. London: Pergamon.

Broadcasters' Audience Research Council (1995) Child's eye view. *Spectrum*, 17, 24.

Bronzaft, A. and McCarthy, D. (1975) The effect of elevated train noise on reading ability. *Environment and Behaviour*, 7, 517–527.

Brophy, J. (1981) Teacher praise: a functional analysis. *Review of Educational Research*, 51 (1), 5–32.

Brophy, J. and Evertson, C. (1976) *Learning from Teaching: A Developmental Perspective*. Boston: Allyn & Bacon.

Brophy, J. and Good, T. (1974) *Teacher–Student Relationships*. New York: Holt, Rinehart & Winston.

Brown, R. (1986) *Social Psychology*, 2nd edition. New York: Free Press.

Brown, R., Cazden, C. and Bellugi, U. (1969) The child's grammar from 1 to 3. In J. Hill (ed.) *Minnesota Symposium on Child Psychology (2)*. Minneapolis: University of Minnesota Press.

Brownell, C. (1988) Combinatorial skills: converging developments over the second year. *Child Development*, 59, 675–685.

Bruges, A. (1988) The outcome of language unit placement: a survey in Avon (1987). *Educational Psychology in Practice*, July, 86–90.

Bruner, J. (1957) Going beyond the information given. In *Contemporary Approaches to Cognition*. Cambridge, MA: Harvard University Press.

Bruner, J. (1961a) *The Process of Education*. Cambridge, MA: Harvard University Press.

Bruner, J. (1961b) The act of discovery. *Harvard Educational Review*, 31, 21–32.

Bruner, J. (1966a) On the conservation of liquids. In J. Bruner, R. Olver and P. Greenfield (eds) *Studies in Cognitive Growth*. New York: Wiley.

Bruner, J. (1966b) *Towards a Theory of Instruction*. Cambridge, MA: Harvard University Press.

Bruner, J., Olver, R., Greenfield, P. and collaborators (1966) *Studies in Cognitive Growth*. New York: Wiley.

Bruner, J. (1983) *Child's Talk: Learning to Use Language*. Oxford: Oxford University Press.

Bryant, P. (1994) Children's reading and writing. *The Psychologist*, 7 (2), 61.

Buchanan, L. and Besner, D. (1995) Reading aloud: evidence for the use of a whole word nonsemantic pathway. In J. Henderson, M. Murray Singer and F. Ferreira (eds) *Reading and Language Processing*. Hillsdale, NJ: Lawrence Erlbaum.

Budge, D. (1996a) Size does matter: medium is best. *Times Educational Supplement*, 19 April, p. 19.

Budge, D. (1996b) Special needs anomaly revealed. *Times Educational Supplement*, 13 September, p.17.

Burden, R. (1978) Schools' systems analysis: a project-centred approach. In B. Gillham (ed.) *Reconstructing Educational Psychology*. London: Croom Helm.

Burt, C. (1921) *Mental and Scholastic Tests*. London: King.

Butler, D. and Winne, P. (1995) Feedback and self-regulated learning: a theoretical synthesis. *Review of Educational Research*, 65 (3), 245–281.

Butler, R. (1988) Enhancing and undermining intrinsic motivation: the effects of task-involving and ego-involving evaluation on interest and performance. *British Journal of Educational Psychology*, 58, 1–14.

Bynner, J. and Parsons, S. (1997) *Does Numeracy Matter? Evidence from the National Child Development Study on the Impact of Poor Numeracy on Adult Life*. London: Basic Skills Agency.

Byrne, B. (1981) Deficient syntactic control in poor readers: is a weak phonetic memory code responsible? *Applied Psycholinguistics*, 2, 201–212.

Cahan, S. and Coren, N. (1989) Age versus schooling effects on intelligence. *Child Development*, 60, 1239–1249.

Cairns, R., Cairns, B., Neckerman, H., Ferguson, L. and Gariepy, J. (1989) Growth and aggression. 1. Childhood to early adolescence. *Developmental Psychology*, 25, 320–330.

Cameron, J. and Pierce, W. (1994) Reinforcement, reward and intrinsic motivation: a meta-analysis. *Review of Educational Research*, 64, 363–423.

Campbell, S. (1995) Behaviour problems in pre-school children: a review of recent research. *Journal of Child Psychology and Psychiatry*, 36 (1), 113–149.

Canter, L. and Canter, M. (1992) *Assertive Discipline*. Santa Monica, CA: Lee Canter Associates.

Caplan, N., Choy, M. and Whitmore, J. (1992) Indochinese refugee families and academic achievement. *Scientific American*, 266 (2), 18–24.

Carey, S. and Bartlett, E. (1978) Acquiring a single new word. *Papers and Reports on Child Language Development*, 15, 17–29.

Carmichael, L., Hogan, P. and Walter, A. (1932) An experimental study of the effect of language on the reproduction of visually perceived forms. *Journal of Experimental Psychology*, 15, 1–22.

Carroll, J. (1963) A model of school learning. *Teachers College Record*, 64, 723–733.

Carroll, J. (1993) *Human Cognitive Abilities: A Survey of Factor-Analytic Studies*. Cambridge: Cambridge University Press.

Carver, C. and Moseley, M. (1994) *Word Recognition and Phonic Skills Test*. London: Hodder & Stoughton.

Cashdan, A., Pumfrey, P. and Lunzer, E. (1971) Children receiving remedial teaching in reading. *Educational Research*, 13, 98–105.

Cassidy, S. (1999a) Pass marks 'fiddle' is strenuously denied. *Times Educational Supplement*, 4 June, p. 6.

Cassidy, S. (1999b) Inquiry discounts rigged test allegations. *Times Educational Supplement*, 16 July, p. 9.

Castellanos, F., Giedd, J., Marsh, W., Hamburger, S., Vaituzis, C., Dickstein, D., Sarfatti, S., Vauss, Y., Snell, J., Lange, N., Kaysey, D., Krain, A., Ritchie, G., Rajapakse, J. and Rapoport, J. (1996) Quantitative brain magnetic resonance imaging in attention-deficit hyperactivity disorder. *Archives of General Psychiatry*, 53, 607–616.

Cattell, R., Barton, K. and Dielman, T. (1972) Prediction of school achievement from motivation, personality, and ability measures. *Psychological Reports*, 30, 33–43.

Cattell, R. and Beloff, H. (1960) *The High School Personality Questionnaire*. Champaign, IL: IPAT.

Cattell, R. and Child, D. (1972) *Motivation and Dynamic Structure*. London: Holt, Rinehart & Winston.

Cattell, R., Eber, H. and Tatsuoka, M. (1970) *Handbook for the Sixteen Personality Factor Questionnaire (16PF)*. Champaign, IL: IPAT.

Cattell, R. and Horne, J. (1978) A check on the theory of fluid and crystallized intelligence with description of new subtest designs. *Journal of Educational Measurement*, 15, 139–164.

Cazden, C. (1965) Environmental assistance to the child's acquisition of grammar. Unpublished doctoral dissertation, Harvard University.

Ceci, S. (1990) *On Intelligence . . . More or Less: A Bioecological Treatise on Intellectual Development*. Englewood Cliffs, NJ: Prentice-Hall.

Chapman, J. and Tunmer, W. (1997) A longitudinal study of beginning reading achievement and reading self-concept. *British Journal of Educational Psychology*, 67, 279–291.

Charlton, T. and O'Bey, S. (1997) Links between television and behaviour: students' perceptions of TV's impact in St Helena, South Atlantic. *Support for Learning*, 12, 130–136.

Chazan, M., Laing, F. and Davies, D. (1994) *Emotional and Behavioural Difficulties in Middle Childhood*. London: Falmer Press.

Chen, Z., Yanowitz, K. and Daehler, M. (1995) Constraints on accessing abstract source information: instantiation of principles facilitates children's analogical transfer. *Journal of Educational Psychology*, 87, 445–454.

Chi, M. (1976) Short-term memory limitations in children: capacity or processing deficits? *Memory and Cognition*. 4, 559–572.

Chiang-Soong, B. and Yager, R (1993) Readability levels of the science textbooks most used in secondary schools. *School Science and Mathematics*, 93 (1), 24–27.

Children's Society (1998) *No Lessons Learned*. London: Children's Society.

Chisholm, B., Kearney, D., Knight, G., Little, H., Morris, S. and Tweddle, D. (1986) *Preventive Approaches to Disruption: Developing Teaching Skills*. London: Macmillan.

Chmielewski, T. and Dansereau, D. (1998) Enhancing the recall of text: knowledge mapping training promotes implicit transfer. *Journal of Educational Psychology*, 90, 407–413.

Chomsky, N. (1965) *Aspects of the Theory of Syntax*. Cambridge, MA: MIT Press.

Chorney, M., Chorney, K., Seese, N., Owen, M., Daniels, J., McGuffin, P., Thompson, L., Detterman, D., Benbow, C., Lubinski, D., Eley, T. and Plomin, R. (1998) A quantitative trait locus associated with cognitive ability in children. *Psychological Science*, 3, 159–166.

Claiborn, W. (1969) Expectancy effects in the classroom: a failure to replicate. *Journal of Educational Psychology*, 60, 377–383.

Clark, C., Dyson, A., Millward, A. and Robson, S. (1999) Theories of inclusion, theories of schools: deconstructing and reconstructing the 'inclusive school'. *British Educational Research Journal*, 25, 157–177.

Clark, E. (1973) What's in a word? On the child's first acquisition of semantics in his first language. In T. Moore (ed.) *Cognitive Development and the Development of Language*. London: Academic Press.

Clark, R. (1983) *Family Life and School Achievement. Why Poor Black Children Succeed or Fail*. Chicago: University of Chicago Press.

Clarke, A. M. and Clarke, A. D. (1974) Genetic–environmental interactions in cognitive development. In A. M. Clarke and A. D. Clarke (eds) *Mental Deficiency*. London: Methuen.

Clay, M. (1985) *The Early Detection of Reading Difficulties*. London: Heinemann.

Cleare, A. and Wessely, S. (1996) Chronic fatigue syndrome: a stress disorder? *British Journal of Hospital Medicine*, 55, 571–574.

Clegg, A. and Megson, B. (1968) *Children in Distress*. Harmondsworth: Penguin Books.

Clift, P. (1970) Factors affecting the growth of reading skills in children aged 8–9 years who are backward in reading. M.Ed. thesis, University of Manchester.

Closs, S. (1977) *APU Vocabulary Test: Instruction Manual*. Sevenoaks: Hodder & Stoughton.

CLPE (1989) *Testing Reading*. London: Centre for Language in Primary Education.

Cockburn, J. (1961) Psychological and Educational Aspects. In J. Henderson (ed.) *Cerebral Palsy in Childhood and Adolescence*. Edinburgh: E. & S. Livingstone.

Coe, R. and Fitz-Gibbon, C. (1998) School effectiveness research: criticisms and recommendations. *Oxford Review of Education*, 24, 421– 438.

Cohen, L. (1976) *Educational Research in Classrooms and Schools*. London: Harper & Row.

Cohen, L., Manion, L. and Morrison, K. (2000) *Research Methods in Education*. 5th edition. London: RoutledgeFalmer.

Cohen, S., Tyrrell, D. and Smith, A. (1991) Psychological stress and susceptibility to the common cold. *New England Journal of Medicine*, 325, 606–612.

Coie, J. and Dodge, K. (1983) Continuities and changes in children's social status: a five-year longitudinal study. *Merrill-Palmer Quarterly*, 29, 261–282.

Coleman, J., Campbell, E., Hobson, C., McPartland, J., Mood, A., Weinfeld, F. and York, R. (1966) *Equality of Educational Opportunity*. Washington, DC: US Government Printing Office.

Collins, A. and Quillian, M. (1969) Retrieval time for semantic memory. *Journal of Verbal Learning and Verbal Behaviour*, 8, 240–247.

Collins, A. and Stevens, A. (1982) Goals and strategies of inquiry teachers. In R. Glaser (ed.) *Advances in Instructional Psychology*, vol. 2. Hillsdale, NJ: Lawrence Erlbaum.

Coltheart, M. (1978) Lexical access in simple reading tasks. In G. Underwood (ed.) *Strategies of Information Processing*. London: Academic Press.

Connell, R. (1989) Cool guys, swots and wimps: the interplay of masculinity and education. *Oxford Review of Education*, 15, 291–303.

Conners, C. (1973) Rating scales for use in drug studies in children. *Psychopharmacology Bulletin*, special issue: *Pharmacotherapy of Children*, 24–29.

Conrad, R. (1977) The reading ability of deaf school-leavers. *British Journal of Educational Psychology*, 47, 60–65.

Conrad, R. (1979) *The Deaf School Child*. London: Harper & Row.

Cooper, H. (1983) Teacher expectation effects. In L. Bickman (ed.) *Applied Social Psychology Annual*, 4. London: Sage.

Cooper, H., Nye, B., Charlton, K., Lindsay, K. and Greathouse, S. (1996) The effects of summer vacation on achievement test scores: a narrative and meta-analytic review. *Review of Educational Research*, 66 (3), 227–268.

Coopers & Lybrand (1996) *The SEN Initiative: Managing Budgets for Pupils with Special Educational Needs*. London: Coopers & Lybrand.

Coopersmith, S. (1967) *The Antecedents of Self-Esteem*. San Francisco: Freeman.

Cordova, D. and Lepper, M. (1996) Intrinsic motivation and the process of learning: beneficial effects of contextualisation, personalisation, and choice. *Journal of Educational Psychology*, 88, 715–730.

Coren, A. (1997) *A Psychodynamic Approach to Education*. London: Sheldon Press.

Cornwall, K. and France, N. (1997a) *Macmillan Group Reading Test (Revised)*. Slough: NFER-Nelson.

Cornwall, K. and France, N. (1997b) *NFER-Nelson Group Reading Test*, 2nd edition. NFER-Nelson.

Cotterell, J. (1984) Effects of school architectural design on student and teacher anxiety. *Environment and Behaviour*, 16, 455–479.

Covington, M. and Crutchfield, R. (1965) Experiments in the use of programmed instruction for the facilitation of creative problem solving. *Programmed Instruction*, 4.

Craske, M. (1988) Learned helplessness, self-worth motivation and attribution retraining for primary school children. *British Journal of Educational Psychology*, 58, 152–164.

Creemers, B. and Reezigt, G. (1996) School level conditions affecting the effectiveness of instruction. *School Effectiveness and School Improvement*, 7, 197–228.

Crispin, L., Hamilton, W. and Trickey, G. (1984) The relevance of visual sequential memory to reading. *British Journal of Educational Psychology*, 54 (1), 24–30.

Crocker, A. (1974) *Predicting Teaching Success*. Slough: NFER.

Croll, P. and Moses, D. (1990) Sex roles in the primary classroom. In C. Rogers and P. Kutnick (eds) *The Social Psychology of the Primary School*. London: Routledge.

Crooks, T. (1988) The impact of classroom evaluation practices on students. *Review of Educational Research*, 58, 438–481.

Crowne, D. and Marlowe, D. (1964) *The Approval Motive: Studies in Evaluative Dependence*. New York: Wiley.

Crowther, D., Dyson, A. and Millward, A. (1998) *Costs and Outcomes for Pupils with Moderate Learning Difficulties in Special and Mainstream Schools*. Research Report RR89. Sudbury, Suffolk: DfEE Publications.

Crozier, W. (1997) *Individual Learners: Personality Differences in Education*. London: Routledge.

Csikszentmihalyi, M. (1975) *Beyond Boredom and Anxiety*. San Francisco: Jossey-Bass.

Cuckle, P. (1997) The school placement of pupils with Down's syndrome in England and Wales. *British Journal of Special Education*, 24 (4), 175–179.

Cumberbatch, G. (1991) Is television violence harmful? In R. Cochrane and D. Carroll (eds) *Psychology and Social Issues*. London: Falmer Press.

Dabbs, J. and Morris, R. (1990) Testosterone, social class, and antisocial behaviour in a sample of 4,462 men. *Psychological Science*, 1, 209–211.

Dale, E. and Chall, J. (1948) A formula for predicting readability. *Educational Research Bulletin*, 27, 11–20.

Daneman, M. and Stainton, M. (1991) Phonological recoding in silent reading. *Journal of Experimental Psychology: Learning, Memory and Cognition*, 17, 618–632.

Daniels, S. (1995) Can pre-school education affect children's achievement in primary school? *Oxford Review of Education*, 21 (2), 163–178.

Davie, R., Butler, N. and Goldstein, H. (1972) *From Birth to Seven*. London: Longman.

Davies, B. (1989) The discursive production of the male/female dualism in school settings. *Oxford Review of Education*, 15 (3), 229–241.

Davies, J. (1999) Standards in mathematics in Year 6: what do the Key Stage 2 tests tell us? *Educational Psychology*, 19 (1), 71–77.

Davies, J. and Brember, L. (1992) The ethnic composition of nursery classes and its effect on children's adjustment to nursery. *Educational Psychology*, 12 (1), 25–33.

Davies, J. and Brember, L. (1994) The first mathematics standard assessment tasks at Key Stage 1: issues raised by a five school study. *British Educational Research Journal*, 20 (1), 35–40.

Davies, P. and Williams, P. (1975) *Aspects of Early Reading Growth*. Oxford: Blackwell.

de Bono, E. (1970) *Lateral Thinking: A Textbook of Creativity*. London: Ward Lock Educational.

Dean, C. and Rafferty, F. (1996) Survey concludes size does matter. *Times Educational Supplement*, 31 May, p. 4.

Dearing, R. (1996) *Review of Qualifications for 16 to 19 Year Olds*. Middlesex: SCAA Publications.

Deaux, K. and Wrightsman, L. (1988) *Social Psychology*, 5th edition. Pacific Grove, CA: Brooks/Cole.

DECP (1999) *Dyslexia, Literacy and Psychological Assessment*. Leicester: British Psychological Society.

DeHirsch, K., Jansky, J. and Langford, W. (1966) *Predicting Reading Failure*. New York: Harper & Row.

Delethes, P. and Jackson, B. (1972) Teacher–pupil interaction as a function of location in the classroom. *Psychology in the Schools*, 9, 119–123.

Dempster, F. (1981) Memory span: sources of individual and developmental differences. *Psychological Bulletin*, 89, 63–100.

Denham, C. and Lieberman, A. (eds) (1980) *Time to Learn*. Washington, DC: National Institute of Education.

DES (1962) *The Report of the Chief Medical Officer, 1960–1*. London: Department of Education and Science.

DES (1985) *Education for All: Report of the Committee of Inquiry into the Education of Children from Ethnic Minority Groups* ('The Swan Report'). Cmnd 9453. London: HMSO.

Desforges, C. (1995) How does experience affect theoretical knowledge for teaching? *Learning and Instruction*, 5, 385–400.

DFE (1994a) *Statistical Bulletin Issue 10/94*. London: HMSO.

DFE (1994b) *Code of Practice on the Identification and Assessment of Special Educational Needs*. London: DFE.

DFE (1995a) *Statistics of Education*. London: HMSO.

DFE (1995b) *The National Curriculum*. London: HMSO.

DfEE (1994) *Bullying: Don't Suffer in Silence. An Anti-bullying Pack for Schools*. London: HMSO.

DfEE (1996a) *Results of the 1995 National Curriculum assessments of 11 year olds in England*. London: Department for Education and Employment.

DfEE (1996b) *205/96 Statistics of Schools in England*. London: DfEE.

DfEE (1997a) *158/97 Statistics of Schools in England*. London: DfEE.

DfEE (1997b) *Excellence for All Children; Meeting Special Educational Needs*. London: The Stationary Office.

DfEE (1997c) *Excellence in Schools*. London: The Stationery Office.

DfEE (1997d) GCSE/GNVQ and GCE A/AS examination results for young people in England, 1996/7. Press release 386/97.

DfEE (1998a) *Autumn Package of Pupil Performance Information*. London: DfEE.

DfEE (1998b) Blunkett welcomes literacy boost and details plans to improve maths teaching. Press release 463/98.

DfEE (1998c) *Circular 10/98. Section 550A of the Education Act 1996: The Use of Force to Control or Restrain Pupils*. London: HMSO.

DfEE (1998d) *Education and Training Statistics for the United Kingdom 1998*. London: HMSO.

DfEE (1998e) GCSE/GNVQ and GCE A/AS/ADVANCED GNVQ results for young people in England, 1997/98 (provisional), Press release 557/98.

DfEE (1998f) *Meeting Special Educational Needs: A Programme of Action*. London: The Stationary Office.

DfEE (1998g) *Statistical Bulletin, Special Educational Needs in England: January 1997*. London: The Stationery Office.

DfEE (1998h) *Statistical Bulletin, Survey of Information and Communications Technology in Schools, 11/98*. London: The Stationery Office.

DfEE (1998i) *Statistics of Education, Public Examinations*

GCSE/GNVQ and GCE in England 1997. London: The Stationery Office.

DfEE (1998j) *Statistics of Education, Schools in England, 1998*. London: The Stationery Office.

DfEE (1998k) Statistics of schools in England – January 1998 (Provisional). Press release, 311.98.

DfEE (1998l) *Teachers: Meeting the Challenge of Change*. London: HMSO.

DfEE (1998m) *The Implementation of the National Numeracy Strategy*. London: DfEE.

DfEE (1998n) *The National Literacy Strategy; Framework for Teaching*. London: Department for Education and Employment.

DfEE (1999a) Blunkett congratulates primary heads and teachers on significant boost in test results for 11-year-olds. Press release, 408/99.

DfEE (1999b) Blunkett welcomes 3 per cent drop in school exclusions. Press release, 272/99.

DfEE (1999c) Boys narrow results gap in reading and writing. Press release, 436/99.

DfEE (1999d) *Social Inclusion: Pupil Support*. Circular 10/99. London: HMSO.

DfEE (1999e) *Statistical Bulletin, Youth Cohort Study: The Activities and Experiences of 16 year olds: England and Wales 1998*. London: The Stationery Office.

DfEE (1999f) *Statistical First Release. Special Educational Needs in England: January 1999*. SFR 10/1999.

DfEE (1999g) *Statistical First Release*. GCSE *GCSE/GNVQ and GCE A/AS/Advanced GNVQ Results for Young People in England, 1998/99*. SFR 31/1999.

DfEE (2000) *Statistical First Release. Class Sizes in Maintained Schools in England. January 2000*. SFR 15/2000.

Digest of Education Statistics (1995) Washington, DC: US Government Printing Office.

Dipboye, R. (1989) Threats to the incremental validity of interviewer judgements. In R. Eder and G. Ferris (eds) *The Employment Interview*. London: Sage.

Dockerell, B. (1995) Assessment, teaching and learning. In C. Forges (ed.) *An Introduction to Teaching*. Oxford: Blackwell.

Dockrell, J. and Messer, D. (1999) *Children's Language and Communication Difficulties*. London: Cassell Education.

Dodge, K., Petitt, G., McClaskey, C. and Brown, M. (1986) Social competence in children. *Monographs for the Society for Research in Child Development*, 51 (2).

Dollard, J., Doob, L., Miller, N., Mowrer, O. and Sears, R. (1939) *Frustration and Aggression*. New Haven, CT: Yale University Press.

Dowling, E. (1985) Theoretical framework: a joint systems approach to educational problems with children. In E. Dowling and E. Osborne (eds) *The Family and the School*. London: Routledge & Kegan Paul.

Dowse, E. and Colby, J. (1997) Long-term sickness absence due to ME/CFS in UK schools: an epidemiological study with medical and educational implications. *Journal of Chronic Fatigue Syndrome*, 3, 29–42.

Drew, D. and Gray, J. (1990) The fifth year examination achievements of Black young people in England and Wales. *Educational Research*, 32 (3), 107–117.

DSM-IV (1994) *American Psychiatric Association: Diagnostic and Statistical Manual of Mental Disorders*, 4th edition. Washington, DC: American Psychiatric Association.

Duncker, K. (1945) On problem-solving. *Psychological Monographs*, 58 (5), no. 270.

Dunn, J. (1984) Changing minds and changing relationships. In C. Lewis and P. Mitchell (eds) *Children's Early Understanding of Mind: Origins and Development*. Hove, East Sussex: Lawrence Erlbaum.

Dunn, J. and McGuire, S. (1992) Sibling and peer relationships in childhood. *Journal of Child Psychology and Psychiatry*, 33, 1, 67–105.

Dunn, L. (1968) Special education for the mildly retarded: is much of it justifiable? *Exceptional Children*, 35, 5–22.

Dunn, L., Dunn, L., Whetton, C. and Burley, J. (1997) *The British Picture Vocabulary Scale*, 2nd edition. Slough: NFER-Nelson.

Dunn, L., Horton, K. and Smith, J. (1968) *The Peabody Language Development Kit*. Circle Pines, MN: American Service.

Dweck, C. (1975) The role of expectations and attributions in the alleviation of learned helplessness. *Journal of Personality and Social Psychology*, 31, 674–685.

Dweck, C. (1986) Motivational processes affecting learning. *American Psychologist*, 41, 1040–1048.

Dweck, C. (1999) *Self Theories: Their Role in Motivation, Personality and Development*. Hove, East Sussex: Psychology Press.

Eaves, L., Silberg, J., Meyer, J., Maes, H., Simonoff, E., Pickles, A., Rutter, M., Reynolds, C., Heath, A., Truett, K., Neale, M., Erikson, M., Loeber, R. and Hewitt, J. (1997) Genetics and developmental psychopathology. 2. The main effects of genes and environment on behavioral problems in the Virginia twin study of adolescent behavioral development.

Journal of Child Psychology and Psychiatry, 38 (8), 965–980.

Echols, L., Stanovich, K., West, R., and Zehr, K. (1996) Using children's literacy activities to predict growth in verbal cognitive skills: a longitudinal investigation. *Journal of Educational Psychology*, 88 (2), 296–304.

Eckblad, G. (1981) *Scheme Theory*. London: Academic Press.

Effective Reading Tests (1985) Macmillan/NFER-Nelson.

Egan, D. and Greeno, J. (1974) Theories of rule induction: knowledge acquired in concept learning, serial pattern learning and problem solving. In W. Gregg (ed.) *Knowledge and Cognition*. Hillsdale, NJ: Lawrence Erlbaum.

Elliott, A. and Hewison, J. (1994) Comprehension and interest in home reading. *British Journal of Educational Psychology*, 64, 203–220.

Elliott, C., Smith, P. and McCulloch, K. (1996) *British Ability Scales II*. Windsor: NFER-Nelson.

Ellis, A. McDougall, S. and Monk, A. (1996) Are dyslexics different? Individual differences among dyslexics, reading age controls, poor readers and precocious readers. *Dyslexia*, 2, 59–68.

Ellis, N. (1990) Reading, phonological skills and short-term memory: interactive tributaries of development. *Journal of Research in Reading*, 13, 107–122.

Ellis, N. and Cataldo, S. (1990) The role of spelling in learning to read. *Language and Education*, 4, 1–28.

Elman, J. (1991) Distributed representations, simple recurrent networks, and grammatical structure. In D. Touretzky (ed.) *Connectionist Approaches to Language Learning*. Dordrecht: Kluwer.

Entwistle, N. (1972) Personality and academic achievement. *British Journal of Educational Psychology*, 42, 137–151.

Equal Opportunities Commission (1995) *Men and Women in Britain*. London: HMSO.

Eron, L. (1982) Parent–child interaction, television violence and aggression of children. *American Psychologist*, 37, 197–211.

Evans, E. and Waites, B. (1981) *IQ and Mental Testing*. London: Macmillan.

Evans, G. and Lovell, B. (1979) Design modification in an open-plan school. *Journal of Educational Psychology*, 71 (1), 41–49.

Eysenck, H. and Cookson, D. (1969) Personality in primary school children. *British Journal of Educational Psychology*, 40, 117–131.

Eysenck, H. and Eysenck, S. (1975) *Manual of the Eysenck Personality Questionnaire (Junior and Adult)*. Sevenoaks: Hodder & Stoughton.

Eysenck, H. and Kamin, L. (1981) *The Intelligence Controversy*. New York: Wiley-Interscience.

Eysenck, M. (1979) Depth, elaboration and distinctiveness. In L. Cermak and F. Craik (eds) *Levels of Processing in Human Memory*. Hillsdale, NJ: Lawrence Erlbaum.

Eysenck, M. and Keane, M. (1995) *Cognitive Psychology*. London: Lawrence Erlbaum.

Farrell, M. (1997) *The Special Education Handbook*. London: David Fulton.

Farrell, P., McBrien, J. and Foxen, T. (1992) *EDY: Teaching people with severe learning difficulties*, 2nd edition. Manchester: Manchester University Press.

Farrington, D. (1978) The family backgrounds of aggressive youths. In L. Hersov, M. Berger and D. Shaffer (eds) *Aggression and Anti-social Behaviour in Childhood and Adolescence*. Oxford: Pergamon Press.

Feingold, A. (1988) Cognitive gender differences are disappearing. *American Psychologist*, 43, 95–103.

Feingold, B. (1975) Hyperkinesis and learning disabilities linked to artificial food flavors and colors. *American Journal of Nursing*, 75, 797–803.

Feingold, B. (1976) *Why Your Child Is Hyperactive*. New York: Random House.

Fergusson, D. and Lynskey, M. (1997) Early reading difficulties and later conduct problems. *Journal of Child Psychology and Psychiatry*, 38 (8), 899–907.

Fergusson, D., Lynskey, M. and Horwood, J. (1997) Attentional difficulties in middle childhood and psychosocial outcomes in young adulthood. *Journal of Child Psychology and Psychiatry*, 38, 633–644.

Ferreira, F. and Henderson, J. (1995) Reading processes during syntactic analysis and reanalysis. In J. Henderson, M. Singer and F. Ferreira (eds) *Reading and Language Processing*. Hove, East Sussex: Lawrence Erlbaum.

Festinger, L. (1957) *A Theory of Cognitive Dissonance*. Evanston, IL: Row Peterson.

Fisher, C., Berliner, D., Filby, N., Mariave, R., Cahen, L. and Dishaw, M. (1980) Teaching behaviours, academic learning time, and student achievement: an overview. In C. Denham and A. Lieberman (eds) *Time to Learn*. Washington, DC: National Institute of Education.

Fisher, J. and Byrne, D. (1975) Too close for comfort: sex differences in response to invasions of personal space. *Journal of Personality and Social Psychology*, 32, 15–21.

Fisher, P. (1996) Long odds on survival. *Times Educational Supplement*, 2 February, p. 7.

Fiske, R., Ward, T. and Smith, S. (1992) *Creative Cognition: Theory, Research and Applications*. Cambridge, MA: MIT Press.

Flanders, N. (1970) *Analyzing Teacher Behavior*. Reading, MA: Addison Wesley.

Fleming, M. and Chambers, B. (1983) Teacher-made tests: windows on the classroom. In W. Hathaway (ed.) *New Directions for Testing and Measurement*, vol. 19, *Testing in the Schools*. San Francisco: Jossey-Bass.

Fletcher, J., Shaywitz, S., Shankweiler, D., Katz, L., Liberman, I., Steubing, K., Francis, D., Fowler, A. and Shaywitz, B. (1994) Cognitive profiles of reading disability: comparisons of discrepancy and low achievement definitions. *Journal of Educational Psychology*, 86 (1), 6–23.

Flynn, J. (1984) The mean I.Q. of Americans: massive gains 1932–1978. *Psychological Bulletin*, 95, 29–51.

Folkard, S., Monk, T., Bradbury, R. and Rosenthal, J. (1977) Time of day effects in school children's immediate and delayed recall of meaningful material. *British Journal of Psychology*, 68, 45–50.

Forge, K. and Phemeister, S. (1987) The effect of prosocial cartoons on preschool children. *Child Study Journal*, 17, 83–88.

Forrester, M. (1996) *Psychology of Language: A Critical Introduction*. London: Sage.

Foster, P., Gomm, R. and Hammersley, M. (1996) *Constructing Educational Inequality*. London: Falmer Press.

Foucault, M. (1978) *Power and Knowledge: Selected Interviews and Other Writings, 1972–1977*, ed. C. Gordon, C. and trans. C. Gordon, L. Marshall, J. Mepham and K. Soper. New York: Pantheon Books.

France, N. (1979) *Primary Reading Test*. Windsor: NFER-Nelson.

Fraser, B. (1986) *Classroom Environment*. London: Croom Helm.

Frazier, L. and Fodor, J. (1978) The sausage machine: a new two-stage parsing model. *Cognition*, 6, 291–325.

Frederickson, N. (ed.) (1995) *Phonological Assessment Battery, Research Edition*. London: University College.

Freedman, J., Klevansky, S. and Ehrlich, P. (1971) The effect of crowding on human task performance. *Journal of Applied Social Psychology*, 1, 7–25.

Freeman, J. (1991) *Gifted Children Growing Up*. London: Cassell.

Freeman, J. (1998) *Educating the Very Able: Current International Research*. London: The Stationery Office.

Freud, A. (1964) *The Psychoanalytic Treatment of Children*. New York: Schocken.

Freyberg, P. (1970) The concurrent validity of two types of spelling test. *British Journal of Educational Psychology*, 40, 68–71.

Frisch, H. (1977) Sex stereotypes in adult–infant play. *Child Development*, 48, 1671–1675.

Frith, U. (1989) *Autism: Explaining the Enigma*. Oxford: Blackwell.

Frostig, M. and Horne, D. (1964) *The Frostig Programme for the Development of Visual Perception: Teacher's Guide*. Palo Alto, CA: Consulting Psychologists Press.

Fry, E. (1968) A readability formula that saves time. *Journal of Reading*, 11, 513–516.

Fry, E. (1977) *Elementary Reading Instruction*. New York: McGraw-Hill.

Fuchs, L. and Fuchs, D. (1986) Effects of systematic formative evaluation: a meta-analysis. *Exceptional Children*, 53, 199–208.

Fuerstein, R., Rand, Y., Hoffman, M. and Miller, R. (1980) *Instrumental Enrichment*. Baltimore, MD: University Press.

Fuller, M. (1980) Black girls in a London comprehensive school. In R. Deem, (ed.) *Schooling for Women's Work*. London: Routledge.

Funding Agency for Schools (1998) *Cost and Performance Comparisons for Grant-Maintained Schools*. York: Funding Agency for Schools.

Fundudis, T., Kolvin, I. and Garside, R. (1979) *Speech Retarded and Deaf Children: Their Psychological Development*. London: Academic Press.

Fusaro, J. (1988) Applying statistical rigor to a validation of the Fry readability graph. *Reading Research and Instruction*, 28, 44–48.

Gagné, R. (1965) *The Conditions of Learning*. New York: Holt, Rinehart & Winston.

Gagné, R., Brigg, L. and Wagner, W. (1988) *Principles of Instructional Design*. New York: Holt, Rinehart & Winston.

Galaburda, A. (1991) Anatomy of dyslexia: argument against phrenology. In D. Duane and D. Gray (eds) *The Reading Brain: The Biological Basis of Dyslexia*. Parkton, MD: York Press.

Galloway, D. (1976) Size of school, socio-economic hardship, suspension rates and persistent unjustified absence from school. *British Journal of Educational Psychology*, 46, 40–47.

Galloway, D. (1982) A study of persistent absentees

and their families. *British Journal of Educational Psychology*, 52, 317–330.

Galton, M., Simon, B. and Croll, P. (1980) *Inside the Primary Classroom*. London: Routledge & Kegan Paul.

Galton, M., Hargreaves, L., Comber, C., Wall, D. and Pell, A. (1999) *Inside the Primary Classroom: 20 Years On*. London: Routledge.

Galvin, P. and Costa, P. (1994) Building better behaved schools: effective support at the whole-school level. In P. Gray, A. Miller and J. Noakes (eds) *Challenging Behaviour in Schools*. London: Routledge.

Galvin, P., Mercer, S. and Costa, P. (1990) *Building a Better Behaved School*. Harlow: Longman.

Gapadol Reading Comprehension Test (1973) London: Heinemann Education.

Gardner, H. (1983) *Frames of Mind: The Theory of Multiple Intelligence*. New York: Basic Books.

Gavienas, E. (1997) Seating arrangements for group teaching in the primary classroom: a study of the relationship between the group teaching strategies teachers employ and the kind of tasks they provide for pupils. Paper presented at the Scottish Educational Research Association Annual Conference, September.

Gay, L. (1973) Temporal position of reviews and its effect on the retention of mathematical rules. *Journal of Educational Psychology*, 64, 171–182.

Geen, R. (1968) Effects of frustration, attack and prior training in aggressiveness upon aggressive behaviour. *Journal of Personality and Social Psychology*, 9, 316–321.

Getzels, J. and Jackson, P. (1962) *Creativity and Intelligence*. New York: Wiley.

Gewirtz, S. (1998) Can all schools be successful? An exploration of the determinants of school 'success'. *Oxford Review of Education*, 24, 439–457.

Ghouri, N. (1998) Literacy guru goes her own way. *Times Educational Supplement*, 26 June, p. 3.

Gibson, A. and Asthana, S. (1998) Schools, pupils and examination results: contextualising school 'performance'. *British Educational Research Journal*, 24 (3), 269–282.

Gibson, E. and Levin, H. (1975) *The Psychology of Reading*. Cambridge, MA: MIT Press.

Giles, D. and Terrell, C. (1997) Visual sequential memory and spelling ability. *Educational Psychology*, 17 (3), 245–253.

Gill, C., Jardine, R. and Martin, N. (1985) Further evidence for genetic influences on educational achievement. *British Journal of Educational Psychology*, 55, 240–250.

Gill, D., Mayor, B. and Blair, M. (eds) (1992) *Racism and Education: Structures and Strategies*. London: Sage.

Gillberg, C. (1989) Asperger syndrome – some epidemiological considerations: a research note. *Journal of Child Psychology and Psychiatry*, 30 (4), 631–638.

Gillborn, D. (1990) *'Race', Ethnicity and Education: Teaching and Learning in Multi-ethnic Schools*. London: Unwin Hyman/Routledge.

Gillborn, D. and Gipps, C. (1996) *Recent Research on the Achievements of Ethnic Minority Pupils*. London: HMSO.

Gillham, B. (1981) *Problem Behaviour in the Secondary School*. London: Croom Helm.

Gipps, C. and Murphy, P. (1994) *A Fair Test? Assessment, Achievement and Equity*. Buckingham: Open University Press.

Gipps, C. and Stobart, G. (1990) *Assessment: A Teacher's Guide to the Issues*. London: Hodder & Stoughton.

Gipps, C., Steadman, S., Blackstone, T. and Stierer, B. (1983) *Testing Children: Standardised Testing in Schools and LEAs*. London: Heinemann Educational Books.

Glaser, B. and Strauss, A. (1967) *The Discovery of Grounded Theory*. Chicago: Aldine.

Goffman, E. (1959) *The Presentation of Self in Everyday Life*. Harmondsworth: Penguin.

Gold, K. (1995) Hard times for Britain's lost boys. *New Scientist*, 145, 12–13.

Goldfield, B. and Reznick, J. (1990) Early lexical acquisition: rate, content, and the vocabulary spurt. *Journal of Child Language*, 17, 171–183.

Goldstein, H. (1995) *Multilevel Statistical Models*. London: Arnold.

Goldstein, H., Huiqi, P., Rath, T. and Hill, N. (2000) *The use of value added information in judging school performance*. London: Institute of Education.

Good, T. and Brophy, J. (1977) *Educational Psychology*. New York: Holt, Rinehart & Winston.

Good, T. and Brophy, J. (1978) Teachers' expectations as self-fulfilling prophecies. In H. Clarizio, R. Craig and W. Mehrens (eds) *Contemporary Issues in Educational Psychology*. Boston: Allyn & Bacon.

Good, T. and Grouws, D. (1977) Teaching effects: a process–product study in fourth grade mathematics classrooms. *Journal of Teacher Education*, 28, 49–54.

Good, T. and Grouws, D. (1979) The Missouri Mathematics Effectiveness Project: an experimental study in fourth-grade classrooms. *Journal of Educational Psychology*, 71, 355–362.

Goodacre, E. (1979) What is reading: which model? In M. Raggett, C. Tutt and P. Raggett (eds) *Assessment and Testing of Reading*. London: Ward Lock.

Goodman, K. (1968) *The Psycholinguistic Nature of the Reading Process*. Detroit: Wayne State University Press.

Goodman, K. (1986) Basal readers: a call for action. *Language Arts*, 63, 4.

Gorard, S. (1998) Four errors . . . and a conspiracy? The effectiveness of schools in Wales. *Oxford Review of Education*, 24, 459–472.

Gotlib, I. and Hammon, C. (1992) *Psychological Aspects of Depression*. Chichester: Wiley.

Gottfried, A., Fleming, J. and Gottfried, A. (1994). Role of parental motivational practices in children's academic intrinsic motivation and achievement. *Journal of Educational Psychology*, 86 (1), 104–113.

Gottlieb, M., Zinkus, P. and Thompson, A. (1980) Chronic middle ear disease and auditory perceptual deficits. *Clinical Paediatrics*, 18, 725–732.

Graesser, A., Singer, M. and Trabasso, T. (1994) Constructing inferences during narrative text comprehension. *Psychological Review*, 101, 371–395.

Gray, J. (1975) *Elements of a Two-Process Theory of Learning*. London: Academic Press.

Gray, J. (1979) Reading progress in English infant schools: some problems emerging from a study of teacher effectiveness. *British Educational Research Journal*, 5, 141–157.

Gray, P., Miller, A. and Noakes, J. (eds) (1994) *Challenging Behaviour in Schools: Teacher Support, Practical Techniques and Policy Development*. London: Routledge.

Greenfield, P. (1998) The cultural evolution, In U. Neisser (ed.) *The Rising Curve*. Washington, DC: American Psychological Association.

Gregory, R. (1970) *The Intelligent Eye*. London: Weidenfeld & Nicolson.

Gresham, F. (1984) Behavioural interviews in school psychology: issues in psychometric adequacy and research. *School Psychology Review*, 13, 17–25.

Grissmer, D., Williamson, S., Kirby, S. and Berends, M. (1998) Exploring the rapid rise in black achievement scores in the United States (1970–1990). In U. Neisser (ed.) *The Rising Curve*. Washington, DC: American Psychological Association.

Guilford, J. (1950) Creativity. *American Psychologist*, 5, 444–454.

Hackett, G. (1998) An ordeal that still upsets teachers. *Times Educational Supplement*, 20 November, p. 9.

Haddon, F. and Lytton, H. (1968) Teaching approach and the development of divergent thinking abilities in primary schools. *British Journal of Educational Psychology*, 38, 171–180.

Hall, E. (1966) *The Hidden Dimension*. New York: Doubleday.

Hall, V., Chiarello, K. and Edmondson, B. (1996) Deciding where knowledge comes from depends on where you look. *Journal of Educational Psychology*, 88 (2), 305–313.

Hallam, S. (1999) Set to see a rise in standards. *Times Educational Supplement*, 23 July, p. 19.

Hammill, D. and Larsen, S. (1978) The effectiveness of psycholinguistic training: a reaffirmation of the position. *Exceptional Children*, 44, 402–414.

Haney, C., Banks, C. and Zimbardo, P. (1973) Interpersonal dynamics in a simulated prison. *International Journal of Criminology and Penology*, 1, 69–97.

Hansford, B. and Hattie, J. (1982) The relationship between self and achievement/performance measures. *Review of Educational Research*, 52, 123–142.

Haralambos, M. and Holborn, M. (1995) *Sociology: Themes and Perspectives*. London: Collins Educational.

Harding, L., Beech, J. and Sneddon, W. (1985) The changing pattern of reading errors and reading style from 5 to 11 years of age. *British Journal of Educational Psychology*, 55, 45–52.

Hardyck, C. and Petrinovich, L. (1970) Subvocal speech and comprehension level as a function of the difficulty level of reading material. *Journal of Verbal Learning and Verbal Behaviour*, 9, 647–652.

Hargreaves, D. (1967) *Social Relations in a Secondary School*. London: Routledge & Kegan Paul.

Harley, T. (1995) *The Psychology of Language: From Data to Theory*. Hove, East Sussex: Psychology Press.

Harris, J. (1984) Teaching children to develop language: the impossible dream? In D. Muller (ed.) *Remediating Children's Language*. London: Croom Helm.

Harris, R. (1965) The only disturbing feature . . . *Use of English*, 16, 197–202. [Summary of research in: An experimental enquiry into the functions and value of formal grammar in the teaching of English, with special reference to the teaching of correct written English to children aged twelve to fourteen. Unpublished Ph.D. thesis, University of London, 1962.]

Harris, R. (1978) Relationship between EEG abnormality and aggressive and anti-social behaviour: a critical approach. In L. Hersov, M. Berger and D. Shaffer (eds) *Aggression and Anti-social Behaviour in Childhood and Adolescence*. Oxford: Pergamon.

Harrison, M. (1992) Information technology (IT): using computers as a tool. In G. Verma and P. Pumfrey (eds) *Cultural Diversity and the Curriculum*, vol. 4. London: Falmer Press.

Harrop, A. and Williams, T. (1992) Rewards and punishments in the primary school: pupils' perceptions and teachers' usage. *Educational Psychology in Practice*, 7 (4), 211–215.

Hart, B. and Risley, T. (1995) *Meaningful Differences in Everyday Parenting and Intellectual Development in Young American Children*. Baltimore: Brookes.

Hasan, P. and Butcher, H. (1966) Creativity and intelligence: a partial replication with Scottish children of Getzels and Jackson's study. *British Journal of Educational Psychology*, 57, 129–135.

Hatcher, P. (1994) *Sound Linkage: An Integrated Programme for Overcoming Reading Difficulties*. London: Whurr.

Hatcher, P., Hulme, C. and Ellis, A. (1994) Ameliorating early reading failure by integrating the teaching of reading and phonological skills: the phonological linkage hypothesis. *Child Development*, 65, 41–57.

Hattie, J., Marsh, H., Neill, J. and Richards, G. (1997) Adventure education and outward bound: out-of-class experiences that make a lasting difference. *Journal of Educational Research*, 67 (1), 43–87.

Hay, I., Ashman, A. and van Kraayenoord, C. (1997) Investigating the influence of achievement on self-concept using an intra-class design and a comparison of the PASS and SDQ-1 self-concept tests. *British Journal of Educational Psychology*, 67, 311–321.

Heath, S. (1989) Oral and literate traditions among black Americans living in poverty. *American Psychologist*, 44, 367–373.

Heller, J., Groff, B. and Solomon, S. (1977) Toward an understanding of crowding: the role of physical interaction. *Journal of Personality and Social Psychology*, 35 (3), 183–190.

Herrnstein, R. and Murray, C. (1994) *The Bell Curve: Intelligence and Class Structure in American life*. New York: Free Press.

Hicks, C. (1980) The ITPA visual sequential memory task: an alternative interpretation and the implications for good and poor readers. *British Journal of Educational Psychology*, 50 (1), 16–25.

Hicks, D. (1968) Short- and long-term retention of affectively varied modelled behaviour. *Psychonomic Science*, 11, 369–370.

Higgins, E., Lee, J., Kwon, J. and Trope, Y. (1995) When combining intrinsic motivations undermines interest: a test of activity engagement theory. *Journal of Personality and Social Psychology*, 68, 749–767.

Hill, J. and Schoener, E. (1996) Age-dependent decline of attention deficit hyperactivity disorder. *American Journal of Psychiatry*, 153 (9), 1143–1146.

Hill, L. (1981) A readability study of junior school library provision related to children's interests and reading abilities. *British Journal of Educational Psychology*, 51, 102–104.

Hillerich, L. (1976) Towards an assessable definition of literacy. *English Journal*, 65, 50–55.

Hinshaw, S., Henker, B. and Whalen, C. (1984) Self-control in hyperactive boys in anger-inducing situations: effects of cognitive-behavioural training and methyl-phenidate. *Journal of Abnormal Child Psychology*, 12, 55–77.

Hinson, N. and Smith, P. (1993) *Phonics and Phonic Resources*. Stafford: NASEN.

Hiroto, D. and Seligman, M. (1975) Generality of learnt helplessness in man. *Journal of Personality and Social Psychology*, 31, 311–327.

HMI (1991) *The Teaching and Learning of Reading in Primary Schools*. London: HMSO.

Hoffman, C., Lau, I. and Johnson, D. (1986) The linguistic relativity of person cognition. *Journal of Personality and Social Psychology*, 51, 1097–1105.

Holmes, E. (1982) The effectiveness of educational intervention for pre-school children in day or residential care. *New Growth*, 2 (1), 17–30.

Honey, J. (1983) *The Language Trap: Race, Class and 'Standard English' in British Schools*. Kenton, Middlesex: National Council for Educational Standards.

Hornsbaum, A., Peters, S. and Sylva, K. (1996) Scaffolding in reading recovery. *Oxford Review of Education*. 22, 17–35.

Hornsby, B. and Miles, T. (1980) The effects of a dyslexia centred teaching programme. *British Journal of Educational Psychology*, 50, 236–242.

Hornsby, B. and Shear, F. (1974) *Alpha to Omega*. London: Heinemann.

Hoste, R. (1981) How valid are school examinations? An exploration into content validity. *British Journal of Educational Psychology*, 51, 10–22.

Howe, M. (1980) *The Psychology of Human Learning*. London: Harper & Rowe.

Howe, M. (1984) *A Teacher's Guide to the Psychology of Learning*. Oxford: Blackwell.

Howe, M. (1988) Intelligence as an explanation. *British Journal of Psychology*, 79, 349–360.

Howe, M. (1989) Separate skills or general intelligence: the autonomy of human abilities. *British Journal of Educational Psychology*, 59, 351–360.

Howe, M. (1990) *The Origins of Exceptional Abilities*. Oxford: Blackwell.

Howe, M. (1997) *IQ in Question: The Truth about Intelligence*. London: Sage.

Howlin, P. (1998) Practitioner review: psychological and educational treatments for autism. *Journal of Child Psychology and Psychiatry*, 39, 307–322.

Howson, J. (1998) Is the glass ceiling beginning to crack? *Times Educational Supplement*, 30 October, p. 24.

Hudson, L. (1966) *Contrary Imaginations: A Psychological Study of the English Schoolboy*. London: Methuen.

Hudspeth, W. and Pribram, K. (1990) Stages of brain and cognitive maturation. *Journal of Educational Psychology*, 82, 881–884.

Huesman, L. (1986) Psychological processes promoting the relation between exposure to media violence and aggressive behaviour by the viewer. *Journal of Social Issues*, 42 (3), 125–139.

Huesman, L. (1988) An information processing model for the development of aggression. *Aggressive Behaviour*, 14, 13–24.

Hughes, M. (1975) Egocentricity in children. Unpublished Ph.D. thesis, Edinburgh University.

Hughes, M. and Westgate, D. (1997) Assistants as talk-partners in early-years classrooms: some issues of support and development. *Educational Review*, 49 (1), 5–12.

Hui, E. (1991) Using Data Pac for Hong Kong Chinese children with reading difficulties. *Educational Psychology in Practice*, 7 (3), 180–186.

Hull, C. (1943) *Principles of Behavior*. New York: Appleton Century Crofts.

Hunt, J. McV. (1971) Intrinsic motivation and psychological development. In H. Schroder and P. Suedfeld (eds) *Personality Theory and Information Processing*. New York: Ronald Press.

Hunter, J. and Hunter, R. (1984) Validity and utility of alternate predictors of job performance. *Psychological Bulletin*, 96, 72–98.

Hutt, C. (1976) Exploration and play in children. In J. Bruner, A. Jolly and K. Sylva (eds) *Play: Its Role in Development and Evolution*. London: Penguin.

ICD-10 (1993) *International Classification of Diseases and Related Health Problems*. Geneva: World Health Organization.

International Energy Annual (1996) Appendix B. Energy Information Administration.

Jackson, P. (1968) *Life in Classrooms*. New York: Holt, Rinehart & Winston.

Jamison, D., Suppes, P. and Wells, S. (1974) The effectiveness of alternative instructional media: a survey. *Review of Educational Research*, 44, 1–68.

Jay, P. (1968) Primate field studies and human evolution. In P. Jay (ed.) *Primates: Studies in Adaptation and Variability*. New York: Holt, Rinehart & Winston.

Jemmott, J., Borysenko, M., McClelland, D., Chapman, R., Meyer, D. and Benson, H. (1985) Academic stress, power motivation and decrease in salivary secretory immunoglobulin A secretion rate. *Lancet*, 1, 1400–1402.

Jencks, C., Smith, M., Ucland, H., Bane, M., Cohen., Ginitis, H., Heyns, B. and Michelson, S. (1971) *Inequality: A Reassessment of the Effects of Family and Schooling in America*. New York: Basic Books.

Jenkins, J. and Dallenbach, K. (1924) Obliviscence during sleep and waking. *American Journal of Psychology*, 35, 605–612.

Jensen, A. (1963) Learning ability in retarded, average and gifted children. *Merrill-Palmer Quarterly of Behaviour and Development*, 9 (2), 123–140.

Jensen, A. (1973) *Educability and Group Differences*. London: Methuen.

Jesness, C. (1966) *Manual – The Jesness Inventory*. Palo Alto, CA: Consulting Psychologists Press.

John, O. (1990) The 'Big Five' factor taxonomy: dimensions of personality in the natural language and questionnaires. In L. Pervin (ed.) *Handbook of Personality Theory and Research*. New York: Guilford.

Johnson, D. and Johnson, R. (1987) *Learning Together and Alone*. Englewood Cliffs, NJ: Prentice-Hall.

Johnson, D., Cox, M. and Watson, D. (1994) Evaluating the impact of IT on pupils' achievements. *Journal of Computer Assisted Learning*, 10, 138–156.

Johnson, M. and Kress, R. (1964) Individual reading inventories. In *Proceedings of the 21st. Annual Reading Institute*. Newark, DE: International Reading Association.

Jones, M. (1997) Trained and untrained secondary school teachers in Barbados: is there a difference in classroom performance? *Educational Research*, 39, 175–184.

Jones, P. (1992) The timing of the school day. *Educational Psychology in Practice*, 8 (2), 82–85.

Josephson, W. (1987) Television violence and children's aggression: testing the priming, social script, and disinhibition prediction. *Journal of Personality and Social Psychology*, 53, 882–890.

Joy, L., Kimball, M. and Zabrack, M. (1986) Television and children's aggressive behaviour. In T. Williams (ed.) *The Impact of Television: A Natural Experiment in Three Settings*. New York: Academic Press.

Judd, J. (1998) Earlier start to lessons leaves British children behind. *Independent*, 28th January, p. 13.

Just, M. and Carpenter, P. (1992) A capacity theory of comprehension: individual differences in working memory. *Psychological Review*, 99, 122–149.

Kagan, J., Rosman, B., Day, D., Albert, J. and Phillips, W. (1964) Information processing and the child: significance of analytic and reflective attitudes. *Psychological Monographs*, 78 (1) (whole issue).

Kamin, L. (1995) Behind the Curve. *Scientific American*, February, 82–86.

Kaufman, B. (1981) *A Miracle to Believe In*. New York: Doubleday.

Kazdin, A. (1987) Treatment of antisocial behaviour in children: current status and future directions. *Psychological Bulletin*, 102, 187–203.

Keil, F. and Batterman, N. (1984) Characteristic-to-defining shift in the development of word meaning. *Journal of Verbal Learning and Verbal Behaviour*, 23, 221–236.

Kelley, H. (1967) Attribution theory in social psychology. In D. Levine (ed.) *Nebraska Symposium on Motivation*, vol. 15. Lincoln: University of Nebraska Press.

Kellogg, R. (1988) Attentional overload and writing performance: effects of rough draft and outline strategies. *Journal of Experimental Psychology: Learning, Memory and Cognition*, 14, 355–365.

Kelly, G. (1955) *The Psychology of Personal Constructs*. New York: Norton.

Kennedy, M. (1978) Findings from the follow through planned variation study. *Educational Researcher*, 7 (6), 3–11.

Khanum, S. (1995) Education and the Muslim girl. In M. Blair, J. Holland and S. Sheldon (eds) *Identity and Diversity*. Clevedon: The Open University.

Kimble, G. (1961) *Hilgard and Marquis' Conditioning and Learning*, 2nd edition. New York: Appleton.

Kintsch, W. (1994) The psychology of discourse processing. In M. Gernsbacher (ed.) *Handbook of Psycholinguistics*. London: Academic Press.

Kintsch, W. and Vipond, D. (1979) Reading comprehension and readability in educational practice and psychological theory. In L. Nilsson (ed.) *Perspectives in Memory Research*. Hillsdale, NJ: Lawrence Erlbaum.

Kintsch, W., Welsch, D., Schmalhofer, F. and Zimny, S. (1990) Sentence memory: a theoretical analysis. *Journal of Memory and Language*, 29, 133–159.

Kivilu, J. and Rogers, W. (1998) A multi-level analysis of cultural experience and gender influences on causal attributions to perceived performance in mathematics. *British Journal of Educational Psychology*, 68, 25–37.

Klare, G. (1975) *The Measurement of Readability*. Ames: Iowa State University Press.

Klein, R. (1996) A steering hand away from trouble. *Times Educational Supplement*, 12 January, p. 5.

Kleinman, R., Murphy, J., Little, M., Pagano, M., Wehler, C., Regal, K. and Jellinek, M. (1998) Hunger in children in the United States: potential behavioural and emotional correlates. *Paediatrics*, 101, e3.

Knight, G., Chisholm, B., Kearney, D., Little, H. and Morris, S. (1989) Developments in the use of 'Preventive Approaches to Disruption'. *Educational Psychology in Practice*, October, 148–154.

Knowles, W. and Masidlover, M. (1982) *Derbyshire Language Scheme*. Private publication, Ripley, Derbyshire.

Kounin, J. (1970) *Discipline and Group Management in Classrooms*. New York: Holt, Rinehart & Winston.

Kuhn, T. (1962) *The Nature of Scientific Revolutions*. Chicago: University of Chicago Press.

Kulik, J. and Kulik, C. (1988) Timing of feedback and verbal learning. *Review of Educational Research*, 58, 79–97.

Kulik, J. and Kulik, C. (1992) Meta-analytic findings on grouping programs. *Gifted Child Quarterly*, 36 (2), 73–77.

Kulik, J., Kulik, C. and Bangert-Drowns, R. (1990) Effectiveness of mastery learning programs: a meta-analysis. *Review of Educational Research*, 60, 265–299.

Labov, W. (1979) The logic of non-standard English. In V. Lee (ed.) *Language Development*. London: Open University.

Landauer, T. and Bjork, R. (1978) Optimum rehearsal patterns and name learning. In M. Gruneber, P. Morris and R. Sykes (eds) *Practical Aspects of Memory*. London: Academic Press.

Lange, G. and Adler, F. (1997) Motivation and achievement in elementary children. Paper presented at the Biennial Meeting of the Society for Research in Child Development, 62nd, Washington, DC. ERIC: ED413059.

Laslett, R. (1977) *Educating Maladjusted Children*. London: Crosby Lockwood Staples.

Latane, B. and Darley, J. (1970) *The Unresponsive Bystander: Why Doesn't He Help?* New York: Appleton Century Crofts.

Law, G. and Sayer, C. (1983) Short term memory and reading ability. *Remedial Education*, 18 (1), 24–29.

Lawrence, D. (1971) The effects of counselling on retarded readers. *Educational Research*, 13 (2), 119–124.

Leach, D. and Tan, R. (1996) The effects of sending positive and negative letters to parents on the classroom behaviour of secondary school students. *Educational Psychology*, 16 (2), 141–154.

Lees, S. (1987) The structure of sexual relations in school. In M. Arnot and G. Weiner (eds) *Gender and the Politics of Schooling*. London: Hutchinson.

Lefrancois, G. (1994) *Psychology for Teaching*. Belmont, CA: Wadsworth.

Leiter, J. and Johnsen, M. (1997) Child maltreatment and school performance declines: an event-history analysis. *American Educational Research Journal*, 34 (3), 563–589.

Lepper, M. and Greene, D. (1978) *The Hidden Costs of Reward*. Hillsdale, NJ: Lawrence Erlbaum.

Lepper, M., Greene, D. and Nisbett, R. (1973) Undermining children's intrinsic interest with extrinsic reward: a test of the overjustification hypothesis. *Journal of Personality and Social Psychology*, 28, 129–137.

Leutwyler, K. (1996) In focus: Paying attention. *Scientific American*, August, 12–13.

Levitt, E. (1957) The results of psychotherapy with children: an evaluation. *Journal of Consulting Psychology*, 21, 181–196.

Levy, A. and Kahan, B. (1991) *The Pindown Experience and the Protection of Children. Report of the Staffordshire Child Care Inquiry*. London: HMSO.

Levy, F., Hay, D., McLaughlin, M., Wood, C. and Waldman, I. (1996) Twin–sibling differences in parental reports of ADHD, speech, reading and behaviour problems. *Journal of Child Psychology and Psychiatry*, 37 (5), 569–578.

Lewinsohn, P. (1974) A behavioural approach to depression. In R. Friedman and M. Katz (eds) *The Psychology of Depression: Contemporary Theory and Research*. New York: Wiley.

Lewis, A. (1972) The self-concepts of adolescent educational subnormal boys. *Educational Research*, 15, 16–20.

Lewis, C. (1995) Improving attendance – reducing truancy: a school based approach. *Educational Psychology in Practice*, 11 (1), 37–40.

Lindsay, G. (1981) *Manual: Infant Rating Scale*. Sevenoaks: Hodder & Stoughton.

Lindsay, G. and Desforges, M. (1998) *Baseline Assessment: Practice, Problems and Possibilities*. London: David Fulton.

Linton, R. (1945) Present world conditions in cultural perspective. In R. Linton (ed.) *The Science of Man in World Crisis*. New York: Columbia University Press.

Lloyd, S. (1998) *The Phonics Handbook: Jolly Phonics*, 3rd edition. Chigwell, Essex: Jolly Learning.

Lloyd-Smith, M. (1985) Off-site, out of mind? *Times Educational Supplement*, 13 September, 53–54.

Locke, A. (1985) *Teaching Spoken Language: The Living Language Handbook*. Windsor: NFER-Nelson.

Long, M. (1984) An investigation of learning ability in a primary school population. M.Ed. thesis, University of Exeter.

Long, M. (1988) Goodbye behaviour units, hello support services. *Educational Psychology in Practice*, April, 17–23.

Lonigan, C., Burgess, S., Anthony, J. and Barker, T. (1998) Development of phonological sensitivity in 2- to 5-year-old children. *Journal of Educational Psychology*, 90, 294–311.

Lovaas, O. (1996) The UCLA young autism model of service delivery. In C. Maurice (ed.) *Behavioural Intervention for Young Children with Autism*. Austin, TX: Pro-Ed.

Lovaas, O., Koegel, R., Simmons, J. and Long, J. (1973) Some generalisation and follow-up measures on autistic children in behaviour therapy. *Journal of Applied Behavior Analysis*, 6, 131–166.

Lowe, M. and Costello, J. (1976) *Manual for the Symbolic Play Test*. Windsor: NFER-Nelson.

Lubart, T. and Sternberg, R. (1995) An investment approach to creativity: theory and data. In S. Smith, T. Ward and R. Fiske (eds) *The Creative Cognition Approach*. Cambridge, MA: MIT Press.

Lucky Duck (1998) *Holding Back, Rarely and Safely*. Bristol: Lucky Duck Publishing.

Lunn, J. (1970) *Streaming in the Primary School*. Slough: NFER.

Luyten, H. and de Jong, R. (1998) Parallel classes: differences and similarities. Teacher effects and school effects in secondary schools. *School Effectiveness and School Improvement*, 9, 437–473.

Mac an Ghaill, M. (1988) *Young, Gifted and Black: Student–Teacher Relations in the Schooling of Black Youth*. Milton Keynes: Open University Press.

McCaffrey, I. and Cumming, J. (1969) Persistence of emotional disturbances reported among second and fourth grade children. In H. Dupont (ed.) *Educating Emotionally Disturbed Children*. Holt, Rinehart & Winston.

Maccoby, E. and Jacklin, C. (1974) *The Psychology of Sex Differences*. London: Oxford University Press.

McGarrigle, J. and Donaldson, M. (1974) Conservation accidents. *Cognition*, 3, 341–350.

McGee, R., Williams, S., Share, D., Anderson, J. and Silva, P. (1986) The relationship between specific reading retardation, general reading backwardness and behavioural problems in a large sample of Dunedin boys: a longitudinal study from five to eleven years. *Journal of Child Psychology and Psychiatry*, 27 (5), 597–610.

McGuigan, F. (1970) Covert oral behaviour during the silent performance of language tasks. *Psychological Bulletin*, 74, 309–326.

McGuiness, C. (1999) *From Thinking Skills to Thinking Classrooms*. Research Brief no. 115. Nottingham: DfEE Publications.

McGuinness, C. and McGuinness, G. (1998) *Reading Reflex*. London: Penguin.

MacIntosh, H. and Hale, D. (1976) *Assessment and the Secondary School Teacher*. London: Routledge & Kegan Paul.

McIntyre, D. and Brown, S. (1978) The conceptualization of attainment. *British Educational Research Journal*, 4 (2), 41–50.

Mackay, D., Thompson, B., Schaub, P. and Knowles, F. (1970) *Breakthrough to Literacy. Teacher's Manual*. Harlow: Longman.

MacKenzie, I. (1990) Courseware evaluation: where's the intelligence? *Journal of Computer Assisted Learning*, 6, 273–285.

Mackinnon, D., Statham, J. and Hales, M. (1995) *Education in the U.K.: Facts and Figures*. London: Hodder & Stoughton.

Macmillan Graded Word Reading Test (1986) Basingstoke: Macmillan Assessment.

McNamara, E. (1979) Pupil self-management in the secondary school: the goal of behavioural intervention. *AEP Journal*, 3, 1.

McSporran, E. (1997) Towards better listening and learning in the classroom. *Educational Review*, 49, 13–20.

Madsen, C. (1994) Prevalence of food additive intolerance. *Human and Experimental Toxicology*, 13 (6), 393–399.

Mael, F. (1998) Single-sex and coeducational schooling: relationships to socioemotional and academic development. *Review of Educational Research*, 68, 101–129.

Maier, N. (1931) Reasoning in humans. 2. The solution of a problem and its appearance in consciousness. *Journal of Comparative Psychology*, 12, 181–194.

Maier, N. (1933) An aspect of human reasoning. *British Journal of Psychology*, 24, 144–155.

Maines, B. and Robinson, G. (1991) Don't beat the bullies! *Educational Psychology in Practice*, 7 (3), 168–172.

Male, D. (1996) Who goes to MLD schools? *British Journal of Special Education*, 23 (1), 35–41.

Mandler, G. (1967) Organisation and memory. In W. Spence and J. Spence (eds) *The Psychology of Learning and Motivation*, vol. 1. London: Academic Press.

Mandler, J. (1987) On the psychological reality of story structure. *Discourse Processes*, 10, 1–29.

Markman, E. (1987) How children constrain the possible meanings of words. In U. Neisser (ed.) *Concepts and Conceptual Development: Ecological and Intellectual Factors in Categorisations*. New York: Cambridge University Press.

Marland, M. (1993) *The Craft of the Classroom*. London: Heinemann Educational.

Marra, M. (1982) How are you doing now? A follow-up study of 48 ex-pupils of an ESN(M) day special school. *Remedial Education*, 17 (3), 115–118.

Marsh, A. (1997) *Current Practice for Resourcing Additional Educational Needs in Local Education Authorities*. EMIE. Slough: NFER.

Marsh, H. and Yeung, A. (1997) Causal effects of academic self-concept on academic achievement: structural equation models of longitudinal data. *Journal of Educational Psychology*, 89, 41–54.

Marsh, H. and Yeung, A. (1998) Longitudinal structural equation models of academic self-concept and achievement: gender differences in the development of math and English constructs. *American Educational Research Journal*, 35, 705–738.

Marshall, P. (1995) *The experiences of gifted children growing: triangulation with the GULB*. Ph.D. dissertation, University of Manchester.

Marton, F. and Saljo, R. (1976) On qualitative differences in learning. 1. Outcomes and process. *British Journal of Educational Psychology*, 46, 4–11.

Martorano, S. (1977) A developmental analysis of performance on Piaget's formal operations tasks. *Developmental Psychology*, 13, 666–672.

Maslow, A. (1954) *Motivation and Personality*. New York: Harper & Row.

Maxwell, W. (1994) Special educational needs and social disadvantage in Aberdeen city school catchment zones. *Educational Research*, 36 (1), 25–37.

Mayer, R. (1979) Can advance organisers influence meaningful learning? *Review of Educational Research*, 49, 371–383.

Mayer, R. (1987) *Educational Psychology: A Cognitive Approach*. Boston: Little, Brown.

Mead, G. (1934) *Mind, Self and Society*. Chicago: University of Chicago Press.

Measor, L. and Woods, P. (1988) Initial fronts. In M. Woodhead and A. McGrath (eds) *Family, School and Society*. London: Hodder & Stoughton.

Medcof, J. and Roth, J. (eds) (1979) *Approaches to Psychology*. Milton Keynes: Open University Press.

Mehrabian, A. and Ferris, S. (1967) Inference of attitudes from nonverbal communication in two channels. *Journal of Consulting Psychology*, 31, 248–252.

Meichenbaum, D. (1977) *Cognitive Behaviour Modification: An Integrative Approach*. New York: Plenum.

Meltzer, L., Levine, M., Karniski, W., Palfrey, J. and Clarke, S. (1984) An analysis of the learning style of adolescent delinquents. *Journal of Learning Disabilities*, 17, 600–608.

Merrett, F. and Wheldall, K. (1984) Classroom behaviour problems which junior school teachers find most troublesome, *Educational Studies*, 10 (2), 67–81.

Meyer, L., Stahl, A., Linn, R. and Wardrop, J. (1994) Effects of reading storybooks aloud to children. *Journal of Educational Research*, 88 (2), 69–85.

Milgram, S. (1974) *Obedience to Authority*. New York: Harper & Row.

Miller, A. (1996) *Pupil Behaviour and Teacher Culture*. London: Cassell.

Miller, A. (1997) *Business and Community Mentoring in Schools*. Research Report no. 43. London: Department for Education and Employment.

Miller, G. and Gildea, P. (1987) How children learn words. *Scientific American*, 257, 86–91.

Miller, L. and Dyer, J. (1975) Four pre-school programs: their dimensions and effects. *Monographs of the Society for Research in Child Development*, 40, 162.

Mirza, H. (1993) The social construction of black womanhood in British educational research: towards a new understanding. In M. Arnot and K. Weiler (eds) *Feminism and Social Justice in Education*. London: Falmer Press.

Mischel, W. (1968) *Personality and Assessment*. New York: Wiley.

Mitchell, D. (1987) Reading and syntactic analysis. In J. Beech and A. Colley (eds) *Cognitive Approaches to Reading*. Chichester: Wiley.

Modbury (1995) *National Curriculum Assessment Made Easy*. Modbury, Devon: Modbury Marketing.

Money, J. (1986) *Venuses Penuses: Sexology, Sexosophy, and Exigency Theory*. Buffalo, NY: Prometheus Books.

Montessori, M. (1936) *The Secret of Childhood*. Calcutta: Orient Longmans.

Moore, T. (1966) Difficulties of the ordinary child in adjusting to primary school. *Journal of Child Psychology and Psychiatry*, 7, 17–38.

Moreno, R. and Mayer, R. (1999) Cognitive principles of multimedia learning: the role of modality and contiguity. *Journal of Educational Psychology*, 91, 358–368.

Morss, J. (1996) *Growing Critical: Alternatives to Developmental Psychology*. New York: Routledge.

Mortimore, P., Sammons, P., Stoll, L., Lewis, D. and Ecob, R. (1988) *School Matters: The Junior Years*. Wells, Somerset: Open Books.

Mortimore, P. and Whitty, G. (1997) *Can school Improvement Overcome the Effects of Disadvantage?* London: Institute of Education.

Moseley, D. (1975) *Special Provision for Reading*. London: NFER.

Moseley, D. (1989) How lack of confidence in spelling affects children's written expression. *Educational Psychology in Practice*, April, 42–46.

Mueller, C. and Dweck, C. (1998) Praise for intelligence can undermine children's motivation and performance. *Journal of Personality and Social Psychology*, 75, 33–52.

Munro, J. (1999) Learning more about learning improves teacher effectiveness. *School Effectiveness and School Improvement*, 10, 151–171.

Murphy, K. (1976) In H. Oyer (ed.) *Communication for the Hearing Handicapped*. Baltimore: University Park Press.

Murphy, R. (1978) Reliability of marking in eight GCE examinations. *British Journal of Educational Psychology*, 48, 196–200.

Murray, H. (1938) *Explorations in Personality: A Clinical and Experimental Study of Fifty Men of College Age*. New York: Oxford University Press.

Murray, L. and Maliphant, R. (1982) Developing aspects of the use of linguistic and graphemic information during reading. *British Journal of Educational Psychology*, 52, 155–169.

Mussen, P., Conger, J. and Kagan, J. (1990) *Child Development and Personality*, 7th edition. New York: Harper & Row.

NAGC (1989) *Help with Bright Children*. Milton Keynes: National Association for Gifted Children.

Naglieri, J., LeBuffe, P. and Pfeiffer, S. (1992) *Devereux Behaviour Rating Scale – School Form*. Sidcup, Kent: The Psychological Corporation.

Nagy, W., Anderson, R. and Herman, P. (1987) Learning words from context during normal reading. *American Educational Research Journal*, 24, 237–270.

NCE (1995) *Standards in Literacy and Numeracy: 1948–1994*. London: National Curriculum on Education.

Neale, M. (1989) *Neale Analysis of Reading Ability*. NFER-Nelson.

Neill, S. and Caswell, C. (1993) *Body Language for Competent Teachers*. London: Routledge.

Neisser, U., Boodoo, G., Bouchard, T., Boykin, A., Brody, N., Ceci, S., Halpern, D., Loehlin, J., Perloff, R., Sternberg, R. and Urbina, S. (1996) Intelligence: knowns and unknowns. *American Psychologist*, 51, 77–101.

Nelson, K. (1988) Constraints on word learning. *Cognitive Development*, 3, 221–246.

Newton, M. and Thomson, M. (1976) *Aston Index Handbook*. Wisbech, Cambridgeshire: Learning Development Aids.

NFER (1997) *Examination Results in Context 1997*. Slough: NFER.

Nicholson, T. and Hill, D. (1985) Good readers don't guess: taking another look at the issue of whether children read words better in context or in isolation. *Reading Psychology*, 6, 181–198.

Nicolson, R. (1981) The relationship between memory span and processing speed. In M. Friedman, J. Das and N. O'Connor (eds) *Intelligence and Learning*. New York: Plenum Press.

Norman, D. (1978) Notes towards a complex theory of learning. In A. Lesgold, J. Pellegrino, S. Fokkema and R. Glaser (eds) *Cognitive Psychology and Instruction*. New York: Plenum Press.

Norwich, B. (1997) *A Trend towards Inclusion*. Redland, Bristol: Centre for Studies on Inclusive Education.

Nuffield Science Teaching Project (1967) Harmondsworth: Penguin.

Nuttall, D. (1990) *Differences in Examination Performance, RS 1277/90*. London: Research and Statistics Branch, Inner London Education Authority.

Oakhill, J. and Beard, R. (eds) (1999) *Reading Development and the Teaching of Reading*. Oxford: Blackwell.

Ofsted (1996) *The Gender Divide*. London: HMSO.

Ogilvy, C. (1994) Social skills training with children and adolescents: a review of the evidence on effectiveness. *Educational Psychology*, 14 (1), 73–86.

O'Leary, D. and O'Leary, S. (1977) *Classroom Management: The Successful Use of Behavior Modification*. New York: Pergamon.

O'Leary, D., Kaufman, K., Kass, R. and Drabman, R. (1970) The effects of loud and soft reprimands on the behaviour of disruptive students. *Exceptional Children*, 37, 145–155.

Olson, M. (1971) *Identifying Quality in School. Classrooms: Some Problems and Some Answers*. MSCC Exchange, 29, 5, New York: Metropolitan School Study Council, Institute of Administrative Research, Teachers College.

Olweus, D. (1993) *Bullying at School*. Oxford: Blackwell.

Oppenheim, C. (1993) *Poverty, The Facts*. London: Child Poverty Action Group.

O'Sullivan, J. and Pressley, M. (1984) The completeness of instruction and strategy transfer. *Journal of Experimental Child Psychology*, 38, 275–288.

Ounsted, C. (1969) Aggression and epilepsy: rage in children with temporal lobe epilepsy. *Journal of Psychosomatic Research*, 13, 237–242.

Pagani, L., Boulerice, B., Tremblay, R. and Votaro, F. (1997) Behavioural development in children of divorce and remarriage. *Journal of Child Psychology and Psychiatry*, 38, 769–781.

Page, E. and Grandon, G. (1979) Family configuration and mental ability: two theories contrasted with U.S. data. *American Educational Research Journal*, 16, 257–272.

Paivio, A. (1969) Mental imagery in associative learning and memory. *Psychological Review*, 76, 241–263.

Parnes, S. (1967) *Creative Behavior Guidebook*. New York: Scribner's.

Parsons, C. and Howlett, K. (1996) Permanent exclusions from school: a case where society is failing its children. *Support for Learning*, 11 (3), 109–112.

Patterson, G. (1982) *Coercive Family Process*. Eugene, OR: Castalia.

Patterson, G. (1986) Performance models for antisocial boys. *American Psychologist*, 41 (4), 432–444.

Patterson, G., Littman, R. and Bricker, W. (1967) Assertive behaviour in children: a step toward a theory of aggression. *Monographs of the Society for Research in Child Development*, 32, 1–43.

Pavlov, I. (1927) *Conditioned Reflexes*. Oxford: Milford.

Peers, I. and Johnston, M. (1994) Influence of learning context on the relationship between A-level attainment and final degree performance: a meta-analytic review. *British Journal of Educational Psychology*, 64, 1–18.

Pennington, B., Johnson, C. and Welsh, M. (1987) Unexpected reading precocity in a normal preschooler: implications for hyperlexia. *Brain and Language*, 30, 1, 165–180.

Peterson, P., Swing, S., Stark, K. and Wass, G. (1984) Students' cognition and time on task during mathematics instruction. *American Educational Research Journal*, 21, 487–515.

Piaget, J. (1951) *Play, Dreams and Imitation in Childhood*. London: Routledge & Kegan Paul.

Piaget, J. (1959) *The Language and Thought of the Child*, 3rd edition. London: Routledge.

Piaget, J. (1966) *The Origins of Intelligence in Children*. New York: International Universities Press.

Piaget, J. (1967) *Six Psychological Studies*. New York: Vintage Books.

Piaget, J. (1972) *The Principles of Genetic Epistemology*. New York: Basic Books.

Piliavin, J., Dovidio, J., Gaertner, S. and Clark, R. (1981) *Emergency Intervention*. New York: Academic Press.

Pinker, S. (1984) *Language Learnability and Language Development*. Cambridge, MA: Harvard University Press.

Pinker, S. (1994) *The Language Instinct*. New York: W. Morrow.

Pintrich, P. and Schunk, D. (1996) *Motivation in Education: Theory, Research and Applications*. Englewood Cliffs, NJ: Prentice-Hall.

Plewis, I. (1991a) Using multilevel models to link educational progress with curriculum coverage. In S. Raudenbush and J. Willms (eds) *Schools, Classrooms, and Pupils: International Studies of Schooling from a Multilevel Perspective*. San Diego: Academic Press.

Plewis, I. (1991b) Pupils' progress in reading and mathematics during primary school: associations with ethnic group and sex. *Educational Research*, 33, 133–140.

Plewis, I. and Goldstein, H. (1997) The 1997 Education White Paper: a failure of standards. *British Journal of Curriculum and Assessment*, 8, 17–20.

Plewis, I. and Veltman, M. (1996) Where does all the time go? In M. Hughes (ed.) *Teaching and Learning in Changing Times*. Oxford: Blackwell.

Plomin, R. (1995) Genetics and children's experiences in the family. *Journal of Child Psychology and Psychiatry*, 36, 33–68.

Plowden Report (1967) *Children and Their Primary Schools: Report of the Central Advisory Council for Education in England*. London: HMSO.

Porter, R. and Cattell, R (1992) *Children's Personality Questionnaire*. Champaign, IL: IPAT.

Prais, S. (1996) Class size and learning. *Oxford Review of Education*, 22 (4), 399–414.

Presland, J. (1991) Explaining away dyslexia. *Educational Psychology in Practice*, 6 (4), 215–221.

Pumfrey, P. (1979) Which Test? In M. Raggett, C. Tutt, and P. Raggett (eds) *Assessment and Testing of Reading*. London: Ward Lock.

Pumfrey, P. and Elliott, C. (1991) National reading standards and Standard Assessment Tasks. *Educational Psychology in Practice*, 7 (2), 74–80.

Pyke, N. (1998) OFSTED figures support failing schools poverty link. *Times Educational Supplement*, 31 July, p. 3.

QCA (1998) *The Grammar Papers: Perspectives on the Teaching of Grammar in the National Curriculum*. Middlesex: QCA Publications.

Ramey, C., Yeates, K. and Short, E. (1984) The plasticity of intellectual development: insights from preventive intervention. *Child Development*, 55, 1913–1925.

Rampton, A. (1981) *West Indian Children in Our Schools*. Cmnd 8273. London: HMSO.

Randall, P. (1997) *A Community Approach to Bullying*. Stoke-on-Trent: Trentham Books.

Rapoport, J., Buchsbaum, M., Zahn, T., Weingartner, H., Ludlow, C. and Mikkelson, E. (1978) Dextroamphetamine: cognitive and behavioural effects in normal prepubertal boys. *Science*, 199, 560–563.

Rathus, S. (1988) *Understanding Child Development*. New York: Holt, Rinehart & Winston.

Raven, J. (1993) *Manual for Raven's Progressive Matrices and Vocabulary Scales*. Windsor: NFER-Nelson.

Ray, B. and Wartes, J. (1991) The academic achievement and affective development of home-schooled children. In J. Galen and M. Pitman (eds) *Home Schooling: Political, Historical and Pedagogical Perspectives*. Norwood, NJ: Ablex.

Rayner, K., Inhoff, A., Morrison, R., Slowiaczek, M. and Bertera, J. (1981) Masking of foveal and parafoveal vision during eye fixations in reading. *Journal of Experimental Psychology: Human Perception and Performance*, 7, 167–179.

Rayner, K. and Pollatsek, A. (1989) *The Psychology of Reading*. Hove, East Sussex: Lawrence Erlbaum.

Rayner, K. and Sereno, S. (1994) Eye movements in reading: psycholinguistic studies. In M. Gernsbacher (ed.) *Handbook of Psycholinguistics*. New York: Academic Press.

Reading 360 (1978) *The Ginn Reading Programme*. Aylesbury: Ginn.

Reezigt, B., Guldemond, H. and Creemers, B. (1999) Empirical validity for a comprehensive model on educational effectiveness. *School Effectiveness and School Improvement*, 10, 193–216.

Reynolds, D. (1987) The effective school: do educational psychologists help or hinder? *Educational Psychology in Practice*, 3 (2), 22–28.

Reynolds, D. and Farrell, S. (1996) *Worlds Apart: A Review of International Surveys of Educational Achievement Involving England*. London: The Stationery Office.

Reynolds, D. and Sullivan, M. (1981) The effects of school: a radical faith re-stated. In B. Gillham (ed.) *Problem Behaviour in the Secondary School*. London: Croom Helm.

Rhodes, J. (1993) The use of solution-focused brief therapy in schools. *Educational Psychology in Practice*, 9 (1), 27–34.

Rhodes, J. and Ajmal, Y. (1995) *Solution Focused Thinking in Schools*. London: BT Press.

Richards, M. (1979) Sorting out what's in a word from what's not: evaluating Clark's semantic features acquisition theory. *Journal of Experimental Child Psychology*, 27, 1–47.

Riding, R. (1991) *Cognitive Styles Analysis*. Birmingham: Learning and Training Technology.

Riding, R. and Anstey, L. (1982) Verbal-imagery learning style and reading attainment in eight-year-old children. *Journal of Research in Reading*, 5, 57–66.

Riding, R. and Cheema, I. (1991) Cognitive styles: an overview and integration. *Educational Psychology*, 11 (3 and 4), 193–215.

Riding, R. and Douglas, G. (1993) The effect of cognitive style and mode of presentation on learning performance. *British Journal of Educational Psychology*, 63, 297–307.

Riding, R. and Mathias, D. (1991) Cognitive styles and preferred learning mode, reading attainment and cognitive ability in 11-year-old children. *Educational Psychology*, 11 (3 and 4), 383–393.

Riding, R. and Pearson, F. (1994) The relationship between cognitive style and intelligence. *Educational Psychology*, 14 (4), 413–425.

Riding, R. and Rayner, S. (1999) *Cognitive Styles and Learning Strategies*. London: David Fulton.

Rigley, L. (1968) Reading backwardness. *Isle of Wight Educational and Medical Survey, Research Bulletin, no.* 9.

Riley, J. (1995) The relationship between adjustment to school and success in reading by the end of the reception year. *Early Child Development and Care*, 114, 25–38.

Rips, L. (1983) Cognitive processes in propositional reasoning. *Psychological Review*, 90, 38–71.

Rivlin, L. and Rothenberg, M. (1976) The use of space in open classrooms. In H. Proshansky, W. Ittelson and L. Rivlin (eds) *Environmental Psychology: People and Their Physical Settings*. New York: Holt, Rinehart & Winston.

Robbins, C. and Ehri, L. (1994) Reading storybooks to kindergarteners helps them learn new vocabulary words. *Journal of Educational Psychology*, 86 (1), 54–64.

Robinson, G. and Maines, B. (1994) Assertive discipline: jumping on a dated wagon. *Educational Psychology in Practice*, 9 (4), 195–200.

Robinson, P. (1997) *Literacy, Numeracy and Economic Performance*. London: Centre for Economic Performance.

Robinson, R., Smith, S., Miller, D. and Brownell, M. (1999) Cognitive behaviour modification of hyperactivity-impulsivity and aggression: A meta-analysis of school-based studies. *Journal of Educational Psychology*, 91, 195–203.

Robitaille, D. and Garden, R. (eds) (1989) *The International Association for the Evaluation of Educational Achievement (IEA) Study of Mathematics II*, vol. 2. Oxford: Pergamon Press.

Rodgers, B. (1983) The identification and prevalence of specific reading retardation. *British Journal of Educational Psychology*, 53, 369–373.

Rogers, B. (1994) *Behaviour Recovery: A Whole School Program for Mainstream Schools*. Melbourne: Australian Council for Educational Research.

Rogers, C. (1951) *Client-Centred Therapy*. Boston: Houghton Mifflin.

Rogers, W. (1990) *You Know the Fair Rule*. Hawthorn, Victoria: ACER.

Rose, S. (1996) *In The Blood: God, Genes and Destiny*. London: HarperCollins.

Rosenberg, M., Schooler, C., Schoenbach, C. and Rosenberg, F. (1995) Global self-esteem and specific self-esteem: different concepts, different outcomes. *American Sociological Review*, 60, 141–156.

Rosenshine, B. (1970) Enthusiastic teaching: a research review. *School Review*, 78, 499–514.

Rosenshine, B. and Meister, C. (1994) Reciprocal teaching: a review of the research. *Review of Educational Research*, 64, 479–530.

Rosenshine, B. and Stevens, R. (1986) Teaching functions. In M. Wittrock (ed.) *Handbook of Research on Teaching*, 3rd edition. New York: Macmillan.

Rosenthal, R. (1985) From unconscious experimenter bias to teacher expectancy effects. In J. Dusek (ed.) *Teacher Expectancies*. London: Lawrence Erlbaum.

Rosenthal, R. and Jacobson, L. (1968) *Pygmalion in the Classroom*. New York: Holt, Rinehart & Winston.

Rotter, J. (1966) Generalised expectancies for internal vs external control of reinforcement. *Psychological Monographs*, 80, 1.

Rowe, M. (1986) Wait time: slowing down may be a way of speeding up. *Journal of Teacher Education*, 37, 43–50.

Rowell, J., Simon, J. and Wiseman, R. (1969) Verbal reception, guided discovery and the learning of schemata. *British Journal of Educational Psychology*, 39, 235–244.

Rowley, G. (1974) Which examinees are most favoured by the use of multiple-choice tests? *Journal of Educational Measurement*, 11, 15–23.

Rumelhart, D. and McClelland, J. (1986) On learning the past tenses of English verbs. In J. McClelland, D. Rumelhart and the PDP Research Group, *Parallel Distributed Processing II*. Cambridge, MA: MIT Press.

Runnymede Trust (1996) *This Is Where I Live: Stories and Pressures in Brixton, 1996*. London: Runnymede Trust.

Rushton, J. (1997) *Race, Evolution and Behavior*. New Brunswick, NJ: Transaction Publishers.

Rushworth, F. (1974) Helping backward readers. *Times Educational Supplement*, 20 September.

Russell, D. (1943) A diagnostic study of spelling readiness. *Journal of Educational Research*, 37, 276–283.

Rutter, M. (1967) A children's behaviour questionnaire for completion by teachers: preliminary findings. *Journal of Child Psychology and Child Psychiatry*, 8, 1–11.

Rutter, M. and Madge, N. (1976) *Cycles of Disadvantage*. London: Heinemann.

Rutter, M. and Smith, D. (1995) *Psychosocial Disorders in Young People*. Chichester: Wiley.

Rutter, M. and Yule, W. (1975) The concept of specific reading retardation. *Journal of Child Psychology and Psychiatry*, 16, 181–197.

Rutter, M., Maughan, B., Mortimore, P. and Ouston, J. (1979) *Fifteen Thousand Hours: Secondary Schools and Their Effects*. Wells, Somerset: Open Books.

Rutter, M., Tizard, J. and Whitmore, K. (1970) *Education, Health and Behaviour*. London: Longman.

Rye, J. (1982) *Cloze Procedures and the Teaching of Reading*. London: Heinemann.

Sachs, J., Bard, B. and Johnson, M. (1981) Language with restricted input: case studies of two hearing children of deaf parents. *Applied Psycholinguistics*, 2, 33–54.

St James-Roberts, I. (1994) Assessing emotional and behavioural problems in reception class school-children: factor structure, convergence and prevalence using the PBCL. *British Journal of Educational Psychology*, 64, 105–118.

Salisbury, J. and Jackson, D. (1996) *Challenging Macho Values*. London: Falmer Press.

Salmon, P. (1988) *Psychology for Teachers: An Alternative Approach*. London: Century Hutchinson.

Salmon-Cox, L. (1981) Teachers and standardised achievement tests: what's really happening? *Phi Delta Kappa*, May.

Sammons, P. (1995) Gender, ethnic and socio-economic differences in attainment and progress. *British Educational Research Journal*, 21 (4), 465–485.

Samson, G., Strykowski, B., Weinstein, T. and Walberg, H. (1987) The effects of teacher questioning levels on student achievement: a quantitative synthesis. *Journal of Educational Research*, 80, 290–295.

Samuels, S., Schermner, N. and Reinking, D. (1992) Reading fluency: techniques for making decoding automatic. In S. Samuels and A. Farstrup (eds) *What Research Has to Say about Reading Instruction*. Newark, DE: International Reading Association.

Sawyer, C., Ferguson, I., Hayward, M. and Cunningham, L. (1991) On reading and the GCSE. *The Psychologist*, 4 (5), 221–222.

SCAA (School Curriculum and Assessment Authority) (1996) *External Marking of the 1996 Key Stage 2 Tests in English, Mathematics and Science*. London: SCAA Publications.

SCAA (School Curriculum and Assessment Authority) (1997) *Report on the National Curriculum Assessment for 11-year-olds*. London: SCAA Publications.

Scales, J. (1999) Home PCs delete hope for poorest. *Times Educational Supplement*, 22 January, p. 30.

Scarr, S. and Weinberg, R. (1976) IQ test performance of black children adopted by white families. *American Psychologist*, 31, 726–739.

Schank, R. and Abelson, R. (1977) *Scripts, Plans, Goals, and Understanding*. Hillsdale, NJ: Lawrence Erlbaum.

Schlesinger, I. (1988) The origin of relational categories. In Y. Levy, I. Schlesinger and M. Braine (eds) *Categories and Processes in Language Acquisition.* Hillsdale, NJ: Lawrence Erlbaum.

Schmidt, M., Esser, G., Allehoff, W., Geisel, B., Laucht, M. and Woerner, W. (1987) Evaluating the significance of minimal brain dysfunction: results of an epidemiological study. *Journal of Child Psychology and Psychiatry*, 28, 803–821.

Schon, D. (1983) *The Reflective Practitioner.* London: Temple Smith.

Schonell, F. (1955) *Schonell Graded Word Reading Test.* Edinburgh: Oliver and Boyd.

Schopler, E., Mesibov, G., Devellis, R. and Chort, A. (1981) Treatment outcomes for autistic children and their families. In P. Mittler (ed.) *Frontiers of Knowledge in Mental Retardation: Social, Educational and Behavioral Aspects.* Baltimore: University Park Press.

Schwebel, A. and Cherlin, D. (1972) Physical and social distancing in teacher–pupil relationships. *Journal of Educational Psychology*, 63, 543–550.

Schweinhart, L. and Weikart, D. (1993) *Significant Benefits: The High/Scope Perry Preschool Study through Age 27.* Ypsilanti, MI: High/Scope Press.

Scott, V. (1990) Explicit and implicit grammar teaching strategies: new empirical data. *The French Review*, 63, 779–789.

Scottish Council for Research in Education (1956) *Hearing Defects of School Children.* London: University of London Press.

Sears, R., Maccoby, E. and Levin, H. (1957) *Patterns of Child Rearing.* Evanston, IL: Row, Peterson.

Secord, P. and Backman, C. (1964) *Social Psychology.* New York: McGraw-Hill.

Sejnowski, T. and Rosenberg, C. (1987) Parallel networks that learn to pronounce English text. *Complex Systems*, 1, 145–168.

Self, J. (1987) IKBS in education. *Educational Review*, 38 (2), 147–154.

Seligman, M. (1975) *Helplessness: On Depression, Development and Death.* San Francisco: W. H. Freeman.

Selye, H. (1956) *The Stress of Life.* New York: McGraw-Hill.

Share, D. and Stanovich, K. (1995) Cognitive processes in early reading development. *Issues in Education*, 1 (1), 1–57.

Sharp, C. and Hutchinson, D. (1997) How do season of birth and length of schooling affect children's attainments at Key Stage 1? A question revisited. Paper presented at Annual Conference of the British Research Association, 10–14 September 1997, University of York.

Sharp, S., Cowie, H. and Smith, P. (1994) How to respond to bullying behaviour. In S. Sharp and P. Smith (eds) *Tackling Bullying in Your School.* London: Routledge.

Shavelson, R., Hubner, J. and Stanton, G. (1976) Self-concept validation of construct interpretations. *Review of Educational Research*, 46, 407–441.

Shavelson, R. and Russo, N. (1977) Generalizability of measures of teacher effectiveness. *Educational Research*, 19 (3), 171–183.

Shayer, M. (1996) *The Long-Term Effects of Cognitive Acceleration on Pupils' School Achievement, November 1996.* London: Centre for the Advancement of Thinking, King's College.

Sheridan, M. and Peckham, C. (1975) Follow up at 11 years of children who had marked speech defects at 7 years. *Child Care and Health Development*, 113, 157–166.

Sherif, M., Harvey, O., White, B., Hood, W. and Sherif, C. (1961) *Intergroup Conflict and Co-operation: The Robbers Cave Experiment.* Norman: University of Oklahoma Press.

Shinn, M. and Hubbard, D. (1992) Curriculum-based measurement and problem-solving assessment: basic procedures and outcomes. *Focus on Exceptional Children*, 24, 1–20.

Shute, R., Foot, H. and Morgan, M. (1992) The sensitivity of children and adults as tutors. *Educational Studies*, 18 (1), 21–36.

Silcock, P. (1993) Can we teach effective teaching? *Educational Review*, 45, 13–19.

Simonoff, E., Bolton, P. and Rutter, M. (1996) Mental retardation: genetic findings, clinical implications and research agenda. *Journal of Child Psychology and Psychiatry*, 37 (3), 259–280.

Skaalvik, M. and Rankin, R. (1994) Gender differences in mathematics and verbal achievement, self-perception and motivation. *British Journal of Educational Psychology*, 64, 419–428.

Skinner, B. (1938) *The Behavior of Organisms.* New York: Appleton Century Crofts.

Skinner, B. (1954) The science of learning and the art of teaching. *Harvard Educational Review*, 24, 86–97.

Skinner, B. (1957) *Verbal Behavior.* New York: Appleton Century Crofts.

Skinner, N. (1985) University grades and time of day instruction. *Bulletin of the Psychonomic Society*, 23, 67.

Slater, B. (1968) Effects of noise on pupil performance. *Journal of Educational Psychology*, 59, 239–243.

Slavin, R. (1990) Achievement effects of ability

grouping in secondary schools: a best-evidence synthesis. *Review of Educational Research*, 60, 471–499.

Slobin, D. (1966) Grammatical transformations and sentence comprehension in childhood and adulthood. *Journal of Verbal Learning and Verbal Behaviour*, 5, 219–227.

Slobin, D. (1985) Crosslinguistic evidence for the language-making capacity. In D. Slobin (ed.) *The Crosslinguistic Study of Language Acquisition*, vol. 2, *Theoretical Issues*.

Smith, C. and Ellsworth, P. (1987) Patterns of appraisal and emotion related to taking an exam. *Journal of Personality and Social Psychology*, 52, 475–488.

Smith, D. and Tomlinson, S. (1989) *The School Effect: A Study of Multi-racial Comprehensives*. London: Policy Studies Institute.

Smith, F. (1973) *Psycholinguistics and Reading*. New York: Holt, Rinehart & Winston.

Smith, G. (1975) *Educational Priority*, vol. 4. London: HMSO.

Smith, M. and Glass, G. (1980) Meta-analysis of research on class size and its relationship to attitudes and instruction. *American Educational Research Journal*, 17, 419–433.

Snow, C. (1987) Relevance of the notion of a critical period to language acquisition. In M. Bornstein (ed.) *Sensitive Periods in Development: Interdisciplinary Perspectives*. Hillsdale, NJ: Lawrence Erlbaum.

Snow, R. (1969) Unfinished Pygmalion. *Contemporary Psychology*, 14, 197–199.

Social Exclusion Unit (1998) *Truancy and School Exclusion*. London: The Stationery Office.

Social Trends (1996) London: HMSO.

Social Trends (1997) London: The Stationery Office.

Social Trends (1998) London: The Stationery Office.

Solity, J., Deavers, R., Kerfoot, S., Crane, G. and Cannon, K. (1999) Raising literacy attainments in the early years: the impact of instructional psychology. *Educational Psychology*, 19 (4), 373–397.

Sommers-Flanagan, J. and Sommers-Flanagan, R. (1996) Efficacy of antidepressant medication with depression in children. *Professional Psychology: Research and Practice*, 27, 145–153.

Sonstroem, A. (1966) Manipulating, labeling and screening in the learning of conservation. Unpublished Ph.D. thesis, Harvard University.

Spaulding, C. (1992) *Motivation in the Classroom*. New York: McGraw-Hill.

Spearman, C. (1904) General intelligence, objectively determined and measured. *American Journal of Psychology*, 15, 210–293.

Special Educational Needs (The Warnock Report) (1978) London: HMSO.

Spence, S. (1995) *Social Skills Training: Enhancing Social Competence with Children and Adolescents*. Windsor: NFER-Nelson.

Spender, D. (1982) *Invisible Women: The Schooling Scandal*. London: Writers and Readers Publishing Cooperative.

Sprafkin, J. and Rubinstein, E. (1979) A field correlational study of children's television viewing habits and prosocial behaviour. *Journal of Broadcasting*, 23, 265–276.

Squire, L. (1987) *Memory and Brain*. New York: Oxford University Press.

Stanovich, K. (1986) Matthew effects in reading: some consequences of individual differences in the acquisition of literacy. *Reading Research Quarterly*, 21, 360–407.

Stanovich, K. (1991) Discrepancy definitions of reading disability. *Reading Research Quarterly*, 26 (1), 7–29.

Stanovich, K. (1994) Annotation: does dyslexia exist? *Journal of Child Psychology and Psychiatry*, 35 (4), 579–595.

Steinberg, D. (1986) Psychiatric aspects of problem behaviour: a consultative approach. In D. Tattum (ed.) *Management of Disruptive Pupil Behaviour in Schools*. London: Wiley.

Sternberg, R. (1988) Explaining away intelligence: a reply to Howe. *British Journal of Psychology*, 79, 527–533.

Stevenson, H., Parker, T., Wilkinson, A., Hegion, A. and Fish, E. (1976) Longitudinal study of individual differences in cognitive development and scholastic achievement. *Journal of Educational Psychology*, 68, 377–400.

Storfer, M. (1990) *Intelligence and Giftedness*. San Francisco: Jossey-Bass.

Stott, D. (1971) *Manual of the Bristol Social-Adjustment Guides*. London: University of London Press. (Note: this was subsequently published by the NFER but is now out of print. Behavioural checklists and diagnostic forms can be obtained from Hodder & Stoughton.)

Stott, D. (1981) Behaviour disturbance and failure to learn: a study of cause and effect. *Educational Research*, 23, 163–172.

Strand, S. (1997) Pupil progress during Key Stage 1: a value added analysis of school effects. *British Educational Research Journal*, 23, 471–487.

Strand, S. (1999) Ethnic group, sex and economic disadvantage: associations with pupils' educational progress from baseline to the end of Key Stage 1. *British Educational Research Journal*, 25, 179–202.

Stroop, J. (1935) Studies of interference in serial verbal reactions. *Journal of Experimental Psychology*, 18, 643–662.

Stuckless, E. and Birch, J. (1966) The influence of early manual communication on the linguistic development of deaf children. *American Annals of the Deaf*, 111, 499–504.

Subotnik, R., Kassa, L., Summers, E. and Wasser, A. (1993) *Genius Revisited: High I.Q. Children Grown Up*. Norwood, NJ: Ablex.

Sue, D., Sue, D. and Sue, S. (1990) *Understanding Abnormal Behaviour*, 3rd edition. Boston: Houghton Mifflin.

Sukhnandan, L. and Lee, B. (1998) *Streaming, Setting and Grouping by Ability*. Slough: NFER.

Swann, Lord (1985) *Education for All: Final Report of the Committee of Inquiry into the Education of Children from Ethnic Minority Groups*. Cmnd 9453. London: HMSO.

Swinson, J. and Melling, R. (1995) Assertive Discipline: four wheels on this wagon – a reply to Robinson and Maines. *Educational Psychology in Practice*, 11 (3), 3–8.

Tajfel, H. (1981) *Human Group and Social Categories*. Cambridge: Cambridge University Press.

Tannock, R. (1998) Attention deficit hyperactivity disorder: advances in cognitive, neurobiological, and genetic research. *Journal of Child Psychology and Psychiatry*, 39 (1), 65–99.

Tattum, D. (1982) *Disruptive Pupils in Schools and Units*. Chichester: Wiley.

Tattum, D. (1986) *Management of Disruptive Pupil Behaviour in Schools*. Chichester: Wiley.

Tennant, M. (1988) *Psychology and Adult Learning*. London: Routledge.

Terman, L. (1925–9) *Genetic Studies of Genius*, vols 1–5. Stanford, CA: Stanford University Press.

TES (2000) Ritalin rise blamed on teachers. *Times Educational Supplement*, 14 April, p. 9.

TGAT (1988) *National Curriculum. Task Group on Assessment and Testing. A Report*. London: HMSO.

Thackray, D. (1974) *Reading Readiness Profiles*. Sevenoaks: Hodder & Stoughton.

Tharp, R. and Gallimore, R. (1988) *Rousing Minds to Life*. Cambridge: Cambridge University Press.

Third International Mathematics and Science Study (1996) Boston: Boston College.

Thomas, A. (1994) Conversational learning. *Oxford Review of Education*, 20 (1), 131–142.

Thomas, A. and Chess, S. (1977) *Temperament and Development*. New York: Brunner/Mazel.

Thomas, E. and Robinson, H. (1982) *Improving Reading in Every Class*. Boston: Allyn & Bacon.

Thomas, S. (1995) Considering primary school effectiveness: an analysis of 1992 Key Stage 1 results. *Curriculum Journal*, 6, 279–295.

Thomas, S. and Mortimore, P. (1996) Comparison of value added models for secondary school effectiveness. *Research Papers in Education*, 11 (1), 5–33.

Thorndike, R., Hagen, E. and France, N. (1986) *Cognitive Abilities Test*, 2nd edition. Windsor: NFER-Nelson.

Thrupp, M. (1998) The art of the possible: organising and managing high and low socio-economic schools. *Journal of Educational Policy*, 13, 197–219.

Thurstone, L. (1938) Primary mental abilities. *Psychometric Monographs*, no. 1.

Tizard, B. and Hughes, M. (1984) *Young Children Learning: Talking and Thinking at Home and at School*. London: Fontana.

Tolman, E. (1932) *Purposive Behavior in Animals and Men*. New York: Appleton Century Crofts.

Tomlinson-Keasey, C., Eisert, D., Kahle, L., Hardy-Brown, K. and Keasey, C. B. (1979). The structure of concrete operational thought. *Child Development*, 50, 1153–1163.

Topping, K. (1983) *Educational Systems for Disruptive Adolescents*. London: Croom Helm.

Topping, K. (1992) Co-operative learning and peer tutoring: an overview. *The Psychologist*, 5 (4), 151–157.

Topping, K. and Whiteley, M. (1990) Participant evaluation of parent-tutored and peer-tutored projects in reading. *Educational Research*, 32 (1), 14–27.

Torgesen, J., Wagner, R. and Rashotte, C. (1994) Longitudinal studies of phonological processing and reading. *Journal of Learning Disabilities*, 27, 276–286.

Torrance, E. (1963) *Education and the Creative Potential*. Minneapolis: University of Minnesota Press.

Torrance, E. (1974) *Torrance Tests of Creative Thinking*. Lexington, MA: Ginn.

Torrance, E. (1988) The nature of creativity as manifest in its testing. In Sternberg, R. (ed.) *The Nature of Creativity*. New York: Cambridge University Press.

Tough, J. (1977) *Talking and Learning*. London: Ward Lock Educational.

Tough, J. (1981) *A Place for Talk: The Role of Talk in the Education of Children with Moderate Learning Difficulties*. London: Ward Lock Educational.

Trabasso, T. and Sperry, L. (1985) Causal relatedness and importance of story events. *Journal of Memory and language*, 24, 595–611.

Tulving, E. (1983) *Elements of Episodic Memory*. Oxford: Oxford University Press.

Turner, M. and Vincent, C. (1986) Are speech and language units effective? *Educational Psychology in Practice*, April, 36–41.

Ullman, L. and Krasner, L. (1975) *A psychological approach to abnormal behaviour*. Englewood Cliffs, NJ: Prentice-Hall.

Unger, R. and Crawford, M. (1992) *Women and Gender: A Feminist Psychology*. London: McGraw-Hill.

Unis, A., Cook, E., Vincent, J., Gjerde, D., Perry, B., Mason, C. and Mitchell, J. (1997) Platelet serotonin measures in adolescents with conduct disorder. *Biological Psychiatry*, 42 (7), 553–559.

Uzguris, I. and Hunt, J. McV. (1975) *Assessment in Infancy: Ordinal Scales of Psychological Development*. Urbana: University of Illinois Press.

Veldman, D. and Brophy, J. (1974) Measuring teacher effects on pupil achievement. *Journal of Educational Psychology*, 66 (3), 319–324.

Verma, G. (1986) *Ethnicity and educational achievement in British schools*. London: Macmillan.

Vernon, P. (1977) *Graded Word Spelling Test*. Sevenoaks: Hodder & Stoughton.

Vygotsky, L. (1962) *Thought and Language*. Cambridge, MA: MIT Press.

Vygotsky, L. (1978) *Mind in Society*. Cambridge, MA: Harvard University Press.

Wagner, P. (1995) *School Consultation: Frameworks for the Practising Educational Psychologist*. Kensington and Chelsea Education Psychology Service.

Waldfogel, S., Tessman, E. and Hahn, P. (1959) A program for early intervention in school phobia. *American Journal of Orthopsychiatry*, 29, 324–333.

Walker, B. (1998) Meetings without communication: a study of parents' evenings in secondary schools. *British Educational Research Journal*, 24, 163–179.

Wallace, A. (1986) Giftedness and the construction of a creative life. In F. Horowitz and M. O'Brien (eds), *The Gifted and the Talented: Developmental Perspectives*. Washington, DC: American Psychological Association.

Wallas, G. (1926) *The Art of Thought*. London: Cape.

Wang, A. and Thomas, M. (1995) Effect of keywords on long-term retention: help or hindrance? *Journal of Educational Psychology*, 87, 468–475.

Wang, M., Haertel, G. and Walberg, H. (1990) What influences learning? A content analysis of review literature. *Journal of Educational Research*, 84, 30–43.

Ward, M. and Baker, B. (1968) Reinforcement therapy in the classroom. *Journal of Applied Behaviour Analysis*, 1, 323–328.

Wasik, B. and Slavin, R. (1993) Preventing early reading failure with one-to-one tutoring: a review of five programs. *Reading Research Quarterly*, 28 (2), 179–200.

Waters, M. (1996) Success in the primary classroom: we are all in it together. *Support for Learning*, 11, 68–73.

Watson, J. (1925) *Behaviorism*, New York: Norton.

Watson, J. E. and Johnston, R. (1999) *Accelerating Reading Attainment: The Effectiveness of Synthetic Phonics*. Edinburgh: SOEID.

Webster, A. (1985) Deafness and reading. 1. Children with conductive hearing losses. *Remedial Education*, 20 (2), 68–71.

Webster, A. and Ellwood, J. (1985) *The Hearing Impaired Child in the Ordinary School*. London: Croom Helm.

Webster, A. and McConnell, C. (1987) *Special Needs in Ordinary Schools: Children with Speech and Language Difficulties*. London: Cassell.

Webster, A. and Wood, D. (1989) *Children with Hearing Difficulties*. London: Cassell.

Wechsler, D. (1992) *Wechsler Intelligence Scale for Children*, 3rd edition, UK. New York: The Psychological Corporation, Harcourt Brace Jovanovich.

Weiner, B. (1985) An attributional theory of achievement motivation and emotion. *Psychological Review*, 92, 548–573.

Weinstein, C. (1979) The physical environment of the school: a review of the research. *Review of Educational Research*, 49 (4), 577–610.

Weisberg, R. (1995) Case studies of creative thinking: reproduction versus restructuring in the real world. In S. Smith, T. Ward and R. Fiske (eds) *The Creative Cognition Approach*. Cambridge, MA: MIT Press.

Wender, E. and Lipton, M. (1980) *The National Advisory Committee Report on Hyperkinesis and Food Additives: Final Report to the Nutrition Foundation*. Washington, DC: Nutrition Foundation.

Wendon, L. (1980) *Letterland: Teachers Manual*. London: HarperCollins.

Wendt, H. (1955) Motivation, effort and performance In D. McClelland (ed.) *Studies in Motivation*. New York: Appleton Century Crofts.

Wheldall, K. (1991) Managing troublesome classroom behaviour in regular schools: a positive teaching perspective. *International Journal of Disability, Development and Education*, 38, 99–116.

Wheldall, K., Merrett, F. and Borg, M. (1985) The Behavioural Approach to Teaching Package (BATPAK): an experimental evaluation. *British Journal of Experimental Psychology*, 55, 65–75.

Wheldall, K., Merrett, F. and Russell, A. (1983) *The Behavioural Approach to Teaching Package*. Birmingham: Centre for Child Study, University of Birmingham.

Whitehead, F. (1977) *Children and Their Books*. London: Macmillan.

Whitehead, M. R. (1997) *Language and Literacy in the Early Years*, 2nd edition. London: Paul Chapman.

Whitehurst, G., Arnold, D., Epstein, J., Angell, A., Smith, M. and Fischel, J. (1994) A picture book reading intervention in daycare and home for children from low-income families. *Developmental Psychology*, 30, 679–689.

Whittaker, E. (1992) Specific learning difficulty (dyslexia) and neurological research. *Educational Psychology in Practice*, 8 (3), 139–144.

Whorf, B. (1956) *Language, Thought and Reality: Selected Writings of Benjamin Lee Whorf*. New York: Wiley.

Whyte, J., Deem, R., Kant, L. and Cruickshank, M. (1984) *Girl Friendly Schooling*. London: Methuen.

Wicks-Nelson, R. and Israel, A. (1991) *Behavior Disorders of Childhood*, 2nd edition. Englewood Cliffs, NJ: Prentice-Hall.

Widlake, P. (ed.) (1996) *The Good Practice Guide to Special Educational Needs*. Birmingham: Questions Publishing Company.

Wilgosh, L. and Paitich, D. (1982) Delinquency and learning disabilities: more evidence. *Journal of Learning Disabilities*, 15 (5), 278–279.

Wiliam, D. (1995) 'It'll all end in tiers'. *British Journal of Curriculum and Assessment*, 5, 21–24.

Wiliam, D. (1996) National Curriculum assessments and programmes of study: validity and impact. *British Educational Research Journal*, 22 (1), 129–143.

Williams, H. and Mallon, F. (1997) The Birmingham criteria for statutory assessment: a non-psychometric approach. *Educational Psychology in Practice*, 12 (4), 203–209.

Williams, P. (1961) The growth of reading vocabulary and some of its implications. *British Journal of Educational Psychology*, 31, 104–105.

Williams, S. and McGee, R. (1994) Reading attainment and juvenile delinquency. *Journal of Child Psychology and Psychiatry*, 35, 441–461.

Wilson, J. and Hernstein, R. (1985) *Crime and Human Nature*. New York: Simon & Schuster.

Wing, L. (1996) The history of ideas on autism. *Autism*, 1, 13–23.

Wing, L. and Gould, J. (1979). Severe impairments of social interaction and associated abnormalities in children: epidemiology and classification. *Journal of Autism and Childhood Schizophrenia*, 9, 11–29.

Withers, R. and Eke, R. (1995) Reclaiming 'match' from the critics of primary education. *Educational Review*, 47, 59–73.

Witkin, H. (1962) *Psychological Differentiation: Studies of Development*. New York: Wiley.

Witkin, H., Moore, C., Goodenough, D. and Cox, P. (1977) Field-dependent and field-independent cognitive styles and their educational implications. *Review of Educational Research*, 47, 1–64.

Wolfe, R. and Johnson, S. (1995) Personality as a predictor of college performance. *Educational and Psychological Measurement*, 55 (2), 177–185.

Wolfendale, S. (1998) *Meeting Special Needs in the Early Years*. London: David Fulton.

Wollin, D. and Montagne, M. (1981) College classroom environment. *Environment and Behaviour*, 13, 707–716.

Wood, D. (1998) *How Children Think and Learn*. 2nd edition. Oxford: Blackwell.

Wood, D., Bruner, J. and Ross, G. (1976) The role of tutoring in problem solving. *Journal of Child Psychology and Psychiatry*, 17, 89–100.

Wood, R. (1991) *Assessment and Testing*. Cambridge: Cambridge University Press.

Wood, S. and Shears, B. (1986) *Teaching Children with Severe Learning Difficulties: A Radical Reappraisal*. London: Croom Helm.

Woodrow, H. (1946) The ability to learn. *Psychological Review*, 53, 147–158.

Woolford, H. and McDougall, H. (1998) *The Teacher as a Role Model: The Effects of Teacher Gender on Boys' vs Girls Reading Attainment*. Swansea: University of Wales.

Word, E., Johnston, J., Bain, H., Fulton, B., Zaharias, J., Achilles, C., Lintz, M., Folger, J. and Breda, C. (1994) *The State of Tennessee's Student/Teacher Achievement (STAR) Project: Technical Report 1985–1990*. Tennessee: Tennessee State Department of Education.

Wragg, E. (1984) *Classroom Teaching Skills*. London: Croom Helm.

Wrench, J., Hassan, E. and Owen, D. (1996) *Ambition and Marginalisation: A Qualitative Study of Under-*

achieving Young men of Afro-Caribbean Origin. London: The Stationery Office.

Wright, A. (1992) Evaluation of the first British reading recovery programme. *British Educational Research Journal*, 18 (4), 351–368.

Wright, C. (1986) School processes: an ethnographic study. In J. Eggleston, D. Dunn and M. Anjali (eds) *Education for Some: The Educational and Vocational Experiences of 15–18 Year Old Members of Minority Ethnic Groups*. Stoke-on-Trent: Trentham Books.

Yerkes, R. and Dodson, J. (1908) The relation of strength of stimulus to rapidity of habit-formation. *Journal of Comparative Neurology and Psychology*, 18, 459–482.

Young, D. (1968) *Manual for the Group Reading Test*. London: University of London Press.

Young, S. (1998) The support group approach to bullying in schools. *Educational Psychology in Practice*, 14 (1), 32–39.

Youngman, M. (1979) Assessing behavioural adjustment to school. *British Journal of Educational Psychology*, 49, 258–264.

Youngman, M. and Szaday, C. (1985) Further validation of the Behaviour in School Inventory. *British Journal of Educational Psychology*, 55, 91–93.

Yule, W., Gold, R. and Busch, C. (1981) WISR-R correlates of academic attainment at 16½ years. *British Journal of Educational Psychology*, 51 (2), 237–240.

Yule, W., Rutter, M., Berger, M. and Thompson, J. (1974) Over- and under-achievement in reading: distribution in the general population. *British Journal of Educational Psychology*, 44, 1–12.

Zajonc, R. (1976) Family configuration and intelligence. *Science*, 192, 227–236.

Zajonc, R. and Mullally, P. (1997) Birth order: reconciling conflicting effects. *American Psychologist*, 52 (7), 685–699.

Zigarelli, M. (1996) An empirical test of conclusions from effective schools research. *Journal of Educational Research*, 90 (2), 103–110.

Zillmann, D. (1988) Cognition–excitation interdependencies in aggressive behaviour. *Aggressive Behaviour*, 14, 51–64.

Zimbardo, P. (1970) The human choice: individuation, reason and order versus deindividuation, impulse and chaos. In W. Arnold and D. Levine (eds) *Nebraska Symposium on Motivation*, vol. 16. Lincoln: University of Nebraska Press.

Zimmerman, B., Bandura, A. and Martinez-Pons, M. (1992) Self motivation for academic attainment: the role of self-efficacy beliefs and personal goal setting. *American Educational Research Journal*, 29, 663–676.

Zirpoli, T. and Melloy, K. (1993) *Behaviour Management: Applications for Teachers and Parents*. New York: Macmillan.

Index